COLLECTED WORKS OF ERASMUS

VOLUME 10

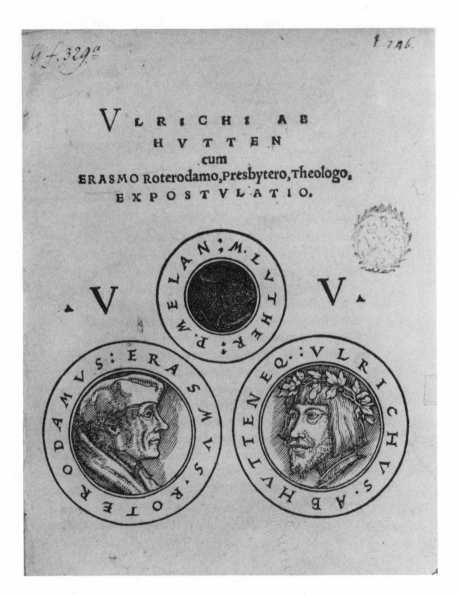

Ulrich von Hutten *Expostulatio cum Erasmo Roterdamo*
title-page
Strasbourg: Johann Schott 1523
Centre for Reformation and Renaissance Studies,
Victoria University, University of Toronto

THE CORRESPONDENCE OF
ERASMUS

LETTERS 1356 TO 1534

1523 TO 1524

translated by R.A.B. Mynors and Alexander Dalzell

annotated by James M. Estes

University of Toronto Press

Toronto / Buffalo / London

The research and publication costs of the
Collected Works of Erasmus are supported by the
Social Sciences and Humanities Research Council of Canada.
The publication costs are also assisted by
University of Toronto Press.

ISBN 0-8020-5976-7

Printed on acid-free paper

Canadian Cataloguing in Publication Data

Erasmus, Desiderius, d. 1536.
[Works]
Collected Works of Erasmus

Partial contents: v. 10. The correspondence of Erasmus:
letters 1356 to 1534, 1523 to 1524 /
translated by R.A.B. Mynors and Alexander Dalzell;
annotated by James M. Estes.
Includes index.
ISBN 0-8020-5976-7 (v. 10)

1. Erasmus, Desiderius, d. 1536. I. Title.

PA8500 1974   876'.04   C74-006326-x rev

Collected Works of Erasmus

The aim of the Collected Works of Erasmus
is to make available an accurate, readable English text
of Erasmus' correspondence and his
other principal writings. The edition is planned
and directed by an Editorial Board, an Executive Committee,
and an Advisory Committee.

Contents

Illustrations

Preface

The letters in this volume cover the period April 1523–December 1524.[1] Despite repeated and debilitating recurrences of Erasmus' old complaint, the stone, it was a period rich in literary production: a new edition of the *Ratio verae theologiae* (June 1523); the paraphrase on Luke (August); the *Spongia* against Hutten (September; second edition in October); an edition of Cicero's *Tusculanae quaestiones* (November); the *Precatio dominica* (c November); the paraphrase on Mark (December); commentaries on Ovid's *Nux* and Prudentius' hymns for Christmas and Epiphany (published together early in 1524); the paraphrase on Acts (February); the *Exomologesis* (February or March); an apologia against his old adversary Diego López Zúñiga (published with the *Exomologesis*); the *Compendium vitae* (not published at the time but embedded in Ep 1437 of 2 April); the first three volumes of the revised edition of Jerome (August); an expanded edition of the *Colloquia* (August–September); *De immensa Dei misericordia* (September); an expanded version of the *Virginis et martyris comparatio* (published with *De immensa Dei misericordia*); *De libero arbitrio* (September); and the *Modus orandi Deum* (October).

Despite the impressive volume and quality of this literary output, only two of the works listed figure significantly in the correspondence of the period taken as a whole: the *Spongia* against Hutten and *De libero arbitrio* against Luther. This is because the predominant theme of the letters, here as in volume 9, is 'the sorry business of Luther,' a business in which the controversy with Hutten marked a turning-point and to which the publication of *De libero arbitrio* was a long-delayed climax.

The Luther problem continued to involve Erasmus in a struggle on two

* * * * *

1 One very important letter of this period, the much expanded second edition of the *Catalogus lucubrationum* (September 1524) has already been published as Ep 1341A in CWE 9. For further details, see the introduction to that letter, and see also CWE 9 xvi–xvii.

fronts: against the conservative theologians who were determined to prove
that he had 'laid the egg [that] ... Luther hatched'[2] and who interpreted his
moderate attitude towards Luther as secret collusion with him; and against
the reforming zealots who interpreted his reserved attitude towards Luther
as secret collusion with the pope and who believed that only cowardice and
greed for financial reward kept him from siding publicly with Luther.[3]
Erasmus' most relentless Catholic detractors, Nicolaas Baechem (Egmon-
danus) in Louvain and Diego López Zúñiga in Rome were no longer as
dangerous as they had seemed to be in 1522, although it took some months
for this to become clear. Both had been silenced by Adrian VI.[4] When Zúñiga
took advantage of the interregnum after Adrian's death in September 1523
to return to the attack, Erasmus appealed directly to the new pope, Clement
VII, to silence him.[5] Clement, who was well disposed toward Erasmus and
who had been greatly pleased by the dedication to him of the paraphrase on
Acts, did as requested; by 25 March Erasmus knew that his tiresome
adversary had been silenced.[6] As for Baechem, he took somewhat longer to
return to the attack after Adrian's death, perhaps because of his involve-
ment in the events that led to the disgrace and dismissal of his colleague
Frans van der Hulst, the chief inquisitor of the Netherlands, in the spring of
1524. In July Erasmus triumphantly reported the downfall of both men,[7] but
by the autumn was once again complaining that Baechem was up to his old
tricks.[8] He appealed both to Pope Clement VII and to the Netherlands
government to silence him.[9] Though the appeal to the pope was successful,
the mandate silencing Baechem was not sent to Louvain until July 1525.[10]

However, silencing his two noisiest Catholic critics did not by itself
solve Erasmus' problem with Catholic conservatives in general. He knew
that he could never be secure against their attempts to persuade the mighty
of church and state that he was a secret Lutheran unless he took an
unambiguous public stand against Luther. For some time already, friendly
princes and prelates had been urging him to publish something against

* * * * *

2 Ep 1528:19 is the earliest known source for this famous slogan.
3 See CWE 9 x–xvi.
4 Epp 1359:2–3, 1415:18–20
5 Epp 1410, 1415, 1416, 1418
6 Ep 1431:13–14, 1443B
7 Ep 1466:14–16, 1467:11–15
8 Ep 1481:67–76
9 Epp 1509 introduction, 1515:11–29
10 Ep 1589

Luther,[11] and the pressure continued in the period in question here.[12] Erasmus nevertheless remained reluctant to yield to that pressure. He was motivated in part by his disinclination to face the furore that an attack on Luther would arouse and, even more, by the fear that the overthrow of Luther would entail the victory of the reactionaries and the quashing of all wholesome reform.[13] Two developments worked to overcome this reluctance. One was the choice of an ideal topic, free will. Not only was this an issue at the very heart of Luther's theological system on which he and Erasmus were in fundamental disagreement,[14] it was also an issue on which Erasmus could write in a moderate, scholarly tone without having to attack Luther's practical reforms, many of which he approved of. The other development plays a far more prominent role in the correspondence: the campaign waged against him in 1523–4 by some of Luther's supporters. This not only aroused his genuine indignation, it also gave him the opportunity to justify his book on free will less as an attack on Luther, about whom his feelings were ambivalent, than as a settling of accounts with Luther's followers, about whom his feelings were unequivocal and whose behaviour was in fact an embarrassment to Luther.

Erasmus had long since developed an aversion to many of Luther's supporters because of their unruly behaviour and their misguided attempts to manoeuvre him into their camp. In the long letter to Marcus Laurinus (Ep 1342) published in February 1523, he loftily declared that he would not join them in their attempt to establish 'universal confusion.'[15] But when those partisans of Luther launched a public, personal attack on him as someone who had betrayed the gospel for base reasons, his aversion and disdain turned into bitter, vehement anger at the 'many-headed hydra' that was 'Luther's party.'[16] It all began in the summer of 1523 when Ulrich von Hutten, 'a friend all at once turned into an enemy,' reacted to the reading of the letter to Marcus Laurinus by publishing his *Expostulatio cum Erasmo Roterodamo*,[17] which was in circulation by the first half of July. Although a quarrel had been brewing between him and Hutten for some time, Erasmus was genuinely surprised and shocked by the *Expostulatio*, which he saw as a

* * * * *

11 Epp 1298:24ff, 1324:24ff, 1324A
12 Epp 1367:11ff, 1408:25–7, 1415:62–4
13 Epp 1313, 1369, 1386, 1526
14 Epp 1342:1022–78, 1384:11–16; cf Ep 1419 introduction.
15 Ep 1342:1112–13; cf CWE 9 xv–xvi.
16 Ep 1410:5
17 Ep 1356 n9

baseless attack by someone he had always treated generously.[18] He was even more indignant when it turned out that the *Expostulatio*, which he answered with the *Spongia*, was only the first in a series of 'wild and libellous pamphlets' aimed at him by supporters of Luther. The next to appear (sometime between 19 January and 13 March 1524) was the *Responsio ad Erasmi Spongiam*, a defence of the now-deceased Hutten by Otto Brunfels,[19] whom Erasmus described as even 'more ignorant and more raving mad' than Hutten himself.[20] A second edition of the *Responsio* appeared in July. At about the same time, Johann Schott, the Strasbourg printer who had already published the pamphlets by Hutten and Brunfels, published Erasmus Alber's *Iudicium de Spongia Erasmi Roterodami*,[21] which Erasmus called 'the stupidest thing ever.'[22] Meanwhile, a month or two earlier Erasmus had had a personal confrontation with Guillaume Farel, a Frenchman 'even madder than the Germans,'[23] who had migrated to Basel and who had begun to call Erasmus 'Balaam,' that is, someone hired to curse God's people. In the wake of this confrontation, 'Phallicus,' as Erasmus almost invariably called him, attacked Erasmus in a number of pamphlets that are now lost.[24]

Erasmus soon persuaded himself that the authors of these 'venomous pamphlets' were not working alone but had accomplices. Very soon after the publication of the *Expostulatio*, he concluded that another friend turned false, Heinrich Eppendorf, had incited Hutten to write it and had supplied the malicious gossip that was in it.[25] Eppendorf's original aim, Erasmus claimed, had been to extort money from Erasmus' friends in return for preventing publication of the *Expostulatio*.[26] In mid-September Erasmus reported that Hermannus Buschius, whom he described as 'much more virulent than Hutten,' was publishing attacks on him.[27] Buschius in fact published no attacks, though Erasmus later attributed the authorship of Alber's *Iudicium* to him.[28] By the time Brunfels published his *Responsio*, Erasmus was convinced that Eppendorf had not acted alone in engineering

* * * * *

18 See Ep 1331 n24.
19 Ep 1405
20 Ep 1432:64–5
21 Ep 1466 n19
22 Ibidem line 29
23 Ep 1483:7–8
24 Epp 1341A n305, 1477A, 1496:146ff, 1510:11ff
25 Epp 1283 n4, 1341A n297, 1376:27–9, 1437:10ff
26 Ep 1383:2–9
27 Ep 1386:31–2
28 Ep 1466:29–34

the breach with Hutten but that a conspiracy of many Lutheran 'lunatics' had encouraged Hutten to attack him and had supplied 'lies' for use in the *Expostulatio*.[29] Perhaps most painful of all for Erasmus was the frequent discovery that leaders of the reform movement, all of them (at least until recently) supposed friends, were giving support to the lesser Lutherans who had written or published such 'palpable falsehoods and devilish lies' about him. Zwingli gave Hutten asylum in Zürich and Oecolampadius in Basel maintained close contact with him.[30] In Strasbourg, Capito 'was taken in by Eppendorf's tricks' and was, Erasmus believed, the moving spirit behind the publication of Brunfels' *Responsio*.[31] Capito's colleague, Caspar Hedio, came to the defence of the printer Schott when Erasmus demanded his punishment for having published the 'libellous' pamphlets by Hutten, Brunfels, and Alber.[32]

By the spring and summer of 1524 Erasmus' initial shock and anger had developed into a towering rage. Men like Hutten and Brunfels, he insisted, 'are not human beings at all, but raging demons' who fear neither God nor man. For that reason, neither pope nor emperor can offer protection against the lies and blasphemies in their 'raving pamphlets.' They claim to be 'evangelicals' but are really 'diabolicals' whose scandalous conduct renders the gospel loathsome and destroys good literature. They seem to aim at nothing less than universal chaos, and the measures necessary to counteract their subversion may well produce bloody civil strife.[33] In short, they are 'a new sort of men: headstrong, impudent, deceitful, foul-mouthed, liars, scandal-mongers ... no good to anyone and a nuisance to all – subversive, crazy, noisy rascals ...'[34] Despite all that they have the support of leaders like Capito, Hedio, Oecolampadius, and Zwingli. But such 'perverted creatures' as these will never restore the gospel or become 'the pillars of a renascent church.' How could anyone make common cause with them?[35]

In the letters, Erasmus' mounting anger at these pamphleteers, their accomplices, and their patrons almost invariably appears in a causal relationship to his decision to take the field against Luther. No sooner was the *Spongia* off the presses in early September 1523 than Erasmus confided to Henry VIII that he had something in the works 'against the new doctrines.'[36]

* * * * *

29 Epp 1432:50–4, 1437:27–30, 73–4
30 Epp 1376:32 with n21, 1437:59–64
31 Epp 1437:106–8, 1485, 1496:120–2, 1477B:74–8
32 Epp 1429, 1477, 1477B
33 See Epp 1432, 1437, 1445, 1477, 1483, 1488–9, 1496–7 passim.
34 Ep 1522:96–9
35 Epp 1445:67–9, 1497:17–23
36 Ep 1385:15–16

However, the earliest surviving evidence of his motives for writing and the
first indication that the book would be on the topic of free will are found in a
letter of 21 November to Johannes Fabri.[37] Erasmus says that his resentment
is directed not so much at Hutten as against those who have encouraged him
in their own interest. They will no doubt soon betray themselves, for 'some
monstrous business' (that is, the publication of pamphlets attacking him) is
being hatched in Strasbourg. Then, without a break, he notes that Luther
has denounced the *Spongia* and has also belittled him in a letter to
Oecolampadius, saying that he is like Moses, who will never enter the
promised land but must be buried in the wilderness, and that little weight
should be given to Erasmus in spiritual matters. 'This sort of thing means
war' is Erasmus' terse comment. A few lines further on, after having listed
his current literary endeavours, he adds: 'If my strength holds out, I shall
add a book on free will.'

By about February 1524 a first draft of *De libero arbitrio* had been
completed and a copy was soon dispatched to Henry VIII.[38] News of the
impending attack caused joy in Rome[39] but considerable consternation in
Germany, where Luther and his supporters were aware of the damage that
an attack by the great humanist could do to Luther's cause. On 2 April
Erasmus reported having learned from Johannes Fabri that the policy of
Luther's supporters was to use threats to frighten him off from attacking
Luther in print.[40] In mid-April Luther himself wrote to Erasmus warning
that he would respond personally to any attack upon him but promising to
restrain his pen if Erasmus would remain silent.[41] Undeterred by these
threats, Erasmus continued to work on the treatise. Replying to Luther on 8
May, he wrote that 'these people [Luther's supporters, described at length
in the terms summarized above] are driving me into the opposite camp –
even if pressure from the princes were not pushing me in the same
direction.'[42] On 13 May Erasmus told Oecolampadius in conversation that
De libero arbitrio had been completed.[43] At first Erasmus seems to have
considered keeping it in manuscript only, but on 21 July he announced to
Willibald Pirckheimer that he had decided to publish it because rumours of

* * * * *

37 Ep 1397
38 Epp 1419, 1430
39 Ep 1443B:8–12
40 Ep 1437:108–10; cf Ep 1341A:1114–17.
41 Ep 1443:23–5, 48–50, 74–8
42 Ep 1445:33–4
43 WA-Br III 294:19–20

his having written it were widespread and people might 'suspect it to be worse than it is.'[44]

In the letters of 2–6 September that accompanied presentation copies of *De libero arbitrio*, Erasmus speaks more of 'taking the field against the Lutherans' than of writing against Luther, and it is them rather than Luther whom he denounces to justify his decision to publish.[45] The most succinct example of this is the letter of 6 September to Duke George of Saxony.[46] Erasmus says that he has not written against Luther sooner for two reasons. The first is that he felt unequal to so dangerous an undertaking and that he was repelled by the prospect of a gladiatorial combat to the death. The second is that he had believed that Luther, whatever the faults of his teaching, was a necessary evil in a church 'so deeply and universally corrupted' and that he had hoped that such bitter medicine might somehow prove beneficial to the health of the body of Christ's people. As it is, however, most people interpret his moderation as collusion with Luther. Moreover, 'a new race is growing up of brazen and shameless men, relations with whom are out of the question. Such men, in a word, as Luther himself would find intolerable ...' And so Erasmus has decided to enter the arena with a small book on the freedom of the will. The pope and the king of England had encouraged him to write the book, but he 'was far more forcibly moved [to do so] by the villainy of some of these brawling ruffians, who unless they are restrained will end by overthrowing both the gospel and the humanities.' At their worst, popes and bishops are to be preferred to these mean and petty tyrants.

In other letters of the same period Erasmus justifies the decision to publish *De libero arbitrio* in somewhat broader terms.[47] Certain theologians had persuaded all the monarchs that he was in close alliance with Luther. Seeing this, Erasmus' friends had given pope and princes reason to hope that he would publish something against Luther, and he himself had encouraged that hope. Meanwhile, the Lutherans had begun to attack him with 'a hail of pamphlets.' There was thus no option but to publish what he had written. Otherwise the monarchs, feeling that they had been duped, would have turned against him, while 'the party of disorder' would have concluded either that they had frightened him into silence or else that he had decided to publish something even worse and would attack him even more fiercely. Finally, since Luther's letter promising to refrain from attacking

* * * * *

44 Ep 1466:64–6
45 See especially Epp 1481, 1483, 1488–9, 1495–7.
46 Ep 1495
47 See especially Epp 1488–9, 1496.

Erasmus unless Erasmus attacked him had been widely circulated, failure to publish would have given the impression that he had been restrained by some sort of agreement with Luther.

The reaction of Erasmus' Catholic patrons to *De libero arbitrio* was gratifying,[48] even if Duke George of Saxony observed, in effect, that it was high time.[49] Moreover, while at least one member of the reform party close to home reacted negatively,[50] the initial reaction from Wittenberg was muted. Melanchthon wrote that the work had been received there with complete equanimity and that Luther would doubtless reply in a moderate tone.[51] Erasmus professed to prefer that Luther would reply 'in his own way,' lest there be any suspicion of collusion between them,[52] but he nevertheless reported the calm reception of the work in Wittenberg to several friends with evident satisfaction.[53] In any case, Erasmus had to wait more than a year to find out what Luther's reply would really be like.

Meanwhile, the 'endless perfidy' of the Germans, that is, Luther's supporters, and the supposed danger of writing against Luther while living in Germany had revived Erasmus' desire to leave Basel and take up residence outside Germany.[54] But where should he go? Clement vii invited him to Rome with generous offers.[55] Francis i, who wanted him to be the head of a new trilingual college in Paris, invited him to France with the offer of a lucrative treasurership at Tours.[56] And Margaret of Austria, regent of the Netherlands, so badly wanted Erasmus back in the Netherlands to help her combat the Reformation that she made the payment of his imperial annuity conditional upon his return to Brabant.[57] But for one reason or another all three possibilities were out of the question. Rome was unsafe because of Aleandro[58] and the rest of Italy was unsafe because of the plague.[59] Besides, the 'crazy evangelicals' would decry any move to Italy as betrayal of the gospel for money.[60] France was out of the question because,

* * * * *

48 See Epp 1503, 1509, 1513.
49 Ep 1520:17–20
50 Ep 1523:118–23; also Epp 1522:93–4, 1523:110–17, 1526:242–3
51 Ep 1500:45–6, 50–1
52 Ep 1523:128–32
53 See Ep 1500 n8.
54 Epp 1385:16–17, 1386:13–15, 18–20, 1437:104–6, 114–15, 1522:99–100
55 Epp 1408:11, 1409:5
56 Epp 1375, 1434:1–37
57 Ep 1380 introduction
58 Ep 1437:119–22, with n55 on Aleandro
59 Epp 1479:201–2, 1514:10
60 Ep 1437:188–90

with the Hapsburg-Valois wars in full swing, no imperial councillor to
Charles v could enter royal service there without seeming to desert to the
enemy.[61] As for the Netherlands, it had Baechem and Hulst and a policy of
religious persecution that was not to Erasmus' taste.[62] Besides that, in all
three places Erasmus would have had to play the courtier, accept the
burdens of office, and thus lose his cherished independence.[63] He probably
could have settled in England had he wished, but for reasons that were
unclear even to himself, he did not want to.[64] So at the end of 1524 he was
still in Basel, 'in a state of siege, pitifully longing to move somewhere else,'
but with no place to go.[65]

Of the 179 letters presented here, 122 were written by Erasmus and 56
were written to him. One other (Ep 1361) was written by Thomas Lupset to
Johann von Botzheim with the request that he pass the contents on to
Erasmus. These letters contain references to more than 165 others that are no
longer extant; because so many of the references are to an unspecified
number of letters, an exact figure cannot be given, but 180 would be a
conservative estimate. Only 81 of the surviving letters were published by
Erasmus himself, 57 in the *Opus epistolarum* of 1529, 1 in the *Epistolae floridae*
of 1531, and 23 as prefaces to various works. One further letter, Ep 1397, was
published without Erasmus' authorization in 1524. Of the remaining 97
letters, 5 were published by their authors and the rest were published by a
variety of scholars in the period from Erasmus' death to 1926. Ten of them
were first published by Allen. To allow the reader to discover the sequence
in which the letters became known, the introduction to each letter cites the
place where it was first published and identifies the manuscript source if one
exists.

Except for Epp 1445, 1469, 1479, 1480, 1512, 1523, and 1526, which were
translated by Alexander Dalzell, all the letters in this volume were translated
by R.A.B. Mynors. Allen's text and his ordering of the letters have been
followed, with a few exceptions. First, Allen Ep 1412 has been redated to
January 1523 and has already appeared as Ep 1337A in CWE 9. Second, Allen
omitted the *Compendium vitae* from his text of Ep 1437, publishing it instead
as a separate item at the beginning of his volume I. We have restored the
Compendium to the text of the letter in which Erasmus embedded it. For
further details, see the introduction to the letter. Third, Allen based his Ep

* * * * *

61 Epp 1408:23–4, 1411:10–12, 1432:76–7, 1434:14, 1437:116–19, 191–3
62 Epp 1408:21–2, 1411:14–17, 1417:20–4, 1434:45–59
63 Epp 1434:59, 1484
64 Epp 1386:17–18, 1432:73–5
65 Ep 1514:9–14

1438 on a manuscript that bore the date 3 April 1524; we have used instead the slightly different text published as Ep 101 in de Vocht *Literae*, which represents the letter actually sent and is dated 30 April. It is given here as Ep 1443B. Fourth, Allen Epp 1508 and 1459 have been assigned new dates and appear here as Epp 1477A and 1477B respectively. Fifth, just as this volume was going to press it was learned that Allen's conjectural dating of Ep 1436 is untenable and that the letter really belongs in volume 11. It was too late to remove the letter from this volume, but a new introduction explaining the situation has been provided; see pages 214–15.

The index to this volume, prepared by Howard Hotson, contains references to the persons, places, and works mentioned in the volume, following the plan for the correspondence series. When that series of volumes is completed, the reader will also be supplied with an index of classical and scriptural references. Because the three volumes of the CEBR are now available, the biographical annotation of this volume has been kept to an absolute minimum. So has the citation of biographical sources. Wherever information is supplied without the citation of a source, the reader is tacitly referred to the appropriate article in the CEBR and to the literature there cited.

I should like to acknowledge here the debt that I owe to those colleagues who have given me their expert assistance in the difficult task of annotating this volume. Alexander Dalzell of Trinity College, University of Toronto, not only provided the classical and biblical annotations for the letters that he translated but also provided much invaluable help with many of the classical references in the other letters. Erika Rummel of the CWE editorial staff gave me the benefit of her wide and detailed knowledge of Erasmus' writings. Moreover, when I had to assume responsibility for making such revisions and corrections as were necessary in the translations of the late Sir Roger Mynors, Prof Dalzell and Dr Rummel came to my aid and found the solutions to all the really difficult problems. James K. Farge CSB of the Pontifical Institute of Mediaeval Studies read the entire manuscript and made a number of suggestions that led to improvements in both the translation and the annotations. The following individuals generously responded to my requests for information on specific issues within their field of competence: Calvin Pater of Knox College in the Toronto School of Theology; James K. McConica CSB of St Michael's College, University of Toronto; John C. Olin of Fordham University; Jaroslav Pelikan of Yale University; Moshe Idel of The Hebrew University, Jerusalem; David J. Halperin of the University of North Carolina; and Rainer Heinrich of the Bullinger-Briefwechsel-Edition, Zürich. The notes on currency were supplied by John H. Munro of the University of Toronto. The assistance of certain other scholars has been acknowledged at the appropriate places in the notes. As usual, the copyeditor, Mary Baldwin, did her job with tact, a sharp eye, and a genuine spirit of collaboration.

Most of the work on this volume was done using materials in the library of the Centre for Reformation and Renaissance Studies at Victoria University in the University of Toronto, especially the Centre's splendid Erasmus Collection. For patristic and medieval texts I had recourse to the library of the Pontifical Institute of Mediaeval Studies on the campus of St Michael's College, University of Toronto. I am deeply grateful to both institutions and their staffs.

Finally, the editors wish to record once again their gratitude to the Social Sciences and Humanities Research Council of Canada, without whose generous assistance the Collected Works of Erasmus could not be published.

JME

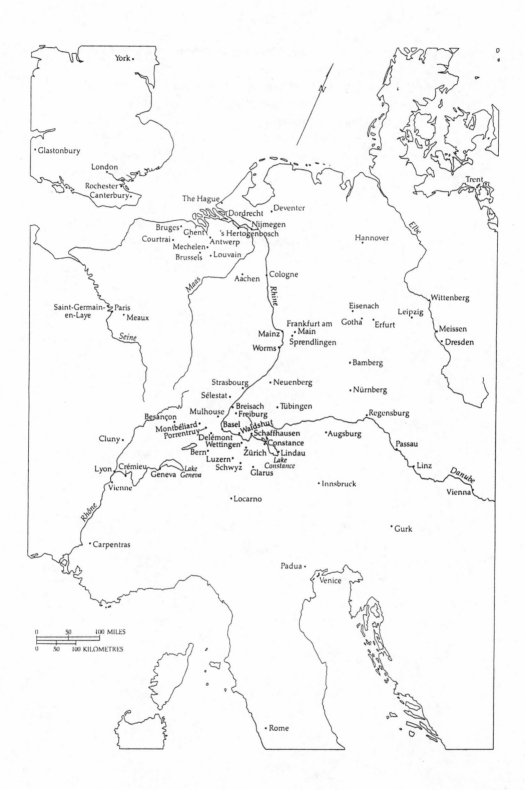

THE CORRESPONDENCE OF ERASMUS

LETTERS 1356 TO 1534

1356 / To Ulrich von Hutten　　　　　　　　　Basel, 3 April [1523]

This is the last surviving letter in the correspondence between Erasmus and
Hutten, whose life was drawing to a close and whose relations with Erasmus
were moving rapidly towards a bitter, public rupture; see Ep 1331 n24. The
letter was first published in the *Epistolae floridae*, where the year-date is
strangely inaccurate (line 73). The letter obviously falls between Hutten's visit
to Basel in December/January 1522–3 (line 9) and his death at the end of August
1523. Hutten was now in Mulhouse (Mülhausen) and Heinrich Eppendorf (Ep
1283 n4) was carrying messages back and forth between him and Erasmus.
Fragments of two letters that Hutten wrote to Erasmus early in 1523 are found
in Allen Ep 1934:275–89. Further echoes of their correspondence in the same
period are found in the *Spongia* (ASD IX-1 130:193–131:229, 204:950–65). The
same source (ibidem 125:75–126:94) indicates that Hutten replied promptly to
this letter, promising that the *Expostulatio* (line 74) would appear shortly, and
that there was at least one more exchange of letters before Hutten's pamphlet
appeared.

ERASMUS OF ROTTERDAM TO ULRICH VON HUTTEN, GREETING
Heinrich Eppendorf, who is well disposed towards me and at any rate a very
good friend of yours, has given me a hint that your intentions towards me
are not as friendly as I could wish, to the extent that you are planning to
write something fairly bitter. This, I must say, surprised me all the more,　　5
inasmuch as my feelings towards you, which have hitherto been friendly, as
friendly as they have towards any man, have so far not changed at all,
although fortune has for a time grudged us our former intimacy. Nor did I
think it beneath me to have a talk with you while you were here,[1] but I sent
you a message by Eppendorf in the most civil terms possible, asking you not　　10
to come, even if it were only a greeting, because of the burden of hostility
which I have now suffered for a long time, even to the extent of personal
danger. What is the point of acquiring fresh hostility for one's pains, if one
can be no use to a friend? Had I been you, my dear Hutten, I should have
asked Erasmus in similar circumstances not to invite fresh unpopularity to　　15
no purpose. And yet I made it clear to Eppendorf that, if you could keep
clear of rooms with stoves,[2] which I cannot endure at any price, I should find
a talk with you not unwelcome.

* * * * *

1356
1 During Hutten's visit to Basel in December 1522, Erasmus had declined to
　receive a visit from him. On this incident, see Ep 1331 n24.
2 See Ep 1258 n18.

It may be that I have done you no service that I can speak of here, and if I had, it would be tactless of me to recall it. This much I could truly affirm, that I have always stoutly maintained my ancient good will towards you, and that I have never said or done anything that could hurt you in the least. My feeling is that a close friendship of the sort that arose between us in the cause of the humanities should scarcely be disrupted even by bloodshed. Perhaps there are people who provoke you against me, with the object of diverting your powers as a writer to the satisfaction of their own personal spite. Should you lend yourself to this, let me tell you, first, that your victim will not have deserved it – that I have deserved well of you, I cannot claim – and at any rate wishes you well; and secondly, that you will do something which will give the greatest possible pleasure to Jacob of Hoogstraten[3] and Nicolaas Baechem[4] and plenty of other people whom you regard as your worst enemies, and in other ways highly damaging to the supporters of the humanities, men whose champion you claim to be. What fresh life it will give those monstrous figures, if they find Hutten mobilizing against Erasmus that strain of brilliance which Erasmus so much admires and that eloquence which Erasmus has so often praised!

It will therefore be sensible on your part if, before the signal is given to advance, before the harsh note of the bugles breaks the air[5] and the trumpet sounds its terrible *tarantara*,[6] the note of battle, as though the *pater patratus* and the *fetialis* had performed their mission,[7] you were to write to me privately with a full account, free and friendly, of the stories you have heard about me, or what it actually is that makes you so bitter. For I myself, as I hope for God's mercy, cannot guess. I have no doubts that I shall be able to satisfy you on every point, unless you have begun to be quite a different person from what you were in the old days. How I wish, my dear Hutten, that you had no enemies except myself! How I wish the prayers of that one enemy on your behalf might be answered! Remember this is said to you in all solemnity.

Further, if you can be recalled from your intended course neither by respect for long-standing friendship nor by the thought of the pursuits we have in common nor by the pleasure it will give your enemies, remember

* * * * *

3 Ep 1299 n25
4 Ep 1254 n6
5 Cf Virgil *Aeneid* 8.2.
6 Cf Ennius *Annales* 452, apud Priscianus; Virgil *Aeneid* 9.503.
7 The *fetiales* were an old Roman priesthood whose duties included the formal declaration of war. Their spokesman was known as the *pater patratus*. According to Varro, he was accompanied by three other *fetiales* when he performed the prescribed rituals for making such a declaration.

that this has no small relevance to your own reputation too. Who will not
regret the absence in Hutten of civilized behaviour, worthy of his lineage
and his learning, if, though unprovoked by any wrong he has suffered, he
draws a blade dipped in deadly venom in order to attack a friend? There will 55
perhaps be no lack of people who, when they consider the state your affairs
are in at the moment, may suspect that the object of these tricks of yours is
plunder, from no matter where, and there is some danger that the
suggestion may strike root with many men, who know of course that you are
a fugitive, deeply in debt, and reduced to extreme penury in all respects. 60
You know well enough what stories are in circulation about you, and you are
not ignorant of the causes of the resentment and the threats of the count
palatine, who has executed one of your servants.[8] And so I should not like
you to think that this protest of mine stems either from fear or from a bad
conscience, rather than from affection for you, and that I am pursuing my 65
own interests rather than yours. Write as offensively as you please: in the
first place you will be attacking someone not unused to trouble of this kind
nor wholly tongue-tied. Secondly, suppose I were to keep silence, even so
you will do more damage to your reputation than to mine. And so I urge you
most sincerely, my dear Hutten, to follow at this point the advice of your 70
own common sense, rather than be a tool for the greed of worthless
wretches.

> Farewell. Basel, Good Friday 152[7]
> I await your expostulation.[9]

1357 / To Bernhard von Cles Basel, 5 April 1523

Member of an ancient Tyrolese family, Bernhard von Cles (1485–1539) studied
at Bologna (LLD 1511) and then embarked upon an ecclesiastical career in his
native diocese of Trent. In 1514 he entered the service of Emperor Maximilian.
He subsequently became one of the most trusted advisers and diplomats in the
service of Archduke Ferdinand, who made him supreme chancellor in 1528. In
1530 Clement VII created him cardinal. Bernhard was a faithful patron of
Erasmus, who in 1526 dedicated the *editio princeps* of Irenaeus to him (Ep 1738).
    The letter was first printed by B. Bonelli in volume 3 of the *Monumenta*

* * * * *

8 See Ep 1341A:1071–2 with nn293–4.
9 This word may well have suggested to Hutten the title that he gave to his attack
    on Erasmus, *Expostulatio cum Erasmo Roterodamo*, which was published during
    the summer by Johann Schott at Strasbourg; see Ep 1341A n283. Erasmus had,
    of course, invited (lines 37–42) and was expecting a private 'expostulation,' not
    a published attack; cf ASD IX-1 125:75–126:90.

ecclesiae tridentinae (1765). The autograph is in the Nationalbibliothek at Vienna
(Cod 9737c, f 3).

Cordial greeting, my Lord Bishop. His most serene Highness Prince
Ferdinand had asked me, in a letter addressed to me personally,[1] to send
him the book containing my paraphrase on St John's Gospel, which is
dedicated to him.[2] I did so, and sent with it the paraphrase on Matthew
which I dedicated some time ago to the emperor Charles.[3] It was however   5
the opinion of Johannes Fabri,[4] canon of Constance and suffragan of the see,
a man of learning and piety who on these grounds, and especially on
account of his enthusiasm for the restoration of peace in Christendom, is
high in favour with the pope, that my modest offering should be tendered to
his serene Highness by you; for he thought it would prove more acceptable   10
with some added support from a man of the highest reputation. If your
lordship will be so kind as to do this, I shall gladly acknowledge myself your
debtor; and I wish I might be favoured with your esteem and closer
acquaintance. My feelings are shared by Fabri, who is your lordship's
particular admirer and openly proclaims your virtues. May Christ the   15
almighty Lord long preserve you for our benefit in health and wealth.

    Basel, 5 April 1523
    Your lordship's most devoted servant Erasmus of Rotterdam
    To the right reverend father in Christ Bernhard, lord bishop of Trent

1358 / To Pierre Barbier   Basel, 17 April 1523

Pierre Barbier (Ep 1294) was chaplain to Adrian vi. On Erasmus' relations with
Barbier at this time, see Ep 1342:698–706. See also Ep 1386 introduction. This
letter was first published in the *Opus epistolarum*.

ERASMUS OF ROTTERDAM TO PIERRE BARBIER, CHAPLAIN TO
POPE ADRIAN, GREETING
You give me an admirable picture of the pope's most pious intentions. I read

* * * * *

1357
1 Ep 1343
2 Ep 1333
3 Ep 1255
4 Fabri (Ep 386), vicar-general of the diocese of Constance, was an ardent
   champion of the papacy against Luther (Epp 1260:81, 99–119, 1335:39–59,
   1382:74–7). On Pope Adrian's high opinion of him, see Ep 1324:129–33.

that part of your letter,[1] my dear Barbier, with heartfelt pleasure, you may be
sure. I shall shortly publish a brief exhortation,[2] urging men to leave this 5
godless quarrelling for Christian concord. In this I shall express the pope's
religious and single-minded policy in such terms that I hope my insistence
upon it will have no small influence in bringing this business to a conclusion,
especially once the Germans feel that he is not opposed to the abolition of
things which even devout people find hard to bear,[3] and which lay traps for 10
the consciences of all men for the profit of a few; and also, once they feel that
even Luther will not find in him a judge without mercy. For what Luther
writes about the tyranny and the greed and the immorality of the Roman
curia – I wish, my dear Barbier, that there were no truth in it! I am still made
wretched by the fear that things will end in open conflict. We hear a great 15
deal about the liberty of the gospel; but they have different things in view.
Under this screen some seek a frenzied freedom to become the slaves of their
own carnal appetites; some cast envious eyes at the resources of the
priesthood; and some bravely lavish their own wealth on drinking,
wenching, and gambling and are agape for the chance to plunder others. 20
Some men's affairs are in such a state that there can be no safety for them in
peace. Yet even among these there are some who would wish to see the
abuses which have crept into the church, and done so much harm,
corrected, if it were possible, without open conflict. When things are in such
confusion, it is like a house on fire: everyone will seize what he had set his 25
heart on.

It is therefore of the first importance to see that open conflict does not
once break out, as I hear has happened at Erfurt,[4] where every day some
people are killed. Among us, although that pitiless fool Baechem[5] and his
colleague[6] have treated some men disgracefully, yet I rejoice that things 30
have not yet come to blows, though in other ways they are unceasingly at
each other's throats. Cornelis Hoen,[7] an excellent man they tell me, had

* * * * *

1358
1 Not extant
2 See Ep 1352 introduction.
3 Cf Ep 1344:178–82.
4 In 1521–2 there were frequent, often violent conflicts between adherents and
    opponents of the Reformation in Erfurt. See Carl Krause *Helius Eobanus Hessus*
    (Gotha 1879; repr Nieuwkoop 1963) I 330–42.
5 Ep 1254 n6
6 Frans van der Hulst (Ep 1345 n8)
7 Cornelis Hoen (d 1524) was a lawyer in the employ of the Council of Holland at
    The Hague. The influence of Wessel Gansfort's *De sacramento eucharistiae* led

been reinstated by the court. They dragged him back by a trick into some castle, and there would have convicted him of heresy (for in such a place Baechem's arguments carry much more weight than in the lecture-room), but he was set free immediately by the chief men of Holland. What made him a heretic was his audacity in disputing with Baechem. So Cornelis[8] was reinstated, but after disgraceful treatment. And now my friend Nicolaas,[9] a man of the highest character, has at last been reinstated too. I have no doubt that the pope's intention to be fair has helped these men; but he would be more effective if he would disarm those whose character makes them universally detested by good and bad alike, especially in such an arduous business. To arm that Carmelite[10] with such authority – I ask you, was it not simply to put a sword into a madman's hand? For my part, I shall behave consistently in such a way that the outcome will prove me to have had no end in view except Christ's glory and the common good. 35

40

45

The other day, having chanced upon a certain provost,[11] a canon of St Donatian's at Bruges, who is trustworthy but was leaving very shortly, I wrote to the pope very much on the spur of the moment,[12] rather outspokenly and I daresay rashly, but at least it was heartfelt. I hardly had time to reread what I had written. I am full of hope that with his natural kindness he will not resent the confidence I placed in him without misgiving. The bearer of this does not strike me as a man who can be trusted, and so I am rather shorter, but will write at length when I find someone to whom I can safely entrust it. Farewell, my honourable friend. 50

55

Basel, 17 April 1523

* * * * *

Hoen to reject transubstantiation and to interpret the words 'This is my body' symbolically. In 1521 he included these views in a famous letter on the Eucharist that was circulated in Germany and Switzerland. Zwingli, who found his own views anticipated in Hoen's letter, published it in 1525 under the title *Epistola christiana admodum* (n p); see Allen Ep 1621:17–19. In February 1523 Hoen was arrested and prosecuted for heresy by the inquisitor Frans van der Hulst (Ep 1345 n8). He was released briefly in March, but was soon back in custody, where he remained until October (Ep 1394:10–12). Erasmus, who seems to have been an old friend of Hoen, followed these developments with interest. Allen believed that Hoen might have been the person to whom Ep 1166 was addressed.

8 Schrijver (Ep 1299 n24)
9 van Broeckhoven (Ep 1299 n23)
10 Ie, Baechem
11 Unidentified, but a friend of Erasmus; Ep 1353:269–70. See also Ep 1352:1–2.
12 Ep 1352

1359 / To Herman Lethmaet   Basel, 17 April 1523

On Herman Lethmaet, see Ep 1320. The autograph of this letter is lost, but Lethmaet's copy survives in the Librije (Town Library) at Gouda (MS 959). It was first printed in Theodor J. van Almeloveen's *Amoenitates theologico-philologicae* (Amsterdam 1694).

Greeting. What men say is not in our power; what is in our power is to pursue what we know to be right. Baechem has been silenced, on orders from the pope;[1] and I wish he would disarm the man altogether, as he is plainly mad. I rejoice at your new position. Honours and wealth will come your way. Be ready for great things; be sincere, be upright, and set Christ's 5 glory above everything. Do not go out for presents that do you no credit. Like Delphius,[2] you must often say no; but always courteously – a proper refusal is something in itself. This will bring you more profit and more of an honourable name. To accept great gifts from great men does, you will find, no harm at all. It is their good will you must aim at. 10

The archbishop[3] has done all he could for me by thinking well of my work, for I was aiming at nothing beyond his approval. Archdeacon Frederick[4] I knew in Rome too; I shall not be ungrateful for his attitude towards me. Hilarius[5] went to Besançon in August, mainly in search of wine, in which lies my hope of prolonging life. 15

* * * * *

1359
1 There is, understandably, no mention of this in Epp 1338–9, but the news had probably been relayed by Hezius (Ep 1339) or Barbier (cf Ep 1358:1–2). See also Epp 1341A:956–8, 1383:25, 1433:16–17, 1481:72–3, 1515:16, 1518:31–2.
2 Possibly a reference to the customary refusal of the Delphic oracle to give clear answers to questions, in which case one must assume that Erasmus or the copyist carelessly wrote 'Delphius' instead of 'Delphicus.' This seems more likely than a reference to the theologian Gillis van Delft or Delphus (Ep 456:98n).
3 Jean de Carondelet (Ep 1276), archbishop of Palermo (cf lines 23–4), to whom Erasmus had dedicated his edition of Hilary (Ep 1334)
4 Unidentified
5 Allen's emendation for 'the impossible reading of all the sources': *Hungariae.* Hilarius Bertholf (Ep 1257 n10) was Erasmus' servant. Bertholf's movements in August 1522, after his return from the Netherlands (cf Ep 1306:6–7), cannot be traced. But when Erasmus returned from Constance in September, his wine was waiting for him (Ep 1316); and his desire not to receive it as a gift (Epp 1342:505, 1353:288–94) suggests that he had sent someone to get it. On Erasmus' newfound devotion to Burgundy wine, see Ep 1342:504–41.

I am already weary of this sedition in Germany.[6] Have no hesitation in this business of Luther in pursuing justice, and set good men free who are oppressed by the injustice of others.[7] This is what the pope himself wishes, as you will see from a letter of his that one can trust.[8] Farewell, dear Herman, and reckon me among your real friends.　　　　　　　　　　　　20

　　　Basel, 17 April 1523
　　　Erasmus, written in haste
　　　To the accomplished theologian Herman van Gouda, in the household of the archbishop of Palermo

1360 / From Thomas Lupset　　　　　　　　Constance, 21 April [1523]

> The manuscript of this letter (=Ep 14 in Förstemann/Günther) was in the Burscher Collection at Leipzig (Ep 1254 introduction). Lupset (Ep 270:69n) was currently on his way to Italy, where he helped edit the Aldine Galen.

Botzheim's[1] devotion to you, if he never showed it anywhere else, he made clear enough at least on this occasion, for as a result of your letter of recommendation[2] he gave me such a welcome that I do not see what more kindness he could have showed me had it been his brother or his father. The moment we met he carried me off to dinner, and in all he said or did on my　5 arrival it was just as though I were an expected guest closely linked by the ties of old friendship; he was reluctant to let me stay in any hostelry except his own house. Yesterday he gave a splendid supper for me and (for my benefit) Master Fabri.[3] I know absolutely nothing I can compare with his kindness. Master Fabri has made the most thoughtful arrangements for　10 everything to do with my journey. His Holiness' nuncio[4] expects Pace's arrival here any day.[5] There is a Swede here,[6] recommended by Hilarius[7] to

* * * * *

6 See Ep 1353 n33.
7 Cf Ep 1358:32–9.
8 Not extant

　1360
1 Ep 1285
2 Not extant
3 Ep 1260 n22
4 Filonardi (Ep 1282)
5 See Ep 1342 n83. Pace was at the moment detained in Venice (LP III 2870, 3023, 3103, 3140). Filonardi had expressed his wish for Pace's support in dealing with the Swiss (ibidem 2941).
6 Unidentified
7 Bertholf (Ep 1257 n10)

Thomas my companion,[8] who for some unknown purpose does not leave us
alone. He waited at Basel for our departure, and does not mean to leave here
until we do; he complains that he is unhappy, and has no money. He looks   15
like a soldier full of self-confidence and ready for anything, and I doubt if his
company will do us much good. Farewell, most learned of teachers.

    Constance, 21 April

    Your devoted humble servant (and rightly so) Lupset

    To that most learned and admirable man, Master Erasmus of Rotter-   20
dam, my most respected teacher. In Basel

1361 / From Thomas Lupset to Johann von Botzheim   Innsbruck, 27 April [1523]

This letter was first published in Johann Fecht's *Historiae ecclesiasticae seculi XVI
supplementum* (Frankfurt and Speyer, Durlach 1684). On Lupset and Botzheim,
see Ep 1360.

Cordial greetings, my revered Botzheim, kindest of all the men I have ever
met in my life. I enjoyed your Johann's[1] company as far as Innsbruck, and
his charming manners made it easy for me to believe that you had sometime
been his master. Master Hieronymus Baldung[2] was just the same to me on
your introduction as you were when I was introduced by Erasmus. He at   5
once nominated an official courier of the city to be my guide on the journey
with no expense to myself. How deeply I am obliged to you for these kind
services you shall discover if the moment ever comes when my own efforts
or trouble or resources can be of any use to you or your friends.

    There is something I want to have passed on to Erasmus, and just now   10
I haven't a free moment, but with your devotion to Erasmus you will not
mind doing this as soon as you can. The day before yesterday his paraphrase
on John was first handed to Ferdinand,[3] with no letter or recommendation of
any kind. All the same, the prince received it most graciously, and gave it to
your friend Hieronymus[4] as a present. He promised me that he would   15

* * * * *

8 Probably Thomas Winter (d 1543), Wolsey's bastard son, who was about
  thirteen years old at this time. Winter crossed the Alps via the Brenner Pass
  and Trent and was in Padua with Lupset c 8 May 1523; see W. Gordon Zeeveld
  Foundations of Tudor Policy (Harvard University Press 1948) 51–2, and LP III 3594.

    1361
1 Apparently a servant
2 Ep 400
3 See Epp 1333, 1376:13–17.
4 Baldung; see line 4.

arrange for the book to be handsomely bound and given back to the prince.
Had I not recognized Erasmus' hand, I should not have believed that
Erasmus had sent it; it is inescapable that in this matter the messenger,
whoever he was, has made a bad blunder, through negligence at least if it is
not treachery or spite, for it has taken till now to present the book, and   20
Erasmus, if I am not mistaken, had sent it just as it was, unbound, on
purpose that the prince might be the first person to enjoy his new
production.

Please thank your Johann for taking such faithful care of me. I am
suffering from such a shortage of funds that apart from his expenses I have   25
nothing to give him.

Farewell, from Innsbruck, in bed, 27 April

Your most devoted Thomas Lupset

To the most learned Doctor Botzheim Abstemius, general benefactor of
scholarship. In Constance   30

1362 / From Juan Luis Vives   Bruges, 10 May 1523

For the source of this letter, see Ep 1256 introduction. The new paragraph at
line 85 indicates that this letter, like Ep 1281, was written in stages. Since his
last extant letter to Erasmus (Ep 1306), Vives (Ep 927) had made a fruitless trip
to England (autumn 1522) in search of employment and was now planning to
return to Spain (line 112) in answer to a call from the University of Alcalá.
However, visiting England on the way, Vives attracted the attention of
Wolsey, who appointed him to a lectureship in Greek at Oxford. For the next
five years Vives divided his time between England, visiting there six times,
and Bruges, where he married in April 1524.

FROM VIVES TO ERASMUS

On this question of accounts, to save Froben from making a mistake, the
facts are as follows. Franz[1] had given me twenty gold florins before the book
came out,[2] and near the end of January he gave me six. This sum I received

* * * * *

1362
1 Franz Birckmann, Antwerp bookseller and an untrustworthy character (Ep
  258:14n); see Ep 1388 n23.
2 If, by his reference to Froben in Basel, he meant Rhenish florins (then
  theoretically containing 2.53 g fine gold when newly struck), they would have
  been worth about £4 16s 8d gros Flemish. If they were instead Florentine florins
  (with 3.54 g fine gold), then this sum would have been worth £6 13s 4d gros (or
  £4 10s 0d sterling, or £41 10s 0d tournois). See CWE 1 316–17, 321; and Ep 1295
  n1.

myself at the time, and three copies of the book. He said he had been   5
instructed by Froben to give me thirty-two gold florins,[3] but had deducted
eight, which were due to you.[4] What he wrote to you[5] about me and on my
behalf did not move me in the least. Believe me, no one is more conscious of
my inexperience than I am myself, or less anxious to conceal it. So I am not
seriously hurt if reputation does not come my way, for I know I did not   10
deserve it. Let me forfeit Christ's favour if this is not true: I think I have
acquired greater repute than I deserve, and am constantly surprised to find
the public estimate of me unreasonably high. So I do not resent what he said,
since I am more successful in this way than I can fairly expect if I judge my
performance impartially. Even if I had the highest opinion of my own merits   15
and supposed the books I write to be very good and very learned, I am not
unaware all the same that it is the special blessing of some genius that
breathes life into works of literature, and that it is fortune which endows
things with value and with immortality; we are responsible for designs, but
not results. It is therefore the part of a wise man, once he has ordered the   20
things that are in his control with all the industry and diligence at his
command, to show himself resigned to all that comes by chance; for a good
man can be responsible for nothing else in his life except what is his own
fault.

These thoughts would console me were I truly learned and wise, and   25
yet obscure. As it is, I am actually better known than I could mostly wish,
from fear that so many people might observe and be well aware of my
deficiency in all respects. And I perceive my ignorance to be such, that I am
compelled for shame to admit it, so as to earn less blame by advertising
myself what others are sure to detect. Yet I have been an author, impelled at   30
first by youthful fire, and then because 'So many grips / That itch to write
that knows no remedy.'[6] But I shall find a remedy for mine, I hope. For as
soon as ever I have got out the book which I have lately put together for the
queen of England,[7] I shall bury myself in a long vacation and in harmless
leisure, partly because this is a shorter route to a comfortable and happy life,   35
and partly to avoid giving myself away so often, like a shrew, by my own
voice and challenging possible risks to my station in life and my reputation;

* * * * *

3 If Rhenish florins, a sum worth about £7 14s 8d gros Flemish
4 Cf Ep 1303:37.
5 Letter not extant
6 Juvenal 7.51–2
7 *De institutione foeminae christianae* (Antwerp: M. Hillen 1524), with Vives'
preface to Queen Catherine dated 5 April 1523. The long interval between the
date of the preface and that of publication suggests that Vives had initially tried
to get the book printed without Birckmann's help but had finally had to employ
his services.

last but not least because, as Atilius recommended,[8] it is better to take a
holiday than to do nothing. At that stage I shall cause no trouble for those
who measure and reckon up our reputations by the profit they themselves   40
can make. And this is so, let what Franz wrote be as true as you please; for
whether it is in fact true, time I hope will show, and Froben can enquire from
Hilarius.[9]

As for the Augustine,[10] I know he[11] has sold a number of copies, and
am aware myself of people who have bought it. How dare he utter such   45
shameless lies about London? – where, as he told me himself, he sold over
thirty copies of the Augustine in a few days. Lupset[12] at any rate said he had
not seen one copy of my Augustine on sale in England. In England too he[13]
assured me that he had sold over forty copies of my *Somnia*.[14] I suppose he
does not think my name will sell a book, because he compares it with yours   50
or Budé's.[15] Are we really to think there is no one else here whom Froben can
take into business as a partner? A poor lookout for the reputation of our
gifted authors, if it is likely to rest solely on the good will of rascals like this!
Personally, I am resigning from all thought of reputation and all literary
work immediately, if this is the only way. I hate to think of the state of   55
literature, if a book cannot come out unless it commends itself to the greed of
some illiterate, with the result that men like Kempo[16] and Brecht[17] and
Torrentius[18] are on every shelf, and hardly anyone owns a Cicero. Immortal
God has never, you will find, treated learning so scurvily that it cannot raise

* * * * *

8 Pliny *Epistles* 1.9
9 Bertholf (Ep 1257 n10)
10 See Ep 1309.
11 Birckmann (n1 above)
12 Ep 1360
13 Birckmann
14 Ep 1108 n28
15 Ep 403
16 Kempo of Texel (documented 1505–22) studied at Paris, taught school in
   Zwolle and Alkmaar, and then (1522) became rector of the Latin school at
   Zwolle. In 1505 he published a commentary on the second part of the *Doctrinale
   puerorum* of Alexander de Villa Dei (Cologne: H. Quentel). This complemented
   the commentary on the first part of the *Doctrinale* written by Kempo's friend
   and colleague Hermannus Torrentinus (see n18 below). Kempo also wrote and
   published numerous poems.
17 Johannes Custos of Brecht (Ep 573:17n), now head of his own Latin school in
   Brecht, was the author of an *Etymologia* (Antwerp: M. Hillen 1515) and a
   Syntaxis (also published by Hillen, probably in the same year). Both volumes
   were reprinted throughout the sixteenth century.
18 Hermannus Torrentinus was the name taken by Herman van Beek (or van der
   Beeke), a native of Zwolle (d c 1520). A member of the Brethren of the Common
   Life, he taught school at Groningen and later at Zwolle. His works included the

its head unless X[19] makes his profit on it. He is, I believe, more severe on me   60
after what happened in Antwerp: when he had given me the slip by lying in
hiding for several days because of some money, I know not what, that was
still due on the account, I told his servants that I was now tired of submitting
to the cheating and trickery with which he was barefacedly leading me such
a dance. Farewell reputation, if it means the sort of slavery that does not let   65
one utter a single word without constraint, while those who do not pursue
reputation say whatever they please!

I could wish you had said in your letter whether Froben means to print
those *Opuscula*;[20] if not, let me know in the first letter you write, and I will
send them elsewhere. For I am not so unreasonably pleased with myself that   70
I should be happy for anything of mine to appear from his press that he will
lose money on. His kindness to me does not deserve that. So let him not
think I shall be annoyed with him if he has not published my work; I would
rather he did whatever he thinks best in his own interests.

But I write at much too great length about trifles, and to you too! As for   75
the title, I am afraid that my book[21] falls somewhat short of my intentions.
You will see I have committed hundreds of full-grown mistakes in the
writing, such as even Baechem[22] will find laughable; I only hope his Majesty
makes none in the gift department;[23] I am not so piteously afraid of the
schoolmasters. In Rome I have no doubt that you will find general confusion   80
and tumult,[24] especially since the fall of Rhodes.[25] Fear of the Turks is
universal; it is thought they will turn their offensive against Sicily and Italy.
This is good news about Budé's appointment,[26] but not as good as the news
of his health is bad; I wrote to him a few days ago.[27]

Since I wrote this, my friends have written to tell me that my *Opuscula*   85
have not been printed by Froben, and that X says you are responsible for

* * * * *

Elucidarius poeticus (Deventer: R. Pafraet 1498) and a commentary on book one
of the *Doctrinale* of Alexander de Villa Dei (third ed, Zwolle: A. Kempen 1504);
cf n16 above.

19 Birckmann (n1 above); cf Ep 1306:42.
20 No Froben edition of the *Opuscula varia* (Ep 927 introduction) is known.
21 See n7 above.
22 Ep 1254 n6
23 Henry VIII, from whom Vives presumably expected a gift in return for the
dedication to Queen Catharine; see n7 above.
24 On Erasmus' determination to leave Germany, see Ep 1353 n33.
25 The Turks attacked Rhodes in June 1522; it fell to them on 28 December (LP III
2324, 2841). Rumours of this reached Rome on 3 January 1523 and Antwerp on
15 February (ibidem 2758, 2833). In Rome it was felt that Italy and even Rome
itself were no longer safe (ibidem 2771, 2839).
26 See Ep 1328 nn1 and 7.
27 Letter not extant

Froben's rejection of the book, and will be writing to me about it by a servant whom you will be sending here in a few days' time. And though it does not make much difference to you what I myself think about this, yet I should like you to know, if you can ever believe what I say, that I cannot credit this of you, even had it been stated by someone of well-tried veracity, much less when it comes from X. I added it only to show that X's character still remains unchanged. If I were to say that I am not somewhat hurt, I should not be speaking the truth; but less hurt, maybe, than other men are by such things. Your letter[28] gave me some hope, for you wrote that Froben would more gladly print my work, if X would come in as a partner, as though you were suggesting that he did mean to print it. I now perceive that I am not important enough, nor is what I write, for there to be any room in all the great variety of books for so small a book, unless it sells off the moment the seller opens his mouth; although Froben's printing-house would have made it more saleable, as he did my *Somnium*,[29] and all this in Germany, a wide market full of interested people where surely everything sells. Beatus[30] arranged for some of my short pieces to be printed there,[31] of which here I have never even seen a copy. I see now that I had got it wrong. I knew I did not sit in the orchestra, but I supposed that by now I had risen to the next fourteen rows, or wished I might have, and as it is, I perceive that I am among the plebeians in the rows at the very back.[32] How true it is that property divides the classes in this city as in others! Ah well, so all those fine phrases, 'a distinguished scholar and a man of universal learning,' have come down to this! But this too is Fortune's business; and those who have the least to do with her are alone truly happy.

I have been quite unable to get out of a journey to Spain, on which I expect to set out tomorrow or the next day; and may it be Christ's will that all goes well. I shall go to England first, and both there and in my native country I will do anything for you that a friend can. I pray that Christ may long, long preserve you in health and wealth. Wherever I am, I will let you know how I am getting on. Farewell, my dear teacher, and always be mindful of our friendship, and commend me to Christ, whom you serve with such energy. Give my greetings to Beatus and to Froben.

Bruges, 10 May 1523

* * * * *

28 Not extant
29 See n14 above.
30 Rhenanus (Ep 327)
31 In June 1520 Lazarus Schürer of Sélestat published a selection of pieces from Martens' edition (Ep 927 introduction) of Vives' *Opuscula varia*. These included the *Adversus pseudodialecticos* (cf Ep 1106 n5) and the *Pompeius fugiens*.
32 In the Roman theatre the senators sat in the orchestra, the knights in the next fourteen rows, and the plebs behind.

1363 / To Ennio Filonardi   Basel, 25 May 1523

On Filonardi, papal nuncio to Switzerland, see Ep 1282. This letter and Ep 1364
survive in copies in a sixteenth-century secretarial hand in the Vatican
Archives (Vat 6559, f 79). They were first published by J.A.F. Orbaan in his
Bescheiden in Italië omtrent Nederlandsche kunstenaars en geleerden (Kingdom of the
Netherlands, Departement van Binnenlandsche Zaken: Rijks geschiedkun-
dige publicatiën, 1911) 56–7.

Greeting, right reverend prelate. I am delighted for my own sake that you
have been restored to us,[1] and if this is in your interests equally, for your
sake too. But I pray that there may be good grounds for my delight. The
bearer of this letter[2] wishes to be released from the company of unworthy
monks, of whom there is everywhere a plentiful supply, and to be enrolled   5
in the society of worthy men. He has been described to me as deserving of
your support, which is given to worthy men everywhere. If you find he
answers that description, please treat him kindly as a fellow creature. Best
wishes to your lordship, as whose devoted servant I shall always regard
myself.   10
     Basel, the morrow of Pentecost 1523
     Erasmus, your lordship's obedient servant
     To the right reverend father in Christ Ennio, lord bishop of Veroli,
apostolic nuncio. In Constance

1364 / To Ennio Filonardi   Basel, 25 May 1523

On the source of this letter, see Ep 1363 introduction.

Right reverend prelate. With your usual kindness you will forgive me for
interrupting you with my trifling letters. I have today recommended a man
to you who is well spoken of by others,[1] I hope not without good reason; and
the German temperament is such that, when they desire something very
much, they will not take no for an answer, considering not what the man is   5

* * * * *

1363
1 Filonardi had gone to Rome in November 1522 to pay homage to Adrian vi and
  had been sent back to Constance in April 1523; see Wirz 58–9.
2 Possibly the Antonius of Ep 1388:20. Cf Ep 1364:2–4. Filonardi was unable to
  do anything for him; Ep 1392:17–18.

1364
1 See Ep 1363:3–8.

able to perform from whom they insist on an introduction, but what they want themselves. But the young man who brings you this, Konrad Heresbach,[2] I gladly commend to your lordship of my own free will; what he asks for,[3] you will learn from him. In Freiburg he teaches Greek at a respectable salary. He has a most gifted mind, rare learning, great   10
judgment, and a wonderfully fertile and fluent style of writing spoiled by no artificiality; he is also of such high character that one could not hope to find anything more congenial and modest and straightforward. Either my forecast is quite wrong or one day he will be one of our great men and famous men. I suppose that what he will ask you for is nothing of great   15
importance, and I could wish that he may find in you the sort of person I believe and maintain you to be. I should be glad to have an opportunity of making clear that I am one of those whose wish is to oblige your lordship in any way possible.

Some sort of rumour is going the rounds in Germany to the effect that I   20
am sharpening my pen to attack Luther; which, to be sure, I am not doing, nor do I see that any result would come of it if I did, except to make the disorder more severe. And already certain men are making such angry noises that I have decided to bid a final farewell to Germany;[4] though that is a decision I had taken long ago. If I make for Italy, I shall take advantage of   25
your kindness for some days where you are now,[5] which illness did not permit me to do when I was lately in Constance.[6] I see no end to our present troubles unless the princes make it clear that in the near future they will pursue justice and do away with the abuses of which the world rightly complains. On this topic I have written something to the supreme pontiff,[7]   30
and the imperial edict recently published seems to hold out hopes of the same kind.[8] May the Lord Jesus preserve your lordship in health and wealth.

From Basel, the morrow of Pentecost 1523

* * * * *

2 Ep 1316
3 Perhaps, as Allen suggests, a degree or some title of honour. As *legatus de latere*, Filonardi had many such in his gift: doctorates and licences in both laws, master's degrees in theology and arts, and titles of poet laureate, papal notary, golden knight, etc. See Wirz 29–30.
4 See Ep 1353 n33.
5 Ie, in Constance (Ep 1363 n1)
6 In September 1522; see Ep 1316 introduction.
7 Ep 1352
8 The imperial mandate of 6 March 1523 (RTA III 447–52) based on the reply (5 February) of the Estates at the Diet of Nürnberg (ibidem 435–43) to the breve of Pope Adrian VI (ibidem 399–404; cf Ep 1344 n10). The mandate provided that,

1365 / To Albert of Brandenburg Basel, 1 June 1523

This is the preface for a new edition of the *Ratio verae theologiae*, the first separate edition of which had also been dedicated to Archbishop Albert; see Ep 745. In the 1524 edition of the *Catalogus lucubrationum*, Erasmus specifies as the final text of this work 'the edition of 1523 published by Michaël Hillen' (Ep 1341A:1579–80), but no such edition has even been identified with certainty. On the other hand, the *Bibliotheca Erasmiana: Bibliographie des oeuvres d'Erasme* IX (Ghent 1914) 83–4 lists an edition containing no date or place of publication but described on the title-page as having been revised and enlarged 'for the last time' (*postremum*) by the author himself and containing this letter as 'a new and elegant preface.' The final page was filled out by the inclusion of Ep 1346. Allen conjectured that this undated edition had been printed for Hillen by one of the Basel printers, pointing out that its type closely resembled that being used by Froben at the time and arguing that the insertion of Ep 1346 would have been easy only if the book were being printed within reach of Erasmus. With this justification, Allen made the undated edition in question the archetype for this letter and for Ep 1346. There was no other authorized version of the *Ratio* in Erasmus' lifetime.

TO THE MOST REVEREND FATHER IN CHRIST ALBERT,
CARDINAL PRIEST OF SAINT CHRYSOGONUS, ARCHBISHOP OF
MAINZ AND MAGDEBURG, PRINCE ELECTOR, PRIMATE, ETC,
ADMINISTRATOR OF HALBERSTADT, MARGRAVE OF BRANDENBURG,
FROM ERASMUS OF ROTTERDAM, GREETING 5
The apostle Paul does not disapprove of wedlock, but he threatens that those who involve themselves in matrimony will have tribulation according

* * * * *

pending the outcome of a council, which was to convene in Germany within a year, Luther and his followers were to write or publish nothing new; that all works were to be approved for publication by censorship commissions, which were to make special efforts to stem the tide of 'abusive writings'; and that preaching should be closely monitored to insure, first, that nothing were preached save 'the gospel according to the interpretation of the writings received and approved by the church' and, second, that preachers would avoid anything that might cause 'agitation, disobedience, disunity, or tumult in the Empire' or lead Christians into error. The promised council did not materialize, and the territorial rulers, upon whom the enforcement of the decree depended, interpreted the ambiguous language of the decree as they saw fit. No generally effective control of preaching or publishing was established. Luther and his followers were not silenced, and the flow of theological billingsgate continued unabated on both sides.

to the flesh,[1] alluding no doubt to the anxieties which parents are obliged to undertake in the birth, nurture, and education of children and in placing them and promoting them in the world. And this, it seems to me, applies no less to those of us who, though physically barren, yet give birth from time to time to something in the way of books instead of children – except that our lot might seem not a little harder than theirs. For St Paul threatens them with nothing worse than tribulation of the flesh, while we are pursued by a twofold tribulation, of flesh and spirit. For we do not write our books without considerable expenditure both in resources and in health; though what a small part of our expense this is, when weighed against the cares of the mind! In fact, the lot of writers deserves more pity than the lot of parents, not only because they carry a double burden, but because in each field our troubles weigh heavier.

How much easier it is for a woman to conceive her baby than for us to conceive a suitable subject! How much less danger in her birth-pangs than in our publication! If her offspring is ill-starred, deformed, or monstrous in some way, public opinion imputes the fault not to the mother but to the stars or to some physical defect or to chance or to God. In the offspring of our intellects, if any fault is detected, there is no excuse; it is ascribed solely to us who are the parents, and for our offspring's sake we are placed in peril of our lives. Besides which, in respect of the same child a mother cannot suffer the pains of childbirth more than once, while we are obliged to produce the same offspring so many times over. In my case indeed it happens for the most part – I make no statement about other people – as it does to pregnant women, who in their eagerness to become mothers too quickly bring on an abortion, and give birth to an offspring that is immature; or rather, what happens to some living creatures, who bring forth shapeless lumps, and are obliged therefore to mould their production by prolonged licking into shape, – the class to which bears belong. This fault I see that I share with some other men, but at the same time recognize most clearly that it is my own fault. I am like that; I cannot endure the tedium of gestation. The result is that, in my eagerness to be set free more quickly from my labours, I have to stomach the same labour more than once.

Add to all this that they who produce the children of the body produce a daughter for one bridegroom only; and if she has secured one who is satisfied with her, it does not matter how well she satisfies everyone else. But we authors produce for the multitude, which is a beast with many

* * * * *

1365
1 1 Cor 7:28

heads, whose eyes are satisfied by very different things; so that it is   45
impossible to give universal satisfaction, even if you produce something
that is by nature very beautiful. This is the suitor, so hard to please, whose
slaves we are. And in our day, to be sure, this is far harder than it ever was;
for nowadays men's tastes differ so widely that what appeals to one party
must of necessity be violently disliked by the other. And it often happens   50
that a book is unpopular or popular for no other reason than the
unpopularity or otherwise of the author.

And we suffer from a further disadvantage. A girl's suitors must as a
rule seek to win the approval of her parents; but we must curry favour with
the multitude, to whose convenience our whole way of life is enslaved.   55
From this point of view we are somewhat more unfortunate than actors – for
I think I have said enough about women in childbed – who do indeed dance
for hire, but none of them ever has to face a house so difficult to please or so
unjust that the player is pelted with stones if his play goes too badly. The
worst disaster is to be driven from the stage with hisses and catcalls. But we   60
act our play to the end in peril of our lives, and even at our own expense.

Your Highness, I am sure, will for some time have been saying to
yourself 'Hey! That will do for metaphors. Be brief and to the point!' And so I
will. It is now some years since I published this pamphlet, *De ratione
theologiae*, still in the rough, so that it was more a collection of notes than a   65
book.[2] Since however even thus unadorned it found suitors to whom it gave
satisfaction, I added a certain amount of ornament, and with the attraction
of your name as a sort of dowry put the same daughter once again on the
market.[3] When this had happened two or three times and, thanks if I am not
mistaken to your presiding genius, had gone rather well, at length in this   70
year 1523 I recalled the thing into my own control, and have spent so much
work on it that it can now almost be reckoned as a book. Though the fact that
it is now popular reading and thumbed by everyone with an interest in the
subject I consider to be due to your genius entirely. If anyone does not like it,
I attribute this to the destiny of our generation, in which the opposites in any   75
question generate such heat that the most brainless and even impious
publication can rely on finding someone to support it, thumbs up, and on
the other hand the most happy and well-judged performance can find no
remedy against the venomous tooth of false accusers. It is one of my
misfortunes that my old age has coincided with this epoch. We must   80

* * * * *

2 In the *Novum instrumentum* of 1516, f bbb, with the title *Methodus*. Cf Ep 1372
n1.
3 In the first separate edition, published by Dirk Martens in November 1518; see
Ep 745 introduction.

beseech our Lord Jesus that by his spirit he, who alone has the power, may turn the hearts of Christian people to a love of peace and concord. For as long as we are led by our own spirit into disorder, the more we strive to free ourselves, the deeper we shall become involved.

How much others approve of this generation, I do not know; I at least 85 find it most unattractive. The heat of faction is such that a true judgment is impossible. The world is full of quarrelling and strife. The former liberties and delights of scholarship have been quite taken away; indeed, good authors are neglected, and nothing finds readers except what smacks of subversion.[4] What a disaster this means all the time for Christian concord! 90 How hard it is to find anywhere that old-fashioned genuine and straightforward friendship that nothing sour can spoil! Fellow conspirators you may find, but no friends anywhere. Yet what becomes of our religion if you do away with peace? I suppose things will look just as they would if you took the sun out of the sky. I would rather be a gardener, enjoying the tranquillity 95 of a Christian and rejoicing in the simplicity of the gospel spirit, than the greatest of theologians three or four times over who must be involved in this kind of strife. As far as I am concerned at any rate, I shall make it my business with all my might to strip this yeasty poison out of the inmost fibres of my mind, to restore myself to the simplicity and tranquillity of the spirit of the 100 gospel, and to compose myself into a state of mind in which I can appear with confidence before the judgment-seat of Jesus Christ, before which I may perhaps be summoned tomorrow or the day after. Though all men must arrive in that same place, nor can this life be long for any man, even were it certain. And as it is in fact uncertain, all ought so to live as though in 105 this same night our souls were to be required of us.[5]

I would however gladly encourage all men to pursue for themselves by a serious course of study the ends which I pursue. We should find it a stage of some sort on the road to restoring peace if everyone, seriously and as though in the presence of God, were to purge his mind of the poison of 110 hatred, jealousy, and strife. The single eye looks at nothing save the glory of Christ.[6] Let those who preach before popular congregations treat of the gospel text in purity and sincerity, currying favour with no man but at the same time refraining as far as they can from all that makes for subversion rather than salvation. Let there be no condemnation of one's neighbour or 115 even of an unfair opponent. Let every man express himself about the writings of others as he would wish them to speak of his own. Apart from

* * * * *

4 Cf Ep 1359:16.
5 An allusion to Luke 12:20
6 See Matt 6:22, Luke 11:34.

that, let the definition of what all men must of necessity be compelled to believe be reduced to the least possible compass, which it will be lawful to do without prejudice to the sincerity of our Christian profession.[7] Let all else either be outlawed as a subject of inquiry or be left to the judgment of the individual. This will not only ensure that fewer disputes arise in future; it will also make it easier to spread the Christian religion through all the nations of the world. And then let those abuses be corrected of which the world has rightly complained for so long. For if that unjust judge in St Luke's Gospel did not altogether despise the appeal of the downtrodden widow,[8] how much less ought we to ignore the complaints of those for whom our Lord Jesus Christ shed his own blood! For it was not only the great ones of the earth for whom he died, and he takes special care of the little and the lowly. These are of all men his first choice, and it was through them that the kingdom of the gospel took its rise and grew.

All this will come to pass even without disorder if the monarchs and princes in whom rests authority, their human passions for the time set aside, will serve wholeheartedly the public good and the glory of Jesus Christ, the leader of them all, and if those men can be removed from any part in this business whom the world has already endured for far too long – those who pursue their own glory, their own appetites, their own worldly power and who think that their own kingdom cannot stand if the common people are allowed to have any mind or any brains. Let us therefore with one voice implore Almighty Jesus in our prayers to put this mind into the leaders of both church and state; among whom you not only occupy a leading place but will be able to make a very great contribution in restoring tranquillity to the church. That you will do this with energy, and are doing it even now, I have no doubt. Farewell.

Basel, 1 June 1523

1366 / From Polidoro Virgilio   London, 3 June 1523

On Polidoro Virgilio, see Ep 1175. This letter was first published by S.A. Gabbema in his *Epistolarum ab illustribus et claris viris scriptarum centuriae tres* (Harlingen 1663). Erasmus presumably received it with Ep 1367. It appears that he had commissioned Algoet (line 7) to inquire through Zacharius Deiotarus (line 1) whether Polidoro had seen Ep 1175, which by now had been in print for over a year.

* * * * *

7 Cf Ep 858:148–58.
8 Luke 18:2–6

My dear Erasmus, greeting. A couple of days ago our friend Zacharias[1] brought me greetings from you; he told me you had done much for the reputation of my books,[2] and ended by asking whether I had known about this. I replied that I had no doubt of your friendly feelings towards me, and the facts were that your friendship and the warmth of your feelings towards   5 myself were exactly the same as mine towards you. After that, he brought your servant[3] to see me yesterday, and from him I learned in detail how you were, which gave me the greatest pleasure; for your health and wealth are of extreme importance to the republic of letters, since it is clear that you were designed by nature to promote its interests above all other men.   10

For the way your kindness to me continues unbroken I am most grateful; in this way you respond to my own feelings, and actively maintain the friendship which has existed between us for so long. I do the same myself, and am very far from attempting to belittle your very great reputation, as is shown by my letter to our friend Cuthbert,[4] bishop of   15 London, to whom I have lately dedicated two centuries of sacred adages. I also wrote you a letter[5] after the last occasion of your leaving us,[6] and gave it to our mutual friend More; but having had no reply, I though it best thereafter to remain silent until chance should bring us together again somewhere, which will happen one day, sooner or later. In the mean time, if   20

* * * * *

1366
1 Deiotarus (Ep 1205 n1)
2 Cf Epp 1175:7–9, 124–30, 1210:1–11.
3 Lieven Algoet (Ep 1373 n1)
4 Cuthbert Tunstall (Ep 207:25n), bishop of London since 9 October 1522. The letter mentioned was probably the preface to a supplement to Polidoro's *Adagia sacra*, an edition of 431 adages already having been published by Froben in July 1519. It appears that neither the supplement, containing an additional two hundred adages, nor the prefatory letter was ever printed, since they are not in the second Froben edition of 1525. Presumably they were sent to Tunstall in manuscript. Erasmus evidently saw them in manuscript as well; Ep 1494:32. The praise of Erasmus in the lost letter was perhaps essentially the same as that found in the *Apologia* appended to the above-mentioned Froben volume of 1525 (folio b3). After praising the scholars who were teaching in Italy and England, Polidoro adds: 'And no man, by Hercules, has performed that office for his countrymen more magnificently than our Des. Erasmus of Rotterdam, who, after some of the arts had been enriched by his eminent genius, thought nothing preferable to making his Germany, formerly less skilled in literature, by far the most accomplished: in which undertaking he indeed achieved so much that nowhere today does the genius of the human race flourish with greater learning.'
5 Not extant
6 In April 1517; see Ep 577.

I can be of any use to you, your friend Polidoro is at your service, and would be glad to contribute pecuniary help as well; when you put this to the test some time in the future, you will not be disappointed, as your servant can explain to you.

Farewell, from London, 3 June 1523.   25

Please give my greetings to Johannes Oecolampadius,[7] if he is living in your part of the world, and to our friend Beatus Rhenanus.[8]

Sincerely yours, Polidoro Virgilio

To the reverend Master Erasmus, his very dear friend. In Basel

1367 / From Cuthbert Tunstall   London, 5 June 1523

Cuthbert Tunstall (Ep 207:25n) had been made bishop of London in October 1522. This letter was first published in the *Opus epistolarum*. Erasmus' reply is Ep 1369.

CUTHBERT TUNSTALL, SERVANT OF THE CHURCH IN LONDON,
TO ERASMUS OF ROTTERDAM, GREETING

I cannot tell you with what joy I read your letters,[1] especially those written to the king and to the legate,[2] in which you clear yourself of the suspicions regarding Luther's published reply to the king,[3] and the suggestion that you   5
had some share in it, which several people told you had arisen here.[4] I do not mean that this suspicion had taken such deep root in men's minds that it needed a letter from you to dislodge it; for the whole book is so full of calumnies and breathes so much of Luther's peculiar poison from every page that one only has to read the book itself, and it betrays the workshop   10
from which it comes. But I was absolutely delighted, because it was clear to me from the letters that you disagree with Luther's party and that, having been invited by the pope to undertake the duty of confronting Luther,[5] you

* * * * *

7 Oecolampadius had moved to Basel in November 1522 (Epp 1258 n4 and 1308 n7), but there were rumours that he either had moved on or intended to do so; see Ep 1401 n9.
8 Rhenanus (Ep 327)

1367
1 Not extant. They were probably written at about the end of April (see n15 below) and delivered by Lieven Algoet (Ep 1373:1). See Ep 1383 n17 for references to answers that Erasmus received.
2 Wolsey
3 See Ep 1308 n3.
4 Cf Ep 1383:28–31. See Epp 1218–19 for similar suspicions two years earlier.
5 See Epp 1324, 1338.

will agree to do so almost at any moment now. This is what all your friends
so much look forward to and want to see, a confrontation after all this time   15
between you and that Protean,[6] or it would be truer to say, Athean monster.[7]

'In any case,' you say, 'I shall be very unpopular with Luther and his
Lutherians.' Not more unpopular than God himself, whom Luther makes
the only begetter of all wickedness by abolishing the freedom of the human
will and roundly maintaining that everything happens according to fixed   20
laws of necessity,[8] so that it is not open to any man to act rightly even if he
would. Abuse heaped on you in the cause of Christ will bring you far more
credit, you may be sure, than the most elaborate panegyrics from every side;
so you have nothing to be frightened of on that score. Personally, I think this
is above all your duty to your country;[9] for, unless counter-measures are   25
taken as soon as possible, it is in grave danger of being infected by this
contagious pestilence, which will spread more widely if no one comes
forward to oppose it.

Never, down to this day, was there a man with the equipment in
theology who saw the rise of a pernicious heresy during his lifetime and   30
failed to attack it. To what, I ask you, does your favourite Jerome owe more
of his reputation than to his vigorous refutation of the heresies of his time?
The sacred books of Moses and the prophets, revised against their genuine
Hebrew original, and all those many commentaries to which he devoted
such immense labour – it is not these that have made him famous, so much   35
as the way he descended into the arena and fought with Helvidius,
Jovinianus, the Luciferians, Vigilantius, or the Pelagians. Where does the
learning of Origen seem greater or more brilliant than in his attack on
Celsus? Where is Basil a greater scholar than when attacking Eunomius? Or
Cyprian: think of the reputation earned by the vigour of his attacks on   40
Demetrianus, Novatianus, and Novatus! Or what Hilary won from his
conflict with Constantius! And what Augustine wrote against Pelagius,
against Julianus, against the Arians, against the Manichaeans, against
Gaudentius, against Petilianus, against Faustus, against Fulgentius gives
that great man's saintly yet passionate nature such expression that I doubt   45

* * * * *

6 Proteus, the old man of the sea who guarded Poseidon's flocks of seals, could
   foretell the future but would change his shape repeatedly to escape those who
   wanted to force him to do so. Here he is the image of a fickle and cunning man,
   ie, someone who changes his shape to avoid telling the truth.
7 'Atheus' is just the word *atheus* (atheist) turned into a proper name to match
   'Proteus.'
8 See Ep 1419 introduction.
9 Germany; cf Ep 1366 n4.

whether even his burning love for the church of God and equally his
immense theological learning are more clearly displayed in any of his other
works. In a word, was there ever a scholar of any distinction in the church
who kept silence after the rise of some new heresy? Here if anywhere, in the
defeat of heresy, is true Christian warfare. Can we think it a noble enterprise   50
to pursue barbarians who invade our borders and carry off some negligible
spoils, while we allow heretics to fight against us for our religion and our
altars and remain unmoved? Surely a victory in this field is far more glorious
than in the other. If we conquer heretics, an eternal triumph awaits us in the
heavens; if we drive off the invader, we get a very brief and trifling share of   55
glory in this life.

   And what should rouse you more than anything is the thought that
when Luther's party falsely reckon you among their number, they are
preparing to deprive you of the glory you have won by all the labours you
have undertaken for the benefit of the church. Besides which, those who are   60
jealous of you, if such there are, and nibble away at your reputation, having
no better pretext on which to do you harm, maintain that you are a member
of that faction. Then what encouragement it must give you that Adrian,
supreme pontiff and your fellow countryman, and one who has such a
concern for the Lord's flock, should invite you so warmly to undertake this   65
task! – an office for which both he and everyone else think you supremely
fitted, and for which you ought to put forward your own name even without
waiting to be asked; for you must see how heresies are sprouting
everywhere which, once they are full-grown, will bring down the whole
church. It is not merely that two or three pernicious novelties are being   70
forced upon us: a vast swarm of Wycliffite heresies[10] has acquired new
weapons – vulgar abuse, false accusations, innuendoes, and tongues
dipped in poison, so that one might well think that the poison of asps is
under their lips and now gushes forth. These are the arms with which, in
default of any other way, they prepare to take the church by storm. The   75

* * * * *

10 The fourteenth-century English reformer John Wycliffe (c 1330–84) and his
   followers, who came to be called Lollards, held views that in many instances
   anticipated (but did not influence) those of the sixteenth-century reformers.
   They held that Scripture is the sole authority for faith and practice and that
   simple lay Christians are able to comprehend the true meaning of Scripture,
   which they should read and have taught to them in English. On this basis the
   Lollards protested against many established doctrines, institutions, and
   practices as unscriptural. Among these were: images in churches, pilgrimages
   to shrines, invocation of the saints, priestly mediation, the authority of popes
   and bishops to go beyond the letter of the Bible, transubstantiation, clerical
   celibacy, and most of the traditional sacraments.

institutions founded by the apostles, which have been maintained in the Catholic church without a break since Christ's incarnation, are rejected by them one and all, the traditions of the holy Fathers, the liturgy of the church, all that is sacred; and what they propose to set up in their place they are not yet agreed on. All Christians, men and women alike, are equally priests, so 80 they maintain, with an idiot philosophy that recalls the Stoics,[11] and for that matter equally kings too; for such is the outcome of that famous liberty of Christians, which they assert is subject to no human laws. What else can they produce by this but anarchy? – although the princes of Germany do not yet fully see this. Such an attempt was made once before, in this kingdom, 85 by the Wycliffites, who collected an army of their partisans and were defeated with some difficulty by the royal forces in a pitched battle and put to flight, as our historians record.[12] Luther has had the effrontery to publish a book on the abolition of the mass,[13] which he has never understood. What more remains, unless he has determined to write one on the abolition of 90 Christ himself? – for that might seem to be the goal towards which his frenzy is shaping; for we hear that the Blessed Virgin has already been sent packing by his followers. Must we endure such godless wickedness any longer?

I adjure you by all the toils that Christ endured in his mortal body, by the blood which he shed in death to redeem the world, and by the glory 95 which you look for in the heavens when your course in this life is run: I beg and beseech you, dear Erasmus, or rather it is the church that begs and beseeches you, to grapple after all this time with the hydra-headed monster.

* * * * *

11 In *Freedom of a Christian* (1520) Luther taught that all Christians are priests and kings because by faith they share in Christ's priesthood and kingship. This reminded Tunstall of the Stoic doctrine that 'the wise are the only priests' and that 'the wise ... are also kings.' See Diogenes Laertius 7.119 and 122.

12 The reference is to Oldcastle's rebellion of January 1414. Sir John Oldcastle (c 1378?–1417) was a knight of Herefordshire who in September 1413 was accused of heresy before Convocation, where he stubbornly maintained Lollard views. Given forty days to recant (at the request of his old friend, King Henry v), he escaped from the Tower of London and placed himself at the head of an incipient Lollard rebellion. The extent and aims of the uprising are not clear. It collapsed almost before it began and the 'pitched battle' in which it was put down was more like a minor skirmish. But orthodox contemporaries were thoroughly frightened. The indictment of captured conspirators charged them with plotting 1/ to kill the king and his brothers as well as prelates and other magnates of the realm; 2/ to force the religious to take up secular occupations; 3/ to despoil and destroy all cathedrals, churches, and monasteries; and 4/ to elevate Oldcastle to the position of regent. Oldcastle himself remained in hiding until 1417, when he was captured and executed. See the *Dictionary of National Biography* 42 86–93.

13 *De abroganda missa privata* of January 1522

Courage is all, and the world is confident that you will win. Think of the guilt
that can not unfairly be heaped upon you if you do not fly at the first moment   100
to the assistance of your native country in peril and the church in danger of
collapse. No less is the immortal glory in store for you, if the religion of your
country is kept safe by you and the church supported by your scholarly
exertions. Last but not least, those very labours which you have expended
on the beautification of sacred literature ought to be a great inspiration; for   105
you see the texts which you have tried to purify with so much effort polluted
with foul heresies by these men, who would like to be credited with some
purity of style themselves; the result of which is to make most men hate the
thought of correctness in the Scriptures. Is there any field, I ask you, in
which you can more profitably expend a spirit which already begins to fail   110
through advancing years, than to draw the sword of the Spirit and drive
back into his lair that Cerberus[14] whose hideous yelping attacks every order
in the church? And the general confidence that you will do this has been
increased by the book which you yourself have lately published,[15] which has
aroused universal expectation.   115

    Farewell. From London, 5 June 1523

1368 / From Wolfgang Faber Capito   Strasbourg, 18 June 1523

> This letter, which survives in a contemporary copy in the Öffentliche
> Bibliothek of the University of Basel (MS Ki.Ar.25a.100), was first published in
> Hess II 555.
>
>   Capito (Ep 459) had been with Archbishop Albert of Mainz at the Diet of
> Nürnberg in the winter of 1522–3. After returning to Mainz in February, he left
> the service of the archbishop and settled in Strasbourg, where he had already
> acquired a tenuous hold on the provostship of the collegiate church of St
> Thomas (see lines 20–1). Strasbourg was on the eve of the series of crises that
> would result in the city's adherence to the Reformation. The process of
> Capito's own gradual conversion to the evangelical faith (see Ep 1308 n4)
> would be completed in the interval between this letter and Ep 1374 (see the
> introduction to that letter).
>
>   * * * * *

14 Cerberus was the dog that guarded the entrances to Hades. He was
   multi-headed, venomous, and had a voice of bronze.
15 The *Catalogus lucubrationum* (Ep 1341A), published in April 1523 together with
   Ep 1342. The *Catalogus* mentions projected dialogues about Luther (Ep
   1341A:1338–1416). In Ep 1342 Erasmus makes plain his disagreement with
   Luther on many points and especially deprecates his attack on Henry VIII (lines
   870–90). Erasmus very likely sent a copy of this volume to England with the
   letters mentioned in lines 1 and 2 of this letter.

Greeting. If I have not written hitherto, the reason is that I respect you too much and am conscious of my own limitations. Tossed to and fro as I have been in endless business, endless tricks and stratagems, I have lost more than half of my energy, of which in any case the surplus runs very thin. And now fresh trouble appears again. Luther's party are hawking me around in libellous cartoons and pamphlets.[1] The pope's people on the other hand, having either bribed their witnesses or at any rate secured them by flattery, present me in Rome as, of all things, a passionate supporter of Luther.[2] And there are people ready to listen gladly to calumnies like this, although I have never written a line on the subject or even given helpful advice to the cause of those who are really keen on revolution; just as in the same way I have never frequented the society of those who mix up everything sacred and profane for their own private profit. I thought I had done well enough and to spare by keeping out of both camps, since both are rent by feuds which are worse than deadly.

My master the cardinal has sent three times to summon me; but feeling myself the object of these attacks I have asked at this juncture for leave, and asked in such terms that he cannot honestly or conveniently refuse it. Besides which they say that Adrian has deprived me, by the issue of letters executory directed to me, of the provostship which I defended with so much unpleasantness while Leo was alive.[3] But they have not yet been served on me; nor am I willing to believe this of such a great pope, who has started promoting penniless lovers of the humanities, except that I very much fear that slanderous accusations have their place even in Rome. I know you must wonder what my plans are, if when deprived of my provostship I deprive myself at the same time of access to a court like this, as though I were passionately determined to choose the path of poverty, since I haven't a farthing left. But I have made up my mind: I am no longer prepared to try this very unreliable position at court. I would really rather starve than change the expression on my face so often. Please commend me to the pope when you have an opportunity.

* * * * *

1368
1 See Ep 1374:106–10.
2 Encouraged, no doubt by Capito's rivals for the provostship; see following note.
3 For Capito's long and difficult campaign to secure the provostship, first from Leo x and then from Adrian vi, see James M. Kittelson *Wolfgang Capito: From Humanist to Reformer* (Leiden 1975), chapters 3 and 4 passim. There is no record of the sequestration reported here.

Hutten's book has been printed,[4] they tell me. I don't know what came
into the man's head that he should decide that you are the person to attack,
you, the founder of the rebirth of learning and no less of the return of
personal religion. Maybe the man cannot stand your moderate attitude,   35
which others think too statesmanlike to do much good in this generation,
when everything tends towards innovation, nor is there much hope that
everything we have accepted up to now will have equal force among
posterity. Farewell in the Lord, O most respected teacher.
Strasbourg, 18 June 1523   40

1369 / To Cuthbert Tunstall   Basel, [end of June 1523]

This letter was first published in the *Opus epistolarum* with the date 1525 (line
92). Allen rejected the date, with good reason. The letter is clearly Erasmus'
reply to Ep 1367, to which there are specific references in the text (eg, lines
27ff). It is inconceivable that Erasmus would have waited two years before
writing such a reply. It is also inconceivable that, writing in 1525 after the
publication of *De libero arbitrio*, Erasmus would have continued to adduce
reasons for declining to write against Luther (lines 33–8). On the other hand,
the catalogue of heresies in lines 41–56, beginning with the reference to
'Anabaptists,' cannot have been written in 1523. The phenomenon of
Anabaptism did not emerge until January 1525 in Zürich when the radical
group known as the Swiss Brethren separated themselves from Zwingli's
church and began to practice adult baptism. The pejorative term *Wiedertäufer*
(rebaptizers) was soon applied to them in the city records. The Greek loan-
word *Anabaptistae*, which Erasmus uses here, was not common before 1527.
Moreover, the denials of the real presence and of the necessity of baptism
(lines 44–8) first emerged in 1524, and some of the other views referred to (lines
50–3) probably surfaced only in the period 1527–9. One must conclude,
therefore, that the original letter to Bishop Cuthbert was indeed written in the
summer of 1523 as Allen insisted but that, when preparing the letter for
publication, Erasmus inserted the passage in question in order to show what
new horrors 'human temerity' had led to in the interim.

ERASMUS OF ROTTERDAM TO CUTHBERT TUNSTALL, BISHOP OF
LONDON, GREETING
Such religious devotion and such burning zeal as you show for the church of
God, most honoured prelate, must command my heartfelt admiration, and I

* * * * *

4 The *Expostulatio;* see Ep 1356 n9.

do not doubt that in adopting this energetic attitude you have used your   5
judgment. But I and others like me have to act with caution for fear that, in
the Apostle's words,[1] we may have zeal but not according to knowledge; we
are bound to fear, as Parmeno puts it in the comedy,[2] that it may be too hot
that way. For I see it happens to certain people that while they act with more
zeal than discretion they not only pull up wheat as well as tares, which   10
Christ forbade in the gospel,[3] but instead of tares pull up wheat, either
condemning what they do not yet understand or distorting something said
in a religious spirit by the sense they put upon it; and this they wish to be
taken as zeal for religion and hatred of heresies, when it is a major threat to
piety and concord. Just so those who are deeply in love with someone   15
admire everything about that person, while those who feel a deep hatred
condemn everything. Take Luther's writings: I hear that some points are
condemned in them, the sober discussion of which in a disputation between
scholarly and honest men might make a useful contribution to that spiritual
and evangelical force in which the world has clearly fallen far behind; and   20
this should be done with the help of those in particular who teach canon law
in Italy, earning a great reputation for ability and hard work and I wish one
could say with a proportionate harvest of true piety. The decrees of men,
being drafted usually for the uneducated multitude, have as their object a
reduction in the frequency of sin; the philosophy of Christ calls us to far   25
more exalted objectives and sets about its task on different principles.

    It is, I agree, very true, as you suggest with equal eloquence and
learning, that the early leaders of the church nowhere displayed their
resources, intellectual, doctrinal, and literary, more clearly than in their
conflicts with heretics and won more solid reputation from them than from   30
anything; and you challenge me to take up this task citing the examples (and
splendid indeed they are) of Origen, Basil, Cyprian, Jerome, and Augustine.
But when I compare myself with them, I am sorry to say, my heart, as Homer
puts it,[4] sinks at once into my boots. How I wish that the many people who
speak as though I had great powers could really confer them on me! One   35
thing I do promise, that so far as my small talent allows I shall not fail the
church's cause. I only wish that as regards the outcome your forecast[5] may

* * * * *

1369
1 Rom 10:2
2 Terence *Eunuchus* 380
3 Matt 13:24–30
4 *Iliad* 15.280; cf *Adagia* I viii 70.
5 Ep 1367:68–70

prove you mistaken! I myself, though no great statesman, have long
suspected something of the sort. And if it does come about, I fear that in
return for driving out popes, bishops, and princes we shall be given some   40
dreary masters far more merciless than they. The so-called Anabaptists have
been muttering anarchy for some time now, and other monstrosities are
hatching in the way of doctrine which if they once break out into the open
could make Luther look almost orthodox. There are murmurs too to the
effect that baptism is unnecessary for adults and for children alike.[6] And if   45
they succeed in persuading men, as some are trying hard to do, that there is
nothing in the Eucharist but bread and wine,[7] I do not see how much they
will leave us of the sacraments of the church. There has arisen another form
of madness: they wish to be taken for prophets,[8] but everyone laughs at
them. It is true that no sect has yet arisen which holds impious views about   50
Christ;[9] but many have gained from this turmoil of opinions the courage to

* * * * *

6 All the radical reformers denounced infant baptism, but not all insisted on
  adult baptism. In particular, those in the Spiritualist camp – Thomas Müntzer,
  Hans Denck, and others – attached little importance to outward baptism with
  water as opposed to inner baptism by the Spirit. Müntzer's *Protestation oder
  Entbietung ... von der Taufe* (January 1524) was the earliest published denial of
  the necessity of outer baptism, though Erasmus may be referring to the views
  of Denck, who died in Basel in November 1527 (cf n10 below).
7 Andreas Karlstadt (Ep 1258 introduction), who in December 1521 had
  celebrated the first evangelical Lord's Supper (Ep 1258 n12), two years later
  (December 1523) became the first to abandon the doctrine of the real presence
  in both its Catholic and Lutheran forms. Then, in November 1524, he
  published at Basel five pamphlets attacking the real presence (cf Epp
  1522:60–4, 1523:102–4). See Barge II 151–2. Although he did not much like
  Karlstadt's arguments, Zwingli adopted the same position, which he expressed in his *Epistola ad Mattheum Alberum*, written in November 1524 but not
  published until March 1525. In Basel, Johannes Oecolampadius (Ep 1258 n4)
  quickly became an ardent champion of the Zwinglian view. Beginning in 1525,
  the question of the real presence was the focal point of a prolonged and
  rancorous controversy between the Lutherans and the 'Sacramentarians.' The
  Anabaptists were in essential agreement with the Zwinglians on this point.
8 Eschatological prophecies and the attribution of prophetic status to individual
  leaders were common features of the radical Reformation in its early years.
  Erasmus had heard reports of the 'Zwickau prophets' by February 1522 (Ep
  1258:14–16 with n13). In the period 1525–9, many Swiss Anabaptists made
  eschatological prophecies; for some examples, see Claus-Peter Clasen *Anabaptism: A Social History, 1525–1618* (Ithaca and London 1972) 119. Numerous
  reports of such incidents would doubtless have reached Erasmus.
9 Erasmus presumably means that none had denied Christ's role as redeemer,
  though, as the rest of the sentence makes clear, some had erred on the question
  of the redeemer's divinity.

dare not only to speak blasphemy about Christ's divine nature but even to
have doubts about the authority of the whole of Scripture.[10] This is what
always happens when once the dams have burst and human temerity floods
headstrong over the field of licence: its madness knows no end until it   55
involves itself and all else in perdition.

Those men reject everything, as you most truly say;[11] but there are
certain people on the other side who hold on to everything tooth and nail,
unwilling to change even abuses which have crept into the church and are
an abundant source of what more than anything else corrupts Christian   60
people. And when we say to the other party that it is monstrously wrong to
tear up what is right because of human faults, they habitually answer with
their usual flood of words that those by whose absolute discretion the
church is governed have for so many centuries down to this day resisted all
correction by the fear of God, the lessons of Scripture, or the authority of 65
princes, and that there is no other way of curing this except by throwing
everything into confusion. Each side draws unto itself the rope of contention. This evil is made more incurable by the undying hostility between
princes,[12] which I should like to see done away with root and branch to such
good effect that after being suppressed for a time it cannot burst out again   70
soon afterwards and cause even greater disasters. A pattern for the
restoration of the church is given us in the book of Ezra.[13] There would be
good grounds for hope if the Lord in his mercy would send us a prince like

* * * * *

10 This is quite possibly a reference to the Anabaptist Spiritualist Hans Denck, or
   to Ludwig Haetzer, whose final theological position was deeply influenced by
   the thought of Denck, or both. Both men were accused of antitrinitarianism
   (with more solid evidence in the case of Haetzer), and both held that the
   immediate witness of the Spirit is superior to the external word in the form of
   Scripture. Denck had been residing at Basel for several weeks when he died
   there in November 1527. Haetzer was tried and executed at Constance in
   February 1529. See the articles on Denck and Haetzer in *The Mennonite
   Encyclopedia*, and see also J.F. Gerhard Goeters *Ludwig Hätzer, Spiritualist und
   Antitrinitarier: Eine Randfigur der frühen Täuferbewegung* Quellen und Forschungen zur Reformationsgeschichte 25 (Gütersloh 1957) chapter 12.
11 Ep 1367:75–9
12 A reference to the Hapsburg-Valois wars between Charles v and Francis i,
   which lasted, off and on, from 1521 until 1544, only to be revived again in the
   1550s under Francis' successor, Henry ii
13 As the quotation in lines 76–9 shows, Erasmus is referring to the books of Ezra
   and Nehemiah, which anciently were one book and are called 1 and 2 Esdras in
   the Vulgate.

Ezra,[14] a pope like Jeshua,[15] a prophet like Haggai,[16] and a people ready, while resisting irreligious doctrines, to amend their evil lives and to build by the good works the city and the house of God. For so we read: 'With one hand they performed the work and with the other held the sword. For each of them as they built was girt about the loins with a sword, and they built and sounded the trumpet.'[17] As things are now, if all our hope lies in the none too sober rantings of a handful of theologians and monks and in the armed forces of bishops and cardinals, I shall be surprised if they make it possible to cure an evil which is an abundant source of what is chiefly wrong. But we do not yet deserve that the great ones of the earth should be aroused by the inspiration of the Spirit. In the Lord is my trust, who is not angry forever;[18] and now we can truly say with the psalmist 'Thou hast rejected and destroyed us.'[19] Oh that we might also add 'Thou wast angry, and hadst mercy on us.' This at least we can say: 'Thou hast shaken the earth and thrown it into confusion; heal its sore places, for it has been moved.'

But how remarkably impudent I am to say all this to you! The Lord preserve you in true religion and prosper you for all time to come, most honoured prelate.

From Basel, 152[5]

1370 / From Guillaume Budé   [Paris, c June 1523]

Like Ep 1328, which was written in December 1522, this letter was first published in *G. Budaei epistolae* (Paris: Bade 1531). The reference here to an earlier letter concerning Budé's appointment as master of requests (lines 35–7)

* * * * *

14 Ezra was not a prince, but rather a fifth-century BC priest and scribe who, with authority granted by King Artaxerxes I of Persia, played a crucial role in the restoration of strict religious observance and the revival of national identity among the Hebrews who, under his leadership, had returned to Judea from exile in Babylon (Ezra 7–10; Neh 8–10). Erasmus, doubtless relying on his memory, evidently confused Ezra with Zerubbabel (see following note).

15 Jeshua (also called Joshua), son of Jozadak, was high priest at the time of Zerubbabel, prince of Judah, who led the return of the Jews from Babylon in the reign of king Cyrus of Persia (sixth century BC). Jeshua and his fellow priests, together with prince Zerubbabel and his kinsmen, recommenced the rebuilding of the temple in Jerusalem (Ezra 3).

16 Haggai and his fellow prophet Zechariah provided the moral pressure behind the resumption of work on the destroyed temple under Zerubbabel and Jeshua (see preceding note); Ezra 5:1–2, Haggai 1 and 2.

17 Neh 4:17–18

18 Ps 103 (Vulgate 102):9

19 The following three quotations are from Ps 60:1–2 (Vulgate 59:3–4).

indicates that this is the later of the two letters. In his *Répertoire analytique et chronologique de la correspondence de Guillaume Budé* (Toulouse 1907; repr New York n d) no 140, Louis Delaruelle assigned the date 'beginning of 1523,' to which Allen objected that the wording of lines 3–4 implies a longer interval between the letters. Allen therefore placed the date in the summer of 1523, assuming that Erasmus' letter of 1 April (lines 1–2) belonged in the same year. Moreover, since Budé apparently wrote from Paris (line 89), the letter must have been written before the end of July, when the court departed for the provinces; see Marichal VIII 440.

BUDÉ TO ERASMUS

I had just had a letter from you when I wrote this; it was the one you wrote on the first of April.[1] This surprised me, for I had written to you twice, I think, since then, but it happens like this sometimes; those who deliver letters take so little trouble. I am grateful to you on account of Morelet the   5
treasurer's son,[2] whom you had so kindly been ready to see for my sake; though I have not yet set eyes on him since I gave him a letter of recommendation to you. I congratulate you, most fortunate of men; no, I am downright envious of you and your kidney troubles, for my own trouble concerns the rule of mind over body. Yes, I am jealous of you, suffering from   10
the stone as you sometimes do, but enjoying unbroken and cheerful leisure and keeping up your spirits, as is clear from the way you go on writing with such success; while I, poor fellow, having had a bad head for a long time now,[3] have lately started having trouble with my heart and my conscious-ness in general, even to the point of fainting. And I lose heart every other   15
hour almost; for I am so overwhelmed and oppressed by a host of responsibilities that I can get no respite, much less find time for a visit to my beloved mistress, those liberal studies from which in the old days I had habitually been inseparable. How much time, pray, do you of all people suppose I can snatch for reading a good book, when I am one hundred per   20
cent, one hundred and fifty per cent chained to the treadmill of public business? – God having consigned me to this bondage, I suppose, to teach me a lesson. But as one of the two needs a man's whole efforts and the other

* * * * *

1370
1 Not extant; nor are the two written by Budé since 1 April (lines 2–3).
2 Antoine Morelet du Museau (c 1500–52), son of Jean (?) Morelet (d 1529), *général des finances* and treasurer of the army. Antoine, who became a royal secretary in 1523, had to flee France in 1533 or 34 because of his evangelical convictions. He settled in Basel, where he was admitted to citizenship in 1555.
3 Cf Epp 1073:6–8, 1328:6–7.

even more than full time, more than one man can do, at any rate as things are
now, I divide time and a half between both as best I can, so much is my spirit   25
sorely pulled in opposite directions. 'Oh, your poor mind!' I hear you say, 'if
you have never a moment off even to look after your body, which is
suffering already.' But such is the punishment men must normally expect
who put their heads all ignorant and unsuspecting into the noose. To be
sure, this present state of affairs has been disastrous for me, and these last   30
two wretched years have upset all my plans, all those at any rate that
concern reading and writing.

But is this disastrous collapse of my literary life to be blamed on the
love of money? It will be worth hearing the story from the beginning before
you pass judgment. This post of a master of requests had come to me from   35
the king's liberality,[4] or rather from his good nature, as I remember I wrote
and told you.[5] For I was at home at the time, and the king with his retinue
was at Lyon,[6] from which I had stolen away about a month before[7] without
asking for leave of absence, for I was quite unable to endure the longing for
my darlings any further, and the king had been unwilling to give me   40
permission to revisit my home. About that time it happened that news
arrived from there of the death of one of our body,[8] and at the same time
most people were telling me that common gossip forecast that this honour
was destined for me. As for me, my sudden departure from the court had
been such that I knew I had left no one behind who could act as my agent or   45
give me support – only the prince's generosity and his pledged faith, for he
had promised me the honour long ago; there was only a foreboding in my
mind, something close to hope and expectation, though I kept this dark.
And even when the question had been in suspense for some time, because
the king had gone off into the Allobrogian country[9] for a bit of hunting and a   50
holiday, while his retinue and the queen mother[10] were still in Lyon, no one
could induce me to write to the court, not even to a friend of mine there who

* * * * *

4 Ep 1328 n1
5 See Ep 1328:9–10.
6 See Ep 1328 n11.
7 See Ep 1328 n10.
8 Jean Caluau (Ep 1328 n12)
9 The *Allobroges* were a people of Gallia Narbonensis who lived to the east of the
   Rhône and north of the Isère, in present-day Savoy, the Department of the
   Isère, and part of the Department of the Ain. During the residence of the court
   at Lyon in the summer of 1522 (see Ep 1328 n11), King Francis was twice absent:
   between 8 and 13 June at Crémieu, east of Lyon; and between 14 and 21 July in
   the country east and southeast of Vienne; Marichal VIII 437. The latter occasion
   must be meant, since Budé had been absent from court in June (lines 37–8).
10 Louise of Savoy, 1476–1531

has a lot of influence. In the end, when most people thought the whole thing had blown over through my own inactivity, and some actually declared this was so, lo and behold a bundle of letters brought by a courier in livery, in which were the royal warrant and a letter to me from the king. For the prince, soul of courtesy that he is and such an admirer of the humanities, himself wished the warrant to be sent to me actually at my own home, which seldom happens. This was no mean distinction, not so much for my humble self as for the whole name and nation of devotees of good literature, and so it was understood by everyone; but they also saw that it would mean no small advancement for me and my position, such as it is.

We are a body of *octoviri*, eight members, whose functions and activities cover a very wide range of public affairs, for in nearly all the most distinguished of official circles the office to which by the king's kindness I have been promoted enjoys the first place and prestige. First and foremost, in the prince's great council, in the court of one hundred,[11] and in a word in all the highest courts with which the ultimate decision of cases rests, it has the right to sit in the place of honour and next after the presidents, unless princes or prelates are present. In expressing opinions it enjoys precedence over all members of the council. The great council is the name for the tribunal that travels round with the court. It is a kind of bodyguard of lawyers, and you might call it a regular appanage of the palace and the royal household, whose head is the chancellor, the keeper of the great seal. But the chief and most important duty of this committee of eight is to wait on the prince when he issues from his privy chamber and finds time to listen to the requests of his petitioners. This duty falls in rotation to us in pairs or often singly, while otherwise we hold our ordinary sessions in that workshop (if I may so describe it) of justice and equity which our people call the chancery; where a place is set apart for the consideration of questions referred by the prince, which are commonly appeals on grounds of equity and the public interest against the full severity and rigour of the law. Besides these matters referred there are the humble petitions of those who have committed any violation of the *lex Cornelia de sicariis*[12] or any other capital offence against the law; and we normally grant them a pardon in the king's name if they humbly appeal against their penalty, provided of course that we think they deserve mercy and forgiveness. These royal pardons can be granted by two of us, or even singly, if one of us happens to be sitting by himself; and this is part of our daily business in this city and at court in the chancellor's quarters.

* * * * *

11 The Parlement of Paris, which had a nominal membership of one hundred
12 The section of the *Corpus juris civilis* dealing with murder (*Codex* 9.16; *Digest* 48.8)

Moreover these duties, manifold as they are, are a point of honour and   90
leave one some freedom of choice, instead of being obligatory and
demanding a man's whole time, unless we are summoned to sit on more
serious cases, the documents in which are unusually full of matter, and this
does not happen very often. As a result, I can perform my duties without a
heavy loss of leisure for my studies. But when people who are friends of   95
mine and also devotees of good literature congratulated me on this as
though an office highly desirable in itself and entirely appropriate for
someone like me had fallen unasked into my lap – I who, as they knew, had
always valued my independence – lo and behold, another office descended
upon me out of the blue,[13] a city one this time, when I least expected it,   100
which was conferred on me in my absence as a great compliment by an
almost unanimous vote (it is conferred as a rule on magistrates, and those of
the highest rank), and this swept me out of my backwater into high and
stormy tides. This was popularly supposed to be a second distinction, a sort
of bonus from Fortune, who had been generous enough to me already, and   105
was looked on as a cause of rejoicing both for the family of our lady Philology
and all her relatives and kindred; but things soon took such a turn that I
realized I had let a flood of troubles into my house or taken on a sort of
harvest of cares and anxieties, the reaping of which will last for two years
(for that is my tenure of the office), unless some accident befalls in the mean   110
time, as accidents will.

I entered on this new position not so very long after issuing on one
occasion from my retreat to revisit after a very long interval the scene of life's
little ironies, summoning myself out of retirement from the beginning and
with other purposes in view; but yet gradually feeling the pressure of the   115
oath I had sworn and having hired myself for a stipend periodically, and all
of it authorized by honourable ambition. If I now begin to withdraw from the
duties of it, I foresee that intelligent and cultivated people, and those who as
candidates for a more distinguished position in the world wear the dress of
civilized men, will complain that I am a backwoodsman at heart, and have   120
done an absurd and paradoxical disservice to the cause of the humanities
and to my own family. I shall be thought, not to take philosophy as my
guide, but to be contracting out of my legal obligations to society and its
honourable bondage, not so much because my spirit detests a life of slavery
as because it is lazy and faints at the burden and heat of the day. This will be   125
acceptable and praiseworthy only when the moment comes, as it does to a
soldier who has fought his battles and has now gone sick, when I have at

* * * * *

13 See Ep 1328 n7.

length earned some modicum of good will even at court, and can apply for
my discharge. If, with the minority, you insist on a different interpretation,
consider whether I do not at least deserve sympathy, if not full absolution,   130
for having somehow or other signed away my freedom, so that I am now
punished like a galley-slave and often thrown to the wild beasts. Farewell.

1371 / To Heinrich Eppendorf   [Basel, June 1523?]

> Allen was the first to publish this letter, using the autograph in the
> Germanisches Museum at Nürnberg (Autographensammlung κ.44). The date
> is a guess, Allen speculating that the letter falls 'perhaps in the period when
> Eppendorf's quarrel with Erasmus was beginning.' On Eppendorf and his
> relations with Erasmus up to this point, see Ep 1283 n4.
>
> This is evidently Erasmus' answer to a letter in which Eppendorf com-
> plained that two of the servants in the house where Erasmus was living had
> defamed Eppendorf in some matter involving a horse.

Greeting. I have had a letter from a knight, a knightly letter on the subject of
horseflesh, though I am nowhere more out of my element than in anything
to do with horses. You are the most straightforward of men, and you have
some kind of warm feeling for me that is out of the ordinary and beyond
anything I deserve; so naturally I am most seriously concerned for your   5
reputation, though I do not think that in this case it is at risk. Who the men
are whom you call my retainers, I do not know. They are so far from being
mine that I have no legal power over them, and it's little enough power that I
have over my own servants. This house belongs to Froben,[1] it is not mine.
And if it were mine, I have no legal authority over the man whom I suppose   10
you are thinking of, beyond rebuking him or even giving him a piece of my
mind, which I have no real right to do; and I did this before there was any
mention of the horse. I have now done it again, which was even more
unpopular.

If it is at all relevant, I have never set eyes on this Hannoverian,[2] and   15
had no reason to take notice of him, except that I began to find him very
unpleasant. And this was my chief reason for dismissing one of my
servants, though in other respects that Hannoverian has done me no wrong;
while you know him as a familiar acquaintance. So you must make up your

* * * * *

1371
1 See Ep 1316 n10.
2 Unidentified. Allen thought he might be the horse-thief mentioned in
  connection with Eppendorf in Allen Ep 1934:412–15.

own mind what to do about him. I shall restrain my own people as far as I   20
can. He of course is not one of mine. And if my Margaret[3] were to say some
foolish things, surely a man of your common sense would not expect me to
take responsibility? And yet he solemnly swears that it was not he who
spread the story. If one of my own household had done wrong – and this
you do not complain of – I had all the same an ancient legal right to hand   25
over the offender for punishment. I therefore hand over to you the Hannoverian in his entirety, and also the other person you are annoyed with, in
so far as I have any legal interest in them. If gossip has got about, how shall
I be expected to control it? If the Hannoverian cannot get away unless the
thing has been gone into, how will it be possible to keep the business dark?   30
In a word I rebuked him more than once, and abused him in a way that made
me unpopular. He swears he is innocent. Write and tell me what else I can
do, and I'll do it. Farewell, my distinguished friend Eppendorf.
　　　To the honourable Heinrich Eppendorf

1372 / From Bartolomeo Villani   Locarno, 3 July 1523

The autograph of this letter (=Förstemann/Günther Ep 15) was in the Burscher
Collection at Leipzig (Ep 1254 introduction). This letter seems to be the only
surviving evidence that Bartolomeo Villani of Pontremoli ever existed. The
Villani family is found in Pontremoli, in the Appenines between Parma and La
Spezia, from the fourteenth to the seventeenth century. No one knows what
Bartolomeo was doing in Locarno, whence he sent this letter. There is no
evidence for Allen's hypothesis that he was a canon of the collegiate church of
San Vittore Mauro in Locarno.

Were I not convinced, most thoroughbred champion of our Christian
calling, and at the same time unchallenged leader of the whole world of
letters in our generation (I beg that your modesty will allow me briefly to
give vent to my inmost feelings) – were I not quite convinced, as I say, that
your life and character correspond to your style and scholarship, I would not   5
dare at this present moment to interrupt the exalted business on which you
are engaged with this nonsense of mine. I have long known, both from
general report and more precisely from the books which go to and fro so
successfully under your distinguished name over, I take it, the whole of
Europe, how great are the treasures of your erudition and what rich and   10
various stores of knowledge of every kind you must possess. Being

* * * * *

3 Apparently Erasmus' housekeeper, Margarete Büsslin.

reminded therefore, fairly enough, of the proud looks which knowledge like
yours in any man can breed in the faces of those that have it, I should never
have presumed, I will not say to write, but even to think of writing, had not
the fear natural in a man of no account like myself been balanced on the   15
other side by growing confidence, as I considered what an eminent
philosopher Erasmus was himself in the school of Christian philosophy, a
creed which possessed above all the peculiar power of making lambs out of
wolves and doves out of serpents. Relying therefore on this assurance, I was
not afraid to approach the presence of such a distinguished man by way of   20
this ill-educated letter. And what I would wish you to learn from it above all
else is this, that I give thanks continually to Almighty God that he has
thought fit to produce such a man at this juncture, by whose incomparable
and truly celestial labours the gospel field, smothered for so long with
weeds, tangled in so many thorns and briars, and impoverished by all those   25
worthless tares, is hoed and cleaned and weeded. So that of the flour
derived from it everyone may most conveniently make his own daily bread.
As for me (if I may say this much about myself – and may God himself be my
witness that I do not lie), I am not wholly untouched by certain humane
subjects, having spent some time in the perplexities of dialectic, bathed now   30
and again in the deep river of Aristotle and Plato, and followed day by day
the footsteps of Hippocrates, though I found the knowledge of these things
more congenial always than the practice; but in the desire to achieve some
form of the religious life it was the food of theological truth that I always
sought with the greatest eagerness. I was however deterred from entering   35
by the thorny hedge which the common run of theologians have set up
round the field that bears so flourishing a crop. It seemed that no path was
left through their hair-splitting pedantry along which one did not first have
to work one's way entirely by solving sundry very knotty and quite
irrelevant questions of small importance, before it should be possible even at   40
an advanced age to reach the point of gathering that harvest with its most
delicious fruit.

But now you, honourable sir, have as it were pointed out to us a short
cut,[1] by which we can very easily make our way quickly through to the

* * * * *

1372
1 The word that Villani uses for 'short cut' is *compendium*, which is a direct
  reference to Erasmus' *Ratio verae theologiae* (Epp 745, 1365). When first printed
  in the *Novum instrumentum* of 1516, the *Ratio* was entitled simply *Methodus*. But
  in Marten's edition of November 1518, which was reprinted in the *Novum
  Testamentum* of 1519, the title-page reads *Ratio seu Methodus compendio perveniendi ad veram theologiam*, while the heading in the text reads *Ratio seu
  Compendium verae theologiae*.

summit of the truest theology and the solid ground of the surest philosophy.   45
I speak of Christ's heavenly teaching, the essence of the gospel, as you have
very lately expounded it in paraphrase in such a gentle, slow-moving, open
way that anyone, even one half a pagan, can in a short time turn out a
finished theologian with a very moderate amount of work. For this, then, we
all owe undying thanks to immortal God; and to you, as the tool chosen for   50
this purpose by divine providence, we ought to be greatly indebted, and to
rejoice with you very much, except that our joy is greater, as the ancient
Romans used to rejoice with those who came home in triumph after a victory
over foreign kings and crowned their country's name with a transient gleam
of earthly glory. What others propose to do in this regard, I know not; as far   55
as I am concerned, I should like Erasmus to know that I am so much devoted
to his name that as I read his works, the *Methodus* especially, I have repeated
to myself a hundred times those words 'I have found a man after my own
heart.'[2] Do not therefore despise, most merciful of men, one who comes to
you with small resources but the best intentions. Receive a fellow Christian   60
of pious and open-hearted disposition, who is wandering in your third
circle,[3] not bound as yet to anything by any worldly chain, and waiting
eagerly for the charity of that fifth epoch of yours,[4] which has grown cold, to
grow warm again, and for its fallen state to be restored. To this end our
industrious Erasmus must labour with all his might; and he need have no   65
fear that Christ, who is deeply concerned in the outcome, will not assist his
most pious endeavours and those of all men of good will. In the mean time,
pray be mindful of me, if there is any corner in the Lord's house where my
earthen vessel can be of use; at any rate I can undertake to serve such a good
cause to my dying breath. Farewell, champion of the gospel; fare as well as   70
you yourself would wish, and reckon me in the number of your humble
followers. From Locarno, 5 July 1523

    Bartolomeo Villani of Pontremoli

    I have given this letter to the treasurer[5] to be conveyed to you.

* * * * *

2 Acts 13:22, echoing 1 Sam 13:14
3 See the *Ratio verae theologiae* LB v 88D: 'The third circle may be assigned to the
   common people, as the rudest part of this world that we are imagining [ie, the
   world divided into several concentric circles having Christ as their centre].' Cf
   Ep 858:310–12.
4 See LB v 88B: 'We may regard as the fifth age the decline and degeneration of
   the church from the pristine vigour of the Christian spirit: concerning which I
   believe that what our Lord says in the gospel is applicable, namely that
   "because iniquity shall abound, the charity of some shall wax cold" [Matt
   24:12].'
5 Possibly an official in the financial administration of the Ticino

Anything for these parts from Basel your reverence will be able to entrust to   75
him in return, if you have leisure (and do not think it simply beneath your
notice); for he promised to see that I got it. Farewell again, and best wishes.

There are some rumours here of the calling of a council in Strasbourg;[6]
if there is any truth in this, I should be very glad if you could tell me.

To the celebrated Master Desiderius Erasmus of Rotterdam, etc. In   80
Basel

1373 / From Antonius Clava   Ghent, 5 July 1523

> The autograph of this letter, first published as Ep 21 in Enthoven, is in the
> Rehdiger Collection of the University Library at Wrocław (MS Rehd 254.53).
> Antonius Clava (Ep 176:13n), whom Erasmus had known since 1514, was a
> member of the Council of Flanders.

ANTONIUS CLAVA TO THE MOST DISTINGUISHED THEOLOGIAN
DESIDERIUS ERASMUS, CORDIAL GREETINGS

That Lieven of yours[1] could have done nothing to give me greater pleasure
than to turn aside on his way back from England and bring me greetings
from you. I could not let him depart without a letter from me; but I have   5
nothing to say except just this, that I am still your same old friend Antonius
and always shall be, and that I am at your service for anything you wish. I
pray every day for your happiness and prosperity, but long greatly for the
looked-for day when you will visit us, if only that could happen without
putting you out in any way. But if that is impossible, or if you or the gods   10
above have other views, I shall live with my Erasmus as I always have
hitherto; every day, I mean, as far as I am allowed to, I shall spend some time
among your lively conversations and your most eloquent addresses and all
your other works, which are so brilliantly written and so good for one's
spiritual health. And though long ago you left me many of these, you do not   15
cease even so to produce and publish more things every day, and greater

* * * * *

6 The rumour probably had its origin in the demand of the German Estates of 5
   February 1523, at the Diet of Nürnberg, that a general council be summoned to
   meet within a year 'in Strasbourg, Mainz, Cologne, Metz, or some other
   convenient place in Germany' (RTA III 440), a demand incorporated in the
   imperial mandate of 6 March (ibidem 449; cf Ep 1364 n8).

1373
1 Erasmus' servant-pupil, Lieven Algoet (Ep 1091), who frequently carried
   Erasmus' letters; cf Epp 1366:7, 1367 n1, 1383:29.

things; you have put the whole human race under such obligations, that
every one of us ought not merely to feel undying gratitude but to express it
in word and in deed too, as best we can, if we wish to be thought not
unmindful of such great benefits. I commend myself most especially to you,   20
most famous of men, with all the warmth at my command. Farewell, glory of
us all.

From my house in Ghent, 5 July 1523
Your worship's most devoted Antonius Clava
To the distinguished theologian Desiderius Erasmus of Rotterdam, his   25
most respected patron. In Basel

1374 / From Wolfgang Faber Capito   Strasbourg, 6 July 1523

This letter, which survives in a contemporary copy in the Öffentliche
Bibliothek of the University of Basel (MS Ki.Ar.25a.123), was first published in
Hess II 557.

As Allen observed, this letter 'marks the beginning of Capito's critical
attitude toward Erasmus.' Though at the moment Capito had reason to be
annoyed with Luther and his supporters (lines 106–10) and was particularly
eager to be on good terms with the papal party in order to secure his hold on
the provostship of St Thomas' (lines 80–7, 100–5), he had also become impatient
with Erasmus' failure to join the party that restricted 'the freedom of
Christianity within the wide limits of Scripture' (lines 45–6) and he bluntly
admonishes Erasmus that he 'must be ... either a clear friend of the truth or a
dissembler' (lines 70–1). Indeed, the contrast between the critical and
sometimes resentful tone of this letter (lines 19–29) and the still friendly,
deferential tone of Ep 1368 is so marked that the two letters are assumed to
establish the *termini* between which Capito's transformation from an Erasmian
into a reformer was completed. In the following year this transformation
produced a bitter breach in Erasmus' relations with Capito; see Ep 1485.

CAPITO TO ERASMUS

Greeting. I have more frequent couriers to the most distant destinations
than (of all places) to Basel; the answer I wrote to your last letter is still by
me,[1] for I had no one I could give it to for delivery. I have kept silence for so
long not by any means because I was offended but merely from awareness of   5
my own ignorance and the respect that is due to you. For in these three years

* * * * *

1374
1 Presumably Ep 1368

the flow of my mother wit, which in any case was as you know below the average and ran very thin, has been dried up completely by all the tedious business of the court, which I was finding daily more and more burden- some, but especially while I was thirsting to get leave. Not a moment was 10 available from official duties at court so that I could even look up freely at the heavens, though all the time in such intervals of leisure as I had I have not failed to keep in touch with the public state of learning; and in the daylight of society and to one tossed on the waves of public affairs this has not been altogether very difficult, since it depends more on the feelings of ordinary 15 people and popular standards of value than on the views of those who are truly scholars. I have found things starting up here and there that look like arousing some tragic uproar in the future, of which a good part seemed likely to be very much your concern. And yet I was forbidden to call your attention to them, as my duty was, by embarrassment, of which I was made 20 acutely conscious not only by experience but by your criticism of me; for you were said with good reason to make fun of me among your cronies, if my name ever came up, as a complete courtier[2] and quite a stranger to the humanities. At any rate by keeping silence I have guarded against the risk of giving everyone a handle to laugh at me for my ill-timed zeal, although I do 25 not grudge you any pleasure you may derive from my barbarisms and easily bear it with no suspicion that our friendship is not what it was, having no reluctance to be told the truth to my face unless, to the extent that my spirit has grown cold, I am found less capable of keeping up such an important friendship. 30

Besides that, I was deterred by the weakness of my own judgment, for I am quite content to await from your wisdom remarks that go far beyond what I myself expect. What was I to do then? Is not Erasmus, I thought to myself, already well informed about the state of things and the emerging future? Has he not surveyed it all and thought about it? Are you the man to 35 bring him up to date? Can you of all people show the way to such great wisdom? I wrote however to some of our common friends and said there was a risk that you might run into danger through excess of caution and that wiser friends than I were afraid of this; but as they did not pass the facts on to you, I suppose they smiled and thought their poor Capito had no eyes in his 40 head. And even now, were I not urged to do so by so many letters, I simply would not dare take up such a shameless task and have the impudence to instruct you. Our native Germany in general, my dear Erasmus, is rousing itself, but aiming at anarchy almost. Such men of good will as there are

* * * * *

2 See Ep 1158:22–3, which Capito had no doubt seen in the *Epistolae ad diversos*.

meanwhile restrict the freedom of Christianity within the wide limits of   45
Scripture, and their vote, being the better one, begins to win the day. Those
people suspect you of having changed your views because to some extent
you deliberately cast aspersions on the name of Luther, while glorifying the
papal majesty more than once and exalting it in the most elaborately argued
panegyrics. Although I and a few like-minded people have ascribed this to   50
prudence, since as a rule it is his way of going to work[3] rather than his matter
and the substance of his arguments[4] that you attack. They say however that
you have gone so far as to charge him with impiety quite falsely, for you
have written that much of what Luther says is impious;[5] but this I have not
yet been able to see.   55
      The rumour that you have published a dialogue in which you were said
to attack particularly the importance ascribed to faith[6] was going the rounds
at Nürnberg among important people;[7] but the story was untrue as the facts
proved. Yet it is surprising how unpopular even a breath of rumour made
you and with what suspicions it made even your friends both speak and   60
think about you, which was not least among the reasons for their silence at
Nürnberg. When I got here I heard the same rumour but more circumstan-
tial. I thought it foolish to be an Epimetheus after the event,[8] but it was my
intention to defend a friend who was endangered by silence, and this had
long been my whole inclination. There were some points which I will freely 65
bring to your attention sometime, if you will allow me to do so (if, that is, you
care to listen to my foolishness) – and maybe they will serve a purpose –
with the idea of defending your reputation against attacks from Luther's
party, by which even then you were hard pressed. For you are set in the
theatre of the world whether you will or no, and you must be and be seen to 70
be either a clear friend of the truth or a dissembler – such are the times now.
      Just see, dear Erasmus, how much wiser your Capito would have been
to say nothing! As I say this in writing I realize what a fool I am to have
acquired no polish from all this experience at court. For I cannot rely on mere

* * * * *

3 See Epp 947:41–3, 980:45, 1033:55–8, 1342:834–91.
4 See Ep 1033:154–6.
5 Erasmus had done no such thing. Quite the opposite, in fact; see Epp
  1143:14–19, 1167:138–57, both published in the *Epistolae ad diversos* (August
  1521). Cf Ep 1342:833–4: 'I have made no public utterance on Luther's
  opinions.'
6 This rumour may have been based on the new edition of the *Colloquia*; see Epp
  1262 and 1296 n10.
7 At the imperial diet: see Ep 1368 introduction.
8 Epimetheus was the brother of Prometheus and Atlas. His name means 'one
  who reflects after the event.'

phrases, especially writing to my friend and benefactor. I am sincerely sorry   75
that the virulence of Luther, who spares no one on any pretext of
Christianity, should extend to you as well, no less for the cause of liberal
studies than for your own sake. His pamphlet,[9] they tell me, is now on sale
here. It is of no importance and absurd that he should attack me so
contemptuously, if what they say is true; but it will do me some good I   80
suppose in the eyes of the pope. For the court people are now proceeding to
turn me out of my provostship,[10] and for this purpose letters executory,
which had been directed to my predecessor[11] after his death, have recently
been served on me; which troubles me, and I am now the subject of general
discussion, with some discredit to the pope. Will anyone make himself   85
agreeable to the Roman pontiff after this, they ask, if that poor Capito has
entirely lost three whole years of labour and lamp-oil spent in buttering him
up? Let a man flatter and worm his way in, but suitably, or he will find, as
this man has, that he will be worse off. Although in public I have always
been steadfast and reasonable in adapting my advice in the direction of   90
peace with no respect of persons, as you in your wisdom can perhaps
confirm and the states of the Empire can testify. And so in that quarter they
will find one day (but too late, I fear) that there was some foundation in what
in my small way I so often publicly maintained; and even now they will not
be able to dislike me for it, unless they prefer soft words to good advice.   95

I have sent the courier back to the court after receiving three letters
from the prince summoning me to return; and this I did in hopes of
recovering my spirits after all this worldly business and even more after the
intolerable crowds, though of course by shutting myself out from all
preferment. Oh, your poor Capito! How he will hate going hungry, still   100
more having no roof over his head, and most of all to be turned adrift
without such small offices as he possesses and above all with such a load of
debt! If you are willing to help me with the pope and with the very reverend
Francesco Chierigati[12] I foresee that I may make my peace. That already
gives you something you can say with truth to please those folk in Rome.   105
Luther's party are vilifying me in libellous pamphlets and cartoons.

* * * * *

9 The *Iudicium de Erasmo Roterodamo* (Ep 1341A n315)
10 See Ep 1368 introduction and n3.
11 Jacobus Fabri (d 1520) of Reichshoffen near Haguenau. See Paul Kalkoff
  W. *Capito im Dienste Erzbishof Albrechts von Mainz* (Berlin 1907; repr Aalen 1973)
  7–8.
12 Francesco Chierigati (Ep 1336), the papal nuncio, whom Capito may have met
  in Nürnberg (see n7 above)

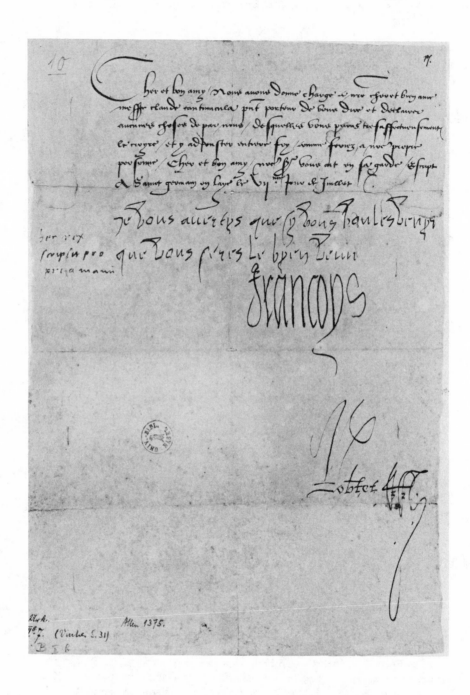

Letter, partly autograph, from Francis I to Erasmus, Ep 1375
Öffentliche Bibliothek, University of Basel, MS Erasmuslade B, Urk.IIb 7

There is Luther's letter[13] and Hutten's,[14] and a parody of our Lord's passion in which they make me the traitor Judas, and a pretty offensive cartoon entitled 'Capito keeps his mouth shut.' Several dialogues too.[15] I have all this to endure, and I get no credit for it, but am being forced into exile. But I write 110 this in a mood of some disorder; I have been stewing in my own juice, as they say, and am worked up. For I do not seriously expect poverty as a result of this if I am allowed to reckon things up in detail, and if it does overwhelm me, I seem unlikely to bear it with such a lack of fortitude. I shall perhaps write an answer to Hutten if you approve, but based on the facts, showing 115 what benefits you have conferred with so much genius on the world and now and then attacking that man's ingratitude and impertinence.

Farewell in the Lord. 6 July 1523

Let Oecolampadius[16] reimburse Trucksess[17] for the ten gold pieces[18] which Cratander[19] will pay over. Greetings to Frau Rottperger[20] and 120 Cratander.

1375 / From Francis I   Saint-Germain-en-Laye, 7 July [1523]

The manuscript of this letter, partly autograph (the postscript is in the king's own hand), is in the Öffentliche Bibliothek of the University of Basel (MS G2.I.36.10). It was first published in Wilhelm Vischer *Erasmiana: Program zur Rektoratsfeier der Universität Basel* (Basel 1876) 31. For Erasmus' earlier plans to migrate to France, see Ep 1319 introduction. For his response to this invitation, see Ep 1400:3–13.

* * * * *

13 A letter of 17 January 1522 (WA-Br II 430–34), published with the *Iudicium de Erasmo Roterodamo* (n9 above) by Hans Schott in Strasbourg. In the letter, written while Capito was still a courtier at Mainz, Luther chided Capito for his readiness to compromise the truth of essential articles of faith for the sake of peace and unity. Its publication was inspired by opponents who wanted to expose Capito as a spineless Erasmian foreign to Luther's spirit: WA-Br II 436.

14 It is not clear from the text that Capito means a *letter* of Hutten. Allen thought that the reference was to derogatory remarks about Capito in Hutten's *Expostulatio*; Böcking II 199–201 (sections 85–7, 93).

15 References unidentified

16 Ep 1258 n4

17 This obscure individual has never been satisfactorily identified. For guidance to the learned guesses, see the entry 'Trucksess' in CEBR.

18 Possibly Rhenish gold florins, which would have been worth about £2 8s 4d gros Flemish. See Ep 1362 n1.

19 Andreas Cratander (also Cartander) of Strasbourg (d 1540) was a printer and bookseller at Basel 1515–36. A supporter of the Reformation, he was a friend of Oecolampadius and the principal publisher of his works.

20 Unidentified

Dear and good friend. We have given instructions to our dear and well-beloved Master Claudius Cantiuncula,[1] the bearer of this letter, to give you certain information and assurances on our behalf, and beg you most cordially to accept his word for them and give him entire credence, as you would to ourselves in person. Dear and good friend, our Lord have you in 5 his keeping.

Written at Saint-Germain-en-Laye, the seventh day of July

I want you to know that if you are willing to come you will be most welcome.

François   10
Robertet[2]

To our dear and good friend, Master Erasmus of Rotterdam

1376 / To Willibald Pirckheimer   Basel, 19 July [1523]

On Pirckheimer, see Ep 318. This letter was first published in the *Pirckheimeri Opera*.

Greeting. I congratulate our friend Dürer with all my heart;[1] he is an artist who deserves to be immortal. He started a picture of me in Brussels; how I wish he had finished it![2] I have been in the same state[3] as he, the cause of my

* * * * *

1375
1 Ep 852:85n
2 Florimond Robertet (c 1461–1527), *secrétaire des finances* and virtual head of government under Louis XII and Francis I

1376
1 The renowned scholar and the great artist (1471–1528) had met in Antwerp and Brussels in August 1520 and February 1521 during Dürer's sojourn in the Netherlands (Epp 1132 and 1136 introductions), to the immediate and enduring delight of both parties. For Erasmus' high praise of Dürer, see Allen Ep 1558:34–6; ASD I-4 40.
2 Dürer made two drawings of Erasmus in August 1520; see *Dürer: Schriftlicher Nachlass* ed Hans Rupprich I (Berlin 1956) 156:100–1. Only one of them survives, a charcoal drawing of his head and shoulders in the Louvre. Erasmus' comment here suggests that one of the drawings was intended to be the preliminary study for an engraved or a painted portrait that was not completed at the time. In 1525 the project was revived (Allen Epp 1536:11–14, 1558:47–9, 1603:117–18), and the result was the famous engraving of 1526, which Erasmus did not much like (Allen Ep 1729:11–13).
3 Erasmus' Latin in this clause is ambiguous: 'Nos eodem in statu fuimus quo ille …' This can be read in two ways: either 'I was in the same state as he was' or, as in our text, 'I have been in the same state as he.' The first version implies that

trouble being a thing of no importance.[4] I felt at heart a kind of happiness at
the prospect of departing from this most unruly world, to be with Christ.   5
This pestilence gets worse every day, and I see no way out. I did send the
pope my advice in a letter;[5] but Eck writes[6] that his proposal[7] was very well
received, and that he has very great influence with the pope. I am
withdrawing from these conflicts, in favour of more peaceful pursuits. As I
work on my paraphrases,[8] I seem to myself to become a better man, and no   10
one is hurt.

Sylvius Egranus[9] has given me the *Gravamina*,[10] but I have not read

* * * * *

Erasmus is still referring to Brussels in 1520 and is saying that, because both he
and Dürer were ill at the time, the portrait was not finished. The second
version implies that Erasmus has shifted his attention to the current year, 1523,
which is clearly the temporal focus of the letter, and is saying that he, like
Dürer, has recently been ill. Although at least one authority has read the
passage in the first way (see CEBR I 414), the extant evidence is entirely on the
side of the second version. There is nothing in Dürer's journal of his trip to the
Netherlands (*Schriftlicher Nachlass* as cited in the preceding note), in Erasmus'
other accounts of his encounter with Dürer in Brussels (Allen Epp 1536:11–14,
1558:47–9), or, as far as one can tell, anywhere else, to indicate that work on the
portrait of Erasmus was interrupted by the illness of either man in 1520. On the
other hand, there is ample evidence that both Erasmus and Dürer were ill in
the summer of 1523 (see the following note). One presumes that Pirckheimer
had informed Erasmus of Dürer's illness in the same letter from which
Erasmus learned of whatever it is that he is congratulating Dürer for in line 1.
4 In July Erasmus had a severe attack of the stone, of which he nearly died: Epp
  1411:20–1, 1422:17–19, 1426:16–19, 1434:38–40. For Dürer's illness at approximately the same time, see his letter of 4 September 1523 in the *Schriftlicher
  Nachlass* (see n2) I 96:25–6.
5 Ep 1352
6 Letter not extant
7 In March 1523 Johann Eck (Ep 769) arrived in Rome to settle certain matters of
  ecclesiastical policy for the duchy of Bavaria. At the same time, he presented to
  Adrian VI a comprehensive plan for the elimination of abuses in Rome and the
  reform of the clergy in Germany. Among the measures recommended for
  Germany were a new bull against Luther and his principal supporters, the
  suppression of the University of Wittenberg, and the establishment of
  provincial and diocesan synods to organize and execute the struggle against
  the Lutheran movement. Eck remained in Rome until January 1524 and
  repeated his recommendations to Pope Clement VII (elected 19 November
  1523). See Pastor IX 108–11, X 107; Pfeilschifter 102–8.
8 See Ep 1381.
9 Ep 1377
10 'The Grievances (*Gravamina*) of the German Nation' (against the Roman see
   and the clergy), adopted by the diet at Nürnberg in February 1523; RTA III
   645–88. Cf Ep 1344:178–82.

them through yet. If you are well, I have every reason to rejoice. As I now see, some other person usurped the office of giving my books to Ferdinand,[11] in hopes of extracting something from him. I sent the books later,   15 having had them gilt. Ferdinand not only sent me a most friendly letter[12] of thanks but added a present of a hundred gold florins.[13]

My life upon it, dear Willibald, I could never have believed that in the whole of Germany there was as much barbarism and impudence and vanity and venom as there is in this one pamphlet of Hutten's.[14] I have spoken   20 highly of him so often.[15] I have recommended him so often to the cardinal[16] his master and all the other princes.[17] I never thought so highly or spoke so fair about anyone. I never said a single word that might injure him. On the contrary, when he was here,[18] I offered to have a discussion with him on any serious topic. I promised him my help if there was anything he wanted from   25 me. Nothing was further from my thoughts than this assault on the part of Hutten. From many indications I am led to believe that Heinrich Eppendorf is the skilled hand behind this story;[19] he became a supporter of Hutten so suddenly. None the less, I will not cease to be what I always was. I have not yet decided whether I am willing to answer him or not.[20] He is raving mad,   30 and has nothing to lose. He is on the run, and is now lying hid in Switzerland, not without some risk. Zwingli supports him in Zürich,[21] but in secret. Farewell, my dear Willibald. You will hear all our other news from Egranus.

Basel, 19 July [1522]   35
Your most sincere friend Erasmus
To the honourable Master Willibald, councillor to his Imperial Majesty

* * * * *

11 See Ep 1361.
12 Ep 1343
13 See Ep 1341A:1738–41 and cf Ep 1386:41–2. On the motive for the gift, see Ep
   1382:33–4.
14 The *Expostulatio* (Ep 1356 n9)
15 See Ep 1341A:1043–51.
16 Albert of Brandenburg (Ep 661); see Epp 745:18–21, 968:24–6, 1009:78–83.
17 Ep 967:115–21
18 Ep 1331 n24
19 See Epp 1283 n4, 1371, 1377.
20 For Erasmus' reply, the *Spongia*, see Ep 1378.
21 On 21 July 1523 Hutten wrote to Eobanus Hessus from Zürich that he had fled
   Germany to Switzerland and instructed that letters be sent via Zwingli in
   Zürich or Oecolampadius in Basel; Böcking II 252–3.

1377 / To Johannes Sylvius Egranus   [Basel, July 1523?]

Johannes Sylvius Egranus was the name taken by Johann Wildenauer (d 1535) of Cheb (Eger) in Bohemia. He had been pastor at Zwickau in Saxony (c 1516–21) and Jáchymov (Joachimstal) near Cheb (1521–3). At this time he was in the process of visiting Basel and Nürnberg (Epp 1376:12, 34, 1383:1). He later served as pastor in Kulmbach on the Main (1524), Zagań (Sagan) in Silesia (1526), and Chemnitz in Saxony (1530). In 1533/4 he returned to Jáchymov, where he died. Although at first attracted to Luther, Egranus was an ardent Erasmian who expressed strong disapproval of Luther's *De servo arbitrio* (Allen Ep 872:12n).

This letter was first published, inaccurately, by Johann Gottfried Weller in *Altes aus allen Theilen der Geschichte* 1 (Chemnitz 1762) 156. Allen's version is based on a manuscript (a contemporary copy) in the Ratsschulbibliothek at Zwickau. A precise date being impossible, the letter has been placed conjecturally in the period of Egranus' visits to Basel and Nürnberg, when Erasmus' quarrel with Eppendorf was in full progress (Epp 1371, 1376).

TO HIS FRIEND EGRANUS

I meant to write more, but this man was off suddenly. Eppendorf denies everything to do with the published book.[1] He has sent me a letter threatening me with a duel,[2] and then in another he threatens me with the noose. He says his parents belonged to the high nobility,[3] and he would   5
rather die a thousand deaths than have one drop of commercial blood in his veins. He is angry with you for writing something about him, I know not what. He said to Froben's son Hieronymus,[4] 'I believe he was cut to pieces by my brother.' Has he such a brother,[5] one who cuts men up like that? Farewell. No time for more.   10

Yours ever, Erasmus

* * * * *

1377
1 Probably Hutten's *Expostulatio* (Ep 1356 n9)
2 Not extant; nor is the other one mentioned in this sentence.
3 Cf Ep 1283 n5.
4 Ep 1226
5 Apparently there was such a brother. Nothing is known of him except that he seems to have been living at Jáchymov (Joachimstal) in Bohemia in 1529 (Allen Ep 2216:28–30).

1378 / To Huldrych Zwingli [Basel, early August 1523]

This is the preface to Erasmus' *Spongia adversus aspergines Hutteni* (Basel: Froben, September 1523); cf Ep 1341A n284. Hutten's *Expostulatio* (Ep 1356 n9) was in circulation in the first half of July. On 19 July Erasmus had still not made up his mind whether or not to reply (Ep 1376:29–30). He soon decided to do so, however, and, despite his recent illness (Ep 1376 n4), completed the work in six days (ASD IX-1 210:140–1), finishing before the end of the month (Ep 1389:77). In Epp 1341A:1023–4 and 1437:74–7, Erasmus states that his decision to defend himself was taken on the advice of friends. Printing began on 13 August and was completed on 3 September (Ep 1389:83–4; cf Ep 1383:14–15). An unusually large number of copies was evidently produced (Ep 1397:3–4). The preface was doubtless the last part of the book to be written, but the continuous pagination indicates that, unlike many prefaces, it was probably not postponed until after the rest of the text had been set up in type. It may therefore be placed in early August, a date further supported by the numerous verbal resemblances to Ep 1379 (cf Zw-Br Ep 316, where the date is put at the beginning of September).

Hutten died while the *Spongia* was still being printed (Ep 1388 n12), a circumstance that robbed the work of much of its welcome. Erasmus was impelled to write a new preface (Ep 1389) for the second edition, and in 1524 he inserted into the second edition of the *Catalogus lucubrationum* a long passage justifying his decision to write the *Spongia* (Ep 1341A: 1019–1105, 1181–91).

ERASMUS OF ROTTERDAM TO THAT EXCELLENT SCHOLAR ULRICH ZWINGLI, PREACHER IN THE CELEBRATED SWISS CITY OF ZÜRICH, GREETING

The poison having been brought from here to your part of the world first, my most learned Zwingli, it seemed appropriate that the antidote should set off 5 first in the same direction, not that I fear any damage to my reputation from Hutten's attack in your mind or in the minds of any intelligent men; my purpose is to cure other people too, who have a prejudice against me, or by some defect of nature would rather believe what is to a man's discredit than the opposite. Is there anyone of any character or intelligence who would not 10 repudiate the precedent set by Hutten? – I never did him any harm in word or deed;[1] I have so often praised him[2] even in my published work more generously, more freely, and more frequently than I have anyone else, and

* * * * *

1378
1 Cf Ep 1379:6–8.
2 See Ep 1341A:1043–51.

so often written him letters of recommendation to persons in high place; and
now suddenly, as though he had been lurking in some sort of ambush, he   15
has published a book like this, attacking a friend who at the very moment
when he was writing it was still speaking of him most openly and
affectionately, and expecting nothing in the world so little as any unpleasantness started by Hutten. Could one imagine anything more alien to the
courtesy and loyalty one expects of a German,[3] more exactly what the   20
enemies of good literature enjoy and hope for, more likely to hurt literature
itself and damage the cause of the gospel,[4] or, if you like, of Luther even, of
which he boasts himself a supporter? He had declared war on the supporters
of Rome; and he attacks a friend who has a most sincere regard for him and
was expecting nothing, with no previous complaints, and in a pamphlet so   25
bitter that he has never yet written anything more venomous even against
an enemy. And since then, I hear, he has added to the book,[5] as though
there were not enough venom in it already; nor does it look as though he
would ever stop, now that he has once declared war on the Muses and the
Graces.   30

For my part, I do not grudge him his generous reception by the Swiss,
who give him a refuge in which he can for the moment be safe from the
pursuers who mean to punish him.[6] All the same, steps should be taken to
see that he does not abuse Swiss kindness by living in safety under their
protection while he fires off pieces like this[7] – personal attacks on anyone   35
who has served the cause of public enlightenment, sparing neither pope nor
emperor[8] nor the princes of Germany nor even the most honourable men
among the Swiss themselves, in which number I include Ludwig Baer.[9]

* * * * *

3 See Ep 1341A n102.
4 Cf Ep 1379:15–16.
5 Erasmus reported this on the authority of Oecolampadius (Ep 1384:83–4), who
   was in close contact with Hutten (Ep 1376 n21).
6 See Ep 1376 n21.
7 Cf Ep 1379:14–15.
8 Cf Ep 1379:11.
9 Ludwig Baer, professor of theology at Basel (Ep 488), and his colleague Johann
   Gebwiler are described in the *Expostulatio* as 'those two deadly plagues of Basel
   who are sunk in avarice, blinded by ambition and of all the flatterers of Rome
   the most abominable and who alone in that city have for a long time now most
   obstinately opposed the renascent sciences and the emerging studies of the
   fine arts' (Böcking II 213, section 139; translation from *The Polemics of Erasmus of
   Rotterdam and Ulrich von Hutten* trans and ed Randolph J. Klawiter [Notre Dame
   1977] 93). Baer, a good friend of Erasmus, was a convinced opponent of the
   Reformation; Gebwiler, whom Erasmus knew only slightly, a rather vociferous
   one. His public denunciation of Zwingli led the Basel city council to dismiss

Since he writes this from a refuge in Switzerland, it is to be feared that one
day some unpopularity, some unpleasantness may befall the Swiss them-   40
selves,[10] whom we wish to see flourishing in public peace and every other
blessing. Nothing is easier than to sow discord, while it is a most difficult
task to cure the evil once it has started. Farewell.

1379 / To the Town Council of Zürich   Basel, 10 August 1523   45

The surviving manuscript of this letter is a contemporary copy in German in
the Staatsarchiv Zürich (MS E.i.1.98). It was first published in Hess II 572. The
letter must have been translated for Erasmus for presentation to the council.
The Latin original evidently bore a close resemblance to Ep 1378. On 15 August
1523 Hutten addressed a letter to the council (Böcking II 257–8) stating that he
had heard of Erasmus' letter and requesting to be informed of its contents.

ERASMUS FROM BASEL
Greeting, my most worshipful lords of the council. Your worships are well
aware, I have no doubt, of the efforts I have hitherto expended, not only to
advance the common good and the cause of the humanities, but in particular
the knowledge of the gospel, to the benefit of all men and to no man's hurt.   5
Now, all of a sudden, Ulrich von Hutten has appeared on the scene, a man
whom I have assisted in every way and have never done any harm in word
or deed,[1] who has published a pamphlet not merely attacking my reputation
but also deliberately filled with palpable falsehoods and devilish calumnies,
in which at the same time he assails other worthy persons who have done   10
nothing to deserve it, and spares neither the pope nor the emperor.[2] My
object in writing this is not to debar him from enjoying the permission you
have generously given him to live in your city, in order not to fall into the
hands of his relentless enemies, but to prevent him from misusing that same
generosity[3] by writing reckless, arrogant stuff that can do great damage to   15
the gospel cause,[4] to the liberal arts, and to public morals; with the further
hope that his boundless audacity may not perhaps in the future bring your

* * * * *

him from his professorship in April 1523. For Erasmus' defence of both men in
the *Spongia*, see ASD IX-1 158–9.
10 Cf Ep 1379:17–18.

1379
1 Cf Ep 1378:11–12.
2 Cf Ep 1378:36–7.
3 Cf Ep 1378:33–5.
4 Cf Ep 1378:22.

state into disrepute or even damage it,[5] for he himself has nothing left to
lose. If therefore you do something to control his arrogance, you will do a
great service not so much to me as to the humanities, to which he does so   20
much harm. You will also take a step which is of great value to your state, in
whose continuing prosperity I am deeply interested.

God give you his protection, my most honoured lords; and if there is
anything in which I can be of service to you I shall gladly be found ready and
willing.   25

From Basel. St Lawrence's day 1523

To the right worshipful and excellent lords, the magistracy and regents
of the city of Zürich

1380 / From Charles v to Margaret of Austria   Valladolid, 22 August 1523

This letter was first published by Alexandre J. Pinchart in the *Messager des
sciences historiques de Belgique* for 1858, page 394, using an original manuscript,
now lost, in the Royal Archives at Brussels, Archives de l'Audience.

Erasmus' pension as councillor to Charles v (Ep 370:18n) had not been paid
since his departure from Louvain in October 1521; Epp 1342:100–2, 1319:21–4,
1408:13. His earlier reminders to patrons at court are found in Epp 1273:50–1,
1275:58–9, and 1276:9–10, but no trace survives of the later petitions, which
reached the emperor and caused him to issue these instructions to his aunt
Margaret, regent in the Netherlands, to pay the pension to Erasmus.

Margaret of Austria (1480–1530), who had been regent under Maximilian I as
well, was one of the most astute governors of either sex in sixteenth-century
Europe. She was also a patron of the new learning who had made available to
Erasmus a valuable manuscript of the Gospels for use in the preparation of the
first edition of the New Testament (Ep 373:25–8). Now she wanted to lure
Erasmus back to the Netherlands to assist her in her efforts to combat the
Reformation. So she made the payment of his pension conditional upon his
return to Brabant; Epp 1408:11–12, 1416:43–4, 1417:19–20, 1431:11–12,
1471:12–14. Indeed, she offered support in excess of the pension if he would
return; Allen Epp 1553:21–3, 1871:11–14, 2792:15–16. But Erasmus would not
do so. He cited as his reason the hostility of Baechem (Ep 1254 n6) and the other
Louvain theologians; see Epp 1417:20–4, 1434:41–56, and cf Ep 1342:638–47.
But fear of being once again subject to pressures from the court to abandon his
mediating role between papalist and Lutheran zealots also played an important role; see Allen Ep 2792:17–23 and cf CWE 9 ix–x. Erasmus persisted in the

* * * * *

5 Cf Ep 1378:39–41.

Margaret of Austria
Portrait by Barend van Orley
Koninklijk Museum Schone Kunsten, Antwerp

hope that the pension would be paid despite his continued absence from the
Netherlands: Allen Epp 1585:7–12, 1645, 1682:1–-7, 1757:32–3, 2364:15–17,
2716:167–9, 2810:41–8. But Margaret stuck to her demand that Erasmus should
return, and so did her successor as regent, Mary of Hungary (Ep 1297 n8); Ep
2820. In 1533 it seemed for a time that Erasmus would indeed return to his
homeland, but poor health made the journey impractical; see Allen Ep 2820
introduction. So the hopes initially raised by this letter were ultimately
dashed. Erasmus never received the more than three thousand 'French
pounds' (ie, livres tournois, as defined in CWE 1 328, 331–2, 347) of back
pension that he calculated were due him in the summer of 1533; Allen Ep
2860:27–9.

FROM THE EMPEROR
Madame, my worthy aunt. Affectionate and loyal greetings. Representations have been made to us on behalf of our well-beloved master Erasmus of
Rotterdam that he is unable to secure any payment of the annuity which we
had previously given instructions that he should receive from us every year,   5
despite all the attempts that he has caused to be made for this purpose, and
begging us to write to you on the subject. In consequence, and because we
desire that the same Erasmus should receive favourable treatment on
account of his great learning and literary skill, we request and require you to
see that he is paid and given satisfaction for all of the said annuity that may   10
be due to him down to this date, in order that he may have no excuse
through default on this payment to leave our service.

Given in our city of Valladolid, this twenty-second day of August 1523
Charles

1381 / To Henry VIII   Basel, 23 August 1523

This is the preface to Erasmus' paraphrase on St Luke (Basel: Froben, 30
August 1523). Erasmus had commenced work on it by 23 April (AK Epp
915:23–4, 916:12–13) and on 22 June it was already being printed (ibidem Ep
924:10–11). The preface appears to have been written in haste and set up
somewhat carelessly. As a result, a good deal of correction was necessary in
the second edition of 1523–4.

TO THE MOST INVINCIBLE KING OF ENGLAND AND FRANCE,
LORD OF IRELAND, DEFENDER OF THE CATHOLIC FAITH, HENRY,
EIGHTH OF THAT NAME, FROM ERASMUS OF ROTTERDAM, GREETING
I send you Luke the physician, most noble king – no different from him you
had before, but speaking now to Latin ears more clearly and more fully. Nor   5

do I think that at this point I need to take trouble to satisfy those who are always dinning into us the excellent principle, handed down by men of long experience, that in making presents it ought to be our first concern that what we give should be appropriate. I followed this rule not long ago when dedicating Matthew to the emperor Charles;[1] and before my time it had been shown by eminent scholars on the authority of ancient custom that any subject can properly be dedicated to princes. Even if we know that they will never read what is presented to them, the presentation has this good result, that the work is recommended to the interest of the learned public by their distinguished names; for there is a point in Pliny's remark that certain works of art are highly thought of solely because they stand as offerings in temples.[2] Now there are people so difficult to please in regard to newly written books that they reject them before sampling their quality; and thus the author loses the profit he hoped for and the reader the benefit that should be his. Such critics will concede this much at least to the style and title of the greatest princes printed on a volume's opening page: they cannot condemn it, spurn it, spit upon it before they have read it. Though in any case the piety of certain princes means that he does nothing patently ridiculous who sends a Gospel as a present to a king. I have been told by men of no mean authority that the emperor Charles gladly devotes to a volume of the Gospels such leisure as is allowed him in this time of public turmoil, and that the illustrious prince Ferdinand his brother is often seen with the paraphrase on John, which I lately dedicated to him,[3] in his hands; while that distinguished king Christian of Denmark,[4] as you yourself are in a position to know,[5] frequently has in his hands a Christian book, and is a keen reader of my paraphrase on Matthew. Why therefore should it be thought foolish to send a Gospel to those who read and love the gospel, which ought to be familiar to all those at any rate who bear in mind that they are Christians? And although human reason tells us that as far as possible we should give the gift of which the recipient is most in need, yet according to the gospel principle we should give to him that hath, that he may abound.[6]

* * * * *

1381
1 See Ep 1255:95–111.
2 *Naturalis historia* preface 19
3 Ep 1333
4 Christian II, king of Denmark and Sweden, brother-in-law of Charles V (Ep 1228 n6), had taken refuge in the Netherlands in April 1523 after being expelled from both his kingdoms by his rebellious subjects.
5 King Christian and Queen Isabella had visited England in late June–early July 1523; LP III 3075, 3141–2, 3153, 3155, 3165–6.
6 Matt 13:12, 25:29; Mark 4:25; Luke 8:18, 19:26

And so I thought I should be doing something most appropriate, if I
were to send you this physician of the gospel, for you are so free from any
distaste for sacred literature that your proficiency in it is actually above the   40
average,[7] as your own writings bear witness;[8] so that he who offers you
anything of this kind seems not so much to make you a present as to repay
what we all owe you. And what of your most noble consort,[9] a unique
example in our age of true religion, who with a distaste for the things of no
account that women love devotes a good part of her day to holy reading? –   45
reading a lesson in their duty to all other princes' ladies, who waste the
greatest part of their time in painting their faces or in games of chance and
similar amusements, and at the same time putting to shame for our idleness,
or rather our impiety, those of us who spend the greatest part of our lives on
pagan literature. Indeed, if special care is taken to provide the courts of   50
monarchs with a regular supply of learned and experienced physicians of
unquestioned loyalty to take care of the king's bodily health, how much
more appropriate that Luke the physician should be a familiar figure there,
not to keep his body in good health with scammony or hellebore, but with
heavenly medicines to free his mind from the sickness that perforce leads on   55
to eternal death! – and this means ignorance of the truth, lack of faith in God,
love of this world, ambition, avarice, dissipation, hatred, envy. These are
the diseases to which the whole life of mortals is exposed, as the apostle John
says, lamenting that the whole world is in evil case and is dominated by
nothing save the lust of the flesh, the lust of the eyes, and the vainglory of   60
life.[10] And the greatest princes are more at risk from these diseases for this
reason, because fortune is more indulgent to them and they have the
freedom to do what they please.

It seems to me then that I shall not waste my time if I spend a few words
in recommending to you, first Luke the physician, and then the medicine   65
that he brings with him, although I do not doubt that neither, as is right and
proper, needs any recommendation to a religious person like yourself. This
is, to be sure, the famous Luke who was a native of Antioch. The city of
Antioch was in olden time so famous and powerful that it gave its name to
that part of Syria which borders on Cilicia, and in one respect it was more   70
fortunate even than Rome itself: this was the place where Peter prince of the
apostles first held the see, and it was here that Paul and Barnabas first
assumed the honour of their apostolic office. He was friendly with all the
apostles, but in particular a follower of Paul, and in fact his sole companion

* * * * *

7 See Epp 964:129–41, 1313:80–5.
8 See Ep 1275 n25.
9 Catherine of Aragon (Ep 1313 n12)
10 1 John 2:15–17

Henry VIII at the age of thirty-five
Framed miniature portrait, artist unknown
Reproduced by permission of the Syndics, Fitzwilliam Museum, Cambridge

on his journeys. On the basis of his familiar acquaintance with the apostles   75
he wrote his Gospel, and as an eyewitness of Paul's activity he wrote the
book which he called Acts of the Apostles. This story he brought down to the
second year of Paul's stay in Rome, which was the fourth year of the
emperor Nero, and hence it is supposed that the book was written in that
city. There is general agreement among the learned that he is the man so   80
often mentioned by Paul the apostle in his Epistles, for instance in the
second letter to the Corinthians, 'We have sent also with him our brother,
whose praise is in the gospel throughout all the churches.'[11] Again, writing
to the Colossians, 'Luke the beloved physician greets you.'[12] Again, in his
second Epistle to Timothy, 'Demas hath forsaken me, loving this present   85
world, and is departed unto Thessalonica; Crescens to Galatia, Titus unto
Dalmatia; only Luke is with me.'[13] There is also an ancient tradition that
whenever Paul calls the gospel 'his,' as in the Epistle to Timothy 'Remember
that the Lord Jesus rose from the dead, being of the seed of David, according
to my gospel,'[14] he is thinking of the Gospel of Luke, because Luke is   90
thought to have written his gospel narrative on Paul's authority, as Mark did
on Peter's.

Jerome thinks Luke had a better knowledge of Greek than the others,[15]
and that was why he put his historical narrative together more precisely,
beginning with the conception of John the Baptist and recording in some   95
detail the birth and infancy of Jesus and some facts about his childhood,
together with many parables and miracles which the others omitted from a
desire for brevity. And while none of the others went beyond the time of our
Lord's ascension into heaven, he alone pursued the story of the birth and
growth of the church in a second volume. They add a further point, that   100
while Matthew wrote his Gospel and Peter his Epistles for the Jews in
particular, Luke wrote his Gospel particularly for the Gentiles, being of
course a disciple of Paul, who as the teacher of the Gentiles wrote to Gentiles
all his Epistles except for one to the Hebrews, the authorship of which has
always been in doubt.[16] He wrote after Mark and before John, so that a   105
disciple takes precedence of an apostle. Lastly, as befits a physician, he is
said to have been long-lived. For he took Paul's advice, who wrote that it is

* * * * *

11 2 Cor 8:18
12 Col 4:14
13 2 Tim 4:10–11
14 2 Tim 2:8; also Rom 2:16, 16:25
15 *Commentarii in Esaiam* 3.6.9–10 CCL 73:91–2
16 Erasmus did not raise the question in the preface to his paraphrase on Hebrews
    (Ep 1181), but he had already expressed his opinion in Ep 1171:9–12.

good not to touch a wife,[17] and lived unmarried to the age of eighty-four. His bones after his death were translated from Achaia to Constantinople together with the relics of the apostle Andrew in the twentieth year of Constantius.[18]

Here then is a physician turned physician[19] recommended by his close friendship with the apostles, praised by the apostle Paul in more than one place, and approved by the unanimous verdict of all the churches. For while many men's gospels were rejected, his was accepted by general agreement, so that he completed that sacred and mystical number four indicated originally by Moses when he told us of the four rivers that well up out of a single fount in paradise,[20] which water the whole earth, and afterwards beheld by Ezekiel when he depicts the four mystic beasts and the four wheels in one wheel.[21]

And now allow me to say a few words about the medicine which he has provided for us. Hippocrates[22] had been his customary source for physic with which to relieve the ills of the body; but it was from the apostles who had seen and heard Christ, or rather from the Holy Spirit himself, that he obtained the remedy with which to heal our minds. Among physicians in ancient times a certain sort of most sovereign remedy was in use, skilfully compounded of different ingredients much sought after, which they called θεῶν χεῖρας, the hands of the gods;[23] but no drug has yet been discovered by the physicians which can cure all the diseases of the body, however much they may boast of that famous *panacea*[24] which, they claim, was so powerful

110

115

120

125

130

* * * * *

17 1 Cor 7:1
18 Constantius II (d 361), created caesar in 324 by his father, Constantine the Great, became ruler of the eastern part of the Empire on his father's death in 337.
19 'Habes medicum ex medico ...' A rather obscure play on words that makes sense if one follows Allen's suggestion that 'medicum' should be understood to mean 'medicum evangelicum,' the appellation that Erasmus had used in line 39. Thus Erasmus is saying: 'Here then is a physician turned into a physician of the gospel.'
20 Gen 2:10–14
21 Ezek 1:5–21
22 The ancient Greek physician (c 460–c 357 BC), to whom a considerable body of works on all branches of medicine was attributed
23 Cf *Adagia* I iii 6.
24 In ancient and medieval times, the term *panacea* (heal-all) was applied to a variety of herbs to which were ascribed the power to heal all diseases. See, for example, Pliny *Naturalis historia* 25.30–3. (The *Oxford English Dictionary* cites this passage in Nicholas Udall's translation of the Luke paraphrase [1548] as the earliest use of the term *panacea* in an English text.)

and yet is quite unknown. Old age, at least, is a disease that yields to no prescription. But here we have in truth the hand of God, which by the agency of a true faith does away once and for all with all diseases of the spirit and, what God alone can do, confers immortality.

And there is some point in the old Greek proverb that words are the   135
physicians of a troubled mind.[25] There have been people who thought that diseases of the body could be driven away by some fixed form of words that had magic power. Our Lord Jesus was a physician who, while he lived on earth, drove out with a word diseases of the body, however desperate or of long standing, and with a word brought the dead back to life; for this was no   140
magic formula, but the omnipotent word of the almighty Father. He also puts to flight with a word diseases of the spirit, when he says, 'My son, thy sins are forgiven thee'[26] and 'Go in peace; thy faith hath made thee whole.'[27] In fact, prophecy too had promised that Christ should be a physician; for it says in the book of Wisdom, 'For it was neither herb nor poultice that healed   145
them, but thy word, O Lord, that healeth all things.'[28] This, we may be sure, is the true panacea. A psalm too, full of hidden meaning, has the words 'He sent his word and healed them out of their destruction.'[29] The Father's living word is Christ. He had sent Moses and the prophets, and by them the nation of the Jews was tended but not healed. The Father's word alone had power   150
to heal the diseases of men, and not less serious diseases only but also those which cause death. The deadly diseases you can recognize, when the prophet[30] adds 'out of their destruction.' When the digestion has sunk so low that it refuses and rejects all food, the patient is at death's door. Such was the sickness from which the whole world suffered before the arrival of   155
the heavenly Physician, as the psalmist had said shortly before: 'Their soul abhorred all manner of meats; they drew nigh even unto the gates of death.'[31]

Different drugs had been compounded by the philosophers, Pythagoreans, Academics, Stoics, Epicureans, Peripatetics, who promised spiritual   160
health and happiness as well. Many were compounded by Moses, who prescribed various religious ceremonies, and many by the prophets; but the diseases got worse, and the medicine did no good – it only increased the

* * * * *

25 Cf *Adagia* III i 100.
26 Luke 5:20; also Matt 9:2, Mark 2:5
27 Luke 8:48; also Matt 9:22, Mark 5:34
28 Wisd 16:12
29 Ps 107 (Vulgate 106):20
30 Ie, David; cf Epp 1324:86–7, 1334:903.
31 Ps 107 (Vulgate 106):18

disease and made it obvious. The digestion of the spirit was poisoned by
distorted appetites, as if by noxious humours, and rejected the elaborate   165
precepts of the philosophers; the prescriptions of Moses made men more
superstitious, but no better. The bitter rebukes of the prophets had an
unpleasant taste, and their promises were not believed. Beholding this, our
heavenly Father, who wishes nothing to perish out of all that he has made,
sent forth his Word, to free men one and all by heavenly medicine from all   170
diseases of the spirit, granted only that we recognize we are ill and have faith
in our Physician. We know how friendly physicians, if ever they cannot be in
constant attendance on the sick, often leave some medicine with which the
patient can be his own physician, should the case so require; and in the same
way the Lord Jesus, when he returned to heaven, left for us in the hands of   175
his apostles the medicine of the gospel, simple itself and within the reach of
everyone, but effective if taken as it ought to be; and to take it to good
purpose, the most important thing is confidence in the Physician. Nor will a
taste suffice; it must pass into the organs, that it may be absorbed by the
stomach, and diffuse its power all through the veins. Only then does it begin   180
to agitate the whole man with hatred of his former life; but these convulsions
are followed by great peace of spirit.

Physicians of the body have pharmacists and druggists as auxiliaries in
their art, while they themselves prescribe what should be given to the
patient. In the same way, it is Christ alone who prescribed the remedy that   185
brings eternal health; the apostles and their successors the bishops are only
the auxiliaries: they mix, they grind, they administer drugs not of their
making but Christ's; they bathe with water, but it is Christ who washes the
spirit clean; they teach what Christ handed down to them, but it is Christ
himself who makes the words effective. Physicians of the body often differ,   190
both in their judgment of diseases and in the remedies which they prescribe;
and sometimes even, instead of remedies, they prescribe poison, as the
Greek poet says: 'Good drugs in plenty mixed, and deadly too.'[32] But the
medicine of the gospel knows one prescription only, which ought not to be
corrupted or altered by any mortal man. Last but not least, it is a simple one,   195
so that, if those whose duty it was to administer this drug are slow to act, any
man can take it for himself, provided he has a faithful and true heart and is
eager to get well. For even the supreme Physician, who alone can heal the
whole man, sometimes gave people health himself, and sometimes by the
hands of the apostles and disciples.   200

Again, the whole art of the physician has two aims in particular: the

* * * * *

32 Homer *Odyssey* 4.230

first is to free the body from disease and from its causes, and this division they call the therapeutic art; the other, to maintain good health and give fresh bodily vigour, and their foundation for this is the theory of regimen. Physicians are not always using cautery or the knife, they are not forever 205 pouring in scammony to reduce the vigour of the body, almost killing that they may give life; sometimes they administer cordials to warm the heart, and even allow a sympathetic diet. So it is with us: first we are given a draught of faith, which administers to the spirit a salutary shock of repentance and reduces us and unburdens us of our sins. Then a potion is 210 added of comfort, encouragement, and more advanced instruction. For if a physician, after reducing a patient's bodily state, were suddenly to abandon him, there is a risk that, while he is thus emptied out and deprived of his natural forces, some more severe sickness may attack him, paralysis for example or apoplexy or consumption. In the same way, when repentance 215 has laid us low and our sickness has been driven out and baptism has left us emptied of our sins, treatment is then applied which is capable of replenishing in a health-giving way the spirit that is now well and truly empty. Anger is drawn off, and gentleness and mildness are instilled. Envy is drawn off, and a readiness to think well of all men takes its place. Greed is 220 drawn off, and generosity substituted for it. The love of fighting is drawn off and succeeded by a passion for peace. Desire for the pleasures of the flesh is drawn off and succeeded by desire for heavenly things.

Do you wish to hear the scammony of the gospel? Repent. 'Now the axe is laid unto the root of the tree.'[33] And 'every tree that beareth not good 225 fruit is cut down.'[34] St Paul again: 'Mortify your members which are upon the earth, fornication, uncleanness, lust, evil concupiscence, and avarice.'[35] And thereafter: 'Stripping yourselves of the old man with all his actions.'[36] He has emptied the patient; now how does he fill him again? 'Put on,' he says, 'as the holy and elect people of God, the bowels of mercy, kindliness, 230 humility, modesty, patience, bearing one another in turn and forgiving one another, if anyone has a complaint against his fellow, even as the Lord has forgiven you. But above all things have this charity, which is the bond of perfection, and may the peace of Christ abound in your hearts.'[37] A house like this swept clean with brooms and filled on every side with such 235 ornaments as this will not be occupied a second time by an evil spirit,

* * * * *

33 Luke 3:9; Matt 3:10
34 Matt 7:19
35 Col 3:5
36 Col 3:9
37 Col 3:12–15

returning with seven others worse than himself.[38] Thus the medicine of the
gospel has wine of its own to scour away the corrupting matter from our
wounds. 'Get thee behind me, Satan, for you are wise not in the things of
God but the things of men'[39] – that is its wine. Now hear its oil: 'Trust in me,   240
for I have overcome the world.'[40] 'A hair of your head shall not perish.'[41]
'Fear not, little flock, for yours is the kingdom of heaven.'[42] Paul has food
with which he builds up those who are newly converted to Christ, that they
may not slip back into sickness while they are still weak; he has also food of a
more solid kind with which to keep up the strength of those who are making   245
progress continually towards the measure of the fullness of Christ. Those
men had gained strength of whom it is written in the Acts of the Apostles:
'They went out rejoicing from the presence of the council, because they had
been found worthy to suffer false accusation for the name of Jesus.'[43] He had
gained strength who said 'I can do all things in him who has made me   250
strong.'[44] And so the Lord Jesus in the gospel exhorts men to eat the bread
which has come down from heaven, the eating of which confers immortal
life.[45] He exhorts them to eat his flesh and to drink his blood,[46] thinking of
his teaching, which like bread makes the spirit active and robust and like
strong wine intoxicates it until it despises this life; like flesh offers solid   255
nourishment and like blood offers living force. But though all Holy Scripture
has a healing power, yet there is no drug in it more powerful than the
Gospels. It is the same Spirit in them all, but this is where he wished
particularly to exercize his power, that there might be no difference between
the servants and their Lord, between the cisterns and the fountain.   260

And it is worth while to consider what the power of this drug is. A
commonwealth is a kind of body. Its pests and diseases are the forms of
moral evil, against which men of outstanding wisdom in different countries
have applied laws as a sort of remedy – Solon for instance in Athens,[47]

add to n #4

* * * * *

38 Luke 11:24–6; Matt 12:43–5
39 Matt 16:23; Mark 8:33
40 John 16:33
41 Luke 21:18
42 Luke 12:32
43 Acts 5:41
44 Phil 4:13
45 John 6:51, 58
46 John 6:53–7
47 In 594 BC, Solon, the Athenian poet, businessman, and politician, was
    appointed archon and invested with unlimited power to heal the civil strife
    that had plagued Athens. He introduced sweeping political and constitutional
    reforms and issued a new and humane code of law.

Lycurgus among the Lacedaemonians,[48] Minos in Crete,[49] and the *decemviri*   265
in ancient Rome.[50] None of these however could secure that the code he had
established should be adopted by other nations too. Nor did any of them
even attempt this, for fear that besides the waste of effort he might acquire a
reputation for impudence for his pains. Solon persuaded one city to adopt
his laws by ten years of exile.[51] Plato, a man of great learning and great   270
eloquence as well, never persuaded the Athenians to accept his code.[52] And
yet it is beyond doubt that they were all convinced of the truth of the laws
they had drafted, and would have liked to see them adopted, had it been
possible, by the whole world. Even the laws of Moses did not spread beyond
one nation, although the Pharisees with their great ambitions hunted   275
successfully for a certain number of proselytes.[53] Last but not least, even the
all-powerful authority of the Roman emperors could not secure by force that
their laws should have weight in all nations alike. What they tried to do by
the publication of their codes was also attempted by the philosophers by
publishing their principles with consummate wisdom and great pains. Yet   280
none of them was eloquent or learned enough to convert any one nation, so
weak and ineffectual was the power of the drug they had to offer.

Unlike all else, the truth of the gospel seized, permeated and
conquered within a few years every region the whole world over, attracting
Greeks and barbarians, learned and unlearned, common folk and kings. So   285
effective as a medicine was this new truth that all those thousands of men
left their ancestral laws, abandoned the religion of their fathers, gave up the
pleasures and the vices to which they had been accustomed since the cradle,
and embraced this new and foreign doctrine, leaving their different
languages and different institutions to agree together in a sort of humble   290
philosophy – and this above all things in an age better equipped than any
both with the defensive powers of learning and eloquence and with the

* * * * *

48 The traditional, and doubtless legendary, founder of the Spartan constitution
   and military system
49 According to legend, Minos, son of Zeus and Europa, was king and legislator
   of Crete and, after his death, one of the judges of the shades in Hades.
50 In 451 BC the Roman constitution was suspended and complete power was
   given to a commission of ten patricians, the *decemviri legibus scribundis*, to draft a
   new code of laws. In 450 a second commission of *decemviri* completed work on
   the new law code, which was published the following year.
51 The 'one city' was Athens. According to Herodotus 1.29, Solon left Athens for
   ten years to avoid being compelled to repeal any of the laws he had made. The
   Athenians themselves could not repeal them because they were bound by
   solemn oaths to abide for ten years by all the laws that Solon might make.
52 Books 5–12 of the *Laws*
53 Matt 23:15

might of monarchs. And although the world fought back with all its defensive power against the unarmed truth of the gospel, yet it could not prevent that truth from first occupying Greece, then invading the capital city   295
and court of Nero, and soon spreading through all the provinces of the Roman empire as far as Cadiz and the Indies, as far as Africans and Scythians 'and Britons quite cut off from the whole world.'[54] These nations differed greatly among themselves in language, law, liturgy, customs, institutions, gods, religion, and physical shape; but out of all this discord   300
harmony was born, and they all began to sing the same song, exalting Jesus Christ the only Lord and Saviour of the world.

All the time, confiscations, exile, imprisonment, torture, death meant nothing but the progress of the gospel. Who was ever found ready to face martyrdom for the laws of Solon or the precepts of Zeno?[55] For the simple   305
teaching of Christ what thousands, old and young, matron and maid, were ready to lay their heads upon the block! And yet how much more remarkable, how much further from the common feelings of mankind are the teachings of the gospel than the paradoxes of philosophers! No prince ever attacked their teaching; yet it vanished of its own accord, like the laws   310
and magic and rites of sacrifice. Who sacrifices nowadays to the gods of the Gentiles or slaughters victims according to the Jewish rite? Who nowadays has heard of Zoroaster?[56] Who gives a fig for those puzzling precepts of Pythagoras?[57] Who reads the life of Apollonius of Tyana[58] except as a kind of dream? Or rather, who thinks it worth reading at all? If Aristotle nowadays   315
is famous in our universities, he owes this not to his followers but to Christians; he too would have perished had he not been mingled with Christ. Against the philosophy of the gospel, still young and growing, the world with all its defenders at once came out to fight: Jews battling under the pretext of religion against the source from which all religion flows,   320

* * * * *

54 Virgil *Eclogues* 1.67
55 Zeno of Citium in Cyprus (335–263 BC), founder of the Stoic philosophy
56 Zoroaster (Zarathustra, Zerdusht), dates uncertain, founder of the Zoroastrian religion of the Medes and Persians (ancient Iran)
57 The Greek philosopher Pythagoras (sixth century BC) taught that the soul is a fallen divinity confined within the body and condemned to a cycle of reincarnation from which it could win release by the cultivation of moral purity. Believing that the soul is purified by study, he taught a way of life in which the investigation of nature became a religion. He and his followers were much interested in arithmetic and interpreted the world as a whole through numbers.
58 Apollonius of Tyana in Cappadocia (4 BC) was a Neopythagorean sage and wandering teacher who pretended to miraculous powers. His life was written by Philostratus.

philosophers powerfully equipped in every field of knowledge, sophists
whose toughness in dispute made them invincible, orators with marvellous
force of eloquence, tyrants armed ready for any form of cruelty, kings,
chieftains, magistrates, magicians, conjurers, and the devils who are the
masters of this world.   325
    All these upheavals, this advancing ocean-tide of evil was faced,
withstood, broken, and vanquished by the force of gospel truth. In the light
of the gospel it was to be expected that the whole puppet-show of human
power should vanish, and there shone forth that gospel in its simplicity and
its lowliness that they were all trying to overwhelm. The books of those who   330
published attacks on the gospel, with their great gifts, their marvellous
erudition and their exquisite style, disappeared of their own accord like
dreams, so that no fragments even remain except such as may have been
preserved by Christians. Kings worship what they at first attacked; magic
has vanished; demons are driven out howling. Philosophy has admitted her   335
own ignorance and, abandoning the foolish wisdom of men, has embraced
the wise foolishness of the cross.[59] Orators write their panegyrics on Jesus
Christ, poets send the old gods packing and instead of many hymn one God
only, Jesus Christ. This tremendous change in the world began a few years
after Christ's passion to spread over the whole earth, and without human   340
defenders continually grew greater until the leaven mixed in three measures
of meal affected the whole loaf,[60] until the grain of mustard seed[61] buried in
the ground reached out its branches far over Asia, Africa, and Europe.
    Another feature was that the opponents of the gospel truth possessed
not only various instruments of terror from which the bravest heart might   345
shrink: decrees, tribunals, confiscations, proscriptions, exile, imprisonment, torture, the scourge, the block, the cross, fire, wild beasts, and every
form of death; they also offered various baits by which the most rigid spirit
might be corrupted. An emperor would say, 'Deny Christ and you shall be
first among my magnates; and unless you do, all your possessions will be   350
seized, I shall let loose my wrath upon your wife and children, and you
yourself shall be thrown to the wild beasts.' Who at this time persuaded so
many thousands of men that they should accept it with joy when their
honours were stripped from them and their property was torn to pieces; that
when they saw carried off to savage punishments those who after God were   355
the dearest thing they had they should give thanks; that they themselves in
the end of all, when they might lawfully escape and gain all those great

* * * * *

59 foolishness of the cross] Cf 1 Cor 1:17–25 and Ep 337:499–501.
60 Luke 13:21; Matt 13:33
61 Luke 13:18–19; Matt 13:31–2; Mark 4:30–2

privileges, offered themselves to the tormentor of their own free will? No force of human eloquence could have achieved it; the divine force of truth that lay hidden in that grain of mustard-seed both could and did.   360

Nor did the teaching of the philosophers lack its attractions. The Stoics promised liberty, true riches, health in every form, kingship, and other things that sounded wonderful.[62] The Epicureans commended pleasure to the listening ears of men.[63] The Peripatetics coupled bodily advantages with virtue.[64] But the gospel teaching, though, it is true, it had no human terrors   365 with which to convert anyone, yet at the same time had nothing in it attractive on the surface and indeed much that was quite incredible. It tells the world that a certain Jesus was crucified who by his death had set free the human race; that he was both God and man, a virgin's son, who had risen from the dead and sat at the right hand of God his Father; who had taught   370 that those were blessed who, because in this world they professed his name, were mourners, were thirsty, were hungry, were afflicted, were evil spoken of, and were put to death, but that one day all men should rise again, and then before his tribunal the good would receive as their lot eternal life and the wicked the everlasting pains of hell. What philosopher would have   375 dared to put forward such paradoxical and improbable ideas? And yet the unassuming language of the gospel has made them seem so plausible that a man who does not believe them is thought to be mad, and that all those thousands of people would rather give up their lives than their profession of the gospel truth.   380

Who were they then with whom this great transformation of the world began? A few disciples, unknown, of low degree, poor, and uneducated. Need I say anything of the remainder, since Peter the chief of them was a fisherman and uneducated and Paul a leather-worker, and none of them all was rich or powerful or of high birth? Either they possessed nothing in this   385

* * * * *

62 According to the Stoics, reason teaches that such things as bodily health, wealth, friends, and death are 'things indifferent' that cannot affect us unless we inwardly assent to them or withhold that assent. Thus pleasure is good and pain is evil only if we judge it to be so. This is the basis for the ideal Stoic sage's indifference to the vicissitudes of life and of the Stoic's paradoxical assertion that the wise man alone is true king, rich in spite of poverty, happy and healthy despite physical torments, free even though a slave, etc.

63 The Epicureans taught that pleasure (*hédoné, voluptas*) was the highest aim of man. Properly understood, 'pleasure' was not profligate pleasure but rather freedom from trouble and pain, imperturbability, independence, and peace of mind.

64 Beginning with Aristotle himself, the Peripatetics attached importance to physical well-being and external goods as indispensable means of virtuous activity.

world or, if they had had any possessions, they left them behind. And how could such men be responsible for so great a change? It was, of course, because they carried with them a medicine, its container cheap, its power and efficacy stemming from the power of God. The language of the gospel is simple and artless, and anyone who compares it with the histories of   390
Thucydides or Livy will find much lacking and much to object to. The evangelists leave out so much and mention so much in few words; in how many passages the order does not fit, and in how many they seem to disagree among themselves! These faults might disgust a reader and make him unwilling to believe what he read. On the other hand, what pains are   395
taken by the writers of human history over the choice of a starting-point, and how careful they are to record nothing indecorous or improbable, inconsistent or absurd! How vividly they make us see the thing they tell of, with what arts they beguile and retain the reader's attention for fear he gradually lose interest! And yet the monuments they built with all this toil have mostly   400
disappeared, and what remains is not read universally and without doubts. Who is there credulous enough to affirm that there is no falsehood in the story Livy tells?[65] And yet all those thousands of men have existed who preferred to face death ten times over than to admit that there is one sentence of falsehood in the gospel narratives. Do we not clearly see from   405
this that it is not a matter of human power or human wisdom but of the power of God? There is a hidden virtue in this medicine, and once introduced into the body it spread through all the nations of the earth as it might through all the limbs. We have found the reason why the truth of the gospel spread in so few years through the whole earth in the hands of   410
humble men, while the world reacted with cruelty of every kind. And now it may have occurred to someone to wonder how it has come about that in more recent centuries, when the world had Christian princes and bishops who were learned and rich and endowed with great authority, Christ's kingdom has contracted within such narrow limits. For if we could find the   415
reason for this, perhaps we should more quickly find a remedy.

But I forgot myself long ago, and transgress the limits of a preface. I return now to Luke our physician, who will, I do not doubt, receive a warm welcome from all other men. The wise preacher says, 'Honour a physician on account of necessity.'[66] How much more should we pay this physician   420
the honour that is his due, who gave us so efficacious a medicine, which is a necessity for everyone, unless the man exists who is free from all guilt and has no need to get better! And it will have its effect if we grow really tired of

* * * * *

65 His *History of Rome* (*Ab urbe condita*)
66 Ecclus 38:1

our diseases and bite off some of this medicine constantly, if we chew it
assiduously and pass it down into our spiritual stomachs, if we do not cast   425
up again what we have swallowed but keep it in the stomach of the spirit
until it develops all its powers and transforms the whole of us into itself. I
have learned from my own experience that there is little profit in the gospel if
one's reading of it is idle and perfunctory. But he who grows familiar with it
by continuous and careful thought will find a power in it that is in no other   430
books.

     And now let me confront those who have their suspicions by saying
that, if I have dedicated each of my paraphrases of the Gospels to a different
prince, this is accident and not a plan for my own advantage; the same thing
has happened to me here as with the apostolic Epistles. When I was writing   435
on Matthew[67] the last thing I expected was that I should be asked for John[68]
and then Luke. Now, to avoid an empty gap among the evangelists, I shall
add Mark[69] too. Not but what the man who dedicated different Gospels to
different persons seems to me to do nothing more peculiar than St Jerome
did when he gave separate dedications to each of the prophets, even the   440
minor ones. Elsewhere I have drawn the reader's attention to the fact, and I
now repeat the warning, that he must not attribute more weight to a paraphrase written by me than he would to commentaries written by others.[70]
My purpose in writing paraphrases is not to strike the gospel out of men's
hands, but to make it possible for it to be read more conveniently and with   445
greater profit, just as food is seasoned to make us more willing to eat it and
enjoy it. I must also warn the less intelligent reader that nowhere in a
paraphrase does he hear me speaking; when I speak humbly and truthfully
under the guise of the apostle, he must not think that I am speaking
arrogantly in my own person.   450

     May the Lord Jesus give your Majesty, illustrious king, a share of his
own Spirit, that under a truly Christian prince the gospel truth may reign
and flourish daily more and more.

     From Basel, 23 August 1523

                          * * * * *

67 Ep 1255
68 Ep 1333
69 Ep 1400
70 See Ep 1255:41–2, 1333:422, 1342:1025–6.

1382 / From Johann von Botzheim   Constance, 24 August 1523

The manuscript of this letter (=Ep 16 in Förstemann/Günther) was in the Burscher Collection at Leipzig (Ep 1254 introduction). On Botzheim, see Ep 1285. This is his reply to a letter now lost.

Greeting. I am truly delighted on your behalf, most beloved of teachers, to hear that you should be the man over whom the rulers of the world and the kings of the earth are at strife for the privilege of possessing you and making you happy, sending you official invitations and gifts from every quarter, and ready to give more if you are so disposed.[1] This enthusiasm for you in   5
England[2] has not arisen out of nothing, for you deserve even greater things from them, although one commonly gets the worst deal from those whose gratitude one has done most to earn. But you will remember that something should be left for the divine mercy to reward or pardon. You say in your letter that you have possessed a large body of friends since early days and   10
have added some to their number. These, let me tell you, are very few, the whole lot of them, compared with the friends you will make in the centuries to come. More invite you with the idea of your undertaking some task which will make you very unpopular. The risk is that feelings may run too high, so that they are more keen to avenge an injury done to their king[3] than to   15
advance the glory of Christ.

I like the secretary's plan; whoever he is,[4] he tries to promote your efforts to find a solution, and the pacific approach that you recommend everywhere. You will be called the hired tool of many papists, not without great risk to your books, which will be torn to pieces all over the place by   20
every cobbler, even. If you take my advice you will hold them all up for a year or two, as was your practice hitherto,[5] unless you prefer to be a target at which they can all shoot. You need no one to tell you what to do; you have more than enough intelligence to cope with that.

I like what you write about the theologians at Louvain;[6] eventually   25

* * * * *

1382
1 Erasmus' letter to Botzheim had evidently been similar in content to Ep 1386.
2 Cf Ep 1383:30–1, 1386 n20.
3 By Luther's book against Henry VIII; see Ep 1308 n3.
4 Most likely Hezius; see Ep 1339:78.
5 Botzheim may have been thinking of the unpublished works listed in Ep 1341A:1332–8. He would have known from the same source (lines 57–62) of Erasmus' acknowledged tendency to 'publish in a hurry.'
6 Probably much the same information as is found in Ep 1383:25–6

they will be put back where they belong. As for joining the king of France,[7] I should sleep on it. I suspect there are some of the Germans in the imperial household who are against you, one of whom they think is a certain Balthasar,[8] a provost in Waldkirch and canon of Constance, who is now in Spain with the court. The Lady Margaret is furious about this business of 30 Luther,[9] and among us here Fabri is the same,[10] and thanks to him several bishops and princes; but there are some of them who do not think him worth a straw. I know for certain that it was he who extracted Ferdinand's money[11] – what was sent you to buy you over; for true to yourself, you would have said no. He judges his Erasmus by his own standards; and in one respect he 35 is more reliable than Judas: he never returns money once he has received it, but puts up the price of his convictions every day. He was summoned to Ferdinand's court.[12] Now he is back again, and living in Constance until he can set his affairs in order. For he is deeply in debt,[13] worse even than Eppendorf.[14] 40

A new storm is blowing up here about the dismissal of Wanner,[15] not without disorderly protests, although the campaign is carried on by a few people and in secret. You shall hear the story in my next letter.[16] The common people and most of the city council support Wanner; Fabri and his

* * * * *

7 See Ep 1375.
8 Balthasar Merklin of Waldkirch (c 1479–1531), who was to become bishop of Constance in 1529. He had entered imperial service in 1507 and in 1522–7 he was with Emperor Charles v in Spain. If Merklin was indeed hostile to Erasmus at this time, he did not remain so. In 1529 Erasmus knew him to be sympathetic (Epp 2123, 2166) and in 1530 dedicated an edition of Alger of Liège to him (Ep 2284).
9 Ep 1380 introduction
10 Ep 1260 nn22 and 23, 1324 n14
11 See Ep 1376:13–17.
12 Fabri's appointment to the court of Archduke Ferdinand of Austria had apparently been announced recently. Fabri's letter accepting Ferdinand's offer, dated 7 July, is printed in the *Archiv für Reformationsgeschichte* 5 (1908) 314–16. Cf Ep 1388:9–11.
13 As a result of his visit to Rome in 1521–2; Ignaz Staub *Dr. Johann Fabri, Generalvikar von Konstanz, 1518–23* (Einsiedeln 1911) 170
14 Epp 1283 n4, 1371, 1377
15 Efforts by bishop and chapter to dismiss the popular Wanner (Ep 1335 n5) from his preachership, under way since February 1523, were finally successful in January 1524; Hans Christoph Rublack *Die Einführung der Reformation in Konstanz* (Gütersloh 1971) 21–2, 25–6.
16 No such letter to Erasmus survives, but Botzheim tells the story in a letter of 28 August to Vadianus; Arbenz Ep 360.

party lean heavily on the help of the bishop of Veroli[17] and others who are 45
now in Constance on behalf of the emperor. Riots are in the wind; but within
a fortnight, if anything is on foot, you shall be told. As to Oecolampadius'
disputation,[18] I have not so far been able to learn the final result, nor was I
given a chance to meet the man who brought your letter.

On St Bartholomew's day[19] I had entertained Cronberg,[20] a new arrival 50
whom I had never seen or heard of before. He has departed for Zürich, and I
had used my man Martin[21] that day to act as his guide. On the burning of the
three monks in Brussels a plain narrative has arrived here printed in
Nürnberg,[22] but I hear that a very well written account will appear shortly. I
like your proposal for quieting Hutten,[23] and all the rest I liked.[24] The same 55
hour that the courier brought your letter he had extracted a letter from me, if
I had anything to send you. I now hear that representatives from the whole
of Switzerland have met at Zürich[25] to discuss the business of Luther. The
inhabitants of Luzern[26] rage against the Zürich people and would welcome
their destruction; I understand however that Bern, Schwyz,[27] Glarus, Basel, 60
and Schaffhausen are in collusion with Zürich, for they are said to be not
altogether against the business. We shall see what will happen. As soon as
Froben has anything ready, see that I get it.

What do you mean, dear Erasmus, by saying 'If you were a little
nearer, I would visit you'? If you are well, and fond of your Botzheim, it's no 65
distance; otherwise anything, however short, will be a very long journey.

* * * * *

17 Ennio Filonardi, the papal nuncio (Ep 1282)
18 See Ep 1384 n18.
19 24 August
20 Ep 1331 n23
21 Evidently a servant; cf Ep 1361:2.
22 See Ep 1384 n2.
23 By replying to the *Expostulatio* (Ep 1356 n9)
24 Perhaps a reference to Ep 1379
25 Botzheim's information was incorrect. Nikolaus von Wattenwyl (Ep 1264) had
recently suggested that a national council should discuss the religious situation
(Zw-Br Ep 311), but nothing came of the idea. The invitations to the Second
Zürich Disputation were not issued until 12 October 1523.
26 Luzern (Lucerne) was one of the cantons most vigorously opposed to the
Reformation and bitterly critical of Zürich in the Swiss diet. On Shrove
Tuesday (17 February) 1523, following the First Zürich Disputation, Zwingli's
picture was burned in the market square; Gottfried W. Locher *Die Zwinglische
Reformation im Rahmen der europäischen Kirchengeschichte* (Göttingen and Zürich
1979) 426.
27 Schwyz was in fact hostile to the Reformation, which was completely
suppressed there over the next few years.

Your lodging awaits you upstairs,[28] nicely fitted up, with a fireplace.[29] And
your devoted Botzheim awaits you, who would give you peremptory
orders, if he could, to set out for Constance. The one risk is the wine;[30] but
everything else I know you will take in good part with your habitual   70
kindness. Farewell, with every good wish.

St Bartholomew's day 1523

Yours sincerely, Botzheim

Fabri wanted to deliver a popular sermon in Lindau on Corpus Christi
day,[31] and having climbed into the pulpit or onto the platform, began to   75
build an impregnable tower against some of Luther's doctrines; but while
defending this with too much enthusiasm got himself properly laughed at.
Then a few days later a puff of wind laid the whole of Fabri's tower low; and
one of his friends who saw it wrote the six-line piece which you will find
enclosed.[32]   80

To that most learned of men, Master Erasmus of Rotterdam, his
beloved teacher. In Basel

1383 / To Willibald Pirckheimer   [Basel], 29 August [1523]

On Pirckheimer, see Ep 318. This letter was first published in the *Pirckheimeri
opera*. The year date is established by the reference to the *Spongia*.

Egranus[1] has a habit of exaggerating everything, though I have never had to
face anything more outrageous than what Hutten has done. This trick was
designed by Heinrich Eppendorf,[2] who had concocted all his plans with
Hutten while he was in Basel.[3] They were both at their last gasp; and this
seemed to them a way to extort two hundred florins from Erasmus' friends.[4]   5
And they would have extracted something had I not prevented it; for I got

* * * * *

28 See Ep 1342:378–9.
29 See Epp 1258 n18, 1342:382.
30 See Ep 1342:480–4.
31 4 June. The incident is related in Schiess Ep 55 (25 June 1523).
32 No longer extant

1383
1 Ep 1377
2 See Epp 1283 n4, 1371, 1377.
3 From late November 1522 to 19 January 1523
4 On the efforts of Eppendorf to extract money from Erasmus and his friends in
   order to prevent the publication of the *Expostulatio* (Ep 1356 n9), see Ep
   1437:45–7, Allen Ep 1934:297–338; *Spongia* ASD IX-1 126:95–7.

wind of their trick. When they saw they could extract nothing, they wanted
at least to get a few pickings out of my printer. Neither of them did it out of
hatred of me – I have earned the gratitude of them both; it was love of booty.
As it is, they have extracted from certain other people 630 florins; Hutten has   10
200,[5] a young man[6] in whose name war was declared has 400, Eppendorf as
second-in-command has 30. Gambling went in his favour, and this capital
investment brought him a profit of ninety. These people are taken here for
men of good character. My *Spongia*,[7] in which I reply to Hutten, has now
almost finished printing at Froben's. So your advice comes too late; though I   15
reply in a tone of contempt.

　　Emser[8] I supposed to be dead. Something of the sort happened to me
in Louvain.[9] I had written to Hartmann of Gouda,[10] who besides no ordinary
skill in Latin and Greek obtained first prize at Paris, a frank and friendly
letter about things that concerned him personally, and never thought he   20
would show the letter to any of his friends. A letter is now circulating in
print. In it, so they write and tell me, there are attacks on Frans van der
Hulst[11] and Baechem the Carmelite,[12] to whom the emperor and the pope
have entrusted regal authority for the burning of Luther's supporters. I have
not yet seen the letter. The pope has ordered Baechem to keep silence,[13] so   25
there is grumbling among the theologians.

　　I am not sure whether I wrote to you about the trouble that cropped up
in England. Something had made the king suspect[14] that I gave Luther some
help in his absurd new book.[15] To deal with this I sent my servant,[16] and he
came back crowned with success. The king exonerates himself, and so does   30

* * * * *

5　Probably Rhenish gold florins, which would have been worth about £48 6s 8d
　　gros Flemish. See Ep 1362 n2. This sum was found in Hutten's possession at
　　the time of his death; Zw-Br Ep 320.
6　Unidentified. Possibly Hartmut von Cronberg (Ep 1331 n23)
7　Ep 1378
8　Ep 553
9　Allen suggests that the implication may be that Emser's translation of Henry
　　VIII's *Assertio* (Ep 1275 n25), made for Duke George of Saxony, had been
　　printed without his knowledge.
10　Apparently a reference to Ep 1345 to Herman (not Hartmann) Lethmaet
11　Ep 1345 n8
12　Ep 1254 n6
13　See Ep 1359 n1.
14　Cf Ep 1367:4–5.
15　His reply to Henry VIII's *Assertio*; Ep 1308 n3
16　Lieven Algoet (Ep 1373 n1)

the cardinal.[17] My old friends have grown in both warmth and numbers.[18] They gave my servant over thirty florins.[19] Buschius,[20] who is more raving mad than Hutten, though I have always spoken well of him, and received him courteously in Basel, and in any case never uttered a single word that might offend him, has printed some sort of an attack on me,[21] which will 35 appear perhaps at the next fair. Such things get Germany a poor reputation. Nothing could be more idiotic. The princes all urge me to attack Luther.[22] But I shall write nothing; or write in such terms that those who fight for the kingdom of the Pharisees would rather I had kept silence.

Farewell, 29 August. Your sincere friend Erasmus   40
To the honourable Master Willibald, town councillor of Nürnberg

1384 / To Huldrych Zwingli   Basel, 31 August [1523]

This letter (=Zw-Br Ep 315) is the last in the correspondence between Zwingli and Erasmus to survive, though Erasmus is known to have written another shortly afterwards (see Zwingli's report of it in Zw-Br Ep 319), and Ep 1496:134–5 bears witness to a further exchange of letters. It is clear from this letter that Zwingli was now openly critical of Erasmus and that their friendly relationship was coming to an end (cf Ep 1314 introduction).

Allen's text is based on the autograph in the Zentralbibliothek Zürich (MS F.42.70). The first substantially complete version to be published, that in Hess II 566, was not based on the autograph, which was presumed to have been lost, and had gaps. The autograph, written in haste, is difficult to decipher, so much so that the text in Zw-Br is, according to Allen, not perfect. The final paragraphs, starting at line 91, are a postscript written on 1 September. The year-date is obvious from the contents. In the address (line 107), Zwingli's first name is incorrect.

Greeting, my excellent Zwingli. I enjoyed a little talk with you in the shape of your letter.[1] A rumour has reached us here that the third of those

* * * * *

17 On these letters, which must have been written at about the same time as Epp 1366–7, see Epp 1386:37–8 and 1408:25–7.
18 Cf Ep 1382:5–11.
19 Presumably also Rhenish florins. See Ep 1362 n2.
20 Ep 1291 n4
21 Cf Epp 1386:31–2, 1406:53–7, 1437:186–8. No such work was printed, but Erasmus subsequently attributed Erasmus Alber's *Iudicium de Spongia Erasmi Roterodami* to Buschius; Ep 1466:29–30.
22 See Epp 1324, 1338, 1341A:1362–70, 1386:5, 1387.

1384
1 Perhaps the letter mentioned in Ep 1496:15–16

Augustinians was burned on the morrow of the Visitation; for two of them were burned on the eve.[2] Whether I ought to deplore their death or not, I do not know. At any rate, they died with exemplary and unheard-of determina-　5 tion, not for the articles of the faith but for Luther's paradoxes; for which I should not be willing to die myself, because I do not understand them. It is a glorious thing, as well I know, to die for Christ's sake. The godly have never been exempt from affliction, but the ungodly are afflicted too. He is a master of many wiles, that creature who sometimes transforms himself into an　10 angel of light;[3] and rare indeed is the gift of discerning of spirits. Luther puts forward a number of riddles which are on the face of it absurd: 'that all the works of the saints are sin which lack the pardoning mercy of God';[4] 'that free will is mere words';[5] 'that man is justified by faith alone and that works are nothing to the point.'[6] To argue about these things and how Luther　15 wishes them to be understood brings no profit that I can see. And then in most of his adherents I observe an astonishing obstinacy. And in what Luther writes there is so much abuse, often off the point. These things force

* * * * *

2　Cf Ep 1382:52–4. The feast of the Visitation of Mary is 2 July. On 1 July 1523 in Brussels, two young Augustinian friars from Antwerp, Hendrik Vos and Jan van den Esschen, were burned as Lutheran heretics, the first victims of Charles v's new state-run inquisition in the Netherlands. Among those prosecuting the case were Erasmus' old adversaries Jacob of Hoogstraten (Ep 1299 n25), Jacobus Latomus (Ep 934:4n), and Nicolaas Baechem (Ep 1254 n6). A third friar, Lambert of Torn (Thoren), who had been condemned with the others, was not executed at the same time, and his fate is not clear. One contemporary account, the presumed source of the rumour referred to here, indicated that he had been burned on 3 July; *Der actus und hendlung der degredation und verprennung der Christlichen dreien ritter und merterer Augustiner ordens zu Brussel*, in Paul Fredericq ed *Corpus documentorum inquisitionis haereticae pravitatis Neerlandicae* 5 vols (Ghent and The Hague 1889–1903) IV no 142. Another account, which circulated widely in southern Germany (WA 12 74) and is probably the one referred to in Ep 1382:52–4, voiced the suspicion that Friar Lambert had been secretly killed in prison; *Historia de duobus Augustiniensibus ob Evangelij doctrinam exustis Bruxellae* (Fredericq IV no 148). This is the version of events that Erasmus subsequently gave in a letter of 1 July 1529 (Allen Ep 2188:58–71). Other evidence, however, indicates that Lambert was still alive in January 1524 (WA-Br III 237–9) and that he died in prison on 15 September 1528; Fredericq v no 371.

3　Cf 2 Cor 11:14.

4　See WA 2 416 (*Resolutiones Lutherianae super propositionibus suis Lipsiae disputatis 1519*) and ibidem 7 136–8 (article 31 of the *Assertio omnium articulorum M. Lutheri per bullam Leonis x. novissimam damnatorum 1520*).

5　See WA 7 142–9 (article 36 of Luther's *Assertio*, cited in preceding note) and ibidem 1 354 (thesis 13 for the Heidelberg Disputation of 1518).

6　This is, of course, Luther's central teaching and is found virtually everywhere in his writings from 1518 on.

me to entertain some doubts about the spirit that moves them; which for the
sake of the cause I support I would gladly think sincere. They take advice   20
from no one, and if they are given advice they adopt the opposite position,
and make a personal matter of it on every opportunity. You call me a
slowcoach.[7] I ask you, what would you wish me to do? Hitherto whatever I
have written, I have written as I chose. If I am sometimes rather conciliatory,
I do not betray the truth of the gospel; I maintain it where I can. Of our   25
present pope I had good hopes,[8] but now I fear he may let me down. And yet
I reminded him of his duty, in conciliatory terms, but I thought that would
do good. I wrote him privately a long letter with the greatest freedom.[9] He
does not answer,[10] and I fear he may be offended.[11] If you had read it, you
would say I am not conciliatory when need arises, and I would write more   30
freely if I thought I should do any good. It is madness to seek your own
destruction, if you can be of no use to anyone. I abandoned a most
prosperous part of the world[12] for fear of being mixed up in their Pharisaic
policy.[13] On any other conditions I should not have been allowed to live
there. And the state of my health is such that I cannot live wherever I choose. 35
Papal tyranny is not liked, either, by those who dislike Luther's. The
bishops are no longer fathers in God; they are temporal princes and hand in
glove with monarchs: this all men see, and all men regret it.

   All this I have said in more places than one. What is happening now, I
can see, is heading straight for civil strife. And how it will end I know not.   40
The world is full of very wicked men, and they always break out when a
tempest arises in public affairs. I have warned the bishops, I have warned
the princes, not least in my book on the ideal prince;[14] and I am a mere man
of no authority. What else would you have me do? Even if I set no value on
my own life, I do not see what further could be done. You yourself disagree   45
on some points with Luther. So does Oecolampadius.[15] Am I, for the sake of
his teaching, to expose myself and my books to dangers? I have refused all

* * * * *

7 In Latin *contator* (=*cunctator*). Glareanus (Ep 440), writing from Basel to
   Zwingli on 20 January 1523, had used the same word in his analysis of
   Erasmus' position vis-à-vis the reformers; Zw-Br Ep 270.
8 Cf the introductions to Epp 1304 and 1324.
9 Ep 1352
10 Cf Ep 1416:30 and Allen Ep 1690:59–61.
11 Cf Ep 1496:61–5.
12 Brabant
13 See Epp 1242 introduction, 1342:57, and Allen Ep 2792:13–23.
14 *Institutio principis christiani* (Epp 393, 853)
15 Ep 1258 n4

the offers made to me on condition that I would write against him.[16] The
pope, the emperor, kings and princes, even the most scholarly and the
dearest of my friends challenge me to do so.[17] And yet I am resolved either   50
not to write, or to write in such a strain that my writing will not satisfy the
Pharisees. There is no need for you to cite witnesses in support of your claim
to the right to correct me. Correction by the learned I have always warmly
welcomed. Oecolampadius had proposed certain questions for debate, and
had already issued notices. He was instructed to postpone it to another   55
occasion. Now he is allowed to dispute when he pleases.[18] He is an excellent
man, but cannot accept advice, however friendly. Luther wrote to him,[19]
saying he had heard a story that Oecolampadius was expounding Isaiah,
and that I had stoutly opposed this, although no one thinks more highly of
him than I do. He added that I ought not to carry much weight in the things   60
of the spirit. What this means I do not understand. He adds that, like Moses,
I have brought Israel out of Egypt, but shall die in the wilderness. I only wish
he himself were the Joshua who is to bring us all into the promised land!

Hutten's *Expostulatio*[20] did not reach me until it was already circulating
in many copies and was going the round of the printers. I do not envy him   65
his popularity with your fellow citizens.[21] All the same, I wonder what
makes them so fond of him. Because he's a supporter of Luther? No one
does more harm to the gospel cause. Because he's a learned man? No one
has done sound learning so much damage. On the contrary, that pamphlet,
that baseless attack on a friend, will make all who call themselves Germans   70
very unpopular. What could be more barbarous than to assail with all those
trumped-up charges a friend who wishes him well and has done him
service? I know that he was put up to do this by other people, and that some I
could name began all this with a view to extorting money from my friends.[22]
The other things he has done I need not discuss; they are common   75
knowledge. But even pirates like to keep their friends. I have written an

* * * * *

16 Cf Epp 1477:26–9, 1477B:64–7, 1510:23–5.
17 See Ep 1383 n22.
18 Oecolampadius had proposed to defend a list of *Conclusiones* in debate on 16
   August, but the town council and the university intervened. The council
   withdrew its opposition on 30 August and the disputation was held the
   following day; cf line 91 below. For details, see Staehelin 250–2.
19 Erasmus here provides a fairly accurate summary of WA-Br III 96:12–25, which
   clearly caused him considerable annoyance. He returns to it in the postscript
   (lines 92–3 below), in Ep 1397:10–12, and in Ep 1522:43–7.
20 Ep 1356 n9
21 Cf Ep 1379.
22 See Ep 1383 n4.

answer to him[23] – not so much answered him as utterly rejected his shameless calumnies. I am more concerned for the cause of the gospel and of sound learning than for any wrongs done to myself. I set no store by the friendship of men who can take pleasure in a mind like that. Everyone here   80
is persuaded that any support he has in your part of the world he secured through you,[24] however much you may turn and twist. He may do some harm to your city; he can do it no good. Furthermore, he has enlarged his scurrilous pamphlet, as Oecolampadius himself told me.[25] Though, if I rightly read his mind, he will not stop raving, which will not hurt me so   85
much as it will the humanities. If he does not desist, 'seeking to drive his tooth into the crumb / He'll strike it on a stone.'[26] Kindly arrange to restrain the man, if you think this will be to the advantage of sound learning, of the gospel cause, and of the reputation of Germany, for the public nowadays call everyone a German who speaks German.   90

Oecolampadius held a disputation yesterday,[27] and it was a success; he will do so again next Sunday.[28] Luther has said in a letter to Oecolampadius that I ought not to be given much weight in the things of the spirit.[29] I should be glad to learn from you, dear Zwingli, my most learned friend, what this spirit may be. For I am under the impression that I have maintained almost   95
all that Luther maintains, only without his violence and abstaining from some riddles and paradoxes; and I should like to see this doing a lot of good eventually, but I prefer the good to be more immediate. Those people are made very unpopular by the way in which you provide opportunity of openly contradicting everyone.[30] May the Lord Jesus direct and prosper   100
your spirit!

If my man Hilarius[31] said that you might have suppressed Hutten's pamphlet had you so wished, this was his own idea; he did not say so on instructions from me. Farewell.

* * * * *

23 See Ep 1378 introduction.
24 Cf Ep 1376:32–3.
25 Cf Ep 1378 n5.
26 Horace *Satires* 2.1.77–8
27 31 August; see n18 above.
28 It is not clear in what sense Oecolampadius' disputation was a success, since no opponents seem to have shown up to debate his *Conclusiones*. Moreover, nothing is known of a continuation of the disputation on the following Sunday, 6 September; see Staehelin 251.
29 See lines 57–62 above.
30 The Latin of this sentence is unclear.
31 Hilarius Bertholf of Ledeberg, near Ghent (d 1533), was in Erasmus' service 1522–4.

From Basel, 31 August   105
Your more than short-term friend Erasmus
To the right learned Master Johann Zwingli. In Zürich

1385 / To Henry VIII   Basel, 4 September 1523

This letter, first published in the Opus epistolarum, *was written to accompany a presentation copy of the paraphrase on Luke (Ep 1381).*

ERASMUS OF ROTTERDAM TO HENRY, KING OF ENGLAND, GREETING
May it please your serene Majesty. Your Majesty's kindly feelings towards
me were reported to me by Thomas More,[1] and the fact was extremely
welcome, though by no means novel. I see all the more clearly that I must
strive with all my might to offer your Majesty some day what you both   5
deserve and desire. Great changes are under way in this part of the world; or
rather, all is in great travail, and what will be born I do not know, nor is one
simple question at issue. There is much devious activity by the emperor's
supporters, and on the other side by those of the king of France. Luther's
party moreover seem to have taken fresh heart; and on the other side, the   10
princes are losing patience. May Christ grant a happy outcome!
    With this there comes to you Luke the physician, who has the secret of
eternal life. I hope your Majesty will give him a kind reception, and will
think of me as one of those whose wishes and prayers are all for your
prosperity and happiness. I have something on the stocks against the new   15
doctrines,[2] but would not dare publish it unless I have left Germany first,[3]
for fear I prove a casualty before I enter the arena. My respectful best wishes
to your Majesty.
    Basel, 4 September 1523

1386 / To Theodoricus Hezius [?]   Basel, 16 September 1523

*The surviving manuscript of this letter is a sixteenth-century copy, in
secretarial hand, among the papers of Jacopo Sadoleto in the Vatican Archives
(Reg Lat 2023, f 151). The manuscript bears the endorsement 'Exemplum
Erasmi' in Sadoleto's hand. The similarity to Ep 1383 leaves no doubt that the*

* * * * *

1385
1 More's letter is lost.
2 Perhaps *De libero arbitrio,* the first draft of which was later sent to King Henry;
   see Ep 1430:15–16 and cf Epp 1358:5–6, 1386:24–6, 1397:15–16.
3 Cf Ep 1353 n33.

letter is by Erasmus. The addressee cannot be identified with certainty. It was surely someone closely connected with the curia, but it can scarcely have been Sadoleto, who was not in Rome at the time. P. de Nolhac, who first published the letter in his *Erasme en Italie* 2nd ed (Paris 1898) 112–18, suggested Pope Adrian's chaplain, Pierre Barbier (Ep 1294). But Allen, calling attention to the deception practised by Barbier upon Erasmus during Adrian's lifetime (Allen Ep 2961:53–81), thought Theodoricus Hezius (Ep 1339) the more likely addressee.

I cannot give you an adequate idea in a letter of the present state of affairs in this region and these times we live in. Either I am quite blind, or some monstrous thing[1] is hatching between many regions and certain of the leading cities. The servant[2] who brings this will be able to tell you much that it is not safe to entrust to a letter. You urge me to write against Luther; but   5 this I have already done, having gone on record more than once that I have always been, and always shall be, the most complete stranger to that faction.[3] I assure you that I have dissuaded everyone I could from joining it and shall always do so;[4] I have done this, and continue to do it assiduously and not without results. This is why Luther's party are furious with me   10 particularly. They had promised themselves a glorious victory if I had simply kept my mouth shut, so that they could use my name as they pleased in their propaganda. I had scarcely started writing a book against him[5] when they got wind of it and began to fly into a perfect fury, such that I have to leave Germany.[6] How I wish I had never set eyes on it!   15

Nor have I any place of refuge. France, to which I am invited with generous promises from the king himself,[7] is ruled out by the war;[8] England I have no wish to live in;[9] here I am not allowed to live. They cannot bear to hear a single word uttered against Luther; there is some risk that I may become a martyr before I earn the martyr's crown. Those people write   20

* * * * *

1386
1 Cf Ep 1406:64–7.
2 See Ep 1387 n3.
3 See Epp 1033:210–11, 1143, 1275 n9, 1342:1106–18, 1352:72–4.
4 See Ep 1275 n8.
5 See Epp 1275 n7, 1358:5–8, 1385 n2.
6 See Ep 1353 n33.
7 See lines 39–40 below.
8 The Hapsburg-Valois Wars (Ep 1369 n12); see Ep 1342:614–37.
9 Cf Epp 451:22–3, 597:57 and note, 1432:73–5.

everything in German;[10] I have a whole nation to contend with. I knew pretty well what determined enemies I had in those parts; and yet, rather than join the strife of factions, I took the risk of rousing all Germany against me, for I would rather perish than fan the flames of civil strife. I shall have no objections to writing against Luther;[11] but I fear that anything I write may   25 put me in danger of my life and arouse fresh uproar. For all their venom will be turned against me; even now they think it principally my fault that things do not go entirely as they wish. We should have been victorious by now, they say, if Erasmus had not roused the princes against us. From Hutten's pamphlet[12] one can guess what abuse they would have poured on my   30 devoted head. Buschius is much more virulent than Hutten;[13] and he publishes attacks on me,[14] and all the time in Brabant and in Cologne theologians and monks call me publicly a heretic. All the same, no libellous attacks have ever been able to move me from the cause of truth.

Meanwhile I have managed my activities so as to secure the approval of   35 all honourable men, and even to receive the thanks of princes for the good they have derived from my books. The other day I had a letter from the king of England, and one from the cardinal of York,[15] to say nothing of many bishops; more recently still, the king of France, adding two lines in his own hand;[16] the emperor wrote some time ago;[17] Ferdinand lately has written   40 twice[18] and also sent me a present with no strings attached.[19] In Germany I should be a god if I were willing to dispute papal authority, which most of them clearly have made up their minds to overthrow. For my part I defend it always in all I say or write. Is it then in return for labours such as these, for this steadfast upholding of the cause of truth, for sacrificing the friendship of   45 so many scholars in Germany, for calling down so many perils on my head, that I am to be rewarded by being thrown to the beasts in Rome – to Zúñiga and mischief-makers like him?

As for me, whatever happens, I will not tamper with the integrity of my conscience or turn from my course to join any faction; nor will I be   50

* * * * *

10 Which Erasmus claimed to be unable to read; see Ep 1313:93–4 with n16.
11 Cf Ep 1385:15–17.
12 The *Expostulatio* (Ep 1356 n9)
13 See Ep 1383:32–3.
14 See Ep 1383 n21.
15 See Ep 1383 n17.
16 Ep 1375
17 Ep 1270
18 Ep 1343 is the only letter still extant.
19 See Ep 1376:16–17 with n13.

separated from the church of Rome or implore the aid of any human prince. I
might have been able to injure the pope's reputation; God forbid that I
should so use the power of Satan! My wish – would that I could fulfil it – is to
do good unto all men, and especially to those whose authority upholds the
good of all.   55

My worldly position causes me no serious anxiety. The English
contribute as much as I wish;[20] the king of France offers me two thousand a
year in a letter written partly in his own hand.[21] In the sincerity of our most
Holy Father I have the greatest confidence;[22] pray promise him in my name
that, whether I do or do not come to Rome, I shall remain steadfastly in the   60
Catholic camp. At least, Rome has my heart; and nowhere would I more
gladly lay down the burden of this wretched body.

Basel, 16 September 1523

1387 / From Ennio Filonardi   Constance, 23 September 1523

The manuscript of this letter (=Ep 17 in Förstemann/Günther) was in the
Burscher Collection at Leipzig (Ep 1254 introduction). On Filonardi, see Ep
1282. As Ep 1392:1–3 shows, the news of Pope Adrian's death on 14 September
had not yet reached Switzerland.

Reverend and honoured sir, respectful greeting. It was the greatest comfort
to receive your letter[1] today, with those attached which are bound for
Rome;[2] and I will arrange for the letters, as you request and require, to be
forwarded to Rome by safe hand with all possible diligence, together with

* * * * *

20 In the form of occasional gifts in addition to his regular annuities from the
benefice at Aldington (Epp 188 and 255 introductions) and from Lord
Mountjoy (Ep 296:136–8). One frequent donor was John Longland, bishop of
Lincoln (Allen Ep 2961:36–7). On the generosity of Erasmus' friends in general
at this time, see Ep 1341A:1767–74.

21 Ep 1375 (see lines 39–40 above). The offer mentioned is not in the text of the
letter but was probably conveyed orally by its carrier, Claudius Cantiuncula
(Ep 852:85n). The two thousand would have been French livres tournois. See
CWE 1 328, 347; and also Ep 1434:25 and n13.

22 The news of Pope Adrian's death on 14 September had, of course, not yet
reached Basel. Cf Ep 1387 introduction.

1387
1 Not extant
2 One of these was Ep 1386.

others of my own. What I have given your servant[3] came to less than I could   5
wish, for I owe one so excellent and so distinguished as your reverence far
more than that.

If you really could think of any suitable remedies which might
extinguish the Lutheran heresy as soon as possible, and would impart them
to our Holy Father, and inform me, if you would be so good, at the same   10
time, I should think it would greatly help the state of things, and enhance
your reputation with his Holiness.

Should anything else arise in which I can be of assistance to your
reverence, pray do not overlook my readiness to oblige, and you will find me
daily more keen to do what I can for you; for I have set very great hopes on   15
you, if I can once see you in Rome in the high position which is your due, as
is the pope's intention and the general wish. And so I commend myself to
you body and soul and devote myself to your service and pray for your
prosperity.

From Constance, 23 September 1523   20
Your reverence's most obliged brother
E., bishop of Veroli
To my much respected master, the reverend Dr Erasmus of Rotterdam,
doctor of divinity without peer. In Basel

1388 / To Conradus Goclenius   Basel, 25 September 1523

On Goclenius, see Ep 1209. This letter was first published in Paul Merula's *Vita
Des. Erasmi* (Leiden: T. Basson 1607).

ERASMUS OF ROTTERDAM TO CONRADUS GOCLENIUS, GREETING
As I am expecting Hilarius[1] to bring a letter from you,[2] my dear Goclenius,
there is no call for me to write at length now. Do not be tormented by other
men's success, but wait for better things – though I do not see why you
should be greatly dissatisfied with your present position.[3] I am surprised   5

* * * * *

3 Probably Johannes Hovius (Ep 867:189n), who is mentioned in Ep 1424:7 as
  someone known to Filonardi. Hovius had already left Erasmus' service (Ep
  1349 n6) but may have visited Erasmus in September 1523 and agreed to carry
  some letters and messages for him.

1388
1 Bertholf (Ep 1384 n31)
2 No such letter has survived.
3 For Goclenius' dissatisfaction with his position at the Collegium Trilingue in
  Louvain, see Epp 1435:1–6, 1457:3–6.

about Vives.[4] He wrote to me that he was thinking of returning to Brabant.[5] If this is true, I suppose he must have been offered sixty livres instead of sixty angels.[6] They say that in Paris too a man has been burned.[7] Ferdinand also is surprisingly severe against Luther's supporters.[8] My friend Fabri, vicar-general of Constance, has been invited to join his court at a huge 10 salary.[9]

I was grateful to you for writing to send me news.[10] My *Spongia* no doubt has already reached you.[11] Hutten departed this life on 29 August,[12] and his death has largely destroyed the appeal of my *Spongia*.[13] The rising disorder everywhere obliges me to go on sitting here this winter.[14] If the 15 letter I have just had from Rome[15] had reached me earlier, I should already have set out on my journey. This winter, I hope, will put an end to our

* * * * *

4 After writing Ep 1362 Vives had gone to England, where he was appointed to one of Wolsey's lectureships at Oxford.

5 Letter not extant

6 The English gold angel-noble (with 5.157 g fine gold) was still worth 6s 8d (80 pence) or one third of a pound sterling, with an exchange value of 9s 8d gros Flemish and 60s tournois. Thus 60 angels = £20 sterling = £29 gros Flemish = £180 tournois. As Allen observed (in his n5), the 'sense requires a smaller coin [or sum of money] than the angel ...' He suggested the French livre [tournois]; but, since Vives was then dividing his time between Oxford and Bruges, these *libras* were more likely the Burgundian-Hapsburg *livres d'Artois* or *livres de quarante gros* (40d gros Flemish), then worth just slightly more than the French livre tournois. If so, sixty such *livres* would have been worth £10 gros Flemish, or £6 17s 10d sterling, or just over 20 gold angels (20.69 angels = £62 1s 4d tournois). See also CWE 1 312, 325–6, 336–7, 345.

7 On 8 August 1523, Jean Vallière, an illiterate hermit from Normandy, was burned at Paris for declaring that Jesus was the son of Joseph and Mary; see *Journal d'un bourgeois de Paris sous le règne de François Ier*, ed V.-L. Bourilly (Paris 1910) 397–8.

8 At the diet held in Nürnberg in the winter of 1522–3, Ferdinand, who attended as imperial viceroy, had manifested great hostility to the Lutherans and eagerness to enforce the Edict of Worms (Ep 1313 n7); see Planitz 211, 232, 245, 354, 387. In July 1523 Planitz (477) reported that Ferdinand had ordered the 'inhuman torture' of a Lutheran monk in Rattenberg am Inn.

9 See Ep 1382 n12.

10 The letter is not extant.

11 Ep 1378

12 Cf Ep 1389:7. The exact date of Hutten's death is uncertain. In other letters written from Basel at about this time, Claudius Cantiuncula says 31 August (Böcking II 352) and Basilius Amerbach says 1 September (AK 935:13).

13 Cf Ep 1389:2.

14 Instead of leaving Germany as planned; see Ep 1353 n33.

15 Perhaps that answered by Ep 1386

troubles.[16] I am full of fear for the French king.[17] My own prince[18] I approve of; but I see no end to it if this expansion of his empire[19] continues.

Antonius,[20] who brings you this, is a simple-minded fellow who has   20
made me laugh. He came here in order to buy books, and get rid of his habit, and even with some idea of marriage; and he hadn't a halfpenny. Take my advice, and do not have much to do with this unauthorized kind of accusation. I advised you long ago not to get deeply involved in friendships with Germans;[21] they are a Sejanus' horse.[22] My best wishes. Fight the   25
Muses' battle with a good courage; worldly success will shine upon you from some other source. As for Franz,[23] let me repeat my warning not to entrust him with any business of mine.

Basel, 25 September 1523

1389 / To the Reader   [Basel, c October 1523]

> This is the preface to the second edition of the *Spongia*; see Ep 1378. The conjectural date is based on Ep 1397:3–5, which also indicates that the edition consisted of 3,000 copies.

ERASMUS OF ROTTERDAM TO THE FAIR-MINDED READER, GREETING
Hutten's death has removed some of the appeal from my *Spongia*,[1] if works of this kind possess any appeal at all. Had I known of it in time, either I

* * * * *

16 Cf Ep 1345:3–6.
17 Francis I had been driven out of northern Italy by Charles V in 1521–2 (cf Ep 1342 n31) and now faced the prospect of an invasion of France by Emperor Charles and Henry VIII in collusion with the French traitor, Charles of Bourbon, constable of France; see Knecht 152.
18 Charles V
19 Erasmus writes 'imperii dilatatio.' *Imperium* here evidently refers not to the Holy Roman Empire, which was not expanding, but rather to Charles' own *imperium* (power, authority, dominion), which was expanding, especially in Italy, in a way that threatened a 'world monarchy' of the sort not seen since the time of Charlemagne. French resistance to this Hapsburg *imperium* caused bloody conflict until 1559; cf Ep 1369 n12.
20 Perhaps the person mentioned in Ep 1363:4. Ep 1437:225–6 indicates that he was a Franciscan.
21 Cf Epp 1258:30–2 with n15, 1389:39, 1437:104–5, 1512:30–2.
22 Ie, a horse that brings disaster to its possessor; *Adagia* I x 97
23 Franz Birckmann (Ep 1362 n1). Cf Epp 1362:59–60, 1437:414, 1488:49–51, 1494:37–9, 1507, 1513:46–52, 1531:29–30.

1389
1 Cf Ep 1388:14.

should not have replied, or my reply would have been different; as it is, there are some things in it which only Hutten was likely to understand.[2] I do 5 not suppose he had yet read the *Spongia* through, though certain people have asserted as much, for Hutten died on 29 August,[3] and Froben ended work on the *Spongia* just about the same time that he met his end. How I wish that death, which came to Hutten almost as a blessing – for it relieved the poor man from the pressure of so much misfortune, or removed him 10 from the threat of more – had been granted him somewhat sooner! – before he had so far lost his reason as to write such a venomous book, productive of so much ill will and so much discredit not only for himself but for the humanities, and for the cause of the gospel, and for all who call themselves Germans; for the very lightest sufferer in all this is myself. Not but what, if 15 men were led entirely by reason and judgment, it would not be fair for anyone to be prejudiced against the humanities by the appearance of a man who uses them perversely, or against the gospel cause, which Hutten has attacked so brazenly, seeing that even Luther has turned against him as an enemy of his party;[4] and it would be far more unfair to assess the nature of a 20 whole nation by the faults of one individual. Scythia produced its Anacharsis,[5] and Athens gave birth to many silly fools. From falling into this disgrace, overlooking any question of the breaches he had made in our friendship, I would have rescued my friend, had not certain persons I could name deliberately seen to it that we should never meet and talk.[6] As it is, I 25 am thankful for one thing at least, that so far I have been able to preserve my old moderation in replying. For even had Hutten attacked me again,[7] as he would I suppose have done, had he lived, either because he had once and for all lost all sense of decency or because there was no lack of people to give the cart a push downhill, as the saying goes,[8] he would have felt my reply to 30 be really just a sponge and no more.

* * * * *

2 See Ep 1341A:1084–5 and Ep 1033 introduction.
3 Cf Ep 1388 n12.
4 There is no direct statement from Luther to this effect, but in several letters whose contents quickly became known to Erasmus (Ep 1341A n299), Melanchthon expressed the Wittenbergers' displeasure over Hutten's *Expostulatio* and the 'great ill will' it had brought to Luther's cause.
5 The Scythian prince Anacharsis rose above the general barbarity of his people by travelling widely in Greece and gaining a reputation for wisdom. C 592 BC he went to Athens, where he became a friend of Solon and was included among the Seven Sages. Later he was credited with the invention of the potter's wheel, the bellows, and the anchor.
6 But cf Ep 1331 n24.
7 Cf Ep 1378:27.
8 *Adagia* I vi 13

Though, as far as I am concerned, Hutten's spirit shall rest in peace, provided that he does not show his teeth against me even after death in some poisonous pamphlet and no one arises to reopen the whole miserable business. It seems to me that this madness has already gone too far. Now 35 that what's done cannot be undone, it remains to bury the damage as far as one can. And since they give us good advice who tell us to pluck what good one can out of evil,[9] I shall learn this as my first lesson from the hard school I have been through: in future I shall be slower to make friends,[10] more cautious in cultivating them, more sparing in singing their praises, more 40 prudent in commending them to others. Why should I not, as Solon's famous saying puts it, learn something every day as I grow old?[11] In fact there is a lesson here for the young, that they should aim to acquire good sense no less than good learning and rein in their mettlesome passions with the bridle of reason; for many are indulgent at first to their own faults, they 45 forgive wenching and drunken revels as the marks of youth and suppose gambling and extravagance to be proper to noble blood. All the time, their property is dwindling and their debts are growing, their reputation is at risk, and they lose the favour of the princes to whose generosity they owed their bread. Then poverty invites them to seize what they want. At first their 50 robberies are excused under the pretext of war;[12] and then they find their appetites, like the urn of the Danaids,[13] insatiable and are reduced to desperate designs, so that the words friend and enemy now lose all meaning in their thirst for prey. In the end, like a horse that has thrown its rider, they are carried headlong to perdition. Though in Hutten this does not greatly 55 surprise me; for how ill-judged almost all his designs were is more notorious than I could wish. Where I am compelled to deplore a lack of judgment is in the men who pushed him forward onto the stage to act this crazy play,[14] and even now applaud such a sorry spectacle. They wish to appear supporters of the humanities,[15] and no man alive has done the humanities more harm 60 than they. They are passionate devotees of Luther, and could not have done more damage to his cause. They loved their Hutten, and his worst enemy did not hurt him more than they did. They hate Luther's enemies, and no

* * * * *

9 Cf *Adagia* I i 29, II v 65.
10 Cf Ep 1388:24–5.
11 Cf *Adagia* I viii 60.
12 Cf Erasmus' description of German junkers in *Adagia* I ix 44 CWE 32 44–5.
13 For their crimes in this world – the murder of their cousins, whom they had just married – the daughters of Danaus were punished in Hades by being compelled forever to pour water into a bottomless urn.
14 See preface xiv–xv, with nn25–9.
15 Cf this passage with Ep 1384:66–71.

SPONGIA ERASMI AD/
uersus aspergines Hutteni.

Erasmus *Spongia* title-page
Basel: Froben, c October 1523
Centre for Reformation and Renaissance Studies,
Victoria University, University of Toronto

one has yet provided those enemies with a spectacle more to their liking.
They are Germans through and through, and in three hundred years no one   65
has done more harm to the reputation of Germany.

Not that I fail to see the design behind this play and who has acted in it.
Straightforward as I am by nature and in no way suspicious, I am not so
devoid of all sense of smell, not such a blockhead, such a mere fungus, that I
alone cannot see what all men see. All the same, if I may be allowed at this   70
point to have finished my part in this life-and-death struggle, my desire is to
be ignorant of what I know and to forget what I remember. But I fear that
certain people who are overfond of this sort of wretched business will not let
me off; for though they know well enough how courteously I treated Hutten
in the *Spongia*, they are yet not ashamed to put it about that I waited till   75
Hutten was dead before publishing my book, as though I meant to do battle
with the dead. I replied to Hutten's *Expostulatio* promptly in July. My
manuscript was seen by Johann Froben and several other men besides. He
would have printed it, but he had no presses idle at the moment, and I
thought it wiser to postpone, for fear that some other attack might come out   80
before the fair,[16] to which I should not be able to reply. And again, as it is
known that Hutten died on the day I mentioned in a small island a long way
beyond Zürich,[17] and known that Froben started on the *Spongia* on the
thirteenth of August and finished it on 3 September, how is it possible
that I could have put out the *Spongia* after Hutten's death? – all the more so   85
since Hutten's death, so they tell me in letters,[18] was sudden. Count up how
long it would take for the news to be brought here even by special courier,
and consider the date on which I had already sent off my parcel; and you will
find I had not four hours in which to write the *Spongia*. That will give you an
idea of the effrontery of those who put this about. If the man whom I   90
suspect[19] makes himself known, he will discover that I did not hate Hutten
with my whole heart.

Farewell, dear reader; learn wisdom from my misfortunes.

1390 / To Johann von Vlatten   Basel, [c October] 1523

This is the preface to Erasmus' edition of Cicero's *Tusculanae quaestiones* (Basel:
Froben, November 1523). Allen judged the surviving manuscript of the

* * * * *

16 Ie, the autumn book fair at Frankfurt (Ep 326A:16n)
17 The island of Ufenau in the eastern arm of Lake Zürich
18 None of these has survived.
19 Either Otto Brunfels (Ep 1405) or Hermannus Buschius (Ep 1383:32–6). Cf Ep
   1406:129–33.

preface in the Librije (Town Library) at Gouda (MS 1324, f 145 verso) to be of 'no great value.' The letter is of great importance for understanding Erasmus' attitude towards Cicero in particular and classical antiquity in general. For Erasmus' earlier work as editor of Cicero, see Epp 152 and 1013.

Johann von Vlatten, or Wlaten (c 1498/9–1562), belonged to a family that took its name from the estates of Vlatten near Düren (between Aachen and Cologne) and that had a tradition of service to the dukes of Jülich. After taking his BA at Cologne (1517), Vlatten studied law, first at Orléans (1520–1) and then, starting in April 1522, under Zasius (Ep 303) at Freiburg. In 1526 he matriculated at Bologna where that same year he received a doctorate in civil and canon law. Meanwhile, in 1524, Vlatten had become a councillor to the duke of Cleves, thus beginning a long career as an influential adviser to the rulers of the united duchies of Jülich-Cleves-Berg.

Erasmus and Vlatten may have met as early as September 1518 during Erasmus' visit to Aachen, where Vlatten was canon of St Mary's. A meeting during Erasmus' later visit to Aachen in November 1520 seems ruled out because Vlatten was presumably in Orléans at the time (see Ep 1170 introduction). In any case, acquaintance evidently flowered into friendship during Erasmus' visit to Freiburg in March 1523 (lines 130–1), and the surviving correspondence between Vlatten and Erasmus (nineteen letters in all) begins with this letter of dedication. In 1528 Erasmus dedicated his *Ciceronianus* to Vlatten (Epp 1948, 2088).

As vice-chancellor (from 1530) and chancellor (from 1554) of Jülich-Cleves-Berg, Vlatten strove, in conjunction with Konrad Heresbach (n9) and others, to implement Erasmian ideals in the ecclesiastical and educational policies of the duchies. In 1532 Erasmus contributed a *consilium* on the revision of the church order for the duchies (Allen Ep 2804 introduction).

ERASMUS OF ROTTERDAM TO THE HONOURABLE
JOHANN VON VLATTEN, PROVOST OF CRANENBURG AND
SCHOLASTER OF COLOGNE, GREETING
When Johann Froben, honoured sir, was preparing to print Cicero's *Tusculan Questions*, and had asked me to put something of my own work into 5
it as best I could, so that the book when it appeared might have some useful novelty to recommend it, I set about the task all the more readily since for some years I had had either no contact with the more humane among the Muses or very little. I therefore entrusted the business of comparing copies of the text to members of my household, and took upon myself the duties of 10
a critic; and having read through the whole work with some attention, I marked off in lines the verse which he collects from Greek and Latin poets, with some precedent, it is true, from Plato and Aristotle, but till one almost

tires of them. Where the copies differed, I either adopted what I thought best
or, if it seemed a difficult decision, maintained both readings, one in the text   15
and the other in the margin. Some places I have restored without the help of
manuscripts, but not very many, and only where there would be no problem
for a good scholar with some experience; and I have also added a few notes.
While so engaged, I was obliged to suffer the loss of two or three days in the
other studies by which I do what I can to advance the gospel cause.[1]   20

And so far am I from regretting this expenditure of time that it is my
ambition, if it is permitted me, to make my way back to those old friends of
mine and spend some months in their intimate society. So great is the profit I
felt I derived from rereading these books, not only in rubbing the rust off my
prose style (though that too is far from negligible, in my view at least), but   25
much more in learning to moderate and control my passions. How often, as I
read, I felt a gush of contempt for those blockheads who are always
repeating that there is nothing notable in Cicero except the splendour of his
language! What a choice of reading he gives us there from the books left
behind them by the best Greek writers on the subject of the good and happy   30
life! What power and plenty in the way of sound and truly moral precepts!
What a range of knowledge and what a memory for ancient and modern
history at the same time! And again, what profound reflections on the true
felicity of man, which clearly show that he practised what he preached! And
in expounding subjects far removed from the sentiments and language of   35
the ordinary man, where many men used to despair of the possibility of
treating them in Latin, the clarity, the openness of mind, the easy
movement, the ready flow of words, and last but not least the lightness of
touch!

Philosophy at first was absorbed in the contemplation of the natural   40
world and had little contact with life; it was Socrates, we read, who first
brought her down to earth and even into the homes of men. Plato and
Aristotle tried to introduce her to the courts of kings, to the legislature, and
even to the law-courts. But Cicero seems to me to have brought her almost
onto the stage, for with his help she has learned to speak in such a fashion   45
that even a miscellaneous audience can applaud. And in this field that great
man wrote so many books in a time of great crisis when his country was in
the utmost confusion, and some of them he wrote when public affairs were
in the most desperate state. Surely we ought to be ashamed of our casual
conversations and our dinner-table talk, when we see how pagans devoted   50
to such high moral considerations even such leisure as they were allowed by

* * * * *

1390
1 See Epp 1391, 1393, 1400, 1414, 1426, 1427.

the downfall of their country, not seeking an anodyne for the mind in brainless pleasures but trying to find a remedy in the most exalted precepts of philosophy.

What others experience, I do not know; but for myself, as I read Cicero, 55 especially when he treats of the good life, he affects me in such a way as to leave me no doubts that something divine dwelt in the bosom whence all this proceeded. And this my judgment seems to me the more likely to be right, when I consider how immeasurable, how far beyond conjecture is the goodness of the eternal God, which some men, judging it I suppose by their 60 own natures, try to constrict within such narrow limits. The present dwelling-place of Cicero's soul is not perhaps a subject for human judgment to pronounce on. I at least shall not be found actively in opposition, as they count the votes, by those who hope that he lives peacefully among the heavenly beings. No one can doubt that he believed in the existence of some 65 supreme power, the greatest and the best thing that can be. And as for his opinions on the immortality of the soul, on the different lots and different rewards in a future life and the great confidence inspired by a clear conscience – if these are not clear enough from all the books he wrote, that one letter at least quite proves the point, which he wrote to Octavius,[2] 70 apparently when his death had already been decided on.

If the Jews before the appearance of the gospel found a kind of rough and confused credulity about divine subjects sufficient for salvation, why should not an even more rudimentary knowledge suffice for the salvation of a pagan ignorant even of the Mosaic law, especially one whose life was of a 75 high standard, and not merely high but holy? Very few Jews before the light of the gospel dawned upon them had any exact knowledge of the Son and the Holy Spirit; many did not believe in the resurrection of the body; yet that was not in the eyes of the older generation a reason for despairing of their salvation. What if a pagan's creed went no further than this, that God, 80 whom he is convinced is almighty, perfectly wise, and perfectly good, will reward the good and punish the bad on some system which seems to him the most appropriate? If someone were to make an objection of the blemishes in his life, I for my part do not suppose that either Job or

* * * * *

2 The reference is to a spurious letter of Cicero to Octavius (or Octavianus) that Erasmus believed to be genuine. See T.O. Achelis 'Erasmus über die griechischen Briefe des Brutus' *Rheinisches Museum* 72 (1917–18) 633–8, especially 634–5. The last two sections of the letter imply a belief in immortality, though one more tentative than Erasmus here suggests; see Robert Y. Tyrrell and Louis C. Purser eds *The Correspondence of M. Tullius Cicero* VI (Dublin and London 1899) 345–6.

Melchizedek was entirely devoid of all faults all his life long.[3] But it is   85
inexcusable that he should have sacrificed to idols. So he did, maybe; only it
was not from conviction but in accordance with public custom, and since
that was established by law, there was no stopping it. That the stories about
the gods were inventions he could learn from, among other places, the
Sacred History of Ennius.[4] But, they say, he should have convinced the public   90
of its folly by the sacrifice of his life if need be. Such stamina was not to be
found among the apostles themselves, before they received the Spirit from
heaven, so that it would be grossly unfair to demand it of Cicero.

But on this topic let each man be free to use his own judgment. I come
back to those blockheads who think that beyond the empty music of the   95
words there is nothing important in the works of Cicero. How can he
possibly expound so many recondite subjects so clearly, so fully, and with so
much feeling, unless he really understands what he is writing? Who ever
took up one of his books without having more peace of mind when he rose
from the reading of it? Who went to him in a time of mourning and was not   100
more cheerful when he came away? What you read seems to be happening,
and your mind feels the breath of a kind of enthusiasm in the style, exactly as
though you had heard it coming from the heart and the eloquent lips of the
living man. This is why I often think that among all the discoveries that
enterprise has made for the profit of mortal life, nothing is more profitable   105
than the use of writing, and no art more valuable than the craft of printers.
What blessing can be greater than to converse at will with the most eloquent
and the most saintly of men, and to have as clear a view of their gifts and
character and thoughts and ambitions and actions as if you had lived in their
company for many years?   110

Never have I more wholly approved of Quintilian's remark that a man
may know he has made progress when he begins to take great pleasure in
Cicero.[5] When I was a boy Cicero attracted me less than Seneca, and I was
already twenty before I could bear to read him at any length, although I liked
almost all other writers. Whether I have progressed with advancing years, I   115
do not know; at any rate, I never enjoyed Cicero more, in the days when I
had a passion for these studies, than I do now in my old age, not only for his

* * * * *

3 On Melchizedek, see Hebrews 6:20–7:17.
4 In his *Sacra historia* or *Euhemerus*, the Roman poet Ennius (239–169 BC) took
  over from the *Sacred History* of Euhemerus, a Sicilian at the court of Cassander
  in Macedon (311–298 BC), the view that the gods were really famous men or
  heroes who had been deified after death. Cicero mentions both works in the *De
  natura deorum* 1.119.
5 *Institutio oratoria* 10.1.112

almost divine felicity of style but for the combination of learning and high
moral tone. I find in him a direct inspiration, and he gives me back to myself
a better man. And so I should have no hesitation in urging the young to   120
spend long hours in reading him and even in learning him by heart, rather
than on the captious and quarrelsome books which abound everywhere
nowadays. As for myself, although now getting on in years, I shall find it
neither embarrassing nor tedious, as soon as I can extricate myself from the
work I have in hand, to resume close relations with my old friend Cicero,   125
and to renew for a few months that original intimacy which has now been
too long interrupted.

   And I decided to dedicate this work, such as it is, to you, dear Vlatten,
man of many and great gifts, partly to make clear by this piece of evidence
that I have not yet forgotten that delightful association through which,   130
when I was in Freiburg,[6] I first learned to know really well your exceptional
kindness and rare subtlety of character, and partly to provide you with a
correct text of these books of Cicero, which you might order to be studied by
the intelligent young; for you used to say that concern for the school was
your special province. In any case, that there should be a chorus of frogs in   135
your part of the world ready to croak against the humanities should surprise
no one, for there is no shortage anywhere of such creatures to interrupt with
their song from the old comedy *brekekekex koax koax;*[7] but you must boldly
pay them no attention, and follow what is most in the interests of the young.
To this end it will be a great help to have in charge of the school a man of   140
good character no less than good education, whose salary can be increased if
he deserves it. Once he has laid the first foundations of both Greek and
Latin, he should read all the best authors with the boys; and this means
Cicero, and the others in proportion as they approach him. Among the poets
he must choose those who are respectable; and in any case those who are   145
worth reading for the amount they can tell us but are objectionable for their
obscenity, of whom Martial is one, must in my view be presented in excerpts
which can safely be read with the boys.

   But of these things I may perhaps say more on another occasion;
though no one will give you better advice than Leonardus Priccardus,[8] a   150
man of various learning and high character, whose great experience makes
his advice of great value. I should be very sorry to see Konrad Heresbach
taken from us[9] – for my life upon it, I never yet saw a more rounded

* * * * *

6 March 1523; see Ep 1353 introduction.
7 Aristophanes *Frogs* 209
8 Ep 972
9 Heresbach (Ep 1316) had just become tutor to young Duke William of Cleves.

character than that young man, whether you consider his knowledge of
Latin and Greek or his fertile intelligence or the courtesy of manners which is   155
a match for his integrity – did I not know what miserly characters he has left
behind him, and what sort of a prince he has for a master.[10] Farewell.

From Basel, 1523

1391 / To Thiébaut Biétry   [Basel, c October 1523]

> This is the preface to Erasmus' *Virginis matris apud Lauretum cultae liturgia*
> (Basel: Froben, November 1523), a mass in honour of the Virgin of Loretto,
> written at the request of its dedicatee, Thiébaut Biétry (see below). During
> Erasmus' visit to Besançon in April 1524 (Ep 1440 n4), the archbishop, Antoine
> de Vergy, issued a diploma granting an indulgence to those in his jurisdiction
> who used the liturgy. This, together with continued prompting by Biétry (Ep
> 1534:23–4), caused Erasmus to enlarge the liturgy by the addition of a sermon.
> This enlarged version, together with the archbishop's diploma, was published
> by Froben in May 1525 with a new dedicatory letter to Biétry (Ep 1573).
>
> Thiébaut Biétry (Theobaldus Bietricius), documented 1516–26, was the
> parish priest in Porrentruy, a little town in the Jura about 40 kilometres
> southwest of Basel where the bishop of Basel had a residence. One assumes
> that Biétry's acquaintance with Erasmus had begun in Basel, though date and
> circumstances are not known. The two were together during Erasmus' visit to
> Porrentruy and Besançon in April 1524 (see above). Biétry disappears from the
> historical record after his last letter to Erasmus (Ep 1760, 11 October 1526).

ERASMUS OF ROTTERDAM TO THEOBALDUS BIETRICIUS,
PARISH PRIEST OF PORRENTRUY, GREETING

Look at this! In future you can expect to see Erasmus dancing in the
market-place if you tell him to. Only remember that the fewer the people
who agree with your judgment, the larger the debt you owe me for my   5
compliance. I foresee one danger, that our Lady of Loretto may not listen
when you are singing[1] this at Porrentruy. Paul condemns neither hymns nor
psalms, provided that he who sings psalms with the spirit sings also with
the understanding.[2] But you have been summoned to fill the office of a
prophet, which means to be a shepherd. If shepherds thought their flocks   10

* * * * *

10 Duke John III of Jülich-Cleves (1490–1539)

1391
1 Biétry was greatly interested in the use of music in church services; see Ep 1573.
2 1 Cor 14:15; Eph 5:19

would grow fat on singing, they would sing to them and do nothing more. As it is, they take them out to pasture, as you see, every day, and do not leave them at home to starve. A shepherd of sheep ought not to know his job better than a shepherd of souls. You too must lead your flock out and back again, and you will find pastures, for the gospel provides food both   15 privately and in public. You must not say, I am no doctor of divinity. Set before the people with a good courage precisely what Jesus provided, and you will see that today as of old a few loaves and still fewer small fishes can feed many thousands of men.[3] Farewell.

1392 / From Ennio Filonardi   Constance, 22 October 1523

The manuscript of this letter (=Ep 18 in Förstemann/Günther) was in the Burscher Collection at Leipzig (Ep 1254 introduction). On Filonardi, see Ep 1282.

Reverend and honoured sir, respectful greeting. After I had sent a letter from your reverence to Rome with mine,[1] I heard with incredible grief of the untimely death of his Holiness[2] of most sainted memory, a blow which can and should fill us all with mourning, for as yet we do not know whom we are likely to have who will be like him and of equal goodness.   5

If however your reverence would be so good as to expound to me in the mean time the plans for suppressing the Lutheran upheaval[3] which you write that you have already indicated to the aforesaid Adrian vi of most sainted memory,[4] whether I am recalled or continued I would faithfully communicate the whole to the future pope, and would omit nothing that I   10 knew might be for the increase of your reputation; to whom I am at any rate so much attached that I greatly desire an opportunity of being able to do your reverence some exceptional service. And I assure you of my lifelong devotion and would wish you all the prosperity that I would wish for myself.   15

* * * * *

3 Matt 14:13–21; Mark 6:30–44; Luke 9:10–17; John 6:1–13
   1392
1 See Ep 1387:1–4.
2 Adrian vi, on 14 September
3 See Ep 1387:8–10.
4 In his answer to Ep 1387 Erasmus had apparently written much as in Ep 1376:6–7.

As for the business of Master Johann Froben,[5] I greatly regret that I do not possess the needful authority, as I have replied on another occasion in the case of a certain monk.[6] Had I the authority, your reverence knows from experience on more than one occasion that I can deny you nothing, for with me you can do even what is impossible; to whom I offer and commend   20 myself wholeheartedly and pray for your long-continued prosperity.

From Constance, 22 October 1523

Your reverence's most obliged

E., bishop of Veroli

To my much respected master, the reverend Dr Erasmus of Rotterdam,   25 doctor of divinity without peer etc

1393 / To Justus Ludovicus Decius   Basel, 24 October 1523

This is the preface to Erasmus' *Precatio dominica in septem portiones distributa* (Basel: Froben [1523]), which had been written at Decius' request (lines 1–18, 40; cf Ep 1341A:780–1). The book quickly became popular and was much translated. The English version (1524) was made by Margaret Roper, Thomas More's daughter.

On Decius, who was secretary to the king of Poland, see Ep 1341A n210.

DESIDERIUS ERASMUS OF ROTTERDAM TO JODOCUS OR JUSTUS
LUDOVICUS OF WISSEMBURG, SECRETARY AND ENVOY OF
HIS MOST SERENE MAJESTY THE KING OF POLAND, GREETING

Not without good reason, honoured sir, have many generations given their approval to the old saw 'When the strong man says "Please," he means "You   5 must"';[1] but I doubt whether it has ever fitted any man better than it fits you, for you have added to your learned letter[2] such an elegant present,[3] a present indeed sent from so far away that it would be impossible to refuse it, unless I had wanted to throw it away. What could not such a letter extract

* * * * *

5 Perhaps a request for a papal privilege to supplement that granted by Archduke Ferdinand; see Ep 1341 n4.

6 See Ep 1363:3–8.

1393

1 One of the *sententiae* falsely attributed to Publilius Syrus; see *Publilii Syrii Mimi Sententiae* ed Otto Friedrich (Berlin 1880) 97, 285.

2 Not extant

3 Among Erasmus' belongings in 1534, when an inventory of his property of this sort was made (Ep 1437 n63), was a gilded goblet listed as 'donum Justi Decii.' It may have been given on this occasion or later. See L. Sieber *Das Mobiliar des Erasmus. Verzeichnis ...* (n p 1891) 6.

from anyone – I will not say from me, for I am too easily won over, but from   10
any man, however hard to move? So well equipped it was with all those
siege-engines of the mind, winning politeness, forcible arguments, convincing erudition, irresistible eloquence; but nothing gave it more power than its
exceptional and lovable modesty, which has such influence over me that it
could make me undertake not only a task like this, which is both congenial   15
and pious, but far more uphill work. And so no sooner had I received your
letter – and it took some time to come and did not reach me till the very end
of August – than I seized my pen and did as you wished. Such as it is, it will
mark the happy opening both of our friendship and of my good will towards
the Polish or, if the ancient name is more to your liking, the Sarmatian   20
people.

      And I congratulate that people, for though in the old days they had a
bad reputation as barbarians, they are now so flourishing in literature and
law, in civilized behaviour and religion, and all else that may protect them
from the charge of barbarism, that they can compete with the most eminent   25
and highly regarded nations. Although even in antiquity, when the
Sarmatians were reckoned among wild and barbarous peoples, that stern
moral critic Juvenal set them none the less for their integrity above the highly
cultivated Athenians: 'Neither Sarmatian nor Thracian he / Who put on
wings, but one in the midst of Athens born.'[4] To say nothing at the moment   30
of the extent of those dominions, embracing White Russians and Lithuani-
ans too, all of which, wide-ranging as they are, from the river Vistula to the
Tauric Chersonese and from the Baltic Sea to the Carpathians, are ruled by
King Sigismund,[5] a monarch who excels in all the gifts that grace a great
prince and has won glory by many great victories over his Tartar and   35
Muscovite enemies, which were I suppose more needful than anything else
for protecting the boundaries of Christendom.

      But we will speak of these things perhaps more appropriately on
another occasion. Let me now offer you the Lord's Prayer, divided into
seven parts, a task which you set me and which I see others have essayed   40
before me; though the last two clauses, 'And lead us not into temptation but
deliver us from evil' lend themselves as little to separation, in my view, as if
one were to try and make two out of what immediately precedes, 'And
forgive us our trespasses as we forgive those who trespass against us.' If
your devotion is not satisfied by taking seven days to complete the whole,   45
you can do as I see our predecessors have done, and divide up every day
with seven moments for prayer. Farewell.

      Basel, 24 October 1523

            * * * * *

4 *Satires* 3.79–80
5 Sigismund I (1506–48)

1394 / From Nicolaas van Broeckhoven   Antwerp, 5 November 1523

The manuscript of this letter (=Ep 19 in Förstemann/Günther) was in the Burscher Collection at Leipzig (Ep 1254 introduction). On Nicolaas van Broeckhoven, see Ep 1299 n23.

Best wishes, dear Erasmus, my master and my patron. Having unexpectedly the offer of a courier, I could not fail to write you a few lines at least to give you my news. I was bound for Lier,[1] but for many reasons my friends made me stay for some time in Antwerp under the eyes of my opponents for fear I might give them a new handle for a triumph over me. And so I shall confine   5
my activities until Christmas to that hive of industry the house of Master Pieter Gillis,[2] and meanwhile shall look out for some convenient place to live. I trust I shall follow your advice, and not try to score off my opponents except by living an honourable life. But their efforts have quietened down very much since the pope's death.[3] Schrijver has been reinstated,[4] and so   10
has Cornelis Hoen,[5] an advocate in The Hague, to the fury of Baechem[6] and his crew.

For the rest, dear master, I wonder that Froben should be so selfish or so thoughtless, if he took seven and a half gold florins off you on my account,[7] when I had paid his son Hieronymus[8] absolutely in full, as I think I   15
told you. I gave him approximately six gold florins. Hieronymus had replied on that occasion that he was grateful to me, and that his father would not have asked for anything had I paid nothing; so I could wish he would return to you the money he ought never to have accepted.

If there is anything you would like me to do for you, I am, as you know,   20
most devoted. You can do nothing that would please me more than to load me with your commands. Many regret the publication of your *Spongia*,[9] but most people admire it, and especially Dorp,[10] because you explain every-

* * * * *

1394
1 About 14.5 kilometres south of Antwerp
2 Ep 184
3 Adrian VI died on 14 September.
4 Ep 1299 n24
5 Ep 1358 n7
6 Ep 1254 n6
7 Presumably Rhenish gold florins, which would have been worth 36s 3d gros Flemish or 25s 8d sterling. Perhaps this was a debt incurred during Broeckhoven's visit to Basel, concerning which see Ep 1431:5–6.
8 Ep 1226
9 See Ep 1378.
10 Ep 304

thing so neatly. Farewell, and prosper in Christ, teacher and patron beyond
compare.   25

Antwerp, 5 November 1523
Nicolaas of 's Hertogenbosch
To the distinguished doctor of divinity Master Erasmus of Rotterdam,
his most respected teacher. In Basel

1395 / To the Town Council of Basel   [Basel, November?] 1523

In this letter, which was first published in the *Opus epistolarum*, Erasmus
appeals to the Basel city council to remit a fine imposed on one 'Benedictus
bibliopola' (Benedict the bookseller). The bookseller in question was Benoît
Vaugris (d by February 1539), a native of Charly near Lyon and a kinsman of
Claudia Vaugris, the wife of the Basel bookseller Johann Schabler, called
Wattenschnee (cf Ep 1335 n2). In 1523 Vaugris opened a bookstore in
Constance.

Apart from its connection in some way with Vaugris' marriage (lines 18–20),
it is not clear what the above-mentioned fine was for. In May 1522 Vaugris was
sentenced to jail for unlawfully wounding a man and on 5 November was
released from jail, bail having been supplied by Wattenschnee and Benoît's
brother Jean, a Basel printer. In the period 1523–6 Vaugris was also involved in
litigation at Basel over his wife's inheritance, which was contested by the
relatives of her first husband.

Given Vaugris' kinship with Wattenschnee and Jean Vaugris, one can
surmise who the citizens were who urged Erasmus to intervene on his behalf.
In a letter of 1 November 1533 (Allen Ep 2874:53–83), Erasmus recounts the
story of this intercession in some detail and accuses Benoît of base ingratitude.

As indicated in the heading, Allen's month-date for this letter is purely
conjectural.

ERASMUS OF ROTTERDAM TO THE TOWN COUNCIL OF BASEL, GREETING
I know well and well remember the many and important reasons I have so
long had to be indebted to such a noble and vigorous body as your worships,
nor am I ignorant that from my slender resources the debt can never be
repaid; and yet your exceptional kindness, of which I have long experience   5
and most certain proofs, ensures that there is no one to whom I would rather
be indebted than yourselves. Nor am I deterred from asking by the
knowledge that I am not the sort of man who could ever repay, unless in
your generosity you will follow the example of the eternal Deity and take it
that an obligation is fulfilled which the recipient admits, remembers, and   10
acknowledges in public. Otherwise, the man who is able to say 'I will repay,

and with interest into the bargain' does not accept a kindness, he borrows one.

I do not deny that it is in the interest of the common weal that the authority of laws and council decisions and magistrates should be inviola- 15
ble. But in this case of Benoît the bookseller, by what I hear, it was from no wish to break the law but by mistake pure and simple that he exposed himself to a fine and (what was the origin of the whole affair) married a young woman. Marriage is normally encouraged everywhere. The young man is in humble circumstances. There will be good hope of a dowry if of 20
your kindness you will remit the fine. I have long been deeply indebted to you, and you will make my debt all the heavier, as well as that of many other citizens not unworthy of your favour, who have urged me to take up Benoît's case and promised moreover a favourable outcome, because no doubt they rely on your generosity. I can promise no service in return; but if 25
anyone can tell me of some way in which I could oblige your distinguished body, you will find that at least I did not lack a ready desire to do so. I pray that the Lord Jesus may keep you all in health and wealth and prosper your commonwealth both publicly and in private. 1523

1396 / From Thomas Blarer   Constance, 17 November 1523

The manuscript of this letter (=Ep 20 in Förstemann/Günther) was in the Burscher Collection at Leipzig (Ep 1254 introduction). On Thomas Blarer and his brother Ambrosius (line 40), see Ep 1341A n430.

Greeting. I have long wished I could find some significant way to put on record my truly affectionate feelings for you; but for a long time no suitable opportunities offered and this was denied me, and now I fear that with the passage of time a new trouble has come between us: I could no longer display my old love for you, but must first remove the suspicion of some 5
new disagreement. For although that letter which you wrote to Laurinus seems to show the two of us at variance, I mean Erasmus and your imaginary Lutheran,[1] and although you do not shake me by your arguments at any point, I should like you to know that my feelings towards you are not altered in the least. My affection for you is such that the more you went 10
astray from the right feelings and obligations of a true Christian, supposing

* * * * *

1396
1 See Ep 1342:807ff. Blarer identifies himself with the imaginary Lutheran whom Erasmus there engages in discussion.

you were to do anything of the kind, the greater would be my longing for my old friend.

You will find me ready to give you a reason for this devotion, if surprise at this concern for you makes you invite me to do so once more.[2] For it was 15 for your sake rather than mine that I thought it better to have it out with you in private letters and not in the market-place. You will find, I think, that there is no call to find fault with me for the ambition of which you accuse me,[3] and that I challenge no man to a mere exchange of scurrilities but much more to a confession of the goodness divinely bestowed upon us. But I do 20 not urge this course upon you by itself alone; who would endanger himself and his position in the world unless he knew the reason why? It is the cause to which I so urgently recall you;[4] and if you and I did not follow different causes, to say nothing of our practical policies, all these exertions of mine on behalf of you and others like you would be wasted.   25

Are we then the only men of sense? Are we alone honest and sane? That is not our objective: we want other people too to have faith and life – faith and life in the spirit of men who reject any suggestion that they are not Christians. This is the object we pursue in Christian singleness of heart, let our adversaries dislike it if they will; and yet they charge us with arrogance 30 and bitterness. Arrogance perhaps, because we despise the things of this world; bitterness because we spoil some people's private profit, for this is how I interpret this pride and venom that they speak of. If you, my dear Erasmus (to whom I am devoted), can show me another interpretation, I shall gladly listen. For my part, I shall never tire of presenting either my own 35 cause or the whole of Luther's cause for your approval and shall receive your verdict on the question; but only on condition that I am allowed to judge in my turn,[5] and on the understanding that the opinions of men must give place to the divine testimonies. And so I bid your reverence farewell. My brother Ambrosius sends you his greetings.   40

From Constance, 17 November 1523

Thomas Blarer

To that most honoured of seniors, Master Desiderius Erasmus of Rotterdam, his sure support. In Basel

* * * * *

2 Cf Ep 1342:838, 856–7, 900–1, 1037.
3 Location of accusation unknown
4 Ie, the cause of Luther; cf line 36.
5 Cf Ep 1342:901, 910–11, 961, 1016, 1037, 1079.

1397 / To Johannes Fabri   Basel, 21 November 1523

Two manuscript copies of this letter survive, both of them in the Forschungsbibliothek Gotha. One (Chart B.26, f 17 verso) was probably made within a
year or two of the letter's having been written. The other (Chart A.399, f 232)
was made c 1553. See Allen's introduction for further details. The second
manuscript copy may have been based on the earliest printed version, which
was appended to Erasmus Alber's *Iudicium de Spongia Erasmi Roterodami* (1524);
see Ep 1466 n19. Allen composed his text out of all three sources.

Fabri, who must by now have joined Archduke Ferdinand's court (see Ep
1382:37–8), was in Linz on 16 November, doubtless en route from Vienna
(where he had been in September) to Nürnberg for the coming diet. Ferdinand
himself entered Nürnberg on 29 November. Fabri's presence in Nürnberg is
not documented until 12 January, but he was probably there much earlier. The
diet opened on 14 January. See pages 382–3 of the article by Koegler cited in n1
below.

Greetings, my honoured friend. The good wishes which you sent me by
Olpeius[1] were a great encouragement, for they were elegantly expressed,
and they came from one friend and were brought by another. A further three
thousand of my *Spongia* have been printed.[2] This was Froben's idea; I myself
hate such productions, nor do I harbour much resentment against Hutten.   5
What I resent is the encouragement the poor fellow got from men interested
solely in what they could get out of it.[3] I do not doubt that they will soon
betray themselves, for some monstrous business is again being nursed in
Strasbourg.[4] Luther passionately abuses the *Spongia*; I have sent you his
letter.[5] He also said in a letter to Oecolampadius that I am like Moses and   10

* * * * *

1397
1 'Olpeius' has been identified as Hans Holbein the Younger by Hans Koegler;
   see his 'Hans Holbein d. J. und Dr. Johann Fabri' *Repertorium für Kunstwissen-
   schaft* 35 (1912) 379–84. The three portraits mentioned in Ep 1452:44–5 are from
   this period. According to Koegler (383), Fabri would have sent his greetings
   from Constance at the end of August or beginning of September, just before his
   departure to join Ferdinand. Holbein made a trip from Constance to Basel at
   about that time.
2 Epp 1378, 1389
3 Cf Epp 1383:2–9, 1389:57–9.
4 Either the expected attack from Buschius (Ep 1383 n21) or that from Brunfels
   (Epp 1405, 1406)
5 See Ep 1341A n298; cf Ep 1415:47–8 with n9.

must be buried in the wilderness and that too much weight should not be given to Erasmus in spiritual matters.[6] This sort of thing means war.

Mark is finished;[7] so are my Lord's Prayer[8] and (this will show you that I am entering my second childhood) Ovid's *Nux* as well.[9] I have started on the Acts of the Apostles,[10] and begun a book on confession.[11] If my strength holds out, I shall add a book on free will.[12] You are a wise man, my dear Fabri, and need no advice from me. I know you will handle the cause of Christ in a reasonable spirit, which will not betray the simple purity of the gospel to the Pharisees and scribes and high priests;[13] this will earn you a solid reputation with posterity. You have a prince who is excellent by nature,[14] and you must prove yourself a loyal counsellor. You know that exceptionally wise man Willibald;[15] please give him my most cordial greetings. I had expected a touch of peace in the air,[16] but you can see what the climate is like now. We have lost our Adrian;[17] if he used his tenure of the Holy See in Christ's service he now has his reward with Christ, and if he used it to serve men he has lost the glorious place that was his in the presence of God. He has his appointed Judge. As for you, my dear Fabri, mind you act as a true steward of the gospel. Pray commend your friend Erasmus to Ferdinand your illustrious prince, whose welfare is always in my prayers. Murner has been sent back from England with his pockets full.[18] How many men are made rich by that penniless Luther![19] Farewell. From Basel, 21 November 1523

* * * * *

6 See Ep 1384:57–62.
7 Ep 1400
8 Ep 1393
9 Ep 1402
10 Ep 1414
11 The *Exomologesis* (Ep 1426)
12 Cf Ep 1385 n2, and see Epp 1419, 1420, 1481.
13 Cf Epp 1382:30–5, 74–80, 1398:5–7.
14 Archduke Ferdinand; cf line 29.
15 Pirckheimer; see Ep 1398.
16 Cf Ep 1400:7–9.
17 Adrian VI, d 14 September 1523
18 Thomas Murner (1475–1537) was a citizen of Strasbourg, a Franciscan, a doctor of theology and canon law, and (since 1512) a prolific writer of satirical poems in German. In 1520 Murner took up the cudgels against the reformers, becoming one of the most prolific and popular Catholic controversialists of his generation. In the spring of 1523 he went to England to visit Henry VIII, whose *Assertio* against Luther (Ep 1275 n25) he had translated into German; WA 10/2 176. Upon his departure from England in September to return to Strasbourg, Henry gave him £100 sterling; LP III 3270.
19 Cf Epp 1352:131–2, 1408:30, 1417:15–17.

Your very sincere friend Erasmus

To the reverend Master Johannes Fabri, canon and vicar-general of Constance, my most respected lord. In Nürnberg   35

1398 / To Willibald Pirckheimer   Basel, 21 November 1523

On Pirckheimer, see Ep 318. This letter was first published in the *Pirckheimeri opera*.

Greeting. Capito has written[1] to say that Varnbüler[2] has a grievance of some sort about being overcharged for a book by Koberger.[3] Tell him not to worry. I will see that whatever it is, is made good. I sent you an effigy in lead,[4] using the licence that exists between friends to do something foolish. I long to know what happened to it. I hope Fabri, the vicar-general of Constance, will   5 find some way to exercise his influence that will not betray Christ to the Pharisees, scribes, and high priests.[5] If only they too were wiser in their generation![6] I warn them constantly, and make a little progress but less than I could wish. Mind you on your side never cease to be my friend; I shall always be my usual self. Farewell, both you and yours, my honourable   10 friend.

Basel, 21 November 1523. Give my greetings to our modern Apelles in return.[7]

Your friend Erasmus

To the honourable Willibald Pirckheimer, right worthy town councillor   15 of Nürnberg

1399 / To Christoph von Utenheim   Basel, [c November] 1523

On Christoph von Utenheim, see Ep 1332. The letter was first published in the *Opus epistolarum*.

Allen's reasons for the conjectural month-date of November are as follows.

* * * * *

1398
1 His letter is not extant.
2 Ep 1344 n27
3 Erasmus writes 'a Conbergio,' but he appears to be referring to the Koberger printing firm of Nürnberg.
4 Possibly a copy of the 1519 medallion by Metsys; see Ep 1092 n2.
5 Cf Ep 1382:30–5, 74–80, 1397:17–19.
6 Cf Luke 16:8.
7 Dürer (Ep 1376 n1). Apelles was a famous Greek painter who did a portrait of Alexander the Great. Cf Ep 1408 n18.

The use of stoves (line 5) indicates that the letter belongs to the cold months of
the year. Erasmus had a serious attack of the stone about Christmas 1523 (Ep
1408 n2); the fairly light-hearted language here (lines 11ff), so different from
the expressions of gloom after Christmas, may indicate the beginning of the
attack. The reference to the third printing of the paraphrase on Matthew (lines
21–2) gives no definite guidance, since there were so many issues in 1522–3
(see Allen's introduction to Ep 1255). However, if one regards the three
octavos of that period as all one impression, then the reference here could be to
the collected volume of the paraphrases on the four Gospels and Acts
published in 1524 (see Ep 1430 n1). Erasmus may have begun to prepare this
volume as soon as the paraphrase on Mark (Ep 1400) was nearly finished and
while work on Acts (Ep 1414) was still in progress. Finally, the reference in line
7 to the current warm weather could indicate that Basel and environs were
experiencing a spell of St Martin's summer, which occurs in November.

ERASMUS OF ROTTERDAM TO CHRISTOPH, BISHOP OF BASEL, GREETING
Most honourable prelate, a week ago I had made up my mind to pay you a
visit, under the guidance of Ludwig Baer,[1] who is wholeheartedly devoted
to your highness. But he thought it uncivil to tempt you away at your time of
life from the warmth of your stoves, and I would not dare expose myself to it   5
once again after having so often experienced the pestilential effect it
instantly has on me. If this warm weather allows you to leave your warm
rooms, I have a great desire to see your lordship and have a talk with you. I
have had trouble for a long time now with the stone,[2] an evil with which I
became all too familiar long ago, but now it recurs either more often or with   10
more dangerous effects. Women grow barren as they grow older; old age
makes me bring forth oftener – conception, birth, or impending birth are
always with me. But the offspring are like young vipers,[3] and will one day I
fear bring about the death of their parent; at any rate I have been delivered
two or three times in the greatest peril. If ever my pains come on when Juno   15
and Lucina are not on my side,[4] all will be over with your poor Erasmus.
They say this complaint is related to the gout, with which I hear (and sorry I

* * * * *

1399
1 Ep 1378 n9
2 Cf Epp 1349 n1, 1376 n4.
3 According to Pliny *Naturalis historia* 10.170, the viper's brood of about
  twenty get so fed up with the delay involved in being born at the rate of one a
  day that they burst open their mother's sides, killing her.
4 Both godesses of childbirth, usually identified with one another. Roman
  women in childbirth invoked Juno Lucina.

am to hear it) that your highness is sometimes troubled. Both take pleasure
in recurring, but my complaint carries greater immediate risk.

If there is anything you do not like in the paraphrase I have lately   20
published on St Matthew,[5] I do beg you most sincerely to be so kind as to let
me know, for the work is now being printed for the third time. I desire to
control what I write in such a way as to make it profitable and pleasant for all
men of good will, if this is possible. Best wishes to your lordship, and may
Christ the Almighty deign to grant you the unbroken peace and happiness   25
which your virtues deserve.

Basel, 1523

1400 / To Francis I   [Basel], 1 December 1523

This is the preface to Erasmus' paraphrase on St Mark (Basel: Froben 1523). The
presentation copy, now in the Bibliothèque Nationale (Rés A.1138), bears on its
title-page an inscription by Erasmus dated 18 December 1523. However, the
book was intended for the spring book fair at Frankfurt, and as late as
mid-February 1524 was still not ready for publication. As a consequence, the
date on the title-page for the edition as a whole was changed to 1524.

The presentation copy and its accompanying letter (Ep 1403) were delivered
to King Francis by Hilary Bertholf (Ep 1384 n31), who received a handsome
reward for his trouble (see Ep 1341A:1743–4).

TO THE MOST CHRISTIAN KING OF FRANCE, FRANCIS, FIRST OF
THAT NAME, FROM ERASMUS OF ROTTERDAM, GREETING
If to this day I have never taken advantage of your Majesty's most generous
encouragement,[1] Francis most Christian king, the fault was neither mine
nor yours. There have been many other reasons against it hitherto; and in   5
particular it is the confusion of the age we live in that has deprived me of this
felicity. I always expected that in the long-continued storms of war[2] there
must be some quarter from which peace, like a spell of fine weather, would
shine upon us. But never did I suppose myself to be one hair's breadth less
indebted to your generosity than if I had already accepted whatever you   10
chose to offer. Even now I am full of hope that the time will soon come when
I may be allowed to establish what my feelings are towards you by more
definite evidence. In the mean time, while that opportunity is slow to arrive,

* * * * *

5 Ep 1255

1400
1 See Ep 1375.
2 See Ep 1369 n12.

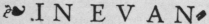

·IN EVAN·

GELIVM MARCI PA,
raphrasis, per D. ERASMVM Ro,
terodamum nunc recens & nata.
& formulis excusa.

IOAN.   FROB.

Basileæ, in officina Io. Frobenij. An. M.D. XXIII.
Cum priuilegio Cæsareo.

Christianiss. Galliarum Regi
Erasmus Roterodamus. dono
misit. 14. Cal. Ian. An. 1523

Erasmus *In evangelium Marci paraphrasis*
Title-page of the presentation copy, with Erasmus' inscription to Francis I
Bibliothèque Nationale, Paris, Rés A.1138

I have decided to send you as a sort of pledge of this commitment my
paraphrase on the Gospel of St Mark. Disposed as I was to accept this idea, I   15
was spurred on like a willing horse already in motion[3] by the perfect
symmetry of the plan. Matthew I had dedicated to my own prince, Charles;[4]
John, which I expounded immediately after Matthew, to Charles' brother
Ferdinand;[5] Luke, my third target, to the king of England;[6] Mark seemed left
for you, so that the four Gospels might be devoted to the four leading   20
monarchs in the world today. I only wish that as your four names are joined
with such symmetry in the one volume of the Gospels, so your hearts may
be closely united in concord by the spirit of the gospel!

Some people credit the Roman pontiff with dominion even over the
nether regions, and some think he can command the angels; I am so far from   25
grudging him this authority that I wish it were wider still. But oh that the
world might feel the life-giving virtue of this power of his in the
establishment and maintenance of concord between kings! – those kings
who have so long put Christendom in extreme peril by conflicts with one
another which are as dishonourable as they are disastrous. We execrate and   30
revile the Turks continually; yet what more agreeable spectacle could be set
before the Turks – or any nation, if one exists, which hates the name of
Christian even more – than the sight of the three most prosperous monarchs
of all Europe engaged in suicidal strife? I can hardly convince myself that any
Turk could be so savage as to call down upon the Christians more evils than   35
they inflict by turns upon themselves. Nor does any peacemaker arise for
the moment with the authority to put an end to these godless upheavals,
though there is no lack of men to encourage them and to pour oil, as the
saying goes, upon the flames.[7]

It is not for me to prejudice or promote the cause of any party by   40
prematurely passing a judgment of my own. I know that every man thinks
his own case most just, and I admit that in judging questions of this kind he
who repels an injury inflicted on him is usually given more support than he
who inflicts it. All the same, I could greatly wish to see all Christian princes
weighing in their hearts at its true value the immense profit that any of them   45
will find he has made who has chosen to accept a disadvantageous peace
rather than pursue the most advantageous of wars.[8] Is anything more

* * * * *

3 Adagia I ii 47
4 Ep 1255
5 Ep 1333
6 Ep 1381
7 Adagia I ii 9
8 Cf Ep 1211:609 and n94.

fragile, more fleeting, more fraught with calamity than this life of ours? I say nothing of all kinds of diseases, of accidents, mishaps, and fatal disasters, the pestilence and the lightning and the earthquakes, fire, flood, and other   50 calamities past all measure and all counting. For among all the evils which torment our mortal life, none is more criminal, none does more harm than war; and it plays worse havoc with men's moral standards than with their possessions or their bodies. He who takes a man's life does him less harm than if he robbed him of his reason. Nor is war any less detestable because   55 the greatest part of the evils it gives rise to falls on the heads of the poor and lowly, of husbandmen, craftsmen, and travellers. The Lord of all men, Jesus Christ, shed his blood no less for their redemption, despised as they may be, than for the grandest monarchs; and when we come before his judgment-seat, where all the satraps of this world, however mighty, must soon take   60 their stand, that stern judge will demand a no less strict account on behalf of those poor unfortunates than he will for the satraps and the great ones of the earth. Those therefore who count the loss a light one when it is the poor and lowly who are robbed, afflicted, exiled, burned, oppressed, and done to death show they think it was folly for Jesus Christ, who is the Wisdom of the   65 Father,[9] to have shed his precious blood that such folk might be saved.

And so I think no sort of men more disastrous than those who supply monarchs with the seeds from which war can grow; and the greater their spirit, the more easily are they imposed on. And greatness of spirit[10] is ranked high among the virtues of a king. Such a spirit won praise in antiquity for   70 Julius Caesar,[11] and by common consent wins it today for Francis. But there is a further point: nothing is more certain evidence of a truly great spirit than the ability to overlook wrongs suffered. The valour of great captains of the past, who fought for power, not for their lives, has won them praise; but they and those who praised them were alike Gentiles. For a Christian prince   75 it is more glorious to secure the peace and tranquillity of the commonwealth by some sacrifice of dominion than to celebrate lavish and luxurious triumphs purchased at such a cost of human misery. So those who have implanted in the minds of monarchs a passion to enlarge their dominions have discovered nothing but a perennial source of war. No less destructive is   80 the effect on the affairs of men of those who plant the seeds of resentment in

* * * * *

9 1 Cor 1:24; cf *Moria* ASD IV-3 188:107–8 / CWE 27 148 and Ep 1381:338.
10 Erasmus uses the word *sublimitas*, but here and in the sentences that follow he is invoking the classical concept of *magnanimitas*, the attribute of a 'great-souled' hero whose conduct is nobler, braver, more compassionate, etc than that of ordinary mortals. The *locus classicus* for the description of this concept is Cicero *De officiis* 1.61–92.
11 See Pliny *Naturalis historia* 7.25.91–4, and cf Cicero *Epistulae ad familiares* 4.4.4.

the hearts of princes and persuade them that a king of spirit cannot fail to seek requital for some remark – which has perhaps been falsely reported or reported as more outrageous than it really was – by declaring war. How much more courage it shows to have regard to the public peace and overlook the insult! If this hurts, it hurts only the individual – nor does it hurt him if it is overlooked. And while in other fields kings may perhaps be allowed to relax their vigilance in one way or another – if indeed they may ever relax who have to be vigilant on behalf of so many – when it comes to engaging in wars which open the floodgates to such enormous evils they must watch with all their powers to make sure that they take no rash decisions.

I say this, your most Christian majesty, with no wish to strike the sword out of the hand of kings. A good prince has perhaps a duty to wage war sometimes; but never until he has tried all other courses and is driven to it by ultimate necessity. The Lord Jesus deprived Peter of his sword,[12] he did not deprive princes of theirs. Paul actually endorses their authority, when he prescribes that those who profess the Christian faith in Rome should not despise the authority of princes, pagans though they were;[13] he goes further, and will not have them deprived of tax or tribute or respect, because they are God's servants. Does he deprive them of the sword who says 'For he beareth not the sword in vain'?[14] The teaching of Peter, prince of the apostles, is no different: 'Submit yourselves,' he says, 'to every human creature for the Lord's sake, whether it be to the king as supreme or unto governors as unto them that are sent by him, for the punishment of evildoers and for the praise of them that do well.'[15] The Lord wished Peter to use no weapon except the sword of the gospel, which is the word from heaven, for this, as Paul tells us in Hebrews, 'is quick and powerful and more piercing than any two-edged sword, penetrating even to the dividing asunder of soul and spirit.'[16] He who gives orders to put up the sword but does not take it away does more than if he were to take it. Why does he give orders for it to be put up into its sheath? Of course, because a shepherd of the gospel must not fight a war. But why does he neither tell him nor forbid him to lay it down? Surely because he wants us to understand that we must not plan revenge, even when our strength is sufficient to avenge the wrong.

The shepherds of the gospel therefore have their sword, the sword of

* * * * *

12 Matt 26:52; John 18:11
13 Rom 13:1–7
14 Rom 13:4
15 1 Pet 2:13–14
16 Heb 4:12

the gospel given them by Christ, with which they cut the throat of wickedness and lop off human greed. Kings have their own sword, which Christ permits them to use to strike terror into evildoers and to do honour to good men. The sword is not taken from them, but its use is delimited; they possess it for the defence of the public peace, not as a safeguard for their own   120 ambitions. There are two kinds of swords, and two kinds of kingship. Priests too have their sword and their kingdom: for crowns and helmets they have the mitre, and for sceptre the shepherd's crook; they have their breastplate and their baldric and, in a word, the whole panoply which Paul, that valiant warrior, describes in more than one passage as being theirs.[17]   125 'Kings' who preach the gospel are called shepherds,[18] but also kings in the secular sphere are called by Homer 'shepherds of the people.'[19] Both priests and kings have the same end in view, though their mode of action differs, like actors playing each his own part in the same play. If each kind of kingship had its own sword always ready, that is, if they used the power   130 entrusted to them as it should be used, we Christians (Christians in name rather than in reality) should not, I suppose, so often draw a godless sword to plunge it in the vitals of our brethren. What is more, while each kind neglects its proper duty and attempts the duty of others, neither maintains its honour or its tranquillity as it ought to do. When has a king more kingly   135 majesty than when he sits in judgment and dispenses justice, curbs wrongdoing, settles disputes, and succours the oppressed, or when he sits in council and takes thought for the prosperity of the commonwealth? When, for that matter, does a bishop enjoy more of his true dignity than when he is in the pulpit, teaching the philosophy of the gospel? At that   140 moment he is truly a gospel king upon his throne.

It was dishonourable for Nero to contend in the theatre with singers and musicians or in the circus with charioteers;[20] and it is no less dishonourable for a king to be immersed in low and sordid business which concerns his own private interest and is prejudicial to the security of the   145 commonwealth. Again, it would be improper for a philosopher with his gown and beard to dance some part in ballet on the stage or carry hook and net in the arena, singing the gladiator's song 'Not you I seek, 'tis fish I seek, why fly me then, Gallus?'[21] – and it is no less improper for a gospel king to wage war or engage in commerce, to mention nothing more discreditable.   150

* * * * *

17 Eph 6:11ff; 1 Thess 5:8
18 See for example, Isa 44:28; Jer 23:4; Ezek 34:23, 37:24.
19 *Iliad* 1.263 et passim
20 Suetonius *Nero* 20–4
21 Preserved in Sextus Pompeius Festus *De verborum significatu* sv 'Retiario'

Why is it now possible to find a bishop who thinks it does him more credit to
have three hundred knights in his train, equipped with artillery, lances, and
guns, than to be accompanied by pious and scholarly deacons and to carry
round with him books of divinity? Why are they great in their own esteem
through a display of those very things which those whose places they now   155
occupy grew great by despising? Why do they find bugle and hunting-horn
sweeter music than the reading of the Bible? Just suppose a king were to put
off his crown and his royal robes and put on mitre and chasuble while a
bishop, on the other hand, in exchange for mitre and chasuble put on crown
and royal robe: would not this seem a monstrosity? If we are so much   160
revolted by an exchange of the emblems of their rank, why are we not more
disturbed to see them exchange their functions? Now if either king or bishop
does anything in his proper capacity, he ought to have no end in view but
the public good. Either he rebukes those who have gone astray or he corrects
the fallen or he comforts those who are cast down or he represses the   165
haughty or he spurs on the idle or he reconciles those who are at variance.

Such is the office of kings, but above all of those gospel kings for whom
it is not fitting to aspire to a kingdom of this world. And seeing that Jesus
Christ embodied both types of kingship in himself, though while on earth he
set an example only of the kingship of the gospel, kings of both kinds must   170
try to imitate their prince to the utmost of their ability. He spent himself
entirely on his own people; and how dare anyone live for his own advantage
who claims that he is the vicar of Christ? All his life Christ played no part
except that of saviour, consoler, benefactor. In the temple or the syna-
gogues, in public on a journey or in the privacy of a home, on shipboard or in   175
the wilderness it was all one: he taught the multitude, healed the sick,
cleansed lepers, restored those sick of the palsy, the maimed, and the blind,
cast out evil spirits, raised the dead, rescued those in peril, fed the hungry,
confuted the Pharisees, was a father to his disciples and to the sinful woman
so lavish of her precious ointment,[22] comforted the sinful Canaanite   180
woman[23] and the woman taken in adultery.[24] Survey the whole life of Jesus.
Never did he hurt any mortal man, although he himself suffered so much
hurt from others, and it would have been easy for him to take vengeance had
he so pleased. Everywhere he was a saviour, everywhere a benefactor. He
restored Malchus' ear, which Peter had cut off;[25] the slightest loss by others   185
was too big a price to pay for his own immunity. Herod and Pilate were

* * * * *

22 Mark 14:3–9; Matt 26:6–13
23 Matt 15:21–8; Mark 7:24–30
24 John 8:3–11
25 Luke 22:51

reconciled through him.[26] As he hung on the cross he promised salvation to one of the two thieves.[27] After his death he brought the centurion to profess faith in Christ.[28] This was truly to play a king's part, to do good to all men and hurt none. His is the example to which all princes ought to come as close   190 as they can. And you, King Francis, more than any other should be inspired by your title of 'most Christian king' to follow Christ your prince to the utmost of your power.

Apart from that, what must be the effrontery of those who while rejoicing in the title of vicars of Christ demand that great quantities of   195 human blood shall be shed in defence, not of their lives and their positions, but of their greed and their pride! And this I say, may it please your Majesty, with no idea of criticizing any bishops or blaming them (and let us hope that none may arise who deserve such words as these), but to show wherein consists the true dignity of kings and bishops, in the hope that both may live   200 and prosper because both recognize that dignity and maintain it as they should. Far indeed from doing their duty are those gospel shepherds whose business it was to reconcile kings at strife with one another and who instead went out of their way to set a match to the fuel that will blaze up into war. And yet, if ever there was a time for a good shepherd to seek the welfare of   205 his flock with the loss of his own life, if ever the supreme Shepherd whose vicegerents they are should be their model, this above all was the moment to hear the call of duty, when such a sea of crime and misery threatens to engulf the world. In that great multitude of abbots, bishops, archbishops, and cardinals why does not one come forward to calm these great upheavals   210 even at the risk of his own life? Blessed indeed are the last hours of a man who by his death has saved so many thousand lives!

Nothing could be more cruel or more inhuman than the single combats and murderous encounters of gladiators in the arena; and yet this spectacle in antiquity gave such insane delight that the vilest precedent left them by   215 the heathen long survived among the Christians too, especially in the city of Rome, which had not yet been able to unlearn its ancient pagan ways. But for the abolition of single combat, as is recorded in the so-called *Historia tripartita*,[29] the credit must go to a certain Telemachus,[30] one of those who because of the simplicity of their life as Christians, their passion for solitude,   220 and their flight from contact with the polluted crowd were in the old days

* * * * *

26 Luke 23:12
27 Luke 23:43
28 Mark 15:39
29 Cassiodorus *Historia ecclesiastica tripartita* 10.2
30 Also called Almachius

commonly called monks, dwellers by themselves. With this purpose in mind Telemachus had left the East and come to Rome, where he entered the theatre and, when he saw two men in armour come forward, each bent on the slaughter of the other, leaped into the arena and thrust himself between 225 the ferocious pair, crying 'What are you doing, brothers? Why rush upon mutual destruction like wild beasts?' To cut the story short, while this man of God in his zeal was trying to save the lives of both, he lost his own life, for the people stoned him to death. Such was the value set by the raving mob on their favourite spectacle. And the sequel? The emperor Honorius,[31] when he 230 heard the story, gave orders that the custom of exhibiting gladiators in matched pairs should cease.

Now pray consider how foul a thing was that gladiatorial show and how many thousands were brought by it to a miserable end, and you will understand how much the world owes to the death of that one man. For this 235 action Telemachus was rightly added to the canon of the saints. But how much more justly would this honour be due to anyone who should separate the world's greatest monarchs when they are locked in conflict one with another! For it is no great loss if gladiator kills gladiator and one criminal acts in his turn as the executioner of another. And yet, while this conflict 240 between princes brings the greatest evils on the whole world, the danger attendant on separating them is less than it was for him who stood between the gladiators. First, because they are Christian princes, and the more noble their temper, the readier they are to comply if some bishop or a person exercising in some other way the authority of the gospel talks to them in the 245 language of truth and reason. Should one by mischance have to deal with a prince who will not listen and flies into a rage, the worst of all the evils that the greatest cruelty can inflict is death. And where, pray, will the successors of the apostles give us an example of the apostolic spirit, if not here?

'What good shall I do,' someone may say, 'if I die without achieving 250 what I have set my heart on?' Christ, who lays down the rules of the game, will not let this heroic player lose his reward. Not but what death often achieves what life could not; for the end of a good man can have a great effect. I will not now repeat examples from antiquity, which are past counting. In England, St Thomas, archbishop of Canterbury,[32] asserted the 255 liberty of the church in a case of no great importance against the king whom he had long served and by whose favour he had received that dignity as a reward for his length of service. There was no question of reconciling

* * * * *

31 Emperor in the West, 393–423
32 Thomas Becket, c 1118–70

princes at variance – though that century witnessed no princes whose
dominions were as widespread as those of the men who nowadays have   260
been disputing for so many years among themselves and draw other and
lesser princes with them into the infectious plague of war. The only question
at issue was a country retreat more suited to a man of God than to a king. The
place is called Ortford.[33] Nor should I have found it very attractive before
William Warham, the present archbishop of Canterbury and primate of all   265
England, a worthy successor on many grounds to that most famous man,
had built there on such a scale that he seemed not so much to have restored
an old house as to have raised a new one from the ground, so little did he
leave of the old palace beyond the walls of some hall or other and of the
church. Thus the objects of the dispute were of little importance; but though 270
that saintly man did all he could, he achieved nothing by it all during his life.
His death, however, gave the priesthood so much authority in England and
brought them such piles of wealth that this has made them seriously
unpopular in our own day.[34] St John was beheaded for speaking his mind;[35]
but not all princes are like Herod and not all have a wife like Herodias.   275
Ambrose, bishop of Milan, had the courage to turn the emperor Theodosius
away from the door of his church on account of the cruel and hasty sentence
he had passed on the people of Salonica,[36] and after rebuking him severely
and instructing him to make amends he dared reduce him to the rank of
penitent.[37] So the majesty of that great prince yielded to a prelate's   280
authority. Babylas, bishop of Antioch, attempted to do the same to a king
who was stained with the blood of an innocent man, and was put to death

* * * * *

33 'Otford' is the correct form. In 1143 Becket was given the living of Otford (Kent)
by Theobald, his predecessor as archbishop of Canterbury. As Allen indicates,
Erasmus' contention that Otford played such an important role in the
controversy between Becket and Henry II probably represents what he had
been told by Archbishop Warham (Ep 188) or someone in his household. The
story is true to the extent that in 1164 two royalist bishops proposed to Becket
that if he were to surrender two of his manors, Otford and Mundenham, to the
king as surety for sums claimed, the king would soon restore the archbishop to
favour. Becket's refusal to compromise the rights of the church in this way only
increased the king's anger against him. See John Morris, *The Life and Martyrdom
of Saint Thomas Becket* (London and New York 1885) 183–4.

34 See A.G. Dickens *The English Reformation* (London 1964) 83–102.

35 John the Baptist; Matt 14:1–12; Mark 6:14–29

36 In AD 390 the mob at Thessalonica murdered the governor and other officials in
a riot following the imprisonment of a popular charioteer. Theodosius' reprisal
took the form of an indiscriminate massacre.

37 Ambrose *Epistulae* 51; Paulinus *Vita Sancti Ambrosii* 24. See also F. Homes
Dudden *The Life and Times of St Ambrose* (Oxford 1935) II 381–91.

for it; but after his death he began to be an object of fear not only to a pagan emperor but to the devils who in those days were still worshipped as gods.[38]

For my part, O best of monarchs, I have such confidence in the   285
emperor Charles and you and the king of England, with your noble natures, as leaves no room for doubt that you would all have followed sound policies long ago had some counsellor arisen in whom a proper respect and freedom of speech could be combined. And all the time there is an immense supply everywhere of those who rouse the spirit of princes to make war, which   290
means those who find it to their personal advantage that the affairs of men should be in turmoil. One of them suggests 'This prince despises you,' 'Another has insulted you thus or thus'; someone else murmurs, 'If you can add such-and-such a province to your dominions, you will easily add that other whenever you please.' Misguided guide! Why suggest how far they   295
can advance the limits of their dominions instead of reminding them how narrow are the limits within which the dominions they have now were once confined? Why not tell them how what they have can be better governed rather than enlarged? Of the extending of dominions there is no end. How true is that remark of Seneca: ' Many a conqueror has set back the bounds of   300
other men's territory, none has set bounds to his own'![39] In any case, good government is the true test of princes. Alexander the Great, having reached the ocean, deplored the absence of another world;[40] for his ambition this world was too narrow. Even Hercules could not pass beyond Cádiz.[41] To our modern ambitions Cádiz is nowhere, the ocean does not exist. Against the   305

* * * * *

38 According to St John Chrysostom, who is evidently Erasmus' source, Babylas, bishop of Antioch in the middle of the third century, barred from his church an unnamed emperor (possibly Philip the Arab, 244–9), who had treacherously murdered a royal hostage. The emperor thereupon had Babylas imprisoned and executed. Subsequently the emperor Gallus (251–3) removed Babylas' remains to Daphne, a suburb of Antioch, where a new church was built in his honour. As a result, the nearby oracle of Apollo fell silent. Later, when Emperor Julian the Apostate (391–3) tried unsuccessfully to consult the oracle, he was told that the silence was due to the presence of corpses buried in Daphne. Julian then had Babylas' coffin moved back to Antioch. Immediately afterwards the temple of Apollo was ravaged by a fire that destroyed the statue of the god. No human perpetrator could be found, and the temple ruins remained a monument to the victory of the martyr over the demon Apollo. See Chrysostom's *Discourse on Blessed Babylas* (PG 50 533–72), and his *Sermon on the Holy Martyr, St Babylas* (ibidem 527–34).
39 *De beneficiis* 7.7.5
40 Plutarch *Moralia* 207
41 Ie, not beyond the pillars (Pillars of Hercules) that he had placed in the Strait of Gibraltar to mark the outer limit of voyaging; see *Adagia* III v 24.

poisonous counsels of such men as they the minds of Christian princes must be diligently fortified in advance by the decrees of Christ, the only antidote, and the ideal of the gospel is the target at which all their policy must aim.

You will ask perhaps why I choose a prince as busy as yourself to play my long and familiar tune to. Indeed, I could wish this tune had been dinned into the ears of every prince, and for no other reason except the torment I suffer from these worldwide and general calamities. I also have a passionate desire to see the state of Christendom more peaceful everywhere, and especially in France, which hitherto has been, I suppose, more pious and more prosperous than any other country. If only these catastrophes recurred more seldom, like floods, earthquakes, and famines, things would be more bearable. As it is, there is no end to struggles of this kind that shake the world. When a new sickness appears, physicians who deal with disorders of the body inquire with all their skill into the causes of the trouble. Once these have been identified it is no great business to devise a cure; and, not content with that, they devise measures to prevent subsequent outbreaks of the same plague. Why is it that in these great and constantly recurring troubles men endowed with the needful wisdom and experience do not investigate the springs from which these tumults break out from time to time over the world, so that it might be possible by cutting them off at the root to cure these dreadful ills? Why are we so clear-sighted in things of much less importance and blind in by far the most important field of all? It seems to me that most wars arise out of a few empty words, invented one might think in order to nourish man's vainglory, as though there were too little ambition in the world already, unless we fed with new formulae an evil which grows too fast among us of its own accord.

These and things like these are the roots of war; and when they have been grubbed up, it will not prove difficult to establish laws of peace between Christian princes such as can prevent these upheavals from sprouting afresh from time to time. In this way we should also secure an increase in the wealth of princes, in which their friendship would ensure that all of them had a share, and at the same time a Christian people governed by prosperous sovereigns would enjoy a delightful state of tranquillity. We should thus secure the blessing of the one true sovereign of the whole world, Jesus our Lord, and he would bestow prosperity on our affairs. We should thus become an object of terror to the enemies of Christianity, against whom we now have difficulty in defending what is ours, so far are we from driving them further away. True, I would rather see them set right than driven off; but how can we set others right when we ourselves are – I should almost say – more corrupt than they are? For I no longer judge Christians by the doctrines we profess in words; I judge them

310

315

320

325

330

335

340

345

by their lives. Wherever ambition and the love of riches and pride and anger and revenge and a passion to hurt others are supreme, there I infer that the faith of the gospel is not to be found.

One further point. Although this pestilence has seized even upon   350
those whose chief duty it was to find a cure for our disastrous state, I yet derive some encouragement from the sight of Christian literature, and especially the New Testament, studied so eagerly by everyone, even laymen in private station, that professional experts in the Scriptures are quite often worsted by them in debate. I find further evidence of the large numbers who   355
now read the New Testament in the fact that, although the printers put so many thousands of volumes on the market every year, yet all those presses cannot keep up with the eager demand of the purchasers. Anything written by anyone on the gospel is a very saleable object nowadays.[42] This medicine, which is so powerful, cannot fail, once taken, to produce its effect. And so   360
the world now seems to me to be in the state of a man who is seriously ill and has taken hellebore or some other effective drug;[43] for his whole body is disordered and shaken and often seems very close to death. If only this gospel hellebore, after it has once purged and penetrated every vein in our hearts, might force its way to the surface so as to cast out the elements of evil   365
and restore us in health and purity to Jesus Christ, and that, after such great upheavals and a disease which has left the world desperately sick it might bring back that universal happiness and peace for which all men pray!

I should, however, have more hope that the prayers of all good men might not be in vain if the great ones of the earth took the trouble, like   370
faithful physicians, to attend the world on its sick-bed, that is to say, if the monarchs on whose decisions rests above all else the future of human affairs were to remember that in a short time (what time in human life is long?) they must give an account of their use of their power to Christ, the supreme prince. Again, if bishops, divines, and monks would bear in mind that they   375
are not the successors of Annas and Caiaphas,[44] or of scribes and Pharisees, who in an ungodly attempt to defend their own kingdom tried to suppress the kingdom of the gospel, who did their best to bury Christ's glory while maintaining their own, and while striving to make their own justice

* * * * *

42 Cf Ep 1349:24–5. This claim is fully justified by the sale of Erasmus' New Testament and paraphrases in both authorized and unauthorized editions; see the appropriate entries in Vander Haeghen and cf Allen's introduction to Ep 1010.
43 Hellebore was a plant much used in the ancient world as a remedy for mental disease, epilepsy, etc. See Pliny *Naturalis historia* 25.21–5.
44 Matt 26:3–4, 57; John 18:13–14, 24

acceptable made God unjust; no, they are rather the successors of the   380
apostles, who even by the loss of their own life-blood rejoiced to maintain
Christ's kingdom and his glory and his justice. Christ suffered once and rose
again to die no more. But what he suffered then he suffers anew whenever
the truth of the gospel is condemned, spat on, scourged, crucified, and
buried. In a word, he considers as inflicted on himself all the evil that is   385
inflicted on his members.

I have spoken perhaps with greater freedom and at greater length,
most Christian king, than was reasonable, but it was the warmth of my
affection that made me both garrulous and confident. As a Christian I wish
well to all my fellow Christians; but towards your Majesty and the most   390
flourishing kingdom of France I am guided by a very special feeling. Now I
pray that Jesus, immortal ruler of the whole world, to whom all power in
heaven and earth is divinely given,[45] may grant his spirit to peoples and to
princes alike. To princes, that all may live together under Jesus their
common prince in concord and therefore in felicity; to peoples, that they   395
may enjoy their new tranquillity under truly religious and flourishing
monarchs; thus we may at length see gospel piety firmly established among
us and widely spread, not by invading or despoiling regions that belong to
others (for this makes them poorer and not better), but by the preaching
everywhere of the true gospel philosophy through men endowed with the   400
spirit of the gospel and by setting such an example in our lives that the sweet
savour of our religion may attract many others to profess the same way of life
themselves. Thus was the kingdom of the gospel born and thus it grew and
thus spread widely and was thus established, though for various reasons we
see it now contracted into a narrow space and almost done away with, if you   405
consider how large the whole world is. Fallen, we must rebuild it;
contracted, we must spread it wide; unsteady, we must uphold it, using the
same resources by which it was first born, increased, and grew strong.

I write this in all simplicity of heart, Francis, most Christian king; I
criticize no man, for I wish well to all, and I seek no man's favour, for I desire   410
nothing from any man. Farewell.

1 December 1523

*   *   *   *   *

45 Matt 28:18

1401 / From Johann von Botzheim   Constance, 3 December 1523

The manuscript of this letter (=Ep 21 in Förstemann/Günther) was in the
Burscher Collection at Leipzig (Ep 1254 introduction). On Botzheim, see Ep
1285.

You will not be surprised at these libellous attacks on your *Spongia*[1] if you
remember that among these supposedly worthy men there are some capable
of trying every form of intrigue when they have once infringed the laws of
friendship. But the good name and honour of Erasmus of Rotterdam are too
soundly based all the world over to be shaken from their place by men like   5
himself, to say nothing of worthless rascals. I know very well, and those
who shamelessly spread rumours of this kind are well aware of it too, that
things are as you describe. But what will men do who have lost all hope, who
spend their time in idleness, drinking, and gaming, and practising virtues of
that description?   10
     The sad story here,[2] which I mentioned in my letter, had a brilliant
start, so far as my friends were concerned, but up to now it has been held up
by the Constance city council, though the bishop[3] and the council are very
busy exchanging emissaries; only, so far as I can see, both cling obstinately
to their own opinions. The bishop has found an excuse which is quite   15
irrelevant, the death of Zwick,[4] who was formerly his steward at Meersburg,[5] and has left Constance. Meanwhile his suffragan,[6] with Michael
Sander and several other people representing the bishop, are very actively
keeping up the pressure on the Constance council; and the more active they
are, the more unpopular they grow every day, I notice, with the good people   20
of Constance. You would be astonished if you knew how passionate
Michael Sander is, who has lately been made a canon of Constance; I hear he

* * * * *

1401
1 See Epp 1378 and especially 1389.
2 The bishop's attempt to dismiss Wanner (Ep 1335 n5), concerning which
   Botzheim had written in Ep 1382:41–7
3 Hugo von Hohenlandenberg, d 1532
4 Konrad Zwick, father of the Constance reformer Johann Zwick (Ep 1519 n9).
   Konrad had a successful career in commerce and was briefly (1485–6) a town
   councillor. It is not known when he entered the bishop's service.
5 Meersburg, the bishop's castle, is opposite Constance on the north side of the
   lake.
6 Melchior Fattlin (or Vechtlin) of Swabia (d after 11 July 1548), suffragan since
   1518 and a vigorous opponent of the Reformation

will shortly be going to Rome,[7] having learned that a new pope has been elected.[8]

I am surprised to hear that Oecolampadius is leaving Basel,[9] for he has, I understand, a good reputation there. And whither will that worthy man betake himself in such a hurry? You must continue to be your true self, a quiet, peace-making writer of paraphrases. Concerning you I hear only this one piece of news, that there are certain people who want to involve you in their own rash behaviour, in fact to make you a champion of unwise and foolish courses. I should be sorry to see you do this, and therefore I urge you to give yourself wholeheartedly to the business of the gospel, as you already do of your own accord. You shall perhaps hear the progress of our sad story on another occasion. Farewell, and best wishes from your friend Botzheim. From Constance, 3 December 1523

Your sincere friend Johann Botzheim

To the incomparable restorer of true theology and the best literature, Erasmus of Rotterdam, his deeply respected master and patron

1402 / To John More

[Basel, c December 1523]

This is the preface to a commentary on the poem *Nux* attributed to Ovid. The commentary was completed in November (Ep 1397:13–14) and published by Froben with Erasmus' Prudentius (Ep 1404) in 1524 for the spring fair at Frankfurt. For John More, son of Sir Thomas, and his sisters (lines 37–8), see Ep 999 n28.

ERASMUS OF ROTTERDAM TO THAT MOST PROMISING YOUNG MAN
JOHN MORE, GREETING

Your kind presents and all those loving letters,[1] my dear John, must not go

* * * * *

7 On 7 September 1523 Sander (Ep 1242 n6) had been appointed to a canonry at Constance, with the support of Filonardi, but at the beginning of 1524 he went to Rome, where Campeggi had named him master of ceremonies.

8 Clement VII was elected on 19 November 1523.

9 In October 1523 it had been reported, evidently without foundation, that Oecolampadius was going to leave Basel because Erasmus was making his position so difficult; Zw-Br Ep 319. In the light of favourable references to Oecolampadius in two recent letters from Erasmus, Zwingli concluded that the report was false; ibidem. One of Erasmus' letters was Ep 1384 (especially lines 56–7). In the other, no longer extant, Erasmus had said: 'Oecolampadius triumphs here.' In January 1524 Willibald Pirckheimer wrote to Oecolampadius, congratulating him on his decision to remain in Basel; BAO no 182 (I 265).

1402
1 Not extant

quite without response; and so I send you a nut-tree. A small gift, but you
must not despise it, for it's a most elegant nut-tree, Ovid's *Nux* – though in   5
any case a man might be thought to send a far from negligible present who
sends a whole tree and a far from worthless one who sends a tree that speaks
such good Latin. Don't be surprised if a walnut-tree in Ovid speaks Latin: in
Lucian there's a voluble argument between the vowels[2] and in Homer the
good ship Argo speaks,[3] and what's more, speaks in verse. Just for a short   10
time then, while you read this, you must turn Pythagorean and believe that
even trees have souls;[4] Ovid gave them a tongue as well, or rather, gave it
back to them, for in the old days at Dodona oaks too used to utter oracles.[5] I
have been very much a stranger in this field of study for a long time now; but
this poem is so gay and so well written that I took a fancy to write a short   15
commentary on it to encourage students to enjoy it. It did not escape my
notice that there would be immediate protests, exactly on the lines of the old
Greek proverb about the old man who is twice a child:[6] here am I in my old
age turned childish and gone back to play with nuts again. Personally, I
think it no waste of time for children, and no discredit to an old man, to play   20
with nuts like this and to use such mental relaxations as refreshment for the
weariness brought on by serious studies.

   In any case, what other people say does not much worry me. I would
like to convince you, my dear John, that a great artist is always himself,
whether he is modelling a colossal statue or a six-inch statuette, whether he   25
is painting a Jupiter or a Thersites,[7] whether he is engraving bronze and
ordinary stone or precious stones and gold – except that when the object is
of small value or small size one can admire the artist's skill all the more.
Ovid's tragedy *Medea* won a great reputation, but even in his *Nux* you will
find him Ovid still. In the play it was the subject that inspired the style, and a   30
good share of the credit must be allotted to the Greeks, who had so often

* * * * *

2 Actually, it is the consonants *sigma* and *tau* that do the arguing in Lucian's *The
  Complaint of the Consonants*. They address their complaint to the vowels as
  judges, who have no lines. Erasmus' memory may have been deceived by the
  common Latin title of the work, *Iudicium vocalium*.
3 Erasmus' memory deceives him here once again: it is not in Homer that the
  Argo speaks but rather in Apollonius of Rhodes *Argonautica* 1.525. Thanks are
  due to Elaine Fantham for providing this information.
4 Pythagoras believed the soul to be a fallen divinity condemned to a cycle of
  reincarnation as man, animal, or plant.
5 Dodona was the site of an ancient oracle of Zeus in the mountains of Epirus.
  The god's will was divined from the rustling of the leaves of a sacred oak.
6 *Adagia* I v 36
7 An ugly, foul-mouthed man who railed at Agamemnon until beaten into
  silence by Odysseus; *Iliad* 2.212ff

treated the same theme; here any credit there is is owed to the genius of the poet.

Now it is not my way to make a habit of whitewashing several walls out of one bucket;[8] but it will make you look generous and me less ungrateful if you share your walnut (you may not want to split the tree itself, but nature has made its fruit part easily into four) with your dear sisters Margaret, Elizabeth, and Cecily, and [Margaret] Giggs, with whom they have such a happy relationship; for they challenge me so often with their letters[9] – so sensible and clear in matter and in such pure Latin – that I can scarcely get my friends here to believe that their letters are their own productions, though I know perfectly well that this is true. And in fact, my dear John, is there any point in my exhorting you to be a good boy and mind your book, when along with such natural gifts you have in your home a father who is not only a model of the well-read man but a most perfect example of all goodness and integrity, from which you could not fall away without great discredit? – especially since he supplies you generously with everything that can contribute to giving you the finish that comes with accomplishments of every kind. You cannot remain in obscurity; your father's great distinction is like a beacon set before you, and you must either be a man like him and win great praise or disappoint to your great discredit the hopes of all your friends.

Not but what, if you were slow to move, the competition of your sisters might well apply the spur. Their beautiful manners, their modesty, their simple ways, the harmony there is between them – confronted with these, anyone might swear they were the three Graces; if he saw the skill with which they play the various kinds of musical instrument, or watched them flitting like honey-bees through every sort of text in the two learned tongues – here jotting down a good phrase to reuse, there gathering some outstanding maxim on which to model their way of life, there learning some merry tale to be repeated to their companions – if you saw all this, you would say they were Muses at play in the flowery fields of Helicon,[10] plucking blossoms and sprigs of amaranth to weave into garlands. They are at any rate so richly adorned with every intellectual gift that beauty, lovely as they are, can add very little to their charms. Such progress do they make in this field of laudable endeavour as though they had formed a plan and wished to leave their brother far behind. All the more therefore must you

* * * * *

8 Cf *Adagia* i vii 3.
9 Not extant
10 The mountain in Boeotia that was sacred to Apollo and the Muses.

devote all your energies to the race so that, nature having given them a start
on the course by making them a little older than you are, you may overtake
them by your keenness in your studies. They will then rival Cornelia,[11]   70
mother of the Gracchi, who distinguished herself in two ways above her sex,
by character and education; and you will be competing with your father,
whom it will be greatly to your credit to equal, though he hopes for nothing
so much as for you to beat him. But more of this perhaps on another and
more appropriate occasion. Now for the *Nux*.   75

1403 / To Francis I   Basel, 17 December 1523

> This is the covering letter for the presentation copy of Erasmus' paraphrase on
> Mark (Ep 1400). The surviving manuscript is part of a volume in the
> Nationalbibliothek at Vienna (Cod 8987, f 35 verso). The volume, apparently in
> the writing of Claudius Cantiuncula (Ep 852:85n), contains a number of
> Cantiuncula's works, including a few letters. Since Cantiuncula had been the
> carrier of Ep 1375 and was at this time in Basel, the presence of this letter
> among his papers is understandable. The letter was first published by Adalbert
> Horawitz in the *Sitzungsberichte der phil.-hist. Classe der kaiserlichen Akademie der
> Wissenschaften* (Vienna 1880).

A LETTER FROM ERASMUS TO THE KING OF FRANCE
May it please your most Christian Majesty. Conscious as I am of the truly
regal generosity of your nature and of the singular favour which your
Majesty has always shown me and which I do not deserve, I had great hopes
on my side of coming closer to you to enjoy them, did not the stormy times in   5
which we live stand in the way of my aspirations.[1] I hope however that God
in his mercy will give us some fair weather after these upheavals, and
without delay. In the mean time, as some sort of evidence of my feelings
towards you, I send you a paraphrase on the evangelist Mark, that the four
Gospels thus set forth by me at greater length may find a welcome in the   10
earth's four quarters under the patronage of the four greatest monarchs in
the world. Matthew I had dedicated long ago to the emperor,[2] and Mark I

* * * * *

11 Cornelia, daughter of Scipio Africanus and mother of the famous reform
   politicians Tiberius and Gaius Gracchus (second century BC), whose education
   in Greek culture she supervised. She was revered as the model of Roman
   matronhood.

   1403
   1 Cf Ep 1400:3–13.
   2 Ep 1255

Portrait of Francis 1 by Titian, 1538
The Louvre, Paris

offer to you now; Luke I have dedicated to the king of England[3] and John to Charles' brother Ferdinand.[4] And I offer my most fervent prayers to the Lord Jesus, in whose hand are the hearts of all kings,[5] that as the four   15 Gospels in one volume now unite your names, so we may soon see the gospel spirit unite your hearts together in enduring concord. I know that of your own nature nothing is more merciful than you are; but war left to itself is a thing that knows no mercy. I know that it is not your fault if that peace is not established which all good men long for; but there is good hope that in   20 future God will turn the emperor's heart to more moderate designs. The more this harmony takes root and flowers, the better both for your felicity and for the peace of the whole world.

Men in my position can do nothing but hope for the best. If these prayers were effective, your Majesty would flourish in the enjoyment of all   25 good things, and so would that most flourishing of all kingdoms over which you rule. While my book is still fresh from the printer[6] I have hastened to send it to your most Christian Majesty by the hand of Hilarius my servant,[7] who is trustworthy and has no mean skill in the humanities, having once taught for a long time at Toulouse. If I hear through him that you have found   30 my work acceptable, I shall be greatly delighted. May the Lord Jesus long preserve your Majesty in health and wealth.

Basel, 17 December 1523

1404 / To Margaret Roper   Basel, 25 December 1523

This is the preface to Erasmus' commentary on Prudentius' hymns for Christmas and Epiphany, printed with Ovid's *Nux* (Ep 1402). For Margaret Roper, daughter of Thomas More, see Ep 999 n28.

ERASMUS OF ROTTERDAM TO THE VIRTUOUS MAIDEN MARGARET ROPER, GREETING

I have been put on my mettle so often lately, my dearest Margaret, by letters[1] from you and your sisters – such sensible, well-written, modest, forthright,

* * * * *

3 Ep 1381
4 Ep 1333
5 See Prov 21:1.
6 The presentation copy (Ep 1400) was so fresh from that press that the ink of folio A2 blotted onto the verso of the title-page.
7 Bertholf (Ep 1384 n31)

1404
1 None has survived.

friendly letters – that even if someone were to cut off the headings I should   5
be able to recognize the 'offspring true-born'[2] of Thomas More. It must not
look as though you had sung your song all the time to a deaf man, and so I
have stolen a brief holiday from the work in which I am buried, and this
Christmas I have put together a small present which I hope will give you
some pleasure.   10

May there be a blessing on it: William Roper,[3] a man of such high
character, such charm, and such modesty that were he not your husband he
might be taken for your brother, has presented you – or, if you prefer, you
have presented him – with the first fruits of your marriage, and most
promising they are; to put it more accurately, each of you has presented the   15
other with a baby boy to be smothered in kisses.[4] And here am I, sending
you another boy, who brings more promise than any other: Jesus, born for
the Jews and soon to become the light of the Gentiles, who will give the
offspring of your marriage a happy outcome and be the true Apollo of all
your reading,[5] whose praises you will be able to sing to your lyre instead of 20
nursery rhymes to please your little ones. For he alone is worthy to be
praised continually on the strings and pipe, with songs and every sort of
music-making, but especially with the harmonious utterance of a true
Christian heart.

Nor will he despise the singing of his praises by such a married pair,   25
whose whole life shows such innocence, such concord, such tranquillity,
and such simplicity that you could hardly find those under a vow of virginity
who would challenge the comparison. A rare sight, especially in this age of
ours; but I foresee it soon spreading more widely. In your own country you
have a queen[6] who might be the Calliope of your saintly choir,[7] and in   30
Germany too there are families of no mean station who practise with success

* * * * *

2 Cf Cyril of Jerusalem *Catechetical Sermons* 19.1.
3 William Roper (c 1496–1578) was the son of John Roper of Kent, a close legal
   associate of Sir Thomas More. A lawyer himself (called to the bar in 1525),
   William became chief clerk of the Court of King's Bench in 1524, an office that
   he retained until 1577. By 1518 he had entered the household of Thomas More,
   whose daughter Margaret he married in July 1521.
4 Thomas Roper (d 1598), his parents' eldest son. He studied law and in 1577
   succeeded his father as chief clerk of the Court of Kings' Bench.
5 Apollo as father of the Muses and patron of all higher learning and culture. The
   image of Christ as the new Apollo was common among the Italian humanists
   but rare in Erasmus, who was uncomfortable with such similes.
6 Catherine of Aragon (Ep 1313 n11)
7 Calliope was the muse of epic poetry and of eloquence.

the life of which you have given hitherto such a successful example.[8] Farewell, not least among the glories of your generation and your native England, and mind you give my greetings to all the members of your choir.[9]

Basel, Christmas 1524   35

1405 / From Otto Brunfels   [Strasbourg? c December 1523]

This is the preface to Brunfels' *Pro Vlricho Hutteno defuncto, ad Erasmi Roterodami Spongiam Responsio* (Strasbourg: Johann Schott n d), which was appended to a corrected edition of Hutten's *Expostulatio* (Ep 1356 n9); cf Ep 1341A n285. The *Responsio*, which answers the second edition of the *Spongia* (Ep 1389), was apparently published sometime between 19 January, when Erasmus was expecting its appearance (Ep 1411:24–6) and 13 March 1524 (Ep 1429:13–15). By 21 July a second edition was in circulation (Ep 1466:27–8). In the light of these dates, it seems reasonable to place this letter and Ep 1406, which appear in both editions, at the end of 1523. This is confirmed by the narrative of events in Ep 1406, where Brunfels describes his long hesitation to take up the pen against Erasmus. Brunfels' exact location at this time is not clear. However, since Ep 1406:17 seems to imply that he had left Neuenburg (see below), and since the book was printed at Strasbourg, it may be that his resettlement there (see below) had already begun.

Otto Brunfels (c 1488–1534) was the son of a cooper in Mainz. After taking his MA in 1510, he entered the Carthusian monastery in Strasbourg, where he became acquainted with the members of the Strasbourg humanist circle. While pursuing humanist studies, he came to know Hutten and Capito (Ep 1368), among others. His earliest pedagogical treatises (1519) show the influence of Erasmus, whom he then sincerely admired. Dissatisfied with monastic life and drawn to Luther, Brunfels fled the monastery in August 1521 under the protection of Hutten and the Strasbourg printer Johann Schott. After a brief period as parish administrator in Steinau (near Frankfurt), he became pastor in Neuenburg in the Breisgau. Then, in 1524, he became a citizen of Strasbourg and opened a school there.

Although his *Responsio* to the *Spongia* was vehement in tone, Brunfels carefully kept open the possibility of a dialogue. Erasmus responded only to the vehemence (Epp 1429, 1432, 1437, 1445) and eventually demanded that the

* * * * *

8 Erasmus probably had in mind not only married couples such as the Peutingers of Augsburg (Ep 1247) but also learned women like Willibald Pirckheimer's sisters and daughters (Ep 409:29n). Cf Epp 1233:112–22 with n21 and 1469:266–7.

9 Of Margaret's sisters and their companions; cf Ep 1402:37–8.

Otto Brunfels, by Hans Baldung Grien
Otto Brunfels *Annotationes ... in quatuor evangelia et acta apostolorum*
(Strasbourg: Georg Ulricher, September 1535) title-page verso
Staatliche Museen Preussischer Kulturbesitz
Kupferstichkabinett, Berlin

Strasbourg magistrates take action against Brunfels and Schott (Epp 1429,
1477). However, when Brunfels offered him an olive-branch in 1525, Erasmus
accepted it, albeit gingerly (Ep 1614).

TO ERASMUS OF ROTTERDAM FROM OTTO BRUNFELS, GREETING
You have dragged in the dirt the reputation of an honourable and
distinguished man, Ulrich von Hutten, with a flood of accusations which are
false, libellous, and fraudulent, directed not only against him but against
men of good will and men who are on the side of the gospel. You must   5
therefore take it in good part if I say a word about you in your turn and give
you some reasons for the charge I bring against you. It was not right for me
to abandon the cause of a friend who cannot defend himself, and still less for
me to express approval of your calumnies, in which you take an impious
attitude to the Scriptures too. Do what you please, paint any picture of me   10
you like in return. I know that I have earned nothing in this life except
unrelieved ignominy and confusion. You can hardly paint me worse than I
am, ignorant, inglorious, obscure, and sinful. Such I am willing to be
thought, and such I am. But this one thing I do not forgive, that you should
use the word impious[1] either of me or of anyone who is devoted to the   15
gospel. And unless you desist from publishing such stuff, I shall tear this
mask from your face once and for all and show you openly in print for the
man you are. Nor shall I lack helpers to lend me their aid and encourage my
efforts; for I know how to touch you in a tender place. You mark my words;
and so farewell.   20

1406 / From Otto Brunfels   [Strasbourg? c December 1523]

This letter, evidently written somewhat later than Ep 1405, was printed at the
end of Brunfels' *Responsio* (Ep 1405).

TO ERASMUS OF ROTTERDAM, PRIEST AND MOST LEARNED
SCRIBE OF THE LAW, FROM OTTO BRUNFELS, GREETING
The preface in which I have addressed you about Hutten's case is shorter
than the facts demand – too short to give adequate space for my defence
before those who will perhaps think it was rash of me to undertake this   5
office. I ought to have done this at the outset, but I deliberately did not. For
one thing I wished to be quit of my task in as few words as possible; and then
the whole sad story was well known, and my only purpose was to satisfy

* * * * *

1405
1 As Erasmus was said to have called Luther; see Ep 1374:53–4.

those who (so my friends told me) had read your *Spongia* with great
indignation; last but not least, I meant to stop you thinking that you have   10
absolute freedom to publish unlimited falsehoods and priding yourself on
being already victorious, because fate has removed the man who started the
battle. But good judgment is not universal, and even you too might suppose
that I was induced to do this by some foolish fancy or a good opinion of
myself; so let me therefore tell you briefly from the beginning how I came to   15
reply and where I feel you have fallen short.

Your *Spongia* first reached me in Neuenburg while Hutten was still
alive,[1] and I cannot describe the pain it gave me to see a friend of mine
attacked and torn to pieces by you with such contempt and ridicule. Then
the news came of the death of that eloquent and honourable man; my sense   20
of loss increased day by day, and what began to make me so wretched was
not so much the death of a very good friend as your most unwise *Spongia*, for
I foresaw that from now on you would abandon all restraint and publish
what lies you might please about the dead man. It was thus that I formed the
idea of taking his part. I got ready my pen, and still the fear of your brilliance   25
would not let me start; I felt it useless to assail a man held in such high regard
by cardinals and bishops – it would be the gnat stinging the elephant.[2] I took
my hand from the picture; I forgave the wrong done to a friend who has now
found life and peace and had himself forgiven it with his dying breath,
although the wrong affected not him alone but all right-thinking men and   30
Christ himself. For Hutten is not the only object of this campaign of yours;
you are rolling together into utter confusion all the lies you have been able to
scrape up, whatever could be found anywhere that might discredit the
gospel and the cause of Luther; so that, being unable to refute the charges he
brought against you with so much truth, you might overwhelm him with   35
your rhetorical tricks, irony, innuendo, question-begging, suggestion,
guesswork, and all the conjuror's devices with which you habitually varnish
over any deception and conceal any unwelcome truth.

Meanwhile you publish a second edition of your misbegotten and
miserable *Spongia*, designed now not so much to wipe off aspersions as to   40
collect and soak up all the lowest filth you can find and disgorge it again
when you squeeze it. You add a letter to sell the book,[3] a bitter, calumnious,

* * * * *

1406
1 The *Spongia*, of course, appeared after Hutten's death (Ep 1378 introduction),
  the exact date of which (Ep 1388 n12) was evidently unknown to Brunfels.
2 Cf *Adagia* III i 27.
3 Ep 1389

poisonous letter. And now a third edition appears at Cologne[4] – I know not whether you are responsible or the people who enjoy watching spectacles like this in hopes of seeing right-thinking men and men who love the gospel universally defamed. Even now I have no plans to issue a reply. By chance I visit some friends; they beg me, they urge me, they exhort me, they appeal to my better feelings: surely I cannot be so stony-hearted as to tolerate the wrong done to a friend to whom I owe so much. They were full, they said, of good intentions, but no one was so well qualified or under such an obligation to do this as myself, for none of our contemporaries has a better knowledge of the facts about Hutten, and especially of his relations with you. I disclaimed the office for the reason I have already given. News came meanwhile that Buschius,[5] who is both a good scholar and an honourable man and is noted for his hatred of impiety and injustice, was considering whether to reply,[6] but was to some extent held back by business and to some extent waiting, as I too was waiting, in hopes that someone would come forward who was Hutten's equal as a writer. There was an exchange of letters, and my own friends suggested that there should be no reply at all. It was improper to treat as worthy of reply what everybody knew to be pure invention; otherwise Luther himself or Melanchthon would have answered long ago. Nothing could confound you more effectively than for you to betray your own true nature without provocation, which with your habitual frankness you were busy doing. You were also writing to friends in Strasbourg and elsewhere to say that some sort of anonymous attack on you was brewing there and that a monstrous birth was hatching which would not dare appear in the light of day;[7] though this at least was not so, unless perhaps you dreamt the impending evil, for the people there are either the sort that dare admit face to face what they are doing or they never mount secret attacks under cover on anyone.

About this time I again visited Basel. There I heard from a friend of mine (and I readily believed it, for I well know that slippery mind of yours) that you had said in so many words, 'If anyone answers, Otto will be the man,' and you added some offensive remark, I know not what, about people who do not suffer from your lack of principle. Whether this is true or no, I do not much care. And yet, at the time when you were secretly uttering this prophecy, I was not yet moved to reply even then. At last, of my own

* * * * *

4 Vander Haeghen lists several editions without place or name of publisher. It is not known which, if any, may have been published at Cologne.
5 Ep 1291 n4
6 Cf Ep 1383:32–5.
7 Eg, Epp 1397:8–9, 1386:2–4

volition, hearing as I did such complaints about you from my friends, I read
your *Spongia* in order to form my own estimate of what this all amounted to.
I found myself reading a piece that was smooth, ingratiating, learned,   80
elegant – and full of deadly poison; and without doubt it was the mirror of a
similar mind, poisonous, ruthless, arrogant, superficial, and bloodthirsty.
For 'as the man is, so is his talk.'[8] I read also your irreligious and
contemptible tirades against the faith, against the Scriptures, and against
the mysteries and the sacraments which today we hold most dear, while you   85
set up for us some sort of supreme super-papacy whose decisions and
decrees and regulations are to rule our lives; and how we ought not to
despise this, put as respectfully and as pompously as befitted such a
champion of men like that.

Soon I plucked up heart (for before that my heart was in my boots[9]),   90
and I cannot describe the all-consuming anger I felt at your cavalier attitude
to the Scriptures and the way you had taken refuge in the enemy camp. No
longer was there any need for my friends to spur me on; I was now driven
forward by my own enthusiasm. I am convinced (and the thought inspires
me) that the man with a good and just cause need have no fear; that he   95
should have no respect for persons when the time has come that not only his
friends were suffering but the cause of God: no, wrongs done to his friend
are intolerable for this very reason, that they were bringing Christ into
disgrace. Piety, I felt, is something greater than eloquence; a show of words
may look fine in the eyes of men, but none the less truth wins the day with   100
pious and Christian souls, and I shall be a poor Christian if I do not refute the
blasphemer. And so I seized pen and ink and made notes of what I could not
stand.

So much for the reasons which impelled me to write; now let me tell
you in what an honourable spirit I have replied. Richly as your folly would   105
have deserved quite different treatment from anyone with a free flow of
words (a spongy flow like yours, for choice) and leisure to go into details, yet
I controlled myself and avoided spite and passion; I have refrained from
calumny and charged you with nothing except what the veriest blockhead
could collect from your *Spongia*. And the style, as you see, is of the simplest, 110
so that you cannot suspect this book of having been got ready to attack you
several months ago and must not induce the innocent to believe any such
invention. There are people here capable of writing a polished attack on you,
but they have better things to do with their time than pit their skill in writing
against yours.   115

* * * * *

8 Greek proverb, cited in *Adagia* I i 98
9 Cf *Adagia* I viii 70.

You are therefore doubly in error if you accuse me hereafter of having undertaken this task in hopes of earning some paltry reputation. I am not the man to make even the slightest claims for myself on grounds of style; and however much I might have wished to do what I could, it must have been on some other subject. Otherwise, what madness it would be to draw the   120
sword on a man who had previously done me no harm, and to seek immortal glory for myself by bringing disgrace on someone else! I am not so stupid and so devoid of judgment as not to know that all these transient things are nothing worth, and that those are the greatest fools who toil away and expose themselves to danger for no other purpose except to win   125
themselves name and fame, which, even if they acquire it, is so quickly over. And I should be the most foolish of them all if instead of glory I achieved repentance and disgrace, if it is disgrace to stand up for the truth and be abused. For of this I am certain, that you will one day do what you promise at the end of your letter:[10] that if the man whom you suspect makes himself   130
known, he will discover that you did not hate Hutten with your whole heart – though whom you mean in saying this I do not really know.

So what moved me to write was not the desire for reputation; what it was, I have already explained above. And indeed I have no fears for myself on this score, that if you do not openly withdraw some statements and cease   135
to maintain them so obstinately, either I shall drive you to a recantation or you will submit to be openly convicted by me of impiety. And you are very, very badly mistaken if you think that this is the sort of trouble you had with Lee[11] or Zúñiga,[12] or that I am a toadstool and blockhead of the Zúñiga type. The last thing I shall tolerate from you is to let myself be imposed upon by a   140
whirling cloud of words. You may be razor-sharp in argument, but unless you fight with that two-edged sword which is the word of God,[13] this leaden dagger of your eloquence does not frighten me at all. Nor do I need very keen wits for my purpose, or the luxuriant charm of style that will win the favour of my readers; the naked truth and nothing else, that is what I shall   145
bring to light in simple and sincere words. Every man of good will has enough judgment already to know what he ought to feel about a man like you when he sees the cunning, shuffling, slippery way you go about everything; it is quite needless for me to point this out. No one alive today, however skilful with the pen, could draw such a detailed portrait of you as   150
you do of yourself: the great scholar, the brilliant writer, but untrustworthy

* * * * *

10 Ep 1389:90–2
11 See Ep 1341A:823–30.
12 See Ep 1341A:868–927.
13 Heb 4:12

and arrogant, always ready, it seems, to be turned aside from your duty or your purpose for a crust of bread; no cause so good that you cannot make it seem abominable, and none so deplorable that you cannot make it look the best of all.   155

And as I sat down to write, there were to be sure some thoughts that made me realize it would do the gospel cause no good if my answer were sometimes too brutally expressed. That Camarina should be left unmoved which when stirred up breathes out and pours forth nothing but poison,[14] unless I want many to fall away from the gospel whom you can turn with   160 your inborn cunning into a different path. These men too put their trust in human reason and were afraid where no fear was;[15] for, granted that you could do so (and do it you cannot, for no man can seize what has once been given to Christ by the Father), why should you wish to attempt anything so frivolous and pointless? It was not my duty to protest when you assumed   165 the censor's rod in order to pass judgment not only on the undeserving but on all good men. Long enough have we looked up to you, and with good reason – that learning of yours, of which you were the pioneer in Germany – and it was a better reason than many even in the first rank of repute can show. But you who were the agent of our salvation, can you now want to   170 offer us a drink of poison and be the agent of our deaths? Do you think we should suffer such treatment at your hands? It is insufferable. As those who are to give someone poison first mix it in some sweet and pleasant drink, so you at first put some sort of spell upon us with your eloquence; we were barbarians, fierce and untameable, and you civilized us; you showed the   175 way by which we could end up not only educated but religious. But when you saw many men taking that path, some of whom were to wrest the victory from you in this field, whether you were overcome by pride, corrupted by bribes, or blinded by jealousy (as some suppose), instead of the old honey, or mixed in with it, you drip poison, and in the end like a   180 scorpion plunge in your sting. Had you not done this, there is not a man to this day who would not reverence you, not one who would not share your

* * * * *

14 Ancient authors had two explanations for the proverb *Ne moveas Camarinam*. The most common was that Camarina, a city on the southern coast of Sicily, had on its northern boundary a swamp (*palus camarina*) whose miasmic vapours made the city unhealthy. When, contrary to the advice of the Delphic oracle, the inhabitants drained the swamp, they thereby opened the way to the successful conquest of the city by its enemies. The other explanation was that camarina was a shrub whose branches gave off a foul odour when shaken. See *Adagia* 1 i 64. Brunfels' reference is closer to the second interpretation. Cf Ep 1523:88–9.
15 Ps 53:5 (Vulgate 52:6)

successes, sing your praises, greet you with honour and respect. But when by your own behaviour you tarnish the record of your eloquence and darken the brightness of your own reputation, who can look up to you, who will respect you? You sin against your own soul, and who shall justify you? If a man dishonour his own soul, who shall give him that honour back?[16]

For my part, it is a most bitter grief to me that you should have come to such a pass, and that a man like myself of no account and no learning should have to do battle with you. Would that I had never been given an opportunity which I could not refuse without losing my peace of mind! Would that you had not sunk to such depths of insanity that you, who ought now to be Christ's mouthpiece and the chosen vessel that should carry the name of God before the children of Israel and before kings and princes and all the people of the earth, have now become the head of those who in secret council have plotted and conspired against the Lord and against his anointed![17] For it is generally agreed that among all the enemies of the gospel none has ever done it more harm than you; for though you never openly attacked it, you wrap things up and slip things in in this extraordinary inconsistent way until all is confusion, trying simultaneously to establish both the papacy and the gospel, wheat and chaff together, darkness and light. What other purpose have you except utterly to overthrow all that you once founded, championed, and spread far and wide? Could any pestilence worse than this attack the gospel, seeing that today no two things have so little in common as Christ and pope, Rome and the church of Christ? While you add at the same time this further point, that there is too much bitterness in some of the things we do, and that even we ourselves are not perfect. It is indeed a pretty saying of yours that mildness is the way to handle the gospel. Yes indeed, when concerned with the infirm, with those whose faith is weak, with such as need milk and cannot take solid food; but not when dealing with the stubborn and stiff-necked, with the desperate and abandoned, with shameless and hardened scribes and Pharisees, who have the key of knowledge yet will not listen to the law, who stop up their ears that they may not hear.[18] If Luther, for instance, says some rather angry things about bishops and monks, there is no cruelty in this; it is demanded by their hardness of heart, their wickedness and their obstinacy – just as I too am rather free in speaking to you now. A tough knot calls for a tough wedge.[19] But when you accuse us too of being sinners, I do not see what that

* * * * *

16 Ecclus 10:29 (10:32 Vulgate)
17 Ps 2:2
18 Zech 7:11
19 Cf *Adagia* 1 i 6, 1 ix 48.

has got to do with it, for no man is able to live without sin. The great thing is
that we are dissatisfied with our sins; but we will try very hard not to be the   220
sort of people that you pretend we are.

So much then in passing for my reasons, though it would have made
more sense had I simply despised you; for why should I make up to you? –
you who by your *Spongia* alone have deserved that the Germans, who first
learned to write under your leadership, should now by squadrons and   225
battalions sharpen their swords against their pestilent instructor. Do you
think it a small thing to shuffle like this and have a double mind, carrying the
burden as they say on both shoulders?[20] The honour and integrity of
Germans does not allow of this, nor for that matter does our Christian
religion.   230

And then for Hutten too, I am astonished at your pitiless attitude, and
at that really poisonous spirit in which they say that you pursue in this
fashion all honourable and distinguished Germans with hidden hatred.
Granted that Hutten treated you with some bitterness too, the difference is
that his anger was just and well deserved and pious and truly Christian,   235
while the false accusations you levelled at him were perverse, offensive, and
mendacious. And when you ought to acknowledge your fault, or at least in
your own defence to produce evidence that you are no enemy of the gospel,
you merely protest that you never wish to have any connection with the men
who under Luther's name embrace the gospel, perhaps in order to repay full   240
measure to the pope, whose slave you are. And another thing points in the
same direction – the way you implicate even innocent people in this
business; for instance, a man right honourable not so much for breeding and
ancestry as for his integrity of life, his character, and his literary gifts,
Heinrich Eppendorf,[21] a German knight, who because he was connected   245
with the man has been rewarded with the same praise from you, a similar
Erasmian tribute of the kind you use so often either to praise the worst of
men or to denigrate the best, and only the best. He too would have some
protests to make to you and a charge to bring against you.[22] This is why I
have preferred to proceed without his knowledge and not to put his case: I   250
did not want to rouse your suspicions that he or anyone else had lent me
their assistance.

And to make an end of my letter once and for all, all I have said so far
was intended to make any future *Spongia* you may write very different and
perhaps more religious. This *Spongia* gave no pleasure even to your dearest   255

* * * * *

20 *Adagia* III vi 84
21 Cf Ep 1376:27–9.
22 Cf Ep 1437:34–5.

friends, and if some people bought it eagerly and waited for it,[23] they bought it not because they found it so attractive but in order to discover how you could wash away the stain that Hutten had inflicted on your reputation, which could never be washed out by wagon-loads of sponges, unless you repent. For there will be no other remedy, no fuller's herb that can put you right.[24] Repent, repent, I beg you in the bowels of Jesus Christ. Draw back; remember you are old; remember your vocation, and the grace that was given you before so many witnesses, for it is infamous to misuse favours received in order to injure the source from which they come. And you do misuse them, as long as you do not fight for the gospel with all your might, as long as you give aid and comfort to its adversaries, as long as you leave the souls of many men in jeopardy who have been attracted by your duplicity and for the time neither believe nor win salvation. In this way you will earn far greater glory (if it was on glory that you had so definitely set your heart) than from the false and feigned friendship of men without hope, who plan to misuse your eloquence that they may pride themselves on your support. Besides which, you deserve a far better fate than to act as a prop for those in whose future there is no ray of hope.

Only, you must act! There is no disgrace in refusing your services to a shameful cause, no loss of face in making good your escape or lying low for a time, if you have renewed the fight. And so far am I from planning further hostile action against you that I shall not be ashamed actually to withdraw any steps I may ever have taken to combat or discredit you. If you persist in your purpose, piling one misdeed upon another, I too shall fight back and strive against you to your face, fearing neither your eloquence nor that magnificent reputation you enjoy among the bishops. Then we shall hear you disgorging your spleen, spouting your rhetoric, launching great clouds of empty words,[25] boasting everywhere of your grand friends and the favour of princes, playing your clever tricks with Holy Scripture, leaning on the broken reed of Egypt,[26] spewing out calumnies of every kind, underpinning the walls of Babylon[27] and rebuilding the ruins of Rome, triumphing in chariots and in horses.[28] But we shall call upon the name of the Lord our God, and shall do our utmost to see that we both say and write what is true

260

265

270

275

280

285

* * * * *

23 Cf Ep 1397:3–4.
24 See Malachi 3:2, where the English Bible has 'fuller's soap.' This was a plant, rich in alkali, used to make soap.
25 Cf Horace *Ars poetica* 97.
26 Isa 36:6
27 Cf Jer 51:58.
28 Ps 20:7 (Vulgate 19:8)

(for true and simple is the language of truth), and moreover to cast out of the camp the false prophet who prophesies in Baal,[29] not with very stylish   290
language but with the holy Scriptures. Nor shall I care very much how far some load me with infamy, how I am sneered at by the dregs of the court, how far you make me a byword, a scapegoat, a theme of ballad-singers, and an example to the world and to all those who have not the mark of the Word written on their foreheads.[30] I shall do what is incumbent on me as my duty,   295
to preserve the glory of our God pure and inviolate. Farewell.

1407 / From Jean Lange   Meaux, 1 January 1524

> The autograph of this letter (=Ep 22 in Enthoven) was in that portion of the Rehdiger Collection of the University Library at Wrocław that perished in World War II. Jean Lange (Johannes Angelus), documented in Paris and Meaux 1522–4, studied under Lefèvre d'Etaples (line 25) at the Collège du Cardinal Lemoine in Paris. He was teaching Greek there in 1522. By the time he wrote this letter, he had joined the entourage of Guillaume Briçonnet (n33), bishop of Meaux.

TO ERASMUS OF ROTTERDAM, A VERY GREAT MAN IN EVERY WAY, ANGELUS WISHES ALL FELICITY
Although I have never dared to write to you hitherto, being conscious of my inexperience and of an idle and stupid ignorance of the art of writing, especially if one has one's eye on a man – Erasmus, no less – who is richly   5
endowed with learning of every kind, my extensive reading in your many books, so characteristic of their author in their peaceful and friendly spirit, has revealed to me your kind and easy nature and your unusually mild and courteous ways. As a result, I have at length lost my fears, I an Angel[1] of you a human being, I a creature of heaven and you of earth, I winged and you   10
featherless, I airborne and you crawling on the ground – which is tantamount, if I may stop fooling, to the fly losing its fear of the elephant, the dwarf its fear of the giant, not to say Achilles losing his fear of Hector.[2] I have also been so much encouraged to this course by a certain Gascon,[3] who is at

* * * * *

29 Cf Jer 2:8, 23:13.
30 Rev 9:4, 14:1

1407
1 'Angelus' in the original, a play on Lange's name
2 See Ep 1481:49–52.
3 Unidentified except as described here

least the scion of a very noble family, being a nephew of the bishop of   15
Condom,[4] and who, for all my reluctance, has spurred me on to the point of
not being afraid to address one letter to you, so that overcoming all timidity I
made up my mind irrevocably (*empedos* they say in Greek) to take the first
chance of writing if a proper opportunity should present itself. This Gascon
is one of those who once lived and ate with you in Padua,[5] at the time when   20
your friend Brie,[6] whom I can never mention without first speaking of his
great kindness and his pure and polished scholarship, was living in Venice.

In the first place, what pains me and torments me most of all and brings
me much unhappiness and bitter regret is the rise of disagreement, even
without cause, between you and that excellent man Lefèvre,[7] slight though   25
it is; for this reason, that the theological faction, a tribe that is bitterly hostile
not only to you but to all men of civilized intelligence, have seized on this as
a handle for false accusations. As a result, every really good scholar is now
such a target for invective, to the great prejudice of literary studies, and
every individual so torn to strips, blackened, and lacerated, and loaded with   30
abuse, that those who formerly held first place with the support and
authorization of bishops, archbishops, cardinals, and the supreme pontiff
himself, in general agreement with no trace of reluctance, and enjoyed
furthermore the good wishes of the emperor, and of kings, dukes, and
counts, are now degraded with great ignominy as though to the bottom of   35
the class and are forced into the ranks of men of no account.

And the source of this is easily discovered. It is the way that insane and
crazy Zúñiga,[8] good scholar though he is, has emptied wagon-loads of
scurrility on you and your *Annotationes* with no motive, as God is my
witness, but hatred and jealousy of your great learning; the way you   40
yourself in several places have criticized Lefèvre excessively, taking his
views to pieces rather too fiercely and sometimes pitching your opinion of
him so low that you deprive that great man, so holy and religious, of all claim
to be considered educated or even a rational being; the way so many others
wage these fierce and bitter battles among themselves, Hutten against   45
Erasmus and Erasmus against Hutten,[9] Brie against Thomas More,[10] and

* * * * *

4 François Du Moulin (Ep 1426)
5 In the winter of 1508; see Ep 212.
6 Epp 212:2n, 569 introduction
7 Ep 597:37n
8 Ep 1260 nn36 and 45
9 See Ep 1378 introduction.
10 Epp 620, 1045

against Budé some German I know not who,[11] and quite often Caelius.[12] May the Almighty lay them all to rest, in such peace that they can rightly be called sons of God. These tumults, these discords, these complicated quarrels, these tedious differences always erupting into perpetual disputes I find so abhorrent, so revolting, so criminal, that there is nothing I would attack more bitterly. No words in the whole body of Holy Scripture are read more frequently than 'Peace be with you.' And rightly so; for as the poet says, 'The love of peace is God; let us love and reverence peace.'[13]

But of this I need say no more, for of all mortals who have ever set down anything about peace,[14] you are the most eloquent. Several of your very keen admirers, myself among them, all Frenchmen who believe they have made some progress in the study of Greek, have come to this resolve, that we should humbly urge upon your unique and incredible learning and your brain that is never weary in the cause of research the task of translating Theodorus' fertile little book on the months,[15] for the general good and specially for the spirit of France, whose welfare you have always had at heart; for though we nearly understand it, we vie with one another in wishing that we had your wording of such a useful author. We cannot see what excuse you can put forward, except the fact that you spend all your

50

55

60

65

* * * * *

11 Zasius (Ep 303), who in a letter to Claudius Cantiuncula, 29 November 1518, printed with his *De origine juris* (Ep 367:37n), had resolved some 'antinomiae' raised by Budé in his *Annotationes in Pandectas* (Ep 403 introduction). Budé took offence and wrote a letter in his own defence on 25 July 1519. Zasius replied on 1 September. See Louis Delaruelle, *Répertoire analytique et chronologique de la correspondance de Guillaume Budé* (Toulouse 1906; repr New York n d) nos 38–9, and Allen's note.

12 Neither Celio Calcagnini (Ep 611:27n) nor Lodovico Ricchieri, called Caelius (Ep 469:10n), seems to have had any controversy with Budé. Allen speculated that Lange may have been thinking of one or the other of two Italians who did (Leonardo de Portis and Giambattista Egnazio; Ep 648:58n) and have pulled the wrong Italian name out of his memory.

13 The reference is to Propertius 3.5.1: 'Pacis Amor deus est; pacem veneramur amantes,' which Lange renders as 'Pacis amor Deus est, pacem veneremur amantes.' The original means 'Love [ie, Cupid] is a god of peace; we lovers venerate peace.' But Lange, who had perhaps encountered the line only in another author or in a florilegium, was apparently unaware of the erotic nature of the original and thus read it in the sense indicated in our translation.

14 Cf Ep 1432:11–13.

15 Theodorus Gaza's treatise on the Greek calendar, first printed by Aldo Manuzio at Venice in December 1495; Emile Legrand *Bibliographie hellénique ou description raisonée des ouvrages publiés en grec par des Grecs aux xve et xvie siècles* I (Paris 1885) no 17. Erasmus did not comply with the wish of his French admirers.

time on much more serious subjects, on theology in fact, and are entirely
devoted to them and immersed in them. You will add also your mature old
age,[16] the sacred anchor (as the proverb puts it[17]) of any well-founded refusal
to take up this task; for, mature as it is, it sets before itself and claims as its
due fields of study far more mature than this. To the first of these objections   70
our reply will be this: the only real, true theology is that which, to Christians'
very great advantage, is ready to attempt anything and produce anything,
all to the unfading glory of Almighty God. For what is put out and published
by human skill, if it is not buttressed by the powerful support of the supreme
Deity, falls easily to the ground and is lost in eternal oblivion. The second   75
excuse we shall rebut without difficulty, and with very great respect for you.
We grant that for your old age you may have selected fields of study far more
mature; though this will be mature enough, given the brilliance as a
translator in which you surpass all other men and Theodorus Gaza's
inexhaustible knowledge of so complex a field; it is equally true that by   80
falling in with the hopes of so many worthy men you will better display your
kindly, generous spirit. And though we all acknowledge and welcome this
eagerly for the moment, the result of your saying yes will be a great increase
in the warmth of our enthusiasm and the constancy of our support, if indeed
you can have any use for the support of Frenchmen such as we are.   85

Apart from those leaders in the literary field who wish you well with all
their heart, Budé, Lefèvre, Deloynes,[18] Ruzé,[19] Bérault,[20] Ruel[21] (and why
you should never have written to him, given some suitable subject, or he
conversely should never have opened a correspondence with you, is a
source of immense surprise to many of us), there are others too of no mean   90
learning who stand ready and waiting to defend you eagerly should any
occasion arise. Among their number is Gérard Roussel,[22] the teacher in

* * * * *

16 Erasmus was in his mid-fifties, either fifty-four or fifty-seven, depending on
   which year of birth (1466 or 1469) one accepts.
17 *Adagia* I i 24
18 Ep 494
19 Ep 493:462n
20 Ep 925
21 Ep 346:13n
22 Gérard Roussel (c 1480–1555) studied arts in Paris and joined the circle of
   Lefèvre d'Etaples as early as 1501. His first published work (1521) was a
   commentary on Boethius' *Arithmetica*. By 1521 he had gone to Meaux to rejoin
   Lefèvre in the circle of reformers around bishop Guillaume Briçonnet (n33
   below). There he became a canon and treasurer of the cathedral chapter.
   Though listed here as a champion of Erasmus, his own letters from this period
   reveal a far greater attraction to Zwingli and Oecolampadius, whose ideas he

dialectic of Guillaume Farel from Dauphiné who now lives in Basel,[23] a man so energetic and experienced in philosophy and mathematics that, with the exception of Lefèvre, he could easily claim first place, and with a very   95 elegant knowledge of Greek and Hebrew too. Then there is Jacques Toussain,[24] now Budé's only pupil apart from his son Dreux,[25] whom Budé accepts and rates as an excellent Greek scholar. In Latin you have the two Dubois,[26] Morel the headmaster,[27] Baventius[28] and Milo.[29] Of theologians, at least those of our own sort, you will find many who would not refuse to die   100 for you. I have left out Brissot the doctor of medicine, excellent philosopher, mathematician, Grecian, and good Latinist.[30] Perhaps you met him lately, when he was returning from Italy to France through Switzerland; if you have spoken with him, I need say no more.

* * * * *

promoted as best he could at Meaux through sermons and Bible-study groups. In October 1525 he fled with Lefèvre to Strasbourg, but returned the following spring to France to become confessor and almoner to Margaret of Angoulême, sister of Francis I and later queen of Navarre, in whose service he remained as an irenic Catholic until his death. In 1536 he became bishop of Oléron.

23 Ep 1341A n305; cf Ep 1477A.
24 Ep 810:497n
25 Dreux Budé (b c 1507) was the eldest son of Guillaume Budé, who in large measure supervised his education. He became a royal secretary and master of requests. His mother and two of his brothers became Calvinists, but he remained a Catholic.
26 François and Jacques Dubois (Sylvius). François (c 1483–1536) taught humanities at Paris and was the author of textbooks on rhetoric and poetics. From 1516 he was one of a team of scholars who helped the publisher Josse Bade with his editions of the classics. Though he was not an exceptionally talented scholar, Erasmus had a high opinion of him; see Epp 1600 and 1677, the only surviving letters in their correspondence. Jacques (1478–1555), was the younger brother of François, who was his teacher in Paris. He later took a medical doctorate at Montpellier (1530) and taught medicine at Paris. Though his contemporary fame rested on his medical works, he also published (1531) the first grammar of the French language.
27 Thierry Morel (documented 1520–6), taught at the Collège de la Marche in Paris and was probably principal of the school. He wrote several school books that show the influence of Erasmus, whom he fervently admired.
28 Baventius studied at Paris. Nothing is known about him save that he edited a small volume of *Epigrammata* published by Bade in 1523.
29 Emile Perrot, also called Milo (documented 1524–1), studied at the Collège du Cardinal Lemoine, where Guillaume Farel (n23 above) was one of his teachers. By 1524 he had become a teacher of grammar at the college. He later studied law and in 1551 became a member of the Parlement of Paris.
30 Pierre Brissot (1478–1525), taught at the University of Paris from 1504, where he received his doctorate in medicine in 1514. Also interested in botany, he went to Portugal in 1518, hoping to proceed to America, but instead practised medicine at Evora for several years.

If it so be that after this recital of distinguished men you still say no to   105
what we ask, hoping to pass this burden on to the first comer, we shall
defend ourselves by the same shield we used before. It is your style that we
passionately desire, your wonderful mastery of the pen, and your Latinity,
which no other man can equal, much less surpass. If it is no trouble, you will
be so good as to send a few lines to let us know your decision in this matter.   110
You will do this the more readily if you convince yourself that we shall
preserve any letter that comes from your treasure-house as something more
valuable than the copy of Homer kept long ago by that prince of Macedon in
a rich and jewelled casket.[31] Pray give my greeting to Glareanus,[32] that witty
scholar and wisest of men.   115

Meaux, from the lodging of Lefèvre in the household of the lord bishop
of Meaux,[33] 1 January 1524
    Sincerely, Lange

1408 / To Willibald Pirckheimer   Basel, 8 January 1524

On Pirckheimer, see Ep 318. This letter was first published in the *Pirckheimeri
opera*. Ep 1417:2–3, 38–9 indicates that delivery may have been delayed.

Greeting. Your letter[1] was most uncommonly welcome, because for one

* * * * *

31 Alexander the Great; see Plutarch *Alexander* 26.
32 Ep 440
33 Guillaume Briçonnet (1470–1534), son of Charles viii's finance minister,
   pursued a career in the church and royal service. He was appointed bishop of
   Lodève in 1489, abbot of St Germain-des-Prés at Paris in 1505, and bishop of
   Meaux in 1516. In 1507 he was sent to Rome on a mission to Julius ii; in 1511 he
   attended the Council of Pisa; and in 1516–18 he represented Francis i in Rome.
   He was an enthusiast for learning and moderate reform and attached great
   importance to the translation of the Bible into French. In 1518 he began the
   reform of his diocese at Meaux and in 1521 he summoned Lefèvre (n7 above),
   Roussel (n22 above), and others to assist him. He maintained close ties to the
   royal court through Margaret of Angoulême, sister of Francis i (ibidem). But in
   1525, while the king was engaged in a disastrous campaign in Italy,
   conservatives brought legal charges against Lefèvre, Roussel, Briçonnet, and
   others for spreading heresy. Lefèvre and Roussel fled the country (ibidem), but
   Briçonnet remained and was rebuked and fined by the Parlement of Paris.
   Though quickly restored to royal favour, he henceforth preached and acted in a
   conservative manner. Erasmus, who had met Briçonnet while the latter was
   bishop of Lodève, spoke a word on his behalf at the time of his trial; Allen Ep
   1581:317–19.

   1408
 1 Not extant; it may have been in reply to Ep 1398. Its contents are referred to in
   Ep 1417:1–2.

thing it carried an air of cheerfulness about it. As for me, during these
Christmas holidays the combination of the stone[2] with the painful complaint
they call the colic came very near indeed to releasing me from these evils of
life. And my poor body is still in such a low state that I fear I may not   5
complete what I have in hand – my work on the Acts.[3] I have no fear of
death, for I have lived long enough. I could wish for death in another,
gentler shape. As it is, imagine how many deaths I die in giving birth to a
single stone! And how often I must taste death afresh. But it is God's will,
and we must submit.   10

Clement VII[4] invites me to Rome with generous offers. The illustrious
Lady Margaret and the emperor call me to Brabant;[5] otherwise it is all over
with my annuity, which has not been paid now for over two years.[6] Here
Luther's party, the more gifted ones, are indignant with me, and Luther
writes about me to his followers in an unfriendly spirit.[7] As for Rome, I can   15
guess what will happen; for there are people there who plan my final
destruction in a spirit of do or die.[8] They had nearly succeeded before
Adrian's death; but after I had written and told him part of my proposals,[9] as
requested in a secret letter from himself, I soon felt a change in the powers
that be.   20

In Brabant a sword has been put into the hands of madmen who hate
me more than they hate Luther.[10] Here my illness dominates everything. I
have already had frequent invitations from the king of France.[11] But it will
look like deserting to the enemy,[12] and was so represented to the emperor by
my opponents; but he is still pretty well disposed towards me. The king of   25
England urges me so hard to write against Luther that it looks as though he
would take offence if I persist in saying no.[13] What a crazy world we live in!
You will do me a great service if you send me a full report of everything else

* * * * *

2 For this bout of the stone at Christmas, see Epp 1409:7–8, 1411:3–8, 1415:108–9,
  1416:11–13, 1418:62, 1422:18–26, 1423:2–6, 1426:16–23, 1434:38–40. See also
  AK Ep 945:26–8.
3 Ep 1414
4 The new pope, elected on 19 November 1523
5 Cf Epp 1416:42–3, 1417:18–20, 1418:59–60, 1422:38–40, 1431:11–12, 1434.
6 See Ep 1380 introduction.
7 See Ep 1384:57–62, 92–3.
8 An apparent reference to Zúñiga; see Epp 1410, 1415.
9 Ep 1352
10 Baechem (Ep 1254 n6) and Hulst (Ep 1345 n8); cf Epp 1411:15–17, 1417:20–3,
   1434:45–8.
11 See Epp 1375, 1403, 1434:18–25.
12 Cf Epp 1411:10–11, 1432:76–7, 1434:14, 1437:191–2.
13 Cf Epp 1415:65 and 1419 introduction.

that happens in your part of the world, and what our friend Lee has been up
to.[14] How Luther makes all his enemies famous and rich![15] I wonder very   30
much what will be the outcome of this diet,[16] and of the preparations for war
that are on foot everywhere. There will be a clash of mountains, I suppose.
May God turn our tumults to the good of us all!

On that Erasmus in cast metal your guess was correct.[17] It normally
comes out better in an alloy of copper and tin. And the Terminus on the   35
reverse makes it more difficult to get a good impression of the face. I should
like your people to try their hand. I am glad our friend Dürer has met his
cobbler.[18] Give him my warmest greetings, and Varnbüler too.[19]

* * * * *

14 Erasmus' former antagonist, Edward Lee (Ep 1341A n224), was now royal
   almoner to Henry VIII. In August 1523 he, Lord Morley, and others had been
   instructed to carry the Garter to Archduke Ferdinand. Setting out in September, the mission reached Nürnberg in mid-October, where it awaited Ferdinand's arrival (29 November) for the impending diet. The Garter was delivered
   on 8 December. See LP III 3275, 3373, 3546, 3611, 3619, 3630.
15 See Ep 1397 n19.
16 The new diet that had been gathering at Nürnberg since November and
   opened on 14 January 1524.
17 Cf Epp 1417, 1452, 1466, 1480, 1536, 1558. It seems that at Pirckheimer's request
   Erasmus had sent to Nürnberg a copy of the medal cast by Metsys in 1519 (Ep
   1092 n2) so that more copies could be struck (cf Ep 1398:3–5). But the high relief
   of the head of Terminus (Ep 604:4n) on the reverse side caused problems (Ep
   1417:39–42). As a remedy, Erasmus suggested that Terminus be turned to
   profile so that he would project less (Ep 1452:34–6). This implies that the
   original medal showed Terminus in full face. However, all surviving copies of
   the medal show Terminus in profile, a circumstance which indicates that those
   copies do not entirely conform to the original intention of the artist. See L.
   Smolderen 'Quentin Metsys médailleur d'Erasme,' *Scrinium Erasmium: Mé-
   langes historiques publiées sous le patronage de l'Université de Louvain à l'occasion du
   cinquième centenaire de la naissance d'Erasme* ed J. Coppens 2 vols (Leiden 1969) II
   513–25, especially 515–16. For pictures of both sides of the medal, see ibidem
   520; Gerlo 8–9.
18 Allen found the word 'cobbler' (*sutorem*) incongruous here, concluded that it
   was probably a textual corruption, and suggested that one should perhaps
   read *fusorem* (caster) instead (because of the reference to the Erasmus medal in
   lines 34ff). However, as Erwin Panowsky has pointed out (*Journal of the
   Warburg and Courtauld Institutes* 14 [1951] 34 n1), 'cobbler' is the correct reading.
   Since Erasmus habitually referred to Dürer as 'noster Apelles' or 'Apelles tuus'
   (eg, Ep 1398:12), it seems clear that he is here making a jocular reference to the
   famous anecdote about the painter Apelles and the critical cobbler (Pliny
   Naturalis historia 35.85) as well as to the associated proverb 'ne sutor ultra
   crepidam judicaret' – 'let the cobbler stick to his last,' ie, not criticize things he
   knows nothing about; *Adagia* I vi 16. Ep 1417:1–2 makes the circumstances
   clear. While at Nürnberg, Lee (n14 above) had sharply criticized some of

I have written this with some difficulty, my hands being still shaky
from my complaint, and I was told of the courier's departure at the last   40
minute. All my best wishes to our friend Fabri.[20] Let me know the details.
Justus,[21] the envoy of the king of Poland, has not yet received my *Precatio
dominica*,[22] which I think is already on sale in your part of the world.
Farewell. From Basel, two days after Epiphany 1523
        Erasmus   45
        To the honourable Willibald Pirckheimer, counsellor to his Imperial
Majesty.

1409 / To Bernhard von Cles   Basel, 16 January 1524

> The manuscript of this letter, which was first published in the *Opus epistolarum*,
> is in the Nationalbibliothek at Vienna (Cod 9737c, f 5). On Bernhard von Cles,
> adviser to Archduke Ferdinand of Austria, see Ep 1357. Since the content of
> this letter is virtually identical to that of paragraph two of Ep 1408, no
> additional annotation is required here.

Greeting, my Lord Bishop. I must say, your generous and Christian spirit is
worthy of a man whose intellectual gifts and physical vigour could be equal
to anything. My own advancing years, and still more the state of my health,
which gets worse every day, make my company unsuitable for any purpose.
Clement VII most kindly bids me come to Rome, the emperor invites me to   5
return to Brabant, the king of France invites me to join him with the promise
of mountains of gold. I fear however that King Stone will soon translate me
to another world. And yet I do not refuse your most generous offer. If I live
till Easter, I shall try and see whether I can stand the effort of a journey. If
that goes well, I long to see Italy, and on the way I shall visit your kingdom.   10
May the Lord Jesus keep your lordship in prosperity, and in kindly feelings
towards my humble self.
        Basel, 16 January 1524
        Your lordship's devoted servant Erasmus of Rotterdam

        * * * * *

> Dürer's paintings. In the lost letter to which Ep 1408 is the reply, Pirckheimer
> had reported this to Erasmus, no doubt with great glee. One can imagine
> Erasmus' amusement at learning that the 'new Apelles' had fallen victim to the
> same 'cobbler' as had he himself some years earlier.

19 Ep 1344 n27
20 See Ep 1397 introduction.
21 Decius (Ep 1341A n210)
22 Ep 1393

1410 / To Lorenzo Campeggi [?]   Basel, 19 January 1524

This letter was first published in the *Opus epistolarum*, where the heading, doubtless in obedience to the manuscript, identifies the addressee as Matthäus Cardinal Schiner (Ep 1295). However, as Allen argued, the date of Schiner's death at Rome, September 1522, makes it impossible to believe that Erasmus could still have been ignorant of that event in January 1524. Thus the heading is inconsistent with the date. On the other hand, the letter bears a close verbal resemblance to Epp 1411, 1418, and 1428; and the articles defended in the second paragraph are identical to some of those defended in the *Apologia* to which Ep 1428 is the preface. Thus the major portion of this letter must be assigned to January 1524, which means that it must have been written to someone other than Schiner. The only passage that corresponds to the heading is the bracketed sentence at the end. In the absence of any evidence of such an offer from any other friend of Erasmus in Rome, Allen and CWE have treated the passage in question as a separate letter that was somehow conflated with the other letter and have printed it as Ep 1295.

Allen concluded that the main portion of the letter, obviously written to Rome, had probably been addressed to Cardinal Campeggi (Ep 961). The date agrees completely with that of Ep 1411, also written to Rome. Moreover, we know from Ep 1415:2–4 and 1423:6–11 that at about this time Erasmus, who was ill, sent Campeggi a letter, dictated to a secretary, in answer to a letter from Campeggi conveying Pope Clement's VII's invitation to come at once to Rome (cf lines 9–14 here).

Allen framed the following supposition to explain the conflation of the two letters. If Erasmus had abandoned Ep 1295 after writing only the introduction and a few lines, the paper would most likely not have been thrown away but rather saved for future use. Eighteen months later the secretary to whom Erasmus was dictating could have used it to take down the rough draft of the letter to Campeggi. The editors of the *Opus epistolarum* may then have combined the two texts, treating the lines in Erasmus' own hand as a postscript to be inserted at the end. If, as is most likely, Erasmus did not correct the proofs, that would explain the inconsistency between the date and the heading.

In December 1523 Clement VII (Ep 1414) had chosen Campeggi as legate *a latere* for Germany. Campeggi's most pressing task was to represent Catholic interests at the coming diet at Nürnberg (14 January–18 April 1524). He left Rome on 1 February, reaching Nürnberg on 14 March. See Pastor x 109–11. Erasmus only learned of these developments about a month after this letter was written; see Ep 1422:8–9.

ERASMUS OF ROTTERDAM TO MATTHÄUS, CARDINAL OF SION,
GREETING

My honoured lord, I find I now experience just what in ancient mythology is
said to have happened as a rule to Hercules.[1] While I am wrestling here with
the many-headed hydra which is Luther's party, a great crab in your part of   5
the world crawls up and fastens tightly on my foot. Once again Zúñiga[2] after
so many prohibitions pours out his pamphlets,[3] and makes me a Lutheran
whether I will or no. It simply is not fair, if I am to be torn to pieces by both
sides. To fight with the hydra was a large enough assignment in itself. I
know, I well remember, the friendly advice and wise counsel that your   10
Eminence gave me, saying I ought to go to Rome; and such indeed was my
intention. But in the mean time I have come within an ace of departing for
another world,[4] and my affliction is of such a kind that I hold myself
constantly in readiness for that day. I will creep slowly towards you all the
same when the milder weather comes, for once in Rome I am quite prepared   15
to die, particularly if I may have your protection against those who, believe
me, show more indulgence to their personal ambitions than concern for the
dignity of the Holy See. What can give this party greater satisfaction than if
Zúñiga were to persuade the world, monstrous falsehood though it is, that
Erasmus agrees at all points with Luther?   20

　　　Personally, I can perceive no single point so far in which he and I
agree.[5] And yet all the accusations levelled at me by Zúñiga are collected
from books published before I had ever heard Luther's name.[6] As to the
sovereignty of the pope I have never doubted;[7] but whether that sovereignty
was recognized in Jerome's day or exercised is a doubt I do raise somewhere   25

　　　＊ ＊ ＊ ＊ ＊

1410
1 See CWE 31 420:36ff (*Adagia* I v 39).
2 Ep 1260 n36
3 Popes Leo x and Adrian vi as well as the college of cardinals had frequently
   denied Zúñiga permission to publish his attacks on Erasmus. But after the
   death of Adrian (14 September 1523), while the cardinals were preoccupied
   with the election of a new pope, Zúñiga published at Rome his *Conclusiones
   principaliter suspectae et scandalosae quae reperiuntur in libris Erasmi Roterodami*; see
   Ep 1341A:914--27. Erasmus replied with his *Apologia ad Stunicae Conclusiones*
   (Ep 1428), which may already have been in preparation at this point.
4 Because of the most recent attack of the stone; see Ep 1408 n2.
5 Cf Ep 1384:95–6.
6 Cf Epp 1418:33–4, 1434:44–5.
7 Cf Ep 1342:981–8 with n175.

when prompted by the context, I think in my published notes on Jerome.[8]
But this has two sides: in one passage I set down what happens to support
this view, and again in others I record in the same notes what leads to a
different opinion. And there are so many other places where I call Peter first
in rank among the apostles, Roman pontiff, vicar of Christ, and head of the   30
church, assigning him the chief power after Christ himself. All this is
concealed by Zúñiga, who picks out only what can be distorted to my
discredit. Leo's bull[9] and the emperor's edict[10] launch no thunderbolts
against what has preceded; they look to the future. On confession I had
observed in passing that I thought this had arisen out of the practice of   35
private consultation; and when I say confession, I mean the kind that is now
customary with all its attendant features. And yet I admit that it ought to be
accepted as though Christ had instituted it, not denying at this stage that it
was of his institution, but raising the question.[11] On marriage my position in
the argument is this: I admit that I accept marriage as one of the sacraments 40
properly so called, a view which all the same was not held by the early
Fathers. And this I set down seven years ago in the New Testament.[12]

These are Zúñiga's principal points, and not one of them could justify
all this commotion, especially since all this was written before anyone
dreamt of the rise of Luther, since I make no positive assertions, since I have 45
always submitted my opinion to the judgment of the church, and since in
later editions I have deleted or modified many things which might be able, it
seemed, to give an opening to the rascals for whom an opening is all they
require. I would not strive to make my views acceptable to everyone; I have
no doubt they will be accepted by fair-minded and right-thinking men. My   50
whole heart is set on the glory of Christ; and in both parties I see things I do
not like, much of the spirit of the world on one side, much that is subversive
on the other. In all this tumult, had I seen something better than the policy
which I have followed, I should without doubt have followed that.

* * * * *

8 See Erasmus' scholia to Jerome's letters to Marcella (Ep 41), Damasus (Ep 15),
and Evangelus or Evagrius (Ep 146) in the *Hieronymi opera* (Basel: Froben 1537)
II 129, 132, 330. Cf Ep 843:565–7; LB VI 88C–F (annotation to Matt 16:18); and
Apologia ad Stunicae Conclusiones LB IX 385F–389A.
9 See Ep 1313 n6.
10 See Ep 1313 n7.
11 Cf Ep 1299:66–74.
12 The matter is discussed briefly in the annotation to Eph 5:32 in the *Novum
instrumentum* of 1516. Criticism by Edward Lee (Ep 765 introduction) caused
Erasmus to expand that annotation greatly in the *Novum Testamentum* of 1519.
Cf LB IX 225–8 (*Responsio ad annotationes Lei* 1520).

[The five hundred ducats[13] a year which you so generously offer me I   55
feel as though I had already received, and am no less grateful than I should
be if they were already mine.] With every good wish for your Eminence's
prosperity.

Basel, 19 January 1524

1411 / To Paolo Bombace   Basel, 19 January 1524

This letter, first published in the *Opus epistolarum*, duplicates much of the
content of Ep 1408. It, along with Epp 1410 and 1412, was part of a packet of
letters to Rome sent via Constance in the care of a stuttering Lorrainer; Epp
1416:5–6, 1423:51–2. On Bombace, see Ep 210.

ERASMUS OF ROTTERDAM TO PAOLO BOMBACE, GREETING
Your long silence, my dear Bombace, has made me more than a little anxious
whether all can be well with you. Here I am in constant peril from the stone;
but I was nearly reduced to abandon all hope of life in July, which is a time
of year when as a rule I am pretty well. And then around Christmas I was so   5
ill for a whole month that I prayed for death; life was insupportable.[1] Any
man would rather die once than have a taste of death over and over again in
its most cruel form. And yet during this time I have got out numerous
books.[2] How else should a man like myself face death? The king of France
tempts me to join him with mountains of gold; but I do not like to go, for fear   10
of seeming to take sides with an enemy of the emperor,[3] to whom I have
sworn an oath of allegiance as a councillor[4] – and you know well what a poor
warrior I am. And yet all this time my annuity as a councillor is not paid, nor
will it be paid, I suppose, unless I return to Brabant.[5] And there, besides the
disorder which is universal, a sword has been put into the hand of a certain   15
Carmelite who is quite raving mad,[6] who hates me more than he hates
Luther, the reason being that the ancient tongues and the humanities in
general are growing in our part of the world far faster than those gentry

* * * * *

13 A sum officially worth £166 13s 4d gros Flemish, £112 10s 0d sterling, and
   £1,037 10s 0d tournois. See Ep 1295 n1.

   1411
   1 See Epp 1376 n4, 1408 n2.
   2 See Epp 1378, 1381, 1389–91, 1383, 1400, 1402, 1404.
   3 See Ep 1408 n12.
   4 See Ep 370:18n.
   5 See Ep 1380 introduction.
   6 Baechem (Ep 1256 n6), who was an inquisitor; see Ep 1408 n10.

would wish. In Rome some make me out to be a supporter of Luther,[7] in
Germany I am an arch anti-Lutheran, and there is no one they rage against   20
more than myself because they think it is entirely my fault that they are not
triumphant.[8] My life upon it, I would rather die outright than kindle such a
blaze of hatred round me. I expect you have heard of the scandalous
pamphlet in which Hutten has let fly at me.[9] But he is not the only one: many
have pamphlets at the ready,[10] to be fired off at the first opportunity if they   25
find I have written anything against Luther. All the same, under pressure
from kings and friends everywhere I have set my hand to the task,[11] by
which I know I shall achieve no result except to renew the uproar on their
side. They are the most obstinate thing imaginable, and they're past
counting; you would hardly credit it. And meanwhile during this vacancy   30
Zúñiga, they tell me, has resumed his hysterics in Rome.[12] Such is the fate of
your poor friend Erasmus.

Of our new pope I have great expectations,[13] and I shall crawl slowly
towards your part of the world if I can, even though half dead. Write and tell
me how you spend your time, and commend me to your patron,[14] who will I   35
am sure help the business I have in hand. I learn from letters that the pope is
well disposed towards me.[15] Farewell.

Basel, 19 January 1524

1412 / To Silvester Prierias

This letter has been assigned a new date and is found as Ep 1337A in volume 9.

1413 / From Philibert de Lucinge   Geneva, 20 January 1524

The autograph of this letter (=Ep 23 in Enthoven) was in that portion of the
Rehdiger Collection of the University Library at Wrocław that perished in
World War II. Philibert de Lucinge (documented 1522–9) was a close relative,

* * * * *

7 Ie, Zúñiga; see lines 31–2 below.
8 Cf Epp 1415:26, 1422:57–8.
9 Ep 1356 n9
10 Such as Brunfels' *Responsio* (Ep 1405)
11 Ie, the composition of the *De libero arbitrio*; see Ep 1419 introduction.
12 See Epp 1410, 1415.
13 Ep 1414 introduction
14 Lorenzo Cardinal Pucci (Ep 860), in whose service Bombace remained until 5
    September 1524, when he became secretary to Pope Clement VII
15 Cf Ep 1414:73–5, 1415:102–5, 1418:9–11.

probably the son, of Bertrand de Lucinge, a councillor of the duke of Savoy. In 1522 Philibert was sent to Basel where, on 10 November, he was Erasmus' dinner-guest. By this time he was already a canon of Geneva.

Dear Erasmus thrice greatest of men, I shall not be too frightened to interrupt you briefly with my nonsense as perhaps I do (I hope not), such is my trust in your goodness and mercy, and also because I have made friends with your Hilarius,[1] perfect Frenchman as he is and perfect courtier, and he has given me some news of your most recent success: how he had offered   5 your paraphrases to the king of France[2] and how the king had accepted your gift so splendidly and with such lively looks and how high the name Erasmus stands not only with the king himself but with all the princes, bishops, abbots, and in fact everyone, scholars and ordinary folk equally. At this happy state of things I rejoice with my Erasmus and I think that heaven   10 has done well too; and I hope for still better to follow. Then there is the way Hilarius himself has been received and the terms of the invitations he has been offered!

Apart from that, I have no news here to offer your reverence, for I live in a most pitiful backwater, deprived of educated men in almost any form,   15 where one cannot expect in the ordinary way to hear a word that is religious and is not debased. The theologians here are madmen in monkish cowls, crazy, conceited, and rejoicing in their own ignorance, who are interested only in nonsense and despise nothing so much as the commandments of Christ, while they observe nothing more faithfully and religiously than the   20 orders they get from the pope. And so nothing torments me more than to be compelled to live in the society of men like them. I am obliged from time to time to follow this court[3] and mix with this sort of ass-eared Midases,[4] pretending that I do not notice their piety, their fasts, their sham devotion and self-denial; and I have always found this much against the grain, for you   25

* * * * *

1413
1 Bertholf (Ep 1384 n31)
2 See Epp 1400 and 1403.
3 Apparently the court of the prince-bishop of Geneva, the Savoyard courtier Pierre de la Baume (1477–1544). The prince-bishop and the duke of Savoy were joint overlords of Geneva.
4 Asked to judge a musical contest between Apollo and Pan, King Midas of Phrygia voted for Pan, whereupon Apollo changed the king's ears into those of an ass. Midas was able to hide the ears under his Phrygian cap, but the disgrace was known to his barber, to whom the knowledge was an oppressive burden. See *Adagia* I iii 67.

know no one less apt at pretence than I am. But through some freak of destiny I have lighted on a generation in which no man has any dearer object than to make black white and white black, and the highest reputation goes to the expert in pretence.

Luther has replied to our illustrious prince,[5] to which the prince on his side has sent no answer; all the same, he did not make light of the letter, but, as I see it, he will carry out very few of Luther's suggestions. For Luther told him to bring his subjects back to the true faith by good works, and by the gospel teaching, rejecting the shams and the place-seeking which flourish here so much. I reckon Germany fortunate to have been released from so many errors and so many false inventions and brought back to a great extent to the way of life of the apostles. Would that Christ the Almighty might grant my native Gaul the power to receive a spark of that true light!

I gave your letter[6] to the abbot,[7] and though he is in poor health he received it with most lively feelings and was relieved of much depression by the news that you are well and flourishing.[8] I do not know whether he has answered it, for I could not stay with him more than three days. Since then I have not seen him, and so I do not know if he has recovered or not. I am grateful to your reverence for speaking so warmly of me to the abbot in question; not that I suppose myself to deserve the recommendation of a great man like Erasmus, but such is and always was his inexhaustible sympathy and kindness. And so, dear Erasmus, my powers are unequal in every respect to the task of rendering thanks even in the slightest degree for your kindness to me. You will however take the will for the deed; and I beg you to believe that nobody is a more passionate admirer of you than your friend Philibert. Please therefore write his name in the list of your friends. He will not weary of being ready to serve you in every possible way. Farewell, great glory of the world of scholars.

From Geneva, 20 January 1524

Your sincere friend Philibert de Lucinge, canon of Geneva

* * * * *

5 The reference is apparently to Luther's letter of 7 September to Duke Charles III of Savoy (WA-Br III 148–54). The letter, inspired by the receipt of reports of the duke's alleged evangelical leanings, is a summary of the chief points of Luther's teaching.

6 Not extant

7 Probably Aymon de Gingins, seigneur of Divonne (c 1465–1537), abbot of the Cistercian house of Bonmont, west of Nyon on Lake Geneva. He was a friend of the Lucinge family and a patron of Philibert.

8 But see Ep 1408 n2.

IN ACTA APOSTOLO/
rum Paraphrasis ERASMI Rote
rodami, nunc primum recens
& nata & excusa.

Basileæ, in officina Ioan. Frobenij. Anno
M. D. XXIIII.
Cum priuilegio Cæsareo.

Erasmus *In Acta apostolorum paraphrasis* title-page
Basel: Froben 1524
Centre for Reformation and Renaissance Studies,
Victoria University, University of Toronto

1414 / To Clement VII   Basel, 31 January 1524

This is the preface to Erasmus' paraphrase on Acts (Basel: Froben 1524). The printing of the volume was not yet complete on 8 February. However, to take advantage of an available messenger, Erasmus sent a copy of the preface in advance (Epp 1416:38, 1423:16). On 17 February the printing had still not been completed (Arbenz Ep 380) but within days it was possible to dispatch a copy of the paraphrase to Rome (Ep 1418:54ff, 1422:78–9, 1423:19). It was received favourably by the pope (Ep 1443B), who sent Erasmus two hundred florins (Epp 1466:4–7, 1467:16–17, 1486:13–15, 1488:18–19; cf Ep 1341A:1683–90 and Allen Ep 1796:17–18). In subsequent editions, 1534 onwards, the preface was omitted, a circumstance for which there is no satisfactory explanation.

Like his cousin and patron Leo x, Clement VII, elected 19 November 1523, was a friend of humanist learning and showed much favour to Erasmus, as many of the remaining letters in this volume will attest. In this letter, Erasmus, punning on the name Medici, comments on the need for a distinguished physician with a new medicine to cure the disorders of Christendom. Clement was indeed well informed about the dangerous spread of heresy in Germany and personally in favour of reform. On the other hand, he was not only preoccupied with Medici family politics and the conflict of the great powers in Italy but was also chronically indecisive. He was therefore unable to overcome the papacy's fatal subordination of spiritual to secular interests and did not, as a consequence, fulfil Erasmus' high hopes of him.

TO HIS HOLINESS CLEMENT, SEVENTH OF THAT NAME,
PONTIFF TRULY SUPREME, FROM ERASMUS OF ROTTERDAM, GREETING
At one and the same moment, most holy Father, I was writing this paraphrase of the book called Acts of the Apostles and the printers were striking it off; and it is the last task of this kind that I have decided to   5
undertake. As I worked at it my mind was not wholly free from something like melancholy, for I could not fail to compare the very turbulent and corrupt state of the church in our own day with the kind of church of which Luke has given us such a wonderful picture in this book. My gloom was intensified by the news of the death of Adrian vi;[1] for a figure at once so   10
learned and so deeply religious had given us some hope that he might be destined to restore the ruined state of things, Leo the Tenth having been jealously snatched from the world by an early death.[2] Not but what, when I

* * * * *

1414
1 14 September 1523
2 Leo died on 1 December 1521, just ten days short of his forty-sixth birthday.

thought of Adrian, my mind had always foreseen that we might be leaning
on a tottering wall; for his age and his health never seemed likely to cope   15
with the great turmoil of the world. But it was not long before my spirits
were refreshed by letters from several cardinals and learned men,[3] bringing
the news that Clement VII had been raised to the summit of human affairs
and at the same time giving me a picture of the man you are, so rarely gifted
and cast in a heroic mould, as worthy of such a lofty position as you are equal   20
to it. I was at once attracted by your adopted name of Clement, to which men
say your character is admirably suited. But what seemed to me above all a
most happy omen was your family name of Medici, one of the best known
and most popular names in the world. Serious, even desperate, sickness
demands some outstanding, some predestined master of the medical art;   25
and no sickness is more dangerous than one in which the patient is very ill in
both halves of his being, both in body and in spirit. Surely it is some sickness
such as this from which the world now suffers. These chaotic enmities
between one monarch and another,[4] so fraught with disaster, so implacable,
so long-continued, so far beyond all cure – are they not like some desperate   30
sickness of the whole body? Can we discern any part of the world that is
immune from the infection of this dread disease? But this makes even more
destructive this pestilence, which with its astounding and insoluble conflict
of convictions has overmastered all men's minds.

Great efforts to resolve the conflicts of war which were already   35
spreading have been made by the invincible king of England, Henry, eighth
of that name;[5] but it came to nothing. Our own Adrian tried to do the same,
and his labours were in vain.[6] Has anything in fact been left untried, has
anyone not attempted to reconcile the conflict of convictions which is a sort
of sickness of the mind? And down to this day all have laboured in vain,   40
while the disease has constantly grown more severe. But now we have a
Medici with his new medicine, and at his appearance, as at some god from
the machine, the spirits of all men rise high in hope. Oh may this hope of all
Christian people not prove an illusion, if only we might deserve that such
should be God's will! At any rate, there are many indications that smile upon   45
our hopes and promise us that here if anywhere we shall find the truth of
Homer's saying that 'a physician is a man worth many men.'[7] For it is a

* * * * *

3 Not extant
4 See Ep 1369 n12.
5 The reference is to Cardinal Wolsey's grandiose but ill-fated plan, embodied in
   the Treaty of London, 2 October 1518, to establish perpetual peace on the basis
   of a new international order; see Scarisbrick 70–4; LP II 4468–71.
6 See Ep 1353 n30.
7 *Iliad* 11.514

greater achievement to heal disorders than to suppress them. For when I contemplate the picture of things as they are today, there come into my mind at once those lines of Virgil: 50

> As oft in some great city riot spreads,
> The vile mob rages, brands and boulders fly,
> Rage finds them arms,[8]

55

except that any riot is more disastrous which affects not one city but the whole world and not some vile mob but every class in the community. But then, when I watch how Clement, a Medici, a member of that family of destiny,[9] has been posted at the helm of affairs, there seems to me to be a happy omen in the lines that follow: 60

> Some grave and reverend senior should they spy
> Of merit proved, they silent fall, and stand
> With pricked ears listening, while his kingly words
> Their spirits rule and soothe their raging hearts.   65
> So all the roaring of the mighty deep
> Sank, as its lord surveyed the waves, then drove
> His willing steeds beneath an open sky
> And gave free rein to his fast-flying car.[10]

70

And so, although I had decided to dedicate this work that I had in hand to another person,[11] a man of the highest rank below the papal majesty, when letters[12] arrived from Rome which gave me a lifelike picture of you and added that your Holiness had actually been heard to express a high opinion of myself (an opinion which I shall be unable to justify, but at least I will do   75 my best to show that I have tried), at that point I changed my mind and preferred to dedicate my new work to the new pontiff. It seemed fitting too that Luke the physician, the medico, should go to a Medici, and that the foundations of the newborn church should be offered to the one man through whom we hope that the church in ruins will be reborn. In those   80 days, despite the world's resistance, the kingdom of the church grew none

* * * * *

8 *Aeneid* 1.148–50
9 Cf Ep 335:20–5.
10 *Aeneid* 1.151–6
11 Cardinal Wolsey; see Epp 1415:99–103, 1418:56–8.
12 Cf line 17 above.

the less, for Christ prospered what was achieved through the leaders of his church; so too in our own day we hope, nay, we are confident that Christ will not withhold his blessing from your pious efforts. And may he in his clemency long preserve our Clement in health and wealth.   85

Basel, 31 January AD 1524
Erasmus of Rotterdam

1415 / To Lorenzo Campeggi   [Basel, c 8 February 1524]

This is evidently the second letter to Campeggi mentioned in Ep 1423:12–13, Ep 1410 presumably being the first. The close verbal resemblances to Epp 1416 and 1418, not quite as obvious in translation as in the original, establish the approximate date. Since the letter to Campeggi mentioned in Ep 1424:1–3 is obviously Ep 1422, the present letter may be assumed to be the one sent along with Ep 1416 on 8 February (Ep 1423:12–15). Erasmus is still not aware that Campeggi is on his way to Germany as legate; see Ep 1410 introduction.

The letter was first published in Balan *Monumenta* I 305–7, but with two lines inadvertently omitted. Allen's text is based on the manuscript in the Vatican Archives (Arm 64, vol 17, f 191), a contemporary copy. The letter is followed immediately (f 192 verso) by a copy of Luther's letter to Conradus Pellicanus (see n9) in the same hand, and then (ff 194–9) by Erasmus' *Adversus Conclusiones Stunicae* (lines 9–10, 22, 89–90), copied in another contemporary hand. This last item is apparently the extempore reply, mentioned in Epp 1418:46–7 and 1423:13–14, which was subsequently turned into the published tract sent to Johann Fabri (Ep 1428).

TO CARDINAL CAMPEGGI

Greeting, my most reverend lord. Illness prevented me from answering the letter from your Eminence which reached me together with one from my friend Richard Pace,[1] except for a few lines dictated to a servant at the time and addressed to Pace, for him to pass on to you if he thought fit. For the 5 friendly and generous spirit in which you write I am exceptionally grateful, as I ought to be, and will do all I can show myself worthy of it. There was one small part of your letter which I did not fully understand, in which you say that I know what was going on in your part of the world. Shortly afterwards

* * * * *

1415
1 Cf Epp 1416:1–2, 1418:2–3, 1422:1–6, 1423:7. None of the letters of this period from Campeggi or Pace has survived. At this point, Pace (Ep 211:53n) was in Rome on an embassy from Henry VIII. In late March or early April, Pace left Rome under orders to return to England; Jervis Wegg *Richard Pace, A Tudor Diplomatist* (London 1932) 224–5. Cf Epp 1423:12, 1424:10–11.

Zúñiga's new *Conclusiones*[2] was sent me from Nürnberg,[3] and besides that 10
he promises three pamphlets, the publication of which has been forbidden
on the authority of your college and of Pope Adrian. It must I suppose have
been this that you meant in your letter. I am astonished by the man's
audacity. He began to act this part under Leo, and got nowhere. Then, after
Leo's death, when he went back to his old tricks, he was forbidden 15
repeatedly by an edict of the cardinals, while the cardinal of Sion was still
alive.[4] Even so, in contempt of the edict of your college, he put out two or
three pamphlets surreptitiously. Again, he approached Adrian vi for
permission to publish those three pamphlets, in which he demonstrated his
capacity for insane abuse; and the pope gave him an absolute refusal. Now, 20
in the interregnum, while you were all busy with the choice of a new pope,
he has published his *Conclusiones*, which are full of pure calumny. I wonder
if they can really be Zúñiga's. I suspect they are the work of some supporter
of Luther who wanted either to drag me irretrievably into his party or to
have his revenge on me, for their fury is directed more at me than at anyone 25
else, and they think me solely to blame for their lack of complete success,[5]
though they have not yet abandoned all hope of victory. If however they are
Zúñiga's, I am not surprised, for in his native Spain he has always been
reckoned an idiot, and the man's books show clearly enough that he is
touched in the head and has good reason to bear a chain in his coat of arms.[6] I 30
feel the need of either fair-mindedness or common sense much more in the
men who put him up to it.

Fair-minded? Could anything be less so? I have contributed so much
by my researches to the cause of public enlightenment, and neither
tempting offers from great princes nor any enticements from learned friends 35
nor the hostility of my enemies have ever been able by force or finesse to
move me to make a pact with Luther;[7] with no thought for advantage or
disadvantage I have been true to my own integrity, not without some
danger to my life; and am I now to be abandoned to the private hatred of a
handful of individuals?[8] Must I, who am most bitterly attacked here in the 40
most virulent pamphlets by Luther's supporters, suffer in your part of the

* * * * *

2 See Ep 1341A n263. For an annotated account of Zúñiga's machinations against
   Erasmus in Rome, the details of which are partially duplicated here in lines
   9–22, see Ep 1341A:868–927, especially 900ff.
3 By Johannes Fabri; see Ep 1428:4.
4 Schiner; see Ep 1410 introduction.
5 Cf Epp 1411:21–2, 1422:57–8.
6 See Ep 1416 n7.
7 Cf Epp 1217:118–21, 1418:16–19, 1432A:11–13.
8 Cf Ep 1418:52–3.

world the most palpable calumnies and be called in common report a
Lutheran? And then how little this serves the cause for which they labour! If
they carry their point that I agree with Luther, more people will be the more
ready to agree with him. In Rome Zúñiga rants away that I am a Lutheran;   45
but so many of Luther's own gang, and a number of letters from Luther
himself, maintain the opposite, one of which I send you,[9] written in Luther's
own hand.[10] In no single thing did I feel myself more fortunate than in my
friendships with other scholars, among whom I felt at peace; and the
majority of these are supporters of Luther, though some of them conceal the   50
fact. These are now either openly my enemies, to the extent of attacking me
virulently in print, or they are friends I cannot trust.

Not that I regret my determination: I would rather sacrifice life itself
than join a faction. It is said I have not written against Luther. On the
contrary, I have written a great deal,[11] and deeply do they resent it.[12] Nor 55
have I been ineffective all this time. Believe me, I have restored to sanity
many men who had already joined that league, I have held many back from
going near it, and restrained many from going too near. I have, it is true, put
no one in prison; but to heal the mind does more than to distress the body. In
any case, the main reason why up to now I have not written whole volumes   60
attacking Luther has been the conviction that I should achieve nothing
thereby except to give this confusion a new lease of life.[13] Even so, under
pressure from princes, and especially from the king of England, I shall
publish a book against him on the freedom of the will,[14] not because I think it
will do any good, but to make clear to the princes that what they would not   65
believe when I said it is perfectly true. My state of health is such that I make
ready daily for my last hour,[15] and this makes me all the less willing to do
what Christ would disapprove. Your sense of justice and the wisdom of our
new pope, of which all speak so highly, give me great hopes that you and

* * * * *

9 The reference is clearly to Luther's letter to Conradus Pellicanus, 1 October
  1523 (see Ep 1341A n298), which is found immediately after this letter in the
  Vatican manuscript volume (see introduction). In November, Erasmus had
  sent a copy of it to Fabri (Ep 1397:9–10). It was probably not yet in print (see
  Ep 1341A nn298 and 285).
10 Allen refused to take this phrase at face value, though there seems to be no
  reason not to do so. The copy in the Vatican Archives, like that of this letter,
  was probably based on the autograph sent by Erasmus; see WA-Br III 159.
11 As, for example, in Ep 1342:807ff
12 See Ep 1341A:1020–1215 and Epp 1405–6.
13 Cf Ep 1313:53–66.
14 See Ep 1419.
15 Cf lines 108–9 below.

yours will take no unpleasant decisions affecting me. Should this happen,   70
you will at the same time give the greatest possible satisfaction to the
Lutheran party and the greatest distress to many men in high place, whose
friendship my work has won for me, though I did not set out to seek their
support. Among them are our own Charles and many in his court, the king
of England, the king of France, the king of Denmark, Prince Ferdinand, the   75
cardinal of England, the Archbishop of Canterbury – not to mention all the
princes, all the bishops, all the good scholars, and the honourable men not
only in England and France and Flanders and Germany but even in Hungary
and Poland who think either that they owe a great debt to my exertions or at
least that I have done good service to the cause of education in general. They   80
would be appalled if certain persons inspired by private spite were allowed
to achieve what they have for so long striven to do; and their distress would
hurt me more than my own.

I have written a great deal, but I wrote when the world was at peace;
had I suspected the coming of the age we live in, I should have written much   85
of it quite differently or not written at all.[16] At least, throughout this general
upheaval, I have behaved in a religious spirit, and so I shall behave to my
dying day. No heretic and no schismatic shall draw strength from my
resources. Zúñiga's calumnies (*Conclusions* is no name to call them by) I have
answered one by one.[17] A demagogue like him will fuel the fire of hatred for   90
the see of Rome by his libellous pamphlets, and none greet them with more
applause than your full-blooded Lutheran. If anything were to be found in
my books – and I have published many – which is written with less than
proper care, I might have been rebuked in a private letter and I would gladly
accept the rebuke and make the change. At this moment a fourth edition of   95
my New Testament is in preparation;[18] I am a man, I can make mistakes,
though I take meticulous care to avoid anything in my books that might
provoke subversion or stray from the clear path of Christian doctrine. A
paraphrase on the Acts of the Apostles is now at the printers.[19] I intended to
dedicate it to the cardinal of England, who has lately written to me in the   100
kindest terms, suggesting through his secretary that such an offering would
be welcome;[20] but I preferred to dedicate it to Clement VII, of whom Pace has
given me a wonderful picture in a letter, making clear in addition what

* * * * *

16 Cf Ep 1418:40–1.
17 See introduction.
18 Not completed until March 1527
19 Ep 1414
20 Possibly in the letter mentioned in Ep 1386:38

kindly feelings he has towards me.[21] I shall do my best to show that he has
not given his support to one who is entirely ungrateful.   105

The emperor recalls me to Brabant;[22] the king of France invites me with
generous promises to join him in France;[23] Adrian often invited me to
Rome.[24] I fear however that my special tyrant, the stone, may translate me
to my heavenly home.[25] Should more robust health come my way, which I
do not expect, there is nowhere I would rather breathe my last, such as I am,   110
than Rome.[26] For I have long had enough of Germany, where I cannot really
live in peace on account of the Lutherans, who hate no one more than my
humble self. The king of France is at war with the emperor, to whom I am
bound by oath as a councillor;[27] in Flanders all is war and turmoil. May
Christ the Almighty preserve your Eminence in health and wealth.   115

Your Eminence's most devoted servant Erasmus of Rotterdam

1416 / To Ennio Filonardi   Basel, 8 February 1524

First published by Allen, this letter is one of three (the others are 1423–4) that
Allen found in the Civica Biblioteca Guarneriana at San Daniele in Friuli (MS
217, pages 841–2). All are copies in the same sixteenth-century hand. For
further details, see Allen's introduction. On Filonardi, see Ep 1282.

ERASMUS TO THE BISHOP OF VEROLI
Greeting, my right reverend lord. I had a letter some time ago from Pace and
one from his Eminence Cardinal Campeggi, and here comes a second letter
from Pace[1] enclosed in yours, singing the same old song. In this connection
what your lordship has done could not suit me better. I wrote the other day[2]   5
by a man from Lorraine who could not stop talking,[3] to whom I had given
instructions that if you had a courier who could take letters to Rome with

* * * * *

21 Cf Epp 1411:36–7, 1414:73–5, 1418:10–11.
22 See Ep 1380 introduction.
23 Ep 1375
24 Epp 1324:119ff, 1338:49ff
25 See Ep 1408 n2.
26 Cf Ep 1416:15–16.
27 Cf Ep 1411:10–12 with n4.

1416
1 See Ep 1415 n1.
2 On 19 January; see Ep 1411 introduction. The letter to Filonardi (cf Ep
  1423:51–2) is not extant.
3 Possibly Jacobus Faber of Lorraine (documented 1518–c 1550), a metal
  engraver active in Basel 1518–c 1526.

greater speed and safety, mine should be handed over to him, but otherwise
he should take them himself. I learn from my friends' letters[4] that he has
already been in Constance.   10

The stone is giving me such trouble that I am obliged to consider my
departure, not for Rome so much as for Jerusalem, by which I mean the
heavenly Jerusalem, our native country;[5] and would that Christ the
Almighty might grant me a prosperous journey! Even so, should my health
improve, which I do not expect, there is nowhere I would rather die than   15
Rome, especially under our present pope, although they report that Zúñiga
is tolerated there;[6] and he is quite simply mad, and publishes the most crazy
pamphlets attacking the dignity of the Holy See and the cardinals, in which
he tries to make me a Lutheran, while here Luther's friends and Luther
himself raise a very different clamour. The man bears a chain in his coat of   20
arms,[7] and undoubtedly deserves to be chained up. It is stupid monks who
put forward this mountebank, in pursuit of their own interests, not the Holy
Father's. For my part, whether I come to Rome or no, I shall always maintain
the same open loyalty to Christ and to the see of Rome that I have
maintained hitherto. In matters of such importance to force one's advice on   25
such outstanding men is as unsafe as it is arrogant. Adrian in an official brief
had called on me to do this.[8] I wrote a few things,[9] but in such a form that
they could be regarded as never having been written if they did not meet
with approval. And immediately after that, I felt a change in the powers that
be; he never answered,[10] and Zúñiga began to go back to his old tricks. If the   30
princes are at one with the pope, the subversive and reprobate activities of
certain persons will be restrained without difficulty. But to root out of men's
minds something that in many of them is now firmly established, and to
cure this evil in such a way that it does not grow again – this requires medical
skill of a high order. It is my prayer and my hope that this Medici will be the   35
man; and he will not find me wanting when the moment comes.

* * * * *

4 Not extant
5 See Ep 1408 n2. At about this time Filonardi wrote to Erasmus recommending
  the services of a physician in Constance; Ep 1341A:1814–15 (passage added in
  1524). In September 1522, Filonardi, a fellow sufferer, had given Erasmus some
  remedies sent from Milan; Ep 1342:473–86.
6 See Ep 1415:9ff.
7 Cf Ep 1415:30. The Zúñiga family coat of arms, which is shown on the title-page
  of Zúñiga's *Annotationes contra Erasmum* (Ep 1260 n36), features a chain. See
  Allen's note.
8 See Epp 1324, 1338.
9 Ep 1352
10 Cf Ep 1384:28–9 and Allen Ep 1690:59–61.

If the work is finished before a messenger offers himself, I will send you a paraphrase dedicated to Clement; if not, I will send the preface,[11] so that it can be taken to Rome together with my letters at my expense. On the other hand, if a messenger does appear, he will gladly take on this parcel in hope of reward. Adrian gave the Basel city courier six ducats[12] for bringing Arnobius,[13] and what is more, with his own hand, though in other ways he was not particularly generous. The emperor and the Lady Margaret tell me to return to Brabant,[14] and if I do not, my annuity is at risk; on account of which I am already owed about six hundred gold florins.[15]

How I do go on, pouring out all my secrets into the ear of a prelate who is my dearest friend and patron! It is your kindness that gives me this self-confidence, and I pray for your great and lasting prosperity. If this courier had presented himself a couple of days later, I would have sent the whole work, for the last pages are in the printer's hands. I will send it in a few days' time, and at the same time will write a few lines to our new pope.[16] And so farewell to your lordship, to whom I gladly confess my deep obligation.

Basel, the morrow of Quinquagesima 1524

In the mean time, if you please, your lordship will be able to send this preface[17] in written form and to enlist his Holiness' support for me by your recommendation.

Erasmus, your devoted protégé

To the right reverend father in Christ Ennio, lord bishop of Veroli and right worthy apostolic nuncio. In Constance

1417 / To Willibald Pirckheimer   Basel, 8 February 1524

This letter, first published in the *Pirckheimeri opera*, takes up again many of the topics discussed in Ep 1408. On Pirckheimer, see Ep 318.

Greeting. I have already answered your earlier letter,[1] in which you reported

* * * * *

11 Ep 1414; cf lines 55ff below.
12 See Ep 1341A:1678–82 and n371.
13 Ep 1304
14 See Ep 1380 introduction.
15 Cf Epp 1408:11–13, 1417:26. Probably Rhenish gold florins (worth £145 gros Flemish), but possibly the new Hapsburg Carolus florins (worth £105 gros Flemish). Cf CWE 8 348–50.
16 Ep 1418
17 See line 38 above.

1417
1 See Ep 1408 n1.

Lee's arrival and his criticisms of Dürer's pictures.[2] Whether you have had my letter[3] I could not really make out from yours.[4] As for the business of our lords and masters, I assure you that you write in safety so far as I am concerned, provided you entrust the letter to a safe hand, in which you have 5 succeeded up to now. When you said that Clement VII *renunciat* his agreement with the French, I did not quite know what you meant, for we use the word equally of announcing an alliance and of renouncing one. Nothing is less appropriate than for the pope, who is a father to all men, to make an alliance with this or that party.[5] It was his duty to achieve an agreement 10 between all parties which is fair to them all. And this must be the desire of all men of good will. The French are Christians like the rest of us. I am not so much in favour of the imperial title, for I see it as a perpetual cause of war.[6] But these things are on the knees of the gods.[7]

You are absolutely right when you say that Luther means promotion 15 for many people. It is he who creates canons, bishops, and cardinals, and also enriches a great many whether they will or no.[8] On the other hand he turns many people out of place and property, and I am one of them; for I am promised the regular annuity of a councillor through Margaret and the emperor,[9] but only when I have returned to my own country. But there 20 Baechem is king, a madman with a sword in his hand,[10] who hates me twice as much as he hates Luther. He has a colleague called Frans van der Hulst with an astonishing hostility to the humanities.[11] They start by putting men in jail and only then look for something to accuse them of. The emperor knows nothing of this, and yet it would be worth while to let him know. 25

* * * * *

2 See Ep 1408:37–8 with n18.
3 Ep 1408
4 Not extant
5 Clement was at this time making strenuous effort to maintain neutrality between Charles v and Francis I, in the hope of securing the freedom of Italy and achieving a general peace; Pastor IX 253–9.
6 Erasmus had long been deeply skeptical of the old but persistent notion of a world monarchy under the emperor; see Ep 586:135ff, CWE 27 285 (*Institutio principis christiani*), and James D. Tracy *The Politics of Erasmus* (Toronto 1978) 8, 16–17, 54. Charles v's pretensions to world monarchy, inspired by his chancellor Gattinara (Ep 1150), were at the root of the Hapsburg-Valois wars (Ep 1369 n12), in which the popes, willy-nilly, frequently became entangled.
7 Homer *Iliad* 17.514 and *Odyssey* 1.267
8 See Ep 1397 n19.
9 See Ep 1380 introduction.
10 Ie, Baechem was an inquisitor; see Epp 1254 n6, 1408:21–2.
11 Epp 1345 n8, 1408:21–2

Meanwhile I am owed five hundred gold florins.[12] There is some risk too attached to my other annuity in respect of a prebend I have resigned.[13]

Again and again I am invited to Rome with generous promises if I will wing my way thither. A crab will fly as well as I could, for I keep alive with difficulty,[14] and as I write this the news arrives of Wonecker's death from the stone.[15] I will see that Varnbüler, that very cultivated man, gets what he wants;[16] I owe him a good deal myself. This pope has nominated six cardinals who are very good scholars to answer questions relating to Luther.[17] They tell me too that princes in Germany have begged for the pope's help against Luther;[18] and so they hope the affair will soon be over. I have no doubt that the leader of the six will be Cajetanus[19] – though I have no sooner written this than I hear he is legate in Hungary.

I had written about the cast of myself,[20] which made me think you had never had that letter. If some craftsman were to copy the mould in lead with the edges cleaned up, the casting would be more successful. And then, if the material is a mixture of copper and tin, it gives the likeness more successfully. Last but not least, if the head of Erasmus were cast without the Terminus, I think it would go better, because the thickness of the stone and the pile of earth on the reverse are a hindrance to a satisfactory rendering of the face and neck. It will be possible to try both. If it goes well, let him cast it and sell it for his own profit. If he sends me a few successful copies which I

* * * * *

12 Probably Rhenish gold florins, which would have been worth £120 16s 4d gros Flemish or £85 8s 4d sterling; but possibly Florentine gold florins, with a value of 500 ducats, or £166 14s 0d gros Flemish, or £112 10s 0d sterling, or £1,037 10s 0d tournois. Cf Epp 1295 n1, 1410:55. Cf also Epp 1408:12–13, 1416:45.

13 From the prebend at Courtrai (Ep 436:6n, 470 and 621 introductions). For his difficulties at this time, see Epp 1458, 1470–1.

14 See Ep 1408 n2.

15 Johann Roman Wonecker, a native of Windecken in Hessen, was town physician in Basel and a member of the medical faculty of the university from 1493 to 1523. A fierce opponent of the Reformation, he attracted ridicule in 1522 by posting a series of obscure theses in clumsy, scholastic Latin.

16 See Ep 1344 n27 and lines 155–8.

17 See Pastor x 106–7.

18 Reference obscure. Perhaps it is another allusion to the activities of Eck in Rome (cf Ep 1376 n7). Eck's plan for the restoration of provincial and diocesan synods as a means of combating the Lutheran heresy required the close cooperation of the papacy with the most zealous of the German Catholic territories, especially Bavaria. See Pfeilschifter 107–8.

19 In July 1523, Adrian vi had dispatched Cajetanus (Ep 891:26n) as legate to Hungary, Poland, and Bohemia; Pastor ix 190, 192. At this point he was still in Hungary; csp iii 788, 790.

20 See Ep 1408:34–7 with n17.

can give to friends, I will pay him in cash whatever he wishes. Farewell, distinguished patron.

Basel, the eve of Quinquagesima Sunday 1524

Your sincere friend Erasmus   50

To the honourable Willibald Pirckheimer, counsellor to his Imperial Majesty

1418 / To Clement VII   Basel, 13 February 1524

> The manuscript of this letter, written and addressed by a secretary but signed by Erasmus, is found in the Vatican Archives (Lettere di Principi ii.142). The letter was first published in the *Opus epistolarum*. Clearly intended to accompany the presentation copy of the paraphrase on Acts (Ep 1414), the letter was dispatched with Epp 1422, 1424. Clement's reply is Ep 1443B.

Most holy Father, I can hardly find words to express my delight when I learned, first from common report and then in letters from Cardinal Campeggi and from men of learning,[1] that a seventh Clement, of the illustrious house of Medici, endowed with gifts of mind and body such as these days of storm from every quarter cried out for, has been called to the   5
helm of affairs. Devoted as I am to the public peace, these tempests caused me exceptional distress; and now my spirit felt a sudden joy as I foresaw some new dawn of felicity that made me more disposed to congratulate Christendom as a whole than you as an individual. But my delight increased as I derived a clear impression from my friends' letters how kindly are the   10
feelings of your Holiness towards my humble self.[2]

It would take too long to tell the whole story from the beginning, and you are too busy to have time for prolix narrative. To one thing I dare swear before Christ himself, who knows the secrets of my heart: if your Holiness really knew how faithfully and loyally I have behaved all through this   15
business, refusing to be driven to join a seditious movement and conspire against the dignity of your see by tempting offers from great princes and the enticements of learned friends, or on the other side by the hostility of certain theologians and monks[3] who hate me worse than they hate Luther for the introduction and encouragement in this country of the ancient tongues and   20
of humane studies – did you but know the hatred and the threats I suffer

* * * * *

1418
1 Not extant
2 Cf Epp 1411:36–7, 1414:73–5, 1415:102–5.
3 Cf Ep 1415:34–7.

even now in Germany for that same cause, you would judge that I do not deserve to be the target of the libellous and crazy pamphlets so often launched against me with impunity by that madman Zúñiga,[4] which do little credit to the Eternal City and cast a shadow on the good name of the Holy   25 See. He makes such play the whole time with the name of Rome, although it is common knowledge that in so doing he defies the decrees of the sacred college and the orders of Leo and of Adrian.[5] I do assure you, most holy Father, that those who support that mountebank with his native gift for this style of calumny, following the dictates of their private feuds and using   30 another man's madness as their tool, give no thought to the good name of the Holy See or to the cause of public peace.

He has extracted a number of scraps from all the books I had published before I ever heard the name of Luther;[6] these he distorts and puts the worst possible interpretation on them, but so outrageously that even with no one   35 to put the other side, a reader with any sense of fairness finds the man's type of mind abominable. I could find more material in the works of St Bernard and St Jerome, had I a liking for this kind of scurrilous distortion. When I wrote those passages, nothing was further from my mind than the coming of the age we live in.[7] Had I known it was coming, I should have been silent   40 on many points or should have put them differently; not that what I wrote is irreligious, but because evil-minded men can seize upon anything as an opportunity. And that was why I deleted many passages in later editions a couple of years ago,[8] to leave such people no handle, and would cheerfully have changed the rest as well, had anyone given me a fraternal warning.   45

* * * * *

4 See Ep 1415 n2.
5 For Clement's action, see Ep 1431:14.
6 Cf Epp 1410:22–3, 1434:44–5.
7 Cf Ep 1415:84–6.
8 The latest edition of the New Testament, which was the main target of Zúñiga's criticism, had been published in February 1522. Erasmus' claim to have 'deleted' many passages should perhaps not be taken too literally. He did indeed expunge a number of potentially controversial passages from the Annotationes in the editions of 1519 and 1522, though there is no obvious connection between these deletions and Zúñiga's attacks. See, for example, Anne Reeve ed Erasmus' Annotations on the New Testament: The Gospels; Facsimile of the Final Latin Text With All Earlier Variants (London 1986) 78, 171, 186. However, Erasmus' more common response to criticism from Zúñiga and others was to expand individual annotations to clarify, revise, or retract the point criticized; see Erika Rummel Erasmus' 'Annotations' on the New Testament (Toronto 1986), chapter 4 passim. Some of these changes could be construed as deletions in the sense that the cause of offence or misunderstanding had been removed (or so it was hoped).

But on this subject I have written more fully to his Eminence Cardinal Campeggi, providing at the same time on the spur of the moment some sort of answer to Zúñiga's latest libels.[9] I have always submitted myself and everything of mine to the judgment of the Roman church, and should offer no resistance even if she were to judge me unjustly; for I will suffer anything rather than be a cause of subversion. This makes me all the more confident that your Holiness' sense of justice will not let me be abandoned to the hatred of a handful of maniacs.[10]

As a pledge of my feelings towards you, I send you a paraphrase on the Acts of the Apostles,[11] which happened just then to be in the press. I had intended it for the cardinal of York,[12] whose most cordial support I have long enjoyed. But I have changed my mind, and shall dedicate to him a book on which I am now engaged, on freedom of the will in answer to Luther,[13] which I suspect he will appreciate even more. The emperor and the Lady Margaret recall me to Brabant;[14] the king of France invites me to join him,[15] with the offer of mountains of gold; but nothing shall separate me from Rome except death or (something more cruel even than death) the stone,[16] if only I have reason to feel that your well-known sense of justice will protect me against the iniquity of my detractors. That my learning can be made universally acceptable I am not sure; but my loyalty, at any rate, and the purity of my conscience I am quite sure that I can prove before all right-thinking and fair-minded judges.

And so, most holy Father, I pray it may be the will of the Lord Jesus to make you the champion and founder of a new golden age: such is the fervent wish and the confident hope of all of us who rightly detest our present divisions.

Believe me, your Holiness will surpass all popes in glory, if you can lay to rest these tempests of armed conflict and opposed convictions. The first you will achieve if you show yourself impartial without exception between one prince and another; the second, by inspiring hopes that you are willing to make certain changes which can be made without prejudice to true religion.

* * * * *

9 See Ep 1415 introduction.
10 Cf Ep 1415:39–40.
11 Ep 1414
12 Cf Epp 1414:71–2, 1415:99–102.
13 See Ep 1419.
14 See Ep 1380 introduction.
15 Ep 1375
16 See Ep 1408 n2.

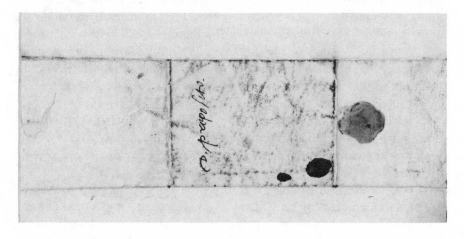

Autograph letter from Erasmus to Ludwig Baer, Ep 1419
Öffentliche Bibliothek, University of Basel, MS AN.III.15.1a

Basel, 13 February 1524

Erasmus of Rotterdam, your Holiness' most devoted servant, signed
with my own hand   80

To his Holiness that truly supreme pontiff Clement, seventh of the
name

1419 / To Ludwig Baer   [Basel, c February 1524]

This is the note that accompanied a first draft of *De libero arbitrio* sent to Ludwig
Baer (Ep 488), professor of theology at Basel and provost of the collegiate
church of St Peter's in the same city. The note, the autograph of which is MS
AN.III.15.1a in the Öffentliche Bibliothek of the University of Basel, was first
published in the *Bibliotheca Historico-Philologico-Theologica* ed T. Hase and F.A.
Lampe II (Bremen 1719) 595. Since the composition of the first draft took only
five days (line 2), the present note may be presumed to be close in date to Ep
1418 (see lines 57–8 of that letter).

In September 1523 Erasmus had informed Henry VIII of his intention to write
against Luther (Ep 1385:15–16; cf Ep 1386:24–6), something that Henry and
Pope Adrian VI, as well as other princes and prelates, had long been urging
him to do (see Epp 1298:24ff, 1324:24ff, 1367:11ff, 1408:25–7, 1415:62–4). The
subject of the book, free will, first mentioned in Ep 1397:15–16, may have been
chosen in response to Cuthbert Tunstall's remarks in Ep 1367:18–22, though
sharp criticism of Erasmus on this point by Lutherans had long since raised the
issue; Epp 1265:14–19, 1268:90–3, 1342:1022–78. In any case, it was a subject on
which Luther and Erasmus were in fundamental disagreement. Luther had
perceived their divergence from the outset; see his remarks in letters of 19
October 1516 (WA-Br I 70–1; cf Ep 501) and 1 March 1517 (WA-Br I 90:25–6).
Erasmus' comments in Epp 1342:1029–31 and 1384:11–16 indicate that no
compromise was possible.

Circa March 1524 Erasmus sent another copy of the first draft to Henry VIII,
inviting his comments (Ep 1430). In May, Erasmus responded to Luther's
solemn warning not to attack him (Ep 1443) by claiming that he had 'so far'
not written anything against Luther (Ep 1445:18). However, rumours of the
existence of *De libero arbitrio* were soon so widespread (Epp 1466:64–5,
1470:55–6) that Erasmus decided, seemingly with some reluctance, to publish
it (Epp 1481:17ff, 1483, 1486, 1487, 1488:30ff, etc). Although he had originally
intended to dedicate the work to Cardinal Wolsey (Ep 1418:56), he finally
decided not to dedicate it to anybody, in order not to rob the book of its
credibility by giving the impression that he 'had been hired to write it to please
the princes' (Ep 1486:9–12).

Three editions of *De libero arbitrio* were published in September 1524: by

Froben at Basel, Hillen at Antwerp, and Cervicornus at Cologne. Despite Epp
1385:15–17 and 1430:19–22, Froben's edition was evidently the original; see
Allen's introduction to this letter.

Incomparable friend, I send you the first draft of a trifling piece about the
freedom of the will. On this I have wasted five days, and very tedious days
they were. I knew I was not engaged in my proper field. May I ask you of
your kindness to run your eye over it and tell me where I have missed the
whole target. I should be sorry, though, if it went any farther. Farewell.   5
     For my lord the provost

1420 / From Ludwig Baer   [Basel, c February 1524]

An autograph letter found in the Öffentliche Bibliothek of the University of
Basel in a manuscript volume entitled 'Variorum Epistolae ad Erasmum,' f 6. A
precise date is not possible, but the letter is clearly a comment on a point in *De
libero arbitrio*, the first draft of which was sent to Baer along with Ep 1419.
Erasmus' final disposition of the matter in *De libero arbitrio* is found in LB IX
1232A–C.

I concede that 'Judas of necessity will betray Christ, if God foreknew that
Judas will betray Christ,' if 'of necessity' refers to the necessity of the
consequence, the sense being 'This is a necessary consequence: if God
foreknew that Judas will betray Christ, Judas will betray Christ.' And this is
true, because a conditional of this type is a good and necessary consequence;   5
for it is impossible for what is signified by the antecedent of this conditional
to be true without what is signified by its consequent being also true.
     But I deny that 'Judas of necessity will betray Christ, if God foreknew
that Judas will betray Christ,' if 'of necessity' denotes the necessity of the
consequent, so that the sense is 'If God foreknew that Judas will betray   10
Christ, this is a necessary proposition: Judas will betray Christ.' And this is
false. For if we assume the truth of the antecedent of that conditional, that
God foreknows that Judas will betray Christ, nevertheless the consequent of
that conditional – that this is a necessary proposition, that Judas will betray
Christ – is false.   15
     In fact, this proposition 'Judas will betray Christ' is a purely contingent
and not a necessary proposition, whether God foreknows or does not
foreknow that Judas will betray Christ. For the state of affairs which it
signifies can be true, and equally can not be true. But a proposition is called
necessary when the state of affairs which it signifies must necessarily be   20
true. When a conditional proposition falls under the second of the two

senses I have explained, the consequence is bad, and therefore the proposition is false and impossible. For if we grant the truth of the antecedent, the consequence is none the less a modal compound proposition which is false. 25

But if we take the proposition already referred to, 'Of necessity Judas will betray Christ, if God foreknew that Judas will betray Christ,' if the words 'of necessity' denote the necessity of the consequent, the sense can also be explained in this way: 'If God foreknew that Judas will betray Christ, Judas of necessity will betray Christ,' so as to make it a conditional of which, 30 if the antecedent is taken to be true (that is to say, 'God foreknew that Judas will betray Christ'), none the less the consequent is a divided modal proposition which is false and impossible (that is to say, 'Judas of necessity will betray Christ'). So that the mode of necessity determines the coherence of the proposition. 35

All these propositions will be more accurately expressed, if for 'foreknew' we read 'foreknows' in the present tense.

This mode 'necessarily' or 'of necessity' indicates the necessity of the consequence, when it denotes a necessary consequence, that is, the obligatory inference of the consequent from the antecedent. For the 40 inference is then obligatory, when the consequence is a good one.

The words 'necessarily' or 'of necessity' indicate the necessity of the consequent, on those occasions when they denote the consequence of one on, or its inference from, the other. The consequent of which is a necessary proposition. 45

The necessity of a consequence is a good and necessary consequence. But every good consequence is a necessary consequence, although sometimes a good consequence may be an impossible proposition, as for instance: 'Man is an ass; therefore man is capable of braying.'

The necessity of a consequent is itself the necessary consequent of 50 some consequence.

Yours, Ludwig Baer of Basel
To the reverend Master Erasmus of Rotterdam

1421 / From Johann Haner   Nürnberg, 17 February 1524

The autograph of this letter (=Ep 24 in Enthoven) is in the Rehdiger Collection of the University Library at Wrocław (MS Rehd 254.82).

Johann Haner (c 1480–c 1545) was a native of Nürnberg. After university studies that probably began in Ingolstadt and ended in Freiburg, he received a number of ecclesiastical preferments in and around his native city. At first sympathetic to Luther, Haner soon drew away from the reformers and

assigned himself the task of reconciling the Lutherans to a church reformed
along Erasmian lines. On 5 January 1524 he wrote to Clement VII proposing a
series of minor reforms and concessions to the Lutherans. A few weeks later he
wrote the present letter. At the same time, he publicly denounced Andreas
Osiander, the leading reformer of Nürnberg, as a heretic. In 1525 Haner
returned to his original support of the reformers and then in 1532 returned
once and for all to the church of Rome. Forced to leave Nürnberg in 1535, he
spent the remaining years of his life at Bamberg, first as a vicar at the cathedral
and then as cathedral preacher. He is the author of several works, none of
which attracted much attention.

Whether I would or no, most learned Erasmus, I am obliged to interrupt you
with a letter, particularly at this moment, when I have a very convenient
opportunity, and my excellent friend Fabri[1] has done much besides to
persuade me of this, and I have someone to carry it who is trustworthy as
well as responsible, to whom I can safely entrust it for delivery to you. I was   5
unwilling therefore to let this opportunity slip and go for nothing.
Moreover, I wished to make a few remarks to you on the unhappiness of the
times we live in. You are aware, if I am not mistaken, in what direction the
drama of the new faction daily develops step by step, and in what
conclusion it is likely to find a most unhappy end, unless limits are set to it as   10
quickly as possible. It has been given more than enough scope hitherto by
both learned men and princes, so that it has already played to a full theatre
and consequently has secured more than one success and won much
support from the spectators; not that it has a very elegant plot, but because
the bedraggled appearance of church discipline, to deal with which it was   15
first started and later widely spread, made this inevitable. This also meant
that I too welcomed it with joy at the start when it first appeared, and even
later, when it led to lamentable disorders, I overlooked them, and took no
steps to protest against its activities.
    Observe, dear Erasmus, the ultimate effect of our laziness or coward-   20
ice. In the mean time, while we look on as idle spectators, this drama has
seized on all men's eyes and hearts, it has carried away the audience in their
serried rows; in fact it rises more lawless every day and breeds I know not
what pestilence with fury as its ensign. Anyone who has made a close study
of this movement recently will soon discover that it works in a spirit of   25
unbridled hatred; nothing is done honestly, there is an ulterior motive in
everything, so that there is no respect and no place on that side even for the

* * * * *

1421
1 Archduke Ferdinand's minister (Ep 1382:27–33).

truth. False doctrine is freely taught; even worse, there is much innovation; worst of all, in many places they live together;[2] so that through the wicked actions of certain people nothing is more sinister than the constant repetition of 'gospel' as a keyword, and nothing more misleading than the frequent use of the name of Christ. Sound gospel doctrine is corrupted into deadly poison, and the true knowledge of Christ is perverted by our impious passions into an abomination, a kind of idol, into Belial himself. And yet we happily close our eyes to all this, and keep silence like dumb dogs that have not the strength to bark. We are in a sad plight! Think of the punishment from God in wait for us, if we take no steps against such a public, worldwide plague! Not to mention the internal troubles caused by this evil thing, what, pray, can be a greater cause of stumbling to the brethren outside than, when so many centuries have passed and when the universal and Catholic faith embraces all nations, that these clefts should for the first time not merely open between us but spread, to the great shame of our religion and our faith?

And so, dear Erasmus, unless we want God to demand at our hands the blood of the brethren whom we have neglected, and ourselves to stand trial for disrespect for God's glory, it will certainly be work well spent to counteract the malevolent zeal of certain of these people; and you are the first person who should have been doing this long ago, or at least should not postpone it any longer. Believe me at any rate: the moment that you blow the trumpet to arouse the world, you will at once see many men bound for a similar enterprise, who will to some extent repeat what you do and devote their energies not without avail to the public good. And what better contribution can you make to the salvation of Christendom? Unless my forecast is quite mistaken, I think that by this one act you will do marvels for your reputation. All that you have done in public on such an immense scale will come to nothing, dear Erasmus, unless you turn your efforts to the calming of this storm; all the more so since many men distort the facts and think you are responsible for it, while most of us defend you meanwhile and vigorously fight back with all our might.

But whether you do or do not bring help to the church in her hour of need, I am sure that the newfangled impieties of our modern enthusiasts cannot last, granted that we also get some light from heaven and that some good fortune, as is thought likely, shines upon us. And so, most generous of men, think of posterity; for I have no doubt whatever that the age to which we look forward will arrive, in which men will take a more reasonable view

* * * * *

2 The Latin of this passage, 'pessime vero passim in commune viuitur,' is such that one cannot tell what Haner is trying to say.

of the Christian religion than this age of ours. And if you are not moved by thoughts of your own reputation, as indeed you ought not to be, at least let the cause of our Saviour and the gospel rouse you to defend her sound doctrine from injury and show the world the perfect and genuine knowl- edge of Christ. In this to be sure, though you had no other helpers, at least 70 my zeal to help will be at your service, or if there is nothing I can do, at least my lasting good wishes. Nor shall I fail meanwhile to bring what help I can to the glory of Christ, the sound doctrine of the gospel and the consciences of brethren who have been led astray. You too, if you will listen to me, will do the same at your advanced age in life, that you may be guiltless as you 75 await the coming of our Lord Jesus Christ. And may he, I pray, preserve you always and bless you too. Farewell, and honour me with a letter from you in reply.

From Nürnberg, 17 February 1524
Sincerely yours, Johann Haner 80
To that distinguished and outstanding man Erasmus of Rotterdam, founder and champion of a more genuine theology. In Basel

1422 / To Lorenzo Campeggi   Basel, 21 February [1524]

This letter, first published in the *Opus epistolarum* with an obviously incorrect year-date, is the third of the letters written to Campeggi in January–February 1524 (see Epp 1410, 1415). As lines 7–9 indicate, Erasmus had just learned of Campeggi's dispatch to Germany as legate (see Ep 1410 introduction).

ERASMUS OF ROTTERDAM TO LORENZO CAMPEGGI,
CARDINAL LEGATE, GREETING
Your earlier letter[1] had filled my heart with great joy at the news that Clement VII, one of that family of destiny the Medici, had been summoned to the helm of affairs.[2] I have never known him except through letters from 5 yourself and Pace,[3] and yet it is surprising how my mind foresees that great felicity will somehow come of this, nor is it (I think) wrong. My happiness was redoubled by your second letter,[4] which reports that you have been dispatched into my native Germany to use your influence and your wisdom to settle the unhappy divisions of this present time, which weigh so heavily 10

* * * * *

1422
1 Not extant; see Ep 1415 n1.
2 Ep 1414
3 Ep 1415 n1.
4 Also not extant; dated 1 February at Rome (see lines 74–5 below).

on every man of good will and fill me at least with such disgust that I am
actually tired of life. And though you have undertaken a task full of difficulty
and unpleasantness, yet I have good hopes that your versatile mind and
your gifts of equal wisdom and sympathy will overcome all that difficulty,
especially if Christ will grant your pious efforts a favourable outcome. How I   15
wish I could contribute something of value at this juncture! There is no task
at which I would more gladly be found working when I die. But my poor
body, weak enough in itself, grows daily weaker from old age. That most
cruel of all pains, the stone, attacks me so often that at any moment my life is
at risk. Indeed in July I suffered from it so long and so severely that I had no   20
hope of survival;[5] but it was even more serious around Christmas, so that
death was my object and I despaired of life.[6] No death can be more agonizing
than this form of torment. The attacks have so much reduced and broken the
strength of my poor body that though I live very carefully I hardly keep
going. I therefore sold my horses some time ago in despair of being able to   25
endure the motion in future.[7]

As it is, even if I had the strength I could not have come to meet your
Eminence at this time of year, since I should have to travel though a land of
stoves, and their stink is death to me if I have to endure it for a single dinner.[8]
This compels me to live in Basel in a house of my own which has a hall-room   30
with an open fireplace,[9] and this means heavy expense for me and no less
heavy responsibilities. Last but not least, until the middle of Lent[10] I shall not
be able to take time off from the things which are now being at the same time
written by me and struck off by the printers.[11] I have decided however to
take a bit of holiday from more serious work this summer; and so if my   35
health is moderately good, when the German stoves have ceased to glow I
shall gladly transfer myself to your part of the world, unless something has
happened to summon me elsewhere. For the emperor and the illustrious
Lady Margaret recall me to Brabant[12] to take part in the mission which they
are getting ready to send to Rome to pay their respects to the new pope.   40

In the mean time however my services will be at your disposal in any
matter where I can be of use. I carry no weight in Germany. I was popular at

* * * * *

5 See Ep 1376 n4.
6 See Ep 1408 n2.
7 Cf Ep 1488:63–4, Allen Epp 1585:37–8, 1702:18–19. But see also Ep 1470:26–7.
8 An old complaint; see Ep 1258 n18.
9 See Ep 1316 n10.
10 10 February–26 March 1524
11 For Erasmus' publications at this time, see Epp 1426, 1427, 1428, 1451. For other
   literary activity, see Epp 1419, 1437.
12 See Ep 1380 introduction.

one time, but my influence vanished completely when I began to be 'an adversary of the gospel,' to use their own language. I brought such hatred on myself that death would have been preferable. But equally I would rather die than abandon the unity of the church and throw myself into some faction. My knowledge is below mediocrity; and yet I will gladly contribute to this cause what little I have of my own, and will moreover take counsel with my learned friends, for example one special friend I have here, Ludwig Baer,[13] provost of St Peter's collegiate church, a man with distinguished gifts of body and mind, who carries a lot of weight among his own people for his noble birth, his upright life, and his more than common scholarship. At Paris he once took first place in the final examination in divinity.[14]

Yet at the same time I must take care not to be torn in pieces by the Germans (not to say maniacs) before I leave Germany. There are many people who boast themselves evangelicals and are diabolicals really and ready to commit any crime. Somehow I am the chief object of their fury, they think it is my fault that they are robbed of their triumph[15] – such is the language they use. And several pamphlets have already appeared, with others ready which they threaten to produce.[16] I do not doubt that with your habitual wisdom you will attack this problem in the best possible way, and I think you most likely to succeed if your keynote is absolute impartiality, and you let it be seen that you are more concerned to cure this trouble than to suppress it; that you have no wish to weed out the tares in such a fashion that you pull up the wheat by the roots at the same time;[17] and that you will not refuse to make certain changes which both can and should be made without detriment to papal authority or to the religion of the gospel. In the meantime they will take a rest from their disorderly pamphlets and subversive activities until under the authority of the pope and the princes some steps are determined on to restore the public peace and make its restoration lasting. Germany is a wide area. If you can restore its peace, it will be a superhuman achievement.

I have sent this letter by the man who brought me yours from Augsburg; he delivered on the eve of St Peter's Chair[18] what you had written in Rome on the first of February. As soon as I know for certain where your Eminence is to be found I will write more fully, relying on your kindness,

* * * * *

13 For Erasmus' reliance on Baer as a theological adviser, see Epp 1419–20.
14 Cf Epp 413:13–14, 852:28–9, and also Ep 305:202–6.
15 Cf Epp 1411:21–2, 1415:26.
16 See Ep 1411:24–6.
17 Cf Matt 13:24–30.
18 21 February

and will send anything I have ready by a safe and reliable hand; or if there is
no chance of that, I will send my own servant. I have also written today to
Pope Clement and sent him his copy of the paraphrase.[19] If you write to him,
and I know you write often, please tell him to control that madman Zúñiga,[20]   80
who in the course of satisfying the itch he suffers from and certain persons'
private passions does much damage to the papal cause. May God Almighty
preserve you in health and wealth.

Basel, 21 February 152[6]

1423 / To Ennio Filonardi   Basel, 21 February 1524

> For the source of this letter (San Daniele MS 217, pages 845–6), which was first
> published by Allen, see Ep 1416 introduction. Erasmus added the last two
> paragraphs in his own hand after receiving Cardinal Campeggi's letter on 21
> February (see Ep 1422:74–5). It may therefore be inferred that the first part of
> this letter was written at about the same time as Ep 1418. The letter was carried
> by a messenger bound for Rome with the paraphrase on Acts and the letters
> enumerated in Ep 1424.
>
> On Filonardi, see Ep 1282.

ERASMUS TO THE BISHOP OF VEROLI
Greeting, my right reverend lord. Just before Christmas I began to suffer so
severely from the stone that death was my object and I despaired of life.[1]
Even now I am not really fit again, so entirely was I shattered and brought
down by the violence of the attack, and I live now very much like a man who   5
is ready for death from one day to the next. At the height of my trouble
letters arrived from Cardinal Campeggi and Richard Pace,[2] urging me in
accordance with the pope's wishes to hurry to Rome at the first opportunity.
I answered these letters at once,[3] uttering words of some sort to my servant
that he could take down. My letter was addressed 'To the right reverend   10
Cardinal Campeggi or to Richard Pace'; I put a double address on it because
it seemed likely that Pace would not be in Rome for long.[4] After that I again

* * * * *

19 Ep 1418
20 See Epp 1431:14, 1443B:16–17.

1423
1 See Ep 1408 n2.
2 Not extant; see Ep 1415 n1.
3 See Ep 1410 introduction.
4 See Ep 1415 n1.

wrote to Cardinal Campeggi[5] and to Pace[6] and sent a reply to the libels of
that madman Zúñiga,[7] and at the same time I wrote to your lordship.[8] These
letters I sent by a servant of Johannes Fabri,[9] the vicar-general of Constance,   15
dressed in motley, and I also sent by him a preface addressed to the Holy
Father.[10] These I suppose you have had by now. Later I received a second
letter from Pace enclosed in one from you.[11]

By the bearer of this I send a paraphrase on the Acts of the Apostles,[12]
together with many letters to be sent to Rome at my expense,[13] whatever it   20
may be. Master Johann von Botzheim,[14] a canon of Constance, will pay you
in cash. For I have a passionate wish to get these things to Rome by safe
hand, and I only wish I could be in Rome myself. And I know there is good
reason for my being there; but in my present condition, even if my life were
at stake, I cannot undertake a journey just now, especially as I should have   25
to go by way of those German parlours with their stoves.[15] I can hardly keep
alive in my own room with constant vigilance and precautions. In May
however, if God grants me a little strength, I will gird myself for the journey
and get to Rome somehow if I die there. Meanwhile I will persevere
single-minded in the cause of Christ as I always have done hitherto.   30

I am astonished that the cardinals allow Zúñiga, who is quite simply
raving mad, to publish such pamphlets in Rome, as he has already done
more than once. He did it, you will say, in the interval between two popes;
agreed, but now that we have a pope he ought to be punished.[16] Take my
word for it, that man's folly is a disgrace to the see of Rome and damages the   35
papal cause; and his behaviour delights Luther's party, who would like
nothing better than to see Erasmus either destroyed or compelled to join
them. For my part, if I must be driven one way or the other, I would rather
choose death than faction.

While I was writing this, a letter reached me from his Eminence   40
Cardinal Campeggi,[17] telling me that he is sent as legate to Nürnberg to

* * * * *

5 Ep 1415
6 Not extant
7 See Ep 1415 introduction.
8 Ep 1416
9 See Ep 1382 nn10, 12.
10 Ep 1414
11 Not extant
12 See Epp 1414, 1418.
13 See Ep 1424:4–9.
14 Ep 1285
15 See Ep 1258 n18 and cf Ep 1422:28–9.
16 See Ep 1415:9ff.
17 The one dated 1 February at Rome; Ep 1422:6, 74–5

pacify the uproar caused by Luther's party. He says he was dispatched by the pope on the first of February, and would like me to meet him or at any rate to go and see him in Nürnberg, or if that too is impossible, at least to write. This third thing I will do, and in every way will help to the best of my 45 power to restore the tranquillity of the Christian commonwealth; for it is still winter and my health is uncertain and it is a long journey by way of the stoves, which I find lethal.[18] I do earnestly beg you of your kindness to help me in passing on what I am now sending to Rome; you could not do me a greater service.   50

I now remember who it was to whom I gave my previous letter:[19] a messenger from Lorraine who stammered.[20] I asked you in the letter I sent you by him, if you happened to have a courier ready, to relieve the Lorrainer of the things I had given him and hand them to the courier. Perhaps he knew I had said so in my letter and therefore did not want to give them to you; and 55 yet I know he was in Constance and delivered a letter of mine to someone else. You are welcome to open the bundle and have a look at the book.[21] Six thousand of them have been printed, three thousand in large print and three in small. If I understand that these efforts of mine are acceptable to the Holy Father, I shall manifest my feelings towards him on a more important 60 subject, and show that I am mindful of my duty. I have written a letter of sorts to his Eminence Cardinal Campeggi,[22] and will write him a longer letter when I know where he is and have the offer of a safe messenger, or I will send my own servant. And so I bid your lordship farewell, most civilized of prelates. I have scribbled this postscript myself.   65

Basel, 21 February 1524. Erasmus of Rotterdam

To the right reverend father in Christ E., lord bishop of Veroli, apostolic legate. In Constance

1424 / To Ennio Filonardi   Basel, 21 February 1524

For the source of this letter (San Daniele MS 217, page 845), which was first published by Allen, see Ep 1416 introduction. The letter was carried by a messenger bound for Nürnberg with Ep 1422.

ERASMUS TO THE BISHOP OF VEROLI
Greeting, my right reverend lord. By the bearer of this letter I have written,

* * * * *

18 Cf line 26 above.
19 On 19 January; see Ep 1416 n2.
20 Cf Ep 1416:5–6.
21 See above, line 19.
22 Ep 1422

or rather, I should say, have sent an answer, to his Eminence Cardinal Campeggi;[1] and on the same day I loaded another courier who proposed to return here, to whom I entrusted a great many letters to the Holy Father,[2] to the cardinal of Volterra,[3] to the cardinal of Lorraine,[4] two to Pierre Barbier,[5] chaplain to our late Pope Adrian of blessed memory, to Michael Sander,[6] to Paolo Bombace,[7] to Hovius my servant,[8] whom you know, to Justus,[9] the secretary and envoy of the king of Poland, whom Cardinal Campeggi mentions in his letter to me.[10] I have not written to Pace, for I suspect he has already left Rome.[11] Cardinal Campeggi is already, I suspect, at Augsburg.[12] My very best wishes to your lordship, on whose good opinion I set great store.

Basel, 21 February 1524

Your lordship's devoted servant Erasmus of Rotterdam

To the right reverend father in Christ Ennio, lord bishop of Veroli, apostolic legate to the see of Constance. In Constance

* * * * *

1424
1 Ep 1422
2 Ep 1418. The remaining letters listed are no longer extant.
3 Francesco Soderini of Florence (1453–17 May 1524) was the brother of Piero Soderini, gonfalonier of Florence from 1502 to 1512. After studying law at Pisa, he undertook a number of diplomatic missions on behalf of his native city, 1480–1503. Meanwhile, he received the bishopric of Volterra in 1478, was ordained priest in 1486, and became a cardinal in 1503. His participation in anti-Medicean politics twice nearly cost him his life, under Leo x in 1517 and under Adrian vi in 1523. In June 1525 Erasmus described Soderini as a learned man who had written to encourage him in his work (Allen Ep 1581:645–6), but no other trace of their relationship survives.
4 Jean de Lorraine (1495–1550), second son of Duke René ii of Lorraine, since 1518 bishop of Metz and cardinal. He had been in Rome since 6 October 1523 (LP iii 3513; CL ii 606) for the conclave that elected Clement vii. The cardinal was known as a patron of poets and scholars. In 1522, when Erasmus contemplated moving to France, the cardinal was one of those who helped arrange for a royal safe-conduct (Epp 1319:26–7, 1342:607–8). The first of the five surviving letters in the correspondence between Erasmus and the cardinal is Ep 1559.
5 Ep 1294
6 Ep 1401 n7
7 Ep 210
8 Ep 1387 n3
9 Decius (Ep 1341A n210)
10 See Ep 1422:1, n3.
11 See Ep 1415 n1.
12 Campeggi is known to have passed through Augsburg on his way to Nürnberg, where he arrived on 14 March, but no precise date can be assigned; see Allen's note.

1425 / From Conradus Mutianus Rufus   Gotha, 23? February 1524

The autograph of this letter (=Ep 22 in Förstemann/Günther) was in the
Burscher Collection at Leipzig (Ep 1254 introduction). One or two lines were
shorn off at the top. On Mutianus Rufus, see Ep 501:9–10n.

... abuse, that even under our prince Frederick[1] they are neither fair nor
friendly towards right-thinking men. Where their headstrong folly and their
perverse desire to shine will end, I do not know. The Camels[2] and the
Scotophiles[3] are no obstacle. The harm is done by the half-converted Jews,[4]
who show wonderful cunning in the air of piety they give themselves and so   5
undermine the credulity of those who know no better. Their criminal
behaviour and the damage they do can easily be brought to book by a man
who writes so divinely as you do, if you will publish something to take the
rust off the prophets and Moses and so stop these crooks of the circumcision
from using the words of Holy Writ as a cloak for administering poison   10
instead of medicine and infringing the public peace. A great mistake is
made, in my opinion, by any state that admits Jews to practise usury. It is a
great mistake to put a baptized Jew[5] in charge of public education. Those
gentry go flocking to Luther; they are his advisers, and are valued in return.
What times we live in and what sights we see! Let the Old Testament be   .15
expounded by men who do not arouse such suspicions, and let us be
allowed to worship Christ as our fathers did and maintain our moral
standards.

On this subject you will have a long talk, if you can spare the time, with
Martin Hune,[6] a graduate of Erfurt, a rather special friend of mine and a   20
man, take my word for it, of the highest character. He loathes a state of
disorder, and the wicked men of whose increasing ferocity you are well

* * * * *

1425
1 Frederick III, called the Wise, elector of Saxony (ruled 1486–1525)
2 Ie, the Carmelites; cf Ep 1254 n6.
3 Ie, 'lovers of [John Duns] Scotus,' the thirteenth-century theologian and
  founder of the Scotist school of scholastic theology, which flourished mainly in
  his order, the Franciscans
4 For Erasmus' views on this subject, see Epp 694 introduction and lines 35ff,
  798:24–6, and 1006:148–50.
5 Mutianus may have had in mind Matthaeus Adrianus (documented 1501–21),
  who had been the first professor of Hebrew at the Collegium Trilingue in
  Louvain (autumn 1517–July 1519) and had then held a teaching post in
  Wittenberg (autumn 1519–February 1521).
6 Ep 1462

aware. He knows that Luther owes his growing celebrity to Philippus and to
no one else.[7] He knows how headstrong Hutten was.[8] He has a very great
admiration for you. He is close to Eobanus[9] and Urbanus,[10] both of whom I   25
commend to your notice. Jonas,[11] Schalbe,[12] Draconites[13] and Crotus[14] have
deserted our circle and joined the Lutherans. Eobanus has taken my advice
and repented;[15] he is really straightforward and fair-minded by nature. Let
others who spend their time hurting their fellow men go their own ways. I
hate these sectarians and their brickbats. In vain I tell them, in the praetor's   30

* * * * *

7 For Mutianus' preference for the gentle humanist Melanchthon over the
   stormy petrel Luther, see Karl Gillert ed *Der Briefwechsel des Conradus Mutianus*
   in Geschichtsquellen der Provinz Sachsen XVIII (Halle 1890) Epp 590, 605.
   Melanchthon's *Loci communes* (Wittenberg, December 1521) had established
   Melanchthon as the authoritative systematizer of Luther's theology.
8 See Ep 1331 n24
9 Helius Eobanus Hessus (Ep 874); for his relationship to Mutianus, see Ep 870
   introduction.
10 Henricus Urbanus (d 1538) was born Heinrich Fastnacht of Orb, north-east of
   Frankfurt. In 1494 he entered the Cistercian abbey of Georgenthal, south of
   Gotha in Saxony. From 1504 he was in contact with Mutianus, soon becoming
   the close friend to whom most of Mutianus' surviving correspondence is
   addressed. In 1510, after completing his university studies in Leipzig, he was
   appointed steward of the house that the Georgenthal abbey maintained in
   Erfurt. From then on he was the principal link between Mutianus in Gotha and
   the humanist circle in Erfurt. Although a personal friend of Melanchthon, he
   never became a Lutheran.
11 Justus Jonas (Ep 876)
12 Kaspar Schalbe (Ep 977)
13 Johannes Draconites (Ep 871)
14 Johannes Crotus Rubianus (1480–c 1545), born Johann Jäger at Dornheim in
   Thuringia, took his BA (1500) and MA (1507) at Erfurt. He belonged to the circle
   around Mutianus, knew Luther from 1501, was a friend of Hutten, and was the
   principal author of the first part of the *Epistolae obscurorum virorum*. In 1520,
   after obtaining a doctorate in theology at Bologna, he became professor of
   theology at Erfurt and, as rector of the university the following year, welcomed
   Luther when the latter was on his way to the Diet of Worms. In 1524 he entered
   the service of Albert of Brandenburg-Ansbach, the last master of the Teutonic
   Knights and soon thereafter the first duke of Prussia, which was founded as a
   Lutheran territory. In 1530 Crotus abandoned Prussia and Lutheranism and
   the following year accepted the archbishop of Mainz's offer of a canonry at
   Halle.
15 This is not true. Eobanus never wavered in his commitment to Luther and the
   Reformation. This did not, however, prevent the continuation of friendly
   relations with Erasmus.

words, 'All violence is forbidden.'[16] They are calling out the vestals.[17] They are as fierce as if they were raving mad. Meanwhile in my peaceful moments I read my Erasmus, and this brings me both profit and pleasure. Farewell, most famous of teachers.

On the feast of Terminus,[18] with the first of March upon us, 1524, from   35
Gotha. Ever your devoted Conradus Mutianus. Tear this up.

To the most learned Doctor Erasmus of Rotterdam, a chief ornament of the whole church, his respected father, in Basel

1426 / To François Du Moulin   Basel, 24 February 1524

This is the preface to the *Exomologesis sive modus confitendi* (Basel: Froben 1524).

François Du Moulin de Rochefort (d before 16 June 1526) rose in royal service as a protégé of Francis I's mother, Louise of Savoy, at whose request he was made grand almoner in 1519. In 1517 he had been one of those who promoted a royal invitation to Erasmus (Epp 523, 537, 568). When he lent strong support to the renewal of the royal invitation in 1523 and 1524 (Epp 1375, 1439), Erasmus responded with the dedication of the *Exomologesis*. Erasmus and Du Moulin continued to correspond until the latter's death (Epp 1484, 1527, 1711, 1719).

Du Moulin's hold on the see of Condom (Gascony) was not as strong as Erasmus assumed in his salutation (line 2). Du Moulin had the royal nomination and, on the death of the incumbent (October 1521), pressed his claim. But a rival candidate with local support appeared and, after two years of litigation, made good his claim to the see.

DESIDERIUS ERASMUS OF ROTTERDAM TO THE REVEREND FATHER
FRANÇOIS DU MOULIN, BISHOP DESIGNATE OF CONDOM, GREETING
When he delivered your letter,[1] most honoured prelate, which was full of a rare sincerity and exceptional kindliness towards myself, my man Hilarius[2] really brought me in full measure the cheerfulness that one associates with   5
his name. And so, since you have been so kind as to tell me how things are in

* * * * *

16 See Cicero *Oratio pro Caecina* 16.45; *Pandects* 43.17 and 31.
17 'Evocant Vestales.' The meaning, apparently, is: 'They are calling the nuns out of their cloisters.'
18 *Terminalia*, the Roman feast of Terminus, fell on 23 February. It was an appropriate day for writing to Erasmus, who had taken the Terminus figure as his personal emblem; cf Ep 1408 n17.

1426
1 Not extant
2 Bertholf (Ep 1384 n31)

your part of the world, it seemed right for me in my turn not to leave you in ignorance of what I was engaged on here when your letter reached me. Horace, when pondering on a subject relating to a life of virtue, uses the words 'I put together and lay up in store what I may later use.'[3] I have a   10 better right to use these lines, for at that moment I was wholly engaged in the preparations for a virtuous deathbed; for this is the most important chapter in philosophy, and the most serious one. It is of course something that all men should be considering all their life long; but somehow or other we are Phrygians most of us,[4] and nothing but blows will make us mend our   15 ways. An affliction of the kidneys, from which I have often suffered before, attacked me so severely last July that I had seriously to consider my departure;[5] but around Christmas it set about me so severely that I despaired of living and actually prayed for death.[6]

The stone is a merciless and rude remembrance, more cruel than death   20 itself. Even so I owe it a debt, or it would be truer to say that I owe it through the stone to the Lord Jesus, for making me now give careful thought to the question how not to be overtaken by death in a state of unreadiness, even if it has not given me space for my *Exomologesis*; which I now send you as a kind of appendix to my letter to you. If you think your letter well repaid, I   25 shall have good reason to be delighted, for I know that nothing I can do for you can ever requite your feelings towards me. Come then, most excellent prelate, let us in the mean time enjoy each other's company in the Lord after this fashion, until the days of peace return and allow a closer intimacy.[7] Farewell.
                                                                                              30
Basel, 24 February AD 1524

1427 / To Melchior of Vianden   Basel, 25 February 1524

This letter consists of the opening and concluding passages of Erasmus' *Paraphrasis in tertium psalmum*, first published with the *Exomologesis* (Ep 1426). According to Allen, the surviving manuscript in the Librije (Town Library) at Gouda (MS 1324, ff 73, 91) does not derive from the printed book and may thus have precedence over it.

Melchior Matthei of Vianden (d 1535) was a teacher at the College of the

* * * * *

3 *Epistles* 1.1.12
4 Ie, we learn wisdom too late; *Adagia* I i 28.
5 See Ep 1376 n4.
6 See Ep 1408 n2.
7 For the political considerations that made it impossible for Erasmus to resettle in France, see Epp 1408:23–5, 1411:9–12, 1415:114–15.

Castle in Louvain whose success in teaching the classics brought him to the attention of Erasmus (Epp 1237:43–7, 1257:1). In 1525 he moved to Tournai to teach at a newly opened trilingual college.

ERASMUS OF ROTTERDAM TO DOCTOR MELCHIOR OF VIANDEN
THE THEOLOGIAN, GREETING

I had lately finished a paraphrase on the Acts of the Apostles,[1] dearest Vianden, and thereafter it never crossed my mind that anyone would arise to take me to task on a question of paraphrases. Lo and behold, out of ambush, as it were, appears your letter,[2] to rob me of this peace of mind; for it leaves no stone unturned to persuade me to do over again for the mystical psalms what I had done for the New Testament. What a well-disciplined phalanx of arguments you advance, sufficient, if you cannot persuade me, to compel me to comply with your suggestion! First you move forward your right wing, and what praises you pile on me! But praise, however ingratiating, is more than anything a means of applying force; while your method of praising is to try to persuade me that all you say is true, so that to contradict you is out of the question. But with your left wing you launch a much more formidable attack. You overwhelm me under arguments like a cloud of arrows, and if I shoot any against you they are either caught on your shield and turned aside or (what makes it still more one-sided) actually turned round and used against me. You block every avenue, that I may have no way of escape. And then, to leave nothing undone, you urge me and adjure me and, as the poet puts it, 'add threats to prayers, as monarchs used to do.'[3] You point out the danger that, if I refuse your request, I may lose all the benefit of my previous efforts, and may in fact reap discredit instead of the reputation I was aiming at. This was presumably the object of that marvellous exaggeration of the worldwide fame achieved by my paraphrases – to make me all the more frightened at the risk of losing so notable an asset, just as a tyrant might say to a father: 'Think of your children: what a good-looking lot they are, so virtuous, so well educated, so clearly born for a glorious future! I will kill them all unless you do as I tell you.' And to leave me no scope to refuse to do what I am urged to do, unless I wish to appear both ungodly and unhelpful, you depict the whole of Christendom prostrate at my feet, making the same request in unison. So you threaten me that, unless I comply, I shall be commonly regarded, and rightly so, as a

* * * * *

1427
1 Ep 1414
2 Not extant
3 Ovid *Metamorphoses* 2.397

creature of silly disclaimers, selfish excuses, and artful dodges back and
forth. The famous exaggerations of Demosthenes, the lightning and
thunder of Pericles – these are nowhere, and all would seem cold and flat   35
when compared with your torrents of rhetoric.

But the way you go on, my dear Melchior, is compulsion, not
persuasion. Who would have thought that our Melchior, a man almost worn
out by the niceties of logic and philosophy, would have had so much
eloquence in him? For my part, my dear Vianden, at my age and in my state   40
of health and in the embittered times in which we live, in which it is not safe
to put pen to paper, if I were to demand my discharge, my freedom, I do not
say from paraphrases but altogether from the whole business of writing, no
fair-minded person would think my demand selfish or my assumptions
unreasonable. Yet, though I see that this subject simply does not lend itself   45
to paraphrase, I cannot risk having this powerful and menacing letter
followed by another even more ferocious; and so I have provided a sample in
the third psalm to show how vain will be the efforts of anyone who attempts
anything of the kind. For in this psalm, short as it is, one is at once
confronted by so many problems, the inversion of historical order (for many   50
psalms have a subject which from a chronological point of view is earlier
than the story of Absalom making war on his father David), the insertion of
selah, the question whether this psalm as a whole can be adapted to the
person of David, which Jerome does not deny, maintaining that it is suitable
to David and Christ and through him to all the saints,[4] while Augustine   55
raises objections[5] – in view of all this, what will the maker of a paraphrase
say about the title, about the complexity of the meaning, which is often
threefold, since it is impossible, once a character has been assumed, to drop
it again? None the less, I will try to give you in one psalm a taste of what I
have tried to do, to make it clear that I did not lack the will to oblige you.   60

When I asked you to put a little work into demonstrating the
corruptions of the logic and philosophy which are now so tediously and
wastefully ground into the young at our universities, and into pointing out
some system of teaching more suitable than this, my reason was that I can
see many gifted minds put off from learning subjects that would be really   65
useful by the dreary and pointless way in which they are taught. In fact, in
many institutions such subjects, together with theology itself, are no longer
taught; and at the same time the ancient tongues too and human studies in
general are neglected. Their youth is wasted solely in quarrelsome disputa-

* * * * *

4 In the commentary on the Psalms printed in volume VIII of Erasmus' edition of
   Jerome (fol 3 in Froben's edition of 1516) but now regarded as spurious.
5 *Enarrationes in Psalmos* PL 36 72–3 / CCL 38:7–8

tions and in bitter polemical pamphlets. This is a great scandal, and no one   70
was better fitted to deal with it than you, who have spent so many years
working in that field and have achieved no mean reputation. You will earn
the gratitude of both sides; for those who have learned nothing except those
traditional subjects, for better or for worse, will prefer to see them lectured
on quite differently in the universities rather than die out altogether, and the   75
young who thirst for a more literary education will express their gratitude to
you for pointing out a more suitable method. Farewell.

Pray give my greetings to your excellent Maecenas[6] and your most
friendly and humane circle, in which I think you highly fortunate. Since you
mention my *Colloquia familiaria* in your letter, it occurs to me to wonder at the   80
part played by fortune in human affairs. What subject could be more
lightweight? And yet you would hardly believe how many thousand copies
have been published[7] and the appetite of purchasers is not yet satisfied. It
appears again this year,[8] enlarged by added matter at the end. Such is the
nonsense I write to please my friends; though there are some grave divines   85
who maintain that these trifles have a serious purpose.[9] You may praise my
Spongia,[10] but you will never persuade me not to hate it; I cannot forgive
those who drove the poor fellow[11] to this. Some people are so misguided. He
died, I think, before he had read my *Spongia*. Farewell once more. Now for
the psalm!   90

So here is your sample, my dear Vianden, taken on the spur of the moment.
If you do not like it, I shall not be disappointed; that is what I expected. But
whether or no, you must for the moment approve my desire to oblige.
Farewell; and farewell too to all those who love the Lord Jesus Christ with all   95
their hearts.

Basel, 25 February 1524

1428 / To Johannes Fabri   Basel, 1 March 1524

This is the preface to Erasmus' *Apologia ad Stunicae Conclusiones* (see Ep 1415
introduction and lines 9–32, 89–92), first published with the *Exomologesis* (Ep

* * * * *

6 Perhaps Pierre Cotrel; see Ep 1237 n8.
7 See Ep 1341A:285–301, and *Bibliotheca Erasmiana: Bibliographie des oeuvres
  d'Erasme. Extrait de la Bibliotheca Belgica* ed F. Vander Haeghen et al I (Ghent
  1903) *Colloquia* 3–134.
8 Ep 1476
9 See Ep 1296 n10.
10 Epp 1378, 1389
11 Hutten; see preface xiv–xv with nn25–9.

1426). There is a noticeable verbal resemblance between this letter and Ep 1410. Fabri (Epp 1260 n22, 1324 n14) had recently joined the court of Archduke Ferdinand (Ep 1382 n12), who was currently in Nürnberg attending the imperial diet.

ERASMUS OF ROTTERDAM TO THE HONOURABLE JOHANNES FABRI,
CANON OF CONSTANCE AND MEMBER OF THE COUNCIL
OF THE MOST ILLUSTRIOUS PRINCE FERDINAND, GREETING

Your servant[1] has brought me Zúñiga's suspicions – *Conclusions*, he calls them. It is clear that I am in just the same position as Hercules was in the   5
story: while I wrestle with a hydra here, a crab has come crawling up from another quarter.[2] At first I suspected that one of Luther's people was up to this game; for Luther has many remarkably stupid friends whose support takes such forms as do his cause the greatest harm. When however both the style of writing and also letters arriving from Rome[3] made it clear to me that   10
this prank was entirely Zúñiga's, I wondered for some time whether I ought to reply, especially as I had answered his *Blasphemies* long ago.[4] At length, seeing that his book has a worldwide circulation, I was afraid that simple people might be taken in by the man's inventions, and spent one day's work on the subject. I fancy his Eminence Cardinal Campeggi is already in your   15
part of the world.[5] If only that man of God could find a solution for these discords of the kind I so much wish! Farewell.

Basel, 1 March 1524

1429 / To the Magistrates of Strasbourg   Basel, 13 March 1524

For the background to this letter, which was first published in the *Opus epistolarum*, see Ep 1405 introduction. It was sent to Hedio (line 24) to be delivered or not, as he saw fit (Ep 1447B:2–9). It appears that Hedio chose not to deliver the letter: in August, Erasmus wrote again to the same purpose (Ep 1477), and the Strasbourg records mention only the second letter (see Allen's introduction to Ep 1477).

* * * * *

1428
1 See Ep 1423:15.
2 See Ep 1410:3–6.
3 Possibly those answered by Epp 1410, 1411, 1412
4 See Ep 1260 n45.
5 Erasmus' surmise was incorrect. Campeggi, the new papal legate, did not reach Nürnberg until 14 March; see Ep 1410 introduction.

ERASMUS OF ROTTERDAM TO THE CITY COUNCIL OF STRASBOURG,
GREETING

Right worshipful and my most honoured lords, I am filled equally with
affection and deep respect by the religious spirit which makes you support
the gospel cause, that gospel for whose advancement I have now expended   5
so many years of hard labour and carry such a burden of hostility on the part
of those who pursue their own advancement with more zeal than they do
Christ's glory. Men have their different ways of showing zeal for this most
sacred cause; but I could name some of them who take a hand in it who
undermine the good work that is done by others. There is in your city one   10
Schott,[1] a printer, who among other things has recently published an attack
on me by Hutten[2] so devoid of sense that even Luther and Melanchthon
highly disapproved of it.[3] Nor was this all: he has printed the same book
secretly a second time, together with a scurrilous tirade by a man who must
be touched in his wits,[4] though its nature is such that it may do very great   15
harm both to the humanities and to the gospel cause. As far as I personally
am concerned, I would not lift a hand to stop him, and this question will
seem to you, I am sure, beneath your notice. At the same time repeated
precautions must be taken to prevent this licence, once overlooked, from
breaking out in a direction which may spell disaster for your common-   20
wealth. It will at any rate do the gospel cause no little harm, if men see that
for the sake of the gospel the moral standards of that commonwealth are
slipping.

    If you wish to find out what this book is worth, send for Hedio[5] or
Capito.[6] I do not grudge Schott his profit, and I know that the writer was put   25

                    * * * * *

1429
1 Since 1499, Johann Schott (1477–c 1548) had been the third generation of his
    family in the publishing business. His deep commitment to the Reformation,
    which led him to publish works by Luther and Hutten when it was still
    dangerous to do so, also produced a conflict with Erasmus that began in 1523
    with his publication of the *Iudicium D. Martini Lutheri de Erasmo Roterodamo* (Ep
    1341A n315).
2 See Ep 1356 n9.
3 WA-Br III 160:7–8, together with n2 (pages 160–1), supplies the views of both
    men with exact citations. Cf Epp 1341A:1099–1106, 1432:60–1, 1437:110–12,
    1477:13–15, 1479:205, 1495:17–18, 1523:9–10, 1528:43–5.
4 Brunfels (Ep 1405)
5 Ep 1477B
6 Ep 1368. The breach between Capito and Erasmus, however, had already
    begun; see Epp 1374 introduction and 1437 n48.

up to it by others.[7] If in your wisdom you think this should be overlooked, I
shall remain unmoved. Nevertheless, my most heartfelt devotion to the
humanities and to the promotion of the gospel make me think I ought to put
you on your guard in this respect; and it may well have some bearing also on
the welfare of your city. That the Lord Jesus may prosper your common-   30
wealth and preserve you all in health and wealth, well-born and highly
honoured members of the council, is the prayer of your worships' for many
years and for many reasons[8] most devoted servant.

Basel, Passion Sunday 1524

1430 / To Henry VIII   Basel, [c March?] 1524

First published in the *Opus epistolarum*, this is the covering letter for a gift (line
5) sent to King Henry. Only an approximate date can be assigned: sometime
between the first draft of *De libero arbitrio* (Ep 1419) and its general circulation in
September (Ep 1481), but doubtless closer to the earlier limit. This letter might
have been carried by the servant whom Erasmus sent to England at the
beginning of April (n7) and who brought back a letter from Henry (Ep
1467:20–1).

ERASMUS OF ROTTERDAM TO HENRY VIII, KING OF ENGLAND,
GREETING
May it please your invincible Majesty. I know how greatly it helps to secure a
welcome for a gift that it should be given at the right moment, nor am I
unaware that this gift of mine is untimely in two respects:[1] it is offered very   5

* * * * *

7 In later letters, Erasmus named Capito as the instigator (Epp 1477B:72–9, 1485,
  1496: 120–2), though such can scarcely have been his view here (see lines 24–5).
  Still later, however, he accused Eppendorf; Allen Ep 1934:59, 63–5, 348–51.
  Eppendorf (Epp 1283 n4, 1371, 1377), or perhaps even Buschius (Ep 1291 n4),
  might well have been the suspected culprit at this point; cf ASD IX-1 112 n133.
8 Erasmus had enjoyed numerous pleasant visits to Strasbourg: in August 1514
  (Epp 302, 305), June 1515 (Ep 337 introduction), September 1518 (Ep 867:24–8),
  and November 1521 (Ep 1342:231–7).

1430
1 Allen suggested that the gift was probably Froben's folio volume (1524) of
  Erasmus' paraphrases on the Gospels and Acts in which the five dedicatees
  (four sovereigns and the pope) are symbolically united. If Henry had
  previously received only his own paraphrase on Luke (Epp 1381, 1385), then
  the collected volume could appropriately be described as sent 'late in the day'
  after widespread dissemination.

late in the day, after a wide popular circulation in every region of the globe, and it is presented to one who is entirely absorbed in the problems of war.[2] I have not previously had the good fortune to find a safe hand by whom I could send it at the proper time. And I shall not be sorry to lose the credit for my whole offering, if by this sacrifice I am able to purchase the agree- 10 ment of monarchs among themselves. As it is, in such severe and long-continued upheavals in human affairs I sometimes feel weary not merely of my labours but of life itself. But God will one day grant an end to these evils, if I deserve it.

I send you the first draft of a book on the freedom of the will directed 15 against Luther.[3] The work is not yet finished, and in fact the ill health which has borne hard on me and almost killed me[4] and the efforts required to clear off other things I had in hand[5] barely allowed me to do as much as this. If your Majesty, and other learned men, approve this sample of my work, I shall finish it and arrange for its printing elsewhere; for here, in my opinion, 20 there is no printer who dares print anything in which a single word reflects on Luther,[6] while against the pope one may write what one likes. This is the present state of Germany. In hopes therefore that what I send may reach your country safely, I have again dispatched a servant of my own whom I can trust,[7] and who is moreover not unknown to your Majesty. May Christ 25 the Almighty long preserve your invincible Majesty in health and wealth.

Basel, 1523

1431 / To Guy Morillon   Basel, 25 March 1524

This letter was first published in volume II of J. Jortin's *Life of Erasmus* (London 1758/60). Allen used the autograph, which was part of the Ortelius Collection in the custody of the Dutch Reformed Church, Austin Friars, London. In 1955 the Ortelius Collection was sold at auction to an American collector and the current location of the manuscript is unknown. On Guy Morillon, see Ep 1287.

* * * * *

2 On the threatened resumption of war with France in the spring of 1524, see Scarisbrick 131.
3 See Epp 1419, 1420.
4 See Ep 1426:16–19.
5 See Ep 1422 n10.
6 Cf Epp 1432:91–2, 1486:3–5, 1493:6–8, 1494:11–12.
7 Possibly Lieven Algoet (Ep 1373 n1), who carried Epp 1431–7 to the Netherlands and England at the beginning of April (Ep 1437:8–9, 200) and returned in July (Epp 1452:51–2, 1467:18–19) bearing Ep 1457–8 and perhaps also Epp 1455 and 1463

Greeting, most sincere of friends. Your letter,[1] written on 21 August but delivered the day before Good Friday,[2] shall have only a brief answer, because I fear you may have left that address already before a letter can reach you there. Barbier's attitude has never caused me a moment's doubt.[3] I will inquire what has been done about the books.[4] When Nicolaas van 5 Broeckhoven was here he and I often spoke about it, but if he received anything, he kept it dark.[5] I have had a letter from Maximilianus,[6] admirably straightforward and friendly, and am sending him an answer, though I am very busy indeed. Doctor de La Roche,[7] my old friend and patron, I am now writing to. Chancellor Mercurino[8] and Jean Lalemand[9] had letters[10] from me 10 some time ago. The illustrious Lady Margaret has written me a letter in which she promises me an annuity if I return.[11] I should not be short of money, if only these scandalous attacks would let me live in peace. Zúñiga rants away in Rome;[12] but the pope has at last told him to be silent.[13] Here there are many who from time to time publish a new pamphlet full of 15 scandalous attacks on me. This can be done in Germany with impunity, thanks to their zeal for the gospel. And yet I have so far written nothing against Luther, except to go on record that I am highly unsympathetic to his party.[14] Here we have a good example of their enthusiasm for the gospel and the behaviour that goes with a revival in the church. Those prebends, and 20

* * * * *

1431
1 Not extant; probably written from Valladolid, contemporary with Ep 1380, and forwarded from Brabant via Sélestat (see Ep 1467:32, and Allen Ep 1553:1–5)
2 24 March
3 See Epp 1294, 1386 introduction.
4 Probably those mentioned in Ep 1507:6, 16
5 Broeckhoven (Ep 1299 n23) apparently had some role in the delivery of the books.
6 Maximilianus Transsilvanus (Ep 1342 n71). Neither his letter, written in 1523 (see Ep 1467 n16), nor Erasmus' reply mentioned here is extant.
7 Ep 1432
8 Gattinara (Ep 1150)
9 Ep 1554
10 Neither letter is extant.
11 See Ep 1408 n5.
12 See Ep 1415:9ff.
13 In response to appeals from Erasmus; see Epp 1422:79–82, 1443B:16–17. Erasmus had apparently received private information in advance concerning the pope's intentions.
14 Cf Epp 1033:210–11, 1041:50–1, 1167, 1217, 1342:807–1118.

the prior rights of which you speak,[15] are not for me. These are long-term
hopes, and I am already at death's door. It must therefore be for you to
choose in whose name you may wish to make the arrangement. I know and
like Nicolas Barbier.[16]

I have now finished paraphrases on the whole New Testament[17] except   25
the Apocalypse. I don't know whether you have seen the latest edition of my
letters.[18] You are mentioned in them by name a few times. And yet I shall see
to it that, if any of my works deserve to survive, the name of my sincere
friend Morillon shall survive with mine. This shall happen shortly, and
would have been arranged already if your letter had arrived in time.   30

I had thought Nebrija more unprejudiced.[19] But none of that is

* * * * *

15 'Primarias preces,' ie, the right of a crowned emperor to appoint one canon to
   every cathedral chapter in Germany; see Du Cange *Glossarium Mediae et Infimae
   Latinitatis* v (Paris 1845) sv 'Preces Primariae.' Cf Ep 1470:44–5.
16 Ep 613. Barbier was evidently next in line if Erasmus were to decline the
   appointment; see Ep 1470:45–6.
17 The last to be completed was that on Acts (Ep 1414).
18 The *Epistolae ad diversos*; see Ep 1206. Morillon's name is mentioned in Epp 695
   and 794, but Erasmus never published any of their correspondence.
19 Elio Antonio de Nebrija (d 2 July 1522) was a renowned Spanish humanist (Ep
   487:17n) of whom Erasmus had otherwise had a good opinion (Ep 1111:43–7;
   LB IX 288A). This ill-humoured reference to him remained a mystery (see
   Allen's note) until the recent discovery by Paul Oskar Kristeller in the Royal
   Library at Copenhagen of an eighteenth-century manuscript of a work by
   Nebrija criticizing Erasmus and Reuchlin. See Carlos Gilly 'Una obra descono-
   cida de Nebrija contra Erasmo y Reuchlin' in *El Erasmismo in España* (Santander
   1986) 195–218; cf Paul Oskar Kristeller *Iter Italicum* III (London and Leiden
   1985) 185. The manuscript bears the title 'Aelius Antonius Nebrissensis Regius
   Historiographicus in Reuclinum Phorcensem et Erasmum Roterodamum,
   quod de *talita* in Evangelio Marci et *tabita* in Luca non bene senserunt.' The text
   is printed in Gilly 204–14. Although the tract, composed shortly before
   Nebrija's death in 1522, was evidently never printed, Erasmus' comment here
   indicates that he was familiar with it. In the absence of any evidence, one can
   only speculate, as has Gilly (196), that a copy might have been forwarded to
   Erasmus via Morillon, perhaps by someone who feared that criticism by so
   eminent a scholar might damage Erasmus' reputation in Spain. In the tract,
   Nebrija charged Erasmus with having made several mistakes in his discussion
   of the word *talitha* in his annotation on Mark 5:41, a charge which Zúñiga (Ep
   1260 n36) had also made. Moreover, Nebrija, having apparently seen the
   second edition of Erasmus' New Testament, remarked (Gilly 213) that Erasmus
   was 'stuck forever in the same mud and never departs from an error once
   conceived.' Although Erasmus here tries to dismiss the issues raised as matters
   of no consequence (line 32), he eventually removed from his annotations the
   errors identified by Zúñiga and Nebrija. See Erika Rummel *Erasmus and His
   Catholic Critics* I (Leiden 1989) 154–5.

anything to do with me, and it is a quarrel over goat's wool.[20] Pray greet my
Spanish friends, the archbishop of Compostela,[21] Doctor Coronel,[22] Master
Guillaume Le Moyne.[23] I wonder you do not mention Guillermo Vergara.[24] I
rejoice to think I have supporters in that country. How I wish I had gone   35
there[25] when I went to Germany, where I have found such pestilent people
that, had I known in advance, I would sooner have gone to live among the
Turks than come here. But fate is to be thanked for this. The Camel[26] is no
concern of yours; but I, whether I will or no, have many a hydra to contend
with. Farewell.   40

Basel, Good Friday 1524
To Master Guy Morillon, secretary to his Imperial Majesty

1432 / To Gérard de Plaine   Basel, 26 March 1524

This letter was first published in the *Opus epistolarum*.

Gérard de Plaine, seigneur de la Roche (c 1480–31 August 1524), followed his
father, the chancellor of Burgundy (n5), in a career in government service. By
1504 he was a master of requests and for a time (1511–15) he was president of
the privy council. Charles v employed him on numerous diplomatic missions.
In the summer of 1524 he died in Rome on a mission to Clement VII.

ERASMUS OF ROTTERDAM TO X[1] DE LA ROCHE, GREETING
Letters from my friends,[2] most honoured sir, and the way they speak of you,

* * * * *

20 *Adagia* I iii 53
21 Alonso de Fonseca (c 1475–1534) had been archbishop of Santiago de
   Compostela since 1508 and archbishop of Toledo since 31 December 1523.
   Erasmus' surviving correspondence with him begins with Ep 1748.
22 Ep 1274
23 A secretary in the chancellery of Charles v
24 Despite the wrong first name, Erasmus is probably thinking of Juan de Vergara
   (Ep 1277).
25 Before his move to Basel in 1521, Erasmus may have been invited, as in 1517
   (see Ep 596 introduction), to accompany Charles on his return to Spain, which
   occurred in May 1522.
26 Baechem (Ep 1254 n6)

1432
1 Erasmus evidently could not remember de Plaine's Christian name.
2 Not extant

Michiel Gillis[3] and Guy Morillon[4] in particular, have taught me what a generous opinion you have of my work. This was indeed no surprise, for many years ago, when I was engaged on some business I forget what with   5
your distinguished father the chancellor,[5] and you were newly married, I could feel that you thought well of me and were kindly disposed. Indeed in all parts of the world my works have won me so many friends, and so distinguished, that in this respect, even were there nothing else, I might have thought myself highly fortunate, had not my lot been cast in my old age   10
upon our generation with its manifold upheavals. How great a hater of war I am,[6] and what a lover of peace, is made clear in all my books, and particularly in my *Pacis undique profligatae querimonia*,[7] which, I hear, has already learned to talk Spanish.[8] And so I am almost tired of life, as I watch the world's two most powerful kings locked for so many years now in mortal   15
conflict,[9] in such a way that no part of the world is free from its share of the evil results. Then there is another split almost more incurable, that between the new gospel and the old, an evil which daily grows and spreads more widely, although so many monarchs vainly strive against it, so many leaders of the church, so many universities, so many learned men. In every way   20
there is a touch of destiny about it, whichever god may be the source of what we see before our eyes.

Personally, as I saw things I disliked in both parties, and as neither party would adapt itself to reach agreement, I had decided to remain quiet and steer clear of both camps, beseeching Christ the Almighty in the mean   25
time (for it was all I could do) that he would one day turn this tempest of ours

* * * * *

3 Michiel Gillis of Antwerp (documented 1520–4) was probably a kinsman of Pieter Gillis (Ep 184). He is known to have been among the secretaries of Maximilian I and Charles V. He attended the Diet of Nürnberg in 1524, and Erasmus expected him to carry some letters back to Spain (Allen Ep 1553:5–7).
4 Ep 1287
5 Thomas de Plaine, seigneur de Maigny (c 1444–1507), chancellor of Burgundy from 1496. Erasmus' business with him probably had something to do with the *Panegyricus* (Ep 179), the heading of which states that the chancellor, de Maigny, replied to it in the name of the prince; see LB IV 507–8 (the heading in question is not found in the texts published by ASD or CWE).
6 See Ep 1225 n52.
7 Ie, the *Querela pacis* (Ep 603)
8 In a translation by Diego López de Cartagena, archdeacon of Seville (Seville: J. Cromberger, 27 April 1520); see Marcel Bataillon *Erasme et l'Espagne* (Paris 1937) 92, 97.
9 See Ep 1369 n12.

into tranquillity. Even so, I did not entirely abandon my researches,[10] but concentrated on subjects which should give no great offence to either party. For besides many other things I have completed all the paraphrases on the New Testament, except the Apocalypse, which entirely refuses to admit of paraphrase and almost of commentary, supposing that I thought it worth the labour.

And for some time this policy worked well enough. But now, while I try as hard as I can to do my best for both parties, the result is that stones are thrown at me by both sides. Baechem[11] and his gang protested loudly that I was a heretic and a Lutheran; nor could he support his noisy protests with one syllable of evidence, except that I published no attack on Luther. In Rome that hydra-headed monster Zúñiga could not be suppressed by Leo or by Adrian or by the college of cardinals,[12] but spewed out a series of poisonous pamphlets furtively from time to time. Just lately Clement VII as well has silenced him with some difficulty as he planned fresh outrages.[13] In Germany I had for some time been a favourite target for the pens of those who now boast themselves gospellers or evangelicals, though there is less gospel in them than anything – not provoked by any harm I had done them, except that in my published work I had gone on record that, as was the plain truth, I had no connection with the Lutheran faction.[14] I had to do this because certain people were using my name to mislead the ignorant, though they knew well that things were different. They were however restrained by some feeling of respect for a man who, as they themselves do not deny for all their prejudices, has done so much for public enlightenment. At length Hutten arrived here, and with encouragement from a number of lunatics unsheathed his pen against me like a weapon,[15] piling up all the calumnies that could be invented against anyone. He had his answer in my *Spongia*,[16] and has now ceased to exist. After him arose another man more ignorant and more raving mad than he was,[17] whom I have not yet answered; and I think it wiser to ignore him, for I hear that a number of other people are girding themselves to rain this sort of venomous pamphlets on me. From storms of this kind neither emperor nor pope can defend me, for these

* * * * *

10 See Ep 1422 n10.
11 Ep 1254 n6
12 Ep 1415:9ff
13 See Ep 1431:13–14.
14 See Ep 1431:17–19.
15 See Epp 1356 introduction, 1437:27–30, 73–4.
16 Epp 1378, 1389
17 Brunfels; see Ep 1405 and 1429:14–15.

people fear neither gods nor men. Such are some of the champions of this
new gospel, so foolish and so crazy that Luther himself and Melanchthon   60
are compelled to attack them in print.[18] Though these men do not even
respect their own bishops, and their contempt for ours is astonishing. No
one here is too mean or too disreputable to pour abuse with boundless
confidence on every man of character and standing; they are ashamed of
nothing and afraid of nobody.   65

　　It was high time for me to be free for my own work; and my old age has
coincided with these upheavals, so that even though on top of the usual
troubles of the aged I suffer cruel torments from the stone,[19] this is
nevertheless the least part of my afflictions. Nor for the moment is there any
escape. In Brabant you know for how many years I did battle with the   70
theologians, who hate the humanities worse than they hate Luther. You are
aware what furies have had the sword put in their hands.[20] In Rome no one
writes but Zúñiga, and Zúñiga is a host of monsters in himself. In England
I have friends in the highest quarters, friends I can really trust; but somehow, I know not why, I do not want to live in England.[21] To France I am   75
invited with enormous offers,[22] but the war stands in the way.[23] People
might accuse me, quite falsely, of deserting to the emperor's enemy,[24]
although the war is none of my business and never was and never will be.
Wherever I live, I shall be the emperor's man. So I have stuck it out here for
some time in hopes of peace; and sorry I am to see even now no glimpse of it.   80

　　I hear that Cardinal Colonna has arrived as legate in your part of the
world.[25] He is a clever man (I knew him in Brussels), and let us hope his
cleverness will secure a truce at least between the monarchs. It is hard to
fight on three fronts at once, with the Turkish menace, the French, and
Luther's crowd, who spread more widely every day. Cardinal Campeggi is   85
here[26] with a commission to settle the business of Luther; he is a really

*　*　*　*　*

18 See Ep 1429 n3.
19 See Epp 1376:n4, 1408:n2.
20 See Ep 1408 n10.
21 See Ep 1386 n9.
22 See Ep 1434:4–25.
23 See Ep 1369 n12.
24 See Ep 1408 n12.
25 Pompeo Colonna (1479–1532), bishop of Rieti (1508) and cardinal (1517). The
　　meeting with Erasmus in Brussels (line 82) probably took place in the winter of
　　1516/17 when Colonna was in Flanders on a diplomatic mission. There seems
　　to be no other evidence that he was sent on a mission to the imperial court in
　　Spain at this time.
26 Ie, in Germany; see Epp 1410 and 1422 introductions.

learned and civilized person, but as I see the state of things in Germany, I
fear he will do no good. If they[27] are cruel and repressive, there is a risk that
the cities will form a league to protect themselves. If they try to put an end to
the split with reasonable offers, I see no hope that either side will give up an   90
inch of its own rights. Printing is useless against that party. If anybody
writes a book against Luther, nobody dares print it,[28] and the books that are
printed elsewhere nobody reads. If only the princes could agree to use their
public authority without civil disturbance to correct what really deserves to
be corrected! But each of them is a slave to his own private advantage, and   95
the common good goes by default. My old age has fallen on this generation
as the mouse in the proverb fell into the pitch.[29] Meanwhile humane studies
are rejected and the cause of literature is abandoned. I at any rate have tired
of all literary work, now that I see the measure of public ingratitude, as those
who have learned from my own books to write fluently[30] vie with one   100
another to sharpen their pens against me.

    Such are the feelings I wanted to pour out into the bosom of a friend. I
have no consolation except that my own conscience is clear in the sight of
Christ, to whose glory I am wholeheartedly devoted. Farewell.

    From Basel, Easter eve 1524   105

1432A / To Conradus Mutianus Rufus   Basel, 28 March 1524

The autograph of this letter was found in the Ratsschulbibliothek Zwickau (MS
xx.iii.9) by the librarian, Otto Clemen, who published it in *Theologische Studien
und Kritiken* (Gotha 1899) 276. Allen printed it as Ep 1432A in his volume VI
(page xxxi). Given its date, the letter could be an answer to Ep 1425, but there is
no clear connection between the two letters.

Greeting. I have always loved my friend Mutianus as a most friendly and
fair-minded person, and now I have a further reason to be fond of him as my
exact contemporary. My old age has coincided with this borderland of great
change in all things. I try to be of use to every man, and every man tears me
to pieces. It would have been safer to serve wild beasts than men like this.   5
But so it has pleased heaven. Posterity will pass, I hope, a fairer judgment.
For my part, to my last day of life I shall be what I have always been. Though
who would not lose interest in all literary work, faced by the perverse

* * * * *

27 Presumably the imperial diet, which was dominated by the territorial princes
28 See Ep 1430 n6.
29 *Adagia* II iii 68
30 See Ep 260.

ingratitude of his fellow men? The cry is that I am a rebel against the gospel: would that they spent as much trouble to promote it! The cry is that I have 10 sold myself for gain[1] – when I have refused all offers, not without some personal risk, rather than show myself indebted to the party of which I did not wholly approve.[2] And now that the insane policies of certain people have brought things to the point where frightful disorders seem to threaten us, they say it is my fault. I have no doubt that Luther himself dislikes the 15 excesses of some of them;[3] but they seem unwilling to listen even to Luther. The Lord Jesus have you, dear friend, in his keeping.

Basel, Easter Monday 1524
Your sincere friend Erasmus

1433 / To Jan de Hondt   Basel, [end?] March 1524

This letter was first published by Peter Scriverius in his *Magni Des. Erasmi Roterodami Vita* (Leiden: G. Basson 1615), an enlarged edition of Merula's *Vita Des. Erasmi* (see Ep 1388 introduction). Although only an approximate month-date is possible, the letter is clearly contemporary with Epp 1431–2, 1434.

Jan de Hondt (Ep 751) held the Courtrai prebend from which Erasmus drew an annuity (Ep 1094 n6). De Hondt was always prompt and reliable in his payments, and Erasmus responded with genuine friendship. Ep 1471 shows that de Hondt had quickly dispelled the suspicions voiced here.

TO THE WORTHY MASTER JAN DE HONDT, CANON OF COURTRAI, GREETING

Another letter to you[1] already sealed had been waiting here for some time, when a letter arrived from Flanders written by a man called Michael Bentinus,[2] which brought news that your feelings towards me were very 5 hostile, and that you had severely reprimanded one young man for reading heretical literature on the ground that he possessed one of my books, I know not which, adding that my books were more pestilential than Luther's, and that you hoped shortly to see me and my books burned. I have no doubt

* * * * *

1432A
1 See Ep 1435 n6.
2 See Ep 1415:34–7.
3 See Ep 1429 n3.

1433
1 An important letter to de Hondt about the payment of Erasmus' Courtrai annuity. Not extant. See Ep 1458:3, 16.
2 His letter is not extant. Michael Bentinus (d 1527) was a Fleming who had worked as a corrector of Latin texts for Froben's press in Basel (1520–3).

these are inventions, unless you have turned into a completely different   10
person or are quite ignorant of what I suffer here at the hands of Luther's
party.

Personally I think death would be more tolerable than what I have to
put up with, and had I known the stage this conspiracy[3] had reached I would
rather have gone to live among the Turks than move here. How different   15
was the verdict passed on my books by Pope Adrian, who laid the
theologians who were vainly tirading against me under a ban of silence![4]
How different that of the cardinals who instructed Zúñiga to remain silent
when he made all those attacks on me[5] – as Clement VII has lately done a
second time![6] How different that of Cardinal Campeggi,[7] who implores me   20
more than he does anyone to help him against Luther! How different that of
the Lutherans themselves, who rage against no man more freely than
against my humble self! I thought you ought to know this, that you may
make no mistake about me. Farewell.

Basel, after Easter 1524   25

1434 / To Jean de Carondelet   Basel, 30 March 1524

First published in the *Opus epistolarum*, this letter was written in response to
letters, no longer extant, from Margaret of Austria, regent of the Netherlands,
and her minister, Carondelet (Ep 1276), intimating that Erasmus' imperial
pension would not be paid unless he returned to Brabant. Because Margaret's
letter had reached Erasmus early in January (Ep 1408:11–12), and because
there are numerous verbal resemblances here to letters of January and
February, especially Ep 1422, Allen concluded that this letter might have been
written several weeks before its date of dispatch.

ERASMUS OF ROTTERDAM TO JEAN DE CARONDELET,
ARCHBISHOP OF PALERMO, GREETING
If I may briefly answer at one blow both your letter and one from the
illustrious Lady Margaret, these French offers are no mirage; long ago

* * * * *

Erasmus had not been pleased with his handling of the *Adagia* (Ep 1437:174–81).
At this time Bentinus was back in Flanders, but by the autumn of 1524 he was
again in Basel working for the presses of Curio and Cratander.
3 Cf Epp 1477:33, 1481:28, 1506:10, 1528:49.
4 See Ep 1359 n1.
5 See Ep 1302:59–61.
6 See Ep 1431 n13.
7 See Ep 1410 introduction.

Bishop Poncher of Paris,[1] when he was in Brussels acting as envoy to King   5
Charles,[2] who was not yet emperor, offered me over and above the king's
bounty four hundred crowns on his own behalf as well as all my expenses,[3]
and promised at the same time that my free time and my liberty of
movement should be unrestricted. And this absence of mine does not
deserve that name, for while I have been away I have published many   10
volumes,[4] which had I stayed in your surroundings I could never have
completed. Even so, when I came away, the treasurers[5] had promised that
my annuity should be kept intact. Besides which, what your highness added
about its not looking as though I were going over to the enemy[6] made me
smile, to tell the truth, at the thought that a man like myself had anything to   15
do with war. Quite the reverse, I do all I can to encourage the monarchs to
agree.

    The reason for these frequent invitations was made clear by the king of
France through his emissary.[7] He has decided to found in Paris a college for
the three ancient languages like the one at Louvain,[8] and he wanted me to be   20
head of it. I made my excuses, however, remembering of course how much

* * * * *

1434
1 Etienne Poncher; see Ep 529.
2 In 1517; Ep 531:618–20
3 The literal translation of Erasmus' words, *coronatos aureos*, is 'gold crowns,' ie,
  the French *écus d'or à la couronne*, which were last struck in 1474–5, with 3.275 g
  fine gold. Since these coins had been replaced by the slightly heavier *écu d'or au*
  soleil (3.369 g fine gold) in November 1475, the coins in question here – and in
  all Erasmus's subsequent references to *coronatos* – were probably the latter.
  Physically unchanged for the next forty-four years, this *écu* had maintained a
  stable value of 36s 3d tournois from 1494 to July 1519, when it underwent a
  modest debasement, which both reduced its weight (to 3.296 g fine gold) and
  raised its value to 40s 0d tournois in silver coin. Thus the 400 *écus*, when Bishop
  Poncher had first offered them in 1517, were then worth £725 tournois, or
  £123 6s 8d gros Flemish, or about £85 sterling. In February 1521, the government of the Burgundian-Hapsburg Low Countries set the value of the new
  debased 1519 *écu au soleil* at 72d gros, but then raised it to 76d gros in the
  following August (CWE 1 315, 321 illustration, 336–7; CWE 8 348–50). Thus,
  when this letter was written (1524) a sum of 400 *écus au soleil* would now have
  been worth £800 tournois, or £126 13s 4d gros Flemish. Cf also Ep 1439:36,
  Ep 1471:13 and n10.
4 See Epp 1390 n1, 1411 n2.
5 One of whom was Jean Ruffault (Ep 1287 n10)
6 See Ep 1408 n12.
7 Cantiuncula; see Epp 1375, 1403.
8 See Ep 522 introduction.

unpopularity and all the trouble I had to face in your part of the world from some of the theologians[9] in respect of Busleyden's college.[10] And yet on his return from France my servant[11] reported on reliable evidence that a treasurership[12] was waiting for me there worth a thousand livres.[13] For my part I have not so far been much of a burden on my prince's exchequer, for my annuity has been paid out of it only once.[14] Another payment I secured by finesse,[15] which cost the exchequer nothing. I live here at great expense, especially as I am constantly ill, though in other respects too I do not husband my resources as I should. And I have already run up a fair amount of debt,[16] so that if my health allowed me to leave, perhaps my creditors would not let me. And so I should be glad if it were possible to pay at least one year's annuity in cash to my servant,[17] the bearer of this letter, to relieve my shortage of funds. I enclose a letter from the emperor,[18] which expresses the same desire. Not but what, payment or no payment, I shall be the emperor's servant, and shall not often trouble you in future with business of such small importance.

On many occasions this year, and particularly in July and December, the stone from which I suffer so tortured me that death was my object and I despaired of life.[19] No death can be as cruel as the stone. And yet these troubles over Luther torment me worse than the stone itself. I will even dare to confess to a friend like yourself that I was not a little dissuaded from returning by the present state of things. You know what an epic struggle I had with certain theologians in support of the humanities, before Luther appeared on the scene. And now a sword has been put into the hand of two men who hate the humanities passionately, Hulst and Baechem.[20] What

* * * * *

9 See Ep 934 introduction.
10 Ie, the Collegium Trilingue at Louvain (Ep 691 introduction)
11 Bertholf; Ep 1400 introduction
12 At Tours; see Epp 1439, 1446, 1471, 1484, 1487, 1488, 1529, 1545, 1553.
13 French livres tournois. See CWE 1 328, 347; and Ep 1471 n10.
14 Paid at Antwerp by Ruffault before Erasmus' departure to Basel in 1521; Epp 1302:29, 1342:100–2.
15 Apparently the 300 florins given him in 1517; Epp 597:30n, 621 introduction, 628:58–60, 695:38–9.
16 Cf lines 66–7 below and Ep 1470:25–30; but for a different view of the matter, see Ep 1518:60–1 and n18
17 Probably Algoet; cf Epp 1430 n7, 1437:8–9, 199–200, 416–17.
18 Not extant, unless the reference is to a copy of Ep 1380 that Erasmus had somehow acquired
19 See Epp 1422:18–22, 1426:16–19.
20 See Ep 1408 n10.

Baechem is like is common knowledge, and he has made clear in many ways
how much he hates me, and still does so. I wrote many books before I ever
heard the name of Luther,[21] and yet nothing has thus far been found in any
of them which agrees with Luther's party. Though it is easy for a personal   50
enemy to pick out the material for calumny, and in your part of the world all
this is done in due theological order. The man they want to hurt is carried off
to jail. There the conduct of business is in very few hands, and the innocent
must be treated vilely for fear their authority may suffer in any way. When
they have lost their way completely, the cry is that we must support the   55
defenders of the faith.

All this did not influence me enough to deter me from returning, but to
be quite honest it did make me less eager to return to Brabant, the more so as
in the emperor's absence there is not much support to be found at court.
Cardinal Campeggi is at present in Nürnberg,[22] charged with a settlement of   60
the dispute with Luther. He has now written three letters most kindly
inviting me to join him there so that I can help him;[23] though what help I
can give I do not know, except that I can see my old age, which has earned a
rest, thrown to the Furies and torn in pieces by both sides while I strive to be
a blessing to all alike. If I can make my excuses to the cardinal, once those   65
German stoves[24] have cooled off I will fly to join you, and also if I can manage
to clear my debts here, in which I am more than usually involved. May
Christ the Almighty long preserve your highness in health and wealth.

Basel, the Wednesday after Easter 1524

1435 / To Jan Robbyns   Basel, 31 March [1524]

The manuscript of this letter, which was first published as Ep 95 in de Vocht
Literae, is a contemporary copy found in the correspondence of Frans van
Cranevelt at Louvain. Jan Robbyns (Robijns), d 1532, was dean of the chapter
of St Rombout, Mechelen, and an influential figure in the affairs of the
Collegium Trilingue at Louvain. Ep 1457 is his reply to this letter.

Greeting, most honoured sir. I am grateful that something in the way of an
honorarium should have been given to my friend Goclenius,[1] not so much

* * * * *

21 Cf Epp 1410:22–3, 1418:33–4.
22 Having arrived there on 14 March; see Ep 1410 introduction and cf Ep 1428:15–16.
23 None of the letters is extant; two of them are mentioned in Ep 1422:1, 8.
24 Cf Ep 1422:27–31, 36–8.

1435
1 Conradus Goclenius (Ep 1209) was professor of Latin at the Collegium
  Trilingue.

for the gift itself as for the knowledge that this kindness on your part keeps him in his proper sphere of activity. Twelve florins, after all, is not a great sum;[2] I myself, from my small resources, have given him more to prevent his abandoning the task he is engaged on,[3] for this I am quite sure – it will not be easy to find a successor like him.

More than once already I have been invited to France with substantial promises from the French king.[4] He wants to set up a college for the three tongues in Paris; but so far I have begged off, foreseeing that I should have a struggle with the theologians, whose tirades against Greek would astonish you.[5] I'm an old man now, and want to retire. If only I could! I find that my old age has coincided with the sort of generation that gives me much to bear whichever way I turn. In both parties there are things I dislike; and all the time, while I commit myself to neither, I am torn to bits by both. Adrian VI was on my side; so is Clement VII, so is the emperor, but I am not allowed to enjoy their generosity and their support. Instantly there is a cry of 'Corruption!' from the Lutheran mob: 'He has shared the spoils and given up the gospel.'[6] In Luther's faction at any rate I can see so many revolutionaries and fanatics that his is a league I could never join. If I see the princes laying aside their private interests and willing to take steps for the glory of Christ, I shall be with them; if not, I shall at least keep my conscience clear in the sight of God. God keep you safe, my honoured friend.

Basel, the Thursday after Easter

Your friend Erasmus of Rotterdam, extempore

5

10

15

20

25

1436 / To X   [Basel, spring 1525]

This letter appears here out of chronological sequence. The circumstances are as follows. First published by Allen, the letter bears a close verbal resemblance to Ep 447 (lines 101–26, 147–243, 360–7, 420–40) and to the *Compendium vitae* (Ep 1437:284–322). But the manuscript, a seventeenth-century copy that Allen's wife, Helen Mary Allen, found in the Öffentliche Bibliothek of the University

* * * * *

2 Either Rhenish gold florins, worth £2 18s gros Flemish; or, since he is referring to Goclenius in Louvain, the new Carolus gold florins, worth £2 2s gros Flemish; or just the Burgundian-Hapsburg money-of-account (1 florin = 40d gros), for a sum of £2 gros Flemish. Cf CWE 1 345; CWE 8 348–50.

3 See Ep 1388 n3.

4 See Ep 1408 n12.

5 The words 'foreseeing ... astonish you' are lined through in the manuscript.

6 Cf Epp 1432A:10–11, 1437:189–90, 1477:11. Cf also Ep 1341A:1196–1215, 1645–1813, 1352:158–9; and Böcking II 332:47–333:3 (Brunfels' *Responsio*; see Ep 1405 introduction).

of Basel (MS G2.1.37.18), bears no indication of the addressee or the date. Allen's speculation that the letter might have been written c April 1524 (ie, at about the same time as Ep 1437) in response to Gerard Geldenhouwer's request for biographical information (Ep 1437:407–10) was never convincing, first, because Erasmus authorized Goclenius to communicate the desired information to Geldenhouwer in person (ibidem, lines 410–11), and second, because the letter was clearly written in response to the 'open and outrageous lies' of the adversary mentioned in line 1 rather than to a friendly request for biographical information. Nevertheless, there being no better conjecture at hand, the annotator decided to leave the letter where Allen had placed it, since that at least had the advantage of bringing it into conjunction with the *Compendium vitae* in Ep 1437. However, just as this volume was going to press, Erika Rummel discovered that the 'lies' in question are found in the *Apologia in eum librum quem ab anno Erasmus Roterodamus de confessione edidit* (Antwerp: S. Cocus, 21 March 1525) of 'Godefridus Ruysius Taxander,' the pseudonym of four Louvain theologians whose ringleader was Vincentius Theoderici (Ep 1196). Thus March 1525 is the *terminus post quem* for this letter. Erasmus first mentions Taxander's work in a letter of 28 April 1525 (Allen Ep 1571:66–8), and it seems likely that this letter was written at about the same time, ie, in the spring of 1525. It is thus out of place in this volume. However, since the trouble and cost of removing it at the last minute were prohibitive, it has been left where it is. It will appear again, with a new introduction and revised notes, at the appropriate place in volume 11.

... A man who is not afraid to tell such open and outrageous lies, and who may be refuted at any moment out of my own writings, which mean something quite different, will be capable of inventing anything. The old story of my changing my style of dress[1] he keeps on repeating with emphasis, adding plenty of falsehoods – the first of which is that Luther   5 never got quit of his monkish cowl, though Luther himself in that book dedicated to his father admits that he laid aside his monastic status while he was in Patmos.[2] Another is to call anyone an apostate who has changed his dress, although the word apostate is used by the orthodox of those who have abandoned the profession of the name of Christ. If one wants to distort   10

* * * * *

1436
1 See lines 119–29 below.
2 In the preface, dated 21 November 1521, to the *De votis monasticis; WA* 8 575–6. The treatise was written during Luther's confinement in the Wartburg, which he often called his 'Patmos' (as, for example, in the *Rationis Latominae confutatio* of 1521; ibidem 44:2).

the word apostate and apply it to monks, it would be better to use the word of those who pile up money, the fornicators and adulterers, the gluttons and greedyguts, who vilify their bishops and attack their own official superiors not only with scandal but with fisticuffs and poison; these are the men who break their vows. The least important thing about a monk is his habit. Such 15
is their everyday behaviour; but when a monk changes his style of dress or place of abode,[3] there are endless cries of 'Apostate!' – as though it were not actually the commonest thing among them for a man to abandon his habit and go off to the wars or wherever he pleases.

Then again, let us grant that canons living under a rule are monks, let 20
us grant that the man who has changed his form of dress can rightly be called an apostate; none of this in any case applies to me, for I never was a monk. It is voluntary, not enforced profession that makes the monk. Consequently, profession made before the age of puberty has no binding force, because will without judgment is worth no more than will which is not free. 25

Our guardians, looking for an easier way to get quit of our affairs, which they had managed so badly, determined somehow to drive us into a monastery. Perhaps they thought they would offer God a highly acceptable service if they had made two proselytes. With this in mind they bought us board and lodging with the brothers who are called Collationers;[4] for they 30
know how to break a boy's spirit, and it is here that monks pride themselves on finding young stock to continue the race, which will otherwise die out. When we were preparing to leave them, I was urged to stay in the same place. My answer was that, being of an age that did not yet know its own mind, I wanted to take no decisions about my way of life. When we had 35
returned to our own country[5] they again purchased a lodging for us in a similar community. I had already been suffering for more than a year from a quartan fever. The elder of our two guardians (the third had died of the plague) began seriously to look about for a permanent place for us. When I realized this, I asked my brother, who was three years older than I, whether 40
he was so minded, and whether he thought it a good idea to get involved in a way of life from which we could not possibly extricate ourselves if we changed our minds, though in what was left of our inheritance there still remained enough to keep us for some years at the university. He did not attempt to conceal that he acted as he did out of fear, and entirely approved 45
my idea, only on condition that I should speak to our guardians on behalf of

* * * * *

3 Erasmus defends himself against this charge in Ep 809:115–81.
4 See Ep 447:108.
5 Gouda, home of Pieter Winckel (Ep 1), the principal guardian

us both, for he dared not do so himself. 'I'll do it,' I said, 'provided you don't change your mind later and let me down.' And he swore he would be loyal.

Our guardians arrived. The elder opened with a long discourse on the trouble he had taken, and how it was only with the greatest difficulty that he   50
had secured an ideal situation for each of us; and he congratulated us on our great good fortune. And I, though I was a child scarcely out of my sixteenth year,[6] replied that we were grateful for the energy and zeal he had shown in doing so much without being asked. At the same time, I said, it did not seem to us a good idea to tie ourselves down to a form of life like that, before we   55
knew our own minds better and had a much clearer notion what the religious life really was. In the mean time we would devote ourselves for two or three years to liberal studies, and after that, at the proper time, would take advice about our way of life. At this point that educated and sensible man (for such he was thought to be), whose duty it was, if we were disposed to tie   60
ourselves down in too much of a hurry, to say the sort of things that would discourage us, took offence at a reply which was so far from childish, flew into a rage, and called me a rascal with no proper spirit, threatening to abandon us and leave us to find a livelihood for ourselves. 'From this moment,' he said, 'I renounce the undertaking I have given for your   65
boarding fees.' I replied that for my part I accepted his resignation of the trust; but that I had not lost my devotion to honourable studies, and was passionately anxious to learn; it would be time enough after that to take advice on the kind of life we wanted. He went away as angry as if he had been beaten black and blue. He then put forward a succession of other   70
people to drive us, when he saw we were likely to refuse, into the net.

For my part, being ruled by reason and not by my feelings, I was unable to change my mind. In the end my brother, who had always been my evil genius, surrendered and was dragged into the opposite camp; he abandoned me, his younger brother, and was beguiled into the net. It was   75
all right for him. He was physically strong, skilful in handling money, a powerful drinker, and pleasure-loving. In a word, in their society he was in heaven. From now on I, who was only a boy, in poor health and alone and lacking all experience of ordinary life (for I had always lived in a school), was daily belaboured with threats; nor was there any lack of people to piece out   80
the threats with blandishments. My brother, who had always managed our financial affairs by himself, carried off with him what little remained, being

* * * * *

6 This conflicts with Ep 447:167–8, 264, where Erasmus states that he had scarcely *entered* his sixteenth year. Allen suggested that perhaps *īgressus* should be read here for *egressus*.

much given to thieving anyway. To finish the story, I did not change my
opinion; I gave in, and entered a monastery.

There at first life was all smiles, and we were given our own way in   85
everything. The day came for assuming the sacred habit. I protested afresh,
and again my protests were rejected with more cruel threats and all hope of
livelihood was taken from me, should I change my dwelling-place. So I took
the habit, or rather, had it forcibly put upon me. Even now there were
blandishments to lure me on; and yet the miseries of that way of life began to   90
taint the air. The year was up for my profession, from which I had the
greatest possible aversion. At that stage they attacked me with every kind of
weapon, internal and external. Among them all what moved me most was
the disgrace, which they grossly exaggerated, if I were to lay aside my sacred
habit. They threatened me with immense dangers from the wrath of   95
Augustine himself, if I were to abandon a garment he held so dear, nor was
there any hope of help from my friends if I did anything so rash. Was not this
clearly an outrageous use of force against an adolescent shy by nature and
without experience, deprived of support of every kind and betrayed even by
his own brother? If this was not 'fear falling on the man of constant heart,'[7] it   100
was at least fear falling on a youth of considerable constancy. And so your
Erasmus became a canon. And in later days that Judas of a brother often
confessed the sin he had committed in pushing me into that trap; but when
he came to his senses, it was too late for me.

Once the halter was round my neck, the mysteries of that life began to   105
be revealed. Yet though I had no hope of making my escape from that kind
of life, yet secretly and against objections from the fathers I found time for
study as far as possible. And while in my heart I had never accepted this
kind of life, I endured it all for fear of scandal, which that time would have
been almost insuperable. This superstitious feeling had taken such deep   110
root in men's minds that a woman suffered a miscarriage because she had
seen a canon who was chaplain to a nunnery walking about in the
neighbourhood in a linen frock not covered by a black cloak. And an elderly
man seriously confessed to me that he was afraid, if he slept without the
protection of a linen frock, of being carried alive by the devil into hell.   115

Meanwhile an opportunity arose by chance, and none of my seeking,
and I was summoned to Brabant, and thence to the bishop of Cambrai.[8] In

* * * * *

7 Source unidentified
8 These words seem to imply that there was an intermediate stage between the
  monastery and employment by the bishop of Cambrai. But in Ep 447:496–7 and
  in the *Compendium vitae* (Ep 1437:339–44) Erasmus states that the invitation
  came from the bishop. The meaning here, as Allen suggests, may be that

this regard nothing was done without the authority of my superiors. I went
to Paris; nor did I change my habit, from a kind of pious respect for it, until
when I was in Italy I was compelled to change it, having twice been put by   120
my habit in peril of my life.[9] At first I concealed it, but did not lay it aside.
Later I secured permission from the pope to be free to wear it or not wear it.[10]
On returning to England I resumed it,[11] but was obliged to change again by
my friends. And so at length, as it seemed to be God's will that I should give
it up, and constant changing would have been even more objectionable, I   125
continued to dress as a priest. The rest I have set out clearly enough in a
letter to Servatius,[12] which certain people stole from him and made public,
though it was written to him alone, and in the first book in which I reply to
the calumnies of Lee.[13]

My first point is then that, if I had on occasion changed my style of   130
dress without papal authority, I should not be an apostate, for I have never
accepted this kind of life. Had I wholeheartedly accepted it and later
changed my life for good reasons, I should not be an apostate, unless
perhaps the supreme pontiff, who sets many people free from this serfdom,
is doing something that he has no power to do. Furthermore, when he says   135
that I am trying to persuade all monks to abandon their profession, I will
admit the truth of this if he can produce one single monk whom I have
encouraged to change his way of life. I on the other hand can produce a
certain number who were wavering, and I strengthened their resolve not to
do so. It is true, I am sorry for many of them; but as things are now, I can see   140
no less unhappiness waiting for them if they abandon their vows.

The facts being as I set them out in my letter, what object can they have
in so zealously ensuring that no one is ignorant of something that is already
very widely known? Do they wish to encourage more people to do without
due thought what I did lawfully and under compulsion? I cannot foresee any   145
other result. Personally, I have never condemned any form of life, but not
every form of life is suitable to just anybody. For me at least no way of life
was less suitable, whether one considers body or mind, than the one into
which I had been driven. Finally, let anyone who so chooses paint me falsely
as a young man determined to get free somehow or other, while I had never   150

* * * * *

Erasmus was summoned to Brabant, likely Brussels or Mechelen, before
learning that it was the bishop whose service he was to enter.

9 See Epp 296:185–202, 447:514–45.
10 See Ep 296:197n.
11 See Ep 296:202–18, 899:15–25.
12 Ep 296:181–218
13 The *Apologia qua respondet invectivis Lei* (1520); see Ferguson *Opuscula* 294–5.
   Cf Ep 1437:383–4.

wholeheartedly accepted my servitude, what sort of civilized behaviour is it
to publish this in print? – unless perhaps they are ready to approve if
someone publishes the things that are perpetrated among them every day.
This is like their pretence that they approve of confession among themselves, as though they have nothing to confess to a priest. I only hope their   155
misdeeds remain unknown at least to the outer world.

   We see the same common sense in his denial that there is any hope of
making our peace with Christ, if there are no celibates – as though all
celibates were chaste, and as though married people cannot make their
peace with God through prayer, and as though nuns and monks need no   160
one to intercede with God on their behalf. He accuses me of brutality,
though I have never mentioned anyone except under savage provocation;
he accuses me of a lust for revenge, though several people have attacked me
like madmen to whom I have not replied. He has doubts about my chastity,[14]
as though I had ever boasted of it or everything on their side was pure and   165
chaste. And here is this hangman ranting about prisons, whatever that
means, when I suppose by prison he means monastery. It is the writers of
these crazy pamphlets who are ripe for fetters, shackles, and prisons, not
those who win the approval of all men by their labours for the public good.
   But enough of this nonsense.   170

1437 / To Conradus Goclenius   Basel, 2 April [1524]

> First published in the *Vita Des. Erasmi* (Ep 1388 introduction), this letter was
> written to accompany the *Compendium vitae*, the autobiographical sketch that
> Erasmus wrote at the request of his close friend and confidant, Conradus
> Goclenius (Ep 1209), who was professor of Latin at the Collegium Trilingue.
> The year-date is indicated by the works mentioned in lines 406–7, 415–16.
>
>   The letter, with its lengthy denunciation of Erasmus' former friend Heinrich
> Eppendorf, is interesting in its own right, and so, of course, is the *Compendium
> vitae*. Allen, in fact, published the two separately, placing the *Compendium* in
> his first volume (46–52) along with other biographical material. But Erasmus
> embedded the *Compendium* in the letter: both begin with Greek headings
> admonishing that the contents be kept secret, and the last paragraph and a half
> of the *Compendium*, which suddenly revert to the first person, are actually a
> postscript to the letter (Allen appended them to his text of the letter). Because
> of its close relationship to Ep 447, the *Compendium*, minus the last one and a
> half epistolary paragraphs, has already been printed in CWE as an appendix to
> volume 4 (400–10). However, fidelity to the text of this letter as Erasmus wrote

* * * * *

14 Cf Epp 296:54–7, 1347:380–3.

it demands that the *Compendium* be included with it (lines 233–end). James K. McConica's textual annotations for CWE 4 have been reproduced here. For his general introduction to the *Compendium* and to the problems that it poses for scholars, see ibidem 400–3.

Read this in solitude and secretly[1]

Greeting. There remains the last act of this drama, and to play out my part in it I need a Pylades,[2] which means someone like you. Such is the confidence I have come to place in you, and I have no doubt at all that you will show the same spirit that you have always displayed hitherto. But on this subject the first thing needed is profound silence; you must reckon no one so close to you that you entrust him with this secret. I would have come myself, but it is a long journey and none too safe, and I think the bearer of this is reliable enough.[3]

Heinrich Eppendorf,[4] whom you know, a rascal born for every sort of chicanery and virulence, is stirring up fearful trouble for me here, though at first I accepted him into the inner circle of my friends, which he admits he found profitable. At any rate, as Petrus Mosellanus writes,[5] it was on a recommendation from me that Duke George first gave him 100 florins to complete his studies.[6] After many wanderings he came at length to Freiburg. There with wenching, drinking, and gaming he became hopelessly insolvent, and ran so deeply into debt that he still cannot go back there. He migrated to Basel and forced himself on my acquaintance,[7] staying for the time in a public lodging-house. No visitor came to see me here without his forcing his way in. When I went to Constance,[8] he forced himself on me unasked as a travelling-companion. He made this out to be pure friendship, but all the time he was plotting trouble. Even at that stage, in Johann Botzheim's house, where for my sake he was most hospitably entertained for several days, he secretly poured out some of his poison.[9]

* * * * *

1437
1 Greek in the original
2 Friend and confidant of Orestes, proverbial for his complete, uncompromising fidelity
3 Lieven Algoet (Ep 1373 n1); cf lines 157, 199–200, 416–17.
4 Epp 1283 n4, 1371, 1377
5 The letter is not extant. On Mosellanus, see Ep 1305.
6 Presumably Rhenish gold florins, worth about £24 3s 4d gros Flemish
7 Cf Ep 1283:16–19.
8 See Ep 1316 introduction.
9 Cf Allen Ep 1934:246–9.

And at this point I was warned by friends that from time to time he was   25
saying very unfriendly things about me.

Meanwhile Hutten arrived.[10] He had been encouraged by many
Lutherans to attack me in print;[11] but it was Eppendorf who supplied him
with a number of calumnies and caused Hutten in no time to lose all respect
for me; for Hutten had always treated me respectfully.[12] Some of these he   30
had picked up in our familiar intercourse, some he had imbibed in your part
of the world from the sad story of Alaard[13] and Paschasius,[14] which is very
familiar to you. This is the source of those designations 'priest and
theologian,' 'priest and scribe,'[15] and of the accusation that Otto[16] threatened Eppendorf could charge me with. But he is such a fool that, though   35
everyone here is well aware that he is the author of this drama, he yet
expressed surprise that anyone should suspect him, as one of Erasmus'
most devoted friends. Nor did he cease all the time from pouring out
remarks to many people which showed what his feelings really were. He
wished me alone to be ignorant of what was common knowledge. In the end   40
a ridiculous letter attacking me was circulated here,[17] though even so it
never reached me.

When Hutten had left here for Mulhouse,[18] whither Eppendorf had
accompanied him, he announced on his return that Hutten was writing
something, and pretended that this caused him great distress. His object in   45
so doing was to extract money from my friends[19] as the price of the book's
not coming out.[20] It was surprising to see the tricks with which he pursued
this in dealing with me, with Froben, with Bentinus;[21] Botzheim had even
been summoned by him from Constance with this in view.[22] Hutten

* * * * *

10 See Ep 1356 introduction.
11 Cf lines 73–4 below, Ep 1432:50–4. See also n34 below.
12 Cf *Spongia* ASD IX-1 130:190–2.
13 For Alaard, see Ep 433. Nothing is known of the 'sad story' referred to here.
14 Perhaps Jan van Paesschen (documented 1504–32), Carmelite and ally of
    Erasmus' enemy Nicolaas Baechem (Ep 1254 n6)
15 Titles attributed to Erasmus. The first is found in the title of Hutten's
    Expostulatio (Ep 1356 n9); the second in the heading of Ep 1406.
16 Brunfels; see Ep 1406:241–9.
17 Possibly the *Iudicium Erasmi Alberi de Spongia* (Ep 1466 n19), which was not
    printed until later but had circulated in manuscript
18 See Ep 1331 n24.
19 See Ep 1383 n4.
20 Hutten's *Expostulatio* (Ep 1356 n9)
21 Ep 1433 n2
22 This is the only evidence that Botzheim (Ep 1285) visited Basel in the spring of
    1523.

meanwhile had sent a copy of his letter;[23] but it was already circulating in   50
several copies. I myself, reckoning (as proved to be the case) that if he
extorted the money, an even more poisonous book would be published
afterwards, warned my friends not to give him anything. They were pitifully
short of money, both of them, as men of that sort often are. They were both
at their last gasp. Hutten consequently was ordered to leave. In Mulhouse   55
he was an object of such universal hatred that unless he left, the citizens
were threatening to break into the Augustinian convent in which he was
hiding. With the support of the town clerk he was let out secretly in the
middle of the night and took refuge in Zürich,[24] a city deeply devoted to
Zwingli's teaching – which is now condemned by Luther,[25] who belatedly   60
remembers the moderation I have recommended so often.[26] There he lay
hidden for a few days, and some days later went to live outside the city with
a certain priest.[27] Everywhere he took money off his friends. At length he
moved to an island in the lake of Zürich,[28] where he died.[29] But before he
died, the Hutten letter was being sent far afield, even into Germany,   65
because they could not find a printer. Nor would they have found one, had
not that rogue Eppendorf, unable to live here any longer because of his debts
and the universal suspicion of him, migrated to Strasbourg on the pretext of
going to the baths at Baden. There with the greatest difficulty he persuaded
a printer that there was nothing libellous in it. And that fellow Schott[30] was   70

* * * * *

23 Not extant. It was a foretaste of the *Expostulatio*, sent through Eppendorf in
   reply to Ep 1356; see ASD IX-1 126:80–7.
24 Ep 1376 n21.
25 This reference is puzzling. As recently as 1 February Luther had expressed his
   unqualified delight at the progress of the Reformation in Zürich (WA-Br III
   241:24) and at this point he had no apparent reason to suspect Zwingli of
   heterodoxy of any sort. Only about five months later, in the autumn of 1524,
   did Luther become aware of Zwingli's denial of the real presence in the
   Eucharist, the issue that would produce several years of bitter controversy
   between them; ibidem 331, 373, 397. So it is not clear what, if anything, was
   behind Erasmus' statement here. It might have had something to do with the
   Wittenbergers' disapproval of the campaign against images in Zürich; cf Ep
   1496 n39.
26 See Ep 980:45.
27 Perhaps Konrad Schmid, commander of the order of St John at Küsnacht, as
   Allen suggests; perhaps Hans Klarer, the priest-physician with whom Hutten
   stayed on the island of Ufenau in the weeks before his death; or possibly
   Johann Jakob Russinger, abbot of Pfäfers. See CEBR sv 'Konrad Schmid.'
28 Ufenau
29 Ep 1388 n12
30 See Epp 1429, 1477.

pitifully jealous of Froben, as they nearly all are. With the result that my friendship with Froben has made me highly unpopular.

At length that mischief-maker's *Expostulatio* came out, packed with lies which had been suggested to him by every Lutheran he came across. I had soon got ready a reply,[31] but in such secrecy that neither Froben nor Beatus[32]   75 knew of it. And I had almost decided to suppress it; but at their instigation I published it. While in the mean time Hutten and I were constantly exchanging letters,[33] one arrived which made Eppendorf's treachery quite clear. Suffering as he did from a load of suspicion, Eppendorf asked Hutten, who was then in Zürich, for a letter[34] confirming that Eppendorf had always   80 dissuaded him from attacking me. But he wrote with such a lack of enthusiasm that the letter did him more harm than good. Meanwhile Eppendorf was suborning people to send me forged letters under false names, which he knew would make me suspect what he was up to, without giving me any handle to complain to him.   85

As for me, I said nothing about all this, and treated him civilly in my *Spongia* when it was necessary to mention him.[35] I wrote that he was a kinsman of Hutten;[36] for he had convinced me of that himself. Petrus Mosellanus however, after reading the *Spongia*, wrote to me, 'How can he be a kinsman, when it is well known that he is a man of humble origin?'[37] On   90 the other hand our half-witted hero was offended because he was described as only an Achates.[38] After the *Spongia* appeared he wrote a letter of protest,[39] pretending great devotion all the time though he was up to his accursed tricks. To show you how great a crook the man is, as a result of a recommendation from me he was given in Basel fifty gold pieces.[40] The   95

* * * * *

31 The *Spongia* (Epp 1378, 1389)
32 Beatus Rhenanus (Ep 327)
33 See Ep 1356 introduction for traces of these letters.
34 A sentence from this letter is found in the *Spongia* (ASD IX-1 202:898–9): 'Nemo instigat Huttenum, nec ille sustinet a quoquam instigari / No one incites Hutten, nor does he permit himself to be incited by anyone.' The letter would doubtless have been written in July 1523; cf Ep 1376 n21.
35 ASD IX-1 123:15–124:29, 126:114–16
36 Ibidem 126:115–16, where Eppendorf is described as *generosus* (of noble birth) and *cognatus* (kinsman)
37 See n5 above. Mosellanus' letter is not extant.
38 ASD IX-1 132:233–4, 163:997. Achates was a companion and friend of Aeneas. Virgil called him *fidus Achates* (*Aeneid* 1.188), so that his fidelity became proverbial.
39 Not extant
40 Probably Rhenish gold florins again, worth about £12 1s 8d gros Flemish

duke[41] was said to have sent me a present worthy of a king,[42] but it never reached me, and I suspected that Eppendorf had intercepted it.[43] For he pretended that his servant had died on a journey,[44] this being his intended excuse, in case I should discover the precise facts; but this one thing I do know, that he is the greatest rascal. He has his spies everywhere under oath,   100
so that nothing can happen without his knowledge.

Melanchthon's judgments on Hutten and Eppendorf[45] I have sent to Nicolaas van 's Hertogenbosch.[46] Mind you keep yourself untouched by any contact with this faction. I fear a bloody outcome. If I had known the true nature of the Germans and their endless perfidy,[47] I should have gone to live   105
among the Turks rather than here. Of Capito[48] I have lively suspicions that he was taken in by Eppendorf's tricks and told him my secrets.[49] The way he makes excuses increases my suspicions. This was the policy of Luther's followers, to frighten me off with threats from attacking Luther in print; that was a story spread by Johannes Fabri.[50] But as it is, Luther writes against   110
himself,[51] seeing things go the way he had not expected, and a tribe arising of men who are not evangelicals but diabolicals, which means the death of all liberal studies.

But I have already said more than enough on these topics. I am resolved to move somewhere from here. I am invited to France,[52] with   115
surprising enthusiasm and great promises; but I am afraid of this spring,[53] for I fear its outcome will be bloodshed and disaster for the French; the emperor's spirit is so implacable, and the motto *Plus ultra*[54] has taken such

* * * * *

41 Ie, George of Saxony (Ep 1283)
42 There appears to be no other trace of this present. For other gifts of Duke George to Erasmus, see Ep 1122:12–14 and Allen Epp 1691:26–7.
43 See Ep 1313 introduction.
44 Cf Ep 1325:6–7.
45 See Ep 1429 n3, and cf line 185 below.
46 Ie, Nicolaas van Broeckhoven (Ep 1299 n23)
47 See Ep 1388 n21.
48 Ep 1374 marks the beginning of Capito's breach with Erasmus, though as recently as Ep 1429:24–5 Erasmus still spoke of him with respect. The further development of the breach is evident in Epp 1477B, 1485, and 1496.
49 See Ep 1496:120–5.
50 Apparently in consequence of the news that Erasmus was working on the *De libero arbitrio* (Ep 1397:15–16); cf Epp 1341A:1114–17.
51 Cf Ep 1432:59–61 and see Ep 1429 n3.
52 See Ep 1434:3–25.
53 See Ep 1430 n2.
54 *Plus ultra* or *Plus oultre*, ie, 'Far beyond [the usual limits]' was the proud motto that young Prince Charles had adopted at the outset of his personal rule as duke of Burgundy.

deep root in him. The pope is my supporter, and so are those round the pope
who have most power. But I would rather leave the arena to the gladiators.   120
Nor do I see how I could be safe where Aleandro rules,[55] however much he
may conceal it. I should like to spend a winter in Padua and Venice. But I
should be summoned from there to Rome. I shall stay on here for eight days
and then make up my mind. Meanwhile it will become clear which way
things are going.   125

Now, since I am in peril of my life from time to time,[56] it remains for me
to commend to you, as the most reliable of my friends, the thing I hold most
dear, which is my posthumous reputation, for I suspect that it will have to
face a lot of calumny. I therefore send you a short account of my whole life,
and an Iliad of ills it truly is,[57] for never was any creature born more unhappy   130
than I. Some people perhaps will make many additions;[58] that will be quite
in order. But if anything should happen to me in the way of mortality, I want
you to have 400 gold florins; 300 Rhenish florins[59] to go to Jacobus Ceratinus;[60]
130 philippics to Melchior Vianden;[61] 50 gold florins and 46 and a half
Rhenish to Cornelis Schrijver,[62] whom I suspect to be in need though he   135
is a man who deserved a better position. About the rest, the vessels and the

* * * * *

55 In August 1522 Aleandro (Ep 1256 n11) had accompanied Adrian vi from Spain
  to Rome: see J. Paquier *Jérôme Aléandre* (Paris 1900) 289. Adrian's successor,
  Clement vii (elected 19 November 1523), was an old patron of Aleandro's who
  in August 1524 made him archbishop of Brindisi.
56 From his recurring attacks of the stone; Ep 1426:16–19
57 *Adagia* i iii 26
58 Erasmus seems to have expected that his terse *Compendium vitae* would be used
  by others as the basis for a formal biography, like those he had composed for
  More (Ep 999) and for Vitrier and Colet (Ep 1211); cf lines 407–12 below. Beatus
  Rhenanus fulfilled this expectation; see Allen i 52–71.
59 The '400 gold florins' and the '300 Rhenish florins' are presumably both
  Rhenish gold florins, worth £96 13s 4d and £72 10s 0d gros Flemish (or £68 6s 8d
  and £51 5s 0d sterling), respectively.
60 Jacobus Ceratinus (Ep 622:34n), who had been an unsuccessful candidate for
  the chairs of both Greek and Latin at the Collegium Trilingue, was now in
  Brussels tutoring the children of Gilles de Busleyden; see Ep 1461:4.
61 On Vianden, see Ep 1427. The philippics would be the older Burgundian-
  Hapsburg St Philip florin (philippus), as struck from 1500 to 1520/1, theoretically with 2.19 g fine gold (vs 2.53 g in the Rhenish florin). In 1524, by relative gold
  contents, this sum should have been worth about £29 7s 0d gros Flemish. See
  CWE 1 318, 321; CWE 8 348–50.
62 On Schrijver, see Ep 1299 n24. These two sums are presumably both expressed
  in terms of Rhenish gold florins, worth £12 1s 8d and £11 4s 9d gros Flemish,
  respectively.

rings,[63] I have not yet made up my mind, but will write shortly. All this you must keep to yourself and not pass on to any mortal man, for fear the man you entrust it to may have a friend whom he may trust as fully as he has himself been trusted, and so the thing gets known to more still. This would   140
have two disadvantages. For one thing my old friends would pounce upon the money;[64] they are a greedy lot. And then, should I need this money myself before my death (and it may perhaps be so, for I see extraordinary changes), this would be a great disappointment to those whose hopes would be frustrated. As it is, it will be safer, and the windfall will be all the   145
more welcome, if it comes to them unexpectedly. Yet as a defence against the harpies, if they manage to sniff the prey, I will protect you with a document which you can produce after my death if need be. Yet it shall have no force until after my death. You see what confidence I repose in you; for you could deceive me. But I fear nothing of the kind.   150

You will ask what services I demand from you all. I will not burden you with psalters[65] and anniversaries;[66] but I do particularly ask that you should divide up my works among yourselves, read through everything I have written, reduce it to order and correct it, and entrust it to Froben to be printed.[67] I knew that you yourself would gladly do this for me as part of   155
your affection for me. I would like you to entrust all the ducats to my man Lieven,[68] provided you think that he can get here safely; he can sew them into his belt, as Hilarius does.[69] If anything happens to you during my lifetime (heaven send this is not a bad omen), you will tear up the document,

* * * * *

63 An inventory of Erasmus' property of this sort, dated 10 April 1534, is preserved in the Öffentliche Bibliothek of the University of Basel (MS C.VIa.71) and was printed by L. Sieber in 1891 (see Ep 1393 n3).

64 The 'old friends' were the Augustinians at Steyn. Although Leo x had given him a dispensation to dress as a secular priest and to live outside the houses of the Augustinian canons, Erasmus was still a member of the order (Ep 517:42–6) and, as such, not entitled to make a will. Thus all his possessions still belonged, strictly speaking, to the order. A dispensation from Clement VII in 1525 (Ep 1588), empowering him to make a will, remedied this situation.

65 A reference to the practice of reciting the psalter one or more times in memory of a deceased person

66 Anniversary masses

67 Later in the year Erasmus included a detailed plan for such a project in the second edition of the Catalogus lucubrationum; see Ep 1341A:1500–1639. In his will of 22 January 1527 he made definite provision for the project; see Allen VI, appendix XIX, 504–6.

68 The Venetian gold coins (even though they were now called zecchini in Venice itself); cf CWE 1 314, 338–9; Ep 1295 n1. On Lieven, see n3 above.

69 Bertholf (Ep 1384 n31)

and hand over the money to Dorp[70] or Gilles de Busleyden[71] or my host 160
Maarten,[72] or any friend you have who is safer than they are. I will not urge
you, my dear Goclenius, to respond to this truly paternal affection for you,
for you have always shown me already the affection of a son. As for the
things I shall leave elsewhere, you shall learn from other sources what I have
decided. For in these too I shall not forget you, knowing that whatever this 165
kindness amounts will be bestowed on a man who will remember and be
grateful.

I have given instructions that you should pay 25 gold florins[73] out of my
money to Ceratinus.[74] If that has been done, I will make up Schrijver's
amount out of the money that is in Antwerp. I will write to Pieter Gillis[75] to 170
pay you those twenty-five, if you have already paid them over to Ceratinus;
if you have not done so, let him pay them, or you can pay them from Pieter
Gillis' money.

I should like you to give some young man the job of reading through
my *Adagia* in the latest edition[76] and comparing it with the last but one.[77] 175
Michael Bentinus introduced a lot of mistakes by taking so much trouble. οἴῳ
'alone' he always turned into οἴῳ,[78] and he collated some passages I had
cited from Homer in Greek with the Homer printed by Aldus, and the same
for the Aldine Cicero, though the Aldine editions are highly corrupt. I
should like the passages which the young man marked to be examined by 180
you when you have the time.

As for my own position, I can tell you, it is fairly confused. I have to
cope here with desperate people – real furies they are, since Hutten first
broke the ice with his mad attacks on me. Luther condemns what has

* * * * *

70 Maarten van Dorp, the Louvain theologian (Ep 1266 n2); cf lines 206, 403 below.
71 Gilles (Ep 686) was the brother of Erasmus' friend, Jérôme de Busleyden,
   founder of the Collegium Trilingue.
72 Maarten Davidts, a canon of Brussels with whom Erasmus usually lodged
   when in that city; see Ep 532:35.
73 Presumably Rhenish gold florins, a sum then worth just over £6 gros Flemish
   or about £4 5s sterling
74 This payment to Ceratinus (n60 above) was doubtless for his work on the new
   edition of Craston's Greek dictionary for the Froben press; see Ep 1460.
75 Ep 184
76 January 1523
77 The edition of October 1520, which had been corrected by Michael Bentinus;
   see Ep 1433 n2.
78 In *Adagia* II iii 53, where Homer *Odyssey* 10.494–5 is quoted. In the Froben
   edition of 1517/18, οἴῳ is given correctly, but Bentinus' lapse in the edition
   of October 1520 is reproduced in all subsequent editions down to 1540.

happened, but Melanchthon has a remarkable hatred for Hutten.[79] And   185
those blockheads boast of it as a splendid achievement.[80] Buschius was
getting ready to print an attack of some sort on me;[81] but Melanchthon
restrained him. If I go to Italy, I shall be pursued with hundreds of
pamphlets by crazy evangelicals, crying that the spoils have corrupted me
and I have betrayed the gospel,[82] when what they call the gospel I have   190
never professed. If I go to France, which has a great desire to see me, they
will accuse me of taking refuge with the emperor's enemy;[83] and I detect a
whiff of Lutherizing in the king's court.[84] In Brabant you know what
monsters have now been entrusted with the sword.[85] You shall know
shortly what I have decided. The king sent me an official letter to say that he   195
has it in mind to found a new college of the three tongues in Paris;[86] he
offered me the headship of it, with an enormous salary.[87] If I do make my
way to France, and have an opportunity of recommending you, I will let you
know. And you meanwhile must write and tell me by Lieven how you feel
about France. In the mean time, while Lieven is away in England,[88] you   200
must write me three lines by another hand to say if he faithfully delivered
the letter.

In writing letters you will be extremely careful, for everything is
intercepted,[89] and Eppendorf has his Corycaeans[90] everywhere. But you
must conceal what I have written about him, and not let it out except among   205
special friends. Dorp, it seems, is hesitating.[91] Something monstrous is
brewing among the theologians, and he is a coward by nature. I have written

* * * * *

79 See n45 above.
80 Presumably the 'desperate people' who rejoiced in the 'achievement' of
   Hutten's attack on Erasmus
81 Erasmus heard and believed all kinds of rumours about Buschius' intentions in
   this period; see Ep 1383 n21.
82 See Ep 1435 n6.
83 See Ep 1408 n12.
84 For examples of reformist sentiment at the French court under the patronage of
   the king's sister, Margaret of Angoulême, see Ep 1407 nn22, 33.
85 See Ep 1408 n10.
86 Not extant
87 See Ep 1434:18–25.
88 See Epp 1430:24–5, 1452:51–2.
89 See n43 above.
90 Ie, spies; Adagia I ii 44
91 Erasmus seems temporarily to have suspected Dorp (n70 above) of wavering in
   his loyalty; cf Allen Ep 1545:36–8.

to the dean and to Gilles de Busleyden[92] to recommend you. Karl Harst[93] is
living with me in place of my servant, for he seems to be a faithful friend.
Nor do I see how he can extricate himself from the labyrinth of marriage, as I   210
see the case. Hilarius I like particularly. Hovius[94] is living in Rome, and has
now at last grown fond of me. While he was here his stubborn ways almost
drove me mad. Nor was Lieven much easier to live with; but both of them
profited greatly from their time with me. The name of Erasmus is the only
thing that keeps Hovius going in Rome. Lieven made splendid progress, in   215
knowledge rather than in character.[95] But I shall do what I can for him,
though I should not wish him to know anything about all this, nor indeed
any mortal except us two. I have no doubts of your honesty; but in case the
unexpected happens, it will be a good plan to send a formal document by
Lieven, in which you go on record that the document I spoke of about   220
distributing the money is invalid during my lifetime, and was invented for
some definite reasons.

　　　After I had written this, Froben delivered two letters from you.[96] I
laughed over our friend Baechem;[97] how he does play the fool! I have not yet
succeeded in hearing from you whether you received the letter[98] I sent by   225
Antonius the Minorite,[99] I began to have my suspicions of him, after he told
me that he wanted to visit Paschasius.[100] Do not write unadvisedly by
anyone. For Eppendorf is in Strasbourg, and intercepts all the letters by
means of his Corycaeans.[101] He has a natural gift for all sorts of crime.
Farewell.   230
　　　Basel, the Saturday after Easter

A BRIEF ACCOUNT OF THE LIFE OF ERASMUS OF ROTTERDAM,
MENTIONED BY HIMSELF IN THE PRECEDING LETTER
The life to be kept secret[102]   235
Born in Rotterdam on the eve of SS Simon and Jude.[103] Reckons he is about

　　　　* * * * *

92 Ep 1435 is the letter to the dean. The letter to Busleyden (n71 above) is not
　　extant, but the answer, Ep 1461, gives some indication of its content.
93 Ep 1215
94 See Epp 1387 n3 and 1424:8.
95 Cf Ep 1470:40–2.
96 Not extant
97 Ep 1254 n6
98 Ep 1388
99 Ep 1388 n20
100 See n14 above.
101 See n90 above.
102 This line of the heading is in Greek.
103 Evidently during the night of 27–8 October; he celebrated his birthday on 28
　　October.

fifty-seven years of age.[104] His mother's name was Margaret, her father a physician named Pieter. She was from Septimontium, commonly known as Zevenbergen, and he saw two of her brothers at Dordrecht who were nearly ninety years old.[105] His father's name was Gerard. He lay with Margaret   240
secretly, in the expectation of marrying her.[106] Some say they were already betrothed. This was received with indignation by Gerard's parents and his brothers. Gerard's father was called Elias and his mother Catherine; both lived to a very great age, Catherine till she was nearly ninety-five. There were ten brothers, but no sister, born of the same parents, all of them   245
married. Gerard was the youngest but one. All agreed that out of so large a family one should be consecrated to God. You know how old men feel. And his brothers wished to have no reduction in their own patrimony, but someone with whom they could always be sure of a dinner. Gerard, finding himself entirely debarred by general consent from matrimony, did what   250
men in despair often do: he ran away, and on his journey sent a letter to his parents and brothers, with two clasped hands on it, and the legend 'Farewell, I shall never see you more.'

Meanwhile the woman he had hoped to marry was left expecting a child. The boy was brought up by his grandmother. Gerard made his way to   255
Rome. There he earned enough to live on as a copyist, for the art of printing as yet did not exist. He wrote a very expert hand. And he lived as young men will. Later he turned his mind to honourable studies. Of Greek and Latin he had a good knowledge. In the law too he was more than commonly proficient. Rome in those days was wonderfully blessed with learned men.   260
He heard Guarino lecture.[107] All the classical authors he had copied with his own hand. His parents, when they learned he was in Rome, wrote to him that the girl[108] he hoped to marry was now dead. Supposing this to be true, in his grief he became a priest, and devoted his whole mind to religion. On

* * * * *

104 On the much-discussed issue of Erasmus' year of birth see R.R. Post 'Quelques précisions sur l'année de la naissance d'Erasme (1469) et sur son éducation' *Bibliothèque d'humanisme et renaissance* 26 (1964) 489–509 and Epp 531:410, 548:5n.
105 Perhaps in 1498; cf Ep 76:19.
106 *spe conjugii*; the theory that Erasmus' father was already a priest cannot be reconciled with this statement. If, however, there was an obstacle of affinity, that obstacle might have been removed by dispensation, a procedure that would have required, in all probability, the cooperation locally of both families. Cf Epp 446, 447, and 517 introductions.
107 Guarino Guarini of Verona (Ep 23:78n) had a younger brother teaching at Ferrara.
108 *Puella*; cf *vidua* in Ep 187A.

returning home, he discovered this was a fraud. But she was never   265
afterwards willing to marry, nor did he ever touch her.

For the boy he arranged to provide a liberal education, and when he
was scarcely more than four years old he sent him to an elementary
school.[109] In his early years the child made very little progress in those
tedious rudiments,[110] for which he had no natural gift. In his ninth year[111] he   270
sent him to Deventer;[112] his mother went with him as guardian and guide of
his tender years. The school there was at that time in a state of barbarism (a
standard text was the *Pater meus*;[113] they were forced to learn the paradigms,
the textbooks being Eberhard[114] and John of Garland[115]), except that
Alexander Hegius[116] and Synthen[117] had begun to introduce something of a   275
higher standard as literature. At length his playmates, of whom the older
ones were in Synthen's class, gave him his first taste of better teaching, and
later he sometimes heard Hegius, but only on high days when he lectured to

* * * * *

109 A school attached to St John's Church at Gouda; cf Ep 1 introduction; Post
    'Quelques précisions ...' 495–6.
110 These studies 'in litteris inamoenis' were apparently in the Dutch vernacular;
    classical studies at Louvain were 'literae amoeniores.'
111 Allen, accepting 1466 as Erasmus' birth-date, placed this arrival in 1475; Post,
    arguing for 1469 as the year of birth, dates the beginning of the Deventer
    schooling in 1478 ('Quelques précisions ...' 497–8, 506).
112 According to Beatus Rhenanus, Erasmus was a chorister in the chapter school
    at Utrecht between his schooling at Gouda and his arrival at Deventer. He
    would have been there at the same time as the famous organist and composer
    Jacob Obrecht; cf Allen I 56 and note; Post 'Quelques précisions ...' 496.
113 According to F.M. Nichols, this is a reference to a set of paradigms (ie 'a
    concord set') for declension in Latin grammar (see Allen I 48:34n).
114 Eberhard of Béthune, a twelfth-century grammarian, author of *Graecismus*, a
    Latin grammar in verse; cf Ep 26:100n.
115 (c 1195–c 1272) An Englishman who taught in Paris and whose *Dictionarius*,
    Compendium grammaticae, and *Accentuarium* became standard works in the
    Middle Ages.
116 Alexander Hegius, rector of the school at Deventer 1483–98; cf Ep 23:59n.
    Erasmus could not have known him there for long; cf Post 'Quelques
    précisions ...' 498.
117 Jan Synthen, born in Delden in the east Netherlands (d 1498). He wrote a
    commentary on the *Doctrinale* of Alexander de Villa Dei which was published
    at Deventer in 1488 and again in 1500 (NK 2276), 1501 (NK 70) and 1503 (NK 2278).
    I am indebted to E.J.M. van Eijl for pointing this out. From the account here it
    would seem likely that he taught only in the first and second forms, given over
    to philosophy. Boys in the third form would be considered ready for
    university. Cf Post 'Quelques précisions ...' 501–2; J.D. Tracy 'Bemerkungen
    zur Jugend des Erasmus' *Basler Zeitschrift für Geschichte und Altertumskunde* 72
    (1972) 227–8.

the whole school. Here he reached the third form; then the plague, which
was raging there, carried off his mother,[118] leaving her son now in his   280
thirteenth year. As the plague grew daily more and more severe, the whole
house in which he lived was deserted, and he returned to his native place.
Gerard when he heard the sad news fell ill, and shortly afterwards died.
Both were not much over forty. He set up three guardians,[119] whom he
thought most reliable. Of these the chief was Pieter Winckel, at that time   285
master of the school at Gouda. He left a moderate estate, had his guardians
managed it in good faith. And so the boy was removed to 's Hertogenbosch,[120] being now old enough for the university. But they were afraid of a
university, for they had already decided to bring up the boy for the life of a
religious.   290

There he spent, or rather, wasted about three years in a house of the
Brethren, as they call them, in which Romboldus was then teaching.[121] This
sort of men now spreads widely through the world, though it is disastrous
for gifted minds and a mere nursery of monks. Romboldus, who was much
struck by the boy's gifts, began to work on him to join his flock. The boy   295
pleaded the ignorance of his youth. At this point there was an outbreak of
plague; and after suffering for a long time from a quartan fever, he returned
to his guardians, having by now also acquired some fluency of style derived
from a few good authors. One of the guardians had succumbed to the
plague; the other two, who had not managed his affairs very skilfully, began   300
to treat with him about the monastic life. The poor youth, who was weak
from the fever which had held him for more than a year, felt no dislike of

* * * * *

118 There was a severe epidemic of plague at Deventer in 1483. From this point to
    'canonical habit' (line 346) the text is adapted from Ep 447, a few passages being
    almost word for word. There are some additions, however.
119 Cf Ep 1 introduction. The chief was Pieter Winckel, master of the school at
    Gouda. The first surviving letter in Erasmus' correspondence was written to
    Winckel evidently in the summer of 1484, shortly after the death of the boys'
    father.
120 Also known as Bois-le-Duc. In reference to speculation about the possibly
    profound influence of the Brethren of the Common Life on Erasmus, it may be
    noted that this is the only period when he is known to have lived in one of their
    hospices, for perhaps two full years. The boarders would have taken most of
    their classes at the municipal school of St John; Erasmus was quite likely by this
    time too advanced in his Latin studies to do so, a circumstance that would
    certainly have added to his boredom and resentment. See R.R. Post 'Studien
    over de Broeders van het Gemene leven' *Nederlandsche Historiebladen* 2 (1939)
    150–1, and Edmund Colledge OSA 'Erasmus, the Brethren of the Common Life,
    and the Devotio moderna' *Erasmus in English* 7 (1975) 2–4.
121 Romboldus is otherwise unknown.

religion, but he did dislike a monastery. They therefore allowed him a day to think it over. All this time the guardian put up people to tempt and threaten him and bring pressure to bear on his innocent mind; and in the mean while   305 he had found a place in a monastery of regular canons, as they are commonly called, in a house near Delft, called Sion, which is the chief house of that chapter.[122] When the day arrived on which he had to answer, the youth answered sensibly, that he did not yet know what the world was, or what a monastery was, or what he was himself; and so it seemed, he said, a   310 better plan that he should still spend some years attending lectures, until he might know his own mind better. When he saw the young man persist in this, Pieter[123] suddenly lost his temper. 'I see,' he said; 'I have wasted my labour in securing you a place like that with so much entreaty. You are a worthless fellow, and have a spirit of perversity in you. I resign my office as   315 your guardian. You can fend for yourself.' The youth replied that he accepted his resignation, being now of an age when guardians were no longer necessary. When the man saw that threats got him nowhere, he suborned his brother, who was also one of the trustees, and a man of business. He set to work with blandishments, and was supported on every   320 hand by those who had put him up to it. The boy had a companion,[124] who

* * * * *

122 The congregation of which Sion was the head included the priory of Steyn (line 324). When Erasmus entered the house at Steyn his older brother (by three years) Pieter, whose existence is not acknowledged in the *Compendium vitae*, was already a monk at Sion. Cf Ep 3 (to Pieter Gerard) introduction and n124 below.

123 Winckel; cf n119 above.

124 The only guarded reference in the *Compendium vitae* to his older brother Pieter; cf n122. The author's reticence about the existence of his brother is regarded by some as a serious objection to accepting the authenticity of the *Compendium vitae*; see for example Roland Crahay 'Recherches sur le compendium vitae attribué à Erasme' *Humanisme et Renaissance* 6 (1939) 137–8. Allen suggests reasons for supposing that Erasmus himself would have wished to suppress his brother's part in his early story; cf Allen I 577. I would add that even if Pieter were still alive there is no evident reason why Erasmus should have wished his brother's name to appear in this account, where it could only have brought embarrassment, even if Erasmus' attitude to their early choice of vocation had been by this time more sympathetic. It should be noticed also that since Pieter was a professed religious (n122), their common defect of birth would have involved him in the same canonical difficulties faced by Erasmus if Pieter had been promoted to any prelacy like that of abbot. In appraising the tone of this account it must be remembered (as with Ep 447) that Erasmus' purpose was less to give a full and impartial history of his early years than to justify his dispensation with the argument that his decision to take vows was neither free nor informed.

betrayed his friend, and the fever still lay hard on him; but even so, a
monastery had no appeal, until by some chance he visited a house of the
same order at Emmaus, or Steyn, near Gouda.[125] There he found one
Cornelis,[126] who had been a friend of his and shared a room with him at   325
Deventer. This man had not yet taken orders; he had visited Italy, but had
returned without learning much. With an eye to his own advantage he
began to draw a most eloquent picture of a very saintly way of life, with
plenty of books, leisure, tranquillity, and a society like that of angels,
everything you can think of. The young man was drawn to his old   330
companion by fond memories of boyhood; he was lured on by some people
and driven forward by others; the fever lay heavy on him. So he chose this
place, being disgusted with the other, and of the moment all was made
pleasant for him, until he should take the habit. Meanwhile, young as he
was, he realized how far the place was from true religion; and yet he inspired   335
the whole community to study harder. Though he made preparations to
leave before his profession,[127] he was restrained partly by natural shyness,
partly by threats, and partly by necessity.

He made his profession. At length he had an opportunity of becoming
known to Hendrik van Bergen,[128] the bishop of Cambrai. The bishop was   340
hoping for a cardinal's hat, and would have had one, had he not been short
of ready money. For the purpose of this journey he needed a good Latin
scholar. So our man was sent for by him, with authorization from the bishop
of Utrecht,[129] which was sufficient by itself, but he also secured the approval
of the prior and of the general of the order. He joined the bishop's household   345
but none the less still wore his canonical habit. When the bishop had lost his
hope of a hat, and perceived that the young man's devotion to them all left
something to be desired, he arranged that he should go to Paris to study. He
was promised an annual subvention, but nothing was ever sent. Great men
are like that. There in the Collège de Montaigu,[130] as a result of rotten eggs   350

* * * * *

125 The priory had been founded in 1419 and was situated within a mile of Gouda
     in the parish of Haastrecht. It was dedicated to St Gregory, but from its
     nearness to Gouda it was known as Emmaus. In 1549 the monastery burned to
     the ground and the site was acquired by the town council of Gouda; it is now
     occupied by a farmhouse; cf Allen I 583.
126 Possibly Cornelis Gerard, who was ordained to a different house in the same
     congregation but who seems to have moved about; cf Allen I 92.
127 In 1488
128 See Ep 446 introduction.
129 David of Burgundy, illegitimate son of Duke Philip the Good (d 1467), bishop
     first of Thérouanne, then of Utrecht
130 Cf Ep 43 introduction.

and infected lodgings, he contracted an illness, a morbid influence on a
constitution until then quite free from taint. So he returned to the bishop.[131]
His reception was complimentary. He recovered his health at Bergen. He
revisited Holland with the intention of remaining with his own people. But
on their unsought encouragement he went back to Paris. There with no   355
patron to support him it was a question of survival rather than study; and as
the plague was continuous there for many years, he was obliged to return
every year to his native country. Theology repelled him, for he felt himself
not disposed to undermine all its foundations with the prospect of being
branded as a heretic. At length, when the plague continued for a whole year,   360
he was compelled to move to Louvain.[132] He had previously visited England
to oblige Mountjoy,[133] who was at that time his pupil and later his Maecenas,
though more of a friend than a benefactor. In those days he won the good
opinion of all men of standing in England, particularly because, although
robbed on the coast at Dover,[134] he not only sought no revenge but   365
published a short work not long after in praise of the king of England and the
whole country.[135] At length he was invited with generous offers to return
from France to England, and it was at that time that he secured the
friendship of the archbishop of Canterbury.[136] When the offers did not
materialize, he set off for Italy, which he had always had a great desire to   370
visit. He spent a little more than a year in Bologna,[137] his life being already at
its turning-point, for he was now about forty. Then he moved to Venice, and
published his *Adagia*; from there to Padua, where he spent the winter;
thereafter to Rome, where a substantial and favourable reputation had
preceded him. Raffaele the cardinal of San Giorgio had a special feeling for   375
him. Nor would he have failed to secure a lucrative position, had he not been
summoned back to England on the death of Henry VII and accession of
Henry VIII by letters from friends, full of generous promises. In England he
had decided to spend the rest of his life; but as these promises were no more
kept now than before, he retreated to Brabant, having been invited to the   380
court of the present emperor, Charles, whose councillor he became through
the efforts of the lord chancellor, Jean Le Sauvage. The rest you know.

* * * * *

131 Cf Ep 76, written from the bishop's library in Brussels in the summer of 1498.
132 Cf Ep 95:51.
133 Cf Ep 79 introduction.
134 Cf Ep 119.
135 The poem 'Prosopopoeia Britanniae,' written in the autumn of 1499 shortly
    after Erasmus' visit to the royal children at Eltham palace; cf Ep 104, C. Reedijk
    ed *Poems of Desiderius Erasmus* (Leiden 1956) 248–53.
136 William Warham; cf Ep 188 introduction.
137 Cf Ep 200 introduction.

The principles behind his change of costume he has explained in the first of the pamphlets in which he answered the attacks of Lee.[138] His personal appearance you will describe yourself. His health was always   385 delicate, and thus he was often attacked by fevers, especially in Lent on account of the eating of fish, the mere smell of which used to upset him. His character was straightforward, and his dislike of falsehood such that even as a child he hated other boys who told lies,[139] and in old age even the sight of such people affected him physically. Among his friends he spoke freely –   390 too freely sometimes, and though often deceived he never learned not to trust them. Having a touch of pedantry, he never wrote anything with which he was satisfied; he even disliked his own appearance, and his friends' entreaties barely prevailed on him to let himself be painted. For high office and for wealth he had a permanent contempt, and thought nothing   395 more precious than leisure and liberty. A charitable judge of other men's learning, he would have been a supreme encourager of gifted minds had his resources run to it. In promoting the study of the humanities no one did more, and great was the unpopularity he had to suffer in return for this from barbarians and monks. Until his fiftieth year he had attacked no man, nor   400 did any man attack him in print. This was his intention: to keep his pen absolutely innocent of what might wound.[140] Lefèvre was the first to attack him; for Dorp's efforts were suppressed.[141] In reply he was always courteous. The sad business of Luther had brought him a burden of intolerable ill will; he was torn in pieces by both sides, while aiming   405 zealously at what was best for both. I will expand the catalogue of my work;[142] you will get a lot together out of that too. Gerard Nijmegen[143] has written to say that some people are planning a life of Erasmus, part in verse and part in prose. He wanted to have some private information, but I did not

* * * * *

138 See Ep 446 headnote; the reply to Lee was the *Apologia qua respondet duabus invectivis Eduardi Lei* (Antwerp: M. Hillen 1520 NK 782).
139 This phrase is taken almost word for word from the *Spongia* (ASD IX-1 192:679ff).
140 Allen describes this passage as 'plainly a reminiscence'; cf Allen I 52.
141 In the second edition of his commentary on the Epistles of St Paul (1517) Jacques Lefèvre d'Etaples had replied to some criticisms made by Erasmus in the *Novum instrumentum* concerning Lefèvre's views on Hebrews 2. In his reply Lefèvre accused Erasmus of holding an 'impious' opinion; Erasmus' indignant rejoinder, the *Apologia ad Jac. Fabrum Stapulensem*, was published at Louvain by Martens in August 1517 (NK 777); cf Allen Ep 597:32n. On the suppressed 'efforts' of Maarten van Dorp (n70 above) in 1514–16, see Epp 304, 337, 347.
142 The second, much expanded edition of the *Catalogus lucubrationum* (Ep 1341A) appeared in September 1524.
143 Gerard Geldenhouwer (Ep 487). The letter is not extant.

dare send it. If you have a chance of a talk with him, you can give him a   410
share. But it is not a good idea to attempt a life, unless things make it really
urgent. But we will speak of this perhaps at another time, or maybe face to
face.

    After I had written this, Birckmann[144] arrived with a load of lies. I know
how hard it is to keep a secret; but you are the one person to whom I entrust   415
everything. I have written in praise of our friend Vianden;[145] Lieven will
show you the book. Tell Ceratinus,[146] if he ever reads a classical author, to
make some notes. We must support Froben;[147] I cannot always be there to
help. And for his sake I have become very unpopular;[148] you know what
potters[149] men are. Farewell once more.   420

    To Master Conradus Goclenius. In Louvain

1438 / From Clement VII

    This letter has been assigned a new date and will be found below as Ep 1443B.

1439 / From Guillaume Budé   Paris, 11 April [1524]

    Except for the opening and closing paragraphs and the date, this letter was
    written entirely in Greek. It was first published in *G. Budaei Epistolae* (Paris:
    Bade 1531). The year-date is the only one that will fit with the movements of
    the court mentioned in line 6.

GUILLAUME BUDÉ TO ERASMUS, GREETING
I have lately had a letter from you[1] and one from Cantiuncula[2] – a long time
after you wrote them, for they were dated 18 December. I would have
answered promptly when it arrived, had I been in my prince's entourage
with the chance of having a man to whom I could entrust a letter.   5

                        * * * * *

144 Epp 1362 n1, 1388 n23
145 Ep 1427
146 See n74 above.
147 For Erasmus' support of him, see Epp 795:1–8, 796:8–19, 1341:3–15.
148 Cf lines 71–2 and Ep 1466:61–2. The other Basel printers probably resented
    Erasmus' policy of publishing only with Froben; cf Ep 1531:34–40.
149 Ie, jealous rivals; *Adagia* I ii 25

    1439
  1 Not extant; apparently sent off with Ep 1403
  2 For his role in efforts to persuade Erasmus to settle in France, see Ep 1375.

The king arrived two days ago,[3] however, quite late at night, though the day before none of us expected him for a fortnight, and left again yesterday unexpectedly, at least as far as I was concerned. So while he was here I happened to be talking to him about something else (for his unforeseen visit gave me a good opportunity), with no one listening and all those present standing some way away. As he was listening to me with attention, I took it into my head to mention the letter I had recently conveyed to him from Erasmus.[4] No sooner had he heard my opening words than he asked, 'Are we to expect that man, and when will it be?' Whereupon I gave various reasons why you had not yet been able to make preparations for your coming, and promised that in any case you would come at the first opportunity; so please fulfil my promise for me, my dear sir, as soon as you can, so that I am no longer responsible for it. For my part I imagine your mind just now is balanced on this question and swinging this way and that, and that you put it off like this deliberately and skilfully. In fact I suppose you to have reached the same position as the man who held the wolf by the ears, as the proverb has it.[5]

And so, as you seem to me cautious and afraid that if you move over here you may lose the modest but dependable position you have now, and at the same time perhaps you fear that, if you come, you may find the conditions of the offer from us not up to expectations, I thought the best thing I could do was to give you some sort of document to guarantee your future in the form of this letter, assuming that you will regard me as a reliable surety for what has been arranged. I myself then would have no hesitation in clearly and definitely giving you these further details. You should know, dear friend, that a specific preferment is earmarked and reserved for you,[6] a position of high repute which will bring you in an independent income – up to five hundred écus au soleil a year,[7] I think, and a little over; and this will be

* * * * *

3 The itinerary in Marichal VIII 442 gives 7–8 April for this surprise visit to Paris. The only source, however, the *Journal d'un bourgeois de Paris*, has the contradictory date 'lundi septiesme avril après Pasques,' 7 April 1524 having been a Thursday and the following Monday the eleventh; see V.-L. Bourilly's edition of the *Journal* (Paris 1910) 183n. Budé's statement here would seem to place the royal visit at 9–10 April but, as Allen points out, that cannot be taken as conclusive because the letter may have been delayed a day or two after it was written and the month-date added only when it was dispatched.

4 Ep 1403

5 *Adagia* I v 25

6 The treasurership at Tours; see Epp 1434 n12, 1446:48–9.

7 A sum then worth precisely £1,000 tournois, or £158 6s 8d gros Flemish, or £106 5s od sterling. See Ep 1434 n3.

secured to you, while you live in peace in a city which is well known and well
situated. So please do not lose such a great opportunity, my dear sir, by thus   35
putting off from day to day; for needless fussing over details is a thing that I
for one find it difficult to admire. People will think you have made a wrong
and foolish decision as regards your own interests, and have been
discourteous and ungrateful to such a great and gifted king. You will, I
think, be blamed by men of taste and feeling for a clumsy rejection of good   40
fortune when it offered of its own accord. For what man, in the name of
prudence itself – what reasonable man will suggest that you ought still to
hesitate, when I give you my assurance that the whole business has been
arranged by your well-wishers and is all safely and securely laid up ready for
you, and that, as far as human foresight can, we have omitted no precaution   45
against the caprice of fortune and the malice of our fellow men.

   And indeed, though I have no great opinion of my other qualities, in
regard to this promise I do think I am really to be trusted. You are aware no
doubt how little pressure I brought to bear on you previously in support of
the offer they made you before,[8] and how I always kept my advice and my   50
opinion in suspense as long as I thought your security of tenure was not
adequately established. I agreed with you at any rate in the view that you
should remain where you were, when bright hopes were spread before you
for the moment with no guarantee for their permanence; for I saw that at that
time, of those who had a proper enthusiasm for your writings, some had   55
already taken this matter in hand and others were very keen and wanted to
have a share with them in the work, in hopes of attracting the famous
Erasmus to our country, the man who is capable with that energy so
immense and so well directed of establishing serious studies, who will soon
no doubt make the revived theology at home in France and will of course   60
eclipse the reputation of those pedantic old wiseacres who have given such
pompous lectures on it.

   When I saw this, I took the line of one who was not concerned, and did
not associate myself with those who were explicitly asking for you and
passionately anxious for this new venture. But I first began definitely to take   65
a hand in the business the moment I knew for certain that your preferment
was definitely allocated and reserved for you, to be given you the moment of
your arrival. And this I learned from the king himself with my own ears,
who told me to confirm the fact to you whenever I might have excuse or
opportunity. Provided then that you are not entirely averse from our way of   70

* * * * *

8 See Ep 522 introduction.

life here, and do not think that our country would be a wholly unsuitable place in which to pursue your search for truth (it is not unknown to you, for you lived here long ago), you may be sure that in the king you will find a man of great courtesy and highly gifted, whose only extravagance is his generosity.   75

Mind you let me know if this letter reaches you as soon as you can, and give my greetings to Cantiuncula, an admirable man with a very high regard for you.

Paris, 11 April

1440 / To Willibald Pirckheimer   Basel, 14 April 1524

This letter was first published in the *Pirckheimeri opera*. On Pirckheimer, see Ep 318.

I am sorry you are having trouble with the gout. If we believe Lucian,[1] this is the time of year[2] when the votaries of that goddess[3] return to their spell-binding. I resent your being ill all the more because it deprives me of the great pleasure of your letters. As for me, I am making an excursion of some days into Burgundy[4] to rub off the staleness I have acquired by doing   5
nothing and lying hidden for so long. I wait to hear what happens in your part of the world,[5] if indeed anything does happen.

The man who brings you this claims some sort of kinship with you; otherwise I would not have written. Farewell, my good friend.

Basel, 14 April 1524   10
Erasmus of Rotterdam

To the honourable Willibald Pirckheimer, counsellor to his Imperial Majesty

* * * * *

1440
1 *Podagra* 42–4
2 In the spring
3 Ie, Podagra (the Gout), personified as a goddess in Lucian's dialogue
4 A visit to Porrentruy, a favourite residence of the bishop of Basel, and Besançon, begun shortly after this date; see AK Ep 955:26. This holiday excursion is described in some detail in Ep 1610, with further information in Epp 1679 and 1956. The first evidence of Erasmus' return to Basel is Ep 1445 of 8 May.
5 Ie, in Nürnberg, where the imperial diet was meeting (14 January–18 April 1524).

1441 / From Ennio Filonardi   Constance, 14 April 1524

> The manuscript of this letter (=Ep 23 in Förstemann/Günther), in a secretary's
> hand and signed by the bishop, was in the Burscher Collection at Leipzig (Ep
> 1254 introduction). On Filonardi, see Ep 1282.

Honoured sir, I have received the enclosed letter,[1] which as usual I faithfully
pass on to your reverence to show that I will never fail you even in things of
little moment. I have no answer yet from Rome,[2] but when I do, I will not
keep it to myself. Meanwhile let me urge you to live as cheerful a life as you
can and to rest assured that I am daily more eager to comply with your   5
wishes, and I offer you my assistance all the more readily as my desire to
oblige you increases. With best wishes for long life and prosperity, I remain
your reverence's most obedient servant and brother.
    E., bishop of Veroli
    Constance, 14 April 1524   10
    To the honoured and reverend Master Erasmus of Rotterdam, the
eminent theologian, etc

1442 / From Ennio Filonardi   Constance, 15 April 1524

> The manuscript of this letter (=Ep 24 in Förstemann/Günther), in a secretary's
> hand and signed by the bishop, was in the Burscher Collection at Leipzig (Ep
> 1254 introduction). On Filonardi, see Ep 1282.

Honoured sir, my agent in Rome tells me that the small book[1] by your
reverence dedicated to the pope and dispatched on the first occasion by
post-horse has arrived safely and has been duly presented by him to the
Holy Father; and that his Holiness was greatly delighted with it, and on the
pope's orders it was immediately bound that he might all the more enjoy   5
reading it through. And he said in reply that he would not forget all the work
it had cost you, and that he had already asked his Eminence Cardinal
Campeggi[2] his legate to bear your reverence's interests in mind before my
letter reached him, in which I had written as best I could about your affairs.

* * * * *

1441
1 Not extant
2 To Ep 1418

1442
1 The paraphrase on Acts; see Epp 1414, 1418, 1423:19–20.
2 Ep 1410 introduction

And so a better man, in the person of his Eminence, now has the duty of   10
introducing your reverence to the friendship of his Holiness and giving you
the most honourable and proper treatment as opportunity may offer. By his
authority I hope to see your reverence invited and convoyed to Rome,[3] for
his Holiness desires to be able one day to have your advice and assistance
near at hand. That this may also contribute to lengthen your life is my   15
earnest hope, and I have no hesitation in forwarding it to the utmost of my
power. And so, with best wishes for your long life and happiness, I beg
leave to sign myself most sincerely your reverence's most obedient servant
and brother.

    E., bishop of Veroli   20
    Constance, 15 April 1524
    To the honoured and reverend Master Erasmus of Rotterdam, the
eminent theologian, etc. In Basel

1443 / From Martin Luther   Wittenberg, [c 15 April] 1524

This letter has also been published in wa-Br III 268–271. The original
manuscript is lost: Erasmus gave it, along with two other letters of Luther, to
Hieronim Łaski, who took it with him to Poland (Ep 1341A:1236–53). But there
are several contemporary copies. The earliest was made in Wittenberg in late
June–early July by Luther's friend Stefan Roth, who sent it to his native
Zwickau along with a copy of Ep 1445, Erasmus' reply of 8 May (Ratsschulbibliothek Zwickau, Rotscher Sammelband 34.264b). Roth's copy is the basis of
the text in wa-Br. Allen, who knew of the Zwickau manuscript but never saw
it, based his text primarily on the copy by Pirckheimer's secretary Andreas
Ruttelius in the Stadtbibliothek Nürnberg (PP.299), taking the postscript about
Camerarius (lines 87–9) from a copy in the Forschungsbibliothek Gotha (Chart
B.26, f 115). For information about the other sixteenth-century copies, see the
introductions in Allen and wa-Br. The letter was first published in Johann
Aurifaber's edition of Luther's *Epistolae* II (Eisleben: Andreas Petri 1565). The
fact that Joachim Camerarius carried the letter to Basel (Ep 1466:19, 1496:29,
1522:32–3) permits the assignment of the approximate month-date: see Ep 1444
n2.

    Rumours that Luther had written to Erasmus were already circulating in
Wittenberg on 17 April, and within two months copies of the letter were in
circulation; wa-Br III 268. By late summer Erasmus knew that the letter had

* * * * *

3 Campeggi had already conveyed to Erasmus the pope's invitation to come to
  Rome; see Ep 1410 introduction. This had been followed by an invitation to join
  Campeggi at Nürnberg; Epp 1422:7–40, 1423:40–4, 1434:60–2.

been widely disseminated; Ep 1489:63–5. He expected it to be printed at Strasbourg (Epp 1496:29–30, 1522:32–4), but it seems that it never was.

LUTHER TO ERASMUS

Grace and peace from our Lord Jesus Christ. I have now been silent for some little time,[1] good friend Erasmus, and though I expected that you as the older and more eminent of us would break silence first,[2] yet after waiting in vain for so long, I am I think obliged by charity itself to make the first move.   5
In the first place, I have no wish to complain if you have kept your distance from me in order to be quite free and uncommitted in opposing my enemies the papists. Nor did I take it much amiss when in some passages in your published work, in order to secure their good will or appease their fury, you have attacked me and criticized me with some bitterness.[3] When I perceive   10
that the Lord has not yet given you the courage, or even the common sense, to join with me in a free and confident confrontation with those monsters I suffer from, I am not the man to dare to demand from you something beyond your powers and limitations. In fact I have put up with your weakness and respected it, and the measure of the gift of God in you.[4] For   15
the extent to which learning flourishes through you and wins the day,[5] thus opening the way to the genuine study of the Bible, is a thing the whole world simply cannot deny, nor that there is a great and special gift of God in you for which we must all give thanks. And so I for my part have never wished to

* * * * *

1443
1 Except for Ep 1127A (Erasmus to Luther, 1 August 1520), nothing survives of the correspondence of Luther and Erasmus between Ep 980 (May 1519) and the present letter.
2 Cf Lucretius 4.583; Virgil *Aeneid* 10.63.
3 The depth to which Luther had been stung by some of Erasmus' remarks about him is revealed in a letter to Oecolampadius of 20 June 1523 (WA-Br III 96:15–18): 'Even though I feel his stings everywhere, nevertheless, because he pretends publicly not to be my enemy, I too pretend not to understand his cunning, although I understand him better than he imagines.' Luther had made a similar statement in a letter to Georgius Spalatinus of 15 May 1522 (ibidem II 527:22–4): 'In his new collection of letters [ie, the *Epistolae ad diversos* 1521] Erasmus at last reveals that he is a wholehearted enemy of Luther and his doctrine, but with deceitful and clever words he pretends to be a friend.' Luther was probably thinking of such letters as Epp 1141, 1143, 1156, 1167, 1202, 1203, 1219. Erasmus' friends were aware of his power to give offence; see Ep 1480:23.
4 Rom 12:3; Eph 4:7
5 '[Erasmus] has accomplished what he was ordained to do: he has introduced the knowledge of languages and has called us away from sacrilegious studies': WA-Br III 96:18–19 (Luther to Oecolampadius, 20 June 1523).

see you abandon or neglect the measure given you and involve yourself in   20
our camp; for though with your abilities and your eloquence you could do
great service to the cause, yet as your heart would not be in it, it would be
safer to serve within your own gift. The one thing to be afraid of was that you
might be persuaded by my enemies to attack my opinions in your published
work, and that I should then be obliged to resist you to your face.[6] I have in   25
fact restrained a number of people who had books ready and planned to
drag you into the fray; and my policy was such that I could have wished
Hutten's *Expostulatio* had never been published, much less your *Spongia*.[7] In
that, if I am not mistaken, you yourself now realize how easy it is to write
about modesty and to complain of the lack of it in myself,[8] and yet how very   30
difficult, if not impossible, it is to be modest oneself, except by some special
gift of the Spirit.

Believe it or not, then, as you please, Christ is my witness how
sincerely I sympathize with you as the target of so much hatred and passion
in so many quarters. That you are not aroused by this, I cannot believe, for   35
your strength is only human and unequal to such burdens; though they too,
maybe, are aroused by justified indignation, and they may think they have
been provoked by you in ways they do not deserve. And, to speak freely,
since their nature is such that, weak as they too are, they cannot endure the
bitterness and dishonesty which you would like to be taken for caution and   40
modesty, they have some cause at any rate for justified resentment, though
they would have none if they were stronger characters. I too, easily roused
as I am, have often been provoked into writing with some bitterness; yet I
have never done so except against the obstinate and the unteachable. For the
rest, my mild and merciful attitude towards the sinful and the irreligious,   45
however insane or unjust they may be, is I think attested not only by the
witness of my own conscience but by many men from their own experience.
Thus I have restrained my pen hitherto, however much you might prick me,
and have written, in letters to my friends which you too have read,[9] that I
shall continue to restrain it until you come out into the open. For however   50
much you may differ from our views, and in an irreligious or deceitful
fashion may condemn or hold in suspense many points of true religion, I
cannot accuse you of stubbornness, and do not wish to.

* * * * *

6 Gal 2:11

7 For Luther's wish, see WA-Br III 160:7–8 (Luther to Conradus Pellicanus, 1
   October 1523). For the *Expostulatio*, see Ep 1356 n9, and for the *Spongia*, see Epp
   1378, 1389.

8 See Ep 980:45, and cf Epp 1437:60–1, 1480:60.

9 Erasmus had seen both the letter to Pellicanus (n7 above; Ep 1397:9–10) and
   that to Oecolampadius (n3 above; Epp 1384:57–62, 92–3, 1397:10–12).

As things are, then, what should I do? Feeling is very bitter on both sides. I should wish, were it possible for me to act as mediator, that they 55 might cease to attack you so fiercely and might allow you in your old age peacefully to fall asleep in the Lord. They would certainly do so, in my opinion, if they took any thought for your weakness, and considered how great are the issues at stake, which have long since exceeded your capacity;[10] especially since things have reached a stage at which there is very little to 60 fear for our cause, even if Erasmus opposes it with all his powers, and still less if he stings here and there sometimes and shows his teeth.[11] But you on the other hand, dear Erasmus, should remember their weakness and refrain from your favourite rhetorical figures,[12] which are so bitter and wounding, so that, if you have neither the capacity nor the courage to maintain the 65 points we make, you should none the less leave them alone and mind your own business. For if they resent the way you use your teeth even in your judgment this is not without justification: human weakness considers Erasmus' authority and reputation and is very frightened of it, and it is a far different thing to be bitten once by Erasmus from having all the papists in 70 league against one.

I wanted to say this, good friend Erasmus, to show that I have an open mind where you are concerned and desire to see the Lord grant you a spirit worthy of your great reputation. And if the Lord is not ready to do so now, I beg you meanwhile, if that is the best you can do, to be no more than a 75 spectator of this trouble in which we are engaged; only do not side with our adversaries and join forces with them, and above all do not publish any attack on me,[13] while I shall refrain from attacking you. And then consider that those who complain that they are attacked under the name of Lutherans are human beings just as you and I are, to whom one must show mercy and 80 forgiveness, bearing one another's burdens, as Paul puts it.[14] There has been enough showing of teeth; we must now make sure that we do not destroy each other,[15] a prospect all the more pitiable as it is most certain that neither party seriously wishes to see religion suffer, and that without stubbornness everyone can be content with his own position. Take my lack of eloquence in 85 good part, and so farewell in the Lord.

I commend to you Joachim,[16] the bearer of this, a young man like our

* * * * *

10 Luther may have been alluding to Ep 1143:59–60.
11 Cf n3 above.
12 Cf WA-Br III 160:8–11.
13 Cf Ep 1437:108–10.
14 Gal 6:2
15 Cf Gal 5:15
16 Camerarius (Ep 1501); cf Ep 1444 n2.

friend Philippus;[17] indeed he will commend himself all the more if you allow
him to see you.

Wittenberg, 1524. Martin Luther   90

1443A / From Gian Matteo Giberti   Rome, 20 April 1524

The manuscript of this letter, which was first published by Allen as Ep 1443A, is
an autograph rough draft among Giberti's papers in the Vatican Archives
(Particolari 154, f 7). The addressee is unquestionably Erasmus. In Allen's
words, 'to no one else could a supporter of the Pope have written with such
admiration for his services in bringing polite learning into Germany and for
promoting sacred studies.' The letter may well have been dispatched with Ep
1443B.

Gian Matteo Giberti (1495–1543) had risen in curial service under the
patronage of Cardinal Giulio de' Medici. When Giulio became Pope Clement
VII in November 1523, Giberti was immediately named datary, with responsibility for distributing benefices, and in 1524 was made bishop of Verona. After
the sack of Rome (May 1527), in which he nearly lost his life, Giberti retired to
Verona, where he became an exemplary bishop whose reforms set the
standard for later bishops of the Catholic Reformation.

This declaration of friendship and offer of support from a learned and
influential patron of art and letters naturally produced a positive response
from Erasmus, the first surviving evidence of which is Ep 1481.

Reverend sir, whom I honour as a brother. Although before now I have
always admired your great qualities, because you alone deserve the greatest
credit for the introduction of polite literature into Germany, and you above
all have shed lustre on our age by writings as religious as they are elegant,
yet hitherto I have refrained from writing to you and have admired your   5
eloquence and your wisdom in silence. This was partly because you were of
such distinction as an author, and only an ambitious man, it seemed, would
try to work his unworthy self into your affections; partly because I saw at
that time that my friendship could be of very little use to you. Now,
however, that our most holy Father has been called by God to that exalted   10
station, and in his kindness has raised my very inadequate and undeserving
self to my present office, which can be, it is thought, of advantage to many
people, I begin to consider that I have a somewhat greater capacity to be of
service to you or, if you should have no need for my assistance, to your
friends on your account. His Holiness has always set the highest value on   15

* * * * *

17 Melanchthon

Clement VII
Portrait by Sebastiano del Piombo
Museo e Gallerie Nazionali di Capodimonte, Naples

you and others like you, and rates you now even more highly, because he
thinks it part of his proper duties to encourage you,[1] who have served so
well the cause of sacred literature, with all the kindness he can show. To my
own good will towards you I have therefore added my master's, which is
now of long standing, and so I honour you most of all men after him, and   20
offer you all I possess. This I do with the greatest readiness. For though I
have no resources, I am none the less a lover of literature, so much so that I
find my thoughts never so happily employed as when they are devoted to
remembering or talking about very learned men. You have acquired great
authority among your fellow men by your most religious researches and   25
your immortal works; and equally great is the power you have over me if you
ever wish to ask for my help.

   And I do most strongly wish that you would do this, not merely for my
own sake (though I would not attempt to conceal that I have a very great
desire to secure your affection), but because if I can carry out in this way the   30
wishes of our most holy Father, my duty tells me and my judgment gives me
the inclination to do so. In my view, whatever can be done for you and yours
ought to be a tribute to your outstanding services to God and the cause of
religion and to no other cause whatever. Farewell.

   Rome, 20 April 1524   35

1443B / From Clement VII   Rome, 30 April 1524

There are four manuscripts of this letter in the Vatican Archives, all of them
bearing the date 3 April. The most important of these is Jacopo Sadoleto's
autograph draft (Arm 44, vol 9, f 23), which Allen took as the basis for his text.
However, the papers of Frans van Cranevelt at Louvain contain a contemporary copy that was clearly supplied to Cranevelt by Erasmus; see de Vocht
Literae Ep 101. It bears the date 30 April. Allen, who published the letter as Ep
1438, gave preference to the Sadoleto draft on the rather feebly speculative
ground that the Louvain manuscript might represent 'a duplicate of the
original letter, sent by another messenger and at a later date.' It is both simpler
and more sensible to conclude, as did de Vocht, that the Louvain copy
represents the letter actually sent and to regard its date as the correct one. We
have therefore taken de Vocht's text as the basis for our version. Apart from the
date, the differences between the Sadoleto draft and the final version of the
letter are of no great significance: the principal one is the omission of ten words
in the second paragraph of the final version (see n5).

   * * * * *

1443A
1 See Ep 1443B.

The letter evidently took a long time to reach Erasmus. Composed in the first week of April, it was not sent off until the last day of the month. It had not yet arrived on 3 June, when Erasmus informed Willibald Pirckheimer that he had written to the pope (Ep 1452). Erasmus does not mention it in his correspondence until 21 July, when he reported his good fortune to Pirckheimer and Johann von Vlatten (Epp 1466–7). By 21 July as well, the news had reached Thiébaut Biétry in Porrentruy (near Basel), either by letter or by word of mouth: Ep 1468:25–6. Since the new papal legate, Cardinal Campeggi (Ep 1410 introduction), was to forward the pope's letter and present, the roundabout route via Nürnberg would explain much of the delay; the postponement of the dispatch of the letter from Rome would explain the rest.

The letter was first published in Balan *Monumenta* I 324 (from Vatican Archives Arm 32, vol 1, f 257, a seventeenth-century copy), and then again in *Monumenta* II 10 (from the Sadoleto autograph).

POPE CLEMENT VII

Beloved son, greetings and apostolic benediction.

Your letter and the book on the Acts of the Apostles[1] which you have sent us give us a clear picture of your devotion to us and no less of the generosity that is coupled with it; and we have formed great hopes that you, 5
who by the will of Almighty God are distinguished for your learning, will take up in God's cause the arms appropriate to your great intellectual gifts and to the piety which you profess. News was in fact reaching us from many quarters that you had it in mind so to do, and that you already planned or had actually started upon a work[2] which would make the light of your 10
learning available for unmasking the errors of many misguided people. This news we were delighted to hear. For we have always had a high opinion of your literary gifts and scholarship; and whether you change your abode to this city[3] or settle in some other place, you are to know that wherever you may be, this our opinion of you and our fatherly affection for 15
you will remain unaltered. As far therefore as concerns your protection from scandalous attacks, we have stepped in to exercise our authority;[4] and as neither our judgment nor our feelings are content to leave unrewarded your merits and the admirable sentiments towards us which you display in the

* * * * *

1443B
1 Ep 1414
2 Doubtless the *De libero arbitrio*, which Erasmus had mentioned in his last letter to the pope; see Ep 1418:57–8.
3 Cf Ep 1418:61–2.
4 See Ep 1431:14.

presentation of this distinguished volume, we have instructed our beloved   20
son Lorenzo Campeggi, cardinal priest of the title of St Anastasia and *legatus*
a latere of ourselves and of the apostolic see, to convey to you on our behalf a
present.[5] Soon, as an honourable opportunity offers, we will take steps to
improve your situation. That we may do so all the more readily and with
even more justification, it will be your duty to please God and ourselves and   25
to lighten our labours by correcting those who have turned aside from the
course of true religion, joining with us in teaching, in preaching, and in
writing, so that we may get the full benefit from your good will, and
Christendom from your learning and scholarship.

Given in Rome at St Peter's, under the seal of the Fisherman, this last   30
day of April 1524, in the first year of our pontificate

Jacopo Sadoleto

To our beloved son Desiderius Erasmus of Rotterdam, doctor of
divinity

1444 / From Heinrich Stromer   Leipzig, 1 May 1524

The autograph of this letter (=Ep 25 in Enthoven) is in the Rehdiger Collection
of the University Library at Wrocław (MS Rehd 254.144). The letter was first
published in Gess I 665.

Heinrich Stromer (Ep 1326) was now a member of the town council and dean
of the faculty of medicine at Leipzig. Despite being a subject of the zealously
Catholic Duke George of Saxony, Stromer was known to be strongly Lutheran
in his views.

Greeting. Although I am sure, most learned and eloquent Erasmus, that you
have recently had a letter from me,[1] carried by Philippus Melanchthon,[2] that

* * * * *

5 Two hundred florins; see Ep 1414 introduction. On the value of the gift, see Ep
1466 n3. In Sadoleto's draft, there were ten additional words after 'a present,'
to wit: 'which will, we think, make some contribution to your ease for the
present.'

1444
1 Not extant; written c 20 April (see n2 below), probably delivered to Basel by
Camerarius (ibidem).
2 In the spring of 1524 Melanchthon, accompanied by Joachim Camerarius (Ep
1501) and Wilhelm Nesen (Ep 1257 n3), journeyed on horseback from
Wittenberg to his birthplace, Bretten in the Palatinate. They left Wittenberg on
about 19 April (Scheible no 319), were in Leipzig on the twentieth (ibidem no
320), and reached Bretten on about the first of May (ibidem no 322).
Camerarius, bearing Ep 1443 and doubtless other letters as well (cf preceding

devotee not of horses but of all good literature,[3] such is my special affection
and respect and admiration for you that I could not refrain from writing to
interrupt you once more when the bearer of this, who is a Basel bookseller,[4]   5
urged me to send you a line.

Among us, our holy religion is divided into three sects. The first of
these flatly rejects all the traditions of men with scorn and contumely, sets
going great upheavals, and confounds earth and sky,[5] fire and water.[6] The
second obstinately maintains and observes those petty human traditions   10
and neglects the majesty of the gospel, trusting to its own invented merits,
neglecting the good works which Christ told us to perform, and setting a
lower value on solid faith in Christ Jesus, our one and only true deliverer and
saviour. The third, which I greatly prefer, teaches the doctrine of the gospel
and urges us to follow it scrupulously. Yet it does not entirely condemn such   15
of the traditions of men as can be seen not to conflict with the word of God,
but sets before us Christ as the sole author of our salvation; it does not
abolish human ordinances, but says that their observance is not a matter of
what is called mortal sin, as the bishops have taught hitherto, who for the
most trifling and ridiculous reason have smitten us with the terrifying   20
thunderbolt of excommunication.

It happened here the other day that a layman (to use the language of
the clerics) who was being abused by a priest struck him lightly on the head
with his fist; he was excommunicated. Another man killed three of the
country folk with a dagger; he was not cast out of the Christian community,   25
for all that Christ said 'Thou shalt not kill';[7] the bishop's version is 'Thou
shalt not strike a cleric.' It is his commandment, not Christ's, that many
mortal men obey. But if the canon law on the devil's instigation has been
burned at Wittenberg,[8] this means that among you the clerics, as they say,

* * * * *

note), went on to Basel to visit Erasmus, returning in a few days to accompany Melanchthon back to Wittenberg, where they arrived on about 8 June
(Scheible no 325). Camerarius' account of this journey is found in his *De
Philippi Melanchthonis ortu, totius vitae curriculo et morte narratio diligens et
accurata* (Leipzig: Ernst Voegelin 1566) 90–5.
3 Melanchthon was apparently not a skilled horseman.
4 Unidentified
5 *Adagia* I iii 81
6 *Adagia* IV iii 94
7 Matt 5:21
8 On 10 December 1520, Luther and a group of students burned a copy of the
canon law outside the Magpie Gate at Wittenberg. This was a reply to the
burning of Luther's books by Aleandro (Ep 1256 n11) at Mainz c 28 November
and also a symbolic rejection of traditional ecclesiastical authority. Cf Ep 1313
n6.

do not enjoy such great privileges as formerly. Perhaps among us too at no 30
very distant date all Christians will be anointed and not those exclusively
who wear formidable garments or a mitre on their bald heads. You for your
part must please support the cause of gospel truth, as indeed you do, and
not allow them to win you over to the opinion of those who seek their own
advantage, not Christ's glory, or who fear the men who can kill the body but 35
not the soul.[9] It is the duty of Christians boldly to profess the word of God,
and on this question not to be always seeking the approval of men, but to
seek the glory of Christ, through whom alone eternal salvation is given to all
men.

It is not necessity that makes me write to you like this; it is the love and 40
reverence that I have for you. Some people are trying to put you in a false
position. They say that Martin[10] and Philippus[11] speak ill of you, their object
being to stir up discord between you by lies if need be, that they may hurt the
majesty of the gospel. I beg you not to give a hearing to mischief-makers
such as they. Philippus was with me after Easter in Leipzig.[12] His feelings 45
about you are by no means what these worthless people say they are, and
unless I am quite wrong, Martin too does not wish you ill. How could a man
possibly pursue you vindictively who loves and respects all champions of
the gospel? – for you are not only one of them, you are their standard-bearer
and the best of them all. 50

On all this I have said more than I meant. Forgive me for rambling on.
Farewell in Christ Jesus, and may he long preserve you for our benefit in
health and wealth to labour with your writings in his vineyard. Pray accept
my humble duty.

From the famous city of Leipzig, 1 May 1524 55
Your sincere friend Heinrich Stromer, physician
To that most scholarly of scholars and of stylists far the most stylish
Erasmus of Rotterdam, true theologian, his special friend

1445 / To Martin Luther Basel, 8 May 1524

This letter, which is Erasmus' reply to Ep 1443, has also been published in
wa-Br 3 284–7. All the surviving manuscripts are copies. The earliest is that by
Stefan Roth in the Ratsschulbibliothek Zwickau (Rotscher Sammelband

* * * * *

9 Matt 10:28
10 Cf Epp 1384 n19, 1397:10–12, 1443.
11 Cf Ep 1313 n3.
12 Easter was 27 March, but Stromer is clearly referring to the visit mentioned in
line 2.

34.266a); see Ep 1443 introduction. Roth's copy is the basis of the text in WA-Br. Allen, who does not even mention the Zwickau manuscript, used as his chief source a somewhat later copy (c 1526) in the Forschungsbibliothek Gotha (Chart B.26, f 117a). For information about the other extant manuscripts, see the introductions in Allen and WA-Br. The earliest published versions of the letter (1692, 1725) were extracts; see Allen's introduction for details. In 1781 a nearly complete version was published by Gottfried Schütze in volume 2 of his *D.M. Luthers bisher ungedruckte Briefe* (Leipzig), and in 1784 H.P.C. Henke and P.J. Bruns included a complete text in volume 2 of their *Annales Literarii* (Helmstadt).

Erasmus' own estimate of the character of this reply to Luther is found in Epp 1452:14–15, 1466:20–1.

ERASMUS OF ROTTERDAM TO MARTIN LUTHER

Cordial greetings. No, I do not concede that your passion for the purity of the gospel is more sincere than my own, for there is no suffering which I do not endure for the gospel's sake; and up to the present I have sought every opportunity to make the gospel available to all. What you describe as 5 weakness and ignorance is partly conscience and partly conviction. When I look at certain passages in your work, I am much afraid that Satan is using his wiles to lead you astray; but there are other passages which so delight me that I wish my fears were groundless. I would refuse to teach any doctrine of which I was not yet convinced in my own mind, much less a doctrine which I 10 do not yet understand. So far I have done more for the cause of the gospel than many who make great play with the word 'gospel.' I see many desperate and disloyal men taking advantage of the present situation. I see humane letters and good learning tumbling into ruin. I see old friendships broken, and I fear a bloody conflict is about to break out. If you are sincere in 15 your heart, I pray that Christ may prosper your work. As for me, nothing will tempt me to yield to human weakness and knowingly betray the gospel.

So far I have not attacked you in writing,[1] though by doing so I could have won the applause of the princes; but I realized that this could not be done without injury to the gospel. All I did was respond to those who tried 20 to convince the princes that you and I were in league, that I was totally in agreement with you, and that everything you taught was to be found in my books. Even now it is hardly possible to uproot these ideas from their minds. I do not greatly care what you write about me. If I were interested in worldly success, I can think of nothing which would turn out more to my advantage. 25

* * * * *

1445
1 But see Ep 1419.

But I want to present my soul to Christ without spot or stain, and I should like all men to act in the same spirit. If you are ready to give an account to every man of the faith that is in you,[2] why should it upset you if someone wants to argue with you in the hope of deepening his understanding? Perhaps Erasmus' opposition will do more for the gospel than all the 30
support you receive from dullards, who will not let me be a spectator and watch the tragedy unfold – I only hope it does not have a tragic ending! These people are driving me into the opposite camp – even if pressure from the princes were not pushing me in the same direction. Because of their scandalous conduct the gospel is becoming an object of derision among 35
sensible people, and the princes will be compelled to check their seditious and disorderly behaviour. That will not happen without injury to innocent people. They listen to no one, not even to you. They fill the world with wild and libellous pamphlets, believing it worth their trouble to condemn the orthodox Fathers of the church.   40

But it would be tedious to go into all this. I pray that the Lord may direct everything to his own glory. You complain that my *Spongia*[3] is lacking in restraint; but, remember, I did not say a word about Hutten's life though he completely ruined himself through extravagance, women, and dice;[4] I said nothing about those silly pretensions of his though no one, not even the 45
most patient of friends, could put up with them; I said nothing about his debts, or about the money he extorted from the Carthusians,[5] or about the two Dominicans who had their ears cut off,[6] or about the three abbots who were assaulted and robbed on the public highway,[7] an outrage which caused one of his servants to be beheaded, or about other crimes of his 50
which have become notorious even among the people. Although I had not uttered a single word to provoke him, he betrayed my friendship simply to curry favour with the greatest scoundrel that ever lived;[8] he also amassed such a heap of false charges against me as would beggar the imagination of the most foul-mouthed rogue. Let me remind you, too, of that letter of mine 55
to the bishop of Mainz which he had the bad faith to publish,[9] though with

* * * * *

2 1 Pet 3:15
3 Ep 1378
4 This denunciation of Hutten closely parallels a passage included in the second edition of the *Catalogus lucubrationum* (Ep 1341A:1063–94).
5 See Ep 1341A n291.
6 See Ep 1341A n292.
7 See Ep 1341A n293.
8 Apparently Eppendorf (Ep 1283 n4)
9 Ep 1033. Cf *Spongia* ASD IX-1 192–3.

the suppression of his own name.[10] I shall say nothing about another act of treachery which he committed against me. He put pressure on me to write several letters of commendation for him to the imperial court, although he had already formed a conspiracy against the emperor – he only wanted to exploit the emperor's name in his hunt for a wife.[11] Under such provocation from one I had served so well, would I not have been justified in speaking with some feeling on these matters? And yet you accuse me of having gone too far. What had Otto[12] to do with Hutten? Yet what a fuss he makes although I never uttered a word to injure him. You say these men are like me. Far from being like me, I think they are not human beings at all, but raging demons. Do you honestly think the gospel will be restored by perverted creatures like these? Are men like this to be the pillars of a renascent church? Ought I to form an alliance with them?

But I have gone on too long on this subject. I found Joachim most congenial.[13] It was a pity there was no opportunity to meet Melanchthon.[14] May the Lord Jesus direct your mind to those purposes which are worthy of his gospel.

Basel, in haste, 8 May 1524
Erasmus of Rotterdam

1446 / From Guillaume Budé   Paris, 8 May [1524]

This letter, written entirely in Greek, is a sequel to Ep 1439 and was first published in *G. Budaei epistolae* (Paris: Bade 1531).

TO ERASMUS FROM BUDÉ

I sent you a hasty letter early in April about your coming to us,[1] and have done this on the king's instructions when he paid a visit here.[2] At that time he spent only one day in the city and even then not a whole day. When he returned the day before yesterday, spending only a day and a half here, he spoke to me again on the same subject, and then hastily set off. If then, my

* * * * *

10 It appears that no such change is found in any of the unauthorized printings of the letter; cf Allen iv 98.
11 See Ep 1341A n296.
12 Brunfels (Ep 1405)
13 Joachim Camerarius (Ep 1501), the bearer of Ep 1443
14 See Ep 1444 n2.

   1446
 1 Ep 1439
 2 Francis was in Paris 3–6 May; Marichal viii 442.

dearest friend, you have had my letter, well and good; but if not, let me repeat the gist of what I wrote.

I urge you to consider which of these two courses you thought would suit you better, to choose to join us here or to stay where you are. If you like our way of life and think that living among us would conduce to your studies into old age, not forgetting your kidney trouble,[3] everything needed to make life easy for you will be ready for you and completely secure. For the preferment offered you by the king,[4] and the house-warming present, so to say, that awaits you the moment you set up house among us – these I myself can guarantee to you with confidence, and I can undertake for the future on my own responsibility, although it is not my way to hazard my reputation lightly, and if I have preserved it intact to this day, it is because I bear in mind the maxim from Delphi 'Stand surety and ruin is at hand.'[5]

What then has now made me so confident that I am ready of my own accord to be bound by this undertaking although it is really beyond me? Quite simple: I know that the king is enthusiastic and devoted to the idea, and I have been reliably told that the presentation is all ready for you which you are to receive the moment you get here. If however you really are permanently attached to Germany, and this makes you afraid that you will be unable to find life here equally agreeable, I find the case very hard to answer. For if I had a similar problem and had a choice to make, I should choose before anything else to follow my own inclination, which is all in favour of the things it is used to and very reluctant to be torn away from them. So, as far as I am concerned, there will be no recriminations if this is how you feel. But if it is because you are equally balanced either way that you hesitate, I do beg you, my good sir, to come down on one side or the other, and preferably on this side. It would be intolerable if you were to postpone a decision a second time, when your reward is guaranteed and awaits your arrival, as I assure you it does – unless of course you think my estate inadequate to underwrite a guarantee of such importance.

So do stop sitting on the fence, my friend, and giving first one excuse and then another and being so needlessly coy, as it might well be called, in your attitude to the king. For inevitably you will be thought by able and intelligent people to be acting very ungracefully, if you seem to be carelessly letting slip this piece of good fortune when you could honourably accept it. If on the other hand, as many suppose, it is the quarrelsome character of our theologians that deters you from moving, your own studies being devoted

* * * * *

3 Ie, the stone; see Ep 1426:16–19.
4 The treasurership at Tours; see Epp 1434 n12, 1439:31.
5 *Adagia* I vi 97

to the restoration of the Scriptures, this fear is groundless. To take it no
further, the distinction of having been invited will provide you with   45
unbroken security and peace, for simply no one would dare make trouble for
you when you have been sent for by the king and enjoy his protection. And
then the preferment that awaits your coming is honourable in itself and
brings in a splendid income,[6] and is not less than five days' journey from
their place of resort,[7] so that you will be able to ignore their criticisms   50
without a second thought. Besides which, the more intelligent of the men
who are now in important positions are already swayed in your favour by
what you have written; and when you are already living here and seem to be
at home among us, this will increase, and will make no small contribution
towards suppressing the faction that dislikes you, especially since not a few   55
intelligent and right-thinking people are convinced they are quite wrong
and are moved by ill will towards all lovers of the humanities for their
admirable and praiseworthy attempts at reform and not by zeal for anything
good and laudable.

In view of all this I am surprised that, though originally you were   60
anxious to move but needed resources, you should hesitate now that you are
splendidly provided for. So make up your mind now about this invitation,
whether it is better for you to accept it or reject it; for the king might well
have second thoughts if he found he was being trifled with.

Farewell, from Paris, 8 May.   65

1447 / To Theobald Hillweg [?]   Basel, 15 May 1524

This letter was first published in the *Opus epistolarum*. The person addressed
was in all probability Theobald Hillweg (c 1450–1535), abbot of Lucelle (Lützel)
in the Jura between Delémont and Porrentruy (south-west of Basel). Lucelle
was the principal Cistercian house in the region and the mother house of the
abbey at Wettingen, whose abbot was Andreas Wengi (see n2). For this reason,
and because the two abbots frequently visited one another, it was assumed
that Hillweg might be invoked to use his influence with Wengi.

ERASMUS OF ROTTERDAM TO A CERTAIN ABBOT, GREETING
Had I not heard so much of your exceptional kindness, reverend father, I
should have been afraid you might instantly protest at the impertinence
with which a man so obscure as myself writes to one in your high position,
being as little known to you as you are to him, and on a subject moreover   5

* * * * *

6 See Ep 1439:33.
7 Tours is about 200 kilometres from Paris.

which has very little to do with me; but as a godly man you will easily excuse
my presumption, which is inspired by Christian charity.

Ambrosius Suagrius,[1] the parish priest of Riehen, is in some danger of
being reduced to starvation, such is the hostility aroused in father Andreas,[2]
abbot of Maris Stella, by reports the source of which I do not know.   10
Ambrosius has satisfied me personally on one point, the report that he said
in the pulpit that there were sinful women among Christ's ancestry. This
was said by Jerome,[3] to Christ's glory and as an encouragement to us, and
his congregation bear witness that he said nothing impious on this subject,
unless what Jerome wrote was impious too. Ambrosius seems to me a man   15
with very little guile in him. He spent quite a lot of money to secure this
living; he has done some very expensive building there, and it will be
impossible for him to be removed without losses which he cannot afford. He
is popular with his congregation. And changes, human affairs being what
they are, are usually changes for the worse.   20

There is an old Portuguese proverb about exchanging one evil for
another.[4] Nowadays we can almost speak of exchanging bad for worse. If
Ambrosius has done anything up to now that he ought not to have done, on
instructions from you he will soon put it right. A man of your godly
disposition ought to wish to settle this dispute between Ambrosius and the   25
abbot of Maris Stella, and a man of your authority will find this very easy. I
have no doubt that Ambrosius will gladly accept any conditions for a
reconciliation. I vouch for that myself.

If in this matter you will be so kind as to help Ambrosius out of regard

* * * * *

1447
1 Ie, Ambrosius Kettenacker (d 1541) of Winterthur, who had studied in Basel
  and become friends with Beatus Rhenanus (Ep 327) and the Amerbach
  brothers (Ep 408), among others. From 1518 he was parish priest at Riehen, just
  north of Basel. He was soon in contact with Oecolampadius and Zwingli and
  clearly committed to the Reformation. This brought him into conflict with
  Andreas Wengi, the conservative abbot of Wettingen (see following note),
  who was patron of the parish at Riehen. In the litigation between Wengi and
  Kettenacker that began in August 1523, Kettenacher enjoyed the support of the
  city council of Basel, which controlled the village of Riehen. With the support
  of the majority of his parishioners, Kettenacker held on to his post, reformed
  his parish, and married a former nun.
2 Andreas Wengi (d 1528), abbot of the Cistercian abbey of Wettingen, near
  Baden in the Aargau (northwest of Zürich). His career was a protracted losing
  battle against the encroachments of the Reformation in the parishes dependent
  on his abbey.
3 *Commentarius in Evangelium secundum Mattheum*, on Matt 1:3
4 *Adagia* II ii 83

for myself, I shall gladly acknowledge my debt to your reverence on this 30
account. If for any reason you decide that what I ask is not right, yet please
put my name among those who wish to serve you in any way they can; and
may the Lord Jesus long preserve you in our midst in health and wealth.

Basel, 15 May 1524

1448 / From Duke George of Saxony   Dresden, 21 May 1524

This letter was first published in Paul Merula's *Vita Des. Erasmi* (Ep 1388
introduction). The surviving manuscript is a rough draft in the Staatsarchiv
Dresden (Loc 10299, f 89). Although Merula probably based his text on the
letter actually sent, his version is marred by errors made either at the time of
copying for dispatch or later at the time of printing. Allen therefore gave
preference to the manuscript.

The letter of Erasmus answered here (line 4) is not extant, but this letter
makes clear that its purpose was to complain about Eppendorf (Ep 1437); cf Ep
1503:24–5. Because the correspondence between Erasmus and Duke George
was still being intercepted by hostile parties (see lines 7–13 and Ep 1313
introduction), this letter was not delivered until 20 September (see Ep
1499:1–2). As Ep 1521 shows, Erasmus did not like the tone of the letter and
wrote to Hieronymus Emser, one of Duke George's secretaries, to complain,
only to be told in reply that the substance of the duke's letters was attributable
to the duke himself, not his secretaries.

GEORGE, BY THE GRACE OF GOD DUKE OF SAXONY, LANDGRAVE OF
THURINGIA AND MARGRAVE OF MEISSEN, TO ERASMUS OF
ROTTERDAM, THEOLOGIAN, GREETING, GRACE, AND FAVOUR
When your letter reached me during the Whitsun[1] holiday it still had no
address, and the man who brought it explained that this should have been 5
added by Mosellanus;[2] but when I read it through, I saw clearly that it was
intended for me and no one else. You say there that you have already
approached me by letter several times but have had no answer, and that this
leads you to suspect that you may have given offence. I have however
replied to every letter of yours that I have received, and to enable you to 10
recognize which it is that I have received, I send you with this a copy of my

* * * * *

1448
1 15 May 1524
2 Ep 1305

last reply,[3] written in answer to the last I had from you.[4] If you have written any others since then, I assure you that they have not reached me. Had they reached me in fact, I should certainly never put you in a position to complain that I had not done what I should in this regard, especially as it is my unvarying custom to send no one away without an answer, however humble he may be, provided that what he writes deserves one.

You say that you regret having praised certain people more warmly than they deserve. Your regret is reasonable; but my opinion is this. Had you not treated these particular individuals of whom you speak in the way you describe, and brought them into prominence by these misplaced tributes, you would have had just as outrageous treatment from them long ago as you have now. We see here of course those famous 'virtuous actions' drawn from this well-spring of true doctrine. These are the 'works of charity,' the charity preached by Luther and by others who boast themselves something more than evangelicals and cling to the letter rather than the spirit. This is the more than German integrity and sense of honour which those noble characters have displayed on all occasions. Whether those who wish to be taken for the heads of this faction resemble those others who are as it were its limbs is not hard to guess. I myself would prefer, if such wishes did any good, that Eppendorf should have started life somewhere else and were not a product of my own dominions; for while he ought to be one of our ornaments, the worthy man's behaviour has been such as to make him a blot on them and a disgrace. When I recall the virtues which you once described him as possessing,[5] it seems to me impossible to imagine a more exquisite example of an abandoned man whose conscience and sense of shame have gone to rack and ruin.

And now how much I wish that God had put you in this frame of mind two years ago, that you might have dissociated yourself from Luther's faction, and to such good effect that by the publication of some work aimed at them you might have gone on record that between you and them there is no common ground, only a major difference of opinion! How much easier it would have been to extinguish a fire that just then was breaking into flame, instead of trying to put it out now when it has grown into such a vast conflagration! The blame for this, to speak my mind freely, falls in the first place on you. If only, while the times pointed that way and this plague had not yet claimed so many victims, you had adopted the attitude towards Luther which you now display, and had descended into the arena and there

* * * * *

3 Ep 1340
4 Ep 1313, a copy of which had been sent with Ep 1325
5 In Epp 1125, 1283, 1325

played the part of a serious and committed combatant, there would be no
reason for our present troubles. As however your method of fighting him   50
hitherto has been never to declare open war, but only to attack from a
concealed position – a very light attack, almost as though you deliberately
did not wish to hit him – the public have come to a quite different
conclusion. Some have decided that you are an enemy of Luther, and some
that you are in collusion with him and that you pretend to differ but really   55
are in agreement. If you wish to be relieved of this burden of error and
misconception, it will be absolutely essential to disclose yourself and come
out at last into the open, to prove to the world by an open confrontation with
Luther what your opinions really are and at the same time to defend the
church from a most abominable heresy. Unless you do this, there will be a   60
universal cry of protest that you have betrayed the supreme position of the
church and paid no heed to the purity of the gospel and to your personal
duty.

Our friend Mosellanus has paid the debt of nature,[6] but of course
before it was due; for that man was the great glory of the University of   65
Leipzig. Would that God had so arranged it that he might have had a longer
experience of what I could do for him! – hardly anything more gratifying
could have happened to me. But since God has decided otherwise, we must
bear his death with resignation, and do what we can to find a man to fill his
place who can bring distinction to our college in Greek and good literature   70
and equip the men of our dominions to perform the obligations of virtue and
social duty. Should you know anyone of the kind, who must however be
entirely free from all taint of the Lutheran faction, I wish you would send
him to me;[7] by so doing you will earn my gratitude, and the man will not
regret it. Farewell.   75

From Dresden, 21 May 1524

1449 / From Kilian Praus   Sélestat, 27 May 1524

The autograph of this letter, first published as Ep 27 in Enthoven, is in the
Rehdiger Collection of the University Library at Wrocław (ms Rehd 254.125).
On Praus, see Ep 1279 n2.

A humble person like myself, Erasmus, owed your eminence the tribute of

* * * * *

6 Mosellanus had died on 19 April 1524.
7 Erasmus ignored this matter in Ep 1499 but corrected the oversight in Ep
  1526:229–37. When the reminder in Ep 1520:47–51 finally reached him
  (February or March 1525), he recommended Jacobus Ceratinus (Ep 623:34n);
  see Epp 1561, 1564–8.

not troubling you with a letter; but there was something that compelled me to write even against my will, and my humility has been overcome by necessity. For necessary I find it to clear my reputation in your mind, which perhaps suffers unduly from the suspicion that some letter of yours has been 5 betrayed by me. That excellent scholar Johannes Sapidus[1] had the same suspicion, and accepted my defence; and when he cleared his name to you, he contrived, I think, not to cast on me the suspicions he had rebutted for himself. But all the same, he said I was a friend of Eppendorf,[2] and I should not like a shred of suspicion to be left in your mind as a result; so I thought I 10 ought to write you this letter as a precaution.

I never had enough of an acquaintance or friendship with Eppendorf to make me immediately divulge to him any letter of yours that I might have chanced on by accident which contained something about Eppendorf that you might not want to get out. I speak the truth, and in Christ's name, 15 Erasmus, I beg you to believe me. I could not behave like that, I could not show such disrespect for you, and set such a high value on being friends with Eppendorf. You see immediately that I should not have wanted to do it, even had I been able. And what if I never was able to divulge anything at all relating to that letter? I spend some time now and again in Sapidus' house 20 with great confidence and great freedom, and use his books as though they were my own, as he with his usual kindness freely invites me to do, but I have never seen any letter from you lying about in his house so much disregarded that I might have found the opportunity to read it secretly and steal any part of it for my own benefit or anyone else's. I have, I confess, read 25 letters from you to Sapidus,[3] but ones that did not mention Eppendorf, because Sapidus, knowing how enormously I enjoy reading your letters, had gladly shown them to me; and then in particular the one in which you protested to Sapidus himself about the divulging of the letter which you had wanted to keep permanently buried. And he showed me that because he 30 thought it concerned me too, since Sapidus suspected that I might have found that same letter by chance in his desk, and might have read it secretly and retailed some of it to Eppendorf. I satisfied Sapidus at the time, and he accepted my explanation without demur, as I have already said. So please accept it also, Erasmus, and be utterly convinced that it was not even 35 possible for anything in that letter of yours to be spread about by me.

What happened then? If neither Sapidus himself nor I leaked (to use a current expression) anything from that letter, what is the source of your

* * * * *

1449
1 Ep 323
2 Ep 1437
3 Neither of the letters mentioned here is extant.

suspicions? And then why did Eppendorf protest to you? The protest has,
believe me, another source, and it may perhaps be something that my   40
kinsman Simon,[4] a man whom you know, wrote to me about before you had
complained to Sapidus about that same letter as having been inadequately
kept secret. I had written to him as a friend about several things which
concerned us both, and while doing so had perforce mentioned Eppendorf,
because he still owed Simon some gold coins. I made it clear that I was sorry 45
for him: that a young man of his gifts and so clever in other ways and so
civilized should be said to follow very unhealthy courses and should
postpone any reconciliation with you. I suggested that he would do well to
beware of your pen, for I heard, I said, from my friends that the eloquence
with which you are beyond dispute more powerfully equipped than anyone   50
would find plenty of material, if you should once have decided to attack
him, and that you had the means to deal with him in a way that would really
hurt. I added to this that it was the considered opinion of men of eminent
character and learning too, and by no means ill-disposed to Eppendorf, that
much the best and most useful thing Eppendorf could do would be to   55
concentrate on paying his debts, which are enormous, rather than carry on a
nasty private war with you and end by provoking the sharp point of your
pen at his expense; for in the one case, I said, he would preserve his
reputation, and in the other his status would suffer a substantial loss.

So I wrote a good deal to my friend Simon Minervius in this strain   60
about Eppendorf with absolutely no hostility towards him but with
particular good will, though admittedly in such terms that had any of it got
through to him, he might perhaps have had some reason to be angry with
me; and finally I inquired whether Simon knew how things then stood
between you. To this last inquiry Simon replied in the following words: 65
'When he was here the other day, Conrad,[5] who used to be Hutten's servant
and is now Eppendorf's, told me that Eppendorf had written a letter of
protest to Erasmus.'[6] When I asked the reason, he said it was a difficult
question. I persisted and went on asking, and at length he reluctantly told
me. 'Eppendorf,' he said, 'is quite clear, from letters he has had from friends 70

* * * * *

4 Simon Schaidenreisser (Minervius), documented 1515–73. Praus and Schaidenreisser had both matriculated at Basel in spring term 1522. Since Schaidenreisser was apparently already known to Erasmus at that time (Ep 1285:57–8),
   he may have been the Simon Hexapolitanus who wrote Ep 482 (see the
   introduction to that letter). Apparently still in Basel at this time, his subsequent
   whereabouts are unknown until 1532, when he was a teacher of poetry in
   Munich. From 1538 to 1573 he was a judge in the same city.
5 Unidentified
6 Not extant

and kinsmen sent to him from home, that Erasmus has set the prince's mind against him.'[7] From these words, Erasmus, you can infer that it was other people, and not me or Sapidus, who started whatever it is that Eppendorf has written to you to protest about. I have never seen him during the whole of this year that I have been away from Basel; meanwhile I have written to him only once and that very briefly, and there was no mention of you in it, and that was when I first discovered that he was in Strasbourg, long before you had written the letter to Sapidus with which we are now concerned. And in Basel I was friendly with Eppendorf at the time when I discovered that he was a great favourite of yours too.

When Hutten left for Mulhouse,[8] and the quarrel between you and him first began to be publicly known, Eppendorf and I left Basel together. Moreover I sometimes paid a call on Hutten while he was in Basel; it was a courtesy I owed the man, for I was personally indebted to him for having given me a letter of recommendation to my patron,[9] who in those days had a high opinion of Hutten, and I had felt the benefit of that testimonial. But Hutten had not yet shown his true colours, and all my meetings with him and my courtesy calls preceded the publication of Hutten's *Expostulatio*[10] by a substantial space of time. In a word, neither Hutten nor Eppendorf ever took me into his confidence. Whatever they said or wrote or did in opposition to you was said or written or done without my knowledge, much less with my approval.

I can also produce reliable witnesses to prove that on more than one occasion and in more than one place I made it clear how much I disapproved of some of their principles and particularly disliked the fact that Eppendorf had a disagreement with you (not to give it at this stage a more serious name), and how much I wished that he would seek an early reconciliation with you. I even discussed this with Conrad his servant, when he happened to be passing here on his way to Strasbourg. I asked him whether Eppendorf still had anything to do with you, and whether you got on all right. He replied that Eppendorf would be quiet in future. I said this was a good idea, and urged forcefully that he should keep it up, and now that Hutten was dead,[11] should not make himself generally unpopular by pursuing his cause; also that he should strive for a reconciliation with you as soon as possible. This, I said, would be much to his advantage; it was the right thing for him to

* * * * *

7 Ie, that of Duke George of Saxony (Ep 1283)
8 18 January 1523; see Ep 1331 n24.
9 Beatus Rhenanus? See Ep 1279 n2.
10 Ep 1356 n9
11 C 31 August 1523; see Ep 1388 n12.

do, and also beyond doubt would do him good in the eyes of all right-thinking men. I spoke on these lines to Beatus Rhenanus too. But when he urged me to write to Eppendorf and try to persuade him to be reconciled to you, I refused; I had no expectation that a letter from me would do any good, and I thought that in taking action, if any, Eppendorf would be guided not by my ideas but those of other people, or more likely his own.

Such then being the state of the case, dear Erasmus, it remains, first, for you to maintain your old feeling for Sapidus, not only because you must now be clear that he divulged nothing from that letter of yours, but equally because whenever you are mentioned he seems to think and speak highly of you. Secondly, you must forget all this suspicion that I have played you false and retain all your friendly feeling for me, now that you know that I too have done no wrong. Last but not least, you must on no account suppose that because some Germans behave towards you in an unfriendly fashion,[12] all Germans think of you in the same way. In my opinion even those who seem to dislike you by no means dislike the whole of their Erasmus, and what is supposed to be dislike proceeds from a warm feeling and a kind of affection for you. For in the days when they were overfond of you, they wanted to have the whole of Erasmus for their own.

But enough of this. The fact is that you can number me among those most devoted to you, and so you ought. Apart from the public benefactions by which you had bound me to you,[13] in common with all who wish to learn, before I ever knew you by sight, I have my private reasons, when I remember how courteous and kindly your language to me was, how I used shyly to come to you to enjoy your society with other learned men, and how even then you never despised a humble creature like myself. As I from time to time turn over in my mind that courtesy and kindness, it is quite impossible that I should not love you and respect you.

This letter is longer than it should be, but it was necessary to write at considerable length. If you give it a kind reception, you will give me more courage to write to you later if there is any need. I pray for your length of life, Erasmus, more for our sakes than for yours. Christ keep you for us in health and wealth as long as possible.

From Sélestat, 27 May 1524

Kilian Praus OSB

To Erasmus of Rotterdam, most famous and best of all doctors of letters both sacred and profane

* * * * *

12 Cf Ep 1437:104–6.
13 Ie, his books

1450 / From Rudbert von Mosham   Passau, 30 May 1524

The autograph of this letter, which was first published as Ep 26 in Enthoven, is
in the Rehdiger Collection of the University Library at Wrocław (MS Rehd
254.113).

Rudbert of Mosham (1493–1543) was descended from a noble family of
Styria. After studies at Vienna and Bologna, he entered the service of Matthäus
Lang, archbishop of Salzburg, whom he accompanied to the coronation of
Charles v in Aachen (1520) and to the Diet of Worms (1521). Soon afterwards
he joined the court of Archduke Ferdinand but by 1524 had retired to Passau,
where he was dean of the chapter. His later years were filled with efforts to
reconcile Catholics and Protestants that were poorly received by both sides.
Driven from his deanery in 1539, he was arrested by Cardinal Albert of
Brandenburg in 1542 and died in prison the following year.

In this letter Mosham reminds Erasmus of their earlier acquaintance (lines
10–12) and pleads for friendship and correspondence. Erasmus replied with
Ep 1512, but no further correspondence survives.

Greeting. In the course of my reading, most learned Erasmus, I happened
lately by pure chance on your letter to Marcus Laurinus,[1] and was much
upset. Thoroughly dissatisfied with my own lot and with my lack of
enterprise, I sighed as they say Julius Caesar did in front of the statue of
Alexander the Great,[2] because although quite grown up he had done   5
nothing worth remembering, while Alexander at that age had subdued the
world. That is just how I was struck to the heart, as I read the list of your
friends which you set down in such a lively fashion, by the high qualities
and the distinction of the people you list in that very long letter. It pointed to
some weakness in myself, if I had known someone as friendly as you for   10
three whole years, by sight first of all in Louvain,[3] and then in Cologne[4] after
the emperor's coronation we saw a lot of each other and made friends, and
yet I had done nothing and so far made no plans to do anything worth
submitting to a scholar like you, not even a letter, in which I could as it were

* * * * *

1450
1 Ep 1342
2 Suetonius *Caesar* 7
3 Erasmus was in Louvain when the imperial court passed through, 1–8 October
  1520, on its way to Emperor Charles' coronation in Aachen (23 October); see Ep
  1155 introduction.
4 In October–November 1520, Erasmus spent three weeks in Cologne (Ep
  1512:26) while the imperial court was there on its way from the coronation in
  Aachen to the diet at Worms; see Ep 1155 introduction.

pay you a visit and confirm or renew the friendship and intimacy I had once   15
begun. I should have thought it a great privilege if I had found some
reference to my name, some agreeable and honourable mention, among
those noble statues that you erect in your letter to Laurinus in honour of
your friends with an encomium for each of them; and equally I found it
disgraceful that I should not have earned a mention, let alone a word of   20
praise, from you among so many of my contemporaries, some of whom had
been my comrades in arms in literary studies and in the universities of Italy,
and some of whom had made their way into your friendship just about the
same time that I got to know you myself. If I have failed to deserve this, the
cause is not so much my own weakness, and a sort of countrified   25
embarrassment that has prevented me from writing to you hitherto; it is
much more the stormy seas of business into which I was plunged by the
death of a kinsman. In these I have been so deeply involved that for almost
three years I have been obliged to give up not only the habit of writing but
very nearly every kind of literary work.   30

The small treatise translated from the Greek on the care of hounds in
health and disease,[5] which I showed you in Cologne, I have still not been
able to publish, thanks partly to that same mass of business, and also
because there are some rather difficult words in it belonging to the technical
language of medicine on which I have found it hard to get any light.   35

If you do not remember me very clearly even now, you will not have
forgotten how, when I was living in the court of his Eminence the
cardinal-bishop of Gurk,[6] who was then known by the even more promising
title of Salzburg and whom you had never known except by reputation, you
had asked for an opportunity to speak with him and pay him a visit. I at any   40
rate have often regretted that I managed this for you, because the cardinal
said very little to you and not really on your level, and sent you away
without a present, which is not the way of other princes. So I have always
had a slight fear that as a result of this a touch of unpopularity might have
rubbed off on me, though I minded the cardinal's lack of courtesy and   45
generosity more than you did yourself. And so in the end, when I too had
secured my freedom from this court and extricated myself from all that
complicated business, I decided to take holy orders.[7] This is not popular just

* * * * *

5 *Kynosophion ac opusculum Phemonis de cura et conservatione canum* (Vienna:
   J. Singriener n d). This was Mosham's translation of a short treatise by a
   thirteenth-century physician of Constantinople, Demetrius Pepagomenos.
6 Ie, Matthäus Lang; see introduction.
7 Allen cites a letter of Mosham to Willibald Pirckheimer, 23 May 1524, which
   shows that Mosham was also considering marriage and a move to Nürnberg
   should he tire of life in the church. He remained in the church.

now, but I chose to aim at a peaceful mode of life rather than be forever tormented by the slavery of life at court.

Another thing that encourages me to take the risk of interrupting you with this letter is the way that when writing to Laurinus you often mention the deans you number among your friends.[8] As I myself have lately acquired the deanery of Passau, I gain confidence from a position with which custom has made you so familiar, and this is a second reason for wanting to be entered in the list of your friends. Last of all, what roused me to some purpose and made me unable to refrain from sending you a letter of respectful greeting (as if to some deity with whom I have enjoyed daily and nightly converse through the medium of your most important works, which I diligently peruse) was the Nürnberg patrician Willibald Pirckheimer.[9] When I went to see him last month to pay my respects and in hopes of getting to know him, among other acts of kindness he paid me the compliment of showing me many letters from you, like a man unlocking his treasures; and it is true that I looked upon them and read them with the greatest joy. And then I sighed again, as I envied him ornaments of this description more than any rare gifts of gold and silver.

And so, most lovable Erasmus, I beg you urgently to take this letter of mine in good part, for it asks nothing of you except to be quite convinced of my great affection for you, to take diligent care of your health, and to despise with lofty determination the calumnies of the wicked. Do not forget that in the eyes of all intelligent judges any ill will, any possible stain on your reputation was overcome and wiped out long ago by the fame of your learning and your brilliant style.

Farewell, from Passau in Bavaria, 30 May AD 1524.

Before I closed this letter your name came up in conversation with our right reverend and most illustrious bishop Ernest,[10] duke of Bavaria and so forth; and remembering the distinguished tribute you pay him in one of your letters,[11] he instructed me to send you his very cordial greetings. Farewell once more.

Your devoted friend Rudbert von Mosham, doctor of civil and canon law, dean of Passau

* * * * *

8 Apart from Laurinus himself, only two deans, those of Speyer and Basel, are mentioned (Ep 1342:223–4, 506), but numerous church dignitaries of both high and low rank are also mentioned.

9 Ep 318

10 Duke Ernest (1500–60), third son of Duke Albert IV of Bavaria and administrator of the see of Passau. In 1516 he had invited Erasmus to accept a chair at the University of Ingolstadt (Ep 386), an offer that Erasmus had to decline (Epp 392, 394) because of his obligations to the future Charles V.

11 Ep 704

1451 / To William Warham Basel, 1 June 1524

This is the preface to *Alter tomus epistolarum Hieronymi* (Basel: Froben, August 1524), which is the second volume of the revised Froben edition of Jerome, 1524–6; see Ep 1465 introduction. On Warham, the generous patron to whom both the original and the revised editions were dedicated (Epp 396, 1465), see Ep 188.

TO THE MOST REVEREND FATHER IN CHRIST WILLIAM WARHAM,
LORD ARCHBISHOP OF CANTERBURY, LEGATUS NATUS OF THE
APOSTOLIC SEE, PRIMATE OF ALL ENGLAND, FROM DESIDERIUS
ERASMUS OF ROTTERDAM, GREETING

Whatever related to the principles of the Christian life, since this must be our 5
first care, I have collected in the first volume,[1] arranged by order of
subject-matter, with the more perfect Christian first and descending by
gradual stages to the lower levels, then to lapsed Christians, and finally to
the awful warnings. The catalogue of authors[2] I have added as a kind of
appendix to a volume which by itself was rather thin, for I could see no more 10
suitable place for it elsewhere. And at this present moment I shall pass over
what in the first edition I had collected in the second volume,[3] since none of
it belonged there and some of it was simply not worth reading, and this
volume will contain two classes of material not unrelated, the refutative and
the defensive. In the first part are the refutations of heretics and in the 15
second the replies to scurrilous attacks, in both of which Jerome is powerful
and spirited and sometimes writes with such heat and such a torrent of
obloquy and biting words that some people might think he had forgotten the
mildness proper to a Christian. But to put a favourable interpretation on this
will be easy for anyone who will consider the man's fiery and essentially 20
forceful nature, which is outspoken rather than malignant, and besides that
his very high character and blameless life; for such a character, while it does
no man an injury, is often intolerant of injuries done to itself. Besides which,
let him remember that the charge of heresy is too outrageous to be tolerated
even by a man of the sweetest natural disposition, to say nothing of that 25
intense conviction in which he so far surpassed all his contemporaries that
even to compare him with any of the rest would be an insult. To which I

* * * * *

1451
1 See Ep 1465.
2 *Catalogus scriptorum ecclesiasticorum*, more commonly called *De viris illustribus*.
3 In the first edition, volume II had been devoted to the many spurious works; cf
Ep 396:324–36. In the revised edition, the *spuria* were placed in volume IV.

would add that there is also something about the imputation of heresy which means that, while in all other contexts to suffer in silence is a virtue, to overlook it here would be irreligious.   30

Again, this whole age in which St Jerome lived was an incredible hotbed of heretical discord and confusion, such that in those days it needed some special gifts even to be a Christian. So many were the names, the nicknames, and the tenets of the leading heretics that scholars have found it hard work even to list them. But the Cataphrygians,[4] the Borborians,[5] the   35 Ophites,[6] the Basilidians,[7] the Manichaeans,[8] and other heretics resembling them, following as they did a sort of nightmare of hallucinations rather than doctrines, not only remote from Scripture but in hopeless conflict with the instinctive feelings of mankind as well, fell easily into senility as though in the course of nature. But the Arian heresy,[9] strongly defended in writing   40

* * * * *

4 Another name for Montanists; see Ep 1334 n52.
5 The Borborians were a sect of libertine gnostics who flourished from the second to the fifth century. Epiphanius described their doctrines and practices in his *Adversus haereses* 1 (haer 26).
6 The Ophites were an early sect of gnostics who regarded the Fall as a positive advantage for mankind and glorified God's opponent, the serpent (*ophis* in Greek).
7 The Basilidians were followers of Basilides, a gnostic who taught at Alexandria in the second quarter of the second century. He appears to have held that the God of the Jews was, as creator, in the lowest rank of spiritual beings and that the supreme God sent his Nous (mind) to dwell in Jesus and free men from bondage to the creator-God.
8 Manichaeism was founded by Manes (Manichaeus), a Persian (c 215–75) who began propagating his views c 240. His system posited a primeval conflict between light and darkness, the aim of religion being to release the particles of light that Satan had stolen from the realm of light and imprisoned in the brain of man. Jesus, Buddha, the prophets, and Manes had all been sent to help in this task, the achievement of which involved the practice of severe asceticism. Manichaeism spread rapidly and, during the fourth century, the sect was established first at Rome and then in Africa, where St Augustine was a member before his conversion.
9 Arianism, the principal heresy that denied the divinity of Christ, was called after its founder, Arius (c 250–c 336). Arians taught that the Son of God was not eternal (and therefore not of the same substance as the Father) but rather a changeable creature, albeit a very special one, adopted as Son of God because of his abiding righteousness and thus worthy of worship. Arian teaching was condemned at the Council of Nicaea (325), but the Arians, who enjoyed the support of Emperor Constantius II (337–61) nearly defeated the Catholics in a series of later councils. Catholic orthodoxy was finally restored under Emperor Theodosius at the Council of Constantinople in 381, though Arianism survived for another century among the Teutonic tribes.

and relying on what seemed impregnable support from Holy Scripture too, not to mention the backing both political and financial of emperors and whole peoples, rocked Christendom with perilous upheavals; so much so that it was long in doubt which way the uncommitted church would turn, and it was more a political movement or a schism than heresy, because the 45 enemy were almost equal in number, and in literary gifts and learning they were superior.

Their pestilence, having somehow been laid at length to rest, was reborn in the school of Origen,[10] a change of name but the same evil thing, only more serious, like some recurring pestilence that often attacks more 50 pitilessly those who have relapsed. A bitter struggle was waged against it with synods and decretals and even with a hundred creeds,[11] in no way the most appropriate weapons in my opinion with which to suppress heresy, unless there is authority behind them all; for without authority the greater

* * * * *

10 The great church Father Origen (c 185–c 254) had been ambiguous on the subject of the Logos, sometimes making it eternal, sometimes making it a creature subordinate to the Father. Arius, following his teacher Lucian of Antioch, developed the latter emphasis into the heretical teaching summarized in the preceding note. It is thus possible to say that Arianism was *born* in the school of Origen. Erasmus' statement here that it was *reborn* in the school of Origen is a reference to the resurgence of Origenism in the last quarter of the fourth century. Although the Origenists claimed to be orthodox on the subject of the Trinity, their opponents, who included St Epiphanius and (from 393) St Jerome, made them guilty, by association, of all Origen's 'blasphemies,' including his proto-Arian views on the Trinity, simply by virtue of their having studied and circulated his works. See Jerome Epp 84.4, 92 and *Contra Ioannem Hierosolymitanum* 8–9; cf Augustine *De haeresibus* 43 (citing the *Anacephalaeosis* of Epiphanius). The controversy reached a climax with the condemnation of Origenism at a council in Alexandria in the year 400. Pope Anastasius I adhered to the condemnation, doing so in language that implicitly charged the Origenists with reviving Arianism; see the *Epistola ad Venerium Mediolanensem episcopum* in Adalbert Hamman ed *Patrologiae Latinae Supplementum* I (Paris 1958) 791–2. When the Origenist controversy flared up again in the sixth century, the charge of Arianizing was once more (unfairly) hurled at them, this time by Emperor Justinian in his *Liber adversus Origenem* of c 542/3 (PG 86 948, 982–4). At Justinian's insistence, Origenism was condemned at a synod in Constantinople in 543 and again at the Second Council of Constantinople in 553. See Franz Diekamp *Die origenistischen Streitigkeiten im sechsten Jahrhundert und das fünfte allgemeine Concil* (Münster im Westfalen 1899).

11 Here Erasmus has apparently taken a step backward chronologically and is referring to the period from the Council of Nicaea (325) to the Council of Constantinople (381). For a survey of the numerous credal statements produced in these decades of bitter controversy, see J.N.D. Kelly *Early Christian Creeds* (London 1950) chapters 8 and 9.

the flow of dogma, the more plenteous the material of which heresies are   55
made. Never was the Christian faith so pure, so simple, so inviolate as when
the world was happy with a single creed and that a very short one.[12] But in
the age of which I speak that faith was found on paper rather than in men's
hearts, and there were almost as many creeds as there were believers. As
often happens, private ambition took a hand, and godless rivalries were   60
pursued under a colouring of the faith. Nor did any evil bring closer to
disaster the see of Peter, always unchallenged hitherto, which was at least
shaken and weakened, though not overthrown; for under Pope Liberius
Rome was not altogether free from Arian errors,[13] and under the emperor
Constantius it maintained a dubious hold upon that rock on which rests the   65
Catholic church. Above all however it was the East and the whole of Greece
that were seething with these troubles; for the greater their admiration for
the genius of Origen, the more the Greeks resented the condemnation of the
opinions of that incomparable man, just as great physical passion sometimes takes delight even in the defects of the beloved.[14]   70

All these upheavals so affected our hero Jerome that he was nowhere
left in peace or given leisure to pursue his studies. Thanks to Rufinus,[15] he
was even suspected and falsely accused of heresy, because at one time as a
great admirer of Origen's genius he had translated some of his work for
readers of Latin and even praised the author.[16] What exposed him yet more   75

* * * * *

12 An apparent reference to the so-called Apostle's Creed, which was much
   shorter and less burdened with theology than the creeds produced at Nicaea
   and Constantinople. In its early form, known as the Old Roman Creed, it dates
   from the second half of the second century. It was used only in the western
   church.
13 Liberius, pope from 352 to 366, was banished after refusing the order of
   Emperor Constantius to assent to the condemnation of Athanasius, the
   champion of Catholic orthodoxy. Liberius was reinstated after having signed
   an Arian formulary, the exact content of which is not known.
14 Horace Satires 1.3.38–40
15 Rufinus of Aquilea (c 245–410), a friend of Jerome from boyhood, was a monk
   known primarily for his translations of Greek theological works into Latin and
   for his dogged defence of the orthodoxy of Origen against the latter's
   fourth-century critics, who eventually included Jerome (see following note).
16 Until the last decade of the century, Jerome was an admirer of Origen,
   translating into Latin dozens of the Greek Father's homilies on books of the
   Old and New Testaments and lavishing praise on Origen's genius. However,
   when Epiphanius, the fanatical bishop of Salamis, launched his campaign
   against the 'arch-heretic' Origen, Jerome, who subsequently claimed that his
   veneration for Origen had been based on the latter's marvellous skills as an
   exegete rather than his controversial views as a theologian, readily delivered

to the attacks of his critics was the wide range of his work. The quality of his scholarship aroused envy; many people resented the exceptional severity of his regime, and even more the freedom with which he criticized the faults of his fellow men. Truth hurts, and everyone with a bad conscience thinks himself the target. Thus it came about that to the very end of his life this most 80 saintly of men had to battle with the viper of malignity, which raved at him so furiously with tongue and pen that some were found to circulate a letter purporting to be written by Jerome himself in which he lamented that he had at one time been a follower of the errors of Origen.[17]

Who will you offer me so meek by nature that when harassed by such 85 treatment as this he does not take fire? And yet, anyone who closely examines and assesses the books in which he seems to attack personal targets without restraint, Vigilantius[18] for instance or Rufinus[19] or Jovinian,[20] will find there is much more wit than gall beneath the surface, and in the full flood of invective will discover clear traces of a most civilized mind. In the 90 comedies,[21] when Demea, unlike his normal self, wants to be courteous and cheerful, there is a touch of boorish bitterness all the same even in his pleasantries; on the other hand, when Micio goes against his nature, which is kindly, in reproving Aeschinus, there is much gentleness even in his

* * * * *

the abjuration of Origenism demanded of him in 393 by agents of Epiphanius. This caused tension in Jerome's friendship with Rufinus (see previous note), who argued naively that Origen's real views were entirely in accordance with late fourth-century standards of orthodoxy. Open breach between the two friends came when Rufinus, in the preface to his translation of one of Origen's most controversial works, *On First Principles* (398), pictured Jerome as the enthusiast for Origen whose example he was following in translating the book and deliberately ignored Jerome's more recent anti-Origenist stand. Feeling that both his orthodxy and his honesty had been impugned, Jerome reacted with bitter invective, and the ensuing controversy lasted until 402. See J.N.D. Kelly *Jerome* (London 1975) chapters 18, 20, 21.

17 In his *Apologia contra Rufinum* 2.24, Jerome complains about a letter falsely ascribed to him. It is not, however, about once having subscribed to the 'errors of Origen' but rather about having translated Old-Testament books from the Hebrew. Erasmus refers to this letter in his *Vita Hieronymi* (Ferguson *Opuscula* 168:919–24) and says that 'in it they have him lamenting the errors of his earlier life' (ibidem lines 921–2).

18 Vigilantius of Aquitaine (fl c 400) attacked Jerome as an Origenist. Jerome replied in his *Contra Vigilantium* (406) and in his Epp 61 and 109.

19 *Apologia adversus Rufinum* (401)

20 Jovinian (d 405) denied that virginity was superior to marriage and also denied the perpetual virginity of Mary. Jerome attacked him in his *Adversus Jovinianum* (392).

21 Ie, in Terence's *Adelphi*

severity. There is nothing more honey-sweet than Christian charity, which,   95
when it is most severe, retains its native sweetness and modifies wine's
medicinal astringency with the blandness of oil. As Cicero, again, is
nowhere more to be admired as an orator than when resentment has, as it
were, struck spurs into his powerful eloquence, so does St Jerome – always
so well read, always so eloquent – yet never speak better than when he is   100
denouncing heresy or misrepresentation, if one can describe as denunciation what is spirited defence of the truth.

My first volume therefore showed us Jerome the master of eloquence;
this one will show his lightning and his thunder. The first established his
outstanding sanctity of life; the second will establish his indomitable   105
courage in the face of all the assaults of evil men. So nature has provided that
exceptional merit will not show its full brilliance until put through its paces
by adversity, like gold that comes refined out of the furnace, or 'the dark oak
with cruel axes trimmed' that shoots again with a thicker growth of branches
and, as Horace puts it, 'gains strength and spirit from the knife itself.'²² The   110
skill and courage of a ship's master are made clear in storms. No one was ever
rated a great general whose valour has not been displayed in adversity. If it
is proper to bring the myths of the ancients into a serious context, when Juno
exposed Hercules to every kind of danger,²³ all she achieved was to make his
courage famous and secure divine honours for her victim. In the same way   115
the Lord allowed his brave servant Job to be tempted by Satan, that through
him he might provide us with an example of invincible patience; in the same
way he tested his beloved Abraham,²⁴ that the world might recognize a
supreme example of man's confidence in God. Nor should we recognize
Jerome's greatness, had it not been polished into brilliance by the calumnies   120
of heretics and detractors.

And so, most reverend prelate, if in the different and difficult kinds of
business in which you are engaged your life has continued its unbroken
tenor down to the old age, green and flourishing as it is, which has been
your happy lot, without involving you in any tragic troubles of this kind,   125
some might perhaps give the credit for this to your integrity and your
prudence; but I would rather give the credit to the favour of heaven, to
which you owe all those gifts of mind and heart. And yet the difficulties

* * * * *

22 *Odes* 4.4.57–60
23 Juno, jealous that Jupiter had fathered Hercules by a mortal woman, sent two
   serpents to attack the infant, who strangled them. Later, Juno drove Hercules
   mad, causing him to murder his own wife and children. To atone for this crime,
   he had to undertake the famous twelve labours.
24 Gen 22:1–14

needed to bring out that high steadiness of purpose allied with integrity to
match it were not entirely lacking. It is a most difficult thing, and in dignity   130
very close to the throne, to play the part of chancellor in England.[25] And
though your conduct of that office was such as to make the task very difficult
for your successor,[26] however distinguished he might be, yet I doubt
whether the way you laid down your office did not display your high
character even more clearly than your conduct of it. Could any man step   135
down from a position so exalted without regretting it? Could any man not be
jealous of his successor? But you, after fulfilling the duties of that most
distinguished office without a trace of pride, laid it down so entirely without
any sign of regret as to make it obvious to all men that you had accepted
office not for your own advantage but for the public good, so readily did you   140
lay down, given an honourable opportunity, the burden which had brought
you so much honour. You thought it an immense advantage that the time
which was saved from almost entirely secular business could be devoted to
the sacred studies in which a bishop should be constantly engaged. For you
did not allow yourself to lose any of the time that was meant for them, even   145
in the days when you were overrun by so many great waves of public
business.

But I will bring this letter to an end, once I have recounted my
experiences as I reread Jerome's works; they are much the same as one has
when looking at pictures. A picture of moderate quality is quite attractive on   150
first inspection; if you study it more often, more closely, and more at leisure,
it gradually loses its attraction. On the other hand, a painting by a
distinguished artist becomes more and more admirable the more often and
more attentively you look at it. Jerome was a favourite in my adolescence,[27]
he was a favourite when I reached man's estate; but never have I enjoyed   155
him more than during this rereading. In heaven's name, how utterly I am
dissatisfied with myself as I watch this man's personal holiness breathing in
all he writes, his burning zeal, his astonishing knowledge of the Scriptures,
and his prodigious memory! Think of such powers of expression and such
intellectual force in a man so far gone in years! It is to your generosity[28] that   160
all lovers of religious literature owe the privilege of reading Jerome with the
errors removed and notes added, not merely legible but intelligible; their

* * * * *

25 Warham was lord chancellor 1504–15.
26 Wolsey, in whose favour Warham resigned as chancellor on 22 December 1515;
   cf Ep 388:93–7.
27 Cf Ep 844:283–8. For examples of Erasmus' high praise of Jerome, see Epp
   126:133–41, 335:232–45.
28 Cf Epp 333:96–9, 334:163–4, 335:252–9, 396:278–82, 361–4.

debt will now be the greater, for they have him better presented in every way. Farewell, most noble of prelates.

From Basel, 1 June 1524

165

1452 / To Willibald Pirckheimer   Basel, 3 June [1524]

This letter was first published in the *Pirckheimeri opera*. The year-date is amply evident from the contents. Pirckheimer's reply is Ep 1480.

Greeting. I think all your letters have been delivered in good faith, and there was not one that did not give very great pleasure. About my own I am not so sure. For about the first medal in bronze that was sent me I know I wrote twice.[1] And now I have received the specimens you had promised me in that letter[2] you sent by the hand of one of your fellow citizens, together with a letter[3] in which you report what has happened in your part of the world since the departure of the princes.[4] Ferdinand has been at Breisach and Freiburg.[5] Fabri[6] summoned me urgently to come and talk to the prince, saying it would mean a lot for me, but I steadily refused. They have got themselves a lot of unpopularity, and want me to share it. When I see the two parties ready to come to terms, I shall not fail to do my duty.

Luther has written to me,[7] but in his usual fashion, promising that he will forgive my weakness provided I do not deliberately attack his views in print. I sent him an answer,[8] but a very brief one, and, in my usual fashion, a polite one.[9] I had no leisure for more, because at that moment Hieronim[10] was here, a Polish nobleman who is the representative of his king, an open-hearted man and very devoted to me, but violently opposed to Luther,

5

10

15

* * * * *

1452
1 Epp 1408, 1417
2 Not extant
3 Not extant
4 At the conclusion of the Diet of Nürnberg (Ep 1408 n16), the recess of which was adopted on 18 April 1524
5 Archduke Ferdinand was in Freiburg on 13 May 1524 and by 16 May he had gone to Breisach to preside over a meeting of the territorial estates of the Breisgau. See Theophil Burckhardt-Biedermann *Bonifacius Amerbach und die Reformation* (Basel 1894) 171 n1; cf LP IV 337–8.
6 Johann Fabri (Epp 1260 n22, 1324 n14), who had recently joined the court of Archduke Ferdinand (Ep 1382 n12).
7 Ep 1443
8 Ep 1445
9 Cf the description of these two letters in Ep 1466:19–21.
10 Łaski (Ep 1341A n310)

as the king himself is.[11] Melanchthon has been on a visit to his native country[12] and would, they say, have been to see me, had he not been afraid of making me unpopular. He sent me a man called Joachim,[13] of whom he 20 thinks very highly, and has written affectionately about me to Pellicanus.[14]

You know, I expect, that Petrus Mosellanus has died.[15] My friend Hedio has married,[16] on 30 May in Strasbourg, a wife with a good dowry. I have written to the cardinal[17] and the pope[18] and also to Fabri,[19] urging them not to take harsh measures or let their hatred of bad men do harm to the 25 good, and they promised they would do as I say. Certain people are taking a hand in this business who seem to have no aim except disorder and subversion.[20] The magistrates here begin to be less favourable to Luther.[21]

I have written this with difficulty, my dear Willibald, being wretchedly burdened with the stone,[22] from which I had been free for some months 30 now, once I had given up eating dried pears, which here means wild ones. Some people I know think that the casting will be more successful in a mixture of copper and tin, the sort of material in which they cast bells. There is another way out, if the head of Terminus were turned to one side.[23] As it is now, there is a corresponding thickness on both sides, which means that the 35 face does not come out very well. Besides which, there is a technique for reducing the size of the subject portrayed (but it is slow and laborious), if a cast is taken in clay within a closed circle of bronze, which is then allowed to dry; this is repeated several times, and the subject then cast from the clay in lead. It would be easier to do this if you had the original, which is in lead; but 40

* * * * *

11 Erasmus had learned this from Łaski himself; see Ep 1341A:1246–69.
12 Ep 1444 n2
13 Camerarius (Ep 1501)
14 The letter is not extant. On Pellicanus, see Ep 1341A n309.
15 19 April 1524. On Mosellanus, see Ep 1305.
16 Ep 1477B
17 Ep 1422:59–67
18 Epp 1414:33–42, 1418:67–71
19 Ep 1397:15–18
20 On this cf the chronicle of the Carthusian Georg Carpentarius of Brugg in *Basler Chroniken* ed Wilhelm Fischer and Alfred Stern I (Leipzig 1872) 384. And on the growing hostility of the reform party to Erasmus, see AK Ep 963 (Bonifacius Amerbach to Alciati, c beginning of August 1524), especially lines 21ff.
21 Cf Ep 1466:25–7.
22 After his severe attack at Christmas (Ep 1408 n2), Erasmus fell ill again in May (Ep 1489:20–1) and was bedridden for a month (Allen Ep 1956:21–2). See also Epp 1456, 1466, 1484, 1488.
23 See Ep 1408 n17.

it is in the artist's hands, though he promised he would send it to me. For he had over thirty florins[24] from me as the price of his work.

He also had the same sum for a painting. And again I have lately sent two pictures of myself to England,[25] done by a very elegant artist. He took a picture of me to France.[26] The king sends a fresh invitation. There is a substantial benefice ready for me.[27] I am periodically at risk here on account of the wine.[28] If we have any gleam of peace, I shall perhaps go there. I had been in April to Besançon.[29] The town authorities and the canons made me generous offers. I thanked them, and replied that I had enough for my simple way of life, and would rather be my own master and enjoy their support without strings, not generosity based on contract. I expect my servant[30] back shortly from England and Brabant. I shall then decide on something. Whatever it is, you shall not be kept in the dark. How I wish my stone and your gout could together be sent packing to the Indies!

I find it just as you say: almost all letters are either suppressed or opened. I wrote some time ago to Duke George,[31] at his instigation. When he did not answer, I sent the same contents by another hand.[32] Still no reply.[33] I wrote again lately about something else.[34] This, I suspect, has been suppressed, though there was nothing in it connected with Luther. Farewell.

I have not read this through. You will make allowances. You know the handwriting.

* * * * *

24 Presumably Rhenish gold florins
25 Two Holbein portraits done in 1523. One of them, now in the Radner Collection at Longford Castle, was sent as a present to Warham (Ep 1488:3–4). The other, whose recipient is unknown, is thought to be the one now in the Louvre. For details, see Allen's note and Gerlo 48–50.
26 The study that was made for the Louvre portrait and is now in the Öffentliche Kunstsammlung Basel. It seems that Holbein took the picture to Bonifacius Amerbach, who in the period May 1522–May 1524 was studying at Avignon. It is possible that Amerbach, who may have been preparing to move on to Montpellier when the portrait arrived, sent it back to Basel with Holbein, which would mean that it was already back in Basel when this letter was written. See Gerlo 50–1.
27 The treasurership at Tours (Ep 1434 n12)
28 Erasmus' supply of Burgundy wine (Ep 1316 n7) had run out, but during the summer he received a new supply; Ep 1484:13.
29 See Ep 1440 n4.
30 Lieven Algoet; see Epp 1430 n7, 1437:199–200.
31 Ep 1313
32 Ep 1325
33 Ep 1340 did not reach Erasmus; see Ep 1313 introduction.
34 The letter, not extant, that elicited Ep 1448

To the honourable Willibald Pirckheimer, town councillor of Nürnberg

1453 / To William Warham   Basel, 5 June 1524

This is the preface to the third volume of the new Froben edition of Jerome (Basel, August 1524), which is the last volume of the letters. See the introductions to Epp 1451 and 1465.

TO THE MOST REVEREND FATHER IN CHRIST WILLIAM WARHAM,
LORD ARCHBISHOP OF CANTERBURY, PRIMATE OF ALL ENGLAND
AND LEGATUS NATUS, FROM ERASMUS OF ROTTERDAM, GREETING
In this volume I have collected the books or letters in which this great scholar
replied to the inquiries of men of many different kinds, following no order   5
except that of the books in which these matters are discussed. A few
particular things, some of which did not fall in this class and some that have
not even the outward form of letters, I have removed in order to incorporate
them in other volumes where they are more at home. I have however
included in this volume the prefaces which in current texts stand at the head   10
of books of the Bible, so that they may be available for the future in a more
correct form and made easier to understand by the addition of notes; but
only those which are really Jerome's. There are among them a certain
number with false ascriptions, which I have referred to but not included, so
that there might be nothing here which does not belong. When however, as   15
my work progressed, I saw that this was a thin volume, I added the Hebrew
traditions,[1] and a few other things which have nothing of the letter about
them. This volume contains therefore the explanatory works – those, that is
to say, which contribute to the exposition of Holy Scripture, my purpose in
choosing to place these last being to relate them more closely to the other   20
works of his which expound the books of Holy Scripture.

Nor is this system of arrangement, I think, a bad fit. The first volume
gives the principles of life and morals, the concern that properly comes first
of all. The next contains the defence of the faith, and the third is for Christian
scholarship. The good life is all men's business; to fight for the faith is for the   25
practised warrior, not for the raw recruit; and then to assume the character
of the scholar demands the authority that is won only by the highest
character and no ordinary learning. And in those days the highest authority

* * * * *

1453
1 The volume included the *Quaestiones sive traditiones hebraeicae* as well as the *De locis hebraeicis* and the *De nominibus hebraeicis*.

was shared by all the bishops, and often prevailed even over the imperial
majesty which then was the greatest thing on earth. There is plenty of   30
evidence to prove this in the writings of the Fathers; and perhaps it would be
the same even now, if the brilliance of a few of them did not throw the
brightness of the rest into the shade, or if most men nowadays did not think
little of the qualities to which the bishops in old days owed their great
influence over the common people. These were integrity of life, sacred   35
learning, and an inexhaustible desire to do good unto all men.

    Jerome, you will say, was not a bishop; and yet his exceptional learning
coupled with great holiness of life gave him an authority such as had hardly
fallen to the lot of any bishop. The name of Jerome was so universally well
known that people gathered to consult that one individual from all parts of   40
the whole world if they found anything obscure or controversial in Holy
Writ. Problems in various fields were referred to him from Italy, Spain,
Africa, Greece, all parts of France, and even from the farthest parts of Gothic
Germany, which began quite late to grow civilized. His sacred learning in all
its power and richness was so ready to hand that, old and isolated as he was,   45
he could cope with all those different subjects. Nor were learned bishops
ashamed to learn from a mere priest; Augustine was one of them.

    And so, most excellent of prelates, I was inspired partly by the merits
of this incomparable man and partly by your wishes, which I know to be
always based on the most authoritative judgment, to revise the first edition,   50
on which great pains were spent. I have set about this task in such a way as
to show the attentive reader without difficulty that I undertook the work
neither without reason nor without result. If he is frank as well as grateful,
he will confess that he is now even more indebted to your highness, to
whom he had long owed a substantial debt; for it is your generosity to which   55
he ought to attribute almost all of it,[2] if I have made any contribution to
public enlightenment. Had such a Maecenas been my good fortune as a
young man, I might have been numbered, for what I am worth, among the
truly fortunate.

    Would that my attempt might succeed! – to make the glory of your   60
name among posterity as great as the affection earned by your lofty
character in the hearts of all good men. I know your saintly character, which
asks no credit for the good you do except from God, and how you are so truly
born to do good to all men that you seem to have received a kindness if you
have done one to another man. I know that your modesty asks for nothing   65
less than the praise of men; but none more truly deserve praise than those

* * * * *

2 See Ep 1451 n28.

who do not ask for it. May the Lord Jesus long preserve your saintly old age for the benefit of learning and the church in England.

Basel, 5 June 1524

1454 / From Johann von Botzheim   Constance, 6 June 1524

The manuscript of this letter (=Ep 25 in Förstemann/Günther) was in the Burscher Collection at Leipzig (Ep 1254 introduction). On Botzheim, see Ep 1285.

As he was recommended by Hummelberg,[1] I gave a kind reception to the young man who brings you this letter; it was his own idea to ask me for a letter of introduction to you. He has been in Constance for three days, and seems to know some Greek and Latin. His name is Magnus,[2] but his first name I have forgotten and he is not at hand as I write this. If it is not 5 inconvenient, please have a word with him, even very briefly. I send this by the hand of a very intelligent young man, and there is no need to burden you with a long letter. There is no news here. They tell me that all the princes of Bavaria, with a few other bishops, not Bavarian, whom they have invited to join them, those of Trier[3] and Strasbourg,[4] have forgathered in Heidelberg 10 under cover of an archery meet.[5] As to what is brewing there, guesses differ

* * * * *

1454
1 Michael Hummelberg (1487–1537) of Ravensburg, north-east of Lake Constance, was an enthusiastic Greek scholar who had studied in Paris and Rome and then settled down in his home town as a teacher. He was a frequent visitor to Constance, where he met Erasmus in September 1522; Epp 1316:17–18, 1342:462–3.
2 Unidentified
3 Richard von Greiffenklau (d 1531)
4 Wilhelm von Honstein (c 1470–1541)
5 A reference to the so-called 'Heidelberg Shooting Match' (Das Heidelberger Schiessen), a congress of twenty-three princes in Heidelberg, 28 May–5 June, held under the cover of a festive shooting match. In attendance were all the members of the house of Wittelsbach, both the Palatine and the Bavarian branches, as well as the archbishop-elector of Trier, the margrave of Ansbach, the landgrave of Hessen, the bishops of Würzburg and Strasbourg, some princes of Württemberg and Braunschweig, and a papal envoy. The highly secret discussions that went on behind this façade caused widespread speculation at the time and are still something of a mystery. The principal subject of discussion seems to have been a decidedly anti-Hapsburg attempt to secure the election of a Bavarian prince as King of the Romans (ie, heir-

widely. Besides which, in the last few days someone newly arrived here reported that in lower Germany, if I remember rightly, there is fresh trouble in Gelderland,[6] stirred up perhaps by the king of France. The bishop of Constance is being very severe on Luther's followers, ten of whom are detained in prisons outside Constance. If what we hear is true, intrigues are being hatched everywhere against the cities which support the gospel and are now labelled Lutheran.[7] These last few days Guillaume Farel was in Constance with a colleague,[8] both of them French. Let me know when you have time what you are doing and how you are, and if you have any news. Farewell, my beloved teacher, and look after your health.

Constance, 6 June 1524

Yours, Johann von Botzheim

To that most Christian and most learned theologian, Master Erasmus of Rotterdam, his most beloved teacher. In Basel

* * * * *

designate to the emperorship). It is not clear how far this project was pursued. The princes also gave audience to an envoy of Archduke Ferdinand, who made an unsuccessful attempt to secure a special grant for war against the Turks. See Walter Friedensburg *Der Reichstag zu Speyer 1526* (Berlin 1887) 112; Walter Müller *Die Stellung der Kurpfalz zur lutherischen Bewegung von 1517 bis 1525* (Heidelberg 1937) 84–6.

6 For half a century (1492–1543) the duchy of Gelderland was a French client state lying astride three of the great rivers that were vital to the commerce of the Netherlands. From 1515, Charles v and Karel van Egmond, duke of Gelderland (d 1528), were incessantly at war, much to Erasmus' distress (cf Ep 628:33n). For the unrest at this time, see LP IV 24, 109, 268, 410. Gelderland was finally incorporated in the Hapsburg Netherlands in 1543.

7 Rumours of such intrigues were perhaps provoked by the preliminaries leading to the formation of the Regensburg Union, an alliance of south-German Catholic princes whose aim was to promote Catholic reform and to stamp out the Lutheran heresy. The members of the alliance, which was concluded at a meeting in Regensburg from 27 June to 7 July 1524, were the archduke Ferdinand, the two dukes of Bavaria, the cardinal-archbishop of Salzburg, and a number of south-German bishops. Invitations to the Regensburg meeting had been issued by Ferdinand and the papal legate Campeggi on 8 May; see Pfeilschifter 301–5.

8 Farel (Ep 1341A n305) and his colleague Antoine Du Blet (Ep 1341A n307) passed through Constance on their way back to Basel from a visit to Zwingli in Zürich; see *Biographie nouvelle* 126. It was at about this time that Farel and Erasmus had the confrontation described in Epp 1341A:1196–1215 and 1510.

1455 / From Juan Luis Vives   Bruges, 16 June 1524

For the source of this letter, see Ep 1256 introduction. On Vives, see Ep 1362.

VIVES TO ERASMUS

I left England in April, solely to get married,[1] and with instructions from the
leading men and the cardinal[2] to return by the end of September. And I will
do so, unless forcibly prevented by some necessity or wholly incapacitating
cause, for those people have treated me so well that it would be wrong not to   5
fall in with their wishes, since they comply in so many things with mine. On
the feast of Corpus Christi[3] I bowed my neck under the yoke of matrimony,
and do not yet feel it at all heavy or the sort of thing I should like to shake off;
but the outcome is in God's hands. So far I have no reason to complain, and
all those who know us are delighted; nothing, they say, has happened here   10
for years that has won such universal approval.

     As for the men whom your friends urge you to attack, they are an evil
past hope of cure, and yet almost a necessary evil[4] in these times, when
everything has gone to the bad; but these things are heaven's doing. In your
position, you will achieve nothing unless you act entirely out of character;   15
and if you do so act, you will spoil the one bad feature in the man which is
really valuable. What great problems you are faced with by your reputation!
So much so that it seems you cannot honourably stand aside without being
involved as a public figure in public affairs; but no skill in management will
save you from offending one side or the other, and maybe both. Do not   20
forget that line of Ennius about Maximus.[5]

     Claymond sends his greetings,[6] and so do almost the whole of that
university. I have heard nothing for a long time more satisfactory than the
news that your works are popular with my fellow Spaniards too.[7] I hope that

* * * * *

1455
1 To his kinswoman Margarita Valdaura (1505–52)
2 Wolsey
3 26 May 1524
4 Cf *Adagia* i v 26.
5 The reference is to the passage cited by Cicero in *De officiis* 1.24.84 and *De
  senectute* 4.10. The line that Vives had in mind may well have been 'noenum
  rumores ponebat ante salutem,' ie, 'he [Quintus Fabius Maximus] valued
  [public] safety more than the applause of the mob.'
6 John Claymond (Ep 990) was the first president of Corpus Christi College,
  Oxford, where Vives had been teaching since 1523.
7 Cf Ep 1488:28–9. This must refer to the circulation of foreign editions of Erasmus'
  works in Spain. At this point there had been no Spanish edition of any of them

as they get used to them and others like them, they will grow civilized, and   25
lose some of the barbaric views on life which are ingrained in them,
sharp-witted as they are but devoid of culture, and which they pass on as it
were from hand to hand.

News reached us in England that you had moved to Burgundy,[8] in
hopes of being cured of the stone by their pure and generous wines. Others   30
assured us you were coming to England,[9] and I heard one man say that you
would undoubtedly have come if you had been invited; which I wish I had
known while I was there. That problem would not have held you up for
long. Your arrival would have been popular and welcome with the king, the
cardinal, and all the nobility. But if you do decide to do so, begin at the same   35
time to write something against the man;[10] for otherwise you will raise a
frown on some faces when it is particularly important for you that they
should be all smiles. But I do not doubt that More, who can give the most
prudent advice about this, will have given you plenty. As for me, dearest
teacher, I am as you know more than ready to do all I can to help; my powers   40
are small, but my good will enormous. My greetings to Froben and
Rhenanus. Every possible good wish, dear master.

Bruges, 16 June 1524

1456 / To Christoph von Utenheim   Basel, 20 June 1524

On Christoph von Utenheim, see Ep 1332. This letter was first published in the
Opus epistolarum. Ep 1464 is Bishop Christoph's answer.

ERASMUS OF ROTTERDAM TO CHRISTOPH, BISHOP OF BASEL, GREETING
Right reverend prelate, while I was recounting the Lord's mercies, his mercy
laid hold upon me. But he hath not given me over unto death,[1] though never
have I been so near death as I was then.[2] I send you a copy of my first draft.[3]

* * * * *

except for a translation of the *Querela pacis* (Ep 1432 n8). See Adolfo Bonilla y
San Martín 'Erasmo en España' *Revue hispanique* 17 (1907) 379–548.
8 See Ep 1440 n4.
9 Erasmus could doubtless have returned to England had he wished to do so (Ep
  1383:30–2), but he did not (Ep 1386:18–19 with n9). He later changed his mind;
  see Ep 1532:39–41.
10 Luther

1456
1 Ps 118 (Vulgate 117):18
2 See Ep 1452 n22.
3 Of the *De immensa Dei misericordia* (Ep 1474)

You are welcome to keep it for some days, so that you can read it through at   5
your leisure. Please be so kind as to tell me if you think anything should be
added or omitted or treated differently,[4] for before I entrust it to Froben to be
printed, I shall put my work back on the anvil,[5] give it a little more polish,
and perhaps also fill it out. If you think fit, I will add a short preface[6] in which
the chapel you have founded shall be mentioned. Let me add, having gladly   10
complied with your most pious wishes in this matter, that I hope all things in
the same way may turn out as you would wish. May the Lord Jesus in his
goodness preserve you full of years and honour.

Basel, 20 June 1524

1457 / From Jan Robbyns   Mechelen, 28 June 1524

> The autograph of this letter (=Ep 26 in Förstemann/Günther) was in the
> Burscher Collection at Leipzig (Ep 1254 introduction). On Robbyns, see Ep
> 1435, to which this is his answer. This is the only letter of Robbyns to Erasmus
> that has survived.

Greeting, reverend father, my much respected master and teacher. A letter
from your reverence sent from Basel on the Thursday after Easter has
arrived safely by the hand of your servant who brings you this.[1] Our friend
Goclenius[2] has not moved from the College of the Three Tongues, although
more agreeable conditions and a better-paid post have been offered him – as   5
tutor to Robert, the new bishop of Cambrai;[3] and I expect that when he does
leave it will be for no trivial reason. He wants to be some use to the
community rather than to a private person, and apart from his other virtues
this is not the least admirable thing about him. I shall always do all I can to
retain him in the post, and with proper maintenance too. The trustees[4] of the   10
will of the late founder[5] of blessed memory are fairly strict and stingy, and do
not consider as they should what a treasure this Goclenius is.

* * * * *

4 Cf Ep 1464:11–20.
5 Cf *Adagia* I v 92.
6 Ep 1474

1457
1 Lieven Algoet; cf Epp 1430 n7, 1458:1.
2 Ep 1209
3 Ep 1256 n28
4 Adrian Josel, canon of Antwerp; Nicolas van Nispern, secretary to Robert de
   Croy (preceding note); Bartholomeus van Vessem (or Wessem), canon of
   Mechelen; and Antoon Sucket (Ep 1331 n11). See de Vocht CTL I 49–62.
5 Jérôme de Busleyden (Ep 205)

If the king of France wants to set up a similar college for the three
tongues in Paris, and invites your reverence to help in staffing it, this does
not surprise me. He now sees clearly what distinction and what advantages   15
it would bring to his own famous university. At the moment, because of the
College of the Three Tongues, Louvain University is flourishing and grows
bigger from day to day; which is highly welcome to most people, nearly all in
fact, but there are some,[6] though few in number, who regret it because this is
the reason.   20
    In this same university and more or less over the whole country there
are people who long earnestly for the day when your reverence will return to
us and wonder how it is that you have deserted them for so long; and for
their comfort and your own peace your friends and keen supporters think
that you ought to leave Basel as soon as you can and move to this delightful   25
part of the world, to live in learned leisure, peaceful and relaxed, even giving
this the preference over grander offers. May the mercy of Almighty God
grant this for your good and ours, and may he preserve your reverence in
unbroken health and wealth into old age, not forgetting always to tell me if
there is anything I can do for you.   30
    From Mechelen, eve of the apostles Peter and Paul 1524
    Your reverence's devoted servant and friend Jan Robbyns.
    To the reverend father Erasmus of Rotterdam, distinguished doctor of
divinity, his most revered master and teacher. In Basel

1458 / From Marcus Laurinus   Mechelen, 30 June 1524

The autograph of this letter (=Ep 27 in Förstemann/Günther) was in the
Burscher Collection at Leipzig (Ep 1254 introduction). On Marcus Laurinus,
see Ep 1342.

Greeting. Your man Lieven[1] did at least choose the right moment to deliver
your letter,[2] dear Erasmus my most learned friend, for if you had not
written, and particularly to master Jan de Hondt,[3] the annuity[4] which was
given me in respect of this quarter-day, St John's Nativity,[5] would have

* * * * *

6 The conservative theologians; cf Ep 1118:13–14.

1458
1 See Ep 1457 n1.
2 Of c 31 March; see Ep 1457:2.
3 The earlier letter referred to in Ep 1433:3. For de Hondt and his role in the
  payment of the Courtrai annuity, see the introduction to the same letter.
4 See Ep 1417 n13.
5 24 June

been paid over to master Johannes de Molendino,[6] canon of Tournai, as   5
attorney for master Pierre Barbier,[7] who also took last Christmas quarter's
and gave me a receipt, of which I send you a copy. He is in charge of the
lawsuit in which Master Pierre Barbier is engaged over the deanery of
Tournai,[8] and when he needs money Barbier has written and told him to
draw on Master Jan de Hondt, and has promised to arrange that money   10
given to de Molendino is reckoned in your accounts as paid.[9] Nor will you
object to this. I see no end to the suit; the annuity will have to be paid him
over a long period, unless you take steps to the contrary. Please therefore let
me know by return what you would like done, and I will see to it that they
faithfully do all you want.   15

      You said in your letter[10] to Master Jan de Hondt that he would not have
to pay you the annuity for very long, and that your death[11] would soon
release him, so dreadful are your attacks of the stone and even worse those
of some of Luther's followers. Master Jan would like you to last for ever for
the benefit of us all; you do so much every day for the republic of letters and   20
promote true Christian theology daily more and more, driving back the false
and sophistical sort. He also declares that your works, to the reading of
which he devotes a good part of every day, have made him not only a better
scholar but a better man. Besides which no advantage would come to him
from your death; it would go to Barbier, who has both livings of his own[12]   25
and an annuity of six livres gros arranged in his own name.[13] This makes me
wonder whether you realize, or is it concealed from you, that all rights to the
compensation paid to you and credited at the same time to Barbier depend
on his title, and if he were to die,[14] both of you – you and de Hondt – will lose
the livings, Jan de Hondt having then first been set free only from the   30

                  * * * * *

   6 Ep 371
   7 Ep 1358
   8 Barbier's appointment to the deanship at Tournai was confirmed by the curia
     in 1523, but a lengthy litigation followed. Not until 1527 or 1528 was he able to
     take up residence in Tournai as dean.
   9 The annuity for the second half of 1523 in fact remained unpaid for many years;
     see Epp 2239, 2407.
  10 See n3.
  11 Cf Ep 1437:126.
  12 See Ep 1094 n6.
  13 £6 gros Flemish, currently worth £4 1s 0d sterling. See CWE 1 347.
  14 Barbier's own account of the scheme is found in Ep 1245:5–22: he had made an
     informal arrangement in Rome about the payment of the annuity to Erasmus,
     but in such a way that, if he should die before Erasmus, the latter could procure
     the necessary bulls with no further difficulty beyond the payment of the usual
     fees.

annuity of six livres gros. Barbier's word, as long as he lives, is your only security; and if he were to break it, you have nothing further to hope for. But I am sure you know Barbier too well to expect any such thing. A certain risk however is involved in his living in Rome, where the plague gets so much worse and spreads more widely every day.[15] I think you would be much 35
wiser to choose someone here who is younger than Barbier and whom you know you can trust and to get Barbier to devolve the livings onto him for your benefit, and the annuity too if that can be transferred, a point which will be fully cleared up by papal bulls. Your man Lieven Algoet would not seem a bad person to take care of this for the future; you know his high 40
character well enough and the sort of man he is. I do not write this out of any mistrust of Barbier; but his age and state of health and his place of residence do cause some anxiety, perhaps needlessly, and this could be met with more confidence by the choice of someone younger and stronger who also lives in more healthy surroundings. 45

Please take my warning in good part, most scholarly of men; you do not need it, for you always have wise counsel ready to your hand. In any case, I have paid over all the money I received from Master Jan de Hondt to Master Pieter Gillis.[16] How I wish he had in safe keeping all the money that is owed you from the court![17] I have pressed your case here with all possible 50
diligence. They all wish you well, and have, they say, the highest regard for you; but it goes no further than regard, and when it comes to money, the war[18] allows no money to be paid out. There are many people here almost reduced to starvation by shortage of money and unlimited plenty of war; and war means such pitiful robbery of the whole population that I fear, if we 55
can get quit of war against our enemies, we may have civil war on our hands as a result. The common people begin to grow restive in two or three places. Troops are ready to move against them, and those who previously were afraid of the enemy now look for some defence against those who ought to have been their defenders. Among these are the Limburgers, approached by 60
way of the upper ferry,[19] who have refused passage to our troops. These are the first tentative moves; God grant better news! If you can come and visit us, however, the war will not prevent you from receiving all the money. For his Grace the archbishop of Palermo[20] (whom I know from experience we

* * * * *

15 There had been a furious outbreak of the plague at Rome since February; see Pastor IX 258n.
16 Ep 184
17 See Ep 1380 introduction.
18 See Ep 1369 n12.
19 Evidently Maastricht
20 Jean de Carondelet (Ep 1276)

can trust) has assured me that on your arrival the treasury-clerks will pay   65
over all the annuity due to you in respect of past dates no less than current
ones. And if you ask to have the rate put up, they will agree handsomely.
Besides which, if there is a vacant preferment, however lucrative, it will be
conferred on you. In all this he will give you his support. He wished me to
write and tell you this in his name, so that you could know it for certain. But   70
you know the court. What you have at home you will not go looking for
elsewhere. So pray do as you think best. Farewell.

The widow ladies[21] send their greetings, and so does Pieter Taelman.[22]
It was you taught him to call a snap of the fingers *talitrum*[23] in Latin, and he
often uses this to annoy the monks, saying they know no Latin because they   75
have never heard of it. He asked me to mention this in my letter. Farewell
once more.

From Mechelen, the last day of June 1524
Your most devoted Marcus Laurinus, priest
To the most learned Master Erasmus of Rotterdam. In Basel   80

1459 / To Caspar Hedio

This letter has been assigned a new date and appears as Ep 1477B below.

1460 / To the Reader   Basel, 1 July 1524

This is Erasmus' preface to the new edition of Craston's *Dictionarius Graecus*
(Basel: Froben, July 1524) prepared by Jacobus Ceratinus (Ep 1437 nn60, 74).

DESIDERIUS ERASMUS OF ROTTERDAM TO ALL WHO WISH TO
ACQUIRE A KNOWLEDGE OF GREEK, GREETING
'As riches grow,' says Horace, 'care follows.'[1] This is much more true in
liberal studies. The deeper you drink, the greater your thirst. One result of
the increasing prosperity of Greek is that the lexicon, though so often   5
republished with additions,[2] does not cease to be in demand. We must be
grateful to all those who have made some contribution, each according to his

* * * * *

21 Laurinus' sisters; see Ep 1342:1123.
22 Unidentified; evidently a boy, perhaps a young relative of Laurinus
23 A rare word meaning a rap or fillip with the finger; cf Suetonius *Tiberius* 68 init.

1460
1 *Odes* 3.16.17
2 For an inventory of the Greek-Latin lexicons published since Craston's in c
1478, see Allen's introduction to this letter.

power; though I think no one has earned less than the man who, in order to
fill out the pages, added many entries like 'Ααρών, proper name' and
Κύπρος, name of an island.' If only Guillaume Budé had been either willing   10
or sufficiently at leisure to spare for this task some portion of his time! –
especially in the adding of Greek metaphors and idioms, for no one is more
richly furnished with Greek than he.[3] We owe no small debt to Du Maine,[4]
and must resent that jealous fever which so much reduced the value of his
contribution for those who wish to learn.[5]   15

In this volume, dear reader, you will find all the additions that had
been made at different times and places by others, not excluding what some
unknown person had added to no purpose, as I have said. The total
previously published has been increased by an immense number of words
chosen out of the best authors by Jacobus Ceratinus, who has the very rare   20
quality of uniting an exact familiarity with Greek and Latin and an incredible
modesty. When I compared his additions with the supplements of other
men inserted in Gourmont's last edition, which my friend Ceratinus had not
seen, I was surprised to find hardly a word added by him in which he had
been anticipated by earlier work. 'He's a poor shepherd that can count his   25
flock,'[6] and it is a sign of greater poverty to count words. Ceratinus has
added a considerable number, but it is a substantial treasure, as you will
agree if instead of counting you weigh the new material.

At this point, I suppose, there will be a protest: 'The brazen impudence
of it! Why do you write a preface for another man's work?' I will tell you.   30
Ceratinus had been urged by me to undertake this work, though otherwise
there is nothing he would have disliked more. Had he not been at such a
distance, you would have a preface with somewhat more meat in it. Though
I too have added a number of words, and would have added a great many,
had I been blessed with even a few days' leisure. I know that there is very   35
little credit to be had from work of this kind, especially since few people
consider how many authors have to be gone through in order to pick out a
few words which others have missed. All the more gratitude is due to those

* * * * *

3 Cf Ep 1233:179–82.
4 Guillaume Du Maine (d 1525) was the tutor of Guillaume Budé's children from
   about 1519 and also Budé's disciple and associate in Greek studies. In 1523 Du
   Maine collaborated with Jean Chéradame in editing a *Lexicon graeco-latinum*
   published by G. de Gourmont at Paris.
5 The verso of the title page in Gourmont's edition of the dictionary (cited in
   Allen's note) states that more than 1,500 of Du Maine's additions had not been
   included because of his poor health and because of the plague that had raged
   the previous summer.
6 Ovid *Metamorphoses* 13.824

who for the public benefit do not refuse a laborious task which brings no
credit and is full of tedium. 40

The former index, which reversed the order and gave Greek equiva-
lents for Latin words, we have omitted as serving no purpose except to
overload the volume. To begin with, such as it was, it was not complete, for
it contained only the words which Aldo gave in his first edition. If it were
completed, the volume would have to be doubled in size. Nor do I see that it 45
would serve any useful purpose, unless one were minded to write in Greek.
But that is a skill which should be acquired by reading the authors, and could
not be got successfully from dictionaries. Aldo himself, when I once asked
him[7] why he had decided to burden the volume with an index as toilsome as
it was useless, replied only that this difficulty had frightened off possible 50
rivals of his edition. So let no one think this volume any less valuable if its
bulk has been somewhat reduced and it has been made much more useful.
Farewell.

Basel, 1 July 1524

1461 / From Gilles de Busleyden   Brussels, 1 July 1524

The autograph of this letter (=Ep 28 in Förstemann/Günther) was in the
Burscher Collection at Leipzig (Ep 1254 introduction). On Gilles de Busleyden,
see Ep 686.

Cordial greeting. Your letter,[1] dearest Erasmus, was most welcome, for I
was exceedingly anxious to hear some definite news of you and your affairs,
for which you have my most sincere good wishes. You say that I and my
children are fortunate to have Ceratinus as their tutor,[2] and I too am
especially delighted to have him, for I find him just the man you describe, 5
open-hearted, very well educated, and admirably adapted to perform a
tutor's duties. I am truly sorry to learn that your annuity has not yet been
paid over to you,[3] and wish there were something I could do to help on that
score. But our hope in this lies in Ruffault the treasurer,[4] who is, I know, a
keen supporter of yours, so that if it is possible in any way to get this money 10
out of the treasury, which is emptied by the war, he will gladly do all you

* * * * *

7 During Erasmus' stay in Venice in 1508

1461
1 Of c 31 March; see Ep 1437:208.
2 See Ep 1437 n60.
3 See Ep 1434.
4 Ep 1287 n10

want. I only hope that invitation from the king of France[5] will bring you as much honour and profit as you have truly deserved and as I would wish for you. It is the greatest pleasure to me to hear that so great a king proposes to imitate at great expense the policy and the foundation of my beloved brother   15
of blessed memory.[6] If it succeeds, I perceive that something in the way of wider fame will come my brother's way, when a king follows his example, and that our College of the Three Tongues here will gain in reputation everywhere.

You say you regret that your old age should have coincided with this   20
generation, in which the Lutheran faction throws everything into confusion; and I too am more than a little sorry that this should be so. Even so I have one source of great joy: thanks to the way you have always acted, with your wisdom and your spirit and your skill with the pen, you have never swerved aside in any direction from the duty of a Christian and of a good theologian   25
into partisanship or hostility towards any man, although your opponents have tried with unbroken pertinacity, one party to lure you or force you to join their faction, the other to drive you, however unwilling and reluctant, into an alien fold. All that remains, my valiant friend, is to go bravely on, never forgetting that the less reward you receive in this unhappy genera-   30
tion, the greater the recompense and the glory that await you at Christ's hands in the world to come. May he grant you not only bodily well-being but the valour to stand against all your opponents, or rather your enemies, and powerful eloquence to teach his people.

Brussels, 1 July 1524   35
Your devoted friend Gilles de Busleyden, with my own hand
To that most excellent scholar Erasmus of Rotterdam, his incomparable friend

1462 / To Martin Hune   Basel, 3 July 1524

The manuscript of this letter, a copy dating from c 1553, is in the Forschungs-
bibliothek Gotha (Chart A.399, f 231 verso). It was first published by Adalbert
Horawitz in the *Sitzungsberichte der phil.-hist. Classe der kaiserlichen Akademie der
Wissenschaften* (Vienna 1880).

Martin Hune (documented 1508–33) of Gittelde in Braunschweig was a
member of the Collegium Maius at Erfurt University. In March 1524 he

* * * * *

5 See Ep 1434:3–25.
6 Jérôme de Busleyden (Ep 205), who in his will bequeathed the money for the
  foundation of the Collegium Trilingue at Louvain. On the plans of Francis I to
  establish a similar college, see Ep 1434:19–21.

travelled to Basel to meet Erasmus, carrying a letter of recommendation from
Mutianus (Ep 1425). After his return to Erfurt, Hune was elected dean of the
faculty of arts. However, as the salutation of this letter shows, he had already
embarked on a career in medicine. In 1525 he left Erfurt and made his way to
Italy, where he became doctor of medicine at Padua in 1531. He subsequently
settled down as a physician in Graz. He and Erasmus continued to correspond
until the summer of 1526 (Ep 1718).

TO MARTIN HUNE, PHYSICIAN, FROM ERASMUS OF ROTTERDAM
Greeting. What really happened about the letter I sent Duke George with no
address I have not yet been able to discover.[1] They write to say that
Mosellanus has passed away,[2] leaving instructions that my letters to him
should be burned.[3] Here there are upheavals of many kinds and rumours   5
more frightful still. Among friends whom I have helped and in whom I
trusted I find both ingratitude and treachery beyond belief. But I shall not
cease to be my true self. The man who came here with you has made me
write this after ten o'clock at night. Johann Moldenfeld[4] sends you his
greetings. Farewell.   10
    The morrow of the Virgin's Visitation. Basel 1524
    Since you left I have had nothing from you in the way of letters, and
nothing from Eobanus.[5]
    Your sincere friend Erasmus

1463 / From Levinus Ammonius   Bois-Saint-Martin, 4 July 1524

This letter was first published by Allen from a manuscript in the Bibliothèque
municipale at Besançon (MS 599, page 98).
    Levinus Ammonius (Lieven van den Zande) of Ghent (1488–1557) was a
Carthusian in the monastery of St Maartensbos, thirty kilometres west of
Brussels. A good scholar and an eager student of the classics, Levinus was both
an opponent of the reformers and an outspoken critic of traditional theolo-

* * * * *

1462
1 The letter was presumably carried from Basel by Hune; see Ep 1448:4–5, Allen
   Ep 1567:1–2. Erasmus did not receive Duke George's reply, Ep 1448, until
   20 September; see Ep 1448 introduction.
2 On 19 April 1524. On Mosellanus, see Ep 1305.
3 Only three survive: Epp 948, 1123, 1305.
4 Johann Moldenfeld of Marzhausen (documented 1520–4), who had probably
   been Hune's companion on the journey from Erfurt to Basel. On his return
   journey to Erfurt, Moldenfeld carried Epp 1495–8.
5 Ep 874

gians. This admiring letter constitutes his first attempt to open a continuing correspondence with Erasmus. His second attempt was successful (Epp 2016, 2062), and five of the letters in their subsequent correspondence survive (Epp 2082, 2197, 2258, 2483, 2817).

LEVINUS AMMONIUS TO ERASMUS OF ROTTERDAM THE THEOLOGIAN, GREETING

For a long time I was full of misgivings, Erasmus most incorruptible of theologians, whether my action would be inexcusable if I were to interrupt you with a letter, I being a monk living obscurely in solitude and you the 5 most distinguished of our whole generation for your outstanding gifts, and if I who enjoy the blessings of leisure were to inflict this tedium on a man who labours for the common good of Christendom. There were many reasons to dissuade me, but one in particular, that to those who had no knowledge of my humble self I might seem to aim at becoming known 10 through you; for that some people have done this is as clear as anything could be. More fools they! – to believe that they can secure renown for themselves through another man's distinction, when they have none of their own.

Besides this there was that small and friendly rebuke uttered by your 15 friend More,[1] in which (quite rightly, to be sure) he discourages someone, I think a member of my order, from writing, on the ground that some people who have an authority by no means to be disregarded have held that hermits are certainly not to be allowed to send and receive letters. That this is so, and for no trivial reasons, I was well aware. But it was my intention to choose a 20 subject on which to write to you far different from that of the man who was rebuked quite rightly for starting his letter with a calumny; and I thought I could see clearly what More meant. It was indeed a mark of arrogance to wish to pass for a judge of matters of which he had as yet no understanding. I hope for my part that on this score your friend More will have no quarrel 25 with me. Nor do I expect to have a very bloody battle with the men of old who might be thought in their constitutions for the order to have forbidden me to write. I only wish they had taken proper steps to prevent any monk in the last five hundred years during which that ruling has been in force from writing in order to catch the ear of the public. To be sure, the affairs of 30 mortals would be in much better shape! But as they did no such thing, and

* * * * *

1463
1 In the so-called 'Letter to a Monk,' first published in the *Epistolae aliquot eruditorum* (Ep 1083 introduction); text in the Yale edition of *The Complete Works of Thomas More* 15 (New Haven and London 1986) 198–311.

on the other hand we see stuff more worthless than the worst Sicilian trash[2] published everywhere, what ground have they left themselves for having the law on me? I saw clearly that in early days, before our new sort of monks (I nearly said Jews) had dawned upon the world, not only were there no   35 laws to forbid the real monks of that time to exchange letters, but letters were often asked for as a great privilege and some of them were a great support to Christianity. You too must be well aware of this after your distinguished labours on the works of Jerome, which have earned you undying praise all the world over.   40

So all this did not move me very much. But that first reason I spoke of just now has kept me hitherto so closely within bounds that though, if it were not for that, I have sometimes as I read been seized with a sudden urge to write and thank you, at first thought of that my impulse has cooled off at once. But in the mean time I have had no misgivings whatever about praying   45 to Christ that he would give you some really substantial recompense in return, instead of me who could only thank you in words. Such then were my feelings towards you; and yet, for fear of being thought to push myself forward, I have so far controlled myself and not run this risk needlessly, although often urged to do so by my friends; though we see (and a sorry   50 sight it is) most men pursuing a far more wicked purpose, and trying to secure a little very empty, not to say very scandalous, reputation by attacking your most godly labours. This is the treatment you have had, apart from other people, from those ringleaders, Lee,[3] Stone,[4] and Camel.[5] Such a spirit as this, the very opposite of our Christian profession, I have always   55 loathed and found abominable. So you ought to expect nothing of the sort from me, and I should not like you to entertain any other idea except that I have sent you this letter solely in order to put on record for you the warm feelings towards you which I have derived from your books and my gratitude. Otherwise I would gladly have refrained from troubling you like   60 this, had there been any other way by which I could have made my feelings known.

But I think I have now made sufficient allowance for modesty; so let me tell you briefly, since I must pluck up my courage, the purpose of this letter. When I see you, Erasmus most honourable of men, toiling with such tireless   65 zeal to produce work which will benefit the Christian world, and receiving from the majority very inadequate thanks for things for which no man could

* * * * *

2 Cf *Adagia* II iv 10.
3 Ep 1037 introduction
4 Jacobus Latomus (Ep 934:4n)
5 Baechem (Ep 1254 n6)

make you an adequate return, I cannot (I confess) conceal my feelings towards you. For I thought it would also be monstrous if anyone who really is grateful were to refrain from acknowledging the kindness you have done 70 him, while I see those ungrateful men so busy repaying you with calumny in place of thanks. Surely I can use the same freedom towards you or before the world at large that they use? They claim the right to vilify all excellence, and to blacken the name of Erasmus in front of the ignorant or even of foolish women with their unspeakable clamour; and shall it be wrong for me to 75 express my gratitude in an ill-written letter if nothing else? You have learned to digest their scurrilities with patience and modesty; and can you refuse to read a letter from a friend, however illiterate? Those men are tolerated by the bishops and the chiefs of Christendom, and in fact by all men of learning – it pains them, but they tolerate it none the less; and will they forbid me to fulfil 80 the duty of all right-thinking men? Last but not least, they boldly assume a licence to vilify, though they are monks; and shall they deny me, though I were a monk many times over – no cause for shame or regret hitherto – the freedom to speak a word of blessing? Quite the reverse: if they listen to me, all men of true good will, whether of high or low or middling degree, will do 85 all that each of them can do, by prayers and blessings and by tributes in writing and in silver and in gold, to leave with you a memorial of their gratitude. What could be fairer than that?

  And so, though I see well enough that you are satisfied with a good conscience and the knowledge that you seek only Christ's glory, I do not 90 doubt that you must find it a little depressing when as a result of their obstinate blindness you sow good seed and reap such an unworthy return. For I know well that you, as a good man, cannot fail to be sorry for their lot; and indeed they deserve to be pitied, because they perish by their own wickedness, rather than hated, because through ignorance of the good they 95 entirely fail to recognize the benefits they have received. At this point however it must console you that there should be so many people all over the world, and those as a rule the men of soundest judgment, who regard their Erasmus with respect and devotion and express their thanks by writing to him from every part of the globe. And if you compare those ungrateful 100 creatures with a recompense like this, they simply do not exist; it is never right to take the wicked into one's calculations, even if they seem to be the majority. I would set more store by the right judgment of even one good man than by many myriads of the wicked protesting in blind ignorance against your sacred labours.[6] Though as far as numbers are concerned, I 105

* * * * *

6 Here Ammonius wrote as follows in the margin: 'Cicero says of himself [*Orator* 13:41]: "When Cato praised me I could easily endure even to be

believe the bad must easily yield to the good; one can hear so many people
not merely giving Erasmus their best wishes but loudly calling down
blessings on his head. That I too am among their number and always was
and ever shall be is a fact of which I should wish you to be thoroughly
assured.   110

But I do not say this with any idea that a letter from me can give you any
pleasure or that you can hope for any advantage from someone like myself
which will mean a great improvement in your circumstances. You do not
seek this yourself, and indeed you would be wasting your time, were you to
expect anything more than a grateful and devoted heart and pure prayers to   115
Christ and whatever else of the kind may be within my power. You would
seek water in vain from pumice-stone, that thirsts itself, as it says in the
play.[7] And yet if anything I could do might be acceptable, I should not
hesitate to offer it most readily and with both hands. But I give thanks to
Christ our Saviour, who raised you up to be a comfort to mortals in their   120
pitiful errors, and through you has opened the eyes of so many men to
embrace the religion worthy of a Christian man. I feel towards you also all
the gratitude of which I am capable, because from your admirable works I
have been fired with the desire first for a right judgment in all things and
then for good authors in both languages, not to learn them through and   125
through, which for one who lives a solitary life would be difficult if not
impossible, but at least to get such a taste of them as I can. The first sparks of
desire to learn both languages I freely confess I caught from you and, thanks
be to God, I have made such progress that I never repented less of anything
in my life than of the task I have undertaken. Hence I can with perfect justice 130
call you my teacher, and so I do, though many may protest and may object to
the way I speak about you. You too know full well, I am sure, how tiresome
the tribe of monks can be. But I have not given way to them hitherto, so far as
I could secure permission, although they have tried from time to time to land
me in serious trouble – excellent men in other ways and sincerely devoted to   135
Christ, but with little sympathy for those who are keen on literary studies.

But I must make an end; it would not be right for you who labour for
the common good to be detained any longer by this unlearned trifling. One

* * * * *

censured by all others. And Isocrates should, I think, make light of the
criticisms of others in comparison with the judgment of Plato [*Phaedrus* 279A]"
... The ancients recount that Heraclitus used to say [Diogenes Laertius 9.16]:
"Why do ye drag me up and down, ye illiterates? it was not for you I toiled, but
for such as understand me. One man in my sight is a match for thirty thousand,
but the countless hosts do not make a single one."'
7 Plautus *Persa* 41–2

thing let me add: there is no task so hard and difficult that I would not gladly undertake it for your sake, if there were anything I could do to give you 140 pleasure. You have my heart, entirely devoted to you, and can use it as you please. Farewell, dear Erasmus, and pray count Ammonius among the least of your dependants.

From my retreat in Bois-Saint-Martin, 4 July 1524

145

Appendix
I thought I might fill in the interval, while the courier[8] is dawdling with his family and there is time to spare, by adding this. Can you imagine, Erasmus, with what pleasure I spend my days in your other writings (of which, to judge by the *Catalogus*,[9] I have almost the lot with me here), but especially 150 the *Enchiridion* and the *Moria*? In these works I can see you aiming with wonderful skill at the same target. Among other things, how elegantly you paint those superstitious folk in their true colours! What a neat and polished mirror you have held up to them, if they want to be wise and repent after all this time! You have laid me under a great obligation, and made not merely all 155 truly religious men but Christ himself your debtor by these books.

If Michael Bentinus,[10] a very learned young man, is living in your neighbourhood, please give him my greetings. A few months ago he was kind enough both to write and to pay me a visit. Please, dear Erasmus, do arrange if possible for something of St Chrysostom's to be printed in his 160 native language, so that we can get a taste of his style.[11] For in our part of the world Greek books that contribute anything to Christian piety are very hard to find and very dear; and anything I have acquired through the generosity of my friends (and I do not have very many), I hold all the more dear, because they were so dear to buy. Christ keep you in health and wealth for 165 the benefit and profit of his church.

1464 / From Christoph von Utenheim   Porrentruy, 13 July 1524

The manuscript of this letter, which was first published as Ep 28 in Enthoven, is in the Rehdiger Collection of the University Library at Wrocław (MS Rehd 254.52). Allen says that the manuscript is 'seemingly in the Bishop's autograph

* * * * *

8 Perhaps Lieven Algoet; see Ep 1430 n7.
9 Ep 1341A
10 Ep 1433 n2
11 In response to this suggestion Erasmus published, beginning in April 1525, a series of small volumes of Chrysostom, some in Greek only, some in Latin translations with the Greek added; see Epp 1558, 1563, 1661, 1734, and others later (see Allen XII 32).

throughout,' but lines 8–9 indicate that the letter was dictated. Did the bishop perhaps dictate first and then copy in his own hand? Whatever the case, he was a clumsy Latinist and his wits had evidently not yet fully recovered from the effects of his illness (lines 5ff), with the result that the present letter is a bit of a shambles. The translation faithfully reproduces the clumsiness and confusion of the original.

CHRISTOPH BY THE GRACE OF GOD BISHOP OF BASEL

Greeting, and the assurance of my sincere wish to oblige you. A short time ago, dear Master Erasmus my most learned friend, when your work on the Mercies[1] was forwarded to me, I sent your reverence a letter[2] in the vernacular and written in another man's hand. The state of my health at the   5
time made this advisable, for I was not fit enough either to dictate so that someone else might have written back or to write myself; but it is now dealing a little more gently with me, and allows me at least to say something in my own clumsy fashion that another man can take down by way of a letter. Such as it is, I know you will take it in good part.   10

Meanwhile I have been thinking over this work on God's mercies, which I like very much. It seems to me at any rate most advisable, and I do urge you to act accordingly, that if this work is to be given public circulation, no further matter should be added beyond what I suggested, and in particular nothing that might excite the Lutherans or those who observe the   15
genuine old-fashioned faith, or even might upset their stomach, and might exhibit us as followers of this or that sect. There seem to me to be some additions at the end of the book, if your reverence will allow me to say so, that are of this nature. And so I do beg your reverence urgently to cancel these and cut them out.[3] I know the reason that prompts me to this, and will   20
one day explain it to you by word of mouth. I hope you will act in this matter so as to justify the great confidence I have in you, and will remember that I am always yours to command in everything. And so farewell in the Lord, to whom let each of us pray for the other.

From my castle of Porrentruy, 13 July 1524   25

To a man beyond compare and very dear to us as a brother in Christ, Master Erasmus of Rotterdam, theologian

* * * * *

1464
1 The draft of the *De immensa Dei misericordia*; see Ep 1456:4.
2 Not extant
3 Erasmus apparently followed this advice. There is nothing at the end of the *De immensa Dei misericordia* that would give anyone in either camp an upset stomach, and the work does not appear to have attracted criticism from anyone.

1465 / To William Warham   Basel, 15 July 1524

This is the preface to the first volume of Erasmus' revised edition of Jerome
(Basel: Froben, 1524–6) in nine volumes, dedicated, like the first edition of 1516
(Ep 396) to Archbishop Warham (Ep 188). The first three volumes are devoted
to the correspondence. Volumes II and III have prefaces (Epp 1451, 1453) dated
six weeks earlier, but each bears the date August 1524 on its title-page. It thus
seems likely that all three volumes were printed at about the same time, in
preparation for the September fair at Frankfurt.

TO THE MOST REVEREND WILLIAM, LORD ARCHBISHOP OF
CANTERBURY, ETC, FROM ERASMUS OF ROTTERDAM, GREETING
Although such trouble had been taken over the first edition, O prelate
beyond compare, that one could scarcely hope for any possible addition
from those second thoughts which are proverbially the best,[1] yet in my great   5
desire to render this work, which I had as it were built as a monument to
your reputation (long may it live!), as perfect and complete as possible, I
have arranged for it to be reprinted separately with more elegant paper and
types; though Johann Froben had already given such an account of himself
in the printing of Jerome that he had not only by common consent surpassed   10
everyone else, but he had left very little scope for improving on his own
performance. For my part, I have found almost nothing in the text of Jerome
that needed correction; in my own notes I have made some corrections and
certain deletions and not a few additions. Places remain however, though
very few in number, where I am not wholly satisfied with my own   15
conjectures; and if anyone can restore these passages more successfully than
myself, either by mother wit or by a plentiful supply of manuscripts, I shall
be happy to salute his industry and give this public service a warm welcome.
    In the course of these labours two new factors have emerged which
have pruned away a large share of the credit I had earned. One is the   20
flourishing state of the ancient tongues and humane studies in general in
every land all the world over, which makes my work seem in many ways not
so necessary as it was. The other is that in our generation most men's
abilities have been diverted to that bloody and internecine battle of words,
so that there has been a falling-off in zeal and numbers alike in those who   25
frequent the life-giving meadows and most delightful orchards of the
ancient authors. I could in any case bear to forego some reputation easily
enough, were not this combined with a lowering of standards, which is a

* * * * *

1465
1 *Adagia* I iii 38

public loss. We must leave the outcome to Christ. I have at least shown my
good will, and so I shall until the day of my death. Farewell.   30

Basel, 15 July 1524

1466 / To Willibald Pirckheimer   Basel, 21 July 1524

This letter was first published in the *Pirckheimeri opera*. Pirckheimer's answer is
Ep 1480.

Greeting, most honoured friend. I sent you a letter[1] the other day by the man
who brought the cast-metal portraits and told you at the same time that so
far your letters to me have been faithfully delivered, since you seemed to
suspect something different. Clement VII has sent me a brief full of
compliments[2] with a complimentary present of two hundred florins,[3] which   5
I would not have accepted had he not said expressly that he sent them in
return for the dedication of my paraphrase.[4] He also makes grand promises
for the future. Cardinal Campeggi has sent me special messengers, by
whom I have sent him in reply what I thought might contribute to the public
peace.[5] Though, as the play is going forward now, I can see, as I hope for the 10
love of Jesus, no solution. The thing spreads more widely every day. Neither
side takes any steps towards reconciliation; most of them in fact have no
other purpose than to pour oil on the flames.[6] In my native Holland nuns
everywhere are leaving the cloister and getting married in the Lord. The
Camel has been disowned by both emperor and pope.[7] His colleague Hulst   15
has barely escaped a death sentence.[8] Literary studies flourish and go

* * * * *

1466
1 Ep 1452
2 Ep 1443B
3 Presumably Florentine or papal florins, then worth about £66 14s gros Flemish,
   £45 sterling, and £415 tournois. See Epp 1295 n1, 1341A n376, 1414 introduction, and 1488 n10.
4 On Acts (Ep 1414)
5 Epp 1410, 1415, 1422
6 *Adagia* I ii 9
7 Baechem (Ep 1254 n6). On his supposed downfall, cf Epp 1359:2–3 with n1,
   1467:11–12. But Erasmus was soon complaining again of Baechem's behaviour
   (Ep 1481:67–76) and seeking to have him silenced (Epp 1509 introduction,
   1515).
8 Frans van der Hulst (Ep 1345 n8) was Baechem's ally and, from April 1522 until
   the spring of 1524, chief inquisitor of the Netherlands. His ruthless persecution
   of the well-connected Cornelis Hoen (Ep 1358 n7) brought about his disgrace

forward,[9] to the impotent fury of the theologians. They proclaim that I am a heretic, but no one believes them.

Martin Luther has written to me[10] by a man called Joachim,[11] quite a civil letter; but I did not dare send an equally civil answer, for fear of those who distort everything. I have however sent a brief reply.[12] Melanchthon,[13] I hear, wanted to talk with me, but did not dare get me into trouble.[14] I at least should have made light of any trouble on that score. He is a very honourable young man.[15]

In Strasbourg there is a great upheaval,[16] even in the city council. Here the authorities begin to be more restrained in support for the Lutherans,[17] for fear of the Strasbourg precedent. Otto's pamphlet has appeared again,[18] revised by the author and, if I am not mistaken, enlarged; I have not seen it yet. There has also appeared a letter from Alber,[19] the stupidest thing ever. I have no doubt it is by Buschius,[20] although he has played down his style as much as he could. But I know the sort of man he is, inside and out. The fellow has always had kindness from me; I never uttered a word that could

* * * * *

and dismissal (cf Ep 1467:13–15). In June 1524, Clement VII confirmed Hulst's successor in office.

9 At Louvain; cf Ep 1467:11.

10 Ep 1443

11 Camerarius; see Epp 1444 n2, 1501.

12 Ep 1445. Cf the description of these two letters in Ep 1452:12–15.

13 During his visit to the Palatinate; Ep 1444 n2.

14 Ep 1496:5–7

15 The anxieties expressed in 1522 (Ep 1313 n3) have evidently evaporated.

16 1524 was a tumultuous year in the history of the Reformation in Strasbourg, with overt and violent agitation against the old ecclesiastical order and demands that the council institute reforms. See Miriam Usher Chrisman *Strasbourg and the Reform* (New Haven and London 1967) 138–44.

17 Cf Ep 1452:28.

18 Ep 1405

19 The *Iudicium Erasmi Alberi de Spongia Erasmi Roterodami adeoque quatenus illi conveniat cum M. Lutheri doctrina*, printed, apparently quite recently, for Johann Schott (Epp 1429, 1477) by Johann Setzer in Haguenau; see WA-Br III 158–9. The text is in Böcking II 373–8. Cf Epp 1397 introduction, 1437 n17, 1477 n12, 1477B n5.

Erasmus Alber (c 1500–53), who had studied theology at Wittenberg, was at this time a schoolteacher in Eisenach. From 1528 to 1539 he was a pastor in Sprendlingen, near Frankfurt. Thereafter he led a rather unsettled existence, eventually dying as pastor in Neubrandenburg. He published numerous pamphlets, primers, hymns, and a German verse version of some of Aesop's fables.

20 By December, Erasmus had learned that Buschius (Ep 1291 n4) was not the author; Ep 1523:108–10.

hurt him. It is flies like this that will ruin the ointment[21] alike of the Gospels and the humanities. This is the sort of monstrous thing that Eppendorf enjoys.[22] He loves to do harm, and wants me to know it, but in such a way that he can deny it before other people. Henceforward I have no intention of answering this kind of rubbish. 35

In Rome two pamphlets by Zúñiga have been published surreptitiously,[23] in one of which he defends the translator[24] against barbarous mistakes I had accused him of but says nothing meanwhile of countless others against which he had no defence. And these forty or so he defends like this. The word in Greek is ὀρθρίζειν,[25] so the translator was right to put *manicare*, for it is permissible to coin new words. He was rendering either a figure of speech or a Hebraism, and therefore he did not commit a barbarism. The Greek has ἐπὶ τρίς, so he rightly rendered this by *per ter* in Acts.[26] In the other piece he displays the corrections I made on the basis of his own annotations without naming him, as though it would not have been enough to answer that book unless I had defiled the entire body of my own annotations with his name, which would ruin anything. In Rome he is a general laughing-stock; and yet the fellow thinks he is wonderful. He promises that he will never rest until Erasmus recognizes Zúñiga as the one great figure born to be his master not only in the Scriptures but in pagan literature as well. Yet the pope had forbidden the printing,[27] and they dare not put them on sale. 40 45 50

* * * * *

21 Cf Eccles 10:1.
22 See Ep 1437:9ff.
23 *Assertio ecclesiasticae translationis Novi Testamenti a soloecismis quos illi Erasmus Roterodamus impegerat; Loca quae ex Stunicae annotationibus, illius suppresso nomine, in tertia editione Novi Testamenti Erasmus emendavit* (Rome: n p 1524). Cf Ep 1410.
24 Ie, the translator of the Vulgate
25 Luke 21:38. In his annotation, Erasmus comments at length on the difficulty of the word; LB VI 315E.
26 In his 1519 edition of the New Testament, Erasmus included a list of solecisms in the Vulgate text, including the *per ter* in Acts 10:16; see LB VI *5 verso. In his *Assertio* (see n23 above), page D1 verso, Zúñiga attempted to refute Erasmus on this point. Erasmus, in an addition to his *Annotationes* made in 1535, made the following comment (LB VI 474E): 'A certain individual has defended this passage against the charge of solecism because the translator rendered the Greek usage. But one should have said *ad ter*. And Latin-speakers say *ad calendas Januarias* for *circiter [calendas Januarias]*. However, the reproduction in Latin of a Greek figure of speech often results in a solecism.'
27 Cf Ep 1470:47–50.

Clement VII has sent to England as legate a Minorite archbishop,[28] who was to tell the princes to come to terms; but he has made no progress. So he 55 has refused to accept a large sum of money offered him by the king. I suppose the king of England has crossed by now.[29] This is how we proceed against the Turks! The emperor had given orders for the payment of my annuity,[30] but they use the burden of the war as an excuse.[31] They promise, however, to pay with interest if I go back.[32] I shall be glad to move 60 somewhere, if only because my friendship with Froben makes me so unpopular with the other printers.[33] I have not yet made up my mind. But I shall decide before long.

Now that rumours have spread about my book on the freedom of the will,[34] I think it best to publish, so that they cannot suspect it to be worse 65 than it is. For I treat the topic with such moderation that I know Luther himself will not take offence.

I have paid a visit to Besançon,[35] but I had such a heavy cold that I could scarcely get back to my nest.[36] When I might have been all right again, I had an attack of the stone,[37] the most dangerous I have ever had. I sometimes 70 take oil of turpentine. Baths I have never been used to, and dare not trust myself to them. Farewell, my incomparable friend.

Basel, 21 July 1524

You know your humble servant's handwriting.

To the honourable Willibald Pirckheimer, town councillor of Nürn- 75 berg

* * * * *

28 Nikolaus von Schönberg (1472–1537) of Meissen in Saxony, who in 1497 became a Dominican (not a Minorite, ie, a Franciscan) at Florence. He subsequently rose to prominence in the order and at the Vatican, becoming archbishop of Capua in 1520. In March 1524 Clement VII sent him on a mission to make peace among the warring monarchs Charles V, Francis I, and Henry VIII, but neither this nor a similar mission in the autumn had any success.
29 To pursue an attack on France in concert with Charles V. The project was much discussed in the early months of the year but ultimately abandoned; Scarisbrick 131–3.
30 Ep 1380
31 Cf Ep 1461:10–11.
32 Ep 1380 introduction
33 Cf Ep 1437:418–19.
34 See Epp 1419, 1481.
35 See Ep 1440 n4.
36 Cf Ep 1488:5.
37 See Ep 1452 n22.

1467 / To Johann von Vlatten　　　　　　　　　　　Basel, 21 July 1524

This letter, which is Erasmus' reply to a letter now lost, was first published in
LB. On Vlatten, see Ep 1390.

TO THE RIGHT HONOURABLE JOHANN VON VLATTEN, PROVOST
AND COUNCILLOR, FROM ERASMUS OF ROTTERDAM, GREETING
You have done so much for me, and in particular have shown yourself so
open and so friendly, that I was already deeply in your debt; and just as
though I was not sufficiently bound to you already, here you are, sending 5
me coins. I do, it is true, take a moderate pleasure in things of this kind; but it
is as a most precious and at the same time most delightful token of your
feelings towards me that I shall treasure them. I am very much pleased with
you, my dear Vlatten, for showing such courage in driving those boars.[1] A
brave spirit indeed! – and you must keep up your high standard. 10

In Louvain the humanities are positively triumphant. The Camel has
been stripped of all his power,[2] both by the emperor and by the pope. His
colleague Hulst[3] faced such a load of accusations that, had not the cardinal of
Liège[4] and the prince of Bergen[5] come to the rescue, he would have suffered
the death penalty. So all the other theologians are growing tame. 15

Clement VII has sent me a laudatory official letter,[6] together with two
hundred florins,[7] in return for my dedicating a paraphrase to him,[8] and
makes grand promises for the future. My man Lieven is back from a
successful trip to England,[9] except that my annuity from the emperor comes
to an end unless I return to Brabant.[10] The king himself has written to me, 20

* * * * *

1467
1 The literary allusion is doubtless to the monster boar sent by Minerva to ravage
  the orchards and fields of King Oeneus of Calydon (cf Ep 396:177). See Homer
  Iliad 9.533ff; Ovid 9 *Metamorphoses* 8.271ff. In the absence of Vlatten's letter, it
  cannot be said who the particular Calydon boars in this case were, but they
  were doubtless enemies of the humanities and true piety.
2 Baechem; see Ep 1466 n7.
3 See Ep 1466 n8.
4 Erard de la Marck; Ep 738
5 Jan (III) van Bergen (1452–1532), a member of the privy council of the regent,
  Margaret of Austria. Erasmus calls him 'prince,' but 'lord of Bergen' would
  have been the appropriate title.
6 Ep 1443B
7 See Ep 1466 n3.
8 Ep 1414
9 Lieven Algoet; see Ep 1430 n7.
10 See Ep 1380 introduction.

and the cardinal too,[11] which (let me tell you) is no less grand. I hear that the cardinal of Liège is not too well disposed towards me,[12] and is in fact on the side of the theologians, though in the old days he could not even bear to hear their names mentioned.[13]

I congratulate you most warmly on this rise in both your emoluments 25 and your position,[14] and may it be the will of the Lord Jesus to make both of them a blessing to you.

Basel, 21 July 1524

Erasmus of Rotterdam, with my own hand, extempore

If Beat Arnold of Sélestat,[15] the emperor's secretary, is there, I should 30 like you to know him; I never saw a more honourable man. Please tell him that all the things he had sent[16] to Sélestat[17] reached me safe and sound, so he must not worry. Farewell once more.

1468 / From Thiébaut Biétry   Porrentruy, 21 July 1524

The autograph of this letter (=Ep 29 in Förstemann/Günther) was in the Burscher Collection at Leipzig (Ep 1254 introduction). On Biétry, see Ep 1391.

Greeting. Your letter was most welcome,[1] and I will come and see you,[2] if all goes well, as soon as we have got our harvest in, that is, in ten days' time. What you write about the indignation at Besançon surprises me extremely. But don't worry: the whole thing is completely imaginary and fictitious. It may be that, after we left,[3] the local lawyers and some of those pedantic 5

* * * * *

11 Henry VIII and Wolsey. Neither of these letters is extant.
12 Cf Epp 1268 n8, 1482:9–16, 1549, 1585.
13 Cf Ep 1038 introduction in both Allen and CWE.
14 Ie, Vlatten's appointment as councillor to the duke of Cleves
15 Also called Batt Arnolt (Ep 399:7n)
16 A package of letters from Spain that Arnold had carelessly left in his trunk to come by sea to Brabant; see Allen Ep 1553:1–5. Since Erasmus was answering them in March 1524 (Ep 1431:7–10), they were probably written in the late summer or autumn of 1523.
17 Probably to Beatus Rhenanus for forwarding to Erasmus

1468
1 Written to inquire about the rumour reported to Biétry by someone in Montbéliard that Erasmus 'had left Besançon on the worst terms with everyone.' See Allen Ep 1610:117–19. The letter is not extant. For Erasmus' visit to Besançon, see Ep 1440 n4.
2 Biétry did in fact visit Basel c August 1524; Allen Ep 1610:125.
3 Ie, after the departure from Porrentruy to Besançon. Biétry was one of Erasmus' companions on the visit to Besançon; Allen Ep 1610:17ff.

divines who are always so jealous of good literature got together a certain number of worthless fellows, of whom they always have a considerable supply, and set this rumour going among the public; but to that too I attach no importance whatsoever. So, when we first arrived in Besançon, there was at once the usual uncertainty in people's minds as to who you were. 'He's a Lutheran,' said some, and others said no, and they all differed, just as happened with Christ and those who maintained his cause. But I merely laughed. I was constantly asked by canons or town councillors and went on record manfully that you were no Lutheran. They took my word for it, and paid you all those honours – would no doubt have paid more, had you been able to meet the council. And things are often said in jest which are sometimes taken seriously by fools trying to understand them. This is a futile waste of time. Consequently, my beloved benefactor, you must not torment your heart about this, but live happy and cheerful and enjoy a venerable and prosperous old age. If you suffer from the jealousy of all around you, so did Jerome and others too; it is a sign of true success, for no one envies the unsuccessful. In any case (and let them all dislike it) you are rated in this our generation (and I speak in all sincerity) the monarch of the literary world.

I am quite delighted that you should be in favour with the supreme pontiff[4] and congratulate you; and I am pleased about the present.[5] I should be very happy to have from his treasury not a like sum – the half would do nicely, and I could make up what we lost in the fire.[6] Give Froben my greetings, and keep an eye on my business, I beg you particularly. My mother too sends you her greeting. And now farewell, and good luck be yours.

From Porrentruy, 21 July 1524

Your devoted bedesman and servant Theobaldus Bietricius of Porrentruy

To the most learned Master Desiderius Erasmus of Rotterdam, his much respected master and friend

1469 / To Nicolaas Everaerts   Basel, 26 July 1524

This is Erasmus' reply to an attack on him by an anonymous doctor of laws who had acted as a mouthpiece for Nicolaas Baechem (Ep 1254 n6). The work

* * * * *

4 Ep 1443B
5 Two hundred florins; Ep 1466 n3
6 According to Allen, who cites an authority that the annotator could not trace, half the town of Porrentruy had burned down on 8 October 1520.

in question, which was written in Dutch, circulated in manuscript and was apparently never printed. A copy was dispatched to Erasmus, anonymously, on 12 September 1523 (Allen Ep 1668:1–4). In February 1526 (Ep 1668) the author was identified as Floris Oem van Wijngaarden, a Dutch jurist who was an intimate friend of Adrian VI and an associate of Baechem and Frans van der Hulst (Ep 1466 n8) in their campaign against heretics in 1522.

The manuscript of the letter, in a secretary's hand but finished and dated by Erasmus, is in volume 79 of the Camerarius collection in the Bayerische Staatsbibliothek München (MS 10429.6). It was first published in the *Opus Epistolarum*. On Nicolaas Everaerts, president of the Council of Holland, see Ep 1092 introduction.

Cordial greetings, distinguished president. I have just received a pamphlet whose author is well known and famous even though it contains no mention of his name. I cannot make up my mind if it was written seriously or as a joke. I am sure you know who the author is.[1] He begins with a remarkable sentence explaining why he chose to write in Dutch rather than in Latin, as 5 though there were a competition between us to determine who had the better command of the Latin language or as if the reader could not guess at once why a brilliant doctor of canon and civil law preferred to write in the vernacular. His purpose is plain enough: he wanted to malign me before ordinary people in a medium where I would be unlikely to reply. It is not 10 difficult to understand what inspired such silliness: he was obviously annoyed by the splendid honour which people did me by placing my name at the head of their work.[2] Does he believe that I should be held accountable for whatever title anyone chooses to bestow on me? He cannot be unaware himself that, before he made the matter public, I knew nothing whatever 15 about the publication of the work or about the reference to myself. Everyone will be quick to realize why he did not put his own name on the work although, he tells us, many people would realize who the author of such an elegant pamphlet was. You can see that he wanted to enjoy the glory without any of the animosity. To those who like this scurrilous pamphlet he 20 would have whispered, 'It is mine!'; but if someone had got out his pen with the idea of revenge, he would have taken refuge in a denial of the charge.

* * * * *

1469
1 This sentence was added when the letter was published in the *Opus epistolarum*, a circumstance which indicates that Erasmus probably did not know the identity of the author when he wrote the original letter.
2 The Latin here is vague and so is the reference. The work in question has not been identified.

But I do not wish to waste time on these trivialities, so let us move on to the substance of the work itself, which on every page betrays itself as the brainchild of Nicolaas Baechem;[3] for no one else could have produced such absurd and silly nonsense and taken it seriously. Moreover I recognize the line of argument which he is accustomed to use. The brilliant doctor is not likely to reap much glory from this production except praise for his command of Dutch.

He begins with a commonplace, which he treats with great ingenuity. He believes that it is absurd to criticize a member of one's own order, that is, for a monk to find fault with other monks or a theologian with other theologians or a priest with other priests. Why then did Jerome, who was a monk, write so much against evil monks? Why is Bernard so often angry with members of his own order? Why does Cyprian attack evil bishops with such bitterness? Or why do the prophets rail so frequently against false prophets? Why does Paul repeatedly do the same thing, an apostle attacking false apostles, a Jew attacking Jews, a Christian attacking Christians, condemning and reviling them for foolishness, frivolity, bickering, drunkenness, laziness, and unchastity? If common membership in one order obliges us to be silent, then it would be wrong for a Christian to speak out against the immorality of other Christians. To malign good men, whatever their order, is a sin. But no one is listened to with more respect when he criticizes the vices of evil men than someone belonging to the same order; for in this case truth has evidently carried more weight than sympathy for one's own community. Suppose, for example, that a Franciscan were to find fault with the Dominicans; even if he did so in all honesty, he would not be able to avoid the suspicion of malice.

If the purpose of criticism is to reform those who are criticized without doing injury to their name, would we not wish our closest friends to be the first to be set on the proper path? For surely he does not think it wrong to offer medicine to an ailing relative. And was it not Nicolaas Baechem himself who attacked his fellow Carmelites at Brussels over some impropriety of theirs involving women[4] – and not just with strong words but with imprisonment and flogging, calling in the civil authorities for that purpose so that there could be no secret about the affair? And if we had asked him why he did so, I am sure he would have replied that the deeper his concern for his order, the less he could tolerate those who were disgracing it by the godless manner of their lives. And yet the man who does this does not allow

* * * * *

3 Ep 1254 n6
4 Either when he was prior there, in 1517–18, or after he was made assistant inquisitor in 1520

a priest or a theologian to utter a word of criticism against the failings of 60
another priest or theologian, even though no one's reputation is being
injured, so that the criticism benefits all and no one is disgraced. Why then
does he rant against Erasmus from his chair of theology and from the pulpit,
attacking him again and again with patent lies?

The passage which seems to have offended him is very modest in the 65
way in which it treats monks and theologians. It is, I think, in the *Paraclesis*,
and runs like this: 'Since baptism, in which we make the first profession of
our Christian faith, is the common possession of all Christians alike, and
since the other sacraments and the reward of eternal life belong to all alike, it
is illogical to believe that dogma alone should be reserved for those few 70
whom the people today call monks and theologians. These men are a tiny
fraction of the people of Christ, but I wish they were more worthy of the title
which they bear. For I am afraid that you will find among theologians those
who are far from deserving the title of their office, that is, men whose talk is
of earthly, not heavenly, things; and among monks who profess to follow 75
the poverty of Christ and to despise the world you find an excess of
worldliness.'[5] It is clear that in this passage I am neither condemning the
order nor hurting anyone's reputation. If no monk ever fails to live up to his
title and no theologian is ever unworthy of his name, then this brilliant
doctor and his Carmelite friend are right to be angry with me. 80

So much for one section of his pamphlet. He is very proud of it, not just
for its style but for its wit, for beneath a mask of modesty he regards himself
as a great humorist. Then he turns to the remark which I make in the same
work, that no one should be prevented from reading Holy Scripture or
drawing from it whatever benefit he can;[6] here he argues that I have failed to 85
notice what is written in John's Gospel, 'The well is deep and you have no
vessel to draw from it.'[7] In fact I remembered the passage well; but since the
words of the woman of Samaria apply to Christ, I could see no reference
there to Holy Scripture – unless you want to interpret it this way: 'The well
of sacred Scripture is deep and Christ has no vessel with which to draw from 90
it'! By the same token we can prove that Christ was a criminal because we
read in the gospel, 'If he were not a criminal, we should not have brought
him before you.'[8] At one time the well was deeper, until the light of the
gospel shone forth and dispelled the shadows and parted the veil of the

* * * * *

5 LB V 140D–E. Erasmus' quotation, though close, is not absolutely accurate.
6 LB V 140B
7 John 4:11
8 John 18:30

law;[9] and yet even in those days the people used to read the sacred books. 95
Now that our Lord Jesus has channelled the water of his gospel truth into
every street, anyone who has faith has a vessel to draw from that stream.
The Jews did not prevent anyone, after his thirtieth year, from reading
Genesis, the Song of Songs, or Ezekiel, although there is much that is
obscure in these books.[10] The eunuch was helped by having read Isaiah,[11] 100
which he did not understand; the pagan Augustine was helped by having
read Paul's Epistles, which he could not yet comprehend.[12] Are we then to
prevent a Christian from having any contact with the Scriptures?

Furthermore in an addendum to the preface on Matthew[13] I describe
the manner in which I would like laymen to read the Scriptures. The brilliant 105
doctor ought to have read it before he made such a fuss about the passage in
John.[14] It is not surprising that he has misunderstood it and used it foolishly,
for I imagine he is more at home with the works of Accorso, Baldo and the
like[15] – though if he cites the laws as ineptly as he cites the gospel, then pity
help his clients! It is more surprising, however, that this great Carmelite 110
theologian should have furnished his puppet with arguments as silly as
these, though admittedly the arguments which he uses in the school of
theology are generally no better and often raise a laugh among the bachelors
of theology. Here too the doctor is pleased with his own wit, when he
pretends to pity me for not seeing something as obvious as the passage in 115
John. But all previous theologians must have been as blind as moles, since
none of them could see that in this passage Christians were being forbidden
to read the gospel, which Christ wished to be the common possession of
every nation. Perhaps a tanner will read the gospel more correctly than

* * * * *

9 2 Cor 3:13–16
10 The idea that the Jews had confined the study of the first chapters of Genesis,
the Song of Songs, and the opening and closing sections of Ezekiel to men 'of
full and mature age' goes back to Origen's *Prologus in Canticum Canticorum*; see
PG 13 63D–64A. But Erasmus' direct source is the introduction of Jerome's
Commentaria in Ezechielem. Jerome's information is apparently taken from
Origen, but he defines Origen's 'full and mature age' as 'the age of priestly
service, ie, the thirtieth year,' a figure taken from Numbers 4:3; see PL 25
17A–C. This testimony of Origen and Jerome had no basis in the Jewish practice
of their day. For further information and bibliography, see David J. Halperin
The Merkabah in Rabbinic Literature (New Haven 1980) 38 n74.
11 Acts 8:27–39
12 *Confessions* 7.21, 8.6–12; *Contra Academicos* 2.2
13 The letter 'pio lectori,' dated 14 January 1522, which follows the preface to the
paraphrase on St Matthew; LB VII **2 verso–**4 verso.
14 See lines 85–7.
15 See Ep 134:30–1n.

either the doctor or his theological mentor, if this is the way in which they 120
interpret it. Isn't it obvious that the reason these men wish the holy
Scriptures to be known to a few is simply so as not to lose any of their present
prestige or income? The lawyers were afflicted with the same sore when the
calendar of business days and feast days was published;[16] now, it seems, it is
bothering some theologians, and since they are greedier and more ambi- 125
tious than the lawyers, the sting is greater.

But let us hear the other arguments with which this fine theologian has
equipped his spokesman. From the Acts he cites the case of the eunuch of
Queen Candace, who, when he was asked if he understood what he was
reading, replied: 'How can I unless someone shows me the way?'[17] He was 130
an Ethiopian, an officer of a barbarian court, totally unfamiliar with Jewish
religion. It is not surprising that he failed to understand a prophecy about
the death of Christ which had not yet passed into common currency. But
today if a sailor read the same passage, he would immediately guess that one
was speaking about Christ. Even so the Ethiopian is praised for having read 135
the Scriptures, and since he was searching for Christ in the mysteries of
Scripture, he deserved to learn about him. No better example than this could
be adduced to inspire the minds of all with a desire to read the sacred texts.

He also adduces the fact that Christ spoke to the multitude in parables.
But Christ also said, 'There is nothing covered that shall not be revealed; and 140
what you hear in the ear, proclaim it upon the house-tops.'[18] Parables were
employed to suit the needs of the time; but with Christ's death the veil was
torn asunder and all mysteries are now revealed. Besides, if nothing is to be
presented to the people except in parables, it will be wrong to expound the
gospel to the laity, and the evangelists, who revealed the mysteries of 145
Christ's teaching in a language known to all, have sinned. For at that time

* * * * *

16 Erasmus is here referring to a quasi-historical tradition about lawyers and the
Roman calendar for which the principal source is Cicero (*Pro Murena* 25; cf
Epistulae ad Atticum 6.1.8). The story is approximately as follows. In Rome, the
dies fasti were the days on which the courts could conduct business, while the
dies nefasti were the holy days on which they could not. The list of all the *dies
fasti ac nefasti* constituted the Roman calendar, knowledge of which was for
centuries a closely guarded secret of priests and a few others, apparently
including lawyers. Consequently, those who wished to transact business in
the courts had to inquire of the privileged few when they might do so and
could scarcely proceed without legal counsel. Thus, when in 304 BC a certain
Gnaeus Flavius published the calendar of business days and feast days, he
thereby deprived the lawyers of the secret wisdom that they had so long
exploited for their own profit.
17 Acts 8:31
18 Matt 10:26–7

even tanners and sailors spoke Greek and Latin as we speak Dutch. But if
Christ used parables when he spoke to an ignorant and hostile multitude
because he thought this was best suited to the task of redeeming mankind, is
that any reason why the people who have been initiated into the mysteries   150
of Christ should hear nothing but parables? If nothing but parables can be
accepted, let them read the parables in the Gospels; but even this they reject,
in flat contradiction to their own beliefs. But, to be serious, if the message of
Scripture is to be reserved to the few, what are we to make of that prophecy
in Isaiah, 'that all men shall be taught of God?'[19]   155
    From the Epistle of Peter he cites the case of those who distorted certain
difficult passages in the letters of Paul to their own destruction.[20] But Peter
does not condemn the reading of Paul's letters, only the fact that they were
being distorted, as were other passages of Scripture also. So if the ordinary
people are to be prevented from reading the sacred texts, then by the same   160
reasoning theologians should also be forbidden to read them; for all heretics,
many of whom have been men of great learning, distort what they read in
order to find support for their wrong-headed views – unless you imagine
that the Arians or the followers of Origen were not heretics;[21] and I say
nothing about Luther, who is in their eyes a heretic a hundred times over   165
and whose peculiar doctrine it is that nothing is to be admitted in argument
except Scripture. But the Carmelite refuses to admit the testimony of the
sacred Scriptures even into theological schools. For when the bachelors
argue, 'Christ said this in Matthew, so your thesis is false,' he cries out, 'That
is how the Lutherans argue; I tell you that I shall not reply.' So what   170
authority is left to Scripture, if even among theologians it has no place? We
shall go, I suppose, to the fountain-head, that is to two Carmelites;[22] and
future generations will learn from them that those who base their arguments
on the sacred books argue heretically.
    But let us put banter aside and return to the issue. If, because some   175
men abuse them, ordinary people ought not to read the Scriptures, which
the apostles have made available so that all may read, then Baechem will not
drink wine (of which he is inordinately fond) because there are very many
who abuse it. In fact no one will preach in church because many teach heresy
there, some stir up sedition, others flatter princes or destroy their neigh-   180
bour's reputation with their lies. If that should happen, where would

* * * * *

19 54:13; cf John 6:45.
20 2 Pet 3:16
21 Cf Ep 1451:40–51.
22 Erasmus is perhaps granting his antagonist honorary status as a Carmelite; cf
   lines 80–1, 120, 212–14.

Baechem hold his court? Where will he exercise that tyranny of which he even boasts? Finally, if no one may wear the Carmelite habit because certain monks abuse it, Baechem will have to take off his own. Such is the brilliant reasoning of those who refuse ordinary people any contact with the 185 Scriptures; but if the people do not understand the Scriptures, who is more to blame for this than those who instruct them every day? After so many years have they taught them nothing? And is this the meaning of evangelical progress – that no one now understands the message of the evangelists?

Finally, in his epilogue, he reaches the conclusion that theologians 190 probably have a more accurate understanding of Holy Scripture than laymen – as if I had ever denied that this is generally true, or forbidden laymen from learning from theologians!

In another passage,[23] where I criticize a perverted sense of values, he finds fault with me for saying: 'If a Franciscan put on a black coat instead of 195 his grey habit, he would be afraid some devil would carry him off alive to Tartarus. But the same man is not afraid when he commits adultery or incest or some other crime which runs counter to God's commands. I do not praise those who thoughtlessly change their habit, but I am opposed to wrong-headed and superstitious beliefs. These men are frightened to violate the 200 ordinances of men, but think it a trifle to violate the laws of God.' My critic took from this what he wanted and omitted those parts which made the argument clear. So our splendid doctor has won a victory and is justified in decking out his triumphal chariot, if it is true that a Benedictine sins more grievously when he happens to put on a brown habit instead of a black one 205 than when he debauches a holy virgin.

As for the remark I made about preachers who seek profit from their preaching,[24] I only wish that what I wrote was untrue. And remember that a general statement is not intended to insult any particular individual. If no one said this sort of thing before me, then I must bear the odium for my 210 remark. If there are no people like that, then I deserve to be laughed at for troubling myself over nothing. And if our splendid doctor is not aware of anyone who fits the description, let him have a look at his friend the Carmelite!

But now our doctor moves from asses to horses,[25] that is, from 215 theologians to princes. He was under the impression that the emperor was threatening the Turks and hoped that he would win great glory for himself.

* * * * *

23 Unidentified
24 Possibly a reference to the comment in the *Ratio verae theologiae* LB V 100F–101A
25 *Adagia* I vii 29

If there are people who twist the phrase *Nolite omnino resistere malo*[26] to mean that one should not resist the Turks, they should remember that the phrase belongs to Christ, not to me. He is the author of these words. In my 220 *Annotationes* I interpret these words in a way which makes such a distortion impossible: for I construe *resistere malo* to mean 'resist with evil,' that is, 'by evil means.'[27] So let the venerable doctor claim, if he can, that it is perfectly proper for the emperor to attack the Turks 'by evil means'! Now you see he is moving from the asses to the dogs! 225

He took exception to the fact that in a private letter,[28] addressed to a particular individual, I mentioned two honourable men, Baechem and van der Hulst, in less than honourable terms. Just how honourable they are, the record itself makes clear. One has had his sword taken from him,[29] the other narrowly escaped conviction.[30] I know Baechem, but I am not the only one: 230 the people also know him for a fool and a madman. Van der Hulst I have only seen,[31] but I have been able to find out about him, just as I can find out about Phalaris and Nero.[32] Because there were one or two words of modest criticism of these men in a private letter, was that any reason to publish a pamphlet and expose to obloquy men for whose reputation he professed 235 such delicate fears?

Finally he criticized my remark about tax-collectors who exact from the people not just what their prince demands, which is a heavy burden in itself, but whatever sum they think fit themselves.[33] He supposes that in this passage I mean to say that the taxes levied by the princes are unjust, and in 240 this way he hopes to make a case against me for *lèse majesté*. And certainly the demands of rulers are sometimes unjust. But I use the word *iniquus* to describe anything which is heavy: thus Virgil wrote *et iniquo pondere rastros* 'and hoes of heavy weight,'[34] and we call a judge *iniquus*, not when he is unjust in his treatment, but when he is strict and shows little mercy to the 245 plaintiff. We call terms *aequus* 'light,' 'fair' when they have been made easy out of kindness, *iniquus*, when they are severe and show little mercy to the defendant. So I described the tax which the princes levied on the people as

* * * * *

26 Matt 5:39: 'Resist not evil' (ASV)
27 See LB VI 30B–C.
28 Possibly Ep 1345
29 See Ep 1466 n7.
30 See Ep 1466 n8.
31 Cf Ovid *Tristia* 4.10.51.
32 Phalaris, ruler of Agrigentum in Sicily (c 570–544 BC), and the emperor Nero (54–68 AD), both of whom achieved proverbial celebrity as cruel tyrants
33 See the annotation on Luke 3:13 LB VI:241D–E.
34 *Georgics* 1.164

iniquus because by itself it was hard enough to pay even if nothing were added to it by the greed of the collectors. You see how dangerous it is to 250 write in Latin when there are readers who are ignorant of the language.

He thinks that he will lower my stock with the emperor if he convinces him that I am critical of the heavy taxes levied by the princes. But the truth is that no one deserves the emperor's disapproval so much as those who support unjust levies from which as a rule very little reaches the emperor's 255 coffers. Paul approves of paying the taxes and tributes which are due to princes.[35] Christ himself, who is the emperor of emperors, paid his assessment. What relevance, then, has this to me? My warning was for the tax-collectors, not the emperor. And as for the emperor, I warned him quite openly about these men in my little book on the Christian prince.[36] The 260 emperor welcomed the work, Ferdinand has it by heart;[37] and both thanked me for it – and there is no doubt that both are more learned than this doctor and more Christian than this theologian. What joy it would give the theologians if they could count me a heretic, and all because some Carmelite and a Baldic doctor[38] are ignorant of the Latin language! Surely it is time they 265 gave way instead to a happier age, an age in which women are competent in Latin.[39]

I have jotted this down in haste, my most learned friend. I congratulate the Christian church in finding such a mighty Atlas. I congratulate our native Holland for having produced such wise men as you. With regard to 270 the pamphlet, I hear he is looking for a printer. May God always be mindful of him.

I wish you and yours every happiness, my good sir.

Basel, the eve of the feast of St James 1524

To the most learned jurist, Master Nicolaas Everaerts, right honour- 275 able president of Holland

1470 / To Pierre Barbier   Basel, [c 26 July 1524]

This letter was first published in the *Opus epistolarum*. The year-date given there (line 60) cannot be correct because the *De libero arbitrio* (September 1524) had not yet been published (lines 56–6). Since the letter was written after the

* * * * *

35 Rom 13:7
36 *Institutio principis christiani* (Epp 393, 853); see CWE 27 260–2.
37 Cf Epp 943:26–8, 970:28, 1323:5–6, 1505:9–10.
38 See lines 108–9.
39 See Ep 1404 n8.

return of Lieven Algoet (Ep 1430:21n) and in accordance with the advice offered in Ep 1458, Allen reasoned that it was roughly contemporary with Ep 1471.

On Barbier, see Epp 1358, 1458 n8.

ERASMUS OF ROTTERDAM TO PIERRE BARBIER, GREETING

I understand from my servant Lieven[1] that Johannes de Molendino[2] has received half this year's annuity[3] from Jan de Hondt,[4] and has done so on the authority of a letter from you in which you had indicated that on this question you had set my mind at rest. And had not Marcus Laurinus,[5] the   5
dean of Bruges, brought my letter in time, Molendino would have swallowed the whole lot. And after all this you say in your letter that the friendship between us will last for ever! The old proverb says 'Anything, short of the altar';[6] experience, which is much older, says 'Anything, short of the money-bags.' What can be more brutal than you are if you strip the naked of   10
their clothes and rob the robber's victim? You know the simple confidence and open heart with which I left this whole business to you as a man of honour; I would with equal confidence have put my life in your hands as well. Among Luther's supporters it is pretty well those who were particular-ly my sworn friends who are now my most deadly enemies; and if my   15
Barbier lets me down, I will never again trust any mortal man. And yet you were promising great lumps of gold out of Paria;[7] and are you now scraping for these little scraps?

But joking apart, my dear Barbier, my annuity from the emperor is past hope unless I return home;[8] and if I do return, I have my doubts whether   20
they will pay what they promise. You remember that remark in the old play (but its real home is the court)? 'Not just this moment. Come again tomorrow. Where were you yesterday?'[9] And you are not unaware what sort of man I am, how far from a shameless beggar. I am owed my annuity for three years now.[10] And life here is expensive;[11] believe me, I cannot live   25

* * * * *

1470
1 See introduction.
2 See Ep 1458:5.
3 See Ep 1417 n13.
4 Ep 1433
5 Ep 1458
6 *Adagia* III ii 10
7 See Ep 913:6n.
8 See Ep 1380 introduction.
9 Terence *Adelphi* 204, 234. Cf *Adagia* IV v 92.
10 Ie, the imperial annuity
11 For Erasmus' financial difficulties during this year, see Epp 1434:28–30, 66–7, 1531:13–14.

on less than six hundred gold florins.[12] I have my household to keep, three servants[13] and the horses.[14] There is always someone away on an errand, and my health gets worse every day. In June I was almost done for; I never brought forth in such a desperate state.[15] I am in pretty low water financially[16] even if there is no reduction. I know that I owe this appoint-   30
ment, for what it is worth, to you; but a right-thinking patron builds on his gift, he doesn't claw back what he has given. My friends write[17] that I was ill advised over that annuity;[18] that I am a mere man, the creature of a day, and that you live in a part of the world with frequent attacks of the plague. If you could put a third prop under it, so to speak, the business would stand   35
steadier. Now I have under my roof a man called Lieven Algoet (Allgood one might call him), who has been my servant for over five years. I should like the annuity to be transferred to him,[19] if anything in the way of mortality should happen to me. And in any case he is a young man who deserves a good appointment of any kind. He has made such progress in both the   40
ancient tongues and in humane studies and scholarship that he is now ahead of me.[20] Last but not least, he was born in Ghent, if I may add this to his pile of qualifications. You will do me a really welcome service if you can put this through at the earliest opportunity. Morillon has written about the prior rights,[21] and I gave him leave to transfer my claim to your brother   45
Nicolas.[22]

Zúñiga's latest offspring has arrived.[23] The man is a serious rival to Pasquil,[24] and he is really a supporter of Luther, for he is a living proof that papal constitutions carry no weight, when after so many official prohibi-

* * * * *

12 But his regular income was only 400; cf Ep 1341A:1760–7, a passage written at just this time.
13 Lieven Algoet (see introduction and lines 36–42 below), Karl Harst (Ep 1437:208–9), and Hilarius Bertholf (Ep 1384 n31).
14 Cf Epp 1422:25–6, 1488:55–66, 1519 n1.
15 See Ep 1452 n22.
16 See Ep 1434:30–2 and n16.
17 See Ep 1458.
18 Ie, from the prebend at Courtrai (see n3 above).
19 Erasmus had earlier expressed his intention to provide for Algoet; Ep 1437:215–18. Cf Allen Ep 1716:8–18.
20 Cf Ep 1437:215–16.
21 See Ep 1431:1, 20–1.
22 See Ep 1431:22–4.
23 See Ep 1466 n23.
24 See Ep 1341A:896–7.

tions[25] he goes on acting out his play just the same. I have decided in future   50
to pay no attention to the man and all his rubbish.

Here there are new gospellers[26] every day loosing off raving pamphlets
aimed at me.[27] But I am in no position to complain, for they have recently put
out some attacks on the pope,[28] such nauseous stuff as no pantomime clown
would launch against a brothel-keeper. I am obliged to publish a book on   55
free will,[29] since its existence has got about already, to stop them thinking it
something too atrocious. I'm sorry the papal legate[30] has done no good in
England. What are these monarchs aiming at, I wonder. Mind you give my
greetings to Hezius[31] and my other friends as well.

Basel [1525]   60

1471 / To Jan de Hondt   Basel, 20 July 1524

> This letter was first published by Scriverius (see Ep 1433 introduction). On Jan
> de Hondt, see Ep 1433.

ERASMUS OF ROTTERDAM TO MASTER JAN DE HONDT,
CANON OF COURTRAI, GREETING

Honoured sir, I am sorry you were upset by my letter.[1] It was not like you,
nor did I ever put much trust in Bentinus. As for the suffragan,[2] he can say
what he likes; at Bruges he has twice made a violent attack on my reputation   5
in a public sermon.

I send you Barbier's second letter,[3] for the first one[4] never reached me.
In it he assures me that it was without his knowledge that the money was
paid over in cash to someone else.[5] What source of income has he, out of
which he will make it good if, as is to be feared, he does not get a benefice?   10
Has he any heirs I shall be able to proceed against? Our friendship can stand

* * * * *

25 See Ep 1341A:914–26.
26 Cf Ep 1483 n2.
27 Cf Ep 1481 n11.
28 See Ep 1477A n6.
29 See Epp 1419, 1481.
30 Schönberg; see Ep 1466 n28.
31 Ep 1339

1471
1 Ep 1433
2 See Ep 1144 n12.
3 Not extant; Ep 1470 is the reply.
4 Not extant; probably contemporary with Barbier's letter to Johannes de
  Molendino mentioned in Ep 1458:9–10.
5 On this trouble with Barbier, see Epp 1417, 1458, 1470.

a loss like this, but as things now are my finances can't.[6] The emperor owes
me six hundred gold florins of my salary,[7] nor shall I receive a penny unless I
were to return to Brabant.[8] And perhaps even then they would not pay cash.
And in the mean time I have made my excuses to the king of France, who   15
offered me a treasurership[9] worth at least five hundred crowns.[10] It is always
the same with our beggarly court!

I write this to prevent any repetition of what has happened, and to ask
for your kind help in seeing that the money given to Molendino[11] comes
back to me as soon as possible. Farewell.   20

Basel, morrow of St James 1524

1472 / To Walter Ruys   Basel, 26 July 1524

The manuscript of this letter is in the Gemeente Bibliotheek at Rotterdam
(Erasmus III.102, page 130). It was first published by Adalbert Horawitz in the
Sitzungsberichte der phil.-hist. Classe der kaiserlichen Akademie der Wissenschaften
(Vienna 1882).

Walter Ruys (d 1534) of Grave, near Nijmegen, was a Dominican living at
this time in Louvain. Although their relations at this point were evidently
friendly, Erasmus later concluded that Ruys was one of the Dominicans of
Louvain who in March 1525 published an *Apologia* against his *Exomologesis* and
De esu carnium (Epp 1603, 1608, 1621, 1624, 1655). At the time of his death, Ruys
was Dominican prior at Nijmegen.

ERASMUS OF ROTTERDAM TO WALTER OF GRAVE OP, GREETING
Why do you strive to make excuses to me for your order?[1] I do not hold the
good ones responsible for the way the bad behave, and however black the

* * * * *

6 Cf Ep 1470 n11.
7 For three years; see Ep 1470:24–5. These were probably Rhenish florins, rather
   than Burgundian-Hapsburg Carolus florins or Florentine florins. If so, a sum
   worth about £145 gros Flemish or £102 10s sterling.
8 See Ep 1380 introduction.
9 See Ep 1434:24–5.
10 Although Erasmus states *quingentorum coronatorum*, the coins in question were
   undoubtedly not *écus d'or à la couronne*, but *écus d'or au soleil*, for the reasons
   stated in Ep 1434 n3. Furthermore, that same Ep 1434:25 (see also n13) explicitly
   states that this 'treasurership' was worth 1,000 livres [tournois], which was
   then precisely the value of 500 such *écus au soleil*. That sum was also worth £158
   6s 8d gros Flemish and £106 5s 0d sterling.
11 Cf Ep 1458:10–11.

   1472
1 See Ep 1006 n1.

habit I delight to find a pure white soul inside it. Your feelings for me, my
dear Walter, are most welcome. All the same, I should not like to think that   5
while you are defending your friend Erasmus against men who are
incurable – insane, I nearly said – you should make yourself seriously
unpopular. Devote yourself instead to something else, to the solid learning
and the character above all reproach by which you can either escape ill will or
overcome it. As for me, my destiny, though it was the last thing I expected,   10
has plunged me in the troubles of our generation, and I must play my part to
the finish. You, who have yet to take the stage, must not fail to prepare
yourself with care for a public appearance.

What you urge should be done with the paraphrases[2] is done already,
in large type and small type too.   15

Farewell. From Basel, the morrow of St James 1524

1473 / To Maarten Lips   Basel, 26 July 1524

The manuscript source for this letter is the same as that for Ep 1472, and first
publication was in the same place. On Maarten Lips, see Ep 750.

ERASMUS OF ROTTERDAM TO HIS DEAR LIPS, GREETING
I can't think where your letter[1] lay hidden for so long. Nothing gave me
greater pleasure. I have written to your friend Walter.[2] Willem[3] seems to be a
good scholar and a friendly person, and he has good judgment. I would
have written to him, but the bearer of this prepares to leave sooner than I   5
expected. I will write another time.[4]

* * * * *

2 Probably a request that they be published in a collected edition. For the folio
  volume containing the Gospels and Acts, see Ep 1430 n1. The companion
  volume containing the Epistles is dated 1523. In octavo there had been four
  collected issues of the Epistles by 1523, but at this time there had apparently
  been no such edition of the Gospels and Acts; see Allen's note.

1473
1 Not extant
2 Ruys (Ep 1472)
3 Evidently Willem Gheershoven (d 1547), also called Willem of Louvain, a
  canon regular of St Augustine at the monastery of Groenendal at Hoeilaart,
  near Brussels. He is known from the seven extant letters of his correspondence
  with Lips (1525–6) dealing with two manuscripts of St Augustine in the
  Groenendal library. One of the letters recalls a visit by the young Erasmus to
  study the manuscripts; see Allen I 590.
4 A letter was finally sent in the spring of 1527 (Allen Ep 1837:50).

The notes you have made on Augustine[5] from ancient codices can be transcribed on paper, if you were to give the edition, page, and line. If you send them here, I will see that you get a little money in return. No time just now to write more. I have written to Goclenius[6] to buy you the paraphrases[7] if you should not possess them. Farewell.

Basel, the morrow of St James 1524

1474 / To Christoph von Utenheim

Basel, 29 July 1524

This is the preface to the *De immensa Dei misericordia concio* (Basel: Froben, September 1524), evidently written to mark the opening of a new chapel (Epp 1341A:782–4, 1456:10, and lines 3–4 of this letter). It was submitted to bishop Christoph for examination (Ep 1456) and at his request (Ep 1464) all controversial material was removed. The work quickly became popular, and by 1526 German, English, and Dutch versions had appeared. Translations into other languages followed in later decades; see Allen's introduction.

TO THE RIGHT REVEREND FATHER IN CHRIST CHRISTOPH,
BISHOP OF BASEL, FROM ERASMUS OF ROTTERDAM, GREETING
Your lordship having, with that piety which we all devoutly admire, established a most elegant chapel dedicated to the Lord's Mercies, I have prepared an offering to it, a panegyric in praise of mercy; nor have I ever complied more readily with your wishes, most honourable of prelates, though it is always a great pleasure to fulfil your commands. No subject could be more appropriate, either to that pious charity which makes you passionately desire that all men through God's mercy should achieve salvation, or to the very wicked age in which we live. Surely in such a deluge of misfortunes it was meet and right to exhort all men to take refuge in the divine mercy. This task I undertook all the more readily from the thought that I should at the same moment fulfil a pious desire of yours and also do something not unpleasing to God. I only wish this passion which we both share may be so effectual among men at large that many, many of them, moved by our pleading, may cast away their ancient wickedness and seek

* * * * *

5 This signals the resumption of work on a new edition of Augustine for Froben; see Epp 1309 introduction, 1531:51–2, 1547. From now on until publication in 1528–9, the topic comes up frequently in Erasmus' correspondence with Lips, who was his principal collaborator on the project.
6 The letter is not extant.
7 Cf Allen Ep 1547:14–16.

the Lord's mercy! And may that mercy ever deign to watch over you in your honourable old age!

Basel, 29 July 1524

1475 / To Helias Marcaeus   Basel, 30 July 1524

This is the preface to the expanded version of the *Virginis et martyris comparatio*, which was printed with the *De immensa Dei misericordia* (Epp 1474). On the first edition, and on Marcaeus, see Ep 1346.

ERASMUS OF ROTTERDAM TO THE MOST WORTHY AND LEARNED FATHER HELIAS MARCAEUS OF THE COMMUNITY OF MACCABAEANS, WARDEN OF THEIR MOST HONOURABLE COLLEGE

I send you a book that is both short and overdue; but you would agree that it is long and finished in good time if you knew how little leisure is left me in 5 which to oblige my friends in such matters by frequent periods of ill health,[1] by almost continuous business,[2] especially in sending and receiving letters, and by the toilsome researches demanded by the subjects I have undertaken. If I have done what you wished, I am delighted; if not, you must at least approve my ready desire to please, if what I hear of your good nature is not 10 untrue. When I have more time to spare, I will meet your pious wishes with something more substantial. My best wishes both to yourself, honoured sir, and to your worthy company of virgins pledged to God's service.

Basel, 30 July 1524

1476 / To Johannes Erasmius Froben   Basel, 1 August 1524

This is the preface to a new edition of the *Familiarum colloquiorum formulae* (Basel: Froben, August–September 1524). It contained six more colloquies than the preceding edition of March 1524 (cf Ep 1341A: 286–301). The dedicatee, Johann Erasmius Froben (Ep 1262), was now about eight years old.

DESIDERIUS ERASMUS OF ROTTERDAM TO A BOY FULL OF PROMISE, JOHANNES ERASMIUS FROBEN, GREETING

The book dedicated to you, sweetest Erasmius, has surpassed my expectations; it will be your task to see that you do not fall short of what I expect of

* * * * *

1475
1 See Epp 1452 n22, 1466:68–70, 1488:5–7.
2 For Erasmus' scholarly work at this time, see Epp 1460, 1465, 1474, 1476, 1502, and 1481 (for the completion of the *De libero arbitrio*).

you. The book is so popular and is in such demand and is so dog-eared by   5
the fingering of the young who wish to learn that your father has had to
reprint it several times and I have had to enrich it from time to time with
fresh additions; you could call it too a kind of Erasmius,[1] and the darling of
all who worship at the Muses' shrine. So you will have to try all the harder to
live up to your name, and this involves being very dear to all good people as   10
an educated, honourable man. It will be a great disgrace if, when this book
has made so many better Latinists and better men, you behave in such a way
as to lose the benefits which for your sake have been open to all men; and
while there are so many young people who are grateful to you on account of
the *Colloquies*, would it not rightly be thought absurd if it should prove to be   15
your own doing that you cannot thank me for the same thing?

The book has grown into a proper large volume; and you too must try,
as you grow in years, to grow likewise in sound learning and uprightness of
character. Something special is expected of you, and these expectations it is
essential to live up to and will be most creditable to surpass, while in any   20
case you cannot fall short of them without great disgrace. Nor do I say this
because I am dissatisfied with your progress hitherto, but to spur a running
horse[2] and make you run all the more eagerly, especially now you have
entered on the time of life when it is most profitable to absorb the elements of
learning and religion. See to it then that these *Colloquies* can truly be called   25
your book; and may the Lord Jesus preserve your boyhood free from all
stain, and lead you on from strength to strength.

Farewell, from Basel, 1 August 1524.

1477 / To the Magistrates of Strasbourg   Basel, 23 August 1524

The manuscript of this letter is an autograph rough draft in the Royal Library at
Copenhagen (G.K.S.95 Fol, f 239).

The content of Ep 1429 is here repeated, though this time, it seems, no one
was given the opportunity to interdict delivery (see Ep 1429 introduction). The
minutes of the Strasbourg council for 27 August 1524, cited in Allen's
introduction, show that in response to this letter, Brunfels and Schott were
summoned before the council to explain themselves. Ep 1481:36–8 indicates
that Erasmus was pleased, at least temporarily, with the outcome, the exact
nature of which is not known. The letter was first published in the *Opus
epistolarum*. Although Brunfels' name was carefully suppressed in the printed

* * * * *

1476
1 Ie, something lovable
2 *Adagia* I ii 47

text, it still seems strange, as Allen observed, that this letter should have been selected for publication long after Brunfels had made his peace with Erasmus (see Ep 1405 introduction).

The information supplied in the notes to Ep 1429 has not been repeated here.

TO THE WELL-BORN AND RIGHT WORSHIPFUL COUNCILLORS OF
THE FAMOUS CITY OF STRASBOURG FROM ERASMUS OF ROTTERDAM,
GREETING

Right worshipful lords of the council, let me not long detain you. There is in your city a printer named Johann Schott. Some time ago this man printed an   5
attack on me by Ulrich von Hutten which is full of palpable falsehoods, and has supplied it with disgusting illustrations.[1] Not content with that, he has secretly printed the same book a second time together with a scurrilous tirade by one Otto Brunfels, in which he heaps upon me all the abuse that one pantomime clown would make bold to throw at another. I am a traitor to   10
the gospel,[2] I have been bribed to wage war on the gospel,[3] I could be hired for a crust of bread to do anything.[4] What need to repeat it all? The whole pamphlet is full of raving abuse and nothing else. This was most strongly disapproved of by Luther himself and by Melanchthon,[5] for both of them can see that such men do more harm than anyone else to the gospel cause.   15
When my friends protested and asked the reason for such behaviour, both of them, Otto as well as Schott, returned an outrageous reply, with threats of something even more spiteful. At length (so they tell me) he was warned, actually by some members of the council, not to try anything of the kind in future. And he, in contempt of the law of the land,[6] which abominates   20
scandalous publications, in contempt of your worships' admirable and necessary regulations, and in contempt of the very well meant warning you had given him, proceeded to reprint the same pamphlet once again.

Whether I have been of service to the public in the work I have done is a matter of common knowledge. For the promotion of the gospel I have   25
supported a great burden of labour and of hostility. I have refused all offers made to me by princes as an inducement to write against Luther;[7] nay more, I have preferred to lose what was mine already rather than write against my

* * * * *

1477
1 See Ep 1477B:31–5.
2 See Brunfels' *Responsio* Böcking II 332:34–5, 341:13–14, 37.
3 Ibidem 341:10–11
4 Ibidem 341:25–9. Cf Epp 1477B nn11–12, 1481:22–3.
5 See Ep 1429 n3.
6 Cf lines 52–3 below.
7 Cf Epp 1477B:64–7, 1384:47–52, 1510:23–5.

conscience to satisfy the desire of certain people. I have shown such
reluctance to lend my name to that league[8] for many reasons, but especially   30
because there were some things in Luther's books which I did not
understand and some of which I did not wholly approve; and particularly
because I saw in that conspiracy[9] some men whose character and enterprises
seemed to me as far removed as could be from the spirit of the gospel. I never
yet did anyone an injury either because he supported Luther or because he   35
gave him too little support. Of neither Schott nor Otto have I ever said a
single injurious word.

     To accuse a man of taking money to betray the gospel of Christ is no
ordinary charge. If in your zeal for justice you allow no thief to go
unpunished, how much more criminal it is so scandalously to attack a man's   40
reputation, which is more precious than life itself! If he who strikes another
man is duly chastised, what does he deserve who pours such criminal libels
on another man's good name? I do not ask your worships to give any weight
to my age or to all I have done to raise the public standard of education, or to
consider the warm feelings I have always entertained towards your city, to   45
which I know myself to be very deeply indebted for many acts of kindness;[10]
I merely warn you in your wisdom to look to the future, and see where the
licence of such men may lead, if they are allowed to do as they please
without penalty. If you support the gospel, these are the men who
undermine it. If you support the cause of public peace, we have here   50
nothing but a hotbed of subversion. If you dislike an open contempt for the
law, as you do with perfect right, the laws of every nation without exception
include criminal libel among the most serious offences.[11]

     The facts speak for themselves. The two persons responsible for this
offence both live in Strasbourg, and both admit their guilt. A second libel   55
upon me has appeared,[12] printed (so they say) in Haguenau, but at Schott's
expense. Nor will they ever end this maniac behaviour, if they can always
take advantage of your clemency. For my part, I can endure injuries done to
myself; but books of this sort earn no little unpopularity for your city, whose
welfare I have so much at heart, in the judgment of all right-thinking men   60
and of the princes, with many of whom I am not unpopular. And so farewell
to your well-born and right honourable worships.

     From Basel, St Bartholomew's eve 1524

          * * * * *

 8 Ie, support the reformers; cf Epp 1481:28–9, 1485:7, 1496:141–2.
 9 Cf Epp 1433:14, 1481:28, 1506:10, 1528:49.
10 See Ep 1429 n8.
11 Cf Ep 1477B:52–3.
12 Doubtless the *Iudicium* of Erasmus Alber (Ep 1466 n19)

Autograph letter from Erasmus to the town council of Basel, Ep 1477A
Staatsarchiv Basel, Handel und Gewerbe JJJ 1

1477A / To the Town Council of Basel   [Basel, late August 1524]

The autograph of this undated letter, in which Erasmus complains to the city
fathers of Basel about attacks upon him written by Guillaume Farel (Ep 1341A
note 305) and published in their city, is in the Staatsarchiv Basel (Handel und
Gewerbe JJJ.1). It was first published by Emil Dürr in the *Aktensammlung zur
Geschichte der Basler Reformation* I (1921) 144–5. Allen published it as Ep 1508.
Scholars have disagreed on the dating of the letter. Because of the numerous
similarities to Epp 1496:145–59 (6 September) and 1510 (27 October), Dürr gave
the letter the date '1524 September/Oktober' while Allen settled on 'October
1524.' There is nothing in the letter, however, that would preclude its having
been written somewhat earlier than September. Two scholars have in fact
argued that the letter should be given an earlier date. In his biography of Farel
in CEBR II, Kaspar von Greyerz has put the date at late June–early July on the
assumption that the letter played an important role in the decision of the Basel
city council to expel Farel from the city (9 July). This assumption, however, is
without foundation. Neither this letter nor any other evidence indicates that
Erasmus made a direct approach to the council in an attempt to have Farel
expelled from the city. Moreover, the real target of the letter is not Farel himself
but rather the Basel printers and booksellers who had published or sold his
works. Finally, nothing in the letter points to Farel's presence in the city, which
would scarcely be the case in a letter written to achieve his expulsion from it. It
thus seems that Dürr and Allen were on the right track when they placed the
letter after Farel's expulsion and close to the dated letters in September–
October in which Erasmus expresses similar agitation about Farel in similar
language. However, as Jean Meyerhoffer pointed out in the *Biographie nouvelle*
130 n1, there are good grounds for concluding that the letter was probably
written in August. In Ep 1481:36–8 (2 September), Erasmus informs Gian
Matteo Giberti that he has warned the city councils of Strasbourg and Basel
that they must control the 'outrageous audacity' of their printers and that both
councils have responded favourably (cf Ep 1510:64–5). The letter to the
Strasbourg magistrates is Ep 1477 (23 August). Might not the present letter be
the one to the magistrates at Basel? Meyerhoffer pointed to certain similarities
of thought and phraseology between it and the letter to Giberti (lines 1–10,
20–1 in this letter, Ep 1481:29–33). Moreover, we also know that by 2 September
Erasmus had already been complaining that Farel was preparing a new book
against him; see Herminjard Ep 121 (page 286), and cf lines 1–6 in this letter.
Thus, while no absolutely certain conclusion can be drawn, the most plausible
reading of the available evidence is that our letter is the warning to the
magistrates at Basel mentioned in the letter to Giberti. Since Erasmus had
already received a reply by 2 September (Ep 1481:38), the letter must have been

written in August. We have therefore redated the letter and placed it immediately after the letter of 23 August to the magistrates of Strasbourg.

Cordial greetings, right worshipful lords of the council. An honourable and learned correspondent writes to me from Lyon that a carver from Lorraine by name Jacques Vérier[1] has brought to that city a pamphlet attacking me,[2] written in French by Guillaume Farel[3] and printed in Basel. Again, a man of honour writes to me from Constance[4] that he has seen two pamphlets[5]   5 attacking me, written by this same Farel. Farel is a subversive character with no control over what he either says or writes, as I shall show whenever the need arises. A pamphlet has been on sale here for a long time in which many individuals are libelled by name,[6] and the supreme pontiff in particular. Neither author nor printer has appended his name, but it is generally   10 suspected, it is in fact more than suspected, that the author is Farel[7] and the printer a man commonly called Welshans.[8] This will easily be established if

* * * * *

1477A
1 Jacques Vérier of Lorraine (documented 1518–c 1550), who was more widely known as Jacobus Faber, was a prolific metal engraver working at this time in Basel.
2 Not extant; cf Epp 1496:153–4, 1510:63, 1519:104–5.
3 Epp 1341A n305, 1496:145ff, 1510:11ff
4 Cf Epp 1496:153–4, 1510:45–6. Erasmus' correspondent was probably Botzheim (Ep 1285).
5 See n2 above.
6 Identified by Nathanaël Weiss as *Determinatio Facultatis Theologiae Parisiensis, super aliquibus propositionibus, certis e locis nuper ad eum delatis, de veneratione sanctorum, de canone missae deque sustentatione ministrorum altaris, et ceteris quibusdam: cum familiari expositione, in qua Hereticorum rationes confutantur* (1524), of which only a handful of copies survive, one of them in the British Library. This was a lampoon of the genuine *Determinatio* (the title of which lacked the words after the colon) published by Jean Petit at Paris in December 1523. See *Bulletin de la Société de l'Histoire du Protestantisme français* 68 (1919) 201–11; cf *Biographie nouvelle* 120–1. Weiss believed that the pamphlet had been published at Nürnberg by Johann Petreius, but recent scholarship has determined that it was in fact published by Cratander (Ep 1374 n19) at Basel in March 1524; see Rodolphe Peter, 'Recherches sur l'imprimeur de la *Determinatio* attribuée à Guillaume Farel' in *Actes du colloque Guillaume Farel* ed Pierre Barthel, Rémy Scheurer, Richard Stauffer (Geneva/Lausanne/Neuchâtel 1983) I 221–5.
7 This attribution, questioned by some scholars, has been convincingly reaffirmed by Peter (see preceding note) 226–8.
8 Johann Bebel (documented 1517–38), often called Welsch-Hans, was a native of Strasbourg who in 1523 set up a small press at Basel. Among his productions were a Greek Galen in five volumes (1538), Sebastian Münster's Hebrew and Latin Bible (1534), and Budé's *Commentaria linguae graecae* (1529–30). But he

Cartrander[9] and Watissneer,[10] in whose shop[11] the book is publicly on sale, are compelled to state on oath where they purchased it. And let enquiry be made what Welshans has recently printed.   15

Every man has a concern for his own reputation; but personally I do not think my reputation suffers much from pamphlets like these. I thought it right however to bring this to your worships' attention, for fear such a pestilent precedent might without your knowledge insinuate itself into your city, to which I am quite rightly devoted and deeply indebted. Those who   20 support Luther are disowned by Luther himself as enemies of the gospel;[12] he writes that they defile the camp of Israel.[13] Farel boasts that he will lose no opportunity of damaging my reputation.[14] And I feel that there is a conspiracy in certain quarters to damage any victim they may choose in pamphlets with no author's name or a false one – which means neither more   25 nor less than a hotbed of sedition. The liberties they now take against me they will soon be taking against you, if their licence continues unchecked. I have given you this friendly warning, as my zeal for your welfare dictated, and shall accept whatever decision you arrive at; for my intention is not to cause trouble in your city but to do it a service if I can. Farewell.   30

Erasmus of Rotterdam, with my own hand

To the right worshipful the lords of the council of the city of Basel

1477B / To Caspar Hedio   Basel, [late August?] 1524

This letter was first published in the *Opus epistolarum*. Probably the reply to a letter now lost, it is the first of the three letters that constitute the surviving correspondence between Erasmus and Hedio. The other two are Epp 2616 and

* * * * *

also published works by reformers, which occasionally got him into trouble. In December 1524 he was briefly imprisoned for having published four pamphlets by the radical Andreas Karlstadt (Ep 1522:61–3, 1523:105–7, 1530:2–4). Bebel and Cratander (see n6 above) often collaborated on projects, which may explain why Erasmus here attributes to Bebel a book published by Cratander.

9 Ie, Cratander (see nn6, 8 above).
10 Ie, Wattenschnee, a name frequently applied to Johann Schabler (d c 1540), who owned bookstores in Paris, Lyon, and Basel.
11 The text says 'shop,' but it should be 'shops.'
12 Allen read this as a reference to those, like Erasmus, who had given Luther moderate support, especially at the beginning; but it can just as well be read as a reference to the more radical supporters of the Reformation, like Hutten. The attempt, in other words, is probably to portray Farel and his ilk as having gone beyond what Luther himself would approve. Cf Ep 1477:13–15; also Ep 1429 n3.
13 The exact passage has not been identified, but see the preceding note.
14 Cf Ep 1510:68–70.

3020. Allen assigned the month-date 'c June?' on the basis of the date of Hedio's marriage, 30 May 1524 (Ep 1452:22–3), and published the letter as Ep 1459. At the same time, however, Allen pointed out that the reference to the wedding in line 1 is so vague that one cannot safely assume that the ceremony had taken place all that recently. He went on to speculate that the letter might have been written at about the same time as Ep 1477 (23 August). Indeed, the first half of the letter (down to line 67) closely resembles Ep 1477 in many respects and gives the impression of having been written at about the same time, ie, before the examination of Brunfels and Schott by the Strasbourg city council on 27 August (Ep 1477 introduction), the apparently gratifying outcome of which was known to Erasmus by 2 September (Ep 1481:38). The problem is the vague comment in lines 94–6 about the abolition of images 'in one city.' If this is a reference to events in Strasbourg, then the letter must have been written no earlier than September or, more likely, even later. Strasbourg was the scene of a popular iconoclastic campaign in the last days of August and the first days of September 1524, with the gradual removal of images from the churches under the supervision of the city council beginning on 22 October; see René Bornert *La réforme protestante du culte à Strasbourg au xvie siècle* (Leiden 1981) 133–4. But placing the date in September, October, or even later would leave as an unsolved riddle the complete absence of any reference to the Strasbourg council's response to Ep 1477. It seems much more likely, therefore, that Erasmus was referring, possibly because Hedio had done so, to the removal of images from the churches in Zürich during June and July, an event that had evidently been much on his mind (see Epp 1496:88–9 with n40, 1522:70–1, 1523:159–60) and would leave its mark on the colloquy *Peregrinatio religionis ergo* of 1526 (see ASD I-3 473–4). Assuming this to be the case, all the internal evidence, such as it is, supports the conjecture that this letter was written at about the same time as Ep 1477. We have therefore assigned the date 'late August?' and placed the letter immediately after Epp 1477 and 1477A.

Caspar Hedio (1494–1552) was the son of a ropemaker at Ettlingen in Baden. He was educated at the Latin school in Pforzheim, where Melanchthon was a fellow student, and at the University of Basel, where in 1519 he completed his licence in theology under the guidance of Capito (Ep 1368), who introduced him into the local humanist circle. Exactly when and how he established personal contact with Erasmus is not known. In October 1520 Hedio followed Capito to Mainz, where he received his doctorate in theology and then succeeded Capito as spiritual adviser to Archbishop Albert. In 1523 he moved to Strasbourg, whither Capito had already preceded him, to become preacher at the cathedral. By 1524 he had identified himself with the Reformation, a move which brought strained relations with Erasmus. As recently as March 1524 Erasmus had still regarded Hedio as a reliable friend (Ep 1429:24), but as this letter and Epp 1496–7 show, Erasmus felt betrayed by Hedio's failure to support his demand for the punishment of the printer Johann Schott, who had published attacks on him by Hutten and Brunfels. Despite the strain, however, relations between Erasmus and Hedio remained civil, in contrast to those with some others, such as Zwingli and Capito, who also deserted to the Reformation.

ERASMUS OF ROTTERDAM TO CASPAR HEDIO, GREETING

I pray that your new marriage[1] will be a happy one. I had sent you a letter addressed to the city council,[2] as being the one friend in whom I had wholehearted confidence. But not wishing to embarrass you even in the slightest degree, I told you to suppress it if you would rather, in such a way   5
that nobody should know of it, the point being that this would leave me free to take what decisions I might think best. But you did not keep the business dark – you told Froben at any rate – and you gave Schott a helping hand to save him from any penalty.

I do not say this because I am annoyed with you. I know that whatever   10
you did was done from the best motives, and I respect your mildness, which is of the gospel. But what is mildness in you is for the moment cruelty to me. Would you call it mildness if someone were to help a murderer or a burglar to escape arrest, and thus give him the confidence to kill more victims in the future? One ought not to withhold forgiveness, but the culprit should first   15
be penitent and change his ways. This man is so far from repenting of his lunacy that he boldly threatens even more dastardly outrages. One ought to love one's enemies, but with the object of making them different. It is not loving a man to let him do wrong with impunity when you are in a position to stop him. The stronger a father's affection for his son, the stricter is his   20
discipline when the son does wrong. It would have been true mercy had he been punished immediately after publishing Hutten's libels;[3] he would not then have piled one new lunacy on another. But he has been warned privately by the mayor, you say, and will be more careful. What tender thought for the man's reputation! – to admonish him privately when he has   25
made such criminal things public. Is there any hope that such a monster can be made more restrained by words alone? Scarcely had he published Otto's

* * * * *

1477B
1 Cf Ep 1452:22–3.
2 Ep 1429
3 The *Expostulatio* (Ep 1356 n9)

ravings[4] when he began to reprint them, and another pamphlet[5] as well by some other noisy rascal; and he would have done so had he not been stopped. And yet, when driven off that, he gave us Otto's letters,[6] very pretty letters designed to throw doubt even on the Gospels. A scandalous drawing was also provided. If they were drawing the prophets of Baal, why did they add the shaven hair, the tonsured crown, the linen garment, and the mitre of our own day? They drew me too,[7] with a cap tied under my chin, a silk scarf on my shoulders, and my arms projecting from my mantle; that is very much how I dress, especially at home, and how I was dressed when Otto came to greet me. I make light of this, of course, but it does show the very wicked spirit of these men whom you think it right to help. Do you and your friends believe that support of this kind can promote the interests of the gospel? I fear much more that the foolish malevolence and malevolent folly of such men will undermine equally the humanities and the gospel, if that is possible, and will one day bring all of you and your city into the gravest peril.

Schott, you say, has a wife and small children. Would this seem a sufficient excuse if he had broken open my chest and removed my gold? I hardly think so. And yet what he is doing here is far more criminal. Unless perhaps you think I count reputation worth less than money. If he has no means of feeding his children, let him beg. He is ashamed to, you will say. And is he not ashamed of outrages like these? Let him sell his wife's virtue, and seem to lie snoring in his cups as he winks at her lover.[8] Monstrous! you cry. What he does now is more monstrous still. No law takes a man's life for selling his wife's virtue; but those who issue libellous publications are faced everywhere with capital punishment.[9] I have never uttered a word that might do him harm, unless he thinks he is harmed when Froben prints good authors while he gives us nothing but raving and rubbish. There are so

30

35

40

45

50

55

* * * * *

4 See Epp 1405–6.
5 Perhaps Erasmus Alber's *Iudicium* (Ep 1466 n19)
6 *Problemata Othonis Brunnfelsii:* i. De ratione Evangeliorum; ii. Quare in parabolis locutus sit Christus (Strasbourg: J. Schott n d), in the form of letters to Schott. There was a second issue, also without date; see Allen's note.
7 Allen, who was able to examine copies of the *Problemata*, reports that each issue had an illustrated title-page. In the second, the prophets of Baal, as described in lines 32–4, are unmistakable. But in neither illustration is there a figure remotely resembling Erasmus, though three in the first and one in the second may fit the description given here. If one of them was really supposed to be Erasmus, he could only have known that from outside information.
8 Cf Juvenal 1.57.
9 See Ep 1053 n62, and cf Ep 1477:52–3.

many old books in the world and so many new ones; let him either reissue
old ones or publish new. Is he the only printer who has no way to feed his
wife and children unless he throws everything into confusion with his
libellous pamphlets? And he will have me on his side, if he would publish
things that might serve a public purpose. I have no need, thank heaven, of   60
money from printers. I take no payment for my work in the cause of
learning, so far is he from the truth, this noisy rascal,[10] in what he has
written about Froben.[11] But his arrogant remarks about profiteering[12] have
far less foundation. Out of the Luther question I have not made a farthing. I
have rejected everything, for fear that perhaps I might inadvertently oppose   65
the spirit of Christ;[13] on the other hand, commending Luther[14] has never
made me richer by a single hair.

You gospellers are supporting that man, who is like an infuriated viper
that has just now emerged from its lair and, intoxicated with its new
freedom, thinks that all must give way before its raging threats. Those who   70
first brought the gospel into this world would not have deigned to speak to
such criminal ruffians. Did Capito, the bishop[15] of your new gospel, have no
other favourite whose society he could enjoy? Only the company of this
wholly disreputable bankrupt,[16] to say no more? I harbour no unfriendly
suspicions of Capito, whom I have always looked on, except for his   75
opinions, as a close friend and towards whom I have always played a
friend's part. And yet there are those who think him not wholly innocent[17]
of this lamentable business. He is not so simple-minded as not to have

* * * * *

10 Brunfels
11 In his *Responsio ad Erasmi Spongiam*, Brunfels had written (Böcking II 343:3–4):
   '[I]n what grand style Froben now supports you at Basel, at the cost of a meagre
   two hundred gold pieces!' Cf Epp 1316 n10, 1528:59–62. It was doubtless such
   criticism that moved Erasmus to add a detailed rebuttal to the second edition of
   the *Catalogus lucubrationum* (Ep 1341A:1776–1813).
12 Also in the *Responsio* (Böcking II 332:47–333:3): 'But if [Hutten] had wished to
   write in return for profit, honours, and fees, he could, like you, have attached
   himself to the Roman pontiff, the cardinals, and the king of England; nor do I
   doubt that magnificent rewards would have been bestowed upon him had he
   wielded his pen against Luther.' Cf ibidem 342:46–343:2; Epp 1342:707–9,
   1435:18–19, 1437:189–90, 1477:10–12.
13 This seems to be a rather obscure version of what Erasmus says much more
   clearly in Ep 1477:26–9; see also Epp 1384:47–52, 1510:23–5.
14 As in Ep 1033
15 The term is used sarcastically. The reformed church at Strasbourg had no one
   who was called 'bishop.' Cf Ep 1482:19.
16 Probably Eppendorf (Ep 1437:9ff). On Eppendorf's presumed connection with
   Capito, see Ep 1437:106–7.
17 See Ep 1429 n7.

detected the bankrupt's machinations and the writer's lunacy. He kept
silence a long time while this monster was growing; then he called me to   80
account at last on points of importance: I had, he said, touched on the topic
of free will[18] before Luther ever wrote on free will, and then that I had
written somewhere that while the law of Moses restrained men's hands, the
gospel restrained their hearts as well.[19] 'Not at all,' says he; 'the law applies
to man as a whole.' These were indeed important points on which to call to   85
account a friend who had already suffered such grievous blows! One is not
allowed to expound the words of Christ's teaching[20] 'It was said by them of
old time, "Thou shalt not kill"'; this is to restrain the hands. 'But I say unto
you, that whosoever is angry,' etc; this is to restrain the heart. Unfold the
law, and it is the same as the gospel. But I speak, as Christ spoke, of the law   90
not yet unfolded. Monstrous behaviour indeed, deserving to be purged by
pamphlets such as these, and indeed by friends like these, to whom I would
have trusted ten lives had I had them. What I do for the gospel cause I should
prefer not to be generally known. They make me out to be a coward.[21] The
gospel has indeed made great strides when images are abolished in one   95
city![22] If only they would cast out the idols of the heart, which I see becoming
more monstrous in those who adopt the gospel as their watchword.

In the old days men who had wives left them of their own free will for
love of the gospel. Now the gospel flourishes if a few marry wives who are
well endowed. I say this, not because I disapprove out and out of the   100
marriage of priests,[23] if it happens of necessity, with the authority of their
superiors, without risk of subversion, and from the highest motives. As it is,
I fear that many take a wife for no reason except that the laws of our
ancestors do not permit it. I know what a scandalous life some men live as
bachelors. But is marriage really a short cut to chastity? Suppose a priest who 105
used to keep a concubine now has a wife and a rival woman? And yet, when
in company with papists (as these people call them) I have always most
freely maintained that priests who are to be ordained in the future need not

* * * * *

18 Cf Epp 1419, 1481.
19 Possibly in the paraphrases on Matt 5:19–20 or Gal 3:24–6 LB VII 29C and
   955E–956A. But the *De libero arbitrio* contains a passage that comes even closer
   (LB IX 1222C).
20 Matt 5:21–2
21 Cf Ep 1384 n7; and see AK Epp 962:209–13, 963:41–3 (both c beginning of
   August 1524), where Amerbach reports that the Lutheran faction condemns
   Erasmus as *timidus* 'faint-hearted,' *pontificis adulator* 'a toady of the pope,' etc.
22 See the introduction.
23 Erasmus had already expressed his views on this matter in the *Epistola de esu
   carnium* ASD IX-1 26–8.

be forbidden to marry, if they cannot remain continent, nor would I change
my view if I were dealing with the pope himself; not that I do not value   110
continence more highly, but because I see almost none who remain
continent. But meanwhile why do we need such a great crowd of priests? I
have never advised a man to marry, but neither have I caused trouble for a
man who wished to marry.

If a monk were to lay aside all wickedness as he lays aside his cowl, I   115
would not stop any man abandoning it who chose to do so. But as it is, they
abandon the cowl in a hurry everywhere and with no leave from their
superiors, and bad monks make worse laymen. The change of garment
means nothing to them except greater impunity in doing just whatever they
choose. There are, I agree, men with natures born for better things who are   120
oppressed by the cowl. On the other hand there are men who are such by
nature that they should be restrained by ten cowls rather than be left to their
own free choice. Many were at least fed and housed by the cowl who now
run the risk of being taught by poverty to help themselves where they ought
not. And what should one say of those who at an advanced age, against the   125
advice of their friends, with full knowledge and their eyes open have
willingly handed themselves over to the cowl? They ought at least to be
ashamed of their inconstancy; as it is, they boast of this as a noble thing to
do, and drag others down to follow their example.

But we will speak of this on another occasion. Farewell in Christ.   130
From Basel. 1524

1478 / To Agostino Scarpinelli   [Basel], 30 August 1524

This letter was first published in the *Opus epistolarum*. On Scarpinelli, see Ep
1169.

ERASMUS OF ROTTERDAM TO AGOSTINO SCARPINELLI,
AMBASSADOR TO ENGLAND OF THE DUKE OF MILAN, GREETING
My generous friend Scarpinelli, that favourite son of all the Graces, is so
graven on my heart that I shall forget my own self first; do not think that any
evidence is needed to refresh my memory of you.[1] I was most happy to learn   5
from my servant[2] that you are well; for I seem to remember that you had

* * * * *

1478
1 Scarpinelli and Erasmus may have last seen one another in Cologne in
   November 1520 (Ep 1169 n1).
2 Evidently Lieven Algoet, who had doubtless brought Scarpinelli's letter from
   England when he returned at the end of June; Ep 1430 n7

picked up some ill health at the Diet of Worms,[3] and I notice that missions on behalf of princes have proved the end of many men through excessive devotion to their duties. But what freak of fortune has taken you to England? How fate tears us asunder![4] The bishop of Chieti has been drawn to Rome;[5] I   10 have become a Swiss and you an Englishman. How I wish England might send you home with your pockets full of gold![6] Poor Milan! After all those disasters in the war[7] to be struck so hard now by the plague.[8]

I would have written at greater length, but you messengers of the gods flit so often from place to place, I was afraid my letter might not find you   15 where you were. But wherever my friend Agostino finds himself, may he always enjoy the good fortune which his uncommon scholarship and that character as upright as it is generous-hearted deserve. I in my turn, whatever part of the world awaits me, shall carry Scarpinelli with me planted deep within my heart.   20

Farewell, 30 August 1524.

1479 / To Haio Herman   Basel, 31 August 1524

This letter was first published in the *Opus epistolarum*. Haio Herman of Friesland (Epp 903:14n, 1131) was now living in Italy, at Padua.

* * * * *

3 In the spring of 1521. Scarpinelli had been there in the entourage of Luigi Marliano, physician to Charles v (Epp 1195:170, 1198:57). In May, Marliano died of the plague that ravaged the imperial household during the diet. Scarpinelli then returned to Italy, where he entered the service of Francesco ii Sforza, duke of Milan.

4 This remark seems to imply that Carafa (see following note), Scarpinelli, and Erasmus had at some point enjoyed close intimacy, most likely in 1516–17 when Carafa and Marliano (and therefore presumably Scarpinelli as well) were in the Netherlands (Epp 411:10, 412:59, 66–9, 539:12, 590:76–7, 591:80–1, 628:63–5, 640) before accompanying Charles to Spain (Ep 695:53–4).

5 Gianpietro Carafa, since 1518 also archbishop of Brindisi, was now in Rome, much preoccupied with the founding of the Order of Theatines (formally established 1524), which took its name from Chieti (*T[h]eate* in Latin). In 1536 Carafa became a cardinal and in 1555 was elected Pope Paul iv.

6 Ie, the customary presents given to ambassadors, which in prosperous England were expected to be substantial (cf Ep 77:15–19). Scarpinelli had no such luck; see CEBR iii 214–15.

7 The period 1522–5 saw a fierce struggle between Charles v and Francis i over the control of Milan; cf Ep 1342 n31.

8 A letter of Alciati, written from Milan on 23 May 1524 and cited by Allen from the *Gudii epistolae* (Ep 1505 introduction) 105, reports that 'the plague has spread greatly.' See also LP iv 570; and cf Ep 1514:10, Allen Ep 1557:6–7.

ERASMUS OF ROTTERDAM TO HAIO HERMAN OF FRIESLAND,
A YOUNG MAN OF EXCEPTIONAL LEARNING, GREETING

My good-natured friend, keep on croaking like a frog[1] until I tell you to be
quiet! For nothing could give me greater pleasure than your erudite and
friendly letters. But to respond in a word or two to the various parts of your   5
letter[2] in turn: I am delighted that Lazare de Baïf[3] has done on the subject of
clothing what Budé did in the *De asse*.[4] I greatly admire that combination of
generosity and exceptional learning which I see in the man, something
which is all too rare among men of letters. I knew that a *laena* 'cloak' was
some kind of garment,[5] and I suspected that it corresponded to the Greek   10
χλαίνη, but I avoided the word first because it was unfamiliar and secondly
because its meaning was unclear. Everybody knows about the *penula hiberna*
'winter cloak.' However I shall alter the passage when I see Lazare's book,[6]
which I hope will happen very soon. With regard to the word ἀναξυρὶν,[7] I

* * * * *

1479
1 Frogs were proverbial for their loquacity; see *Adagia* II i 34, III i 76.
2 Not extant
3 Lazare de Baïf (c 1496–1547) was born into a noble family of Anjou. Trained in
   both law and the humanities, he undertook to investigate the practical side of
   ancient life on the basis of the *Corpus juris*, using methods developed by Budé.
   At this time he appears to have been in Italy working on his *De re vestiaria*
   (Basel: J. Bebel, March 1526), a work that earned him second rank among
   French scholars after Budé. In 1525 Baïf entered the service of Cardinal Jean de
   Lorraine, and in 1529 Francis I made him French ambassador in Venice. His
   extant correspondence with Erasmus begins in 1528 (Ep 1962).
4 Ep 403 introduction
5 Baïf had apparently criticized Erasmus' translation of χλαῖναν by *penulam* in
   Adagia I x 100, and of ἀναξυρίδα by *subligaculo* in *Adagia* III iv 52. According to
   Allen, Baïf gives *laena* as the translation of χλαῖνα in chapter 15 of the *De re vestiaria*; in chapter 16 he cites Erasmus' notes on Jerome's *Adversus Pelagianos* 3.4
   (vol II 308 in the Basel edition of 1537) for the translation of φαινόλην (2 Tim 4:13)
   by *lacernam* or *penulam*; and in chapter 20 he distinguishes *subligaculum* from
   ἀναξυρίδα, which he translates as *brachem* in citing the same adage.
6 Erasmus kept this promise for *Adagia* I x 100 in the edition of 1526 by adding the
   passage beginning 'Quanquam et Latini laenae vocabulo utuntur ... toleran-
   tiam' (CWE 32 281 with n2). As for *Adagia* III iv 52, in the edition of 1533 he
   changed *subligaculo* in the heading to *Anaxyride* and inserted the statement that
   'Eruditi quidam putant Anaxyridem Graecis dici quas Latini vocant brachas
   sive foeminalia / Certain scholars believe that Anaxyride in Greek means what
   the Latins call breeches or thigh-bandages.'
7 Herodotus (*Histories* 1.71) uses this word in the plural for the trousers worn by
   the Scythians.

thought *subligar*[8] meant 'breeches' or something very close to that. I had 15
read in Juvenal, if I remember correctly, *et subligar Acci* 'and the breeches of
Accius.'[9] But whatever the truth of the matter is, surely you don't think a
man should be promptly scolded and abused because he employed the
wrong word in a reference to clothing? I am surprised that anyone today can
be dogmatic about the correct language for ancient garments, since in my 20
own lifetime I have witnessed so many changes of fashion.

I don't take seriously the critics you mention in your letter.[10] If they
published something of their own, they would perhaps have to face their
critics too. I can cheerfully accept the loss of esteem, since I make no claim
myself to the esteem of others. I wrote somewhere that Budé can stand 25
comparison with men like Ermolao and Poliziano and that he has perhaps
gained first place in Greek composition.[11] I have not seen anyone who can
extemporize with comparable facility. He writes me frequently, handling
any subject he pleases wholly or partly in Greek – and without previous
preparation too. 30

When I was in Italy, I showed great respect to all the scholars there and
disparaged none of them. I have never even heard the name of Angelo
Colici.[12] So I am surprised that he has found something to write about in his
invective.[13] I have always felt well disposed to men of talent in Italy and I
have said so.[14] I am not acquainted with Casali[15] either. I wish he had told us 35
the true interpretation of those proverbs where he thinks I have gone astray.
On 'the bad egg of the bad raven'[16] I reported what was in the Greek
commentators. I was greatly puzzled by the 'eyes of the crow.'[17] I consulted

* * * * *

8 In classical usage *subligar* appears to refer to a sort of loincloth worn by actors
  under their costume.
9 *Satires* 6.70
10 A reference to the members of the so-called Roman Academy (Ep 1341A n115).
   For a parallel response to these critics, written at about the same time, see Ep
   1341A:527–66. Cf also Ep 1482:34–67, 1488:13–15, 1489:24–5, 1496:203–4.
11 Ep 531:45–55
12 Undoubtedly a reference to Angelo Colocci (1467–1549), a papal secretary,
   collector of antiquities, owner of a fine library, and leader of the Roman
   Academy
13 The work here attributed to Colocci was probably the 'Invectiva in Erasmum
   Roterodamum' of Colocci's friend Battista Casali (n15). See CEBR svv 'Casali'
   and 'Colocci.'
14 Eg, in Epp 531:51–5, 635:9–11, 809:142–5
15 Ep 1270A
16 Erasmus thought that this proverb referred to cause and effect. In *Adagia* I ix 25
   he gives as an example that a bad teacher produces bad students.
17 See CWE 31 295–7.

one or two people, but could find nothing which satisfied me. Considering
the extent and complexity of the subject, I do not think I need feel   40
embarrassed if someone finds a better explanation for a particular problem
than I have.

Then there is the old man you refer to:[18] nothing would surprise me
about him. He was born with a natural antipathy towards literary studies.
He was like that twenty-five years ago, and this is not a disease which is   45
mitigated by the passage of time. The silliness of his suggestion[19] that ἄνες
means the same as *remitte* and that ἄφες[20] is the word to which *dimitte*
corresponds is proved by the fifth[21] and seventh[22] chapters of Luke, where
the same translator,[23] who elsewhere is fond of the word *dimitto*, translates
ἀφέονται as *remittuntur* not *dimittuntur*. Also in the song of Zacharias[24] *in*   50
remissionem peccatorum 'for the remission of their sins' is ἀφέσει in Greek.
Similarly in chapter 3[25] we have εἰς ἄφεσιν. Again in Leviticus 25[26] the 'year
of remission' [*annus remittionis*] is ἀφέσεως, not ἀνέσεως. You will find
the same usage frequently in Deuteronomy 15.[27] Also in Ezekiel, chapter
46[28] the word is ἄφεσις, not ἄνεσις. From these instances it is quite clear   55
that the translator has taken no account of the distinction which this old man
proclaims as a piece of esoteric wisdom. But it is foolish of me to collect
passages where ἄφεσιν is translated as *remissio*, when it is nowhere

* * * * *

18 Allen believed that this was a reference to Baechem (Ep 1254 n6), which seems
odd in a letter replying to Erasmus' Italian critics. Moreover, there is no evidence
that Baechem knew Greek; and, though Baechem did object to *remitte* for *dimitte*
(Ep 1341A:983–96, 1003), so did many others (see, for example, n20 below).
On the other hand, no Italian critic can be identified here.

19 The issue here is the meaning of two compound verbs from the same root:
ἀφίημι and ἀνίημι. Both have a wide range of meaning, to some extent
overlapping, but the distinction that Baechem wants to make cannot be
sustained.

20 Erasmus' translation of ἄφες as *remitte* in Matt 6:12 had already been attacked
by the monk whom More answered in his 'Letter to a Monk' (pages 235–7 of
the text cited in Ep 1463 n1).

21 Luke 5:20; but in verse 23 one finds *dimittuntur*.

22 Luke 7:47–8; but in verses 47 and 49 one finds also *dimittitur* and *dimittit*.

23 Ie, the translator of the Vulgate

24 Luke 1:77

25 Verse 3

26 Verse 10

27 Verses 1, 2, 3, 9

28 Verse 17

translated in any other way. In 2 Corinthians 8²⁹ ἄνεσιν is translated as
remissio, but in the sense 'relaxation of life,' not 'forgiveness of sins.' But let   60
us suppose that there is a distinction between ἄφες and καὶ ἄνες: must
we then commit the solecism of writing *dimitte* instead of *remitte*, when so
many Latin words are available, *condone*, *ignosce*, *remitte*? You see how
ridiculous these people's ideas about Scripture are.

With regard to the speed with which I produce my works, I admitted   65
this failing long ago,³⁰ and I am paying the penalty for it. The *Letters* of
Jerome are now being printed,³¹ with many corrections. My *Proverbia* came
out a year ago,³² augmented and revised in not a few places, and a further
revision is now ready. This is a practice which I promise to continue as long
as I live.³³ My object is to assist the general cause of scholarship, though I   70
lack the support which manuscripts and other scholars could provide, while
these people, with all their resources, keep what they have to themselves. If
they believe that nothing should be published which is open to criticism, let
them point to a single Italian who meets this criterion. Theodorus Gaza was
rightly criticized by Trapezuntius³⁴ in several places and that great scholar   75
was not ashamed to alter his text. Ermolao, in his translation of the preface of
Themistius,³⁵ ran aground in spectacular fashion while still, as the saying
goes, within the harbour.³⁶ And did not Lorenzo Valla manifestly go astray
in several passages – to say nothing of men like Valla,³⁷ Pio, Beroaldo,³⁸ and
Raffaele?³⁹   80

These people are upset when work which they have laboriously
prepared for themselves is made freely available to the public. Here is an
attitude worthy of that wretched old man! He ought to have been eager to
have the public share in these discoveries so that the labours of so many
years did not go for nothing. For myself, I feel I am enjoying the fruits of my   85

* * * * *

29 Verse 13
30 See Epp 1341A:57–62, 1352:106–7; and see also the concluding passage of
   Adagia III i 1 (LB II 714Eff), found in the Aldine *Adagiorum chiliades* of 1508.
31 Ep 1465
32 Ie, the edition of the *Adagia* published by Froben in January 1523. The next
   edition did not in fact appear until February 1526.
33 For the balance of this paragraph, cf Ep 1341A:520–63.
34 George of Trebizond; see Ep 1341A n121.
35 Ep 1341A:553–6
36 *Adagia* I v 76
37 Ep 1341A n118
38 For both Pio and Beroaldo, see Ep 1341A nn123–4.
39 Ep 450:22n

labours when in my old age I see many young men surpassing me. This was
in fact the reason why I burned so much midnight oil. Some people of course
respond to a good turn with malice. I know this only too well, and I see more
and more evidence of it every day. But it is wrong to disappoint everyone
because of the ingratitude of a few. A virtuous man, much more a Christian,   90
will be ready to do a good turn even if the recipient is ungrateful. These men
publish nothing and so, they claim, they are misleading no one. But who is
doing the misleading? Is it the man who shows that a passage is corrupt and,
when no old manuscripts are available, resorts to conjecture? Do scholars
owe little to inspired guesses of Ermolao Barbaro on the text of Pliny?[40] I do   95
not embark upon such work without the assistance of ancient manuscripts
where it has been possible to obtain them – let those who regard my criticism
as nothing but guesswork[41] make no mistake about that!

     In my work on Seneca I was let down by a friend who was either
unwilling or unable to accomplish what he had undertaken[42] – for I was not   100
responsible for that edition myself. Realizing that the work had been badly
done, he then made away with a manuscript annotated in my hand. I am
delighted to learn that that distinguished Hungarian scholar has removed so
many errors from the *Naturales quaestiones* of Seneca.[43] For there was no
ancient manuscript available for this work. I only contributed to a second   105
edition,[44] and I altered nothing except where the text had been clearly
distorted by the carelessness of the copyists. I added some conjectures in the
margin,[45] several of which, unless I am mistaken, he will not disapprove of.
So if there are errors in his work, they are not my errors.

* * * * *

40 See Allen Ep 1544 introduction and line 38n.
41 Cf Ep 1482:38–40, and see Allen Ep 1544:124 and note.
42 Wilhelm Nesen; see Ep 1341A:447–63.
43 The scholar was Matthaeus Fortunatus (d 1528), about whose life little is known.
   While studying in Italy in 1522 he completed work on a critical edition of
   Seneca's *Naturales quaestiones* (Venice: Aldo Manuzio, February 1523). This was
   based on the 1515 edition published by Erasmus at Basel, but Fortunatus
   corrected a large number of mistakes in the Basel edition. The genuineness of
   Erasmus' admiration for Fortunatus' work is exhibited in the 1529 Basel edition
   of Seneca, where Erasmus names him as co-editor of the volume and praises
   him in the dedicatory letter (Ep 2091).
44 The *Quaestiones naturales* were first published in Seneca's *Opera moralia* at
   Venice in 1490 and thereafter in other Venice editions of 1492, 1495 (?), and
   1503. A separate edition was issued at Leipzig c 1493–5. It is not clear which
   text Erasmus used for his edition of 1515.
45 According to Allen, some of these were cited by Fortunatus in his notes; for
   example, folios 74, 78 verso, 81, 92 verso.

Apropos the edition of Plautus[46] published by Aldo for forty gold   110
pieces,[47] the publisher did not quite come up to his word, for only twenty
crowns[48] were paid to me. Moreover I undertook only to set right passages
where the metre was confused and I did so only in places where the metre
was continuous. In the case of Cyprian,[49] wherever I had the assistance of an
ancient manuscript I did not fall down on the job. My critics observe that not   115
just lines, but whole books have now been added. But I could not be held
responsible for mistakes made through the carelessness of the printer, since
I was living in Brabant at the time. I did not ruin the text of Suetonius,[50] but
followed the evidence of a very old manuscript,[51] and nothing that I did has
blocked the way for others who may have a better suggestion to offer. Far   120
from being apprehensive that I may be humiliated by the efforts of these
scholars, I intend to claim some credit for myself, at least in so far as I
provided the stimulus when they were still asleep.

I have never been excessively troubled over niceties of style.[52] My aim
is to be understood by any means possible, only avoiding offensive   125
language. But what is this ancient model of style from which they think my
work departs? Ancient writers in fact adopt many different styles. What
have Seneca and Quintilian got in common? Or Quintilian and Cicero? Or
Valerius Maximus and Sallust? Or Livy and Quintus Curtius? Or Ovid and
Horace? I have no objections if some people find the style of Pontano[53]   130
admirable; for myself, there is nothing which I particularly admire in him
apart from his fluency, which is not unattractive, and the sonority of his
language. Marullus,[54] I always think, sounds just like a pagan, and perhaps
for this reason is more popular with these people than Mantuanus.[55] They

* * * * *

46 For Erasmus' work on Plautus during his sojourn in Venice, see Epp 589:45n,
   1482:57–60, 1341A:440–3.
47 *Quadraginta aureis*: either Rhenish florins, or, more likely, the *écus d'or* (the
   so-called 'crowns') indicated in the next note
48 Although Erasmus here specifies *viginiti coronati*, these were undoubtedly the
   current *écus d'or au soleil* rather than older *écus à la couronne*, for the reasons
   given in Ep 1434 n3 and Ep 1471 n10. If so, this sum was then worth precisely
   £40 tournais, or £6 6s 8d gros Flemish, or £4 5s od sterling.
49 See Ep 1000, and cf Ep 1482:40–2.
50 See Ep 586.
51 See Ep 586:61–6.
52 Italian criticism of Erasmus' freedom of style is reflected in Ep 914:51–74. This
   criticism eventually led to the composition of the *Ciceronianus*; see CWE 28
   324–7.
53 Ep 337:355n
54 Ep 385:7n
55 Baptista Mantuanus; Ep 47:86n, and cf Epp 49:112ff, 385:6–7.

hate the very name of Christ. I only wish that we barbarians were as   135
sincerely and passionately devoted to his name! But all this is beside the
point. Judgments about men of talent, as about food and drink, have always
differed; so each man is free to judge for himself.

There has been great merriment over the expression 'porro fanatic,'[56]
as though I use it frequently or in such a clumsy manner. When somebody   140
finds me deficient in one quality and somebody else in another, they are
being doubly hard to please, first because they are expecting all good
qualities to be combined in one person and secondly because they are
demanding from a writer something which he does not claim to possess. All
I hope to accomplish when I treat a subject is to make some advance on my   145
predecessors. Even if you had mentioned by name the man who prefers
Aleandro to Erasmus in all respects,[57] there would have been no embarrassment; for I am always ready myself to recognize the merits of Aleandro,
especially in literary matters, and I feel no more put out by superior
scholarship than by superior wealth or superior beauty – unless you   150
consider me such a jealous person that I could scarcely tolerate anyone more
pious than myself. If Aleandro is my friend, then privately I congratulate
myself, for I certainly admire the man's qualities and I count what a friend
has as my own; but if he is not my friend, then publicly I can still
congratulate the world of learning, for there is hope that some day he will   155
share with everyone the rich treasures of his erudition.

And what is this they are saying? They allege that I did not translate the
Hecuba and the Iphigenia[58] myself but claimed as my own what I had come
upon elsewhere. But where? In Italy? But Bade had already published my
work[59] before I reached Italy. In my own country? But has anyone seen   160
anything of the sort there? Luckily there are people still alive who were
present when I was working on the translations – Jean Desmarez[60],

* * * * *

56 Ie, *porrophagus*, literally 'voracious for *porro*.' This is mockery of Erasmus for his
   tendency to start paragraphs with *porro*, 'furthermore.'
57 Possibly Alberto Pio (Ep 1634). In his *Responsio ad epistolam paraeneticam Alberti
   Pii* (1529), Erasmus claimed to have learned from Aleandro (Ep 1256 n11) c 1520
   about Pio's hostility; see LB IX 1099C–D, where Aleandro is referred to as Pio's
   'comrade' (*sodalis*), who 'seven years earlier' had been the papal representative
   'in our country.' In the same connection Erasmus refers to the jokes in which
   he is called 'porrophagus' (see previous note) and 'Errasmus' (Ep 1482:46), and
   to the aspersions upon his orthodoxy (line 176 below); LB IX 1099A.
58 Ep 158:10n
59 Ep 188 introduction
60 Ep 180

Mountjoy,[61] Thomas More, Thomas Linacre,[62] William Grocyn,[63] and William Latimer.[64] It is not my practice to palm off the works of others as my own: I have demonstrated my honesty clearly enough in other instances; far from claiming what belongs to others as my own, I am ready to accept with a good grace the injuries inflicted on me everywhere by my own pen. If there is something unsatisfactory about my translations in the *Proverbia*, no one is in a better position to explain the reason than Aleandro himself, who saw me writing my translation extempore as the printers set the type.[65] Each day they printed six gatherings (that is, a double ternion). If I seem somewhat more felicitous in the tragedies than in the *Adagia*, the reason is obvious. When I translated the tragedies, that was all I did – though even then I often translated a hundred lines at a single sitting. In the *Adagia* I translated prose and verse at the same speed.

Finally they deny my orthodoxy. I shall answer that charge when they tell me what orthodoxy is and when they make their own Christianity manifest. If a man who criticizes priests and bishops is not orthodox, then neither Jerome nor Cyprian will be orthodox. And did anyone ever suspect that I should be found wanting in piety? But then who would have guessed that we should see a generation like this? No one is more to blame for the disastrous state of the Holy See (if that is in fact a just description) than these men, who are so enamoured of pagan literature that they have less Christianity in them than the very authors over whom they swoon with delight.

Let this be my answer to my captious and spiteful critics, whose hostility I hope you will not inflame by incessant debate. I was pleased to read the list of my well-wishers, among whom I found no names that I recognize except Sadoleto,[66] Alcionio,[67] and Corycius.[68] The passages to which you were kind enough to draw my attention I corrected three years ago, and these, my good friend, were not the only ones. I shall write to Mindesius[69] if I have a spare moment. I shall look out for the letter that you

165

170

175

180

185

190

* * * * *

61 Ep 79
62 Ep 118:27n
63 Ep 118:26n
64 Ep 207:25n
65 In the period from about December 1507 to April 1508, when Erasmus and Aleandro shared a room in Venice and Aleandro assisted Erasmus with work on the *Adagia*
66 Ep 1511
67 Ep 450:29n. He had recently become a professor of Greek in Rome.
68 Ep 1342 n90
69 Mindesius has not been identified and no letter of Erasmus to him is known to exist.

have written in Greek. It will be most welcome, I assure you. You have evidently made great progress in this subject. But don't go overboard: I would prefer to see you devote your attention to the study of philosophy. I 195 know how little Christianity there is about those who, in their enthusiasm for literature, are dashing themselves to pieces, as it were, on the rocks of the Sirens, and this is especially so in Italy. They are more pious at Padua, and you have the Venetians close at hand: you will find several among them who possess great learning without pretension, especially Leonico.[70] 200

I had resolved to spend the winter in Italy, but the plague[71] has made me change my mind. My book *De libero arbitrio*[72] is being printed at the moment. I am well aware what a swarm of hornets I have stirred up around my head,[73] men with Christ and the gospel on their lips and Satan in their hearts. Even Luther is trying to restrain them,[74] but without success. 205 Farewell.

Basel, 31 August 1524

1480 / From Willibald Pirckheimer   Nürnberg, 1 September 1524

On Pirckheimer, see Ep 318. This is his answer to Epp 1452 and 1466. Erasmus' reply, written before 12 November, was never delivered (Allen Epp 1536:2n, 1543:1–2). The letter was first published, without indication of source or editor, in volume I of the journal *Literarisches Museum*, founded in 1777 at Altdorf (near Nürnberg). The original of the letter has never turned up.

Greetings. It is good news, Erasmus, my distinguished friend, that you have received all my letters. For there is so much fraud and dishonesty in the handling of letters that I was rather afraid that perhaps mine too had not been delivered. I have just recently received two from you.

You say in your first letter that the medallions did not turn out too 5

* * * * *

70 Niccolò Leonico Tomeo (1456–1531) was a Venetian of Epirote Greek parentage who had taught Greek first at Padua (1497–1504) and Venice (1504–12) and was now at Padua again. He had taught many of Erasmus' English friends, including Linacre and Latimer, at Padua, and this may account for Erasmus' high opinion of him.
71 See Ep 1478 n8.
72 Epp 1419, 1481
73 Ie, the zealots among the adherents of the Reformation; see Epp 1429, 1477, 1477A.
74 See Ep 1429 n3.

successfully.[1] I am well aware of this myself. Although I tried three master craftsmen, none came up to my expectations. They all have silly excuses to offer, but what they lack is patience. They rush their work with an eye to profit and predictably the results are unsatisfactory. I am sending you a medallion of myself,[2] so that you can see that I have had no more success with myself than with others.

I was deeply upset by Petrus Mosellanus' death;[3] the humanities too have suffered no small loss by his passing. He has now paid his debt to nature, while we are still imprisoned in the bonds of the flesh. He was very fond of you and was a good friend to me. May he enter into the joys of eternal life!

Melanchthon was undoubtedly sincere when he sent a good friend of his to see you.[4] He is an honest man and a good Christian, whose considerable learning is matched by the probity of his life. As a consequence his actions square with his words, and he is no dissembler. He has always liked and admired you, as he has made clear on this occasion too. Luther himself, I am sure, is not ill disposed to you, although he can be venomous in his writings. But then you don't lack a barbed tongue yourself,[5] and there are many people who would like to embroil the two of you[6] in a confrontation. That is why I feel more strongly about those meddling friends of yours who make your letters public almost as soon as they are written in the hope that someone will provoke the two of you to anger. It appears from your letter that you have settled some of your differences,[7] which pleases me very much. I am certain that Luther will be true to his word – unless you are the first to raise the call to battle. If your opponents and the enemies of truth and of the humanities could stir up both of you to a fight, there is nothing which would delight them more. I hope God and your friends will avert such a disaster.

But I have never felt any confidence that the two parties could be reconciled. I know the Romans will make no concessions, none at least of any significance, for that would be contrary to the long tradition in which they have been formed. But it is very difficult to hoodwink the people any

* * * * *

1480
1 Ep 1452:32ff
2 Cf Allen Ep 1543:6–7.
3 19 April 1524; cf Ep 1452:22.
4 Camerarius (Ep 1501); see Ep 1452:20.
5 Cf Ep 1443 n3, 62.
6 Reading *vos* for Allen's *nos*, which makes no sense in context.
7 Ep 1452:12–15; cf Ep 1466:19–21.

longer, for now their eyes are open and they know the truth. So these men are now trying what force can accomplish, since bluff has met with little success. Any fool can see where that will lead. They have lately given us at Regensburg some notion of what they are like and shown clearly what goes on inside their heads.[8] On the other side there is no lack of persons who would prefer to settle the issue by blows rather than words. Luther himself, unless I am mistaken, now realizes how unsafe it is to put swords into the hands of fools and children. Sensible people who recognize that old, ingrained habits cannot be eradicated in a single moment, and certainly not without danger or scandal, are now dismissed as temporizers or smooth-tongued impostors by these troublemakers, who have made the freedom of the spirit an excuse for the sins of the flesh. But such is the will of God, who is making us atone for our sins in this way. Everyone can see the dangers and upheavals and squabbles that lie ahead, while the Romans maintain their stubborn attitude and try to defend their manifest errors, and the followers of the gospel, as they call themselves, want to demonstrate the truth in words rather than deeds. But may God's will be done and his name be blessed! I have little doubt that much that is being done in the name of the gospel is displeasing to Luther. But what can he do if things do not always turn out as he hoped? We know what those false brethren did to the Apostle while he was spreading the message of the true faith.[9] There is no wheat without tares, and Satan too once stood among the sons of God.

But someone will say that Luther should have acted more moderately and ought to have foreseen what is happening everywhere. But granted that he was not too experienced in the conduct of affairs and that he was deceived in his expectations, was this any reason for him to hold his tongue and refrain from proclaiming the truth? What if God is hardening men's hearts and robbing those who can see of their vision? Is there anyone so

* * * * *

8 From 27 June to 7 July 1524, the papal nuncio, Cardinal Campeggi (Ep 1410), and the imperial viceroy, Archduke Ferdinand of Austria, held a conference in Regensburg with Dukes Wilhelm and Ludwig of Bavaria and twelve south-German prince-bishops to form a common anti-Lutheran front in their region. The princes and bishops agreed on the strict enforcement of the Edict of Worms (Ep 1313 n7) in their territories, on the elimination of abuses in worship and preaching, and on mutual support in the common struggle against the spread of the Lutheran heresy. Thus was formed the first of the numerous 'confessional' alliances of estates that were to appear in Germany during the Reformation. Though potentially powerful, the Regensburg alliance was from the start weakened by internal divisions (Bavaria versus Austria, ecclesiastical princes versus secular princes). See Pfeilschifter 294–393.

9 Cf Gal 2, Acts 15.

foolish that he does not realize the schemes and tricks and evil designs of those who call themselves religious? It is true that for a time they succeed in covering up their faults; but no one dared even to open his mouth, let alone reprove them for their sins. In any case they themselves are well aware of the errors in which they are ensnared; yet when have they ever made an effort to 70 correct them? Is it any wonder, then, that men cry out, when, if they held their peace, not even the stones would be silent?[10] And yet I know how much could have been accomplished by a more moderate policy. Indeed Luther himself is now aware of this. But how can one deal moderately with obstinate men who know nothing of moderation, who neither fear God nor 75 are moved by respect for men? They have now got what they have long sought, these restless and insolent creatures. Monstrous evils, so numerous as these, cannot be abolished without monstrous remedies. But enough on this subject.

I congratulate you on the gift the pope sent you[11] and on his 80 complimentary letter.[12] I am sure you understand what this means. But I also know that he can use your help but cannot abuse it. People may think what they like, but I have never had any doubts about your integrity. I am not afraid that you will do something unworthy of your name and character. This is what I believe, and it is a view shared by many good men. So let these 85 fools and troublemakers rant and hurl abuse at you and publish their slanderous pamphlets.[13] Surely such things cannot do you any harm – unless you want to win the favour of the populace. Your standing is too secure to be injured by men like that; and you know yourself that the more foul a man is in his heart, the more shameless his tongue. So do not be upset, dear 90 Erasmus, by scurrilous attacks from vicious men. If they discover that their insults bother you, they will never stop nettling you. Their aim is to cause you distress and make themselves famous at your expense. I wish you had followed my advice and refused to reply to certain persons.[14] But one may criticize what is past; one cannot change it for the better: To review the past, 95 however, may make you more cautious in the future, especially if you reflect that no one can be hurt except by himself.[15]

I feel bound to say these things, my dear Erasmus, because of my affection for you. So take them in good part – if a pig may give advice to

* * * * *

10 Cf Luke 19:40.
11 Two hundred florins; see Ep 1466 n3.
12 Ep 1443B; see Ep 1466:4–5.
13 See Ep 1466:27ff.
14 See Epp 747:91–4, 1095:16ff, 1265:20ff.
15 Cf *Adagia* III vi 34.

Minerva,[16] though I do not consider myself inexperienced in these matters, since I have been harried for many years by the calumnies of unprincipled men. But God has been my defender. He can keep us from all adversity if only we place our steadfast hopes in his goodness, remembering that no one in this world can escape trouble and that it is good for us to be chastened from time to time.

You see how things have turned out for the Carmelite and his colleague;[17] in spite of this you are upset by Zúñiga's perversity,[18] although no one is madder or sillier than he is, as Rome itself attests, and his writings have brought you more praise than blame in the scholarly world. So dismiss these wretched, annoying flies who deserve our contempt. We pray, Erasmus, that you may enjoy a long life with every fortune and success and be lauded to the skies to the discomfiture of all evil men.

But I must stop or it will seem that I am trying to flatter you. I hope the move from Basel which you mention in your letter turns out well; but I am sorry that you have chosen this way to avoid the hostility of the printers. I wish I had one of those rings of Aristophanes;[19] I would gladly give it to you to protect you against the sharp fangs of your detractors. I am sending you another ring instead[20] so as not to appear generous only with my promises. Its stone, especially if given as a present, is said to have the power, when worn on the finger, to keep one safe in a fall.[21] Don't put it to the test, however, especially if you plan to leave by ship. But I am only joking. Far from thinking, my dearest Erasmus, that you owe me thanks for this little gift, I should regard it as a compliment if you did not scorn it, but kept it as a token of my affection for you. I know you have no need of my possessions; yet if the necessity arose, I would take second place to none of your friends and you would see that I understood how to be a true friend in deed as well as in word.

I was hoping that you would visit us some time,[22] so that I could

* * * * *

16 Cf *Adagia* i i 40: *Sus Minervam* 'The sow teaches Minerva.'
17 Baechem and Hulst; Ep 1466:14–16
18 Ep 1466:39ff
19 *Plutus* 883–4. The character 'Good man' wears a ring that is an antidote against false accusations.
20 See Allen Ep 1543:6–7. Not in the list of rings that Erasmus drew up in 1534; see *Bodleian Quarterly Record* 2 (1917–19) 143.
21 Perhaps a bloodstone, popularly believed to protect one from falling and, especially, from drowning
22 A hope often expressed; see Epp 318, 375, 527, 555, 747, and cf Ep 856:75–7.

express my feelings for you in person. But since I have been disappointed in
my hopes, I have decided to say in your absence, however inadequately,   130
what I am unable to say to your face – though you and I will never be far
apart, however great the distance which separates us.

I do not think the king of England will make the crossing; for he is
detained by the Scots, who have lately inflicted a serious defeat on him.[23]
This is how we fight against the Turks! I await your book on the freedom of   135
the will.[24] I shall be surprised if it does not stir up quite a commotion; for it is
truly a rock of offence[25] to a lot of people.

Farewell, dear Erasmus, and do not let this over-lengthy screed upset
you.

Nürnburg, 1 September AD 1524   140
Your friend Willibald Pirckheimer, who loves you as himself

1481 / To Gian Matteo Giberti   Basel, 2 September 1524

Most of the letters in the series Epp 1481–98 are concerned with the dispatch to
patrons and friends in Rome, England, and Saxony of copies of *De libero arbitrio
diatribe* (Basel: Froben, September 1524), the book in which Erasmus finally
joined issue with Luther (Ep 1419). On 2 September, the date of this letter,
Pierre Toussain, an aspiring reformer who lived with Oecolampadius (Ep 1258
n4), wrote to Guillaume Farel from Basel that 'Erasmus has written back to the
datary' and indicated that he (Toussain) was familiar with the contents of the
letter; Herminjard Ep 121 (pages 286–7). Since it is most unlikely that Toussain
could have known of the letter to Giberti if it had been written and dispatched
on the same day as his own letter to Farel, one assumes that he had learned of it
during the earlier visit to Erasmus that is also mentioned in the letter to Farel.
This would indicate that the letter to Giberti and the others in the same series
were written in advance and dated when copies of the book were ready to be
dispatched.

On Giberti, see Ep 1443A. His reply to this letter is Ep 1509.

* * * * *

23 Possibly a reference to the events of 5 July 1524, when 1,000 English troops
   returning from a raid into Scotland encountered 2,000 Scots who were
   preparing a raid into England. The outcome of the ensuing mêlée was such that
   both sides could claim a victory. See LP IV 482.
24 See Epp 1419, 1481.
25 Cf Rom 9:32–3; 1 Pet 2:8.

ERASMUS OF ROTTERDAM TO GIAN MATTEO GIBERTI, DATARY OF
CLEMENT VII, BISHOP OF VERONA, GREETING

I sent a letter[1] some time ago by Bishop Ennio of Veroli,[2] and have no doubt
that that distinguished man, who has always professed the warmest regard
for me, will have given me no cause to think him either false or careless. All   5
the same, there are so many mishaps in human life that I take advantage of
the bearer of this, one Hermannus Blauius,[3] whom I know well, to send you
a second copy of the same letter. In the earlier letter there was a mistake in
your name in the heading. I had also added something to that letter in my
own hand, rather outspokenly perhaps, but you would not call my remarks   10
wholly unreasonable if you were to survey the present state of Germany,
which I can hardly find words to describe. They might grow less ferocious, I
think, if certain concessions could be made in the near future. If the thing is
tackled with harsh measures, I cannot forecast the outcome; and yet a great
many parts are played in this by men who seem to aim at nothing short of   15
universal chaos.

I send you a small book on the freedom of the will, and am entering the
arena, having become a gladiator instead of a member of the band, at
roughly the same age as that at which Publius the moralist took to the
boards.[4] This effort, I thought, had better not be dedicated to anybody,   20
though it was hinted that I might dedicate it to the cardinal of York.[5] There
would have been an instant outcry that I was writing thus to please the
princes because I had been hired[6] or was fishing for something. Thus I
should have deprived the work of its credibility, and should have stirred up
the hornets, who are quite crazy enough when left alone. I treat the subject   25
without any personal attacks, so that if they use personalities in reply, it will
be all the more evident what spirit drives them on. I do not fail to see what
storms I have called down on my own head. But I am resolved to go through
with anything rather than put my name[7] to this conspiracy,[8] among whose

* * * * *

1481
1 Not extant; written in response to Ep 1443A. Cf Ep 1509:1–2.
2 Filonardi (Ep 1282), who since 1522 had frequently served as the conduit for
  Erasmus' correspondence with Rome; cf ibidem lines 2ff.
3 Unidentified
4 Erasmus here confuses the rival mime-writers Publilius Syrus and Laberius. It
  is about the latter that Macrobius (*Saturnalia* 2.7) tells this story. Erasmus
  repeats his error in Ep 1495:20, but in Ep 1522:19 has finally got it right.
5 Wolsey; cf Ep 1415:99–102.
6 Cf Epp 1477:11–12, 1477B n12.
7 Cf Ep 1477:29–30, 1485:7, 1496:141–2.
8 Cf Epp 1433:14, 1477:33, 1506:10, 1528:49.

members I see many men of a kind that Luther himself would find   30
insufferable.[9] They have invented a new principle: to overwhelm those who
withstand the gospel (such is their jargon) with raving pamphlets full of lies,
with no author's name or a forged one. They have their own printers,[10]
whom I could name; they have their own salesmen, devoted to the task.
Several pamphlets of this kind have already been launched,[11] attacking me,   35
and every day I expect more. I have however warned the council at
Strasbourg[12] and at Basel[13] that they must control these men's outrageous
audacity; and both have promised to do as one would expect of them.

I fear their knives less than I do their pamphlets, for nothing is easier
than to charge a man with any crime you may choose to invent. And nothing   40
can be invented nowadays so outrageous that it does not find a wide and
gleeful welcome in this frenzy of party zeal. From these storms neither the
pope's authority nor the emperor's dominion can protect me. My age and
state of health moreover are such that neither emperor nor pope can make
me happy. He who gives me a bishopric or any preferment now will find he   45
has merely laid a burden[14] on a man who has not long to live. I must
therefore strive all the harder in all this business to keep my conscience clear;
and in this I shall not knowingly default. If both the parties proceed to
defend their rights tooth and nail, I fear we shall see a battle like that
between Achilles and Hector, when with equal fury on both sides, as Horace   50
puts it, 'rose such deadly rage / Death in the end must sort their
differences.'[15]

I have had a letter[16] from Nicolas de Marville,[17] in which he says that for
some reason or other Clement has taken against the University of Louvain
and is therefore rejecting their petition for the confirmation of their ancient   55

* * * * *

9 See Ep 1429 n3.
10 See Ep 1477.
11 Hutten's *Expostulatio* (Ep 1356 n9), Brunfels' *Responsio* (Ep 1405), Alber's *Iudicium*
    (Ep 1466 n19), and Farel's pamphlets (Ep 1477A)
12 Epp 1429, 1477
13 Ep 1477A
14 Cf Epp 1484:7–10, 1487:23–4, 1523:194, 1526:93–6, 1529:9–10.
15 *Satires* 1.7.13
16 Not extant
17 Nicolas Wary (Varius) of Marville in Luxembourg (now France). Educated at
    Louvain, where he matriculated in 1508, he became one of the most influential
    members of the faculty of arts. He was three times elected dean, held numerous
    other elective offices, and in 1526 succeeded Jan Stercke (Ep 1322) as president
    of the Collegium Trilingue, a post he held until his death in 1529. Erasmus had
    certainly met him before leaving Louvain in 1521, and Erasmus' surviving letters
    to him (Epp 1756, 1806A, 1856, 1973) bear witness to a cordial friendship.

privileges.[18] Allow me to make this point to your lordship first, that in this case I have no axe to grind myself; at the same time, those who provoke the pope to take this line, in pursuit perhaps of their own personal ambitions, are in my opinion not serving his best interests. Quite enough unpopularity has already been created to the discredit of the papacy without adding any   60
more, and nothing is more unpopular than the revocation of some privilege granted by the generosity of our ancestors, which it has been much more the custom to extend. And a Clement ought to live up to his name. Consider too that this university is a unique ornament of the Empire in my country,[19] and so distinguished in every field of study that it does not yield to Paris itself.   65
Nor is any university less infected with this Luther business.

The university is not to be blamed if Nicolaas Baechem[20] bungled his presentation of the papal case. What else could a man do who is a blockhead by nature, none too well informed, unattractive in manner, hasty in temper, uncontrollably rash, and devoted solely to his own advantage? And so I had   70
foretold to Aleandro just what has happened,[21] for I had learned beforehand

* * * * *

18 In June 1522 the faculty of arts at Louvain had sent Wary to Rome to defend its *privilegium nominationum*, the right to nominate scholars to certain benefices. This privilege, bestowed on the faculty by Leo x in a bull of September 1523, had aroused the strenuous opposition of those whose own rights were thereby curtailed, particularly Erard de la Marck, bishop of Liège (Ep 1268 n9), who managed to secure the support of Margaret of Austria, regent of the Netherlands (Ep 1380). In June 1523, Wary managed to secure a confirmation and extension of the faculty's disputed privilege from Pope Adrian vi, himself a former student and teacher at Louvain. However, the necessary bull had not been executed when Adrian died in September 1523. Clement vii took the matter up during his first weeks in office and on 26 November 1523 signed the rough draft of a bull. But the opponents of the faculty's prerogative now remonstrated with the pope, and his old friend Aleandro (Ep 1256 n11), acting as agent for the bishop of Liège, managed to delay the issuance of the bull just as it was about to be promulgated at the end of April 1524. The opponents continued their efforts and by September the faculty believed that its cause had been lost. However, Wary had in the mean time enlisted the support of Erasmus, who responded with the appeal to Giberti in this letter. Erasmus' intervention and Giberti's efforts (Allen Ep 1716:1ff) were apparently decisive in persuading the pope at last to grant the faculty's wishes. Giberti's reply to Erasmus (Ep 1509) announced the faculty's victory as an accomplished fact, although the bull *Rationi congruit* did not reach Louvain until September 1525. See de Vocht *Literae* 381–5, and the same author's CTL II 299–308.

19 Cf Ep 1515:19–21.

20 Ep 1254 n6

21 Possibly at Cologne in November 1520 (Ep 1167 n20), or at Brussels or Louvain in October 1521 (Allen Epp 1238 and 1242 introductions)

exactly what the man was like. He had been ordered by Adrian VI in a papal brief to keep silent where I was concerned;[22] for in his public lectures and his sermons he was ranting in language that Orestes in his maddest moments[23] would not use of anyone. And now, Adrian being dead, he again begins to 75 bray;[24] but he's a public joke. Clement promises in his brief that his present attitude is unchanging;[25] and I promise in my turn any service that a most devoted son can render to a father who has fully earned his gratitude.

Farewell, honoured sir, and maintain the favourable attitude you so generously take towards me. When opportunity offers, I shall take pains in 80 my turn to show that your kindness has not been expended on a man wholly ungrateful.

From Basel, 2 September 1524

1482 / To Girolamo Aleandro   Basel, 2 September 1524

This letter was first published in the *Opus epistolarum*. On Aleandro, see Ep 1256 n11.

ERASMUS OF ROTTERDAM TO GIROLAMO ALEANDRO,
ARCHBISHOP OF BRINDISI, GREETING

Honoured sir. Once more you complain of my defaming you in my letters.[1] This is not so. There are already two or three places in my published work where I mention you in the most honourable terms;[2] and this fact has made 5 me highly unpopular in Germany. If I complained of you sometimes in the old days in letters to my friends,[3] this should be considered nothing new, for I knew well enough the hostile spirit in which you attacked me to begin

* * * * *

22 See Ep 1359:2–3 with n1.
23 Orestes was driven mad by the Furies after he had murdered his mother, Clytemnestra.
24 Cf Ep 1466:14–16.
25 Ep 1443B

1482
1 There is an abundance of defamation in the *Spongia*, where Erasmus surveys his relations with Aleandro over the years; ASD IX-1 148:680–152:760.
2 See Epp 1195 n15, 1256 n26, 1341A:1364–5.
3 See Epp 1195, 1199, 1268.

with. I saw[4] a letter[5] you had written to the bishop of Liège,[6] which referred
to me without reason in rather offensive terms. Soon your mind, which was   10
already prejudiced against me, was still more embittered by that man in
black,[7] who is the biggest rogue alive and the biggest liar; whose own affairs
however were in such a state that a word from me could have ruined him. As
a result you always avoided any talk with me,[8] and the bishop ever since has
been unfriendly. I know well enough what he said at the Diet of Worms,[9]   15
and today he is still his old self. As for the things you were publicly saying
about me in Cologne,[10] they were reported to me by stray Poles[11] and
Hungarians whom I met in the streets. At any rate, that man you know well,
who has long been patriarch of the new church in Strasbourg and is now
newly married,[12] has either written or recounted everything. I have   20
moreover learned from Glapion[13] the monstrous account of me you gave
the emperor, and I have had the same story here from the bishop of
Strasbourg,[14] among others. That you afterwards gave me some support, I
gratefully admit; this too the patriarch told me, but in such terms as to claim
all the credit for himself. Nor is it hidden from me what offensive judgments   25
are passed on me by certain scholars in Rome;[15] but they do not trouble me
over-much. In learning I readily give place to everyone else; though at least
among our own barbarians and at a very unpromising time I have advanced
the cause of liberal studies not wholly without success – which owe no small
debt to you too, as you do equally to them. If you are willing to edify us all   30
with publications of your own as well, you will find me with an open mind,
ready to welcome the glory they will bring you. Nor have I any doubt that we
should get on together well enough, if we had but a chance to live together.

* * * * *

4 Possibly at Louvain or Brussels in the autumn of 1519; see Ep 1038 introduction
  in Allen and CWE.
5 Not extant, written from Rome; see Ep 1496:25–7 and *Spongia* ASD IX-1 149:690–
  150:692. It presumably drew the attention of the bishop (see following note) to
  the indiscreet reference to him in Ep 980:42–3.
6 Erard de la Marck; see Ep 1268 n9.
7 See Ep 1263 n3.
8 Cf *Spongia* ASD IX-1 150:694–704.
9 In April 1521. Cf Allen Ep 1585:41–3; *Spongia* ASD IX-1 150:710–14.
10 In November 1520; Ep 1155 introduction
11 One was possibly Hieronim Łaski (Ep 1341A n310).
12 Capito (Epp 1368, 1374), who had married on 1 August 1524. On the sarcastic
   use of 'patriarch,' cf Ep 1477B n15.
13 Ep 1275
14 Wilhelm von Honstein (c 1470–1541)
15 See Ep 1479:22ff.

There is in your part of the world a man called Angelo[16] who writes
invectives attacking me.[17] Some call Luther an Erasmian.[18] Some most   35
shamelessly put it about that the *Hecuba* and *Iphigenia*[19] are not my versions,
in spite of the number of people who saw me sweating in that particular
treadmill. Some say that my Jerome[20] is nothing but guesswork,[21] though I
constantly cite early copies, and when they fail me and I do have to guess, I
always warn the reader and do not deceive him. In Cyprian[22] they make me   40
responsible for the omission of lines by the printer. For I was not there when
it was printed. In Seneca[23] (so they write and tell me) someone[24] has
corrected thousands of mistakes in the *Naturales quaestiones*. In that work I
had no assistance from any ancient copy. And the whole of this business
was entrusted to a man whom I would have trusted with my life,[25] and he let   45
me down and did the job very badly while I was away. When he found me
full of complaints, he removed my annotated copy so that he might not be
shown up. Jerome's letters have lately gone into a second edition,[26] with
corrections in many places.

I am always in a hurry;[27] I admit my fault and cannot deny it; but the   50
cause of learning makes progress. If anyone will produce more polished
work, there is no call for him to rage against me; I have done what I could. In
Rome they call me Errasmus,[28] as though authors in your part of the world –
I don't mean people like Pio and Beroaldo,[29] but Ermolao Barbaro[30] and
Poliziano[31] – never made a mistake. They make me out to be an enemy of   55
Italy, though no one has spoken out more in favour of the gifted Italians than

* * * * *

16 Colocci (Ep 1479 n12)
17 See Ep 1479 n13.
18 See Ep 1195 n19.
19 Ep 158:10n
20 Ep 396
21 Cf Ep 1479:98, Allen Ep 1544:124 and note.
22 Ep 1000
23 Ep 325
24 Matthaeus Fortunatus; see Ep 1479 n43.
25 Nesen; see Ep 1479:99–100.
26 Ep 1465
27 See Ep 1479 n30.
28 Zúñiga (Ep 1260 n36) used this term in his *Loca quae ... Erasmus emendavit* (Ep
   1466 n23) f D5, suggesting that 'Arasmus' would also be appropriate 'because
   of the crudity of his [Erasmus'] mind. 'Arasmus' is apparently a play on *aro* 'to
   plow' and *arator* 'ploughman' or 'peasant.'
29 See Ep 1341A:556–7.
30 Epp 126:150n, 1341A:553–6
31 Ep 61:154n

I have.[32] They say I was hired for forty gold pieces[33] to edit the text of Plautus[34] and made a mess of it; not a bit of it – I agreed for twenty crowns[35] merely to read it through quickly and mark off the lines in the passages of continuous metre, and for removing the mistakes I had received nothing. 60 Whoever did that job therefore has no bone to pick with me. Many other such comments are made in your city by these critics who are so hard to please, and some of them look as if they emanated from you. If one man I could name ranks you ahead of me in all departments, even in theology,[36] I do not think this means any disgrace for me, any more to be sure than if you 65 were richer or more handsome. I can derive plenty of credit from the fact that I am even compared with you.

But I have said too much on this already. Everyone is welcome to form his own judgment of me, provided they allow that I am orthodox. I have written you a rather frank letter, having secured a messenger whom I know 70 and can trust absolutely.[37] So let there be an agreement between us to forget all this, and you will find Erasmus a steady and well-disposed supporter of your reputation. Farewell.

Basel, 2 September 1524

1483 / To Theodoricus Hezius Basel, 2 September 1524

This letter was first published in the *Opus epistolarum*. On Hezius, see Ep 1339.

ERASMUS OF ROTTERDAM TO THEODORICUS HEZIUS, LONG SECRETARY TO HIS HOLINESS POPE ADRIAN, GREETING
I send you a treatise on the freedom of the will which I have published recently,[1] though well aware how much I was operating in a field that is not mine and what a storm I was raising round my own head. I wanted to show, 5 all the same, that at least I was ready and willing. Support for Luther spreads wider every day. Some Frenchmen I could name[2] are madder already than

* * * * *

32 See Ep 1479 n14.
33 *Quadraginta aureis*: see Ep 1479 n47.
34 See Ep 1479 n46.
35 *Coronatis viginti*: see Ep 1479 n48.
36 Perhaps Alberto Pio; cf Ep 1479:146–7, which seems to indicate that Erasmus did not in fact know his critic's name.
37 Hermannus Blauius; see Ep 1481:7.

1483
1 Epp 1419, 1481
2 Guillaume Farel and his supporters; see Epp 1496:72–3, 145ff, 1510:11ff.

any Germans. They all have on their lips five words: gospel, God's word, faith, Christ, and spirit – and yet I see many among them of a sort that leaves me in no doubt they are moved by the spirit of Satan.[3] If only this upheaval which Luther has aroused might bring us, like some violent physic, a measure of good health! I could have spun you a long yarn of the behaviour of our Lutherans here – for so they are called, though even that name is too good for them – had I the time to spare. Mind you look after your health, my excellent friend.

Basel, 2 September 1524

1484 / To François Du Moulin   Basel, 2 September 1524

This letter was first published in the *Opus epistolarum*. On Du Moulin, see Ep 1426.

ERASMUS OF ROTTERDAM TO FRANQIS DU MOULIN, BISHOP OF CONDOM, GREETING

I only wish I were a rock, as you call me in your letter![1] I would soon roll down to your part of the world, for if this achieved nothing else, at least I could then enjoy the society of the most warm-hearted man I know. As it is, I am entirely made of glass, or some more fragile substance, if there is one. The bishoprics offered me by his Majesty have no attractions;[2] they would exhaust my ready money, of which I have a pretty limited supply, and burden[3] me with debt, involve me in business cares, and rob me of the freedom[4] without which I could not survive for a couple of days. And a treasurer's life[5] is like a bishop's. I know my own weakness, of both body and mind. For two or three months now I have been free from the torments of the stone.[6] This I owe to the wine of which I have lately secured a supply.[7] The king is absorbed in warlike designs,[8] and you too are obliged to follow him; and winter approaches. There are other reasons which pretty well

* * * * *

3 Cf Epp 1495:15–17, 1496:68–73, 1497:9–10, 1510:12–16.

1484
1 Not extant
2 Cf Allen Epp 1545:21–4, 1562:5–6.
3 See Ep 1481 n14.
4 Cf Ep 1488:24–6.
5 Ie, the treasurership at Tours (Ep 1434 n12)
6 See Ep 1452 n22.
7 See Epp 1452 n28, 1489:21–2.
8 See Ep 1478 n7.

convince me that we should wait for the swallows.[9] Till then we will converse by letter. Winter, I hope, will calm the warlike fervour in your part of the world, and then like the halcyons I shall come and nest with you. Pray do not cease to commend me to his most Christian Majesty. I am sorry to hear he has become a widower,[10] as though the storms of wartime were not 20 trouble enough. So good a man deserved better fortune. Farewell.

From Basel, 2 September 1524

1485 / To Wolfgang Faber Capito   Basel, 2 September [1524]

The manuscript of this letter is written in an unknown hand inside the vellum cover of a copy of volume III of the *Opera omnia* (Basel: H. Froben and N. Episcopius 1541) now in the possession of Oxford University. For further details, see Allen's introduction.   The letter was first published in LB, but with the year-date 1529, after Erasmus had already left Basel. Allen assigned the year-date 1524 on the basis of verbal resemblance to letters of this period and in view of Erasmus' relations with Capito at this time; see Epp 1429 nn6–7, 1437 n48, 1477B:72–85, 1496:76–7, 120–2.

On Capito, see Epp 1368, 1374.

ERASMUS OF ROTTERDAM TO WOLFGANG CAPITO, GREETING

So much points to it that I know rather than suspect it is you[1] who stir up Eppendorf[2] to attack me as you did Otto[3] before. Please use these tactics against those who are ill disposed towards you and not against me. You do not know how much I can hurt. I have enough troubles without asking for 5 more. I work for the gospel cause much more wholeheartedly than you suppose. For that church of yours I will never put my name to,[4] unless I see it something very different. Farewell, and pray give that young man[5] better advice.

Basel, 2 September 152[4]   10

Erasmus, once your friend in Christ

* * * * *

9 That is, wait for spring; *Adagia* I vi 59
10 Francis' first wife, Claude de France, daughter of Louis XII, died on 20 July 1524.

1485
1 See Ep 1341A n301.
2 See n5 below.
3 Brunfels; see Epp 1405–6.
4 Cf Epp 1477:29–30, 1481:28–9, 1496:141–2.
5 Eppendorf (Ep 1283 n4), whom Erasmus now completely mistrusted; see Epp 1437:9ff, 1466:34–5, 1477B:73–4, 1496:122–3.

1486 / To Thomas Wolsey   Basel, 2 September 1524

This letter was first published in the *Opus epistolarum*.

TO THOMAS, CARDINAL OF YORK, FROM ERASMUS OF ROTTERDAM,
GREETING

Encouraged by his serene Majesty and by yourself,[1] I at once both finished
and published a small book on the freedom of the will, a rash thing to do in
Germany as conditions are now.[2] I refrained from personal abuse to give   5
them[3] no excuse for resentment. If they reply with the usual calumnies, they
will hurt themselves, not me. Several pamphlets attacking me have already
appeared;[4] but I hope those men will not always be able to do so with
impunity. I chose not to dedicate this work to anyone. There would at once
have been loud protests that I had been hired to write it to please the   10
princes,[5] and thus I should not only have infuriated them but robbed the
work of its credibility. Otherwise I should have dedicated it either to you[6] or
to the pope, who showed his gratitude for the dedication of my Acts[7] by
sending me an official letter[8] in most kindly terms and two hundred gold
florins[9] with it. I thought it a pity to give this opportunity to wicked men, 15
who do quite enough evil without one.

   I am delighted that your Eminence should think well of my Lieven.[10]
While he was with me he made good progress in both Latin and Greek. But
wider opportunities I cannot offer him. He has a natural gift for humane
studies, and though I found him indispensable, I have considered his own   20
good rather than mine. He is capable of assisting your kinsman's studies at

* * * * *

1486
1 Ep 1419 introduction
2 See Ep 1430 n6.
3 The Lutherans
4 See Ep 1481 n11.
5 See Ep 1477B n12.
6 For another work that Erasmus had contemplated dedicating to Wolsey, see Ep
   1415:98–102.
7 Ep 1414
8 Ep 1443B
9 See Ep 1466 n3.
10 Ep 1494:3 shows that Lieven Algoet (Ep 1373 n1) carried Epp 1486–94 to
   England. He doubtless also carried the letter to Vives that was answered by Ep
   1513 (Ep 1513:31).

Louvain University.[11] Your Eminence can very easily make it worth his
while; only I beg you to leave him sufficient leisure for his own reading. The
better scholar he can make himself, the more useful he will be to you and
yours alike.   25

I send one copy of my book on the freedom of the will[12] for your
Eminence, and a second for his Majesty, to whom I beg you to commend me
without fail. Anything you do for Lieven, I shall consider as done for myself.
For the present you sent me I am most grateful.

From Basel, 2 September 1524   30

1487 / To Cuthbert Tunstall   Basel, 4 September 1524

This letter was first published in the *Opus epistolarum*. On Tunstall, see Ep
1367.

ERASMUS TO CUTHBERT TUNSTALL, BISHOP OF LONDON, GREETING
I fear I may seem tiresome and importunate if I send you my thanks every
time you lay me under a duty to do so. The die is cast. I have published a
small book on the freedom of the will,[1] most temperately written but likely,
if I am not mistaken, to excite very serious opposition. Several pamphlets   5
attacking me have already come out.[2] All the same, they are frightened; let
them hate me as long as they fear me too. I have rewritten much of it. I wish
you would read the book through when you have leisure, and write and tell
me what you think of it in the friendly way you often do.

John of Damascus has proved impossible to find here anywhere.[3] I   10
have sent you a present,[4] not gold, of which I know you have a large supply

* * * * *

11 See Ep 1491:22–8.
12 Ep 1481

   1487
1 Epp 1419, 1481
2 See Ep 1481 n11.
3 Very little of the work of the Greek theologian St John of Damascus (c 675–c
   749) had as yet been edited. There had been an Aldine edition of some hymns
   (c 1501); Lefèvre d'Etaples' translation of the *Orthodoxa fides* had been
   published at Paris (1507, 1513, 1520); and in 1514–15 a large volume containing
   those works plus *De preceptis dialectice, De rebus naturalibus, Aphorismi medicine,*
   and *Rudimenta sacrorum dogmatum* had been published at Venice; see Allen's
   note. Tunstall may have inquired after one of these.
4 This passage, including the two following sentences, is obscure. The present,

already, but something quite new. Just as you see it, it flowed in veins of earth. If anything had happened to me as a mortal man, it would have perished; but now I have made it secure. While my servant was in your part of the world,[5] I was in such danger from the stone that I fully hoped for an end to my torments.[6] Now however I have secured a different wine,[7] and for two or three months have been in rather better health.

The king of France shows me such kindness, it is incredible. My arrival is awaited. The treasurership of Tours[8] is ready for me, worth at least five hundred écus.[9] I have sent my man Hilary[10] in advance. But when I consider that the king is wholly absorbed in making war,[11] that winter is approaching, and that my health though somewhat improved could be imperilled again on the smallest provocation, and last but not least that such honourable positions mean nothing for me but pack-saddles on the ox,[12] I have almost made up my mind to spend the winter here. There is the further point that if I were to move now, all the Lutherans would claim loudly that I had run away in a fright. It is better when trouble starts to be on the spot. If you wish your work to be printed,[13] I will talk to Froben about it, but I have not approached him seriously so far. Farewell, best of prelates.

From Basel, 4 September 1524

* * * * *

as Allen suggests, may have been one of the medallions of himself that had been struck at Nürnberg earlier in the year (Ep 1408 n17), the novelty perhaps being the combination of metals used (Ep 1452:32–3). Allen thought that the reference to 'veins of earth' (lines 13–14) was a joke about the medal being something 'dug up from the earth.' On the other hand, the whole phrase is '*flowing* in veins of earth,' which might be an allusion to the process of casting in a clay mold (Ep 1452:37–40).
5 Lieven Algoet (Ep 1486 n10). The reference is to his earlier trip to England in the spring (Ep 1430 n7).
6 Ep 1452 n22
7 See Ep 1452 n28.
8 See Ep 1434 n12.
9 See Ep 1439 n7.
10 Bertholf (Ep 1384 n31)
11 See Ep 1478 n7.
12 *Adagia* II ix 84. See Ep 1481 n14.
13 Perhaps Tunstall's *De arte supputandi* (London: R. Pynson 1522), which was reprinted several times at Paris and Strasbourg but not, apparently, at Basel

1488 / To William Warham   Basel, 4 September 1524

This letter was first published in the *Opus epistolarum*. On Warham, see Ep 188.

ERASMUS OF ROTTERDAM TO WILLIAM, ARCHBISHOP OF CANTERBURY,
GREETING

Most honoured prelate, you will, I think, have received the picture I sent
you.[1] I wanted you to have some piece of your Erasmus, in case God should
call me hence. In April I was dangerously ill with the phlegm.[2] Scarcely had I   5
recovered when the stone took its place,[3] with such severity that I fully
hoped for an end to my sufferings. Now I am in somewhat better shape. I tell
you this so that you can more easily share my relief, for I know my good
health is very near your heart, seeing that, as you say in your letter,[4] when I
am dangerously ill you feel shaky yourself, and then again when I get over it   10
you recover your spirits. You tell me to be of a good courage; and if I had but
one army to fight against I could support the burden of the fray somehow or
other; but as it is, I am engaged on three fronts at once. In Rome there are
some lovers of pagan literature who are pitifully jealous of me,[5] as I learn
from my friends' letters. Certain theologians and monks stick at nothing in   15
hopes to do away with me.[6] But none rage so much or so madly as the
characters who call themselves Lutherans,[7] though their excesses are
offensive even to Luther himself.[8] Clement VII sent me an official letter[9] full
of compliments, and with it a hundred angels[10] and the promise of greater
things; he also imposed a veto on Zúñiga,[11] who seemed likely to go ranting   20
on for ever. The friendship of kings I have kept up to this day in good repair.
King Francis of France shows me such kindness, one can hardly believe it. I

* * * * *

1488
1 See Ep 1452 n25.
2 Cf Ep 1466:68–9.
3 See Ep 1452 n22.
4 Not extant
5 See Epp 1479 n10.
6 Zúñiga (see lines 20–1 below) and Baechem (see Ep 1481:67–76)
7 See Epp 1429, 1477, 1477A.
8 See Epp 1429 n3, 1477A n12.
9 Ep 1443B
10 100 English gold angel-nobles, a sum then worth £33 6s 8d sterling or £48 6s 8d
    gros Flemish. In Epp 1341A:1688 and 1466:5, however, Erasmus had stated that
    Clement sent 200 florins, worth about £45 sterling or £66 14s gros Flemish. On
    angel-nobles, cf Ep 1388 n6.
11 See Epp 1341A:925–6, 1431:14, 1432:40–1, 1433:18–20, 1443 B16–17.

am again invited to France,[12] and for some time the treasurership of Tours has been waiting for me,[13] which carries a substantial income.[14] But such burdens[15] have no attractions for me; I am eager for freedom,[16] and am not 25 long for this world. I enjoy the approval and support of Ferdinand,[17] who has written to me often already and sent me lately a hundred gold pieces.[18] Poland is on my side,[19] and in Spain by some freak of fate I begin to be popular.[20]

As for the Lutherans, I would gladly have avoided taking the field 30 against them,[21] and up to now have put all my efforts into that; but some time ago my friends gave the pope and the kings reason to hope that I might publish something, and I too had somehow made promises that encouraged that hope.[22] Had nothing resulted I should have earned their resentment, for they would have thought I was playing them a trick; while at the same 35 time, as a rumour that the book was coming out was already widespread everywhere, I should have made the Lutherans even more hostile. Either they would have put it about that I had been frightened into suppressing the book,[23] or they would have expected something more ferocious than the reality. At any rate I shall thus have silenced those who try to persuade all 40 the princes that I am in complete agreement with Luther. Some of them do this out of hatred for myself, hoping to make me objectionable to the princes, some in hopes of making it easier to defeat Luther's case by putting me in peril.

I am sending you Jerome;[24] it could not be bound yet, while the ink was 45

* * * * *

12 The invitation tendered in 1523 (Ep 1375) renewed that of 1517 (Ep 522).
13 See Ep 1434 n12.
14 See Epp 1434:25 and n13, 1439:32–3, 1471:16.
15 See Ep 1481 n14.
16 Cf Ep 1484:9–10.
17 See Epp 1376:16–17, 1386:40–1.
18 More than a year earlier; see Ep 1376:17. The *centum aureos* were possibly Rhenish gold florins, and, if so, a sum worth about £24 3s 4d gros Flemish or £17 1s 8d sterling.
19 This confidence in Polish support was doubtless the result of Erasmus' relations with Decius (Ep 1341A n210) and, more recently, with the Łaski brothers (Epp 1341A:1218ff, 1452:15–17, 1496:235–7, 1502).
20 Cf Ep 1455 n7.
21 In *De libero arbitrio* (Epp 1419, 1481)
22 See Epp 1385:15–16, 1386:5ff, 1489:54–7, 1496:190–2, 1522:28–9.
23 See Ep 1496 n84.
24 Ie, the three volumes of the correspondence; see lines 70–1 below and Ep 1465 introduction.

fresh. Preferment has no attractions for me,[25] provided it is God's will that
you, my friend, are still alive. I have received two remittances of ten
pounds,[26] one from Potkyn,[27] delivered if I am not mistaken by a Spaniard
called Dassa;[28] the other was brought here by Franz Birckmann,[29] who had
the money in your part of the world from a bookseller, for I should be   50
reluctant myself to entrust him with any business of mine. I am grateful for
the increase in my annuity. Plague take all these wars, which mean paying
so many tithes! And yet I used to think that annuities were exempt from
levies.

I have received a horse, of no great beauty but excellent character, for   55
he is free from all the deadly sins except gluttony and sloth and is adorned
with all the virtues of a good father-confessor: pious, prudent, humble,
modest, sober, chaste, and quiet; he biteth no man and kicketh no man. I
suspect that through fraud or mistake on the part of your servants another
horse arrived instead of the one you had told them to send. I had given my   60
man[30] no instructions about a horse, unless by any chance someone made
him a present of one that was good-looking and suitable. All the same I am
most grateful for your kind thought. For my part I was considering the sale
of my horses, having now given up riding.[31] I am a little annoyed with my
servant, who did this without any instructions from me, and whose   65
thoughtlessness has meant the arrival here of a most inferior horse. When
you promise something good beyond the evils that fill the scene, I do not
rightly understand what this can be. If God lets me live so long, perhaps next
spring I shall enjoy a conversation with your highness.

It gives me very great delight to have finished Jerome's letters with   70
success, for I have restored the text in many places. The remaining volumes
will follow if the printers can agree, for it is a very expensive undertaking
and too much for one man. May the Lord Jesus preserve you in health and
wealth, best of patrons.

Basel, 4 September 1524   75

* * * * *

25 Cf Ep 1205:48ff.
26 The money-of-account for these sums, given as *decem libras*, is not specified;
    but the 'remittances' would have been in the form of bills obligatory or letters of
    exchange payable in the local Swiss-German currency and money-of-account.
    Basel's silver coinage and money-of-account system, based on Basel's own
    silver pfennig, the *Stäbler*, was then part of a South German-Austrian
    Rappenmünzbund, which also included Freiburg, Kolmar, and Breisach.
27 Ep 782:4n
28 Unidentified
29 Ep 1388 n23
30 Lieven Algoet; see Ep 1430 n7.
31 See Ep 1422 n6.

1489 / To John Fisher Basel, 4 September 1524

This letter was first published in the *Opus epistolarum*. On Fisher, see Ep 1311.

ERASMUS OF ROTTERDAM TO JOHN, BISHOP OF ROCHESTER, GREETING
One phrase in your letter,[1] right reverend prelate, I read with pain and grief.
'I only hope,' you say, 'that the book may find me still alive,' and so forth.
My servant increased my anxiety by reporting that you were troubled with
ill health. You never consider your poor body. I suspect that a large part of 5
your ill health is caused by the place where you live (for I propose to play the
physician, if you will allow me).[2] Your being near the sea and the mud which
is repeatedly laid bare at low tides means an unhealthy climate,[3] and your
library has walls of glass all round, the chinks of which let through an air
which is tenuous and, as the physicians call it, filtered, which is very 10
dangerous for those who are sparely built and not robust. Nor have I
forgotten how you sit continually in that library, which to you is a paradise.
Personally, if I spent three hours together in such a place, I should fall sick.
You would be much better suited by a room with a wooden floor and
wooden panelling all round the walls; some sort of miasma issues from 15
bricks and mortar. I know that for those who live a godly life death is nothing
to fear; but in the present shortage of good men it is important for the whole
church that such a bishop should live as long as possible.

The health of someone like myself is not of the same importance; but in
case you wish to know how I am, I suffered as dangerous an attack of the 20
stone last May as I have ever had.[4] Then I secured a different wine,[5] and the
stone has treated me more leniently for two or three months now. You
congratulate me on my triumphs. What triumph I have earned, I do not
know; I am engaged, at any rate, on three fronts, with the pagans in Rome
who are pitifully jealous of me,[6] with certain theologians and monks who 25
leave no stone unturned to do away with me,[7] and with some crazy
Lutherans who rage against me as the only man (so they say) who stands

* * * * *

1489
1 Not extant
2 Cf Ep 1532.
3 Neither of the bishop's residences – his palace at Rochester and Rochester
  House in Southwark, London – was really near the sea, but both were close to
  estuaries that exposed mud-flats at low tide.
4 See Ep 1452 n22.
5 See Ep 1484:13 with n7.
6 See Ep 1479 n10.
7 See Ep 1488 n6.

between them and victory.[8] And I stand in their way because I am not willing at the risk of my life to accept the whole of Luther's teaching, in which there is much that I do not follow, much of which I am doubtful, and 30 much which, even were it safe to do so, I would not dare accept, for conscience' sake. I could wish that this tumult which Luther has aroused might act like some powerful and bitter drug and be the cause of some degree of good health within the church. And yet, when I see the malignant behaviour of some men who have the name of the gospel always on their 35 lips, my mind forebodes some desperate and bloody outcome.

Faction spreads more widely every day; it has extended into Savoy,[9] into Lorraine,[10] into France, and even Milan. Burgundy, my nearest neighbour, is being thrown into confusion by a Frenchman, Phallicus by name,[11] who came here as a refugee from France, a demagogue as 40 unrestrained in speech as he is on paper. He has left here and will not, I think, return, he has behaved so badly. This is sometimes the way with the champions of the gospel.

I had made a start on the book you ask for (and others ask for it too);[12] but my complaint, which threatened me with the worst, and certain other 45 interruptions obliged me to break off. I will devote this winter to the subject, God willing; although I had decided henceforward to abandon contentious questions of principle and beguile my time in translating Greek or in secular subjects, provided they contribute to the formation of character. But in a theoretical treatment of preaching I am obliged to point out some mistakes 50 made by certain preachers and to touch on several of the theologians' favourite doctrines. Nonetheless, with your encouragement I will gird myself for the task.

I have published a small book on the freedom of the will,[13] though by no means unaware how far I was from my proper field. But I had already 55 roused expectations among the princes,[14] with whom I saw that my position was at risk from my enemies, and had confirmed these hopes in letters. Had nothing been forthcoming, it would have looked as though I had played them false, and with the Lutherans challenging me so unpleasantly, I might

* * * * *

8 See Epp 1429, 1477, 1477A.
9 See Ep 1413.
10 See Herminjard Ep 112 n6.
11 Guillaume Farel, who was now in Montbéliard (Ep 1522 n23); see Epp 1496:72–3, 145ff, 1510:11ff.
12 The *Ecclesiastes sive de ratio concionandi*; see Ep 1321 n1.
13 *De libero arbitrio* (Epp 1419, 1481)
14 See Ep 1488 n22.

have been supposed to keep silence out of cowardice,[15] while they, who had 60
been expecting something pretty ferocious, would have raged even more
fiercely than they do now. And there would have been plenty of people to
put it about that I was keeping my mouth shut by arrangement, because I
already knew that unknown hands had circulated a letter containing
overtures of peace from Luther,[16] but on condition that I should not openly 65
attack his opinions, even if I had sometimes criticized him by name. So
firmly was it fixed in my destiny that at my age I should cease to follow the
Muses and turn gladiator. The Lord Jesus have you in his keeping, best of
prelates and patron beyond compare.

Basel, 4 September 1524 70

1490 / To Richard Bere   Basel, 4 September 1524

This letter was first published in the *Opus epistolarum*. Richard Bere (d 25
January 1525), abbot of the Benedictine house of Glastonbury since 1493, is
remembered primarily as a great builder in and around his abbey. In his own
day he was also well regarded by humanist scholars, as this letter testifies.

ERASMUS OF ROTTERDAM TO RICHARD BERE, ABBOT OF GLASTONBURY,
GREETING

Long ago, when he and I were living in Ferrara,[1] Richard Pace often spoke
highly of your generous attitude towards good literature, and convinced me
that I ought to get to know your reverence; and I was myself on the lookout 5
for a chance to make your acquaintance. But my hunting was unsuccessful,
perhaps because I followed a blind guide, the Frenchman Bernard André,[2]
whom you will remember, who was once that admirable prince Arthur's not
wholly admirable tutor. And so, being blind myself through my not
knowing your reverence, and having chosen a blind man to lead me, the 10
result was that we both fell into the ditch. Besides which your chaplain, who
had come out to greet us, entered into a long and tiresome argument about

* * * * *

15 See Ep 1496 n84.
16 Ep 1443, especially lines 48–50, 74–8. For its circulation, see Epp 1496:29–30,
   1501:56–7, 1522:32–4.

   1490
1 December 1508; see Ep 211:53n.
2 Ep 243:60n

the book I brought with me,[3] for he supposed it to contain St Jerome's *Argumenta* reworked by me in a more polished style, as though I find St Jerome's style lacking in polish. I had translated from the Greek the pieces   15 you can now see added to the New Testament in Greek,[4] in the state in which they then were. When I found my version did not satisfy you, I began to be dissatisfied with it myself. Otherwise I should have given it its final revision and published it, had you not dissuaded me.

But I have been more dissatisfied with myself for having set out,   20 contrary to my nature and my normal practice, to secure the friendship of such an eminent divine.[5] Nothing is more importunate than the class of men who in the meanest way set their caps at the powerful in hopes of a few pickings from them even against their will, nor is there any class of mortals whom I dislike more. It may be that your reverence suspects me of being one   25 of that money-grubbing fraternity. On the contrary, my feeling for you has been unbroken, thanks partly to Richard Pace, the half of my soul, whom you helped so generously with his studies long ago, partly to Zacharius of Friesland,[6] a man of great integrity and very dear to me on many grounds, who has never ceased in his letters to me to speak highly of your kindness to   30 him. What you do for friends such as these, I reckon as done for myself. I pray that Christ may long preserve your reverence in health and wealth.

Basel, octave of St Augustine 1524

1491 / To Zacharias Deiotarus   Basel, 4 September 1524

This letter was first published in the *Opus epistolarum*. On Deiotarus, see Ep 1205 n1.

ERASMUS OF ROTTERDAM TO ZACHARIAS DEIOTARUS OF FRIESLAND, GREETING
This generous spirit you show towards my friends, my dear Zacharias, I should welcome warmly, if only your position in life were worthy of your

* * * * *

3 Evidently Erasmus' translations, now lost, of a set of traditional Greek introductions to the Pauline Epistles. See Ep 894:42–5. One surmises that this attempted interview took place sometime between his return to England in 1509 and his departure for Basel in May 1515.
4 The Greek text of the introductions (see preceding note) had not been published at the time of Erasmus' confrontation with the chaplain, but had since appeared in the *Novum instrumentum* and later editions.
5 For similar disclaimers, see Epp 1326:10–11, 1512:8ff, 1531 n3.
6 Deiotarus (Ep 1205 n1).

virtues. As it is, there was no call for any outlay to be a burden on your   5
purse, which cannot I suppose be well filled, especially as Lieven[1] was not
short of money and had instructions from me not to be in any way a burden
on you on grounds of expense. It is impossible for me not to feel the warmest
affection for that fine old man Thomas Lovell,[2] who renews his youth in the
ancient tongues and in good literature at an age when ordinary men   10
nowadays spend their time normally on amassing money. The present he
sends me is so welcome that, had he sent me a hundred marks, it could not
have been more so,[3] though I felt some misgivings in accepting it. But who
would have the heart to refuse an offer made in such terms? 'Friends have all
things in common,' he says, 'and what I give is not my inheritance, but   15
Christ's; and since it belongs to all men equally, I am the steward of it and
not the owner.' Here to be sure is the true spirit of the gospel, and I reckon
you happy in the possession of such a friend, my dear Zacharias, with all my
heart, I solemnly assure you.

I shall be hard put to it without Lieven, but he is growing up now and I   20
did not think he should waste the best years of his life running errands for
me. I had therefore decided to send him to Louvain at my expense, that he
might have a few years of complete leisure for the humane studies for which
he is naturally fitted.[4] But I should be sorry if he became a secretary to the
cardinal;[5] I don't want him wasted at court. If the cardinal lets him study at   25
Louvain with his nephew,[6] his sister's brother's child, I shall have no
objections. Otherwise, I at least shall disapprove the arrangements Lieven
has made.

Farewell, dearest Zacharias. Mind you give my greetings to Andrew
Smith,[7] to whom I shall perhaps not have time to write.   30

Basel, octave of St Augustine 1524

* * * * *

1491
1 Algoet (Ep 1430 n7)
2 Ep 1138 n3
3 The mark was an English money-of-account, representing two-thirds of the
   pound sterling; and thus 100 marks were worth £66 13s 4d sterling. See CWE 1
   325.
4 For Lieven's progress in these studies, see Epp 1437:215–16, 1470:36–42,
   1486:17–18.
5 Wolsey
6 Doubtless the 'kinsman' mentioned in Ep 1486:21
7 A London notary, documented 1522–9, about whom little is known

1492 / To Robert Toneys   Basel, 5 September 1524

On Toneys, see Ep 1138 n4. This letter was first published in the *Opus epistolarum*.

ERASMUS OF ROTTERDAM TO TONEYS, A MEMBER OF THE COUNCIL
OF THE CARDINAL OF YORK, GREETING
Honoured sir, a letter[1] from William Burbank[2] criticizes me, not without
reason, for my failure hitherto to send a letter of greeting to such a generous
friend, such a courageous patron, and such a distinguished scholar as   5
yourself. The reason for this is the obligation to answer so many letters from
both friends and enemies, of whom I have a very great many, which leaves
me no time to spare. In any case, your exceptional gifts and your special
friendliness in some way towards myself have been extolled to me more
than once by Thomas More, who is as you know an authority both reliable   10
and eloquent. I know this, my dear Toneys, I am well aware of it and do not
forget it. I say thank you now, and it will be a greater pleasure to repay you
when I can. When I have more leisure, I will write at greater length.
Meanwhile, my best wishes for your prosperity.
        From Basel, 5 September 1524   15

1493 / To Henry VIII   Basel, 6 September 1524

This letter was first published in the *Opus epistolarum*.

ERASMUS OF ROTTERDAM TO HENRY VIII, KING OF ENGLAND,
GREETING
May it please your invincible Majesty, I knew very well that the rough-and-
tumble of the arena was not for me, who have spent all my life in the
delightful garden of the Muses. But with the encouragement of your most   5
auspicious Majesty[1] one could face anything. The die is cast: a short book on
the freedom of the will has seen the light of day[2] – a desperate step, believe
me, in the present state of Germany.[3] I await a shower of stones, and several

* * * * *

1492
1 Not extant
2 Ep 1138

1493
1 See Ep 1419 introduction.
2 Ep 1481. Henry's copy was presented to him on 12 November; Ep 1513:7–8.
3 See Ep 1430 n6.

raving pamphlets have already taken wing,[4] aimed at my head. I shall
console myself however with the precedent set by your Majesty, for even   10
you are not immune from these men's savagery.[5] I had made up my mind in
any case to do what your letter[6] encourages me to do, and work to my dying
day for the defence of the Christian religion. But this I shall do with greater
spirit, now that your Majesty has deigned, as they say, to spur the willing
horse.[7] With all my prayers for your perpetual felicity.   15

From Basel, 6 September 1524

1494 / To Polidoro Virgilio   Basel, [c 6 September 1524]

This letter was first published in the *Opus epistolarum*. The date is dictated by
the contents. On Virgilio, see Ep 1175.

ERASMUS OF ROTTERDAM TO POLIDORO VIRGILIO, GREETING

My most learned Polidoro, I had intended to write you a long gossiping
letter; but by mere bad luck I had to provide not only Lieven[1] but four other
couriers at the same time with their burden of letters, and long letters too –
one bound for Rome,[2] the second for France,[3] the third for Frankfurt, and   5
the fourth for Saxony.[4] So I must be brief as any Spartan.

First of all, you know that the printer's copy you sent is in the hands of
Franz,[5] not Froben. I discussed the publication of the work, or rather, works
with Froben,[6] and he says if he were to print it in large type it would make a
very big volume; six hundred gold coins would not cover the costs,[7] and he   10
fears some risk in the sales, Germany being now crazy for things which have

* * * * *

4 See Ep 1481 n11.
5 See Ep 1308 n3.
6 Not extant; cf Ep 1467:20–1.
7 *Adagia* I ii 47

1494
1 Algoet (Ep 1486 n10)
2 With Epp 1481–3 (see also Ep 1511 n1) and perhaps Ep 1479 as well
3 With Ep 1484
4 With Epp 1495–8
5 Birckmann (Ep 1388 n23)
6 The discussions summarized here clearly refer to a folio volume, published by
  Froben in June–July 1525, comprising Virgilio's *De rerum inventoribus* and
  Adagia; see Epp 1175 and 1366.
7 *Sexcentos aureos*: Rhenish gold florins, with a value of about £145 gros Flemish
  or £102 10s sterling

some element of Luther in them.[8] Apart from that he is full of good intentions to oblige us both, and I will myself take steps to encourage him.

There are three ways of getting a book printed. Sometimes Froben undertakes the whole business at his own risk; this he does now and again for smaller books in which the risk of loss is less perilous. Sometimes the whole thing is done at the risk of another party, and he himself stipulates only to be paid for the work he has put into it. Sometimes the risk of the business is shared by a partnership. So far in his contract for the work Franz is offering the most inadequate remuneration. There will now be discussions in Frankfurt whether the thing can be done either at Franz's sole risk or jointly by a consortium; and I will send you a full account of what has happened when Froben gets back from the fair. I hope the business will turn out to your satisfaction.

My view is that you would do well to rewrite the whole of that first preface.[9] To begin with, this will help to recommend the book, because it will be new. Secondly, this will be good for the reputation of both of us, because there are things in that earlier preface to which I personally do not take exception, but all the same they arouse suspicions among the learned that there is some rivalry between us. Besides which, it seems to me more straightforward to dedicate your whole book of proverbs to a single person; at the moment you dedicate the added material to someone else.[10] On these points you will decide with your usual wisdom what you think best; I am frankly telling you what I think myself.

As to X's treachery,[11] words fail me. You seem to have protested to him, and let me tell you the revenge he took on me. In Antwerp he spread a rumour that in Rome I had been burned in effigy with all my books,[12] and that as a result I am now writing attacks on the pope; and he has convinced many people that these portentous lies are true. Far from it: Clement VII of his own accord has sent me a most flattering brief[13] and two hundred gold florins with it,[14] and for my own part I have published at the same time a small book against the Lutherans on the freedom of the will. So much for my being burned in Rome! So much for my attacks on the pope!

* * * * *

8 See Ep 1430 n6.
9 Addressed to Richard Pace, and dated 5 June 1519; see Ep 1175 introduction and n2.
10 See Ep 1366:15–16 with n4.
11 Apparently a reference to Birckmann; cf Epp 1306:42, 1362:44–53, 60–7, 1388:27–8.
12 Cf Ep 1518:36–8.
13 Ep 1443B
14 See Ep 1466 n3.

If you can find a man in the business who would take responsibility for
fifty copies, I could easily arrange the rest with Froben. Farewell.   45
    Basel, 152[3]

1495 / To Duke George of Saxony   Basel, 6 September 1524

The manuscript of this letter, in a secretary's hand but signed and addressed
by Erasmus, is in a volume in the Staatsarchiv Dresden entitled 'Dr Martin
Luthers Lehre und andere Sachen, 1522–49' (Loc 10300). The letter was first
published in the *Opus epistolarum*.
    Communications between Erasmus and Duke George (Ep 1283) had now
been disrupted for two years; see Ep 1313 introduction. Ep 1448 finally reached
Erasmus on 20 September and was immediately answered with Ep 1499.

Greeting, most illustrious prince. If I have not complied hitherto with your
Highness' exhortations,[1] there have been many reasons, and two in
particular. The first is this. I could see that in both age and capacity I was
unequal to this most dangerous undertaking and, what is more, I felt a
surprisingly strong natural revulsion from battles of this kind, in which   5
gladiators fight to the death; for what other purpose is served by these
pamphlets which now pour from the press on every hand beyond that of
gladiators in the arena? In the second place, I reflected that Luther, whatever
one may think of his teaching, is a kind of necessary evil[2] in a church so
deeply and universally corrupted; and indeed I was hopeful that this   10
medicine, bitter and drastic though it is, might be the source of some
element of good health in the body of Christ's people. As it is, I understand
that most people interpret this moderation on my part as collusion with
Luther, with whom I have never had any private understanding of any kind;
and at the same time I see that under the cloak of the gospel a new race is   15
growing up of brazen and shameless men, relations with whom are out
of the question.[3] Such men, in a word, as Luther himself would find intolerable;[4] though to be sure they have the same villainous contempt for
Luther as they have for bishops and princes. And so I have entered the
arena, at roughly the same age as that at which Publius the moralist took to   20
the boards.[5] Whether this move of mine will prosper, I do not know; I hope

* * * * *

1495
1 To write against Luther; see Ep 1298:24ff.
2 Cf *Adagia* i v 26.
3 Cf Epp 1483:8–10, 1496:68–73, 1497:9–10, 1510:12–16.
4 See Ep 1429 n3.
5 See Ep 1481 n4.

at least that it may be for the advantage and prosperity of Christendom.

I send your Highness a small book on the freedom of the will,[6] the subject of a most learned letter from yourself,[7] which I saw some time ago. I was given an additional spur to write this by letters from his most serene Majesty the king of England[8] and from Clement VII;[9] but was far more forcibly moved by the villainy of some of these brawling ruffians, who unless they are restrained will end by overthrowing both the gospel and the humanities. I would prefer the tyranny of the Pharisees to be done away with rather than altered; but if we must be slaves, let popes and bishops be our masters, whatever one may think of them, rather than this or that mean and petty Phalaris,[10] more intolerable than a whole bench of bishops. I await your Highness' verdict, and meanwhile offer my prayers for your entire felicity.

Basel, 6 September 1524

Erasmus of Rotterdam, signed with my own hand

To the most illustrious Prince George, duke of Saxony, etc

1496 / To Philippus Melanchthon   Basel, 6 September 1524

This letter was first published in the *Opus epistolarum*. The day after receiving the letter, Melanchthon sent it on to Spalatinus (Ep 1497) with a copy of *De libero arbitrio* and a note (CR I 673–4) in which he says: 'Erasmus appears to have treated us not at all abusively ... I am desperately eager that this matter, which is certainly the chief point of the Christian religion, should be diligently investigated, and for that reason I almost rejoice that Erasmus has taken the field. I have long wished that it would befall Luther that some adversary would publish on this matter; if Erasmus be not seen as such, I am greatly mistaken.'

ERASMUS OF ROTTERDAM TO PHILIPPUS MELANCHTHON, GREETING

Had Pellicanus shown me your letter to him[1] in good time, Joachim[2] would not have returned to your part of the world without one from me, for though

* * * * *

6 Ep 1481

7 A letter of 9 May 1523 in response to a letter of Henry VIII (20 January 1523) to the princes of Saxony, warning them against Luther. The two letters were printed by W. Stöckel at Leipzig on 23 May 1523; see Gess I 499–500 n1. Duke George's letter is found ibidem 504–9.

8 Ep 1419 introduction

9 Ep 1443B:25–9

10 Ruler of Agrigentum in Sicily c 579–554 BC, proverbial for his cruelty

1496

1 See Ep 1452 n14.

2 Camerarius; see Ep 1444 n2.

it was addressed to him, it looked as though you thought I should read it. One of my friends[3] wrote and told me that you would have come here too,[4] 5 had you not been afraid you would rouse ill feeling which would make me unpopular. My dear Melanchthon, I could easily have met that ill feeling with contempt. It's true, I excused myself from an interview with Hutten,[5] but fear of ill feeling was not the only reason. There was something else, which all the same I did not mention in my *Spongia*. Hutten was penniless 10 and completely destitute; he was looking for some refuge in which to die. I was expected to take this swashbuckler into my house, pox and all, and with him that whole band of evangelicals, as they call themselves, with nothing of the gospel but its name. In Sélestat[6] he took money off all his friends. He had the face to ask Zwingli for money,[7] as Zwingli himself wrote and told me 15 in detail.[8] As for the man's bitterness and his endless boasting, no one, however long-suffering, was able to endure it. In fact,[9] were not Wittenberg so far away, I should not have hesitated to come and spend a few days in your part of the world, for an exchange of ideas with Luther and yourself.

I was further deterred from writing by that first letter to Luther,[10] the 20 publication of which put me in a very dangerous position. For it was that that gave Aleandro,[11] who had long been prejudiced against me, a handle to try to destroy me; he attempted to poison Leo's mind against me,[12] and the same for the bishop of Liège,[13] who before that had had almost a passion for his Erasmus,[14] if you will allow the phrase. The bishop himself showed me a 25 letter which Aleandro had written to him from Rome containing some pretty offensive remarks about myself.[15] So, as I saw that your people can keep nothing to themselves, I judged it better to refrain from writing. What is more, a copy of the letter which Luther sent me by Joachim[16] is available in

* * * * *

3 Possibly Heinrich Stromer, whom Melanchthon had visited on his journey: Ep 1444:1–2. The letter is not extant.
4 See Epp 1452:18–20, 1466:21–4.
5 See Ep 1331 n24.
6 Hutten had visited Beatus Rhenanus (Ep 327) in Sélestat on his way to Basel; see *Spongia* ASD IX-1 130:193ff.
7 For Hutten's visit to Zwingli in July 1523, see Ep 1376 n21.
8 The letter is not extant; cf Ep 1384 n1.
9 Here Erasmus resumes the line of thought in lines 7–8.
10 Ep 980, with the indiscreet reference to Erard de la Marck in lines 42–3
11 Ep 1256 n11
12 To counteract this poison, Erasmus had to write Ep 1143.
13 Erard de la Marck; see n10 above.
14 See Epp 746, 748:23–25, 40–6.
15 See Ep 1482:9–10 with nn4–5.
16 Ep 1443

Strasbourg,[17] and will no doubt soon be published. To make me unpopular   30
they have published your judgment on me,[18] and two letters of Luther as
well. This is the sort of rubbish with which certain starveling, low-class
printers keep the pot boiling. They have added a letter from me to Johannes
Fabri written absolutely on the spur of the moment,[19] which makes clear all
the same how far I am from inciting anyone to violence or to betraying the   35
gospel.

But let us leave this for another time. I have read your *Loci* all
through,[20] and saw in it very clearly how fair as well as fertile your mind is.
Your gifts have always inspired me with respect and affection, and this is the
more true on both counts now that I have read this, so far am I from   40
regretting your work; though as I read I took exception to several passages
which I would gladly have discussed with you, had we been able to meet. I
perceive a fine army of principles marshalled to fight the tyranny of the
Pharisees. But there are some points among them, to speak frankly, which I
do not follow, and some of a kind which, even were it safe to do so, I would   45
rather not profess publicly for conscience' sake, some such that, if I did
profess them, it would do no good. And yet your friends were indignant
with me for not professing things which I either did not understand or did
not accept – and that too when it was against my conscience to do so, and
meant the greatest personal risk not only to me but to friends, for whose   50
safety I am more concerned than for my own.

You will say, why then did you not immediately take me up on those
points of disagreement? Because I was in favour of a policy of restoring the
liberty of the gospel, and hoped that Luther would take advice and follow
more moderate counsels in future. I therefore did what I could to suppress   55
the noisy protests of the theologians and restrained the savagery of the
princes, as I still do to this day. I separated the cause of the humanities from

* * * * *

17 See Epp 1489 n16.
18 Melanchthon's *De Erasmo et Luthero Elogion*, published in the first half of 1523
with his *Ratio discendi*; texts in CR 20 699–704. The same volume included
Luther's *Iudicium de Erasmo Roterodamo ad amicum* (Ep 1341A n315) and his letter
to Capito of 17 January 1522 (WA-Br II 428–35); these are the two letters of
Luther mentioned here. In the *Elogion*, Melanchthon contrasted Luther, who
taught the true biblical doctrine of justification by faith, with Erasmus, who
remained merely a teacher of civic virtue much like the ancient philosophers.
Thus, despite its polite and respectful tone, the *Elogion* was a harsh dismissal of
Erasmus as someone whose life-work had no specifically Christian value.
19 Ep 1397, appended to Erasmus Alber's *Iudicium de Spongia*; see Ep 1397
introduction.
20 Melanchthon's *Loci communes* (Wittenberg 1521). Cf Ep 1425 n7.

Luther's cause.[21] I sought for an opportunity to promote the gospel without disorder, or at least without great disorder. Even now I lose no chance, writing to the emperor[22] and the other princes,[23] acting as a kind of Gamaliel,[24] and hoping that the play will have a happy ending. I had written rather freely to Pope Adrian on the subject.[25] Later I had felt that I was in danger, not that he attacked me himself, but he ceased to protect me against the attacks of others.[26] Nor was it really safe to trust him, however civil his language. None the less I wrote freely to Clement too,[27] and also to Cardinal Campeggi.[28] I know nothing of your church; at the very least it contains people who will, I fear, overturn the whole system and drive the princes into using force to restrain good men and bad alike. The gospel, the word of God, faith, Christ, and Holy Spirit – these words are always on their lips; look at their lives and they speak quite another language.[29] Are we driving out our masters, the princes and the bishops, that we may suffer the more pitiless tyranny of pox-ridden Ottos[30] and madmen like Phallicus?[31] For he is a recent import here from France.

In the old days, you will say, the church had its false apostles, who under a cloak of piety did what their bellies told them. But in our time they are lovingly supported meanwhile by our gospel chiefs – Capito,[32] who always smelled like a rascal, and Hedio,[33] who protected a filthy wretch[34] on the occasion of a letter from me which should have meant that he was punished,[35] and called this an act of mercy because the man had a wife and young children.[36] He thinks of nothing even now except to see that that worthless fellow's reputation and business suffer no loss. Oecolampadius is

* * * * *

21 Cf Ep 1155 n5.
22 Ep 1526 n26.
23 See Epp 1400, 1430, 1499, 1515.
24 Acts 5:34–9
25 Ep 1352
26 Because of Erasmus' unsatisfactory response to the call to write against Luther; see Epp 1384:28–9, 1408:18–19, 1416:27–30.
27 Ep 1418
28 See Epp 1410, 1415, 1422.
29 Cf Epp 1483:8–10, 1495:15–17, 1497:9–10, 1510:12–16.
30 Otto Brunfels (Epp 1405–6)
31 Guillaume Farel (Ep 1341A n305); see lines 145ff below, Ep 1510:11ff.
32 See Ep 1485 and lines 120ff below.
33 Ep 1477B
34 The printer Schott; see Ep 1429 n1.
35 Ep 1429
36 Ep 1477B:43

a little more restrained than the others,[37] and yet there are moments when I find him too lacking in the sincerity of the gospel. As for Zwingli,[38] how subversive his methods are! – to say nothing for the moment of the rest. They do not agree with your lot, nor are they at unity among themselves, and yet they expect us to follow their authority and abandon all the orthodox Fathers and councils. You teach that those who cast out images as something impious are in error.[39] And Zwingli has roused such an uproar over images![40] You teach that a man's fashion of dress is not relevant. Here several people teach that the habit must be utterly rejected. You teach that bishops and episcopal constitutions must be tolerated unless they lead to impiety.[41] Here they teach that all are impious and antichristian.

What could be more crazy than this business that they started here two years ago, put on to it, or at least assisted, by a certain learned man whom I could name?[42] You remember the story of the pig which led to the carving up of that unhappy Sigismund.[43] And yet, though he[44] was no friend of mine, I defended him in friendly fashion to the bishop of Basel, saying things much to his credit though he did nothing but rant against me, while all the time my table and a room in my house were always at his service, invited or uninvited, nor did I ever say a word that could have done him harm. When I was told that he never ceased to use his tongue as an offensive weapon at my

* * * * *

37 For Erasmus' deteriorating relations with Oecolampadius (Ep 1258 n4), see Epp 1510 n5, 1519:75–7, 1522:93–4, 1523:118–26, 1526:242–3, 1538.

38 See Ep 1384.

39 See, for example, BAO no 183 (Melanchthon to Oecolampadius, 14 February 1524), where Melanchthon expresses his disapproval of the campaign against images in Zürich.

40 Starting with the so-called Second Zürich Disputation, 25–8 October 1523, Zwingli argued that the presence of images in the churches was unbiblical and that they should be removed in an orderly way under governmental supervision after the necessity for doing so had been explained to the people by the pastors. Finally, on 15 June 1524, the city council ordered that images be removed forthwith. In the city itself this was done in the period 20 June to 2 July. There was no violence or public disturbance, but the transformation was dramatic – all pictures and images gone and the walls whitewashed – and the defiance of the authority of the bishop of Constance was complete. See G.R. Potter *Zwingli* (Cambridge 1976) 131–42.

41 See the section 'De magistratibus' in the *Loci communes* (n20 above); CR 21 224–5.

42 Buschius; see Ep 1466:29–33.

43 Steinschneider; see Ep 1353 n13. Buschius was one of the participants in the pork feast during Lent.

44 Buschius, as indicated by the resemblance of lines 108–10, 117–19 to Ep 1466:29–33

expense, I challenged him in a friendly way to tell me openly if there was anything that offended him, and I would make it good; and he refused. When he had written a pamphlet[45] in which he criticized some of the authorities, and many had already got to know of this, which put him in   105 some danger, I warned him privately in a most friendly and warm-hearted letter[46] to be careful. When he had left here[47] and was still savagely attacking me, I wrote him a kind and friendly letter.[48] At length a letter appeared over the name of Erasmus Alber,[49] which that scabby fellow[50] had promised,[51] so that you can see the thing was a conspiracy. He disguised his style[52] and   110 imitated some things of yours. But even were there nothing else about it, the way he so often repeats the name Erasmus in contemptuous tones sufficiently points to the author. And a talk with you seems to have given him courage, for he boasts himself a disciple of a man who learns from Luther. I will say nothing here of the chastity of his life, the purity of his   115 vocabulary, his extravagance, and the way he has cheated his creditors. How can people like that recommend this new gospel? And this is a friend of mine, to whom I have done no wrong, of whom I have always spoken in friendly terms, and who was admitted to my inner circle.

As for Capito, many people think very ill of him, and I have some ugly   120 suspicions; it was at any rate from his house that that scabby character[53] issued forth to print his crazy pamphlet. That Thraso from Planodorp[54] has always been a favourite of his; and then the way he made his excuses, with a worried air and in public, was such that the excuses themselves deepened my suspicions. The one man I trusted was Hedio, and of him I do not yet fear   125 the worst. I had sent him a copy of the letter which you wrote,[55] if I am not mistaken, to Hummelberg,[56] in which you expressed surprise that a man you had known twelve years before[57] should not yet consider, and so forth.

* * * * *

45 Not extant
46 Not extant
47 In May 1522
48 Not extant
49 See Ep 1466 nn19–20.
50 Brunfels; cf lines 72, 121, 172.
51 See Ep 1406:53–6.
52 Cf Ep 1466:30–1.
53 Brunfels
54 Eppendorf; see Epp 1283 n4, 1437:9ff. Thraso is the braggart soldier in Terence's *Eunuchus*. Cf this sentence with Ep 1437:106–8.
55 CR I 649 (Ep 267, undated). Scheible no 300 puts the date at 'second half of December 1523.'
56 Ep 1253 n6
57 Presumably at either Heidelberg or Tübingen, c 1511–12

No name was given,[58] but those who sent it gave some sort of hint of our Thraso. I sent it to Hedio with no purpose except to warn him to be careful;   130
he showed it to Capito,[59] and Capito showed it to the braggart soldier. This put him in a rage, and there are threats of sword and gallows.

I sent Zwingli a friendly warning, and he sent a most contemptuous reply.[60] 'The things you know,' he said, 'are no use to us; and the things we know are unsuitable for you,' for all the world as though like Paul he had   135
been caught up to the third heaven and there learned sundry mysteries which are concealed from us dwellers on earth.[61] I know some men of excellent character, who have deteriorated as a result of this business, to say nothing of those utter rascals, as you yourself call them,[62] who have no point in common with the gospel. I see many people, here especially, of such bad   140
character that if I approved everything that Luther writes, I should not care to put my name to this faction.[63] One would be absolutely at their beck and call, and would constantly be giving them money to live on; for the one really evangelical thing about them is that they are always penniless.

As for Phallicus, he and I had a very brief meeting.[64] He wrote an   145
account[65] of it to someone at Constance.[66] A copy has reached me secretly. It's the most self-satisfied, boastful, poisonous thing I ever saw. There are sometimes ten consecutive lines in it without one syllable of truth in them. He has also published a pamphlet about the Paris school and the pope.[67] The coarse jokes in it, the pointless virulence, the slandering of many men   150
by name! And yet the author is the one man whose name does not appear. He has also, I am told, enlarged Alber's stupid *Iudicium*,[68] but this I have not yet been able to see. Two other pamphlets have been seen in Constance which he has written attacking me.[69] And he professes a new doctrine, that this is the way to bring scandal on those who resist the gospel; of whom he   155
reckons I am one, and in several places calls me Balaam,[70] because Pope

* * * * *

58 Melanchthon called him 'philophaebus,' the meaning of which is not evident; see n55.
59 Cf Ep 1437:106–7.
60 Ep 1384 introduction. Neither Erasmus' letter nor Zwingli's reply is extant.
61 See 2 Cor 12:2–4.
62 Where? Not in the letters mentioned in Ep 1341A n299.
63 See Epp 1477:29–30, 1481:28–9, 1485:7.
64 See Ep 1510:19–45.
65 In the form of a dialogue; see Herminjard Ep 121 (page 286).
66 Herminjard (Ep 123 n4) suggests Ambrosius Blarer (Ep 1341A n430).
67 See Ep 1477A n6.
68 See n49 above.
69 Written in French, not extant; cf Epp 1477A:3–6, 1510:63–4, 1519:104–5.
70 See Ep 1510 n7.

Adrian invited me to give him advice.[71] I sent some, but he didn't like it.[72] He offered me a deanery,[73] and I sent a straightforward refusal; he wanted to send me money, and I wrote back and asked him not to send a halfpenny.[74]

So I am Balaam. And it is men like this who expect us to throw over all   160 the Doctors of the church and put our trust in their 'spirit,' when they don't even agree among themselves. How can I convince myself that they are led by the spirit of Christ, when their behaviour is so far from Christ's teaching? In the old days the gospel made the fierce mild, made robbers generous, made the quarrelsome peaceable, taught those who cursed to bless; these   165 men are roused to frenzy, they seize other men's property by fraud, arouse uproar everywhere, speak ill even of those who do them service. New hypocrites I see, new tyrants, and not one grain of the spirit of the gospel. If I were passionately devoted to Luther, I should hate these men even more than I do now, for the sake of the gospel, which their behaviour renders   170 loathsome, and of good literature, which they wipe out. Look at the manifest falsehoods in that book by our scabby friend,[75] in which that gospel-figure writes against his conscience for no reason except that he may burn. And these reverend fathers assembled in senate have passed a decree that Erasmus be buried under a pile of pamphlets. If I reply, what a glorious   175 result! –a confrontation with criminals by which I shall put bread into the mouths of sundry mean and starveling printers who deserve hanging many times over. Look at the blasphemies and lies in that pamphlet of Alber![76] – as if it weren't bad enough to show such contempt for Jerome without accusing him of perfidy as well.[77] I forbid marriage,[78] I have gone over to the papists   180 because I call them 'reverend father,'[79] I run with the thief,[80] I wage war on the gospel!

But away with these complaints. You will wonder why I published my book on the freedom of the will.[81] I had to fight off three ranks of enemies. The theologians and those who hate the humanities were moving every   185 stone for my undoing, not only because of the way I write about them, but

* * * * *

71 See Ep 1338.
72 See lines 61–4 above.
73 See Ep 1324 n13.
74 The letter is not extant, but see Ep 1341A:1686–7.
75 See Ep 1405–6.
76 See n49 above.
77 Böcking II 374:27–30
78 Ibidem 374:44–6, 377:14–33
79 Ibidem 378:1–2
80 Ibidem 375:40
81 See Epp 1419, 1481.

for my bringing that most flourishing new college into Louvain[82] and
defacing (as they call it) a whole province with the ancient languages and
with humane studies. They had persuaded all the monarchs that I was
closely bound on oath to Luther. My friends therefore, seeing I was in 190
danger, gave the pope and the princes reason to hope that I should publish
something against Luther. This hope I myself for a time encouraged.[83] In the
mean time the party in question, without waiting for a book from me, began
to attack me with a hail of pamphlets. There was therefore no course left
except to publish what I had written; otherwise I should have set all the 195
monarchs against me, who would think I had deluded them with mere
words, and the party of disorder would have cried out that I was
suppressing it from fear,[84] and would have attacked me all the more bitterly
in the expectation that there was worse to come. Finally, since a letter of
Luther's is now in general circulation in which he promises that he will 200
restrain his pen in writing of me if I keep quiet,[85] I should be thought to have
abandoned publication under some agreement with him. Besides which,
those who profess pagan literature in Rome are wondrous indignant with
me[86] – jealous, it is clear, of Germany. So, had I published nothing, I should
have given a handle at the same time to the theologians, to the monks, and 205
to those Roman potters[87] whose alpha, if I am not mistaken, is X,[88] so that it
would be easier for them to make popes and monarchs believe what they
wanted to make them believe; and I should have had the crazy evangelicals
even more bitterly against me than before. For I myself have treated the
subject in a very low key; and yet what I write is never written against my 210
convictions; though I should be quite happy to change them too when
anyone convinces me of something better.

    'But meanwhile,' you may say, 'you encourage tyrants to violence
unchecked.' No one has discouraged them from violence more diligently
and more outspokenly than I. Even were I a passionate follower of a narrow 215
papist group, I should discourage the use of violence, because this is the
way by which it spreads wider. It was because he understood this that
Julian[89] gave orders that Christians were not to be killed. The theologians

* * * * *

82 The Collegium Trilingue; see Epp 1221, 1322.
83 See Ep 1488 n22.
84 See Ep 1437:108–9; cf Epp 1488:38–9, 1489:59–60, 1522:31–2.
85 See Ep 1489 n16.
86 See Ep 1479 n10.
87 Ie, envious rivals; see *Adagia* I ii 25.
88 Apparently Colocci; see Ep 1479 n12.
89 Emperor Julian the Apostate (ruled 361–3), who opposed Christianity and
    sought to promote a revival of paganism

supposed that if they burned two or three in Brussels,[90] the rest would mend
their ways; and that death made many new Lutherans. But there are some   220
people in your camp who cry to heaven that the gospel is overthrown if
anyone resists their own mad conduct. The value of the gospel? not in liberty
to sin without penalty, but in keeping us from sin even when no penalty
exists.

But on all this I have written more than enough. Cardinal Campeggi,[91]   225
a man of singular generosity of mind, has sent someone to have a talk with
me on many topics, and among others on the question whether you could be
invited to move elsewhere. I replied that I wished a man of your gifts might
be free from these disputes, but that I had no hope of your undertaking a
recantation.   230

Relying on your good nature, my dear Philip, I have poured all this into
your sympathetic ear; I know that as an honourable man you will see that it
does not get out into the wrong hands. When Joachim[92] was here, I was
so weak from illness that I could scarcely endure to talk to anyone, my
digestion was so enfeebled; and by bad luck I was overwhelmed just at that   235
moment by a Polish baron,[93] of whom you can read in the enlarged catalogue
of my works.[94] Had he been willing to stay longer, we should have had more
talk. But I would have talked it all over with you, had you come to see me.
Farewell.

In haste, from Basel, 6 September 1524   240

1497 / To Georgius Spalatinus   Basel, 6 September 1524

The manuscript of this letter is an early copy (c 1526) in the Forschungsbibliothek Gotha (Chart B.26, f 121). The letter was first printed in C. Schlegel *Historia
vitae Georgii Spalatini* (Jena 1693). On Spalatinus, see Ep 501.

TO GEORGIUS SPALATINUS
Greeting. I have always tried hard to secure that Luther's bitter and violent
medicine, which has so shaken the world, should contribute something to
restore its health; but in this country I observe the rise of certain people who

* * * * *

90 See Ep 1384 n2.
91 See Epp 1410 introduction and 1466:8–10.
92 Camerarius; see Ep 1444 n2.
93 Hieronim Łaski
94 Ep 1341A:1217–78

turn it to their own private profit, and they are the most pestilent and the 5
most difficult to deal with of any kind of men I ever saw. They despise
Luther and are leagued together to pursue their own advantage. When I see
how they behave, it turns me even more against that whole movement; it
turns me even against a liberal education. I hear the word gospel the whole
time, and not a trace of the gospel do I see.[1] They throw off the cowl and 10
marry, and then defend what they have done; and all the time they are
hunting for a safe and comfortable job. They scribble lunatic pamphlets with
no name to them or a false name, and cap this with the principle that this is
the way to defend the gospel. A splendid defence for anything! In this
respect I approve of Luther: he puts his name to what he writes, and teaches 15
that things are lawful which he himself makes no use of. These noisy rascals,
you will say, have nothing to do with the gospel. Rascals as they are, they
have the support of leaders like Capito, Hedio, Oecolampadius, Zwingli.[2]
They provoke the princes to take severe measures, and they rage against me
because I do not profess the name of Luther.[3] Am I expected to profess, at 20
great personal risk, what I do not follow, or have doubts about, or
disapprove of? Am I to join a faction like this, in which I see men of such bad
character that I would rather join the Turks? Of one thing I can assure you: I
shall never cease to support the gospel cause.

Farewell, dear Spalatinus, and help the young man who brings this,[4] if 25
he needs it.

Basel, 6 September 1524. Your sincere friend Erasmus of Rotterdam

1498 / To Helius Eobanus Hessus   Basel, 6 September 1524

The manuscript source for this letter is the same as that for Ep 1462, and it was
first published in the same place as well. On Eobanus, see Ep 874.

TO THAT MOST LEARNED MAN EOBANUS HESSUS FROM ERASMUS
OF ROTTERDAM
Greeting, most learned Eobanus. The young man who brings you this,
Johann Moldenfeld,[1] besought me to write at least a couple of lines to greet

* * * * *

1497
1 Cf Epp 1483:8–10, 1495:15–17, 1496:68–73, 1510:12–16.
2 See Ep 1496:74ff.
3 See Ep 1477B n21.
4 Probably Moldenfeld; see Ep 1462 n4, 1498:4.

1498
1 See Ep 1462 n4.

you and recommend him. Both which I do, and ask you in turn to give my   5
greetings to my friend Hune,[2] that wise and warm-hearted man. I fancy you
take a more moderate line in your part of the world; and for your sake at least
I would gladly think so. Here the pseudo-Lutherans make a terrific uproar,[3]
and will overthrow both Luther and the humanities unless some deity
comes to the rescue. Farewell, dear friend.   10

     Basel, 6 September 1524

     I have written[4] about your books.[5] I don't yet know what has passed
between Froben and Beatus,[6] for he has your poems. Printers nowadays
look for what will sell rather than really good stuff. If you like, I will try the
French.   15

     Your truly sincere friend Erasmus

1499 / To Duke George of Saxony   Basel, 21 September [1524]

The autograph of this letter is of the same provenance as the manuscript of Ep
1495. It was first published by Adalbert Horawitz in the *Sitzungsberichte der
phil.-hist. Classe der kaiserlichen Akademie der Wissenschaften* (Vienna 1878). On
Duke George, see Ep 1283.

Greeting, most illustrious Prince. A letter[1] from your Highness written on 22
May[2] reached me on St Matthew's eve,[3] when I had already sent you my
book on the freedom of the will with a letter from me,[4] which I hope has been
delivered by now. I perceive that both my letters to you and yours to me
have been intercepted;[5] for a friend of mine in Nürnberg wrote some time   5
ago to tell me that a letter of mine to you had been intercepted by the

* * * * *

2 See Ep 1462.
3 See Epp 1495:27–9, 1496:66–73.
4 Letter not extant
5 Eobanus had evidently resumed his attempts, first made in 1519, to get his
  works published by Froben. Once again he was unsuccessful, though Ep 1567
  indicates that the discussions referred to here were carried further. See Allen's
  note.
6 Rhenanus (Ep 327)

  1499
1 Ep 1448
2 A mistake for 21 May; cf Epp 1521:4, 1526:2.
3 20 September
4 Ep 1495
5 See Ep 1313 introduction.

Lutherans,[6] nor had your letter,[7] of which I now have a copy, ever reached me. I now send a brief reply to both your letters, as it must go by a courier who is unreliable, and who departs earlier than he said he would.

The pamphlets you sent me[8] I received with great gratitude, though they are already to be had here publicly. But I retain absolutely nothing of this language,[9] I regret to say. My business is all with authors in Greek and Latin.

Your Highness expresses the wish that I had been minded two years ago to have separated myself from the Lutheran faction and to have put this on record in some published work.[10] But I did do this of my own volition more than five years ago, when Luther's books had first appeared and still enjoyed general approval; and I have recorded the same opinion in hundreds of books and letters, published letters too. Not only have I separated myself from that faction but, what is more, I always most carefully abstained from all contact with it at a time when I could not yet suspect what monsters that faction was to breed; and I not only abstained, I dissuaded as many as I could from joining it.[11] If I have hitherto not refuted any of Luther's doctrines in a book written for the purpose, Hilary had remained silent even longer while the Arians overran the world.[12] And yet, if I had the leisure, I would prove with irrefutable arguments that I ought not to have acted otherwise than I did, and that it would not have been expedient to do so.

Nor have I had any hesitation in the mean while in teaching in my books doctrine very different from the decrees of Luther. I wrote to Pope Adrian about the suppression of this business in a way that might prevent it from shooting up again.[13] How much has been achieved hitherto by public uproar and anti-Lutheran pamphlets, by censures and proclamations, I do not know. But if it has been decided to suppress this evil by putting men in chains, burning, and confiscating, for this my help is not required. Neither by nature nor experience am I fitted for these gladiatorial contests; but to the limits of my power I have never failed the church of God and never shall,

* * * * *

6 The friend was presumably Pirckheimer. No such letter is extant.
7 Ep 1340
8 See Ep 1298:26–33.
9 See Ep 1313:94 with n16.
10 Ep 1448:38–42
11 See Epp 904:20n, 1033, 1143, 1275:25–9.
12 St Hilary of Poitiers (c 315–67) was the church Father who led the fight against the Arian heresy (Ep 1451 n9) in the West. He was still a child during the early years of the spread of Arianism.
13 Ep 1352

especially when I see the princes of the church sincerely committed to a
policy of pursuing Christ's glory and the salvation of the Christian flock. If I
do not see this, at least I shall always remain as much a stranger to Luther's   40
faction as I have always been. And so I bid your Highness farewell.

Basel, St Matthew's day, under pressure from the courier
Erasmus of Rotterdam with my own hand, in haste
To the most illustrious Prince George, duke of Saxony, landgrave of
Thuringia, margrave of Meissen   45

1500 / From Philippus Melanchthon   [Wittenberg], 30 September 1524

First printed in the *Opus epistolarum*, this is Melanchthon's reply to Ep 1496.
Erasmus' reply to this letter is Ep 1523.

In a letter to Oecolampadius, probably dispatched to Basel at the same time
as this one (BAO no 220), Melanchthon writes as follows: 'With the papacy now
almost vanquished, Luther has begun to concern himself with certain new and
thoroughly bloodthirsty Manichaeans [evidently Müntzer and Karlstadt; see
n5]. And Erasmus, whom I had wished to be the author of peace rather than of
new disturbances, renews the papist war. His work on free will has been
received with complete equanimity. Luther of course promises that he will
respond with moderation. And he will, unless everything deceives me. For
what is more unsuitable than what is now openly happening, namely, that one
prefers to crush rather than to instruct the dissenter?'

PHILIPPUS MELANCHTHON TO ERASMUS OF ROTTERDAM, GREETING
You are quite right, dear Erasmus, to complain of the behaviour of our
modern professors of the gospel.[1] The curs who bark at a man of your
importance seem to me entirely oblivious of both civilized conduct and
religion, for someone who has served the common weal as you have and has   5
reached your age deserves more gratitude. And those who rouse the
common people in their churches with subversive sermons, make violent
attacks on learning, and undermine the whole system of society, are
building kingdoms for themselves, not teaching Christ. Luther is quite
unlike them, and often deplores the way in which the name of religion is   10
used as a cloak for personal ambitions, even by those who want to give the
impression of fighting a campaign against the Pharisaical dominion of the
pope. But deeply concerned as he is at these abuses, he believes none the

* * * * *

1500
1 Ep 1496:66ff

less that these scandals are stirred up by the devil himself in order to
overwhelm the gospel somehow or other, and so he thinks it his duty not to   15
turn back or abandon the common cause.[2] You on the other hand seem so
deeply offended by the faults of some of these wretches that you take against
the cause and the teaching too. You may perhaps think you are on the right
lines; but I am afraid that such an attitude may prove a danger to the gospel,
for you cannot deny that Luther's cause has taken to its heart the gospel   20
teaching. All Luther's contentions, taken by and large, either revolve
around the question of free will or involve the use of ceremonies. On the first
of these I have noticed for some time that you disagree. On the second there
is a large measure of agreement; but since this is in your judgment some part
of the gospel, he[3] is afraid that you might allow it to be suppressed. There   25
was a philosopher once who used to say that he offered the precepts of
philosophy with his right hand, but his pupils grasped them with their left;[4]
and how much more true this is in theology! But it is most unfair to make the
teaching responsible for any mistakes made by the class.

So I do beg you, dear Erasmus, first of all not to think that Luther is on   30
the side of those whose character is rightly rejected, and secondly not to be
prejudiced against his teaching by the folly or rashness of any individual.
Luther's own spirit you may gauge without difficulty. To say nothing of the
question of the papacy, he now makes this at any rate abundantly clear, how
much he detests cruelty and self-seeking and all subversive policies; he puts   35
his life and reputation very much at risk by his opposition to a new faction of
bloodthirsty teachers.[5] You draw up a list,[6] in which you collect the greatest
wretches among two-legged creatures in order to bracket them with
Oecolampadius and his like. Now what, I ask you, was the object of that?
Personally, I cannot with a clear conscience condemn Luther's teaching,   40
though I would do so, and boldly too, if Scripture so required. Others can
call this superstition or folly if they like; it makes no difference to me. At least
I shall never allow human authority or any scandals to make me change my
mind.

* * * * *

2 On this aspect of Luther's thought, see Mark U. Edwards jr *Luther and the False
  Brethren* (Stanford 1975) passim.
3 Luther
4 Theodore the Atheist; see Plutarch *Moralia* 467B (*De tranquillitate animi 5*).
5 See Ep 1523:107–8, where Erasmus speculates that Melanchthon had Karlstadt
  (Epp 1258 introduction, 1523 n18) in mind. Melanchthon doubtless also had in
  mind the fiery revolutionary Thomas Müntzer, against whom Luther had
  published a pamphlet at the end of July (see Ep 1523 n39).
6 Ep 1496:74–182

As for your *Diatribe* on the freedom of the will,[7] it had a very mild   45
reception here.[8] It would be tyranny to forbid anyone inside the church to
express an opinion on a religious subject. That ought to be most freely open
to anyone, provided private interests do not come in. Your moderate
attitude gave great satisfaction, though you do slip in a barbed remark now
and again. But Luther is not so irascible that he can swallow nothing.[9] And   50
so he promises to use equal moderation in his reply. It may perhaps be a
good thing for everyone to have this problem of the freedom of the will
thoroughly discussed;[10] and if one wishes to be of use to men's consciences,
what is the point of bringing private feelings into a question of public
importance? Once indignation has begun to carry the mind off its course, I   55
do not see how it can do justice to such an important subject. I personally am
quite clear about Luther's good will towards you, and this gives me hope
that he will make a straightforward reply. In return it is your duty, my dear
Erasmus, to make sure that this discussion is not embittered by any greater
ill will on your side. For one thing, he has Scripture behind him quite clearly;   60
and then you yourself have never yet condemned his cause, so that you
would be thought to act against your conscience if you opposed him bitterly;
last but not least, prophecies, as you know, should be tested, not
condemned.[11] Anything you write to me I shall keep absolutely to myself; I
would rather die than commit a breach of confidence. And I do want you to   65
be sure of this, that I have the deepest respect and affection for you.

Here we have lost Nesen,[12] a man who could be trusted, and much
devoted to you; it is one of the most bitter blows I ever suffered. Luther
sends you his respectful greetings. I did not want to trouble you with a
longer letter, or I would have written more.   70

Farewell, and my very best wishes. 30 September 1524

I wish you could be persuaded to translate the opposing speeches of
Aeschines and Demosthenes.[13]

* * * * *

7 Epp 1419, 1481
8 This news caused Erasmus evident satisfaction; see Epp 1526:241–2, 1528:51–2,
   1529:27–8, 1531:2–3.
9 Cf Ep 1443:42–3.
10 Cf the passage quoted in Ep 1496 introduction.
11 1 Thess 5:20–1
12 Wilhelm Nesen (Ep 1257 n3), who died on 6 July 1524
13 Rival Athenian statesmen and orators in the fourth century BC. The reference is
   to their speeches at the trial of Ctesiphon in 300, where Demosthenes carried
   the day with the jury. In Ep 1523:221–3, Erasmus suggests that Melanchthon
   himself undertake the translation.

1501 / From Joachim Camerarius   Wittenberg, 30 [September 1524]

This letter was first published in the *Opus epistolarum*, where the text undoubtedly is that of the letter actually received by Erasmus. Camerarius' autograph rough draft, which ends in the middle of the paragraph beginning at line 92, is found in the Bayerische Staatsbibliothek Munich (MS Lat 10357.153). The date given in the *Opus epistolarum* (line 124) cannot be correct. Ep 1496, which Melanchthon answered with Ep 1500 on 30 September, is here said to have arrived 'a few days ago' (line 7). Furthermore, Camerarius left Wittenberg c 15 October to visit Nürnberg and Bamberg, where he remained until the following summer; see Camerarius' *Vita Melanchthonis* (Ep 1444 n2) 100, and Scheible Epp 349–416 passim. It would appear, then, that this letter and Ep 1500, which were answered in tandem (Epp 1523–4), also arrived in tandem, thus making 30 September the correct date.

Joachim Camerarius (Kammermeister) of Bamberg (1500–74) studied at the universities of Leipzig, Erfurt, and Wittenberg, where he became a close friend of Melanchthon. He met Erasmus in Basel in the spring of 1524 when he accompanied Melanchthon on a journey to southwestern Germany (see Ep 1444 n2). Although he instantly established cordial relations with Erasmus that were to last until the latter's death, Camerarius' real inclination was towards Luther, who subsequently stated in his Table-Talk that it was Camerarius, along with Frau Luther, who finally moved him to get busy on a reply to Erasmus' *De libero arbitrio*; WA-TR IV no 5069. From 1526 Camerarius devoted himself to a career in teaching, first as rector of the city school in Nürnberg, then as a professor at the University of Tübingen (1535–41), and finally at the University of Leipzig, where he served repeatedly as dean of arts and rector. A devoted classical scholar, Camerarius published many editions and translations of ancient authors. He wrote biographies of Melanchthon and Eobanus Hessus, among others, as well as histories of the Bohemian Brethren and of the Schmalkaldic War. Unfortunately, neither a complete edition of his correspondence nor a collected edition of his *opera* has ever been undertaken.

TO ERASMUS OF ROTTERDAM

I have thought hitherto that I ought not to write to you, partly to protect myself and partly out of respect for the very splendid work that keeps you busy. With nothing to say, I did not want to display how badly I write, or to seem to have forgotten my duty at a point where I least ought to do so. But   5
when Philippus Melanchthon read me two passages in the letter he had from you a few days ago,[1] because I was mentioned in them, I changed my
* * * * *
1501
1 Ep 1496:29–30, 233–8

IOACHIMVS CAMERARIVS.

Joachim Camerarius
Portrait in Theodorus Beza
Icones, id est verae imagines virorum ... illustrium
Geneva: Jean de Laon 1580
Robarts Library, University of Toronto

mind; I abandoned all thought for myself in this regard, and put my trust in your kindness and your sympathetic attitude, for I saw that I could not leave your remarks about me unanswered without betraying my own credit and your kindness to me; and I decided to break in with my chatter (that is the only word for it) and write you a letter. This I have done very briefly, in hopes that by brevity if nothing else I might atone for any faults I have committed elsewhere and make them good. I am most grateful to you, honoured sir, for having formed such a good opinion of me, when after that one meeting[2] (to say nothing harsh about myself) you might easily despise me, that you have not yet entirely forgotten me and add a greeting when you write to an excellent man and a good scholar, who is a very dear friend of mine. I count this as a very great kindness, and am as much pleased by it as I was at my being lately admitted to have a talk with you and discuss any subjects I might have wished to raise.

As I thought over this great generosity, I got a wonderful idea of your modesty, which extends even to accusing yourself unjustly; for you do not hesitate to say in the letter that you did not give me very generous and full treatment.[3] What more, and more agreeable, could you have done for me than that delightful interview? What more could I expect of you, even if I enjoyed being selfish, and what defect could I find in our conversation, except to wish that we had been spared one Russian baron,[4] a distinguished and admirable man no doubt but rather inconvenient for me just then? And so, Erasmus, let me assure you that I have boasted proudly among my friends of the kindness you showed in your reception and treatment of me, and now pride myself on the greeting you sent me as a distinction and an ornament. And I have no fear that you will be annoyed with me for this, for it makes no small contribution to your fame and reputation if other men bask in the reflected glory of your brilliance. So I adapt your eminence to myself in such a way that it makes me greater, yet at the same time the sum of your praises grows no smaller and perhaps is somewhat increased.

Since I had to write to you in any case, I thought it sufficient to touch on this, as you see, for fear of being tiresome if I dwelt on it at more length, or of finding more difficulty in convincing you of my zeal and my affection for you if I said nothing. If I did not feel affection, respect, and veneration for you, Erasmus, I should be a very bad man; for this tribute is due to your learning, your scholarship, and your goodness. Were I to hate you and act as an

* * * * *

2 Ep 1444 n2
3 This is essentially what Erasmus says in the second passage cited in n1.
4 Hieronim Łaski; see Ep 1496:235–7.

enemy of your reputation, what an outrage should I not rightly be thought
to have intended! Satisfied as I am with a good conscience in this regard, I 45
neither advertise my fondness and esteem for you (especially in your
hearing), nor am I meticulous in refuting the calumnies that all men put
upon you. I see that it would have no point if I wanted to do any such thing,
as though it made much difference to you what attitude is taken by
individuals in the lowest class, or as though I believed that anyone could 50
give universal satisfaction.

But what is the point, you will say, of this far-fetched introduction? The
point is this, Erasmus, that I suspect there has been some change in your
feelings toward me, the fault for which lies with the sinister activities of
certain men's misplaced curiosity (I now come to the heart of the matter) 55
who, to Luther's great regret as well as lamentations from Philippus and
myself, divulged[5] Luther's letter[6] and your reply,[7] both of which I had most
faithfully carried and put into the hands of the recipient. 'What,' you will
say, 'do you suspect, or what sort of person do you think I am?' Forgive me,
Erasmus: 'love is all fear and all anxiety.'[8] If it is mere chance that what I read 60
in your letter to Melanchthon about the circulation of the letter should have
been put immediately after the mention of my name,[9] yet my anxiety in this
regard will be additional evidence of my affection for you. But if your kind
feelings for me have in any way received a shock (I do not like to think so, but
I cannot but be anxious), let me restore and strengthen them. To begin with, 65
the facts are these, Erasmus, and you must take my word for them. The
letter I had received from Martin Luther to be delivered to you if I got as far as
Basel[10] I delivered personally into your hands, as I have already said, and
you were the first person who set eyes on it. The letter you wrote in reply[11] I
handed over faithfully to Luther; nor in the mean time did I show anyone 70
except Philippus the bare sheet with nothing on it but your Terminus,[12] until
I had returned to Wittenberg and offered it to Luther. I was myself carefully
brought up by those who educated me from childhood to learn that one
should keep mind, hands, and eyes off other people's property, and from

* * * * *

5 See Ep 1489 n16.
6 Ep 1443
7 Ep 1445
8 Ovid *Heroides* 1.12
9 Ep 1496:29–30
10 Ep 1443
11 Ep 1445
12 Erasmus' personal emblem; see Ep 604:4n.

my own nature I have always detested the idea of inspecting private papers.   75
I always thought a man acted disgracefully who tried to find out, even by
criminal practices, things which were most carefully protected from him by
the folding of the sheets and the defences of wax and seal. I have often
deplored the mad lawlessness of this generation on account of other wild
things they do, but especially for this criminal dishonesty, which means that   80
nothing can any longer be safely entrusted to locked chests and drawers, no
reliance be placed on friends, and nothing be left securely in the secrets of
the heart. Human rascality ferrets out everything, and in our days busies
itself particularly and tires itself out in searching through secret papers. And
so the moment anyone nowadays thinks he has been hurt and wronged, he   85
not only publishes the letters sent him by those who he thinks have done
him harm, and repeats them openly by printing them in hundreds of copies,
but searches through other men's papers with this offence as an excuse, in
hopes of finding even one letter which he can use to make his enemy
unpopular with the reading public. Such men, as Cicero says, are devoid of   90
common humanity, and have no idea how to live in a society.[13]

    If then such are my nature and my feelings, how could I endure (for I
will now imagine that you accuse me of this crime) to divulge most
disgracefully what had been given me and entrusted to my honour? How
could I hope not to be tormented at least by my own conscience and to   95
escape the judgment of the rest of the world, not to mention yours? What
effrontery and treachery for a feeble creature like myself to allow to take root
in his mind! Suppose that I were free from any respect for honour, and took
such determined steps to be a rascal, you could have noticed at once (and I
have no doubt you did so; but even now, as I keep on repeating, I am   100
troubled by empty fears) – you could have noticed, I repeat, that the seal on
the letter from Luther of which you speak was sound and unbroken when I
brought it. As for your letter – for I hear that it suffers a similar fate, that is, it
has been transcribed many times, and well-thumbed copies are in the hands
of the public – I swear by all the Muses, that most sacrosanct of oaths, that   105
Luther saw it in exactly the same state. Unless perhaps you judge that I have
learned those 'cunning ways of opening seals' invented by Alexander.[14]

    Already perhaps I have some idea whose fault it was – or foolish
assiduity, which surely amounts to a fault – that these letters lately got out.
But I am not so keen to defend myself that I would willingly include among   110
my excuses an accusation levelled at others; nor do I think it suits a

* * * * *

13 *Philippics* 2.4.7
14 See Lucian *Alexander the False Prophet* 20.

straightforward man like me, when I do not know something for certain, to
make it up to suit my own convenience out of common gossip and various
rumours. And so, Erasmus, if on this question you have got an idea of me
into you head which is not what I really am (as I say, I do not think this 115
certain, but I fear it), I beg you to correct the opinion you have thought up as
something false, however probable in the present climate of human folly.
And pray be convinced that I am a zealous supporter of your reputation and
your name and fame; nor shall I ever act in such a way as to feel, speak, or act
in any other way than as consideration of your dignity suggests and 120
requires. This may add nothing to your reputation, but it is essential for me
to behave in this way unless I prefer to be regarded as having forgotten and
deserted my duty. Farewell, most distinguished of men.

Wittenberg, 30 November

The man who has brought you my letter is of noble birth and comes 125
from Meissen; he was formerly a pupil of Mosellanus, and is an outstanding
young man.[15] I would recommend him to you, did I not think it would be
arrogance and pride to claim for myself such authority as to hope that a
recommendation from me would have any effect with you. Though here too
this man and his good qualities will be their own best recommendation. 130

1502 / To Hieronim Łaski [Basel, c October 1524]

This letter consists of the opening and closing passages of the *Modus orandi
Deum* (Basel: Froben, October 1524), which has no preface. Since the book was
directed against Luther (Allen Ep 1559:120–2), Łaski was a suitable dedicatee;
see Ep 1341A:1218–69.

TO THE HONOURABLE HIERONIM ŁASKI, BARON OF POLAND
AND IN RYTWIANY PALATINE OF SIERADZ, FROM ERASMUS OF
ROTTERDAM, GREETING
See how the gifts of the Graces, dear Hieronim my distinguished friend,
pass in exchange now this way and now that. You had left in my house a 5
pledge of your affection for me;[1] and here in its turn comes back to you a

* * * * *

15 Probably Christoph von Carlowitz (1507–78), who had studied with Mosellanus (Ep 1305) at Leipzig. In the autumn of 1527 he again visited Erasmus,
whose service he entered for a time. In 1529, with Erasmus' strong recommendation, he entered the service of Duke George of Saxony.

1502
1 The silver cup mentioned in Ep 1341A:1263–5

pledge of that mutual sympathy for which you made a formal request at
your departure[2] ...

Here then is a modest present for you, noble Hieronim. It was yours from   10
the moment of its birth, for it was conceived in order to give me some means
of reminding you in my turn of your absent friend. If you think well of it, you
will be so kind as to share it with your excellent brothers Jan and Stanisław.[3]
If you have any better guidance on this subject, follow the better course; but
at the same time let my ready good will be at least to some extent requited,   15
and if you have something better let me share it.

1503 / From Duke George of Saxony   Leipzig, [October] 1524

> This is Duke George's reply to Ep 1495. The manuscript, a rough draft in a
> secretary's hand, comes from the same source as that of Ep 1495. The letter was
> first published by Adalbert Horawitz in the *Sitzungsberichte der phil.-hist. Classe
> der kaiserlichen Akademie der Wissenschaften* (Vienna 1878). On Duke George, see
> Ep 1283.

GEORGE, BY THE GRACE OF GOD DUKE OF SAXONY, LANDGRAVE OF
THURINGIA AND MARGRAVE OF MEISSEN
Greeting, most learned Erasmus, and the assurance of our support. We have
received your letter, and with it your sermon on the freedom of the will; and
since you await our verdict on it, we cannot refuse to tell you frankly that it   5
gives us great pleasure, nor have we any doubts of its being a lasting
contribution to the glory and advancement of Christendom. What fruit it
will bear, however, among those of the opposite persuasion, is not yet clear;
for we fear they have stopped their ears and are like the asp that will not hear
the voice of the charmer,[1] and it is said that they themselves have almost   10
finished their reply. But the situation is in hand, for the examination of this
case does not rest with them. And to show you that this is our sincere
opinion, we send you Luther's own book on vows,[2] on which he has also

* * * * *

2 Ep 1341A:1267–8
3 Ep 1341A nn319–20

1503
1 Ps 58:4–5 (Vulgate 57:5–6)
2 Because of Erasmus' repudiation of any knowledge of German (Epp 1313:94
   with n16, 1499:11–12), Duke George now sent Erasmus a work by Luther
   written in Latin, the *De votis monasticis* of 1522, in the apparent hope that
   Erasmus would write a reply; cf Ep 1520:38–43. Erasmus subsequently

published impious opinions in the vernacular, with the result that he has
caused countless souls to stumble and driven them from their convents into   15
the brothels. And so, in order to bring help to them and to others who still
observe their vows but hesitate none the less, we strongly urge you to be
ready on this point also to assert the opinion of the Fathers and of the
Catholic church, which has stood for so many centuries, and to be its
defender and champion against these impious and abominable sophistries.   20
Beyond a doubt you will have God himself to support and assist you, and all
right-thinking and religious men will be at one with you and will persevere
until the end. The froward you will either recall to bear a better harvest of
repentance, or you will reduce them to silence. Apart from that, we have
lately replied[3] to your letter about Eppendorf.[4] And so we await a further   25
reply from you.

Farewell, from Leipzig, the year of our salvation 1524.

1504 / To William Warham   Basel, 10 October 1524

> This is the preface to volume IV of the new edition of Jerome (Basel: Froben
> 1525); see Ep 1465 introduction. The volume contains the works falsely
> ascribed to Jerome, divided into three series or classes (lines 38–41). In the
> edition of 1516 these had been in volume II. Erasmus' only contribution to the
> volume was the brief introductions preceding each item (lines 36–7).

TO THE MOST REVEREND FATHER IN CHRIST WILLIAM WARHAM,
LORD ARCHBISHOP OF CANTERBURY AND PRIMATE OF ALL ENGLAND,
FROM ERASMUS OF ROTTERDAM, GREETING
The affairs of men, O jewel among prelates, have sometimes been likened to
the sea, and those who do so have, I would say, a firm grasp of their nature;   5
but those who have made them resemble the Euripus have found a more
vivid image. All other seas are motionless in places, and feel no movement
except when stirred by the force of the wind. But the Euripus,[1] the sea that

* * * * *

acknowledged receipt of the book, pronouncing it 'long-winded,' but did not
agree to write a reply; Ep 1526:243–6.
3 Ep 1448
4 Not extant; see Ep 1448 introduction.

1504
1 In general, a *euripus* (from the Greek εὔριπος) is any narrow channel where the
ebb and flow of the tide are especially violent. In particular, the Euripus is the
strait between Euboea (Negroponte) and Boeotia in the Aegean Sea. The
Euripus off Taormina (line 11) is the Strait of Messina. See Pliny *Naturalis historia*
2.219.

lies between Phocis, a part of Boeotia, and the island of Euboea, recedes with
incredible velocity seven times in the course of a day and a night and flows   10
back seven times, and the Euripus off Taormina does this even oftener; and
it was this impetuous spirit that gave it its Greek name. How great and how
frequent have been the changes we have seen here these last few years in the
leading men of the two estates, both sacred and secular! What a hurricane
has shaken our Christian calling and what an upheaval has followed in the   15
world of learning! On top of that, what a cataclysm of evil in all its forms
seems to menace the world with its last day! Never would I at least have
believed any historian recounting such things as I both see and feel.

But let us leave the problem of warfare and religion to the control of
Christ himself. How prosperous within these few years has been the   20
flowering of the humanities! And at the same time how close we have come
to the sight of all liberal studies buried under barbarism once again
victorious! And none do them more serious harm than those who pursue
them for improper reasons. One can see shady scribblers springing up
everywhere, who have no sooner learned ten words of Latin and two of   25
Greek and half a dozen paradoxes but they write pert pamphlets and with
amazing self-assurance turn up their noses at authors hallowed by the
unanimous verdict of so many centuries – whether more ungrateful in this
or more ungodly I do not yet know. Anything stinks in their nostrils as
illiterate in which they do not find the half dozen paradoxes for which some   30
people now have a mad passion. We are of course to reject the masterpieces
of great authors, in order to read in their place the quarrelsome rubbish of
some noisy hack!

All this has made it a greater pleasure to work on my beloved Jerome,
that he who had seen the light of day polished and neat some time ago   35
should now appear with a higher polish still. In this volume there is nothing
of mine except the critical introductions. Nor should one despise at the
outset what is not Jerome's; for the first series[2] contains many things so
much worth reading that I am very glad they have survived, though falsely
given to him. In the third series I have found almost nothing that deserves to   40
have a godly and educated reader waste his time on it. Anyone who does not
accept my verdict has all the same no grounds to find fault with me. He has
here not only all that appeared in earlier editions by other editors, but much
that has been added, and he has them in better print and a more correct text
than ever before. As far as I am concerned every man is welcome to his own   45
opinion. Those with some critical powers have been warned; those who hate
to see anything omitted have not been given short measure.

* * * * *

2 For the three divisions of the contents, see Ep 396:324–36.

I pray it may be the will of the Lord Jesus that your old age, which is such a singular example of godliness, may equally be prosperous and long continued for the benefit of his church.

Basel, 10 October 1524

50

1505 / From Archduke Ferdinand   Vienna, 12 October 1524

The two surviving manuscripts are contemporary copies. One, which Allen thought might be a rough draft in the hand of Spiegel (see n4), is in the Stads-of Athenaeumbibliothek Deventer (MS 91, f 238). The other, a copy of the letter actually received, was made by one of Erasmus' servant-pupils and sent to Frans van Cranevelt (see Ep 1546). It is part of the Cranevelt collection discovered by Henry de Vocht at Louvain. The letter was first published in *Marquardi Gudii et doctorum virorum ad eum epistolae* ... ed Petrus Burmannus (Utrecht 1697). Erasmus' reply is Ep 1515.

FERDINAND, BY THE GRACE OF GOD PRINCE AND INFANTE OF SPAIN, ARCHDUKE OF AUSTRIA, DUKE OF BURGUNDY ETC, LIEUTENANT-GENERAL OF THE EMPIRE, TO DESIDERIUS ERASMUS, DOCTOR OF DIVINITY, GREETING

Honourable and well-beloved, if you infer from our silence that we have 5 forgotten you, you are mistaken. We do remember you, and rightly so, for you deserve to be thus far remembered and more also. If we address you but seldom, you are yourself responsible.[1] We do not choose to trespass[2] against the public good by interrupting your sacred labours, the results of which we read eagerly,[3] or listen eagerly as they are read to us. We have about us the 10 most zealous supporters of your reputation and your learned labours,[4] men in whose judgment we repose great trust. These men set before us all the books that you bring into the world, in the knowledge that, when such leisure permits as we can steal from public business, there is no one with whom we converse more readily than Erasmus. We do not hear from you of 15 heresies, of schism, and Antichrists, nor do we detect the flattery of which your detractors so shamelessly accuse you. We recognize instead that

* * * * *

1505
1 Possibly an allusion to Erasmus' refusal to visit Ferdinand earlier in the year; see Ep 1452:6–8.
2 Cf Horace *Epistles* 2.1.3.
3 Cf Ep 1369:260–1.
4 Such as Johannes Fabri (Ep 1382:28, n12) and Jakob Spiegel (Ep 1323 introduction), who composed this letter (lines 55–6 below).

well-known mildness and moderation of yours which truly follows Christ's decrees, and at the same time, when it is needed, the censor's rod, with which you demonstrate the character of truly Christian bishops and princes. 20 Since in so doing you use no subversive language, it is thought to be servile flattery of us, but no one thinks so except the most impious heretics, faithless apostates, and perfidious traitors. Remember that you are rightly subjected to the same treatment, not as kings and princes (for you must not think we wish to cry up our own order) but as your most sainted 25 predecessors among the Fathers; you have followed them at all points with the greatest success, and cannot but repeat their experience in this also. You know well the disgrace, the torments, and the agonies they suffered, and the false accusations more bitter than torment and death, until the day should come that relieved them of their sufferings. For this the reward of 30 their deeds is laid up for them in heaven.[5]

Hold on therefore and play the man, until like your own Paul you have finished your course.[6] We see in some passages that this is an end for which you long; but for our part we pray that it may be long delayed, that the authors and the teaching may be able to flourish which are closest to our 35 Christian profession. For you have not only given us corrected texts of several of the holy Fathers who fought successfully against the heresies of the infant church; this generation of ours also, which has been plunged into such misfortunes by the polluted leaders of heresy and thrown into confusion by revolutionaries, gets help from you as it does from few other 40 people (and their number grows less every day), in which you show clearly enough your Catholic sympathies and your views on what should be done. May Christ therefore long preserve you, and may he give us the opportunity of showing you some token of our good will. For if you have received anything in the past, it was to say the least very little in comparison with 45 what you deserve, nor was it given in return for any flattery on your part, such as these men ascribe to you quite falsely, but from the wish to encourage your religious researches for the common good. And today we offer you, not indeed the generous treatment you deserve, but such at least as is within our means. We look forward eagerly to Irenaeus,[7] and what else 50 we wish to see you do, you will learn from Froben.

* * * * *

5 Cf Matt 5:12.
6 2 Tim 4:7
7 Erasmus' edition of Irenaeus, not completed until August 1526, was dedicated to Ferdinand's minister Bernhard von Cles (Ep 1357).

Given in our city of Vienna, the twelfth day of the month of October AD 1524

Ferdinand

On instructions from his most serene Highness the archduke Ferdi-   55
nand, Jakob Spiegel

1506 / To Gian Matteo Giberti   Basel, 13 October 1524

There are two manuscript copies of this letter at the Vatican, one in the Archives (Arm 32, vol I, f 263) in a seventeenth-century hand, and another in the Library (Barb Lat 1499, ff 310–11), perhaps in the same hand. The letter was first published in Balan *Monumenta* I 380, using the first of the two manuscripts listed above.

On Giberti, see Ep 1443A.

DESIDERIUS ERASMUS TO GIAN MATTEO GIBERTI

Greeting, most honoured sir. I sent some time ago a book on the freedom of the will;[1] one is now in the press on the invocation of saints and some other topics.[2] For a long while they were attacking me furiously in frenzied pamphlets[3] and scandalous cartoons,[4] and now an even greater uproar has   5
been started. No one would believe how widely the evil has spread and spreads every day, nor can I fail to see what friends I have lost and what enemies I have provoked.[5] In fact, an upheaval of the most violent description seems to threaten us, and I know not in which direction it will break out. Yet I would endure anything rather than join that conspiracy.[6] I   10
do not doubt that his Holiness will show the same feeling towards me that he promises in his brief;[7] in return, my handling of this business will be such as may make all men understand that to the utmost of my power I have not failed the Catholic church. My book on the freedom of the will has already produced a change of heart in many people who had been wholly   15
committed to the Lutheran view. Pray take every opportunity to increase the

* * * * *

1506
1 With Ep 1481
2 *Modus orandi Deum* (Ep 1502)
3 See Ep 1481 n11.
4 Ep 1477B:31–7
5 A veiled reference to Erasmus' appeal against Baechem (Ep 1481:67–78)
6 Cf Epp 1433:14, 1477:33, 1481:28, 1528:49.
7 Ep 1443B

Holy Father's support for me by your recommendation; for if he deserts me, I have simply exposed myself to be torn in pieces by mad dogs. But Christ, as I hope, will help me; and I rely on the Holy Father to serve his glory in sincerity of heart.   20

I wished at first that this split, which is more dangerous than many people realize, might be healed by a policy of moderation; but now I see that some of the ringleaders of this evil thing have no purpose in view but universal chaos. Thus mere necessity will compel the princes to restrain sedition by force. In this I have good hopes that our Clement in his wisdom   25 will contrive that we do not, as so often happens, while trying to remedy one evil fall into another. You know how many men are wicked by nature, and hope of the spoils can very easily induce them to bring false accusations against the innocent; you know how many are driven to do the same by private malignity and a passion for revenge. We must not open a window for   30 these men so that they can pounce upon the innocent under the shadow of the pope's authority, choosing their victims on some flimsy pretext as they please. Such a thing would embitter the bad feeling aroused against the papacy, while it is important that its popularity should be great and universal, and I myself do all I can to make it more acceptable. We have a   35 plentiful supply of people who by deed and word and in print profess themselves enemies of the Holy See, without proceeding against those who are either innocent or look as though they could easily be cured.

These warnings, my excellent friend, are a waste of your time, maybe; but take my word for it, they are not unfounded. I wish your lordship all   40 felicity under Christ our Saviour. Basel, 13 October 1524

Desiderius Erasmus of Rotterdam, with my own hand

1507 / To Conradus Goclenius   Basel, 13 October 1524

This letter was first published in the *Vita Des. Erasmi* (Ep 1388 introduction). On Goclenius, see Ep 1209.

ERASMUS OF ROTTERDAM TO CONRADUS GOCLENIUS, PROFESSOR OF LATIN IN BUSLEYDEN COLLEGE[1]

Goclenius, my learned friend, Franz Birckmann the Antwerp bookseller[2]

* * * * *

1507
1 Ie, the Collegium Trilingue at Louvain
2 Ep 1362 n1. For recent complaints about his conduct, see Ep 1388 n23.

owes me, among other things, thirteen gold florins,[3] which he deducted
from a sum he was due to pay Froben on my behalf, the pretext for the   5
deduction being that on instructions from me he had supplied books of that
value to Guy Morillon.[4] A letter from Guy[5] however makes it quite clear that
not one page has reached either Guy himself or his wife.[6] I therefore transfer
this sum to you and appoint you his creditor in my place, and am ready to
indemnify you in writing if he puts up any opposition. For the facts on this   10
are beyond all controversy. In witness whereof I have written the enclosed
document with my own hand and sealed it with my seal.

Basel, 13 October 1524

I, Erasmus of Rotterdam, hereby testify that Franz Birckmann,
bookseller, owes me thirteen florins, which he deducted from a sum due in   15
my account with Froben in respect of books which he states that he had
supplied to Guy Morillon, although not a single sheet had been delivered,
and also of seven Tertullians[7] or the price thereof, which he received from
Froben and did not convey to me. These facts he himself admitted to me
personally, nor could he deny them, since he stands to be confuted by the   20
evidence of the two Frobens, and by a letter from Morillon which I have
shown him and of which I have sent a copy to Nicolaas van Broeckhoven.[8]
The right to recover this debt I hereby transfer to Jan van Campen,[9]
professor of Hebrew at Louvain. In fuller testimony whereof I have written
this with my own hand and sealed it with my seal.   25

4 October 1525. In Basel

1508 / To the Town Council of Basel

This letter has been assigned a new date and appears above as Ep 1477A.

* * * * *

3 In all likelihood, Rhenish gold florins again, with a value of about £3 3s gros
  Flemish. Given the reference to the Antwerp bookseller, however, the new
  Burgundian-Hapsburg Carolus florins may have been meant here; if so, a sum
  worth only £2 5s 6d gros Flemish. By 1526 Erasmus had abandoned his effort to
  recover the money; Allen Ep 1666:23–6.
4 Ep 1287
5 Not extant, but see Ep 1431:4–7.
6 Elisabeth de Mil (d 1552). During Morillon's absence in Spain, she would have
  been the recipient of any delivery.
7 Apparently copies of Beatus Rhenanus' edition (Basel: Froben, July 1521)
8 Ep 1431:5–7
9 Ep 1257 n12

1509 / From Gian Matteo Giberti   Rome, 19 October 1524

This letter, Giberti's reply to Ep 1481, was first published by Förstemann/
Günther (Ep 30), using a contemporary copy in the Burscher Collection at
Leipzig (Ep 1254 introduction). The Vatican Archives have the autograph
rough draft of the end of the letter starting in the middle of line 34 (Particolari
154, f 53).

The failure of Giberti to make any reference to Erasmus' appeal concerning
Baechem in Ep 1481:67ff indicates that no decision in the matter had as yet been
made in Rome. It was not until July 1525 that a mandate silencing Erasmus'
detractors was dispatched to Louvain; see Ep 1589.

Greeting, reverend sir. After I had both received and answered[1] your earlier
letter,[2] a second arrived, dated 2 September, with a copy of the first, and in it
I recognized not only the brilliance of style which is so notable in all you
write but also your remarkable affection for me. Every letter that you write is
like this: you always show yourself my loving friend, and I must of necessity   5
increase (if that were possible) and redouble my affection for you. I offered
your book[3] to our most holy Father, and while the author's popularity would
alone be enough to commend it, it had all its other qualities to ensure it the
warmest of welcomes: the style, the religious feeling, the wisdom and – not
to list them all – your other merits. He appreciates your virtues and is well   10
aware of your labours, and so it will not be long, given a suitable
opportunity, before he does something to secure you the resources and
dignity that you deserve.

You mention the privileges of Louvain university.[4] I am sorry you had
not heard the news of what really happened for, fair-minded as you are, you   15
would have decided that Clement has dealt with this, as you wish, in the
spirit that his name suggests. Almost everyone in your part of the world,
even including the princes, was opposed to the claims of Louvain, and
urged with great force not only that Clement should make no concessions
but that what had been conceded by Adrian and not yet issued should be   20
suppressed; but his Holiness, anxious to do what is best for everyone and to
hurt no one, adopted a middle course, and left Adrian's benefaction to

* * * * *

1509
1 This reply is not extant.
2 Not extant, sent by Filonardi; see Ep 1481:3.
3 *De libero arbitrio*, sent with Ep 1481
4 Ep 1481:53–66

Louvain intact. Indeed, with the one exception of the cardinal of Liège, he
has increased rather than reduced it. Thus our Holy Father in person has
paid more attention to that famous university, a nursery of the liberal arts   25
and brilliant with the name of Erasmus, than to its opponents, many and
great though they were.

The representatives of Louvain seemed at the time to accept this
decision quite happily, and I wish they had written to tell you of his
Holiness' sincere good will towards them, and of my own readiness to help.   30
I think, my dear Erasmus, that had you been here, you would have felt as I
did, and would not have wished to ask for anything different from the
concession that was actually made.

I write of this at perhaps needless length, but the reason mainly is that I
found you more concerned on behalf of Louvain than a man would be who   35
had heard what had happened. As I should wish my own actions and my
influence among us here to ensure that you always get what you want, I am
inevitably in some distress when an opportunity arises to do something for
you unless I either grasp it eagerly or, if it eludes me, can show some good
reason for my refusal and give you complete satisfaction, as my affection for   40
you demands. Farewell.

Your man Hovius,[5] if he asks me for anything within my power, will
find that a recommendation from you has great weight with me.

Rome, 19 October 1524

Your sincere friend Gian Matteo, bishop elect of Verona   45

1510 / To Antoine Brugnard   Basel, 27 October 1524

This letter was first published in the *Opus epistolarum*. On Brugnard, see Ep
1318.

ERASMUS OF ROTTERDAM TO ANTOINE BRUGNARD IN
MONTBÉLIARD, GREETING

You give me to understand that you have written to me four times.[1] The first
letter reached me, and the last; the two middle ones I have not had, so pray
do not write except by couriers you can really trust. Your feelings towards   5

* * * * *

5 Ep 1387 n3

1510

1 Unless Ep 1318, despite the lapse of time, is one of the four letters, none of
   them is extant.

me are most gratefully acknowledged. In Besançon[2] I had nothing in the way of an unpleasant dispute, nor did I feel that anyone was against me. I was depressed when I left because my health was really bad. Even so, that rumour you report,[3] when it reached here, cheered up several keen Lutherans surprisingly.   10

What Phallicus[4] is teaching in your part of the world, or what he is up to, I do not know. How I wish he would practise what he preaches! – for he purports to preach the gospel. But I have never seen a man with such arrogant self-confidence, so insanely abusive, such a shameless liar; in a word, I found him the type of man whom I should be sorry to have as either   15 friend or enemy. The Lutherans themselves could not endure his insatiable scurrility. Oecolampadius often protested, even by a letter,[5] and so did Pellicanus,[6] but it did no good; he is too far gone.

I have never argued with him, but I have broken up an argument in which he was at loggerheads with certain other people, because I wanted to   20 protest and ask why he had called me Balaam[7] – a taunt cast at me by a businessman called Du Blet,[8] which pleased Phallicus so much that he constantly referred to me as Balaam, though nobody has yet been able to get me to accept a farthing on the understanding that I would write against Luther.[9] So I wished to learn why the man had taken it into his head to think   25 I deserved the name. The other abuse he poured out at me every day I had

* * * * *

2 In April; see Ep 1440 n4.
3 See Ep 1534:19–20.
4 Guillaume Farel (Epp 1341A n305, 1496:72–3, 145ff), who was now in Mont-béliard (Ep 1522 n23). For another account of his recent actions, see *Epistola ad fratres Inferiores Germaniae* (1530) ASD IX-1 394–6. Cf the following two sentences with Epp 1483:8–10, 1495:15–17, 1496:68–73, 1497:9–10.
5 In the *Epistola ad fratres* (see preceding note) Erasmus states that an informant in Oecolampadius' household had told him of the latter's efforts to persuade Farel to be less violent; ASD IX-1 394:447–396:451. Moreover, two letters dated 3 and 19 August 1524, in which Oecolampadius urged Farel to restrain his intemperate outbursts, survive (Herminjard Epp 111, 115; BAO nos 208, 212). The informant in Oecolampadius' household was probably Pierre Toussain (Ep 1481 introduction) and it is entirely possible that Toussain revealed to Erasmus the contents of Oecolampadius' letters just as he had revealed to Farel the contents of Ep 1481. See Herminjard Ep 126 nn4–5.
6 Ep 1341A n309
7 See Ep 1341A n306. Erasmus was deeply angered by this taunt, which led to the confrontation described here (lines 19–45) and in Ep 1341A:1196–1215. See also Ep 1496:156 and ASD IX-1 396:452–7 (n4 above).
8 Ep 1341A n307
9 Cf Ep 1477:26–7.

Guillaume Farel
Anonymous portrait
Bibliothèque Publique de la Ville de Neuchâtel

ignored. Our skirmish lasted barely ten words. I asked him why he thought it wrong to invoke the saints; was it because there was nothing expressly about it in Scripture? He said yes. I told him to produce clear evidence out of Scripture that it was right to invoke the Holy Spirit. 'If he is God,' he said, 'it 30 must be right to invoke him.' I urged him to demonstrate this from Scripture, assuring him two or three times that I was speaking for the sake of argument, for on this point, I said, we were in complete agreement on the facts. My only object was to show up his incomplete inference, by which he tried to demonstrate that the reason why we should not invoke the saints 35 was that this could not be proved out of Scripture. He produced the passage from that Epistle of John 'And these three are one.'[10] I replied that that passage was thinking not of their having the same nature but of their bearing the same witness, and what follows about blood, water, and spirit can bear no other interpretation. Besides which, that part about the Father, the 40 Word, and the Spirit[11] was not to be found in old days in the ancient manuscripts,[12] nor is it quoted by the principal opponents of the Arians, Athanasius for instance and Cyril and Hilary. We soon broke off our discussion, for night was coming on, and I protested to him as I left, though briefly. 45

On this subject he wrote the most boastful letters to his friends,[13] one of which was sent me from Constance. In this there are sometimes ten consecutive lines without one syllable of truth in them. He was unable to prove that the Holy Spirit is called God, although this can be proved out of Paul; and yet even if he had proved it, he would not have defeated me. It is 50 no personal view of mine that the saints should be invoked,[14] though people are fools who take a tradition which dates back to the first beginnings of the church and is godly in itself, and make an uproar trying to expel it. Had I known him then to be the sort of man I later discovered from experience, I should never have agreed to address a word to him, and if I had met him by 55 chance I should have avoided him. Some men are such sinister figures that even to meet them contributes to one's bad luck. Hence I fear that some great

* * * * *

10 1 John 5:7–8 as found in the Vulgate and the AV. Cf the same passage in the RSV.

11 Ie, verse 7

12 Several years earlier, this perfectly correct assertion had caused an uproar among conservative theologians because it seemed to undermine a standard text in the defence against Arianism. Both Lee (Ep 765) and Zúñiga (Ep 1260 n36) attacked Erasmus on this point. See Erika Rummel Erasmus' 'Annotations' on the New Testament (Toronto 1986) 132–4.

13 Cf Ep 1496:145–8.

14 This is one of the matters discussed in the Modus orandi Deum (Ep 1502).

evil may threaten your city, now that a bird of such ill omen has winged his way to you.

He has made a successful escape from his native France, but he left 60 behind him here a book of exceptional scurrility;[15] he did not in fact put his name to it, but the author is loudly and universally said to be Phallicus. He has also written, they say, another in French which is an attack on me,[16] but it is lurking in the hands of his fellow conspirators. The authorities in Basel[17] are keeping an eye open to see if they can identify the printer.[18] A carver of 65 images from Lorraine[19] boasted about this in Lyon. He also brought with him some of Phallicus' remarks: one was that Froben's wife knows more theology than Erasmus, and another 'I would rather die a martyr's death daily' (this is Phallicus speaking) 'than fail to damage Erasmus' reputation wherever I can.'[20] To Phallicus I shall easily become a great theologian, if I 70 cram in all the time that the pope is Antichrist, that decisions handed down by men are heretical, ceremonies are an abomination, and more of the same sort. He developed this anger at my expense because in my *Spongia* I throw doubt on Luther's spirit;[21] besides which I have stated that certain mean men of immoral life parade under the name of the gospel;[22] and as for promising 75 Adrian a plan for extinguishing the Lutheran conflagration to such a tune that it will not easily be rekindled,[23] Phallicus takes this to mean that I wish to extinguish the gospel. I on the other hand was thinking of excising the sources of this trouble. And on this topic I have written to Adrian, and also to Clement, to Cardinal Campeggi, and to the emperor;[24] but, as far as I can 80 see, they prefer to use those commonplace remedies, fetters and faggots.

Meanwhile the trouble spreads everyday. What the end will be is in God's hand; personally I have always tried as far as I could to restrain the princes from cruelty, except in cases of subversion. Whatever these men teach, it is not the gospel, and their way of teaching sometimes stirs up 85

* * * * *

15 See Ep 1477A n6.
16 See Ep 1477A:3–4.
17 See Ep 1477A introduction.
18 Cratander for the Latin work at least; Ep 1477A n6
19 See Ep 1477A n1.
20 Cf Ep 1477A:22–3.
21 ASD IX-1 163:991–2, 182:437–8
22 In lines 12–13 of Ep 1445, the contents of which were evidently no secret (see Ep 1501:54–8); again in Ep 1341A:1114–15, 1194–6 (ie, the second edition of the *Catalogus lucubrationum*, September 1524); and frequently thereafter (see especially Ep 1496:66ff).
23 Ep 1352
24 For the letters listed here, see Ep 1496:59–66.

subversion, not the gospel. I am on the side of the gospel; but that gospel of theirs I shall never adhere to, unless I have seen different evangelists and a different crowd from what I see hitherto. Scandalous pamphlets come flying out anonymously, and Phallicus approves of them, and all the rest applaud, as though lying and lawbreaking were proper defences for the gospel, and as though the purpose of the gospel were to provide a cloak for sin without penalty. After this they will break into our strong-boxes and say, 'This is how the children of Israel spoiled the Egyptians.' The crime once committed, they will invent some new doctrine. If Luther knew Phallicus, I don't doubt he would unsheath his pen against him. And these are the men who tell us so proudly that they possess the spirit of the gospel. For my part, I know not what Christ's intentions are, but to put the most fitting interpretation on it, I suspect that his plan is to use these monsters to make the priests, who are drunk with the good things of this world and are now sound asleep, wake up. And yet all the ranting and the calumnies, as vain as they are false, that I have hitherto suffered from Phallicus will easily be forgiven, because the man is sick, if only he will behave in future in a way more fitting for a herald of the gospel.

But more than enough of this nonsense; more on another occasion when I have the leisure. I have done a deal with this vintner for three half-casks, one of old wine and two of new. The wine which the dean[25] bought did me a world of good, and so ever since I started drinking it I have been free from the stone. It is now said to have disappeared. Could you please help me and have some sent, a fine wine that is suitable for my digestion; I'm not concerned about the price, if it is the sort of wine I want. Old, provided it's free from acid; young, if it's mature; not sweet, not rough, moderately heating, a light ruby in colour. The vintner has a pretty good idea of the sort I like. Farewell.

Basel, eve of SS Simon and Jude, 1524

1511 / From Jacopo Sadoleto   Rome, 6 November 1524

The autograph rough draft of this letter, which was first published in the *Opus epistolarum*, is in the Vatican Archives (Arm 45, vol 42, f 17).

Jacopo Sadoleto of Ferrara, 1477–1547, was educated in his home town and in Rome, where he became an accomplished humanist scholar. His appoint-

* * * * *

25 Nikolaus von Diesbach, who introduced Erasmus to Burgundy wine (Ep 1258 n17); or possibly Antoine Montrivel, dean at Montbéliard (Allen Ep 1610:102–3), whom Erasmus had met on his visit to Burgundy the previous spring (Ep 1440 n4)

ment by Leo x to the apostolic secretariat in 1513 launched his career in the curia. Shortly before the sack of Rome in 1527 he fled to his bishopric of Carpentras in southern France, where he not only became a zealously reforming bishop but also found time for productive scholarship. In 1536 Pope Paul III called him to Rome to work on the Commission of Nine that produced the *Consilium de emendanda ecclesia* (1537). In 1542 and 1545 he was summoned to Rome again, the first time to assist in the preparations for the Council of Trent and the second time to participate in the council itself.

Erasmus and Sadoleto did not always see eye to eye on the best way to deal with Lutheran heretics or Catholic conservatives. The curia's policies for dealing with Luther, in the execution of which Sadoleto was necessarily involved, drew Erasmus' criticism, and Erasmus' vigorous assaults on the conservative Catholic theologians were a source of dismay to Sadoleto. Nevertheless, no member of the curia during the pontificates of Leo x and Clement VII was a more consistent advocate and defender of Erasmus than Sadoleto, which earned him the wrath of Aleandro (Ep 1256 n11), among others. Although Sadoleto had drafted and signed several friendly papal briefs to Erasmus (Epp 338, 1180, 1443B), this is the first surviving letter in their personal correspondence.

JACOPO SADOLETO, BISHOP OF CARPENTRAS, TO ERASMUS OF
ROTTERDAM, GREETING

It was a pleasure to read your letter[1] – so simple and open-hearted, so full of devotion towards God and respect for our truly supreme and admirable pontiff, who is entirely disposed to do all he can for you. And I am grateful to 5 Bonifacius,[2] who is a very excellent young man and a good scholar, for supplying you with a reason for writing to me and me with a reason for answering. I had the warm feelings for you demanded by your outstanding qualities, but they were pent up in my heart and even now would not have forced their way out into actuality had not Bonifacius, playing the part of a 10 true friend, established the contact between us which has led to this exchange of greetings in pen and ink.

The pope would have shown himself more generous to you,[3] had not he too found himself in straitened circumstances in these very difficult

* * * * *

1511
1 Probably of the same date as the letters (Ep 1481–3) sent to Rome with copies of *De libero arbitrio*. Cf n5 below.
2 Amerbach (Ep 408). For the matter referred to and Amerbach's role in it, see Ep 1519 introduction.
3 See Ep 1443B n5.

times;[4] such is the universal confusion and the daily outflow of funds on   15
costs and expenses that he has difficulty in making both ends meet. But
there will one day be an opportunity to give you the honour and the rewards
that you deserve.

Your book I have not yet read;[5] I have not yet had access to it so far, and
I was hindered by an exceptionally heavy load of business. Even so, I am   20
sure it will be like your other things, many of which I have both read and
enjoyed. I am delighted for your sake that with your outstanding and very
special gifts you should have found the leisure which makes it easily
possible for you to publish for the benefit of posterity those monuments of
your scholarship which will make your name immortal.   25

And so if, as you say in your letter, you are a failure in this world and
only God can make you happy, I accept this as true piety and give it high
praise; what I cannot accept is that you should call yourself a failure, when
your distinction will be remembered in the undying tradition of all time to
come. Such a prize is of far less value than the rewards of heaven, but there is   30
no call for you to despise it. For my own part, if I have any authority and
influence – and what I have amounts to very little – I promise it all and
pledge it to your service; and so, if anything needs to be done on your behalf,
my good will and my efforts will be most readily at your disposal. Farewell.

6 November 1524, from the City   35

1512 / To Rudbert von Mosham   Basel, 12 November 1524

First published in the *Opus epistolarum*, this is Erasmus' response to Ep 1450.

ERASMUS OF ROTTERDAM TO RUDBERT VON MOSHAM, DEAN OF
PASSAU IN BAVARIA, GREETING

I retain a very clear recollection of your features, which reflect so well your
generous nature; I remember too our frequent talks and your personal
kindnesses, and I have not forgotten the short work on hunting which you   5
translated, in my opinion at least, most felicitously. Indeed you stand out so
clearly and completely in my mind's eye that I could even paint a portrait of
you in full colour. The only point I do not remember is the interest I am
supposed to have taken in calling on the cardinal-bishop of Gurk. I do not
look down on the bishops of the church, but, being the sort of person I am,   10
there is nothing which would interest me less than paying that sort of call,

* * * * *

4 News of the French reoccupation of Milan (see Ep 1342 n31) had reached Rome
  on 6 October, causing great consternation; Pastor IX 265.
5 Presumably *De libero arbitrio*; see n1 above.

especially when I am in Germany. If on this occasion I acted frivolously, then clearly I must have done so out of deference for your feelings. If I got nothing from the meeting, that would not trouble me very much. Every day I am called on by men of the lowest sort who, even when they have extorted   15 money from me, make fun of me and ridicule me before their drunken friends. I have no reason, however, to complain about the cardinal: he showed me more civility than I expected.

Whether it is unusual for German princes to send anyone away unrewarded is a question for others to explore. Speaking for myself, I was   20 certainly not offended by such novel and unfamiliar treatment – though I do recall the occasion when I paid my respects to Frederick, duke of Saxony, and the following day[1] Georgius Spalatinus arrived when I was still lying in bed and presented me with some linen cloth, although I never dreamt of any such thing. To make it easier for you to believe what I am saying, let me   25 remind you that I spent three weeks in Cologne[2] and never called on any German prince during all that time. I want to help all men so far as I can, but to be no man's slave. But if one has to be a slave, it is my experience that there is more arrogance in a single German printer than in ten English or French bishops. But the lack of trust and gratitude[3] which I find so   30 widespread does not diminish my affection one iota for my real German friends. I tell you this so that you won't imagine that my friendship for you has cooled for any reason.

You observe what generous references I have made to my friends in my books, more, I admit, out of respect for their attachment to me than in   35 response to my own judgment. You see also how few of these have remained friends and how many have turned into enemies. The failing of the latter, however, do not weigh so heavily with me that I am any the less fond of Willibald and the rest of my true friends. As for the fact that I made no mention of you in my letter, in the first place I remembered everything   40 about you except your name! And secondly there was no suitable occasion to mention you. Some people prefer not to be mentioned in my works and I sometimes take heed of their protests. I approve your freeing yourself from the service of the court, all the more so since you have taken this step early. I shall make sure that you will have no reason in future to be jealous of   45 Laurinus or Willibald, if 'jealousy' is the right word to use. I have known

* * * * *

1512
1 6 November 1520, during Erasmus' sojourn in Cologne with the imperial court; see Ep 1155 introduction.
2 See Ep 1450 n4.
3 See Ep 1388 n21.

Laurinus since he was a boy,[4] and I have received more enlightenment from
Willibald than I have passed on to him. I appreciate very much your advice
to act boldly – though I have been doing so of my own accord. It grieves me
deeply that the cause of the gospel and of the humanities is being ruined by   50
the folly of a few. I was delighted to have my memories of Bishop Ernest
rekindled by your letter.

   If the physician Antonin of Košice delivers this, please get to know
him. When you know him, I am sure you will like him. His departure made
me very sad.[5] Farewell.
                                                                                    55
   Basel, 12 November 1524

1513 / From Juan Luis Vives   London, 13 November 1524

For the source of this letter, see Ep 1256 introduction. On Vives, see Ep 1362.

VIVES TO ERASMUS

Those people have made a professional wrestler of you, whether you would
or no. But you overthrow your antagonist in such style that the spectators
can see you are letting a man off lightly whom you could have laid
completely flat, and this was as it should be, to prevent the other side   5
claiming the victory – and applause from them would mean laments for the
rest of the world. Your book on the freedom of the will was handed to the
king yesterday,[1] and he read several pages of it between services and
showed signs of being very much pleased with it. He says he will read it
through. He showed me a passage with which he says he is particularly   10
delighted, where you discourage mortal men from exploring too intensely
the secrets of the divine majesty.[2] The queen[3] too is quite devoted to you as a
result of this same book and even the same passage in it, and instructed me
to send you greetings on her behalf and to say at the same time how grateful
she is that, though a great man and preparing to speak on a major subject,   15
you should have lowered your style and dealt with the topic in such an
unambitious way. What the king wants you to write by way of a

* * * * *

4 Erasmus may have met Laurinus (b 1488) as early as 1502 in Louvain.
5 Ep 1341A:1821–4 and n425

   1513
1 See Ep 1493.
2 LB IX 1216C
3 Catherine of Aragon (1485–1536)

commentary on the Psalms[4] you will learn from Mountjoy,[5] whom the king instructed to write specially; at the same time he gave me to understand how much he would value a talk with you. On this he has no doubt spoken with   20
More; for More is with him constantly and in high favour, as you will learn from his letter.[6] How happy the state of literature would be if only this storm had not broken! And what a rash and enthusiastic man you have for your new opponent![7] While he enjoys showing off and being clever and the delights of making a name for himself, it is easy to say what harm he has   25
done to the excellent cause which had brought him into the field to start with, so that he has not only lost all plausibility himself but has used a ready-made unpopularity as a defence against all those who have dared to complain of anything wrong in the better things he said before.

I am delighted to hear you have revised Jerome's letters,[8] for there   30
were some slips of memory in them; for instance, in your letter to me,[9] Publius the mime-writer put for Decimus Laberius,[10] another member of the same profession. But who, though he detected this, would not overlook it? – With such erudition as you display and such a record of brilliant and scholarly writing. I should like to see everything you write so accurate that   35
Momus[11] himself could find no handle for complaint; but when I correct you, I myself feel I am being corrected, or admonished rather, like the people who admonished Cato.[12]

Linacre has departed this life,[13] to the great sorrow of all the learned. He wished them all well, and was their sincere supporter; and his opinion of   40
a man's gifts and scholarship carried more weight with him than a suspicion of possible disagreements – you understand in a word. His book on the

* * * * *

4 Possibly a continuation of the series already begun, in part at King Henry's urging; see Ep 1341A:774–80. See also Ep 1535.
5 Ep 1531:15 indicates that Mountjoy (Ep 79) did not write immediately, if at all.
6 Not extant
7 Erasmus was puzzled by this reference and thought that Brunfels might have been intended; Ep 1531:17–18. Another possibility would be Erasmus Alber (Ep 1466 n19).
8 See Ep 1465.
9 Not extant, but doubtless contemporary with Ep 1486–94 and carried by Lieven Algoet; see Ep 1486 n10.
10 See Ep 1481 n4.
11 God of mockery and censure
12 The reference is to the younger Cato (95–46 BC), whose reputation for moral severity was so great that his critics felt embarrassed about criticizing him. See the amusing story told by Pliny in *Epistles* 3.12.
13 Thomas Linacre (Ep 118:27n) died on 20 October 1524.

improvement of syntax is being published;[14] he makes honourable mention of you in it,[15] in a way that will show that he had great respect as well as affection for you.

Franz Birckmann[16] had asked me to revise my books,[17] which he said he wished to be printed by Froben; but now I have heard in a letter that he is making some sort of excuses, and that Froben is too busy. I am sorry for you, who have so often had to do business with a man like that; you were thinking of him, I suspect, when you wrote about lying in your *Colloquia*.[18] I must find someone else, so that I am not forced to lose my temper quite so often with this man after he has let me down. If Froben is willing to take my things for printing, I shall gladly send them to him, provided Franz has nothing to do with it; otherwise, you must please find another man. And I am surprised that so few books by the ancients come out now that are printed in Germany. These things written either for Luther or against him have put all thought for other kinds of literature out of the heads of the reading public, such is the pleasure they get from watching this struggle. Farewell, dear master.

London, 13 November 1524

1514 / To Caspar Ursinus Velius   Basel, 14 November 1524

The only source for this letter, which was first published by Allen, is a manuscript copy in a collection of documents from Wrocław (see Ep 850 introduction) that is now in the Bayerische Staatsbibliothek Munich (Clm 965, page 347). On Ursinus, see Ep 1280A. His reply is Ep 1557.

ERASMUS OF ROTTERDAM TO CASPAR VELIUS, GREETING
I learn in a letter from my friend Landau[1] that you are teaching the

* * * * *

14 *De emendata structura Latini sermonis* (London: Pynson, December 1524)
15 Erasmus had made honourable mention of Linacre in volume I of the 1516 edition of Jerome; see Ep 350:18–19. Linacre now returned the compliment by placing Erasmus in the company of Plato, Virgil, and Budé; f 54 verso.
16 Ep 1388 n23
17 The *Opuscula* (Ep 927 introduction), *Declamationes* (Ep 1082 introduction), *Somnium* (Ep 1108 n28), and *Veritas fucata, sive de licentia poetica, quantum poetis liceat a veritate abscedere* (Louvain: Dirk Martens, January 1523). Froben had published an edition of the *Somnium* in March 1521.
18 In *Pseudochei et Philetymi* 'The Liar and the Man of Honour,' first published in Froben's edition of August 1523; cf Ep 1531:49, Allen Ep 1560:13–14.

1514
1 Jakob Ziegler (Ep 1260). The letter is not extant.

humanities in Vienna on a large salary,[2] and I send my best wishes for your success. You have an elegant sphere of operations, of which you used to give me a good account.[3] Thanks to these new gospellers of ours the humanities are out in the cold more or less everywhere, and we must use every effort to assist them. You will do so with all your might, and I with what little might an old man has. I hear things are none too peaceful even in your part of the world. I am held here in a state of siege, pitifully longing to move somewhere else.[4] I was kept out of Italy by severe threats of plague,[5] for I had intended to winter in Venice. From France I am debarred by these crazy wars,[6] though I have long had an invitation with generous offers.[7] Brabant has much about it to frighten a man who longs to be left alone,[8] and yet it looks as though I might have to go back there.[9] If you have read my *Diatribe*,[10] you will have seen, I expect, that your friend Erasmus has left the band and turned gladiator; such is my destiny. Mind you let me know how you are getting on.

Here is something to make you smile. Your old favourite Michael Bentinus[11] is revisiting his native land. He wandered round from one schoolmaster to another, instilling the teaching of our new gospel into the children: the pope is Antichrist, his decisions are heretical, and so on – you know the form. Luckily for him he made his escape, or he would have been arrested. He is now back here in high spirits, and has married a wife. Now he waits for an invitation to some small town in France where he can preach his gospel. He is working for Valentinus,[12] and being as much of a nuisance to Froben as he can. Farewell, my dear Velius.

Basel, 14 November 1524

* * * * *

2 Ursinus had just been appointed to the chair of rhetoric at Vienna.
3 During his visit to Basel in November–December 1521; Epp 1243, 1252 n1
4 Cf Epp 1316 introduction, 1353 n33.
5 See Ep 1478 n8.
6 See Ep 1369 n12.
7 See Epp 1434, 1439, 1446.
8 See Ep 1434:45ff.
9 Ie, in order to obtain his imperial annuity; see Epp 1434, 1470.
10 *De libero arbitrio* (Epp 1419, 1481)
11 Ep 1433 n2
12 Valentinus Curio (Schaffner) of Haguenau (documented 1516–32) was one of the leading printers at Basel, specializing in Greek grammars and lexicons but also publishing pamphlets critical of the church of Rome.

1515 / To Archduke Ferdinand Basel, 20 November 1524

The manuscript of this letter, which was first published in the *Opus epistolarum*, is an autograph rough draft in the Royal Library at Copenhagen (MS G.K.S.95 Fol, f 243). It is Erasmus' response to Ep 1505.

TO FERDINAND, BROTHER OF THE EMPEROR CHARLES

Greeting, most illustrious prince. Your Highness' sympathetic encouragement, of which I have concrete experience,[1] is something which, even if your most kind letter had not provided fresh evidence of it, I should never be allowed to forget by the many men who speak of it and also by the letters 5 from scholars from which I daily learn of your Highness' generous interest in my researches. Never shall I regret my nightly vigils, now that so great a prince thinks the results are worthy of his eye and ear; and I only wish that they deserved their good fortune.

The scurrility of the Lutherans I can easily despise; but it is hard to be 10 the target of stone-throwing from both sides. Besides the others there is in Louvain a Carmelite called Nicolaas Baechem,[2] a blockhead and a lunatic, as everybody knows. In the lecture-room, at the dinner-table, and in the pulpit he does not cease to attack me with all the rubbish that comes into his head. The educated laugh at him, but not all members of the public are aware of his 15 disease. Pope Adrian had sent an official brief to silence him,[3] but on the pope's death he is once more in a frenzy.[4] If you ask the reason for his hostility, the man hates the ancient languages and the humanities worse than ten Luthers; and the College of the Three Tongues, which now flourishes in Louvain and is a great benefit and ornament to all the 20 emperor's dominions, is seen by him as my responsibility. Hence all these tears.[5] The emperor is far away.[6] If your Highness would ask the illustrious Lady Margaret[7] in a word or two to tell this noisy rascal by her authority to be silent, it would be a very great blessing to myself and of no less advantage to the public peace. Although when it suits him no man's authority carries any 25

* * * * *

1515
1 In Ep 1343, acknowledging the dedication of the paraphrase on John; see Ep 1341A:1738–41.
2 Ep 1254 n6
3 See Ep 1359:2–3 with n1.
4 Cf Ep 1466:14–15 with n7.
5 *Adagia* I iii 68; cf Ep 1258:8, where the reference to the adage was omitted.
6 In Spain. He would not return to the Empire until 1530.
7 Margaret of Austria, regent of the Netherlands (Ep 1380)

Beginning of the autograph rough draft of a letter from Erasmus
to Archduke Ferdinand, Ep 1515
The Royal Library, Copenhagen, MS Gl.kgl.S.95 Fol, f 243 recto

weight. He is made a laughing-stock, and has never learned to be ashamed. He is given orders, and ignores them. He is rebuked, and this makes him more savage. For such a creature there is no treatment but a good sound beating.

As in great storms the management of rudder and sails is then most difficult, so in these days of universal confusion it is hard to maintain the moderation which your Highness thinks I show.[8] At least I have tried in all this business to keep my conscience clear in the sight of Jesus Christ. Every day I beseech him in my prayers continually to increase and prosper your outstanding gifts and at the same time to grant you the tranquillity which your virtues deserve, that under these two brothers, the most sublime spectacle that for many centuries the world has had to show, prosperity may await the Christian religion, the study of honourable subjects, and the public peace, all of which seem to me to be in peril in the great crisis through which we are passing. There is an ancient saying that evil counsel hurts the counsellor most;[9] but in such great upheavals I think it hardly safe even to give good counsel. This business of Luther is very widely spread, and pushes further every day. And so I fear that the common remedies of public recantation, prison, and faggot will not get us very far.

On this subject I had made representations to his invincible Majesty,[10] your illustrious Highness' brother, through Glapion.[11] To Pope Adrian I had done the same.[12] I did the same to Clement[13] and his legate Campeggi.[14] If certain things were changed, which could be changed with no loss to religion and no violent disturbance of the public peace, and if this were done on the authority of popes, bishops, and princes, the world I believe would begin to listen and there would be hope that concord would gradually return. As it is, both parties hold on tooth and nail to what they have. And I fear there are some in both parties who set their own advantage above the cause of Christ. I for my part am not one of those who in this most perilous of all questions dare give advice to the most powerful monarchs; but at least I do what I can. I pray God continually to bestow his Spirit on the princes of the church and of the world, and to turn the hearts of peoples at the same time towards the things that really belong to piety and the peace of Christendom.

* * * * *

8 Ep 1505:18
9 *Adagia* I ii 14
10 Cf Ep 1526 n26.
11 Ep 1275
12 Ep 1352
13 Ep 1418
14 Epp 1410, 1415, 1422

As far as I am concerned, as long as there is any breath and warmth in   60
my poor body, I shall not cease to serve the public good with all my powers,
if not with great success, at least with great sincerity of heart. May God, who
both can turn the evils made by men to a good outcome, and often does,
vouchsafe that out of this violent and bitter medicine which through Luther
has shaken the world like a body corrupt in all its parts, some element of   65
sound health may be born in Christian character and conduct. And may he
preserve your illustrious Highness in health and wealth.

From Basel, 20 November 1524

1516 / From François Du Moulin   Lyon, 21 November 1524

The autograph of this letter (=Ep 31 in Förstemann/Günther) was in the
Burscher Collection at Leipzig (Ep 1254 introduction). Erasmus' reply is Ep
1527. On Du Moulin, see Ep 1426.

Many people send you elaborate epistles, sweetest Erasmus, filled with
recondite words. Your friend the almoner[1] tells you what he wants in the
briefest of notes. Hilarius your heir[2] can tell you how passionately I long to
embrace my Erasmus, but fortune has never allowed me to fulfil my fixed
intention. At the moment I seek the swallow[3] deep in mountain snows; but   5
in a very short time, God willing, I shall find my way back to Basel. For the
rest of my news you can safely trust Hilarius, and he shall do duty for the
long, long letter I had meant to write to you. At least, dear Erasmus, if I am
buried in the snows, you will reflect that you have lost a faithful friend.
Farewell, leading light of our generation, farewell and every good wish.   10

From Lyon, at daybreak, breakfast being already done, 21 November
1524

F. Du Moulin, a friend of Erasmus

1517 / To Jakob Wimpfeling   Basel, 25 November 1524

In his old age, the conservative Alsatian humanist, Jakob Wimpfeling (Ep 224),
was profoundly depressed by the progress of the new faith in his home town of

* * * * *

1516
1 Ie, Du Moulin himself, grand almoner to Francis I
2 An allusion to the gift that Francis I had given to Hilarius Bertholf (Ep 1384 n31)
  as his reward for delivering the paraphrase on Mark (Ep 1400) while Erasmus
  himself received nothing; Ep 1341A:1743–5.
3 Ie, await the coming of spring; cf Epp 1484:16, 1527:29–30, Adagia I vi 59.

Sélestat and elsewhere. In a letter to a friend, dated 2 November 1524, lamenting this situation, Wimpfeling mentioned that he had written to many friends, among them Erasmus' friends Ludwig Baer in Basel, bishop Christoph von Utenheim of Basel, and Johann von Botzheim in Constance, but that no one had answered him, despising in his old age someone whom they had once venerated; see *Zeitschrift für Kirchengeschichte* 16 (1896) 287–89, especially 289. It may be that Erasmus was prompted to write these affectionate lines by being shown one of the letters in question. The letter was first published in the *Opus epistolarum*.

ERASMUS OF ROTTERDAM TO JAKOB WIMPFELING, GREETING

If my dear Wimpfeling is well, I have every reason to rejoice. I myself am in moderate health,[1] and somewhat better than usual. I am no longer a member of the band – I have become a gladiator.[2] Such was my destiny. Do not tear yourself to pieces, dear friend, in the conflict of our generation; 5 enjoy the consciousness that you have done right. Have no doubt that I am devoted to you; if you don't write, no matter, provided you give me your affection – better perhaps, if you return mine, as I have no doubt you do. Give Sapidus my greetings, and let me advise you to keep up your old friendship with him;[3] if anything is amiss be charitable, and blame it on the 10 days we have to live in. Farewell, dearest brother.

Basel, St Catharine's day 1524

1518 / To Paul Volz   Basel, 25 November 1524

This letter, Erasmus' reply to a letter no longer extant, was first published in the *Opus epistolarum*. Volz's reply is Ep 1525. On Volz, see Ep 368.

ERASMUS OF ROTTERDAM TO ABBOT PAUL VOLZ, GREETING

Many thanks for the prayers you offer for my late self,[1] which I will gladly

* * * * *

1517
1 Cf Ep 1518:39–40.
2 Cf Ep 1514:14–16.
3 The enthusiastic adherence of Sapidus (Ep 323) to the Reformation had caused conflict with Wimpfeling, who now referred to him as 'Sathanas'; see page 289 of the letter cited in the introduction. Sapidus also became embroiled with the city council of Sélestat, as a result of which he moved to Strasbourg in 1526.

1518
1 Rumours of Erasmus' death appear to have been widespread in late October and November; see Schiess Ep 85, and *Der Briefwechsel des Conradus Mutianus* ed K. Gillert II (Halle 1890) page 300.

reciprocate when you too are so good as to die. Rumours like this merely
make me laugh, though at the same time I am sick at heart to see so much ill
will between Christians. Personally I do all I can for the common good and   5
hurt no man; and in this I risk, as they say, my own bread and butter – do it
in fact at great personal expense. In spite of this, apart from the other lies
they tell about me they are constantly killing me off. For you, it was a French
mass-priest who told you he had set foot on my grave; and in Heidelberg
there was an Englishman who had spread the news that he had attended my   10
funeral, adding that I was buried in the same grave as Lachner,[2] Froben's
father-in-law; while before that, in Flanders, there had been gleeful reports
of my perishing by some horrible form of death. Others had put it about in
Brabant that my books have been publicly burned in Rome with myself in
effigy.[3] The men who make these things up are well aware that their   15
falsehoods must be immediately detected, but in the mean time they love to
see the bad triumphant and the good cast down. What could be more
criminal than their state of mind? If Satan himself were living in our midst,
what could he do more after his own heart? And those who act like this are
Christians, they are priests and monks and grandchildren of Dominic and   20
Francis. But the opposite happens, thanks to God's protection; never am I in
better health than when these men and their rumours have me at death's
door.

　　　Three years ago when I was living in Anderlecht,[4] in one place I had
had a fall from my horse and broken my neck, in another I had died of a   25
fever, somewhere else I had had a fit of apoplexy and fallen dead on the
spot. And yet within the last four years I had never been so fit as I was just
then. After I left there was a rumour that my books had been publicly
condemned in Rome on the authority of Adrian vi;[5] yet at that same time I
was sent a brief by Adrian in most complimentary terms,[6] and one even   30
more so followed it,[7] and then came a third to order those noisy rascals to be
silent,[8] without any move on my part. At the very moment when they were

*　*　*　*　*

2　Ep 305:198n
3　Cf Ep 1494:36–7.
4　In the summer of 1521. For the rumours mentioned here, cf Ep 1342:25–32.
5　See Ep 1324 introduction.
6　Ep 1324
7　At first glance it seems that Erasmus intends a distinction between this brief
　　and the letter mentioned in line 34 below. But the reference here is clearly to Ep
　　1338; cf Ep 1353:249–51.
8　See Ep 1359:2–3 with n1.

putting it around that the dedication of Arnobius to Adrian[9] had been
unwelcome, a letter arrived assuring me that he had been delighted.[10] And
these official documents were sent to Brabant, where this rumour was rife,   35
before they came to me. Again, it was just when news was spreading that
Erasmus' books and his effigy had been burned in Rome under Clement that
a brief arrived with promises and a complimentary present.[11] Last but not
least, in these last few months, in which they have been so busy burying me,
my health has been such that I have not been so well for three years;[12] and I   40
think I have found a way to be less tortured by the stone in future.[13] And yet
one day it must come about that they have guessed the truth.

Personally, I am not so tired of life as to wish for death, nor yet am I
terrified of it, for my trust is in the Lord's mercy. Meanwhile I shall press on
with my resolution to do good unto all men and hurt no man, so far as this is   45
possible in an age which is much the most turbulent that has ever been. I
have joined no faction, and I never shall; but my one object, which I shall
pursue diligently, is to secure that this hurricane may be followed by some
clear weather. Nor am I much shaken at the moment by that humorous
passage where you call me 'the amphibious wonder of the learned world'[14]   50
in the address on the back of your letter. Let me be 'amphibious' between
faction and faction, provided that I am not amphibious where Christ is
concerned. And whence pray comes your new title of 'ex-abbot'? I recall
what you once said to me about laying down the burden of your title.[15] And
yet, if you wish to avoid all forms of trouble, you must leave this world for   55
good. How much greater the wisdom of your friend Erasmus who, on the
many occasions when he was offered burdens of this kind,[16] constantly and
boldly despised them all! I am now even ex-councillor of his imperial

* * * * *

9 Epp 1304, 1310
10 Ep 1338
11 Ep 1443B; cf Ep 1494:36–41.
12 Cf Ep 1517:2–3.
13 See Epp 1341A:1821–7, 1484:12–13.
14 The proper meaning of 'amphibious' (ἀμφίβιος) is 'living a double life' and
    usually refers to living both on land and in the sea. Erasmus here takes it to
    mean 'ambivalent,' which is stretching the meaning severely. In Ep 1525:15–19,
    Volz seems to interpret it as 'uncertain which world one is living in, this world
    or the next,' which is not what the word means at all; cf Ep 1529:15–20. In 1527
    Erasmus called Vives an 'amphibion' because the latter was living part of the
    year in England and part in Bruges; Allen Epp 1830:1, 1889:9–10.
15 See Ep 1075.
16 See Ep 1481 n14.

Majesty, since beyond complimentary expressions none of my annuity[17] has
yet reached me since I left Brabant. And yet, thanks be to heaven, I feel no   60
lack.[18]

I suppose you have seen by now my books on the freedom of the will,[19]
on the way to pray,[20] and on God's mercy,[21] and therefore I do not send
them. The Lord Jesus be your keeper, reverend Father.

Basel, St Catherine's day 1524   65

1519 / From Johann von Botzheim   Constance, 26 November 1524

The autograph of this letter, which was first published as Ep 29 in Enthoven, is
in the Rehdiger Collection of the University Library at Wrocław (MS Rehd
254.29).

On Botzheim, see Ep 1285. The principal subject of this letter is Botzheim's
anxiety over his citation to Rome; see especially lines 17ff. According to
Botzheim's own account, the denunciation that produced the citation was, at
least in part, an act of petty revenge by the bishop of Constance, Hugo von
Hohenlandenberg, whom he had reprimanded, albeit in private, for his
adulterous relationship with the wife of an aged and ill citizen (AK Ep 991:21ff).
A zealously anti-Lutheran canon of Constance who had recently found
employment at the curia may have played an important role in Rome (Ep
1530:8–9). The summons called upon Botzheim to appear in Rome on 26
November. No charge was indicated, but since Johann Zwick (line 22) had also
been cited, the nature of the charge could be presumed (AK Ep 970:10–17). At
Botzheim's request, Bonifacius Amerbach (Ep 408) wrote to Jacopo Sadoleto
(Ep 1511) to enlist his support (AK 970, 13 September), and Erasmus may have
done the same (see Ep 1555). Thanks to Sadoleto's prompt intervention,
Botzheim was not required to appear in Rome, but the case was referred to the
bishop of Constance (AK Ep 989) which, under the circumstances, did not seem
to Botzheim to be an encouraging development. So he renewed his request for
support from Erasmus (Ep 1530:4–8) and Amerbach (AK Ep 991). However, in
January 1525 the papal brief addressed to the bishop arrived in Constance
(Allen Ep 1540:1ff) and when, a month later, Erasmus and Boniface wrote
again to Sadoleto (Ep 1555 and AK Ep 999), they expressed their satisfaction

* * * * *

17 See Ep 1380 introduction.
18 Cf Epp 1523:192–3, 1526:92–3, 1528:61; but for a somewhat different view of
   the matter, see Epp 1434:28–32, 66–7, 1470:25–30.
19 Epp 1419, 1481
20 Ep 1502
21 Ep 1474

with the outcome, which indicates that some sort of resolution of the matter had been achieved.

Greeting, most beloved teacher. The horse has come,[1] sound and without a fault, and also your letter, by the Constance courier, and then another letter by Hieronymus Froben,[2] but belatedly, for it was the twelfth day since you wrote it; beside which a third has been delivered by a man called Ludwig,[3] a proctor in our consistory court. You had told me in your first letter where   5 Hovius[4] was to be found in Rome, but it was no good; for your letter and mine[5] were both sent to Rome by an Augsburg merchant, at great expense. I divided all the letters into two bundles. For the bishop of Veroli[6] and the datary[7] I put theirs together, and then for Hovius his; and on these I put an address with your name in it, like this: 'To Johannes Hovius, servant of   10 Erasmus of Rotterdam, in care of Master Ludovicus Volterranus,'[8] for he is the physician with whom he has been living hitherto, as I learned some time ago from a letter Hovius wrote me. I fear that by an oversight the word 'physician' was omitted from the address, and nothing put but 'in care of Master Lodovico da Volterra.' But I hope that if he is there he will have had it   15 safely.

I am waiting to see what the great Roman chiefs mean to do with me, whether it is some nice fat bishopric that nobody there is trying for or would accept if it were offered him, or what else they have in mind for me. The morrow of St Catherine is the limit for the day fixed in my citation. I hope   20 that by Christmas I shall know how the business has gone one way or the other. Zwick[9] has taken no steps, and will await the outcome. There is no

* * * * *

1519
1 Sold to Botzheim (see lines 81–2 below, Ep 1530:11), possibly as the result of the recent gift from Warham (Ep 1488:55–6), because Erasmus had decided to give up riding (Ep 1422:25–6)
2 Ep 903:3n
3 Unidentified
4 Ep 1387 n3
5 None of the letters mentioned here is extant.
6 Ennio Filonardi (Ep 1282)
7 Giberti (Ep 1443A); see Epp 1509 introduction, 1530 n3.
8 Unidentified
9 Johann Zwick of Constance (c 1496–1542), a cousin of Thomas and Ambrosius Blarer (Ep 1341A n430), studied law in Freiburg (1509–18) and in November 1520 took a doctorate in both laws at Siena. Meanwhile, in 1516, he had taken holy orders at Constance. In September 1522, after having taught for several months at the University of Basel and having already begun the study of Luther's works, he was secretly married at Constance and then took over as

doubt however that this is a concealed attack mounted by some of those pigs. Our bishop has excused himself on oath and says that whatever it is, it was done without his knowledge; nor can I discover, after calling in my spies 25 as well, that this sort of deception finds more than a very few people to approve it. I have no wish to evade a judge in Constance, however hostile even, where my way of life is well known. But to plead in Rome, where I am a stranger, before unfamiliar judges and counsel, in a place where even the least scrap of suspicion of Lutheranism produces the most blazing prejudice 30 – this I do not think a good idea. But when I have heard my opponent's statement of claim, I shall take advice to more purpose. Even the anti-Lutherans among us disapprove what has happened, with few exceptions. I have written to tell Fabri the whole story,[10] but he has not yet answered. Please recommend me to any friends who you think can 35 forward my business. You will not suffer from any ill feeling yourself, for you can promise freely that I shall appear before any judge they please in Constance. But above all please do not hesitate to approach your friends in Rome, if the time comes that I need a recommendation. If you think it might help with Cardinal Campeggi[11] if I went to see him armed with a 40 recommendation from you, and the case seems to demand that, I will go. But until I get instructions from Rome, what has been done there or has to be done, I see no need to do anything. A letter reached Constance some time ago from the bishop of Veroli[12] about renting lodgings; for he would soon be returning, he said, and we have heard nothing different meanwhile. But 45 more than enough of this for the moment.

You also write in your second letter[13] that an attack on you by Eck[14] is in

* * * * *

parish priest in Riedlingen on the Danube. His enthusiasm for Luther and the reformers of Zürich and Strasbourg soon aroused the disapproval of the bishop of Constance and led to his being cited to Rome along with Botzheim. Although the citation, which he ignored, led to nothing, he was unable to remain much longer in Riedlingen. At the beginning of 1526 he returned to Constance and soon became one of the leaders of the reform movement in that city. Despite his adherence to the Reformation, he retained a friendly attitude towards Erasmus, whom he had probably met in the autumn of 1522, when the latter visited Constance.

10 Because of Fabri's important position at the court of Archduke Ferdinand; see Ep 1382 n12, and cf lines 67–9 below.

11 Campeggi (Ep 1410) was now in Vienna (LP IV 696, 721, 885–6), following his success at Regensburg in July (Ep 1480 n8).

12 Since the summer of 1524 he had been in Rome (cf line 8 above), but in February 1525 he returned to Constance. See Wirz 64–5.

13 Not extant

14 There appears to have been no foundation for this report.

the press at Augsburg. I have never heard anyone speak of this, though that most conceited of men, and a theologian too, is capable of anything. One thing I do know, that the people in Zürich and their accomplices have written some utterly contemptible pamphlets in German against Eck,[15] having been tricked and provoked (so I hear) by him.

You say that Melanchthon writes about a reply by Luther to your *Diatribe*,[16] and I have had almost the same news in a letter,[17] much as follows: 'Luther is replying to Erasmus on freedom of the will, but with the modesty which Erasmus' virtues deserve.' I now understand from your last letter that Luther has answered.[18] I hope he writes to the point, and more like a theologian than he does in his answers to many other people, without scurrility and coarse humour, I mean, which I will never accept on a topic of such importance. Karlstadt writes the sort of thing we are not used to nowadays;[19] I wish he were as wise as he is painstaking! I have things to say to you here if we could meet. If Oecolampadius has given up his project,[20] he has done as I should wish; indeed, I wish he had never started.

* * * * *

15 In August 1524 Eck had offered to debate with Zwingli, who accepted the challenge in a printed reply, *Johannis Eggen missive und embieten* (31 August). Zwingli's associate Sebastian Hofmeister also joined the fray with an abusive letter to Eck. See Zw-Br Ep 344 n1.
16 See Ep 1500:50.
17 Perhaps that by Hummelberg's unnamed correspondent cited in BRE Ep 256. The wording here matches closely that of the first two extracts given there (page 365). Copies or extracts of letters to Hummelberg (Ep 1253 n6) at Ravensburg could easily have reached Botzheim.
18 A misunderstanding apparently based on rumour. In fact, Luther, who was much distracted by other matters, especially the Peasants' Revolt, found the task of replying to Erasmus irksome (WA-Br III 368:30–1) and did not seriously address himself to it until September 1525; see WA 18 580–2. His *De servo arbitrio* (ibidem 600–787) was published only at the very end of the year.
19 See Ep 1369 n7.
20 Oecolampadius was reportedly so eager to get started on a reply to *De libero arbitrio* that he actually fetched sheets from the printer while the work was still in press. Learning of this, Erasmus asked Oecolampadius not to proceed lest the already tense situation in Basel be made even worse. After discussing the matter with some members of the city council, Oecolampadius did in fact abandon the project. See Allen Ep 1804:16–30; Staehelin 257. However, in early December 1524 Oecolampadius did publish, under the title *De libero arbitrio*, a little volume containing brief works by Prosper, Augustine, and Ambrose on the topic of free will (Basel: Thomas Wolff); *Oek-Bib* no 101. In the preface, Oecolampadius stated that his purpose was to stop the mouths of 'our Pelagians,' presumably including Erasmus (cf Ep 1225 n66). See Staehelin 257–9.

They say Ferdinand is back in Innsbruck.[21] Spiegel[22] and I were taught
together when we were young and he is a very old friend; if he could do   65
anything to help in my business, I should hope he would not let me down,
especially if I could add a warm recommendation from you. I hope the same
of Fabri, who likes to have people make up to him; he likes to be asked and
enjoys giving the impression of being able and willing. You will be able to do
much through your friends, if you are willing, for my sake; but I do not want   70
this to be done except in moderate language, so that it does not look as
though you are supporting a nasty and very poor case, for I have never
approved of hasty action or had any part in it. Let me be dealt with at the
proper place and time, and with Christian justice, not cunning and
pretence. I shall use no subterfuge. Who the theologian can be who said in a   75
sermon that you wrote under compulsion, I have no idea, unless you think it
was Oecolampadius.[23] As for Zwingli, I have never heard that he writes
against you,[24] though we get many letters here from Zürich. All this trouble
about my citation was started and organized, I am pretty sure, by a pig,
though one has certain other suspicions too.   80

Most honoured teacher, there is no call for you to think that I am trying
to conceal my receipt of the horse; I never wanted it except as a purchase, nor
do I now. Had I ever found anyone to whom I might have entrusted a letter
or the money, I should not have put it off. A citizen of Constance, whom I do
not know well, was in Basel without my knowledge; and besides him   85
Ludwig the proctor,[25] by whom you sent your last letter, was there, but I
only discovered this after I got your letter. Have no doubts: you will receive
everything as soon as I get a suitable courier. Neither the St Nicholas
pamphlet[26] nor the dialogue has been printed; and the reason is that I had

* * * * *

21 He was currently at Amstetten, but by 6 December he was in Innsbruck; LP IV
   824–6, 912.
22 See Ep 1505 n4. He and Botzheim had been fellow students at Heidelberg.
23 Epp 1523:114–17 and 1526:243 indicate that Botzheim's guess was probably
   accurate.
24 Erasmus' fears of an attack from this quarter were unjustified. Since the breach
   in their relations in 1523 (see Ep 1384), an icy silence had prevailed between
   them. While Zwingli's attitude remained generally respectful but distant, it
   was Erasmus who expressed open hostility, first in letters (eg, Epp 1496–7) and
   then in the *Hyperaspistes* of 1526 (LB X 1263D, 1268F, 1302D, 1308B) and the
   Epistola ad fratres Inferioris Germaniae of 1530 (ASD IX-1 336, 352).
25 See line 4.
26 Wilhelm Nesen's *S. Nicolai vita*; see Ep 1165 n17. It seems that Erasmus had lent
   to Botzheim copies of this pamphlet and of the *Dialogus bilinguium ac trilinguium*
   (CWE 7 330–47) and that Botzheim had proposed to reprint them, perhaps

promised the music.[27] Meanwhile the printer had started to print certain   90
other things, so that there is no danger to be feared on that score. I will send
back your copies, if not by this courier, by the next suitable one I can get, and
the money at the same time. Benoît[28] the bookseller said he would be going
shortly, and I was waiting for him. Had I found another in the mean time, I
would have arranged for them to be taken. You must have no doubts about   95
me; you will not find me deceitful where you are concerned, as long as I live,
for I respect you as you deserve, which is, religiously.

On worldly affairs, all my news is well known to you. They say the
king of France stormed Pavia in great force after entering Milan,[29] and killed
whatever he found there, a terrible story. The duke of Württemberg is said   100
to be in Zürich,[30] getting ready for something. Rumour has it that he will
return to his native land, which has been torn from him. Necessity finds out
the means, just as 'fury finds arms.'[31] But policies and principles often
deceive one, even those which look most reliable. On the pamphlets written
against you in French[32] I can discover nothing, however hard I try. I can do   105
nothing, and I produce nothing; you, who can do so much, produce even
more, for all of which I am openly grateful. Farewell, beloved teacher, and

* * * * *

because of the recent death of their author (Ep 1500 n12). Erasmus, however,
had evidently asked that they not be published.
27 The term here translated as 'music' is 'musicos sonos,' ie, 'musical sounds.'
Given Botzheims's talents and the nature of the works in question, 'music' in
the literal sense cannot be the meaning here. Since, however, 'musicus' can
also mean 'poetic,' the intended meaning might well be 'poetical sounds' or
even 'poetical noises.' If so, then the passage is likely Botzheim's jocular way of
saying that he had promised to supply some kind of literary ornamentation,
possibly introductory verses or perhaps stylistic improvements to the texts.
28 Vaugris (Ep 1395)
29 The French had indeed invaded the duchy of Milan in October 1524, but the
report of the fall of Pavia was false. The siege of Pavia began on 6 November
and was still going on when Francis I was defeated and taken prisoner by
imperial troops on 24 February 1525. See Knecht 164–72.
30 Ulrich (Epp 923:27n, 1030 n18, 1280A n3), who was now living in his county of
Montbéliard and plotting to recapture Württemberg. In 1524 he began to court
the Swiss, was made a citizen of Basel in June, and attended Oecolampadius'
sermons (Zw-Br Epp 347, 352, 356, 362). Leaving Basel on 17 November, he
was in Zürich from 23 November until the end of the month and had an
audience with the council on the twenty-sixth. His attempt in 1525 to recover
Württemberg failed, and he was not to find success in that endeavour until
May 1534. See Ludwig Friedrich Heyd *Ulrich, Herzog zu Württemberg* II
(Tübingen 1841) 145–50.
31 Virgil *Aeneid* 1.150
32 See Ep 1496 n69.

look after your poor body which, apart from continual illness, is burdened
by a load of work.

From Constance, morrow of St Catherine 1524 110

Your most devoted Bivilaqua[33]

To that valiant champion of a more genuine theology and of all good
letters, Erasmus of Rotterdam, his most revered teacher and patron. In Basel

1520 / From Duke George of Saxony   Dresden, 29 November 1524

The surviving manuscript is a rough draft in a secretary's hand in the
Staatsarchiv Dresden (MS Loc 10299, f 87). The letter was first published by
Adalbert Horawitz in the *Sitzungsberichte der phil.-hist. Classe der kaiserlichen
Akademie der Wissenschaften* (Vienna 1878). Delayed in transit, the letter did not
reach Erasmus until February or March 1525; see Ep 1561.

On Duke George, see Ep 1283.

GEORGE, BY THE GRACE OF GOD DUKE OF SAXONY, LANDGRAVE
OF THURINGIA, AND MARGRAVE OF MEISSEN

Greeting, most learned Erasmus, and the assurance of our support. On the
Sunday after the feast of SS Simon and Jude[1] a letter arrived from you,[2] in
which you reply to one from us[3] and to a copy of an earlier letter,[4] which had 5
been sent to you some time ago but not received; and that the Lutherans
should have intercepted your letter to us is not surprising. Is there anything
they are not prepared to do provided that somehow or other it can serve
their plans? If we knew who was responsible for the theft, we should at least
show how greatly we resent it. Apart from that, when you say that of your 10
own accord and more than five years ago you not merely drew away from
the Lutheran faction (as we had wished you would do in our letter) but had
always most carefully kept out of it, and always had been and in future
would be most unsympathetic to it, you need not labour to persuade us of
the truth of this, for we easily believe it. In wishing that you might leave 15
them, we had no mind to accuse you of being a member of that faction or
having any share in the disorders it has aroused; I wished rather to urge you

* * * * *

33 A variant of Botzheim's usual byname, Abstemius (Ep 1341A n1).

1520
1 20 October
2 Ep 1499
3 Ep 1448
4 Ep 1340

once again and rouse you and set you to work somehow or other on the task which you declined two years ago with so many reasons drawn from a wide field[5] – I mean, the defence of the church of God from so many monstrous and abominable doctrines.

You have, it is true, stated more than once that Luther's brazen effrontery, his abuse and coarse jests, and the highly subversive disruption caused by the Lutherans are supremely repugnant to you, and you have rebuked and refuted them with powerful arguments; but until the publication of your address on the freedom of the will nothing had reached us in which we had been able to discover openly any teaching of yours that differed from their declarations and met them on equal terms. In fact it was widely believed that you in fact agreed with him for the most part, and condemned nothing except his impious and violent method of proceeding; and what is more the Lutherans themselves boasted of this, and constantly asserted that you were on their side – a charge which was more than once brought against you by your detractors and rebutted by you. Now however they have come to understand that you have openly spoken against them and seriously offered them battle, and they are greatly disappointed and much cast down. Would that you had taken up this task from the first moment that the heresies showed themselves! That faction would not have increased as it has done. But since you produce an impressive precedent for your silence and promise to give unquestionable reasons, we shall not think you guilty of any neglect, if in the maintenance and defence of vows[6] and other things handed down to us almost from hand to hand by our forbears you still show yourself a vigorous champion and tower of defence in the service of the church and the holy Fathers. Nor do we doubt that, like Hilary, who by breaking his long silence suppressed the Arian heresy, you too will be able to overcome the Lutheran heresy and root out and destroy his pestilent paradoxes.

Why you should have given no answer to the concluding sentence of our letter, and not offered even the hope of finding a successor to Mosellanus,[7] we do not rightly understand, unless you wish it to be ascribed to the unexpected departure of that same messenger. We ask you therefore to let us know about this as soon as you can. And so farewell.

From Dresden, St Andrew's eve, AD 1524

* * * * *

5 In Ep 1313
6 See Ep 1503 n2.
7 See Ep 1448 n7.

1521 / From Simon Pistoris   Dresden, 1 December 1524

The autograph of this letter is in the Uffenbach-Wolf Collection at the Staats-
und Universitätsbibliothek Hamburg (Supellex Epistolica 4.11). According to
Allen, the letter was apparently first published in the *Unschuldige Nachrichten*
(1715), a rare volume that he had not seen.

On Pistoris, Duke George's chancellor, see Ep 1125 n6.

s.t.[1]
Greeting. Hieronymus Emser[2] has shown me the letter you wrote him,[3] in
which you suppose him to be responsible for the rather indignant letter sent
you by Duke George on 21 May,[4] no doubt thinking that he was then
secretary; and you tell him to see that the prince is better informed in future   5
both on the facts and on your own attitude, so that you may get more polite
letters. As however Emser is completely blameless in this and has not
earned any protest, I fear this rod is prepared for my own back and that you
will have the law on me, for I am much more in the position of secretary than
Emser, who has absolutely nothing to do with the prince's correspondence.   10
I should however be very sorry to get into Erasmus' bad books and to have it
suspected by him that I have encouraged rather than prevented anything
that might reflect on his attitude or his reputation; and so I thought it my
duty to write and tell you the facts and deprive you in advance of any reason
for protesting. It is then beyond any shadow of a doubt that in this and in all   15
the other letters that have reached you in the prince's name the views and
the material have originated with and have been thought out by the prince
himself, by his own prowess, as we say,[5] and in accordance with the
judgment which he has formed in each case, he has written them down as a
guide in his own hand (how I wish I could conveniently show you this), and   20
nothing except the wording (which again, I have no doubt, you will easily
recognize is not mine, but you will know whose it is) has been either added
to or taken away. So there is no reason for you to suspect anybody.

There is indeed plenty of further evidence by which I could persuade
you more fully and convincingly that this is so; but one cannot trust the pen,   25
particularly since letters, as you say, are intercepted, and between lawyers

* * * * *
1521
1 *Salvo Titulo*, ie, 'saving your title,' a formulaic apology for the omission of an
  honorific heading. The formula is still used in the Netherlands.
2 Ep 553
3 Not extant; doubtless contemporary with Ep 1499
4 Ep 1448
5 *Adagia* I vi 19

there is still no real agreement, if that happens, with whom an action for theft would lie. In the mean time, pray accept my assurance that in any business in which I think you have any wishes or are an interested party I shall take particular care and pains; and if there is a man anywhere who has a 30 high opinion of Erasmus from every point of view, I declare that I am that person. Farewell.

From Dresden, 1 December 1524

Simon Pistoris

To the most learned and honourable theologian Erasmus of Rotter- 35 dam, his honoured friend

1522 / To Heinrich Stromer Basel, 10 December 1524

This letter was first published in the *Opus epistolarum*. On Stromer, see Ep 1444.

ERASMUS OF ROTTERDAM TO HEINRICH STROMER OF AUERBACH, THE PHYSICIAN, GREETING

Your very amusing letter[1] made me laugh, though the laugh was sardonic at times. That joke of yours refreshed my memory of a charming remark of my friend More. When I published the two books of my *De copia*,[2] 'I hear,' he 5 said, 'that Erasmus has given *Plenty* to the world in both its senses. What has he left at home except Scarcity?' So now, I have sent my *Free Will* into the world,[3] and my will is no longer free. I was hoping to be a spectator of this drama, not that I dislike taking a part in the church's cause to the best of my power, but because I could see this was a dispute about who knows what 10 insignificant paradoxes; and I also foresaw that if I took a part in the action of the play, I should merely embitter things and hurt both myself and the cause. Last but not least, when I surveyed the excessively corrupt life led by Christians everywhere, even had I had the lowest possible opinion of Luther, I should almost have judged him to be a necessary evil[4] that could 15 not be removed without removing the best thing we had in the present state of affairs. But it was written in my destiny that at my time of life I should become a gladiator instead of a member of the band.

* * * * *

1522
1 Not extant
2 Ep 260. On the joke, cf Ep 237:2–4.
3 *De libero arbitrio* (Epp 1419, 1481)
4 *Adagia* I v 26. Cf Ep 1455:12–17.

Laberius the mime-writer laments that at the age of sixty he was forced
by orders from the emperor to go on the stage,[5] so that he left his house a   20
Roman knight and returned a common player. I at almost the same age am
becoming a prize-fighter instead of a devotee of the Muses. Veianius, who
had spent his life in the arena, earned his retirement on the ground of old
age and now, his arms 'safe hanging in the shrine of Hercules, / He tastes the
secret peace of country life';[6] while I, who have spent all my life in the fields   25
of the Muses, am thrust into this bloody fight. I could do nothing else. There
was a constant clamour from the sophisters: 'Erasmus and Luther are in
league; neither attacks the other.' The princes expected something,[7] and it
was not safe to disappoint them much longer. There were offensive
challenges from some of Luther's friends (though they bring Luther nothing   30
but misfortune), so that had I held my peace it would have looked as though
it was fear of their threats that had silenced me.[8] Moreover a letter of
Luther's[9] which he had sent me by Joachim[10] was already in Strasbourg,[11]
and no doubt would be published shortly. In it he promises that he will not
unsheath his pen against me, but makes it a condition that I abstain from   35
deliberately undermining his opinions, as I had done hitherto.[12] At this
point it is not yet really clear whether it would have been more disgraceful
for me to keep quiet from fear or by agreement. So the die was cast, but in
such terms that I did not go one single word beyond what I actually think.

When you say that I am unpopular with the sophisters, there's nothing   40
new in that; that I shall ever enjoy any peace in that quarter I neither hope
nor desire. And as for Luther's feelings towards me, as it is the faith that is at
stake, I attach very little importance to them. That his opinion of me is
nothing very special he makes clear in many letters he has written to my
friends,[13] in which he makes me out to be blind, pitiful,[14] a stranger to   45

* * * * *

5 See Ep 1481 n4.
6 See Horace *Epistles* 1.1.4–5.
7 See Ep 1488 n22.
8 See Ep 1496 n84.
9 Ep 1443
10 Camerarius (Ep 1501)
11 See Ep 1489 n16.
12 Ep 1443:48–50, 76–8
13 Erasmus was particularly exercised by Luther's letter to Oecolampadius of 20
   June 1523 (WA-Br III 96–7) and that of 1 October to Conradus Pellicanus (ibidem
   160–1); cf Ep 1443 n9. Typically, Erasmus' version of Luther's remarks is more
   barbed than the original.
14 WA-Br III 161:38

Christ,[15] far from any understanding of Christian principles,[16] devoid of the spirit[17] and still fast bound to the letter. But if this is what he thinks of me, that is not surprising, when he has a lordly contempt for all the Fathers compared with himself. If only he would devote the qualities he claims to possess to the peace of the church. I do not cease to pursue the same aim I   50 have always had, that true religion and sound learning might flourish together, and I lose no opportunity here, if only I might be allowed some success. But the Lutheran party embitters the feelings of the princes more and more every day. The other party merely use the traditional remedies: prison, public recantation, confiscation, faggots; and I do not see that they   55 will get us anywhere in a trouble like this that is so widespread and daily goes further. If I did not know that God governs the affairs of men and often brings a play which we have started very badly to a happy outcome, I could not imagine any way out from our situation except of the most bloody kind. Karlstadt has been here, but with scarcely a greeting to Oecolampa-   60 dius.[18] He has published six pamphlets;[19] the two men who printed them were thrown into prison the day before yesterday by order of the magistrates,[20] the particular reason being that (so they tell me) he teaches that the true body of the Lord is not present in the Eucharist. This no one can tolerate. The laity are indignant when they see their God torn from them, as   65 though God existed nowhere except under that particular symbol; and the learned are troubled by the words of Holy Scripture and the decrees of the church. This question will stir up great trouble for us, as though we had not more than enough already.

It would be a long job to tell you all that is going on here. You know that   70 in Zürich they have thrown all the saints out of their temples;[21] in Waldshut even out of the glass windows of private houses.[22] Phallicus[23] is king in Montbéliard and does what he likes. But what a fool I am to tell all this to

* * * * *

15 Ibidem 160:34–6
16 Ibidem 160:25–6
17 Ibidem 96:14ff; cf Ep 1384:53.
18 See Ep 1523:102–4. He did not in fact visit Oecolampadius; see BAO no 226 n9.
19 See Ep 1523 n19.
20 See Ep 1523 n21.
21 Ep 1496 n40
22 Waldshut, on the Rhine above Basel, where the future Anabaptist leader Balthasar Hubmaier (1480?–1528) was pastor 1522–5. His vehement opposition to images had been expressed at the Second Zürich Disputation in October 1523.
23 Guillaume Farel (Epp 1496:72–3, 145ff, 1510:11ff). Farel was in Montbéliard, a Burgundian possession of the dukes of Württemberg (cf Ep 1519 n30), from mid-July 1524 until March 1525; see *Biographie nouvelle* 131–50.

you, who hear of it, I suppose, before it happens here. There is a humorous
touch about those who keep saying that I refuse to be a martyr, as though I 75
still had much of this life left to lose, or as if the stone were not such torment
that it might make any death desirable.[24] Does a man refuse martyrdom who
sincerely proclaims what he believes? You assure me that you agree with me
about freedom of the will. What is taught by those men does not instantly
become gospel, and often the way they teach or the teacher's way of life is a 80
cause of uproar. For my part, as I want nothing in this life, I shall try to
arrange that I may be of help to all men so far as I can, princes, prelates, and
Pharisees, sophistic philosophers however unfairly they may treat me, and
noisy gospel-mongers. Perhaps the gratitude denied me during life will be
paid to my memory; before Christ at any rate nothing in the way of duty 85
done can be wasted.

As I was writing this I had not your letter at hand,[25] so do not be
surprised if I have not answered quite everything. Farewell, my valued
friend.

Basel, 10 December 1524 90

Before I sealed this letter, yours happened to come to hand. That's an
amusing story about the physician,[26] and your guess was not wide of the
mark. And yet there's a preacher here who in every single sermon produces
some argument against my book for the benefit of a mixed congregation.[27]
What Luther is like as a person, I do not know. In these parts our new 95
gospel[28] provides us with a new sort of men: headstrong, impudent,

* * * * *

24 See Epp 1408 n2, 1452 n22.
25 See line 1.
26 Details unknown
27 Oecolampadius (Ep 1496 n37); see Epp 1523:114–17, 1526:243.
28 This verbal abuse (down through line 100) naturally offended the reformers. In
his *Epistola apologetica* (May 1530), Martin Bucer, writing in behalf of the
Strasbourg pastors, objected strenuously to Erasmus' description of the
'servants of Christ' as monsters born of the new gospel that they preached,
since that gospel was 'undoubtedly Christ's'; see BOL I 186:5–21. In the *Epistola
ad fratres Inferioris Germaniae* (1530), Erasmus responded by distorting what
both he and Bucer had said (ASD IX-1 400:531–7): 'In the letter to Stromer of
Auerbach I wrote that from this new gospel was born to us a race of men that I
liked not at all. This logician [Bucer] reckons that a grave offence has been
committed because I did not say born by reason of the gospel, since their
gospel is without doubt the gospel of Christ ... Immortal God, how great a lust
for defamation possesses this man who seeks in my words something biting!'
Allen observed that this passage illustrates Erasmus' capacity for self-
deception in controversy.

deceitful, foul-mouthed, liars, scandalmongers, quarrelsome among themselves, no good to anyone, and a nuisance to all – subversive, crazy, noisy rascals; I dislike them so much that if I knew any city that was free of these gentry, I would move there. On the freedom of the will I have written nothing except what I actually think; on many other points I disagreed with Luther, but was afraid to attack him for fear that any benefit to be derived from this uproar might be lost through my fault. And those idiots keep saying that I agree with Luther but am too frightened to say so. I should indeed make a wonderful martyr if to please worthless rogues like them I were to tell lies that would lead to my destruction. In my native country there are a great many who support Luther; had I foreseen that such wretches would be forthcoming, I would have professed myself from the very beginning an enemy of this faction.

I very much liked the look of the young men, both Duba[29] and Haubitz,[30] and shall not fail in my duty if I can be any use to them. Farewell once more.

1523 / To Philippus Melanchthon   Basel, 10 December 1524

First published in the *Opus epistolarum*, this is Erasmus' reply to Ep 1500. The surviving manuscript is a contemporary copy among Camerarius' papers (see Ep 1501 introduction) in the Bayerische Staatsbibliothek Munich (MS Lat 10358.2). It was supplied to Camerarius by Melanchthon, who wrote at the end an admonition to keep it strictly confidential. In his accompanying letter of 22 January 1525 (CR I 722), Melanchthon wrote: 'I am sending to you Erasmus' bitter letter to me ... He has written even more bitterly to Stromer [Ep 1522].'

ERASMUS OF ROTTERDAM TO PHILIPPUS MELANCHTHON, GREETING
If you were here, my dear Philippus, and could see for yourself the tragedy which is unfolding, you would be more ready to admit that it is not without reason that I complain about the behaviour of those who are stirring up trouble in the name of the gospel. For in spite of all I have done they attack

* * * * *

29 Jindřich Berka (Henricus Bircko) of Dubá (Dauba), d 1541, was a member of a large and influential family in Bohemia. He had studied Greek with Melanchthon at Wittenberg (1520–1) before matriculating at Leipzig. He subsequently served as chief justice and captain of Bohemia under Ferdinand I.
30 This Haubitz returned to Saxony early in 1525, bearing Ep 1561. He may have been Valentin Albert von Haubitz, a nobleman who had matriculated at Leipzig in 1520. But since there were three other students named Haubitz at Leipzig in 1521–2, the identity of Erasmus' visitor remains uncertain.

me outrageously in words, books,[1] and drawings,[2] all of which would be tolerable if what they take from my reputation could be credited to the advancement of the gospel; but their reckless conduct obstructs the progress of the humanities and ruins the cause of the gospel. I have no doubt that Luther is offended by these dreadful people.[3] But, when it is to their advantage to do so, they pay no heed at all to Luther's authority. I do not understand it, but the same is true of both sides. No one has done more harm to the pope than those who are the most ardent champions of the papal cause, and no one has caused greater injury to Luther than those who desperately want to be seen as Lutherans. I know what wonders Christ can work, for he knows how to turn the divisions among men to his own good and to the benefit of his people. So, had it been possible, I would have kept clear of these tragic events. While I do not wish to be the cause of trouble, yet I will not fail the interests of the gospel in so far as I see some prospect of success. Luther himself must consider what his own conscience tells him to do.

I have not tried hard to make you change your tune, if only because I realized I would be wasting my time.[4] I am not the judge of another man's conscience or the master of another's faith. Certainly it was always my hope that you should dedicate yourself wholly to the humanities, since that is where your natural talent lies. There would have been no lack of actors for that tragic play, whose ending is still unclear. Far be it from me to be upset by the teaching of the gospel, but there is much in Luther's views which I find offensive. I dislike particularly the extraordinary vehemence with which he treats whatever doctrine he decides to defend and that he never stops until he is carried to extremes. He was warned about this,[5] but far from toning down his invective, he goes even further than before. Perhaps someone will see in his arrogance the confidence which comes of a good conscience and will think his bitterness justified by our behaviour; and to be honest, the general corruption of Christian morals called out for bitter reproof. But my preference was for a temperate frankness so that we might induce even bishops and rulers to share in the endeavour. This was always my aim, nor have I any other aim today. What Luther has in mind I do not know.

* * * * *

1523
1 See Epp 1477, 1477A, 1477B, 1496, 1510.
2 See Epp 1477B:31–7.
3 See Ep 1429 n3.
4 See Ep 1500:40–4.
5 See Ep 980:45–58.

I wrote to Hedio[6] and talked to Oecolampadius[7] and Pellicanus,[8] more than once in fact, to advise them to give a common account of their beliefs to Cardinal Campeggi.[9] Certainly they could have wished for no fairer or kindlier legate. But my words fell on deaf ears.[10] I do not think we would find even Clement[11] as unsympathetic towards restoring the true gospel as some people imagine. But I could get nowhere with any of these suggestions. Their only interest is in seeing their cause creep along by one means or another and they believe the gospel has made fine progress if a few monks divest themselves of their cowls (many of whom, I fear, ought to be behind bars) or if a few priests are on the lookout for a wife or if images have been thrown out of a couple of churches. I wanted to reform the religious life of the priests without lessening their authority and to aid good men who are now buried beneath the rituals of the monks without giving evil men an opportunity to sin more freely; I also hoped that things to which we had grown accustomed through long familiarity might be gradually corrected in such a way that we could avoid throwing everything into confusion and turmoil and that the liberty of the gospel might be the common possession of all mankind. Luther is interested only in things that have gone wrong; he fights to remove whatever offends him, but without being sufficiently careful to avoid some greater evil. Whatever changes heaven may bring about in the state of the world, there will never be any shortage of things to complain about. Our problems can be mitigated, but not removed completely. However many rivers flow into the sea, however much rain falls into it, it always keeps its characteristic savour. Not to mention the fact that the remedy is sometimes worse than the disease. What could be more deadly than the present dissension? How many places are torn by dreadful conflicts? And we anticipate worse to come. Is all this worth it to have a church devoid of images and a few changes made in the rite of the mass?

Now supposing we grant that Luther's teaching is true, since there are many wicked people everywhere who, given the opportunity, are ready for any crime, is there anything which is less likely to foster Christian piety than for ordinary, uneducated people to hear, and for young people to have it drummed into their ears, that the pope is Antichrist, that bishops and priests are demons, that the constitutions of men are heretical, that

* * * * *

6 Not in Ep 1477B, the only extant letter that Erasmus wrote to him at this time
7 For his current relations with Erasmus, see lines 110ff below.
8 Ep 1341A n309
9 Ep 1410
10 *Adagia* I iv 87
11 Pope Clement VII

confession is a pernicious practice, that works, merit, human effort are
heretical ideas, that there is no freedom of the will but all is governed by
necessity, and that it makes no difference what works a man performs? 75
Some people spread such ideas abroad without qualifying them in any way,
and wicked men take them up and turn them to evil ends. I know you will
say that we should not attribute ideas to Luther which spring from the folly
of certain people whom you rightly call fiends, the vilest of creatures to
walk on two feet.[12] But these monsters are encouraged by men whom Luther 80
embraces as the leading exponents of evangelical teaching. In the past the
gospel produced a new race of men in the world. What kind of men this
gospel is producing, I do not like to think. Perhaps things are different
where you live. But the people I know here are of such a character[13] that, if I
had to enter into a contract, I would rather do business with papists than 85
with them. Finally I observe that those whom I once knew to be excellent
people, men to whom you might say virtue came naturally, have changed
for the worse. Whatever the state of things may be, it is highly dangerous to
move the camarina[14] of this world.

Plato, in imagining his ideal republic, realized that people could not be 90
governed without lies.[15] Far be it from a Christian to tell a lie, and yet it is not
expedient to tell the whole truth to ordinary people no matter how it is
done.[16] I could wish that Luther were as successful at turning the minds of
princes and prelates towards the religion of the gospel as he is at raising a
storm against their vices. I do not greatly care what he thinks of me, 95
especially in a matter like this, where private feelings should not be allowed
to count for much. But he has written a great deal about me to his friends
which hardly reveals the sort of attitude you describe. None of this has had
the least effect on me, just as your own judgment on me[17] has not made me
any less appreciative of your abilities. I am prepared for any insults, 100
however cruel, provided the gospel of Christ can flourish.

Karlstadt was here,[18] but he kept his visit a secret. He has published six

* * * * *

12 See Ep 1500:37–8.
13 Cf Ep 1522:95–100.
14 See Ep 1406 n14.
15 *Republic* 414C–415C
16 Cf Epp 1119:45–6, 1167:182–5, 1195:121–4, 1202:137–40, 1219:109–11, 1331:
   23–7.
17 See Ep 1496 n18.
18 Andreas Karlstadt (Ep 1258 introduction), once Luther's colleague in Wittenberg, but now in disgrace because of his increasingly radical views, was
   expelled from Saxony in September 1524. He visited Basel briefly at the end of
   October; cf Ep 1522:60.

pamphlets in German in which he explains that nothing is involved in the Eucharist except the symbols of Christ's body and blood.[19] This caused a terrible commotion at Bern.[20] Here the two men who published the works   105 were thrown into prison[21] on the eve of the Vigil of the Immaculate Conception.[22] I suspect Karlstadt is one of those whom you call bloodthirsty teachers.[23] As for Buschius,[24] I imagine he has hoodwinked many people besides me. Alber,[25] that famous critic of Erasmus, lives in your part of the world – he is a schoolmaster, I think, in the town of Eisenach. I do not   110 include Oecolampadius[26] and men like him among the monsters I spoke of, although there is much about them which I could rightly criticize. So far there is no one for whom I have felt or expressed greater enthusiasm than for Oecolampadius. Yet although he too has professed the deepest friendship for me, not only has he attacked me verbally in conversation and lectures,   115 but he often makes oblique references to me in his writings,[27] even when there is no reason to bring me into the discussion.

You say that my *Diatribe*[28] has not raised any eyebrows in your part of the world. It was not well received, however, by Oecolampadius, who began writing a reply[29] before the work was published. He had taken offence   120 at my *Exomologesis*,[30] imagining that it was an attack on his *Confessio*,[31] when in fact I never read it. Certainly when I was writing that work, no thought of Oecolampadius even entered my head. I could say a great deal more about this, but I have no time for such things; and where friends are concerned,

* * * * *

19 See Ep 1369 n7. Actually seven pamphlets were published, only five of which dealt directly with the Eucharist.
20 There appears to be no other record of this 'terrible commotion.'
21 Thomas Wolff, a printer active at Basel 1519–35, and Johann Bebel (Ep 1477A n8). See Barge II 220.
22 7 December. By 17 December they were out of jail; see Herminjard Ep 130 (p 309).
23 See Ep 1500:37.
24 See Epp 1466:30–7, 1496:96ff.
25 Ep 1466 n19
26 See Ep 1496 n37.
27 The reference is probably to the sermons on 1 John (June 1524; *Oek-Bib* no 95) with their denunciations of 'miserable Pelagians,' and perhaps also to the little volume of sources on free will (Ep 1519 n20); see Staehelin 257.
28 *De libero arbitrio* (Epp 1419, 1481)
29 See Ep 1519 n20.
30 Ep 1426
31 Oecolampadius was the author of two works on this subject, both published in 1521: *Quod non sit onerosa christianis confessio, Paradoxon,* and *De confessionis obligatione;* see *Oek-Bib* nos 38, 42, 43, 50.

there is much to which one must turn a blind eye, although among men who 125
profess the purity of the gospel, such issues should not even arise.

I see that you are anxious that in this reply to me Luther should show
moderation. I should prefer him to reply in his own way. In my own
discussion I adopted a temperate tone, but this was both deliberate and in
keeping with my nature. If he acts out of character, mischief-makers will say 130
that we are in collusion and that the whole thing has been got up between
us. So I hope he will think of the cause and not of me. If, as you seem to
believe, there is an element of bitterness in my *Diatribe*, it is aimed at the
Farels of this world and men like him,[32] as I make clear elsewhere.[33] Besides,
there were things in Luther's *Assertio* which I might justly have taken strong 135
exception to,[34] but I preferred to stick to the point at issue. In other cases I
have made allowance for human feelings, but in this business no insult will
drive me from the proper path. You seem to be worried that, if I continue in
this way, the cause will fall under a greater cloud of hostility and that both it
and the gospel will be placed in jeopardy. In his letters Luther claims that it is 140
of no consequence whether I am with him or against him.[35] I promise you
this, that I shall never knowingly take up arms against the truth of the
gospel. It is for this reason that I have hesitated up to now to demolish those
arguments of Luther's which displeased me, for fear that those which I
approved of would collapse at the same time. Indeed I seize every 145
opportunity to make sure that from the strong and bitter medicine which
Luther has given to the world something helpful may arise for the morals of
the church. Perhaps because of our way of life we have earned for ourselves
such a pitiless physician to cure our ills by cautery and the knife.

Here a few troublemakers are complaining about my lack of consisten- 150
cy, although none of them can point even to a single passage where I
contradict myself. If they think it a sin to disagree with Luther on any point –
though one may ask if Luther is always consistent himself – why do they
permit themselves, when it suits them, to disagree with Luther's teaching? I
am not going to mention here what people said in the course of conversa- 155
tions or at drinking-parties. But did Oecolampadius not publish a work[36]

* * * * *

32 See Ep 1496:72–3, 145ff, 1510:11ff.
33 In *De libero arbitrio* LB IX 1216B
34 Article 36 of Luther's *Assertio omnium articulorum* (Ep 1263 n4) deals with free
   will.
35 See WA-Br III 160:21–3 and Ep 1443:19–24, 60–2.
36 *Quod expediat epistolae et evangelii lectionem in missa vernaculo sermone plebi
   promulgari* (June 1522); see *Oek-Bib* no 65.

when he was staying with Sickingen[37] in which he states that there is no danger in calling the mass a sacrifice? Luther detests that view, so much so that he would rather die ten times over. And what a commotion Zwingli caused when he removed the images of the saints![38] Luther has attacked them both, I am told, in a book that might even be characterized as severe.[39] At Strasbourg, and not only there, they argued publicly that no subject and no language should be studied except Hebrew.[40] Luther answered them in a cutting rejoinder.[41] Need I mention the case of Karlstadt? – for I know what answer I shall get from certain nonentities: 'We do not serve Luther, we serve the gospel.' I am aware that Karlstadt himself wrote that,[42] but he did so in an accommodating spirit to please Melanchthon. Some of these people, my dear Philippus, seem so irresponsible that, if they succeeded, I am afraid that even Luther himself would long for the return of the old tyranny of popes and prelates. For who could keep them in check, since they do not

160

165

170

* * * * *

37 See Ep 1258 n4.
38 See Ep 1496 n40.
39 Allen identified this as Luther's *Wider die himmlischen Propheten, von den Bildern und Sacrament*, part I of which (published 2 January 1525) contains a section entitled 'Von dem Bildsturmen' (WA 18 67–84). This, however, is chronologically impossible, since Luther himself did not know that he was going to write the work until 14 December and did not get to work on it until about the seventeenth (ibidem 18 42–3). On the other hand, Erasmus might well have received from someone some indication of the content of Luther's *Brief an die Fürsten zu Sachsen von dem aufrührischen Geist*, which had been published at the end of July 1524, (ibidem 15 203), and which expressed views on the problem of images similar to those in *Wider die himmlischen Propheten* (ibidem 15 219–20). While the *Brief an die Fürsten* was aimed at Thomas Müntzer and Karlstadt, Zwingli and like-minded reformers would have recognized that their stand on images was implicitly rejected as well.
40 In his *Epistola apologetica* (BOL 1 176:7–177:3) Bucer complained about this remark, which echoed a widespread rumour that the study of Latin was disparaged at Strasbourg. He indicated that all that had happened was that one of the Strasbourg pastors (namely himself) had attempted to help the local Greek teacher find some students by extolling in a sermon the virtues of Greek and Hebrew in comparison with Latin. Despite this and other efforts to set the record straight, the rumour persisted. In his *Epistola ad fratres Inferioris Germaniae* ASD IX-1 392:394–6 Erasmus attributed the view to a single preacher but otherwise stuck to his hostile interpretation of the incident. When Erasmus repeated the rumour in *Hyperaspistes* I LB X 1268F–1269A, Bucer complained directly to him in a letter (Allen Ep 1901:14–16). See the informative notes by Cornelis Augustijn in the passages in BOL and ASD cited above.
41 No such utterance by Luther could be found.
42 The 'answer ... [anticipated] from certain nonentities' appears to be a substantially accurate summary of Karlstadt's attitude rather than a precise quotation.

listen to popes or princes or magistrates or even to Luther himself? Their only theme is the gospel and nothing but the gospel, but they want a gospel of which they themselves will be the interpreters. Even this might be tolerable if their disagreement with the old authorities were matched with agreement among themselves.

With regard to the honesty of your motives, I have no doubt that you are conscientious in what you are doing. But as for Luther's intentions, there is much which makes me hesitate; and if I do not dare to trust my own judgment absolutely, I think, nevertheless, that I can plumb a man's mind as well from his writings as from his company. Luther has a fiery and impetuous temperament. In everything he does you can recognize the 'anger of Peleus' son who knows not how to yield.'[43] You understand, too, what cunning schemes are laid for us by the enemy of mankind. And Luther has won such success in his endeavours, such widespread support, such general applause as would turn the head of even the most modest of men.

Now that I am launched on these troubled seas, consider what a strong anchor, what heavy ballast, what a reliable rudder my ship must have if I am not to be driven from the proper course. Here I see with my own eyes the encouragement which some men take from even the smallest success. If my purpose squares with my conscience, then I have no cause to fear for myself, whatever these men say about my lack of spirit.[44] Neither the emperor nor the pope can free me from the burdens of old age and infirmity. My resources are sufficient to nourish my poor body.[45] I care no more for wealth and office than a winded horse for a heavy load.[46] I have had my fill of glory long since, if glory is anything worth having. And there has been no lack of dangers serious enough to terrify even a bold-hearted man;[47] yet they call one who scorns such hazards a coward. You yourself will not abandon a settled opinion which you have formed: shall I, against my own convictions, profess beliefs which would bring me certain ruin – to say nothing of disgrace? Nothing would be easier for me than to scorn this life, so little of which remains for me – and what little remains is beset with so many ills that I could pray for death if I could present a clear conscience to Christ. My hesitancy[48] and moderation have no other aim than to make myself useful to

* * * * *

43 Horace *Odes* 1.6.6. Peleus was the father of Achilles.
44 Reading *pusillanimus* with the Munich manuscript rather than *pusillanimis* in Allen's text. Cf Ep 1477B n21.
45 See Ep 1518 n18.
46 See Ep 1481 n14.
47 Greek in the original; an expression used by Euripides *Hippolytus* 424
48 *Contatio*; see Ep 1384 n7.

both parties. I hate dissension and I have constantly and steadily counselled
the princes to renounce violence. If I could strangle men's vices without   205
hurting their persons, you would see what a terrible executioner I would be
– beginning at home.

I have no doubts about your good faith, even though I have been
deceived so often in the past by men to whom I was ready to entrust my life
ten times over. But whatever is put on paper becomes public property,   210
whether by the treachery of the couriers or in some other way. If I could have
talked to you, there would have been more which I would have whispered
in your private ear. I have just one wish – that you and your friends honour
and love the gospel with true religious zeal. I have no great concern about
myself.   215

Nesen's death moved me very deeply. He was a dear and faithful
friend, even if his friendship did not turn out very well for me.[49] Everyone
talks of the trustworthiness of the Germans,[50] while the British are spoken of
very differently in this respect. But it has been my fate to encounter the
truest friends among the British and the opposite among Germans; and I am   220
not generalizing from a few instances. I do not understand why you suggest
that I translate the speeches of Demosthenes and Aeschines, since I am sure
there is no one living who could do the job better than you. I have other
things on hand at present and this is the sort of task which is more suited to
your years than to mine. Farewell.   225

Basel, 2 December 1524

I am afraid you won't be able to read this hurried scrawl.

1524 / To Joachim Camerarius   Basel, 11 December 1524

This letter was first printed in the *Opus epistolarum*, doubtless from Erasmus'
rough draft. In 1557 Camerarius published it himself in a volume entitled
*Libellus alter epistolas complectens Eobani et aliorum quorundam doctissimorum
virorum* (Leipzig, in officina Papae). Since Camerarius' text is the more
complete one and is in other respects superior as well, Allen concluded that it
was based on the letter actually sent and gave it preference. On Camerarius,
see Ep 1501, to which this is Erasmus' reply.

Greeting. How I hate this ill health! – not so much for the torments I suffer
from it, but it prevents my doing a kindness to any of my friends; so much

* * * * *

49 See Ep 1479:99–102.
50 Cf Ep 1225:383–90.

harder is it to find oneself uncivil than unfortunate! And it often happens by some fate, I know not how, that several friends descend upon me at once and almost overwhelm me. So it quite often happens that at the same time I 5 have to load with letters men bound for Rome, France, England, Brabant, and Germany. What is more, when you were here[1] I was in such parlous health that I could hardly endure the effort of uttering a word, so that I had not only to make my excuses to a Polish count[2] when he asked me to a party, but to turn him away when he suggested he might come to supper. And so 10 this misfortune compels me to be embarrassed as well as wretched. Could any trouble in one's whole life be harder to bear than one which combines torture with embarrassment? Even so, I know people who do not accept my excuses, which have much more truth in them than I would wish.

As for you, my dear Joachim, when you put such a generous 15 interpretation on the scurvy reception I gave you, it just proves what a straightforward and kindly man you are. When I see you not only taking all my excuses in good part but thanking me so meticulously for our brief talk and for the few words of greeting I added to my letter to Melanchthon,[3] and playing this up in eloquent language as though it were some kindness quite 20 out of the ordinary, I recognize with gratitude the unusual, the extraordinary courtesy of your nature; and not only am I devoted to this quality in you, it makes me sad to think in how few people one can find it nowadays among devotees of the Muses. There ought not to be this distance between the Muses and the Graces. You can find certain individuals in our time who 25 join three Furies with the Muses rather than three Graces – our habits are so barbarous and our writers so spiteful.

And further, while in this business you make me see so clearly your remarkable goodness of heart, at the same time the way you disarm any suspicion that you are responsible for the publication of the letters shows me 30 what powers you have in the way of fertility of wit and readiness of expression. You have left nothing unsaid which skilled counsel ought to bring to bear on such a brief. Let me assure you then, my dear Joachim, that the one thing in all this of which you have convinced me is that you are capable of giving the strongest support even to a case in itself very weak. For 35 my own part, you see, I was entirely persuaded, even before you had said a word, that anything done wrong here was none of your doing; the ugly

* * * * *

1524
1 See Ep 1444 n2.
2 See Ep 1496:235–7.
3 Ep 1496:233–8

suspicion which you try to dispel had never entered the mind of your friend Erasmus. And I can now make a pretty good guess who the people are whose foolish and officious behaviour you criticize. Nor should I have   40 complained about this to Melanchthon, had not this point needed clearing up for the benefit of the discussions that were going on over there. Long ago they had published a letter from Luther to Pellicanus,[4] and also Melanchthon's *Iudicium*;[5] and I did not utter a word of complaint to anyone.

The man who brought your letter needed absolutely no recommenda-   45 tion from you; on the very face of it, as they say,[6] he clearly had intelligence to match his breeding, and besides that, a sort of ready kindliness towards myself. I am sorry that Nesen should have been taken from us,[7] but glad that you have come out safely, for they tell me that you were at risk like everyone else. Farewell.   50

Basel, 11 December AD 1524
Erasmus of Rotterdam, with his own hand, extempore
I fear you may not be able to read this.
To the learned scholar in Greek and Latin, Joachim Camerarius

1525 / From Paul Volz   Hugshofen, 11 December 1524

The autograph of this letter (=Ep 32 in Förstemann/Günther), which is Volz's reply to Ep 1518, was in the Burscher Collection at Leipzig (Ep 1254 introduction). Erasmus' reply is Ep 1529.

Greeting. I have recently sent you three letters,[1] Erasmus dearest brother in Christ, in return for which I have received only one, on the morrow of Our Lady's Conception[2] – and I joyfully put it to my lips, so dear to me is everything that comes from such a gifted man. That my French mass-priest and the many others of whom you write should have exalted you, albeit   5 falsely, above the living, is a great delight to me; not that I set any store by his falsehood, but because your life is not spent in idleness but is laborious and of great value both to the church of God and to our universities. Let it be the will of Almighty God that in future they continue long with their repeated

* * * * *

4 See Ep 1341A:1096–9 with n298.
5 See Ep 1496 n18.
6 *Adagia* I ix 88
7 See Epp 1500:67–8, 1523:216–17.

1525
1 None extant
2 9 December

falsehoods, if they so please, provided only that you by divine mercy live all   10
the longer for the benefit of all who wish to learn. Again, that you should
now be less severely tormented by the stone is great joy. When you say you
have joined no faction, I am bound to approve, although this of itself makes
other men abuse you, who as the Apostle teaches, are yet carnal and walk as
men.[3] What I meant on the back of my letter by coupling together 'the   15
amphibious wonder of the learned world'[4] I cannot say, for I have forgotten
how I addressed it. The only thing I know is that I jokingly slipped into
Greek and used the word 'amphibious' because I was not sure whether or
not you were still alive; and nothing else has occurred to me.

Your book on the freedom of the will I possess and have read, and I   20
greatly prefer this balanced Erasmian view to the meticulous and overly
critical teaching of the Lutherans. The others I have not seen yet. How I wish
your discussion between Thrasymachus and Eubulus might soon appear![5] I
fancy you have already heard the reasons for my being 'ex-abbot.' It began
with the dislike of administration[6] which is almost part of my birthright and   25
was much strengthened by the ambition of the steward of my monastery,
who, though he already has everything in his power, still aims at one thing
more, the crozier and the rings. As he has now been quite unexpectedly
rejected, while I still depend on the approval of the council,[7] I am now called
not 'ex-abbot' but 'twice-abbot.' Such are fortune's merry japes. Forgive me,   30
dear Erasmus, and so farewell.

From my monastery, such as it is, 11 December 1524

Your sincere friend P. Volz

To the honourable Master Erasmus of Rotterdam, his dearest friend in
Christ. In Basel   35

1526 / To Duke George of Saxony   Basel, 12 December 1524

At this point, Erasmus still had not received Duke George's most recent letter,
Ep 1520, which did not reach him until February or March 1525; see Ep 1561.

There are two authentic manuscripts: Erasmus' rough draft in the Royal
Library at Copenhagen (MS G.K.S.95 Fol, f 184), and the actual letter received by

* * * * *

3 1 Cor 3:3
4 See Ep 1518 n14.
5 See Ep 1341A:1338–46.
6 See Ep 1075 introduction.
7 The council (*domini*), located in Ensisheim, that represented the Austrian
   government in Alsace. For evidence of the council's power to intervene in the
   affairs of the monastery, see Ep 1607 and BRE Ep 241.

Duke George, in a secretary's hand, but corrected and signed by Erasmus (Staatsarchiv Dresden, MS Loc 10300). First published in the *Opus epistolarum*, the letter has also been published in Gess I 777–82.

Cordial greetings. Most illustrious prince, I have received three letters from your Highness, one[1] written on 21 May, enclosing a copy of your reply[2] to what, I believe, was my first letter to you.[3] Your third letter[4] has just been delivered, acknowledging the receipt of my *De libero arbitrio*.[5] In the first of your letters you are very angry with me for not taking the field against 5 Luther.[6] You seem to think that if I had acted, things would not have reached their present pass. I replied to this in a brief and hurried note;[7] but we know from experience that letters are frequently intercepted (evidently neither the letter which I sent you[8] in reply to your first letter to me[9] nor that letter of yours[10] of which you recently sent me a copy was ever delivered). So 10 I shall repeat the main points of my argument.

When Luther first appeared upon the stage, the whole world applaud-ed him with one accord; and I believe your Highness was among his supporters. Certainly the theologians, who are now his bitterest enemies, were on his side, as were several of the cardinals, to say nothing of the 15 monks. For it was a worthy cause which he had espoused when he attacked the church and the schools for the corruption of their morals, which had declined to such a point that no decent person could tolerate the situation any longer. He also included in his attack certain men whose evil and deplorable conduct pained the Christian church. Could anyone have 20 foreseen at that time that the affair would have such consequences? If some Daniel had predicted the present outcome, I would not have believed him. I doubt if Luther himself expected such success. And yet, before he had published anything except his *Theses* on papal indulgences,[11] when only one or two pages were circulating among his supporters, I tried to discourage 25

* * * * *

1526
1 Ep 1448
2 Ep 1340
3 Ep 1313
4 Ep 1503. Ep 1520 was still to come; see introduction.
5 Epp 1419, 1481
6 Ep 1448
7 Ep 1499
8 Ep 1313
9 Ep 1298
10 Ep 1340
11 Ie, the Ninety-Five Theses; see Ep 785:39n.

him from proceeding.[12] I thought Luther's scholarship unequal to the task, though practice has now made a fine fighter out of him; I also suspected his campaign would end in trouble and dissension.

At that time I was on intimate terms with men who greeted the prologue to this drama with great enthusiasm; yet none of them was able to change my mind or make me approve what was happening. Certainly I was openly critical of the plot of the play and always made my disapproval clear to everyone; so much so, that when the news came to me in Brabant, where I was staying, that Froben had yielded to the influence of certain scholars (of whom Capito was one) and had printed a few of Luther's books, I wrote to remonstrate,[13] telling him that he could not enjoy my friendship if he persisted in blotting the reputation of his press with work like that. I went further: I wrote a postscript to my *Colloquia*,[14] which were then being printed at Louvain, in which I made it clear that I had no sympathy whatever with the Lutheran party. At this time I advised Luther privately[15] (since he had taken the initiative in writing to me) to pursue his cause in a sincere and honest way and in a spirit of moderation as became one who professed to follow the gospel. Up to that point even the emperor was sympathetic to Luther's teaching. The only protests came from a few monks and in-dulgence-sellers whose profits seemed to be threatened. It was largely the mad turmoil which they created that fanned a tiny spark into such an immense conflagration.

The more I tried to persuade Luther to moderate his conduct, the more savage was his rage. And when I attempted to restrain the other side, all I got for my pains was to be branded as a Lutheran sympathizer. You will say, 'Why did you not take the field when you saw that the evil had already become so serious?' Well, I had formed an opinion of my own abilities, that no one was less suited to the task than I was, and I am far from sure that I was wrong in this assessment. Those who kept telling the emperor and the other leaders that I was the person to put a stop to Luther had reasons for doing so which were by no means innocent. These were the people who maintained – and still maintain – that I know nothing about theology. What, then, did they have in mind? Obviously they wanted to toss me unarmed into a den of ravening beasts and to channel the infamy from this whole affair on to my head. What acclaim would I have earned from that? I should have become

* * * * *

12 See Ep 1143:25–9 with n7.
13 See Epp 904:20n, 1143 n6.
14 Ep 1041
15 In Ep 980

the mouthpiece for the theologians: they would have claimed for themselves the credit for erudition; I would have been given credit only for the style.

Moreover I could never have satisfied them unless, by releasing a torrent of abuse and insults, I had created a general commotion and had used my pen against Luther with a savagery which matched their seething 65 hatred. They had another aim: they wanted to paint me as someone who had earlier been sympathetic to Luther and was now making a public recantation. This was what they proposed: 'You once wrote on behalf of Luther; now write against him.' A fair proposition indeed! I was first to prove myself a liar and then make my pen the drudge of surly, hot-tempered 70 men who have shown themselves my deadliest enemies and who will never cease to be my enemies until they abandon their opposition to the humanities, and that is something they will put off, as the saying goes, till the Greek calends.[16]

Furthermore, unless I had been prepared to defend all their ideas, I 75 would have left myself open to their bitter hatred. I know what these people are like. I should have been nothing but their hatchet man. I have no doubt that what has now come about would have happened at once: all Luther's staunch supporters – and he has many supporters everywhere – would either have ceased to be my friends or would have turned into deadly 80 enemies, as is the case now with some of my oldest and closest friends. There is no part of the world in which my writings have not won for me a host of friends; I count myself a rich man to possess such blessings, however limited my personal wealth may be. Their friendship is a treasure which I greatly prize, and I should have had to give it up without regret and subject 85 myself, unarmed and bereft of the protection of my friends, to those who hate the humanities – or rather I should be offering myself as a victim to be torn to pieces by both sides at once.

At this point you will try to console me by assuring me of the protection of the popes and of the emperor. But will they run to my support when they 90 cannot defend themselves from being pilloried in pamphlets which are full of insults and accusations? As for material support, I have all that I need to nourish my poor body.[17] Anyone who offers an important position to a man of my years and fragile health will not just be strapping a pack-saddle on an ox,[18] but loading an old and winded horse with a burden[19] under which he is 95

* * * * *

16 Ie, forever; see *Adagia* I v 84.
17 See Ep 1518 n18.
18 *Adagia* II ix 84
19 See Ep 1481 n14.

Beginning of the autograph rough draft of a letter from Erasmus
to Duke George of Saxony, Ep 1526
The Royal Library, Copenhagen, MS Gl.kgl.S.95 Fol, f 184 recto

bound to fall. I know that some people say that one should be ready to sacrifice one's life for the Catholic faith. But I am frightened by the fate of Uzzah,[20] who failed in his efforts to support the falling ark. Not every man is called upon to bolster a tottering faith. Even Jerome, in attacking heretics, came close to falling into heresy himself. Surely, then, a man like myself, born for other things and ill equipped for such a fight, had good reason to be afraid? I never doubted that someone would come forward from the serried ranks of the theologians and from the colleges of bishops who would be willing to take on so difficult a task and able to perform it. And my guess has not proved wrong. You see how many distinguished men have risen up to oppose Luther. Yet what have they accomplished? A terrible edict has been issued by the pope[21] and a more fearful one from the emperor,[22] and these have been followed by imprisonments, confiscations, recantations, faggots, and fires.[23] I am not aware that anything has been achieved by this, except that the evil daily spreads more widely. If a pygmy like Erasmus had jumped into the ring, would he have had the least effect on men who take no notice of such mighty giants?

Speaking for myself, what I find particularly distressing about Luther's writings, apart from the extremism of his views, is his bitterness, a bitterness which is equalled only by his arrogance – although those who have now succeeded him make Luther seem comparatively moderate. Yet I hardly dared to trust my own judgment when I reflected on the thousands of supporters who favoured Luther's cause, among whom, even discounting the sheer fact of numbers, I recognized many men of great ability, good judgment, and uncommon learning who had always seemed to me to lead virtuous and godly lives. I often wondered what they saw in Luther's work to make them receive it with such unswerving enthusiasm and cling to it so tenaciously. Yet I never found anyone among them who could satisfy me on all points whenever we had the opportunity for a friendly argument. So the thought sometimes occurred to me that it was my own stupidity which prevented me from seeing what was crystal clear to them and what they defended with such confidence and unanimity.

There is no reason, therefore, why anyone should criticize me for being slow to act: St Hilary hesitated much longer before he lifted his pen against

* * * * *

20 2 Sam 6:6–7; 1 Chron 13:9–10
21 See Ep 1313 n6.
22 See Ep 1313 n7.
23 See Epp 1141 n11, 1157 n3, 1166 n20, 1186 n8, 1299 nn23–4, 1388:8–9.

the Arians.[24] It was not collusion, but religious scruple, which kept him 130
silent so long. A different kind of religious scruple held me back. I often feel
sad when I think of the extent to which Christian piety had declined. The
world had become bewitched by ceremonial, evil monks reigned unchecked, tying the conscience of mankind into inextricable knots. As for
theology, think of the subtle sophistries to which it had been reduced. What 135
dominated the discipline was a reckless passion for definition. I shall say
nothing now of bishops and priests and of those who acted like tyrants in the
name of the Roman pontiff. When I reflected on these things, the thought
came to me: 'What if our infirmities have earned us such a cruel physician,
one who will use cautery and the knife to cure a sickness which will not yield 140
to poultices and salves? Has it pleased God to use Luther, as once he used
the Pharaohs, the Philistines, the Romans, and men like Nebuchadnezzar?
For Luther's successes can hardly have come about without God's help,
especially since many of the actors in the play are vile creatures of
extraordinary depravity and stupidity.   145

I came to the conclusion, therefore, that I should leave the outcome of
this tragedy to Christ. All I could do was dissuade everyone I could from
joining the sect and encourage the opposing parties to try to reach an accord
which was fair to both sides; in this way I hoped that peace might gradually
be restored. To accomplish this end, I thought I had discovered a not wholly 150
ineffective approach. The first attempt was made at the Diet of Worms.[25] A
little later I discussed the matter by letter with the emperor,[26] then with
Adrian vi[27] and Clement vii,[28] and finally with Clement's legate, Cardinal
Campeggi.[29] The leaders of the Lutheran movement were sounded out to
see if they could calm things down.[30] I found them very obstinate and so 155
reluctant to retreat from any of the positions they had taken that every day
they added new bitterness to that which existed before. And it seemed that

* * * * *

24 See Ep 1499 n12.
25 Doubtless a reference to the *Consilium* that was put into circulation just before
    the diet; see Ep 1149 introduction.
26 There is no trace of such a letter to the emperor, but a year after the Diet of
    Worms, Erasmus was at work on another pamphlet on how to settle the Luther
    business (see Ep 1275 n7) and was in lively communication with the imperial
    court (see Ep 1278 n6). Cf Epp 1496:60, 1515:45.
27 Ep 1352
28 Ep 1418
29 Epp 1410, 1415, 1422
30 Erasmus may have been thinking of letters such as Epp 967A and 1202. See also
    Ep 1275 n8.

the leaders on the other side had made up their mind to crush dissent with violence.

I could see that such a plan, even if we agree that it was fair and proper, would need no help from me. One could argue that it is right to send to the stake anyone who opposes an article of faith or any other doctrine which has been accepted by the general consent of the church and therefore has the same status as an article of faith. But it is not right to punish every error with the stake, unless the offence involves sedition or some other crime for which the law prescribes the penalty of death. The gospel should not be used as a cover to allow us to sin with impunity; rather it should teach us to avoid sin altogether even where the law would permit us to sin with impunity. On the subject of the authority of the pope the Paris theologians differ in many of their ideas from the Italians, and one side or the other must be wrong. Neither side, however, calls for the burning of the other. The followers of Thomas differ on many points from those who side with Scotus; and both parties may be represented in the same school. What worries me now is that these common remedies, that is, recantations, imprisonment, and the stake, will simply make the evil worse. Two men were burned at Brussels,[31] and it was precisely at that moment that the city began to support Luther. If the infection had reached only a few, surgery of one sort or another might have been effective. But now it has become so widespread that, I believe, even kings have cause to fear.

The conclusion which I draw from this is not that we should turn a blind eye to the problem; my point is rather that we should not make the evil worse by applying the common remedies. Is anyone impressed by a recantation which has been extorted through terror of the stake? What is achieved by punishing one or two people except to provoke anger in a sect which is far from insignificant in the number of its members? But let us suppose that the evil could be suppressed by remedies such as these. What good will it do to suppress it if it re-emerges soon afterwards more vigorous than before? I could believe that the pope and the princes might be persuaded to accept a fair settlement, if Luther too could bring himself to make concessions. But there are Lutherans here who make me despair of their ever listening to a fair proposal. In these circumstances all I can do is seek with a pure heart for any opportunity to make some useful contribution to the restoration of the public peace; and if it is not possible to achieve the best solution, at least I shall not cease to pray to Christ that he may find it for us. My prayer is not for the owl of Minerva,[32] but for the dove of Christ, that

* * * * *

31 See Ep 1384 n2.
32 A symbol of victory; see *Adagia* i i 76.

it may descend upon us and bring good out of the reckless deeds of certain men. This is what I work and pray for with a pure heart. Whichever side wins, I shall not live to enjoy the victory, since I must soon leave this mortal scene. But I shall leave with a quieter mind if I see Christ's cause winning the palm of victory. Luther has given the world strong and bitter medicine. 200 Whatever we may think of Luther's medicine, I hope it will bring better health to the body of Christ's people, which has been tainted by ills from every quarter.

There are other matters which it would not be safe to entrust to a letter. If your Highness had been aware of them, you would not have written two 205 such letters as you did, so unlike those which I receive from the pope,[33] the emperor,[34] Ferdinand,[35] and the king of England.[36] However, I am not offended by your frankness. Someone must have persuaded you to write as you did, and your own devotion to the Catholic faith made you say those things. But it was very hard to read 'I wish God had put you in this frame of 210 mind two years ago, that you might have dissociated yourself from that faction and to such good effect that by the publication of some work aimed at them' and so forth.[37] In fact, what your most illustrious Highness is advising me to do, so I did four years ago, and I did much more than you are asking for. I never joined those people; I preferred to suffer the loss of many friends 215 rather than have anything to do with that faction despite its general popularity. How often have I testified, both in books and in letters,[38] that I have never had any connection with Luther! How frequently have I set out my disagreements for all to see! I did try to maintain my old friendship with learned men so far as it was possible to do so, though without accepting their 220 views. My courtesy in these matters was praised even by Pope Adrian and by the most reverend cardinal Campeggi, who understood that this was helpful to the cause. Perhaps there will be critics who will attack me for the moderate tone which I adopted in the *Collatio*,[39] although it was enthusiastically approved by many scholars and by the king of England and his 225 cardinal.[40] Such moderation is more troubling to Luther than any number of

* * * * *

33 Ep 1443B
34 Ep 1270
35 Ep 1505
36 See Ep 1467 n11.
37 Ep 1448:38–42
38 For example: Epp 939, 961, 967, 1041, 1342
39 Ie, *De libero arbitrio*
40 Possibly in the letters mentioned in Ep 1467:20–1. A rough draft of the treatise had been dispatched to Henry the previous March (Ep 1430). But see also Ep 1513:7–12.

insults. Some may think that I have been too slow to take the field. But the record will show that I have never failed the cause of the church.

It would have done much for scholarship if Mosellanus had been long spared to live among us.[41] But I accept his death with an easier mind because he has been taken from a world in dreadful turmoil. I imagine you have already made provision for his successor, since the letter in which you raised the question[42] was written a long time ago. It will be difficult to find someone who is an expert in both languages to take Mosellanus' place, and even more difficult to meet your additional requirement, that it be someone who has absolutely no connection with the Lutheran party. If I think of anyone suitable, I shall let you know.

So much for your two earlier letters.[43] Now for the latest.[44] I am delighted that my *Collatio* has met with your Highness' approval. Letters come in from all quarters, congratulating me on my efforts.[45] Some confess to having changed their opinions after reading my work. They tell me also that it has not ruffled any feathers at Wittenberg.[46] Here, however, it has raised a storm. In all of his sermons Oecolampadius takes aim at the book.[47] I have received the *De votis* and begun to read it. It seems a very long-winded work. Josse Clichtove, the Paris theologian, has already written a detailed reply.[48] I suppose the *De modo orandi*[49] has reached your part of the world by now. Otherwise I would have sent you a copy. And perhaps I shall send one if the courier is willing to accept such a heavy parcel.

May the Lord Jesus keep your illustrious Highness in good health for many a year to come.

Basel, 12 December 1524
Erasmus of Rotterdam
Your Highness' most humble servant

* * * * *

41 See Ep 1448 n6.
42 Ep 1448
43 Epp 1340, 1448
44 Ep 1503
45 Epp 1509, 1511, 1513
46 See Ep 1500:45–6.
47 See Epp 1522:93–4, 1523:110–20; also Ep 1496 n37.
48 In book three of his *Antilutherus* (Paris: S. de Colines, 13 October 1524).
49 Ep 1502

1527 / To François Du Moulin   Basel, 12 December 1524

First published in the *Opus epistolarum*, this is Erasmus' answer to Ep 1516.

ERASMUS OF ROTTERDAM TO FRANÇOIS DU MOULIN, BISHOP OF
CONDOM, GREETING

If only Hilarius, my heir as you call him, had the brains to match his good
intentions! I had told him actually in writing to get some modest refuge
ready for me in your part of the world before September; he forgot entirely,   5
intoxicated, I suspect, with the delight of finding himself again in France, to
which he is entirely devoted. I wrote again to say I should not be coming
before next spring,[1] and that meanwhile if France was treating him well he
had better make the most of it; if not, he should return here, where I should
find him useful and he perhaps might not suffer by it. Back he came, with a   10
few letters[2] which he had managed to extract from the writers, with nothing
in them, and soon he means to take wing again for France. If in your
generous way you want to be kind to him, and if you find he deserves it, do
not trust him with much money in hand; let him look out for a chaplaincy,
which cannot run through his fingers. I know what he's like; it isn't that I   15
don't like him.

He tells me that your Excellency has decided to pay us a flying visit
here. Though I suspect the remark was not serious, yet as Hilarius swears it
is so, I see no reason why you should undertake such a laborious journey.
Had it so chanced, I was minded to risk this wretched body of mine on a   20
journey in September. In winter I shall not do so, unless I have previously
made up my mind to die; and even for the spring I cannot promise anything
definite. The war is getting more serious;[3] and my future state of health is
uncertain. Many other things could arise which might at least impede any
plan, even if they did not change it. I do not write this because to have a sight   25
of you would be anything but the greatest possible pleasure to me; only
because I should not like a dear friend to have the expense and labour of a
journey to no purpose. You say something in your letter about seeking the

* * * * *

1527
1 Cf Ep 1484:15–16.
2 Not extant
3 Epp 1369 n12, 1519 n29

swallow[4] in snowy places; please God this may not be a bad omen.[5]
Farewell. 30

Basel, 12 December 1524

1528 / To Johannes Caesarius   Basel, 16 December 1524

On Caesarius, see Ep 374. This letter was first published in the *Opus
epistolarum*, and it is that text that Allen published. A sixteenth-century
manuscript copy of the letter, unknown to Allen, is found in the so-called
Codex Ratzeberger in the Bibliothek des Evangelischen Predigerseminars
Wittenberg (Man 101). This volume, which has no pagination, contains copies,
in two unknown hands, of 102 letters, mostly by Luther and Melanchthon,
from the period 1521–30. Compared to the text in the *Opus epistolarum*, the
manuscript of the letter has many gaps; the first twelve lines, for example (here
down to line 21, 'porridge'), are missing. On the other hand, the manuscript
begins with two sentences that are missing from the *Opus epistolarum* text;
see n4. Thanks are due to Walter Thüringer of the Melanchthon-Forschungs-
stelle in Heidelberg for calling this manuscript to our attention. A version of
the letter similar to that in the Codex Ratzeberger, based on an unidentified
source and with an inferior text, was published by Johann Gottfried Weller in
his miscellany *Altes aus allen Theilen der Geschichte* II (Chemnitz 1766) 643–5.
Allen reports that he had heard of this version but that he had not succeeded in
tracing it, which is odd, since he had managed to find Ep 1377 in the same
source.

ERASMUS OF ROTTERDAM TO JOHANNES CAESARIUS, GREETING
There was a suspicion, not a very serious one, that you had taken some sort
of offence at the letter[1] in which I gave a rather light-hearted answer to your
question about the justified publican[2] – you must not think I had heard
reports of any sharper reaction. That you should pay your friend the 5

* * * * *

4 See Ep 1516 n3.
5 Here Erasmus deliberately misconstrues Du Moulin's comment by reference to
   Adagia I i 2, 'You shall not have swallows unders the same roof' (CWE 31
   44:361ff), where the swallow is the symbol of an ungrateful and untrustworthy
   guest. In other words, he hopes that he will not be an unwelcome guest if he
   visits Du Moulin.

1528
1 Not extant
2 Luke 18:10–14

splendid compliment of saying that he has gone counter to his true self fills me of course with proper gratitude. My enemies too in their foolish way say the same thing that you now tell me seriously as a friend. Yet all this time no one has appeared who could produce a single point on which I have contradicted myself, although so much work of mine is in existence and   10 though my pieces are scrupulously examined by men steeped in prejudice and bent on calumny. I write now what I used to write in the old days, I pursue the same objects so far as I can, and put more effort into doing so than you people suppose.

'I laid the egg, and Luther hatched it.'[3] An astounding statement by   15 those Minorites of yours, which should earn them a fine big bowl of porridge![4] The egg I laid was a hen's egg, and Luther has hatched a chick of very, very different feather. I am not surprised that those pot-bellies should be the source of such remarks, but it astonishes me that you agree with them. And yet you yourself could be the best witness to my constant   20 disapproval of Luther's virulence, afraid as I was that the thing would end in rioting and bloodshed.

You would like me to have kept my mouth quite shut. How can you say such a thing? Was I to remain quite silent on superstition and sophistry and sham bishops and wicked monks for fear someone would twist my words   25 into the wrong sense? Who could have guessed that monstrosities were lurking in Germany like those of the kind we now behold? 'This was the way your writings were thought to lead'; so you tell me. Which way? Towards civil strife, which I have always loathed? Towards subversion, which I have consistently detested? I have advanced as far as the shore; am I thought to   30 contradict myself if I am reluctant to plunge headlong in the waves?

You are sorry that men should speak ill of me. I in my turn am sorry that there should be so many Christians who speak ill of a man who does them good service. To remain silent was out of the question. To please both sides was beyond me. Jupiter himself, they say, has not the privilege of   35

* * * * *

3 This letter is the earliest known source for this famous slogan, which apparently originated with the Franciscans of Cologne.
4 The Wittenberg manuscript (see introduction) commences at this point with the following two sentences that are not found in Allen's text: 'I know and I see that the barbarians, victorious over all the humanities at once, will rage against me especially; this is attributable solely to those who are stupidly raving, to whom everything is displeasing. Melanchthon has been swaying to and fro for a long time now, and Luther too, seeing that things are swept so violently off course, begins to totter.' The Wittenberg version then continues as here: 'The egg I laid was a hen's egg,' etc.

pleasing everyone,[5] whether he rains or smiles from a clear sky. In any case I count it a lesser evil to be ill spoken of by the men you mention than to join some lunatics I know of and go raving mad. Perhaps the outcome will of itself make people speak of me more kindly. At least the most intelligent men in either camp now approve both the moderate line I take and my 40 integrity. It is something, my dear Caesarius, in such a storm not to be blown off course. You would agree all the more if you knew the whole story of what is happening here. I am ill spoken of in the company of some mean characters,[6] whom even Luther hates because their support is embarrassing.[7] I am more kindly spoken of in the hearing of the pope, the emperor, 45 Ferdinand, the king of England,[8] and other great ones to whom I had been falsely reported as having made a compact with Luther. Personally I would rather have abuse rained on me by both sides than be a glorious leader in this conspiracy[9] of rebels. Never will I join a faction, never betray the gospel.

Some people in your part of the world have taken offence at my 50 Diatribe.[10] Yet Melanchthon writes that it has had a mild reception in Wittenberg and that Luther himself was not much put out.[11] Those gods of yours no man can satisfy. I am delighted that you liked my *Misericordia*;[12] my *De libero arbitrio* you must tell me what you think of when you have time, and I shall receive your opinion with great respect. On the business of the 55 printers[13] I have had two letters.[14] What you wanted in the first one I had done already of my own accord, and the object of your second will be achieved in any case unless something unavoidable happens, though I do not mix much in such men's affairs; potters,[15] you know. I have been here for more than two years now,[16] independent of Froben except that we are 60 united by the greatest good will. I pay my own way.[17] For the ten months I lived with him[18] I paid 150 gold pieces.[19]

* * * * *

5 *Adagia* ɪɪ vii 55
6 See Epp 1429, 1477, 1477A.
7 See Ep 1429 n3.
8 See Ep 1526 nn33–6.
9 Cf Epp 1433:14, 1477:33, 1481:28, 1506:10.
10 *De libero arbitrio* (Epp 1419, 1481)
11 See Ep 1500:45–6.
12 See Ep 1474.
13 See Ep 1523:105–6.
14 Not extant
15 Ie, jealous rivals; *Adagia* ɪ ii 25
16 In the house that he had rented from Froben; Ep 1316 n10
17 See Epp 1477B n11, 1518 n18.
18 In 1521–2; Ep 1289 n14
19 See Ep 1341A:1790–1 with n418.

The letter[20] that you wanted not to fall into Froben's hands was delivered to me by him, and the man who delivered it to Froben had told him more secrets than were in the letter; so it had pretty clearly been opened. But that this was not Froben's doing I am quite certain. He is the most honourable of men. It is foolish nowadays to put into a letter what you want not to get out. The veil of the temple is rent in twain;[21] everything is common property, even what you have said to the priest under the strictest seal of the confessional. Let each man look to himself. The Lord is at hand. Farewell, best of men.

Basel, 16 December 1524

1529 / To Paul Volz Basel, 18 December 1524

First published in the *Opus epistolarum*, this is Erasmus' reply to Ep 1525.

ERASMUS OF ROTTERDAM TO ABBOT PAUL VOLZ, GREETING
You too must bear your cross, dear friend, if you wish to reign with Christ; and from this no crozier however historic, no two-peaked mitre, and no rings will ever set you free. It is a poor kingdom that is at stake,[1] and were it a very great one, I know that your spirit is not much attracted by such things. You have learned by experience that even an absolute ruler is not his own master, for he may not abdicate even when he wishes to. I have steadily refused the treasurership at Tours.[2] It was a post with plenty of freedom and perfectly ready for me, worth five hundred crowns at the very least.[3] I am no ox for the pack-saddle.[4] Would you have exchanged your abbatial staff for such a position? Though the income specified may be fair enough, the sum promised is not always paid; and the worst thing of all is that those who wish to hurt one find a good pretext for their malevolence, and the resulting discredit is a heavier burden than the loss of money.

The letter in which you say you have written three times was the third to reach me,[5] so one at least has gone astray. When I read 'amphibious'[6] I

* * * * *

20 Not extant
21 Matt 27:51, Mark 15:38

1529
1 Cf Statius *Thebaid* 1.151.
2 See Ep 1434 n12.
3 See Ep 1471 n10.
4 *Adagia* II ix 84; see Ep 1481 n14.
5 Ep 1525
6 See Epp 1518 n14, 1525:15–19.

suspected what you now say you meant, except that I did not really guess
how 'the learned world' came in. For we call creatures amphibious which
live in both elements, like crocodiles and seals. Moreover, in defiance of the
Muse of grammar you wrote the word in Greek with a short *o*.   20

As for my own life, you wish me a long one; but this is in Christ's hand.
For my own part, I will never knowingly turn aside either to the right hand
or to the left. What will be the outcome of the uproar these men have raised, I
do not know. I keep clear of it myself, no longer out of prudence merely but
as a religious duty. Can it be God's will to use it to correct our obstinate   25
persistence in evil?

Melanchthon writes that my *Diatribe* has had a mild reception even in
Wittenberg.[7] Stupid people are furious. Thrasymachus and Eubulus dare
not raise their heads,[8] expecting to be stoned by both sides if they even look
out of the window. This is an age in which one may not speak either truth or   30
falsehood. I wish you joy and peace in the Lord, reverend father. Beatus I
have not yet seen,[9] nor do I think he will come soon. So much for a very
laconic answer to your letter.

Basel, 18 December 1524

1530 / From Johann von Botzheim   [Constance], 20 December 1524

The autograph of this letter (=Ep 33 in Förstemann/Günther) was in the
Burscher Collection at Leipzig (Ep 1254 introduction). On Botzheim and his
current 'business' (line 7), see Ep 1519 introduction.

Greeting, my beloved teacher. The day after I had written to you, I had the
letter you sent by the Basel courier.[1] The news of their imprisonment does
not greatly distress me, for I see how the art of printing is misused, not
without serious disorder and danger.[2] You say you are sorry for my sake that

* * * * *

7 See Ep 1500:45–6.
8 See Ep 1525:22–3 with n5.
9 Beatus Rhenanus (Ep 327) was away at Sélestat; see Ep 1567.

1530
1 The letter, which is not extant, was probably dated c 10 December, since it
   reported the news of the arrest of the Basel printers, which is also reported in
   Ep 1522–3. The letter was presumably written in response to Ep 1519. If such
   be the case, then the letter mentioned here in lines 1 and 14 must be another
   letter no longer extant.
2 See Ep 1523:105–6 with n21.

you did not get the datary's letter in time,[3] but it makes little difference; a   5
letter from you is always well timed. Do try to help me as far as you can,
though I hope the business can be settled somehow, yet not without some
loss of money on my side. One must expect to put up with something. That
Sander is the instigator of this affair I have many grounds for supposing.[4]
What you say about the airs Fabri gives himself is nothing new;[5] he is a   10
thoroughly conceited man. I have sent the money for the horse[6] and this
letter by a reliable messenger; please send an answer back by him if you have
any news. I have also sent money to Froben for a Jerome[7] and a Lexicon.[8]
Everything else I put in my last letter.[9] Farewell, dearest teacher.

20 December 1524   15
Your sincere friend Johann von Botzheim
To the most learned of all theologians, Erasmus of Rotterdam, his
beloved teacher. In Basel

1531 / To Juan Luis Vives   Basel, 27 December 1524

First published in the *Opus epistolarum*, this reply to Ep 1513 is the first
surviving letter of Erasmus to Vives (Ep 1362) since Ep 1111.

ERASMUS OF ROTTERDAM TO LUIS VIVES, GREETING

My *Diatribe*[1] has had a very mild reception in Wittenberg, as I learn in a letter
from Philippus Melanchthon;[2] but he does not try to conceal his anxiety for
the future of Luther's movement (which he says is tied up with the gospel) if
I go on like this. When you speak, my dear Vives, of a victory which will   5
mean lamentation for the whole world if certain people were to take
advantage of it, you are absolutely right. I am under pressure from both
sides, which is indescribably unpleasant, but in both parties I perceive men

* * * * *

3 Doubtless Ep 1509, which Erasmus apparently wished he had received before
  writing the letter on behalf of Botzheim mentioned in Ep 1519:6–9.
4 On Sander and his passionate opposition to the reform party at Constance, see
  Ep 1401:17–23.
5 Cf Ep 1519:67–9.
6 See Ep 1519:1.
7 See Ep 1465.
8 See Ep 1460.
9 See n1 above.

1531
1 *De libero arbitrio* (Epp 1419, 1481)
2 See Ep 1500:45–6.

who will be insufferable if they win. In these parts things are clearly heading
towards subversion, and some great men are trying to involve me in this　10
business whether I will or no, though I should produce no result except to
stir up both sides against me. To have the approval of such a king, and such a
queen, makes me intensely grateful; but what does this contribute to one's
daily bread?[3] I argue prettily enough, but it costs a lot to keep the pot boiling
here. Not a word from Mountjoy[4] in the way of a message or a letter; I expect　15
Lieven's sudden departure is the reason.[5]

Whom you mean by my new opponent I do not quite understand,
unless perhaps you are thinking of Otto Brunfels,[6] whom Luther himself
abominates worse than I do.[7] And yet Phallicus[8] is madder still. Their
insolence has been restrained by the magistrates with very severe threats;[9]　20
otherwise they were all set to attack me with no restraint of any kind.

In my notes on Jerome I have made many corrections at least, though
perhaps not all that were needed. I had at that time many people urging me
on and no one to help me. How little I knew what the Germans are really
like![10] That mistake about Laberius I detected quite lately, while trying to get　25
more certainty about his dates, though I had my doubts before. Linacre's
death would distress me more if I did not consider the great torments he has
been spared.

As to X,[11] I wrote less than he deserves, for he is a bigger villain than
any Eurybatus or Phrynondas,[12] but as much as I thought suitable for a　30
moderate man like myself or a sensible man like you. He diligently

* * * * *

3 This remark conflicts with Erasmus' claim that he was not a 'hunter of gifts' (Ep
　1326:10–11). However, lately he claimed to have been having difficulty making
　ends meet; see Ep 1434:28–30, 66–7, 1470:25–30. But see also Ep 1518:60–1
　with n18.
4 See Ep 1513 n5.
5 In September, Lieven Algoet had carried a packet of letters to England for
　Erasmus (Ep 1486 n10). The approximate date of his departure from London
　(13 November) is given by Ep 1513, the only extant reply to any of the letters
　delivered in September.
6 Ep 1405
7 Cf Ep 1477:7–15.
8 Guillaume Farel; see Epp 1477A, 1496:72–3, 145ff, 1510:11ff.
9 See Epp 1481:36–8, 1510:64–5.
10 Probably a reference to the similar circumstances that had resulted in so many
　errors in the edition of Seneca: see Epp 1341A:454–8, 1479:99–102, 1482:42–8.
11 Clearly Birckmann; Ep 1513:46ff
12 Eurybatus was one of the Cercopes (ape-like people who robbed Hercules in
　his sleep), 'a man of notable wickedness,' 'notorious for cunning and wicked
　ways;' *Adagia* I ii 86. The other rascal, Phrynodas, is mentioned in the same
　adage but stands on his own in *Adagia* III vii 22.

discourages Froben from printing anything of yours; and Froben, in this matter at any rate, can do nothing without his support. For in Germany hardly anything will sell except Lutheran and anti-Lutheran stuff. My own things however still go pretty well, as is shown by one thing at least, that   35 Froben has so many imitators, which loses him a lot of money. The imperial privilege[13] which discourages competitors is not worth a snap of the fingers to the gentry who inflict the emperor on us; in fact they make money by selling his name. I have been longing for some time to get away somewhere from this strife of potter with potter.[14]   40

Froben has complained to me seriously that he cannot sell a single *De civitate Dei*[15] at Frankfurt, and his expression as he said this was such that I think he is speaking the truth. You see how fortune rules even where the Muses are concerned. In that particular case I am ready to suspect anything; except that, had the book been shorter as I advised you long ago,[16] this   45 would have made it more saleable. And Froben took this business on under compulsion from me rather than persuasion. And it's a thing that demands considerable outlay. I am sorry for him; he is a worthy man and absolutely honest, and that Pseudocheus[17] with his trickery leads him a proper dance. If you could make that *De civitate* more saleable by lecturing on it or in some   50 other way, it would be a help to him. I see no way except to get out a corrected edition of the whole of Augustine.[18] In this I should like to help you by taking on some portion of the work. Weary as I am already, I shall not fail in my duty. I am extremely glad, my dear Vives, to hear that England is going well for you, and I pray that you may always find it so. Farewell.   55

Basel, Nativity of St John the Apostle 1524

1532 / To John Francis   [Basel, c 27 December 1524?]

This letter was first published in the *Opus epistolarum*. Allen's dating is necessarily entirely conjectural. Points of resemblance to Epp 1489 and 1514 suggest this general period, but September is ruled out because the packet of letters sent to England at that time included a letter (Ep 1486) to Wolsey (see line 45 of this letter). Thus this letter was perhaps written sometime after Ep 1489 and sent with Ep 1531.

* * * * *

13 That granted by Archduke Ferdinand in the emperor's name; see Ep 1341 n4.
14 *Adagia* I ii 25
15 Ep 1309
16 Cf Ep 1271:12–13.
17 A name for Birckmann; see Ep 1513:46–50 with n18.
18 For the origin and early progress of this project, see Ep 1309 introduction. For Erasmus' resumption of work on it, see Ep 1473 n5.

A founding member of the London College of Physicians in 1518, John Francis was a long-time friend of Erasmus (Ep 1138:23–4). At this time he was physician to the household of Cardinal Wolsey.

ERASMUS TO FRANCIS, PHYSICIAN TO THE CARDINAL OF YORK, GREETING

I am often surprised and distressed by the question how it can be that England has for so many years now been beset by continual pestilence, and in particular by the sweating-sickness,[1] which almost seems to be its speciality. We read somewhere of a city set free from a pestilence of long standing by rearranging the buildings on the advice of a philosopher.[2] Unless I am much mistaken, a similar policy might set England free.

To begin with, they do not consider which quarter of the sky their windows or doors will face, and then their rooms are as a rule so planned as to make a through draught impossible, which Galen especially recommends.[3] Then a great part of the walls consists of transparent glass panes which admit light in such a way as to exclude air, and yet admit through chinks what they call filtered air, which is considerably more unhealthy and stands there motionless for long periods. The floors too are generally spread with clay and then with rushes from some marsh, which are renewed from time to time but so as to leave a basic layer, sometimes for twenty years, under which fester spittle, vomit, dogs' urine and men's too, dregs of beer and cast-off bits of fish, and other unspeakable kinds of filth. As the weather changes, this exhales a sort of miasma which in my opinion is far from conducive to bodily health.

Besides which, England is not only surrounded entirely by the sea but marshy too in many places and intersected by brackish rivers, to say nothing of the salt fish to which the common people are so surprisingly addicted.[4] I should be confident that the island would be far healthier if the use of rushes were abolished, if rooms were so constructed as to be open to the air of heaven on two or three sides, and all the glass windows were so made that they could be opened fully and fully shut – so shut as to leave no gaping chinks to let in unhealthy draughts. For if it is healthy sometimes to let in the

* * * * *

1532
1 Something with which Erasmus was all too familiar; see Epp 623–4, 1211 n64.
2 Plutarch *Moralia* 515C (*De curiositate* init)
3 *De sanitate tuenda* 1.11, which Linacre had translated into Latin (Ep 502:17n)
4 For Erasmus' views on the evils of salt fish, see the opening passage of Ἰχθυοφαγία 'A Fish Diet,' first printed in the Froben *Colloquia* of February 1526.

fresh air, it is healthy sometimes to exclude it.[5] The common people laugh if   30
anyone objects to a foggy day. For my part, even thirty years ago, if I went
into a room which no one had lived in for several months, I began to feel
feverish immediately. It would help if the common people could be
persuaded to eat less and to be more restrained in the use of salt fish, and
then if local magistrates could be given a public responsibility to keep the   35
streets more free from filth and urine, and if areas near the city could be
taken care of too.

You will smile, I know, to find I have enough leisure to mind about
such things; but I have a kindly feeling for a country that gave me a lodging
for so long, and in which I should be happy to spend the rest of my days[6] if   40
that were permitted.[7] No doubt with your usual good sense you know far
more about this[8] than I do, but I took a fancy to mention it to you so that, if
my judgment agrees with yours, you may persuade the leading men to act
on this. For in the old days this was thought to be the business of kings.

I would have written very readily to his Eminence the cardinal, but I   45
had no time and nothing particular to say and I know how he is distracted
with business. Farewell, kindest of friends, to whom I am much indebted.

1533 / To Eustachius Andreas   Basel, 27 December 1524

This letter was first published in the *Opus epistolarum*. About Eustachius
Andreas nothing is known apart from the information in this letter.

ERASMUS OF ROTTERDAM TO EUSTACHIUS ANDREAS, MONK OF
CLUNY, GREETING
Dearest brother in Christ, the exceptional warmth of your feeling for me,
conveyed not so much in words as by the look in your face (as the phrase
goes),[1] your glance, and your whole demeanour, makes it impossible for me   5

* * * * *

5 The idea seems to have been that when it was windy, the air would be fresh
  and the windows should be kept open, but that when it was still, a miasma
  would rise from the dirty streets and it would be better to keep the windows
  closed.
6 See Ep 1455 n9. Though eager to leave Basel, Erasmus had found that most
  other places of refuge were closed to him; see Ep 1514.
7 Ie, by those who paid his imperial pension; see Epp 1380 introduction,
  1514:13–14.
8 Ie, the causes of pestilence

1533
1 Cicero *Ad Atticum* 14.13b.1

not to return your affection, unless I am ready to be thought a monster of discourtesy. I fear however that you may share the experience of Ixion[2] in the story, who embraced a cloud instead of Juno. It remains that you should give my labours, of which you have such a high opinion, the support of your prayers, while I most gladly admit you into the circle of my friends and will not fail to play my part should anything arise in which I can oblige you. 10

Pray give my respects to those two brothers, the most civilized of lawyers, whose name came up in our conversation, and also to that equally learned and civilized doctor whose acquaintance I made in Mechelen and who came to greet me at Besançon.[3] I remember everything about him except his name. 15

Mind you devote yourself to honourable studies, so as to become both an ornament and an asset to your order. The dignity of an abbot is not a thing to be pursued, but it will come of its own accord to one who deserves it as you do. Farewell. 20

Basel, morrow of the Holy Innocents 1524

1534 / To Léonard de Gruyères   Basel, 29 December 1524

This letter was first published in the *Opus epistolarum*.

Léonard de Gruyères (d 1540) came from a noble family in the region of Fribourg, Switzerland. He had been a canon of Besançon since 1507 when, in about 1520, the archbishop of Besançon made him his official (ie, head of the archiepiscopal court). Erasmus met Gruyères in Besançon during his visit there in the spring of 1524 (Allen Ep 1610:34–5), and from then on they corresponded.

ERASMUS OF ROTTERDAM TO LÉONARD, OFFICIAL OF THE
ARCHBISHOP OF BESANÇON, GREETING
My distinguished friend, I should have resented my state of health less if it

* * * * *

2 After murdering his father-in-law, Ixion, king of the Lapithae, sought refuge with Zeus, who offered him hospitality. But Ixion had the impudence to covet Zeus' own wife Hera (Juno). Zeus thereupon formed a cloud in the likeness of Hera and by this phantom Ixion fathered Centaurus, who in turn fathered the race of centaurs.

3 Erasmus visited Besançon in the spring of 1524 (Ep 1440 n4). The two brothers referred to in line 12 remain unidentified. Allen speculated that the 'civilized doctor' (cf Allen Ep 1610:37) of line 14 might be the Dr Felix of Dôle to whom Ep 1956 is addressed, and that this Dr Felix might have been identical with Petrus Phoenix, professor of law at Dôle. There is, however, no evidence for Phoenix's presence at Mechelen.

meant only torment for myself and did not also make me a tedious burden to
my friends, for it would be easier to bear if it brought pain without   5
embarrassment. As it is, I suffered when I was with you[1] not so much from
my affliction[2] as from a feeling of shame at my enforced inability to respond
to all the very great kindness you showed me. I rather suspect that there are
people who do not share your courteous disposition, who use my calamity
as a basis for calumny, and when I yield to unhappy necessity call me   10
discourteous. After I left you I lay ill here for some time, and thanks to a
severe regime I slowly and gradually returned to life. When I was a little
stronger the stone,[3] which had been lying in ambush, showed its true
colours. I got rid of it, but at very great peril of my life. Later I began to be
somewhat more comfortable, having discovered liquorice water,[4] with   15
which I dilute my wine, for if the wine is bitter the liquorice sweetens it; it
corrects acidity, modifies excessive dryness, softens a hard wine, and cools a
fiery one.

Some sort of rumour has reached here that after I left you there was
some gossip about my being a follower of Luther,[5] but I am hardened now to   20
all this uproar. If only both sides would devote their efforts to a real
flowering in all men's hearts of the purity of the gospel! My own pen would
not fail in its task. Biétry is in a great state of activity, hoping to get the mass
authorized;[6] but I am not keen on the idea, and it is better nowadays not to
give bad men a handle to provoke an uproar.   25

You have in your neighbourhood our new evangelist Farel,[7] the most
poisonous and subversive liar I have ever seen. It seems to me high time for
bishops and princes to put their heads together seriously, to see if they
cannot put an end to this schism, which spreads more widely every day, in
such a fashion that it cannot easily sprout again. The ordinary remedies,   30
recantations, imprisonment, and penance, evidently have no effect except
to make things worse.

* * * * *

1534
1 In April; see Ep 1440 n4.
2 A severe cold; Epp 1466:68–9, 1488:5
3 Ep 1452 n22
4 Cf Pliny *Naturalis historia* 22.9.26. The remedy is more fully described in Ep
1759.
5 Cf Ep 1510:8–9. The origin of the rumour is recounted in Ep 1956.
6 On Biétry and the mass in question, see Ep 1391.
7 Epp 1477A, 1496:72–3, 145ff, 1510:11ff.

Pray give my warmest greetings to the archdeacon[8] and his official,[9] and besides them to François the treasurer[10] and to Désiré[11] and my other respected friends. Farewell.   35

Basel, morrow of the Holy Innocents 1524

* * * * *

8 Ferry de Carondelet (Ep 1350 n6)
9 Guillaume Guérard of Besançon (d 1529) was canon of Besançon since 1514. He played host to Erasmus during the latter's visit to Besançon in April (Allen Ep 1610:29–33), but in the aftermath appears to have instigated hostile rumours questioning Erasmus' orthodoxy (Allen Ep 2895:63ff).
10 François Bonvalot (d 1560), member of a newly rich and powerful bourgeois family of Besançon, became canon of Besançon in 1510 and treasurer of the chapter in 1522. Later he became abbot of St Vincent at Besançon (1532) and abbot of Luxeuil (1542). Well connected at the imperial court through his brother-in-law, Nicolas Perrenot de Granvelle, Charles v's powerful adviser, Bonvalot was in the period 1528–44 sent on a number of diplomatic missions in the emperor's service. Erasmus and Bonvalot continued to correspond until the former's death.
11 Désiré Morel of Besançon (d 1533) was canon of Besançon from 1494 and in 1529 succeeded Guérard (line 28) as official to the archdeacon.

TABLE OF CORRESPONDENTS

WORKS FREQUENTLY CITED

SHORT-TITLE FORMS

INDEX

TABLE OF CORRESPONDENTS

This list provides bibliographical information for works referred to in short-title form in this volume. For Erasmus' writings see the short-title list, pages 485–8. Editions of his letters are included in the list below.

AK	*Die Amerbachkorrespondenz* ed Alfred Hartmann and B.R. Jenny (Basel 1942–)
Allen	*Opus epistolarum Des. Erasmi Roterodami* ed P.S. Allen, H.M. Allen, and H.W. Garrod (Oxford 1906–58) 11 vols and index
Arbenz	*Die Vadianische Briefsammlung der Stadtbibliothek St Gallen* ed Emil Arbenz and Hermann Wartmann (St Gallen 1890–1913) 7 vols
ASD	*Opera omnia Desiderii Erasmi Roterodami* (Amsterdam 1969–)
Balan *Monumenta* I	*Monumenta reformationis Lutheranae, ex tabulariis secretioribus S. Sedis 1521–1525* ed Pietro Balan (Regensburg 1884)
Balan *Monumenta* II	*Monumenta saeculi* XVI. *historiam illustrantia* ed Pietro Balan (Innsbruck 1885)
BAO	*Briefe und Akten zum Leben Oekolampads* ed Ernst Staehelin 2 vols Quellen und Forschungen zur Reformations-geschichte 10 and 19 (Leipzig 1927–34; repr New York/ London 1971)
Barge	Hermann Barge *Andreas Bodenstein von Karlstadt* (Leipzig 1905; repr Nieuwkoop 1968) 2 vols
Biographie nouvelle	*Guillaume Farel, 1489–1565: Biographie nouvelle* (Neuchâtel/ Paris 1930)
Böcking	Ulrich von Hutten *Opera quae reperiri potuerunt omnia* ed Eduard Böcking (Leipzig 1859–61; repr Aalen 1963) 5 vols
BOL	*Martini Buceri Opera Latina* ed C. Augustijn et al (Leiden 1982–)
BRE	*Briefwechsel des Beatus Rhenanus* ed A. Horawitz and K. Hartfelder (Leipzig 1886; repr Hildesheim 1966)
CCL	*Corpus christianorum, series latina* (Turnhout 1954–65) 176 vols
CEBR	*Contemporaries of Erasmus: A Biographical Register of the Renaissance and Reformation* ed Peter G. Bietenholz and Thomas B. Deutscher (Toronto 1985–7) 3 vols
CL	*Calendar of Letters, Despatches, and State Papers, Relating to the Negotiations Between England and Spain, Preserved in the Archives at Simancas and Elsewhere, 1485–1603* ed G.A. Bergenroth et al (London 1862–99) 21 vols
CR	*Philippi Melanchthonis opera quae supersunt omnia* ed C.G. Bretschneider et al *Corpus Reformatorum* 1–28 (Halle 1834–60; repr 1963)
CSP	*Calendar of State Papers and* MSS *Relating to English Affairs, Existing in the Archives and Collections of Venice and in*

Other Libraries of Northern Italy, 1202–1629 ed Rawdon Brown et al (London 1864–1916) 23 vols

CWE   *Collected Works of Erasmus* (Toronto 1974–)

Enthoven   *Briefe an Desiderius Erasmus von Rotterdam* ed L.K. Enthoven (Strasbourg 1906)

Epistolae ad diversos   *Epistolae D. Erasmi Roterodami ad diversos et aliquot aliorum ad illum* (Basel: Froben, 31 August 1521)

Epistolae floridae   *Des. Erasmi Roterodami epistolarum floridarum liber unus antehac nunquam excusus* (Basel: J. Herwagen, September 1531)

Ferguson *Opuscula*   *Erasmi opuscula: A Supplement to the Opera Omnia* ed W.K. Ferguson (The Hague 1933)

Förstemann/Günther   *Briefe an Desiderius Erasmus von Rotterdam* ed. J. Förstemann and O. Günther, XXVII. Beiheft zum *Zentralblatt für Bibliothekswesen* (Leipzig 1904)

Gerlo   Aloïs Gerlo *Erasme et ses portraitistes* (Nieuwkoop 1969)

Gess   *Akten und Briefe zur Kirchenpolitik Herzog Georgs von Sachsen* ed Felician Gess (Leipzig/Berlin 1905/7; repr Cologne/Vienna 1985) 2 vols

Herminjard   *Correspondance des réformateurs dans les pays de langue française ... Tome premier 1512–1526* ed A.-L. Herminjard (Geneva/Paris 1866; repr Nieuwkoop 1965)

Hess   Johann Kaspar Hess *Lebensbeschreibung M. Ulrich Zwinglis* (Zürich 1811) II (= the 'literarisch-historischer Anhang' by Leonhard Usteri)

Knecht   R.J. Knecht *Francis I* (Cambridge 1982)

LB   *Desiderii Erasmi Roterodami opera omnia* ed J. Leclerc (Leiden 1703–6; repr 1961–2) 10 vols

LP   *Letters and Papers, Foreign and Domestic, of the Reign of Henry VIII* ed J.S. Brewer, J. Gairdner, and R.H. Brodie (London 1862–1932) 36 vols

Marichal   *Catalogue des actes de François Ier* ed Paul Marichal (Paris: Imprimerie Nationale 1887–1910) 10 vols

NK   W. Nijhoff and M.E. Kronenberg eds *Nederlandsche Bibliographie van 1500 tot 1540* (The Hague 1919–)

Oek-Bib   Ernst Staehelin *Oekolampadius-Bibliographie* 2nd ed (Basel 1918; repr Nieuwkoop 1963)

Opus epistolarum   *Opus epistolarum Des. Erasmi Roterodami per autorem diligenter recognitum et adjectis innumeris novis fere ad trientem auctum* (Basel: Froben, Herwagen, and Episcopius 1529)

Pastor   Ludwig von Pastor *The History of the Popes from the Close of the Middle Ages* ed and trans R.F. Kerr et al, 6th ed (London 1938–53) 40 vols

PG   J.P. Migne ed *Patrologiae cursus completus ... series graeca* (Paris 1857–1912) 162 vols

Pirckheimeri opera   *Bilibaldi Pirckheimeri ... opera politica, historica, philologica, et epistolica* ed Melchior Goldast (Frankfurt 1610; repr Hildesheim/New York 1969)

PL J.P. Migne ed *Patrologiae cursus completus ... series latina* (Paris 1844–1902) 221 vols

Planitz Hans von der Planitz *Berichte aus dem Reichsregiment in Nürnberg 1521–3* assembled E. Wulcher ed H. Virck (Leipzig 1899)

Pfeilschifter *Acta reformationis catholicae ecclesiam Germaniae concernentia saeculi* XVI ed Georg Pfeilschifter (Regensburg 1959–)

RTA *Deutsche Reichstagsakten, Jüngere Reihe* (Gotha, Stuttgart, Göttingen 1896–)

Scarisbrick J.J. Scarisbrick *Henry* VIII (Berkeley and Los Angeles 1968)

Scheible *Melanchthons Briefwechsel: Kritische und Kommentierte Gesamtausgabe* ed Heinz Scheible (Stuttgart-Bad Canstatt 1977–)

Schiess *Briefwechsel der Brüder Ambrosius und Thomas Blaurer, 1509–1567* ed Traugott Schiess (Freiburg im Breisgau 1908–12) 3 vols

Staehelin Ernst Staehelin *Das theologische Lebenswerk Johannes Oekolampads* Quellen und Forschungen zur Reformationsgeschichte 21 (Leipzig 1939; repr New York/London 1971)

Vander Haeghen *Bibliotheca Erasmiana: Répertoire des oeuvres d'Erasme* ed F. Vander Haeghen (Ghent 1893)

de Vocht CTL Henry de Vocht *History of the Foundation and Rise of the Collegium Trilingue Lovaniense 1517–1550* 4 vols Humanistica lovaniensia 10–13 (Louvain 1951–5)

de Vocht *Literae* *Literae virorum eruditorum ad Franciscum Craneveldium 1522–1528* ed Henry de Vocht, Humanistica lovaniensia 1 (Louvain 1928)

WA *D. Martin Luthers Werke, Kritische Gesamtausgabe* (Weimar 1883–)

WA-Br *D. Martin Luthers Werke: Briefwechsel* (Weimar 1930–78) 15 vols

WA-TR *D. Martin Luthers Werke: Tischreden* (Weimar 1912–21) 6 vols

Wirz J. Caspar Wirz *Ennio Filonardi, der letzte Nuntius in Zürich* (Zürich 1894)

Zw-Br *Huldreich Zwinglis Sämtliche Werke 7–11: Zwinglis Briefwechsel* ed Emil Egli et al / *Corpus Reformatorum 94–8* (Leipzig 1911–35)

Titles following colons are longer versions of the same, or are alternative titles. Items entirely enclosed in square brackets are of doubtful authorship. For abbreviations, see Works Frequently Cited.

Adagia: Adagiorum chiliades 1508, etc (Adagiorum collectanea for the primitive form, when required) LB II / ASD II-4, 5, 6 / CWE 30–6
Admonitio adversus mendacium: Admonitio adversus mendacium et obtrectationem LB X
Annotationes in Novum Testamentum LB VI
Antibarbari LB IX / ASD I-1 / CWE 23
Apologia ad Caranzam: Apologia ad Sanctium Caranzam, or Apologia de tribus locis, or Responsio ad annotationem Stunicae ... a Sanctio Caranza defensam LB IX
Apologia ad Fabrum: Apologia ad Iacobum Fabrum Stapulensem LB IX
Apologia adversus monachos: Apologia adversus monachos quosdam hispanos LB IX
Apologia adversus Petrum Sutorem: Apologia adversus debacchationes Petri Sutoris LB IX
Apologia adversus rhapsodias Alberti Pii: Apologia ad viginti et quattuor libros A. Pii LB IX
Apologia contra Latomi dialogum: Apologia contra Iacobi Latomi dialogum de tribus linguis LB IX
Apologiae contra Stunicam: Apologiae contra Lopidem Stunicam LB IX / ASD IX-2
Apologia de 'In principio erat sermo' LB IX
Apologia de laude matrimonii: Apologia pro declamatione de laude matrimonii LB IX
Apologia de loco 'Omnes quidem': Apologia de loco 'Omnes quidem resurgemus' LB IX
Apologia qua respondet invectivis Lei: Apologia qua respondet duabus invectivis Eduardi Lei *Opuscula*
Apophthegmata LB IV
Appendix respondens ad Sutorem LB IX
Argumenta: Argumenta in omnes epistolas apostolicas nova (with Paraphrases)
Axiomata pro causa Lutheri: Axiomata pro causa Martini Lutheri *Opuscula*

Carmina varia LB VIII
Catalogus lucubrationum LB I
Christiani hominis institutum, carmen LB V
Ciceronianus: Dialogus Ciceronianus LB I / ASD I-2 / CWE 28
Colloquia LB I / ASD I-3
Compendium vitae Allen I / CWE 4
[Consilium: Consilium cuiusdam ex animo cupientis esse consultum] *Opuscula*

De bello turcico: Consultatio de bello turcico (in Psalmi)
De civilitate: De civilitate morum puerilium LB I / CWE 25
Declamatio de morte LB IV
Declamatiuncula LB IV

Declarationes ad censuras Lutetiae vulgatas: Declarationes ad censuras Lutetiae
vulgatas sub nomine facultatis theologiae Parisiensis LB IX
De concordia: De sarcienda ecclesiae concordia, or De amabili ecclesiae concordia
(in Psalmi)
De conscribendis epistolis LB I / ASD I-2 / CWE 25
De constructione: De constructione octo partium orationis, or Syntaxis LB I / ASD I-4
De contemptu mundi: Epistola de contemptu mundi LB V / ASD V-1 / CWE 66
De copia: De duplici copia verborum ac rerum LB I / ASD I-6 / CWE 24
De immensa Dei misericordia: Concio de immensa Dei misericordia LB V
De libero arbitrio: De libero arbitrio diatribe LB IX
De praeparatione: De praeparatione ad mortem LB V / ASD V-1
De pueris instituendis: De pueris statim ac liberaliter instituendis LB I / ASD I-2 / CWE
26
De puero Iesu: Concio de puero Iesu LB V / CWE 29
De puritate tabernaculi: De puritate tabernaculi sive ecclesiae christianae (in Psalmi)
De ratione studii LB I / ASD I-2 / CWE 24
De recta pronuntiatione: De recta latini graecique sermonis pronuntiatione LB I /
ASD I-4 / CWE 26
Detectio praestigiarum: Detectio praestigiarum cuiusdam libelli germanice
scripti LB X / ASD IX-1
De taedio Iesu: Disputatiuncula de taedio, pavore, tristicia Iesu LB V
De vidua christiana LB V / CWE 66
De virtute amplectenda: Oratio de virtute amplectenda LB V / CWE 29
[Dialogus bilinguium ac trilinguium: Chonradi Nastadiensis dialogus bilinguium ac
trilinguium] Opuscula / CWE 7
Dilutio: Dilutio eorum quae Iodocus Clithoveus scripsit adversus declamationem
suasoriam matrimonii
Divinationes ad notata Bedae LB IX

Ecclesiastes: Ecclesiastes sive de ratione concionandi LB V
Elenchus in N. Bedae censuras LB IX
Enchiridion: Enchiridion militis christiani LB V / CWE 66
Encomium matrimonii (in De conscribendis epistolis)
Encomium medicinae: Declamatio in laudem artis medicae LB I / ASD I-4 / CWE 29
Epigrammata LB I
Epistola ad Dorpium LB IX / CWE 3
Epistola ad fratres Inferioris Germaniae: Responsio ad fratres Germaniae Inferioris
ad epistolam apologeticam incerto autore proditam LB X / ASD IX-1
Epistola ad graculos: Epistola ad quosdam imprudentissimos graculos LB X
Epistola apologetica de Termino LB X
Epistola consolatoria: Epistola consolatoria virginibus sacris LB V
Epistola contra pseudevangelicos: Epistola contra quosdam qui se falso iactant
evangelicos LB X / ASD IX-1
Epistola de esu carnium: Epistola apologetica ad Christophorum episcopum Basil-
iensem de interdicto esu carnium LB IX / ASD IX-1
Exomologesis: Exomologesis sive modus confitendi LB V
Explanatio symboli: Explanatio symboli apostolorum sive catechismus LB V / ASD
V-1

Expositio concionalis (in Psalmi)
Expostulatio Iesu LB V

Formula: Conficiendarum epistolarum formula (see De conscribendis epistolis)

Hymni varii LB V
Hyperaspistes LB X

In Nucem Ovidiii commentarius LB I / ASD I-1 / CWE 29
In Prudentium: Commentarius in duos hymnos Prudentii LB V / CWE 29
Institutio christiani matrimonii LB V
Institutio principis christiani LB IV / ASD IV-1 / CWE 27

[Julius exclusus: Dialogus Julius exclusus e coelis] *Opuscula* / CWE 27

Lingua LB IV / ASD IV-1A / CWE 29
Liturgia Virginis Matris: Virginis Matris apud Lauretum cultae liturgia LB V / ASD
 V-1

Methodus (see Ratio)
Modus orandi Deum LB V / ASD V-1
Moria: Moriae encomium LB IV / ASD IV-3 / CWE 27

Novum Testamentum: Novum Testamentum 1519 and later (Novum instrumentum for the first edition, 1516, when required) LB VI

Obsecratio ad Virginem Mariam: Obsecratio sive oratio ad Virginem Mariam in
 rebus adversis LB V
Oratio de pace: Oratio de pace et discordia LB VIII
Oratio funebris: Oratio funebris Berthae de Heyen LB VIII / CWE 29

Paean Virgini Matri: Paean Virgini Matri dicendus LB V
Panegyricus: Panegyricus ad Philippum Austriae ducem LB IV / ASD IV-1 / CWE 27
Parabolae: Parabolae sive similia LB I / ASD I-5 / CWE 23
Paraclesis LB V, VI
Paraphrasis in Elegantias Vallae: Paraphrasis in Elegantias Laurentii Vallae LB I /
 ASD I-4
Paraphrasis in Matthaeum, etc (in Paraphrasis in Novum Testamentum)
Paraphrasis in Novum Testamentum LB VII / CWE 42–50
Peregrinatio apostolorum: Peregrinatio apostolorum Petri et Pauli LB VI, VII
Precatio ad Virginis filium Iesum LB V
Precatio dominica LB V
Precationes LB V
Precatio pro pace ecclesiae: Precatio ad Iesum pro pace ecclesiae LB IV, V
Progymnasmata: Progymnasmata quaedam primae adolescentiae Erasmi LB VIII
Psalmi: Psalmi, or Enarrationes sive commentarii in psalmos LB V / ASD V-2, 3
Purgatio adversus epistolam Lutheri: Purgatio adversus epistolam non sobriam
 Lutheri LB IX / ASD IX-1

Querela pacis LB IV / ASD IV-2 / CWE 27

Ratio: Ratio seu Methodus compendio perveniendi ad veram theologiam (Methodus for the shorter version originally published in the Novum instrumentum of 1516) LB V, VI

Responsio ad annotationes Lei: Liber quo respondet annotationibus Lei LB IX

Responsio ad collationes: Responsio ad collationes cuiusdam iuvenis gerontodidascali LB IX

Responsio ad disputationem de divortio: Responsio ad disputationem cuiusdam Phimostomi de divortio LB IX

Responsio ad epistolam Pii: Responsio ad espistolam paraeneticam Albert Pii, or Responsio ad exhortationem Pii LB IX

Responsio ad notulas Bedaicas LB X

Responsio ad Petri Cursii defensionem: Epistola de apologia Cursii LB X

Responsio adversus febricitantis libellum: Apologia monasticae religionis LB X

Spongia: Spongia adversus aspergines Hutteni LB X / ASD IX-1

Supputatio: Supputatio calumniarum Natalis Bedae LB IX

Tyrannicida: Tyrannicida, declamatio Lucianicae respondens LB I / CWE 29

Virginis et martyris comparatio LB V

Vita Hieronymi: Vita divi Hieronymi Stridonensis *Opuscula*

Index

This book

was designed by

ANTJE LINGNER

based on the series design by

ALLAN FLEMING

and was printed by

University

of Toronto

Press